The
Sir Arthur Conan Doyle
Reader

The
Sir Arthur Conan Doyle
Reader

From Sherlock Holmes to Spiritualism

Edited by
Jeffrey Meyers and Valerie Meyers

Cooper Square Press

First Cooper Square Press edition 2002

This Cooper Square Press hardcover of *The Sir Arthur Conan Doyle Reader* is an original publication. It is printed by arrangement with the editors.

Published by Copper Square Press
An Imprint of the Rowman & Littlefield Publishing Group
200 Park Avenue South, Suite 1109
New York, New York 10003-1503

Distributed by National Book Network

Library of Congress Cataloging-in-Publication Data

Doyle, Arthur Conan, Sir, 1859-1930.
    The Sir Arthur Conan Doyle reader : from Sherlock Holmes to spiritualism / edited by Jeffrey Meyers and Valerie Meyers.— 1st Cooper Square Press ed.
        p. cm.
    Includes bibliographical references (p.).
    ISBN 0-8154-1202-9 (cloth : alk. paper)
    I. Meyers, Jeffrey. II. Meyers, Valerie. III. Title.

PR4621 .M94 2002
823'.8—dc21

                                                                    2002001288

⊚ ™ The paper used in this publication meets the minimum requirements of American National Standard for Information Sciences—Permanence of Paper for Printed Library Materials, ANSI/NISO Z39.48-1992.
Manufactured in the United States of America.

CONTENTS

INTRODUCTION

Born in Edinburgh, Scotland, in 1859, of a poor family of Irish descent, Arthur Conan Doyle became one of the most celebrated English writers of his time. He lived through the late Victorian era and the Boer War (in which he participated as a field doctor), the devastating trauma of World War I and the beginning of literary modernism in the 1920s. He died in Crowborough, Sussex, in 1930. He had trained as a doctor and struggled to establish a practice, but his efforts to supplement his income by writing met with success and he eventually left medicine to be an author.

Immensely productive and hardworking, he published an extraordinary quantity of work in a variety of genres. Though best known today for the Sherlock Holmes detective stories, he also wrote historical novels set in England in the Middle Ages and in the seventeenth and eighteenth centuries, adventure stories of the Napoleonic wars, science fiction, ghost stories, sporting tales, plays, memoirs, travel journals, polemics and war reportage. He pamphleteered about the Boer War and imperialistic exploitation in the Congo, warned of the approaching Great War and reported it from the Western front. In middle age he became profoundly attracted to Spiritualism, a craze that swept Europe and America in the years following the Great War. The stories and nonfiction collected here span the years from 1887 to 1921, and show the range and quality of his work.

Conan Doyle was an instinctive storyteller, with a Dickensian eye for the striking and often macabre detail. He shared Dickens' sense of justice and social responsibility, his warm humanity and delight in the lively individuality of the characters he created. Like Dickens, he published his stories and novels, often in serial form, in the weekly magazines that were the staple of popular entertainment in the late nineteenth century. Like his younger contemporary and friend, H.G. Wells, he used his scientific education and medical training in his fiction, and challenged the prevailing belief in the idea of progress. Like Wells, he also became an important public figure whose opinion was sought on the crucial issues of the day, an influential speaker at a time when the lecture was a popular social event.

Following Edgar Allan Poe, Conan Doyle gave the detective story its modern form. Sherlock Holmes stands among the greatest characters in literature: Achilles and Aeneas, Faust and Hamlet, Don Juan and Don Quixote, Tristram Shandy and Tom Jones. Fond of conundrums and hieroglyphics, the tall, angular Holmes displays a preternatural acumen. He lives in seclusion, excludes sunlight from his chambers and tends to venture outside after nightfall, when his lucid intelligence pierces through the foggy atmosphere. A sexless bachelor, dilettante musician, amateur chemist and cocaine addict, he has erudite tastes. An expert in ciphers and much superior to the plodding police, he attracts suspects to his rooms through cunning newspaper advertisements. He indulges in abstract reflection while meditatively puffing his curved pipe and solves the crimes through crisp logical analysis. He exhibits virtuoso displays of arcane knowledge and identifies with the thoughts of the criminal, has uncanny powers of observation and can deduce occupations from physical appearance. His offhand remark—really an educated guess—in *A Study in Scarlet:* "You have been in Afghanistan, I perceive," provokes Watson's astonished exclamation: "How on earth did you know that?" He's portrayed through the eyes of the dim but devoted Dr. Watson, who (like the reader) struggles to keep up with Holmes' brilliant deductions and remains in the dark until the final startling revelation. Holmes is a pinnacle on the path that leads from Poe's M. Dupin to Umberto Eco's ratiocinative monk in *The Name of the Rose*.

A Study in Scarlet, published in Beeton's *Christmas Annual* in 1887 and brought out in book form a year later, was written while Conan Doyle was still working as a doctor. The title may have been influenced by James McNeill Whistler, who gave his paintings such titles as *Purple and Rose*, *Symphony in White* and *Nocturne in Black*. In the first of the Sherlock Holmes mysteries Conan Doyle introduces Dr. Watson to Holmes—and his readers to both men—in a masterly way. The story begins as the autobiographical reminiscences of "John H. Watson M.D., Late of the Army Medical Department," yet deftly launches into his vivid encounter with Sherlock Holmes. Invalided out of his regiment in India, Watson finds himself in London, convalescent, short of money and looking for lodgings. Young Stamford, a fellow student from his college days, tells him about the eccentric and dubious Holmes. Even the subjects that Holmes studies are mysterious—he spends hours in the chemistry lab and dissecting rooms, but is not a doctor. He's been known to beat corpses to examine their bruises and has a "passion for definite and exact knowledge." Stamford calls him "a compendium of criminal knowledge."

Holmes and Watson quickly meet, agree to share rooms and, when Watson is casually invited to go along, are soon rumbling through grimy streets in hansom cabs, solving the mystery of the dead man in an empty house. Though utterly different in character, they are a complementary pair, for Watson's training gives him an interest in forensic medicine and in Holmes' ruling passion: crime and the criminal mind. Gregson and Lestrade, two of the bumbling London police detectives who ask for help and are always several steps behind Holmes, appear for the first time, as well as the landlady on the staircase and the gang of street urchins Holmes calls the Baker Street irregulars.

The first-person narrator is a hallmark of Conan Doyle's fiction, and his use of Watson as the observer and interpreter of Holmes was a particularly brilliant stroke. He had hit upon a winning combination, and this first novel established a pattern for nearly all the sixty Sherlock Holmes stories and novellas he would write. Holmes once called Watson "my Boswell," and the crime stories also comprise the biography of the detective. Holmes believes that "detection is, or ought to be, an exact science," and always acknowledges Watson's usefulness. Dr. Watson's earnest puzzlement stimulates the detective, elicits his ideas and, not incidentally, pushes the narrative along. Watson is always the student, Holmes the teacher.

Conan Doyle was inspired to create Holmes by one of his instructors at the University of Edinburgh Medical School, Dr. Joseph Bell, a dazzling teacher who used observation and deductive skills to understand the patient and diagnose his disease. Holmes' rivalry with the Scotland Yard policemen was based on Conan Doyle's memories of the sharp debates among the professors.

Watson also describes Holmes' effect on others, recording Gregson's astonishment as Holmes draws yet another decisive yet inexplicable conclusion, and recapitulates the plot at convenient moments. He voices the reader's response (as in "The Sign of Four") by declaring: "This is all an insoluble mystery to me." "On the contrary," comes the reply. "It clears every instant. I only require a few missing links to have a perfectly connected case." And we read on for story after story, wanting to know the details, mundane or exotic.

Conan Doyle was the most devoted of husbands and fathers, and with few exceptions his women characters are domestic angels with minor roles. Mary Marston in "The Sign of Four," whom the susceptible Watson falls for and marries, is very like Louise Hawkins, Conan Doyle's first wife. Most of his stories are structured around male relationships. In the first thirty pages of *A Study in Scarlet* we have not only an intriguing mystery, but the creation of an enduring male friendship that develops before our eyes. Watson expresses his admiration, and notices the effect on Holmes: "I had already observed that he was as sensitive to flattery on the score of his art as any girl could be of her beauty."

Holmes has a dual temperament, energetic and dedicated to detection, but also given to depression and lassitude; if there's no case to challenge him, he can spend days doing absolutely nothing. His interest in crime is all-absorbing and, without the presence of the stolid Watson, would verge on the obsessive and disturbing. His only recreations are music and cocaine. Watson, by contrast, is a bourgeois, sensible, compassionate man. At the crime scene he says, "I followed him with that subdued feeling at my heart which the presence of death inspires." Though Watson is far from the bumbling fool portrayed in films and television—in this story he is young, thin and deeply tanned from his service in India—Holmes is much more intellectual. A coldly practical man of reason, he's interested in the mysteries of human personality and uses motivation as an aid to solving the crime.

Watson, who in so many ways *is* Conan Doyle—the humane biographer of eccentric characters—keeps the reader anchored to a comforting world of firm moral values and commonsense responses. Watson's bluff and hearty attitudes are a necessary foil to the mysterious and mercurial Holmes. Conan Doyle's great admirer, P.G. Wodehouse, paid him the compliment of creating another set of immortal male companions—the dim and accident-prone Bertie Wooster and his shrewd butler Jeeves—a comic variant of Watson and Holmes. And like Conan Doyle, Wodehouse developed a perennially entertaining art.

Part One of *A Study in Scarlet* ends as Holmes arrests the perpetrator. Part Two, omitted here, lacks the swift pace and interest of the first, though we sympathize with the murderer, Jefferson Hope, when he tells his story. This goes back forty years, to Utah and the Mormon pioneers who settled Salt Lake City, and Brigham Young himself makes an appearance. Hope has killed Drebber and Stangerson in revenge for the deaths of John Ferrier and his adopted daughter Lucy. She was promised in marriage to Hope, but was abducted and forced to marry the gross and greedy Drebber (a good name for a villain). Hope, who knew his victims were guilty and would never be convicted, has spent his life pursuing them, but dies of an aneurysm before he can be brought to trial. Conan Doyle was far more at home in Baker Street than in the Utah Desert, and Holmes concludes the story by describing to Watson his process of "reasoning backward" or working out the steps that could have led to the murder. Watson is ecstatic and declares: "Your merits should be publicly recognized. You should publish an account of the case. If you won't I will for you." Gregson and Lestrade are given the credit in the press, and Watson's career as Holmes' Boswell is born.

The second Holmes story, "The Sign of Four," which begins with the remarkable sight of Holmes taking down his hypodermic syringe from its neat morocco case and injecting himself with cocaine as Watson watches disapprovingly, contains a locked-room murder and an exciting chase, worthy of Dickens, along the Thames. But the criminal's long and far-fetched narrative of pursuit and revenge—exacted by means of poisoned darts—makes the story drag. By the time he wrote the third Holmes mystery, "A Scandal in Bohemia," Conan Doyle realized that he excelled at describing the process of detection and the interplay of his two great characters, and could do without exotic crimes and digressions. As long as the solution was interesting and the motivation plausible, his readers had far rather watch and listen to Holmes than anyone else. The much shorter and more satirical "A Scandal in Bohemia," published in 1891 in a new magazine, the *Strand*, shows Conan Doyle hitting his stride. He also saw that he could produce a series of stories about one character more easily and profitably than a serial novel. Over the years the *Strand* grew rich on the popularity of Sherlock Holmes.

Conan Doyle managed his material so economically and circumstantially, and Sherlock Holmes was such a vivid personality, that people began to think of him as a real person living in a real world. In "A Scandal in Bohemia" Watson even gives the date he happened to drop in on Holmes in Baker Street—March 20, 1888. The events take place some years after *A Study in Scarlet*, and the contrast between the two friends is all the greater. Watson is now happily married and working as a doctor, and Holmes, with an established international reputation as a detective, is as cold and precise as ever. A "reasoning and observing machine," he loathes society, cannot feel emotion, and still alternates between cocaine and ambition. But the story centers on Irene Adler, American opera singer and adventuress (quite the opposite of Watson's sweet Mary—but then Holmes would not want such a wife), who belies Holmes' scorn for the intellect of women, and is ever after called *the* woman. By creating a bold exception to Holmes' indifference to women, Conan Doyle makes him a deeper and more complex character, and cleverly sets up his readers' expectations for the sequel.

The pace of the story cracks along, with vivid attention to visual detail, from the marks on Watson's shoes to the Bohemian client's deep blue cloak lined with flame-colored silk, and with an emphasis on sound that makes Conan Doyle's London so atmospheric: "the sharp sound of horses' hoofs and grating wheels against the curb, followed by a sharp pull at the bell." The story displays Holmes' gifts for acting and disguise, and for setting up a situation that will force the guilty party's hand, and ends with a witty flourish as he shows chivalrous disdain for the King.

Conan Doyle was greatly influenced by Poe's *Tales of Mystery and Imagination* and imitated Poe's scientific horror tales. "The Los Amigos Fiasco" (1892), also narrated by a doctor, is a blend of science fiction and tall tale set in the American West. The town of Los Amigos prides itself on its giant electric generators and, hearing of clumsy attempts in the East to execute offenders by this method, sets out to electrocute the next man guilty of a capital crime and do a better job of it. Their grisly attempts meet with comic results. At a time when electrocution was an innovative and controversial method of execution, Conan Doyle used the supernatural to make fun of technological progress.

In "The Case of Lady Sannox" (1893), a horror story, a doctor is once again a main character. The first paragraph boldly tells us the disastrous fate of Douglas Stone. A celebrated surgeon with a society practice, he has suffered some terrible shock that has rendered his brain, in one of Conan Doyle's homely but striking similes, "as valuable as a cap full of porridge." This is the author at his most sophisticated. Everyday social life is cruel enough, he suggests, noting how the gossip goes round "over the teacups in snug little drawing-rooms or with the aid of a cigar in the bow windows of clubs." If the characters are worthy of Oscar Wilde—the sensual, luxury-loving Stone; the man-eating beauty, Lady Sannox; the icy Lord Sannox, with thin lips, heavy eyelids and a Sherlockian talent for acting, who consoles himself with his orchids for the infidelities of his wife—the savage denouement is as sadistic as the stories of Saki. As in so many of his tales, Conan Doyle makes our shudders enjoyable by engaging our sense of justice and creating sympathy for the villain.

Conan Doyle published several lengthy and enormously successful historical novels that are rarely read today. Far more enduring and appealing are the short stories of Brigadier Etienne Gerard, an officer in Napoleon's army. Conan Doyle researched the period exhaustively, based Gerard's exploits on the real-life memoirs of General Marbot, created a classic boys' adventure hero and constructed action-packed plots, with duels, moonlit rides and hairbreadth escapes. In the first of the stories, "How the Brigadier Came to the Castle of Gloom" (1894), the vain,

boastful Gerard narrates in his "French" style. Like an Errol Flynn character, brave, masculine and patriotic, devoted to the regiment and to his
beloved black horse Rataplan, Gerard is as proud of his endurance as of
his legs in the tight-fitting cavalry trousers. Though he constantly refers
to his liaisons with women, in keeping with the genre we never hear
about any of them in detail. Though willing to die anytime—for the
right reason—he is a prudent soldier and resourceful survivor, with his
eye on the chance of promotion. The story has entrapment in a Poe-like
castle, a tiny key and door out of *Alice in Wonderland*, a damsel in distress
and a fiery explosion worthy of a Hollywood epic.

The second story in the volume, "How the Brigadier Slew the
Brothers of Ajaccio" (1895), shows Gerard conversing with great historical figures, and even with the Emperor himself. The statesman Talleyrand and Napoleon come vividly to life through the eyes of the astonished Gerard. The black-clad diplomat contrasts with Gerard's
Colonel, who sits down "with a clash and jangle like a prancing charger,"
and the Emperor is revealed to be still a Corsican at heart. Quartered in
Fontainebleau in 1807 after a peace has been concluded (although "the
old Bulldog over the Channel was still growling"), Gerard is called upon
to help Napoleon. Colonel Lasalle describes Gerard as "all spurs and
moustaches, with never a thought beyond women and horses," but his
capacity to act bravely and without thinking lands him the job.
Napoleon is the brigadier's hero, but the egalitarian Gerard takes pride
in his own skill and his part in the French conquests: "he was the finest
leader in the world, but we did not forget that he had the finest men to
lead." Gerard is tricked once again, but he lives to save his leader from
scandal—as it turns out, the real danger.

In 1895 Conan Doyle published *The Stark Munro Letters*, a series of
autobiographical letters written by J. Stark Munro, a struggling young
doctor, to "Dear Bertie," an American college friend. The novel barely
disguises Conan Doyle's own life—the tall, athletic J. Stark Munro is
clearly A. Conan Doyle—and the writing is fresh, natural and collo-
quial. Munro's job as assistant to an excellent, hard-working doctor with
a huge practice in a mining village corresponds to Conan Doyle's work
in industrial Birmingham as an assistant to the first-rate Dr. Hoare.
Munro is a sympathetic narrator, a compassionate observer of the de-

tails of poverty who shows sympathy and respect for the working people he serves. He says of the miners: "I like the grip of their greasy and blackened hands."

Munro is fired from his job—taking care of a mentally ill young man—for his religious views, a reworking of Conan Doyle's bitter break with his wealthy Catholic relatives in London. They could have helped him start his career, but withdrew their support when he admitted that he had lost his faith. Munro (like Conan Doyle) believes Christ was a human being, not a god, and argues against Christianity and for principled humanism. In this charming book the only longueurs are the religious and philosophical ramblings, though they do suggest the independent-minded and earnest character of the narrator.

Munro's devotion to his mother and her anger with him for associating with the unscrupulous Cullingworth, an unstable and unprincipled young doctor, is also taken from real life. The book's richly comic focus is on Munro's hilarious and disastrous relationship with this man, who advises Munro (like Watson, a solid citizen and caring doctor): "Break your patients in early, and keep them well to heel." He corresponds in real life to the madly eccentric and paranoid Dr. Budd, a medical school classmate who offered Conan Doyle a job in Plymouth when he had absolutely no other possibilities. Cullingworth is said to have left considerable debts behind him in "Avon," as Budd had done in Bristol. Conan Doyle's mother was furious to hear that Budd was making money in Plymouth but refusing to pay off his debts. The two chapters included here describe Budd's fraudulent practice and their break a few months later. When they parted Budd agreed to send him money each month to support him in his new practice, but then claimed to have found an insulting letter from Conan Doyle's mother and withdrew his offer. Budd had evidently gone through Conan Doyle's possessions and had been reading his letters all along—which explained his volatile attitude to his assistant. Conan Doyle saw that he'd been completely taken in by Budd (who meant to get him stranded and penniless), but the only revenge he took was creating the comically evil figure of Cullingworth, the doctor as showman and bully.

Conan Doyle poured his heart into this book, as he looked back from the success and prosperity of his mid-thirties to the joys and hardships of his impoverished early years in Southsea, a suburb of Portsmouth. After the parting with Cullingworth the letters describe Munro's first evening in "Birchespool" (a fictional name for Portsmouth) when—like the muscular and chivalrous Conan Doyle in real life—he got involved in a street fight. He attempts to get clients with the aid of the hard-drinking but well-meaning Captain Whitehall, and sets up home and business with some cheap furniture and a brass nameplate (which he polishes himself at night, so that no one would see that he had no servant). His mother in Scotland, sinking ever deeper into poverty, sends his schoolboy younger brother to live with him, and they both scrape by on bread and potatoes. After subletting to some undesirables, Munro finds the perfect tenant and marries the sister of a dying patient he had taken into his home, exactly as Conan Doyle had done. In a postscript the young Munro and his wife are inexplicably killed off in a railway accident—just as his career as a doctor is launched. Though he later returned to it in his autobiography, it was perhaps Conan Doyle's way of closing off this part of his life.

"The King of the Foxes" (1898), a sporting tale, gives the conventional fox-hunting tall story a macabre and comic twist. For his description of the chase Conan Doyle may have drawn on the great wolf hunt in *War and Peace* (Part 7, Chapters 3–5), in which the wolf terrifies the dogs, but is captured alive and strung up for display with a stick in its mouth. The story was certainly influenced by the fox-hunting novels of Robert Surtees and by Somerville and Ross' *The Silver Fox* (1897); it led, in turn, to Siegfried Sassoon's classic *Memoirs of a Fox-Hunting Man* (1928).

The main character, Wat Danbury, a wealthy young farmer who's advised by the sensible Dr. Middleton that he's on the verge of alcoholism, goes hunting to clear his head. The breathless narrative—whose speed is conveyed by active verbs and present participles—builds excitement and suspense, as no one even glimpses the quarry, and the run of the hounds, longer and longer, goes over the Sussex Downs and nearly reaches the sea. Many of the dogs are lamed and all the other riders gradually fall by the wayside, until Wat, the only huntsman left, "has tasted the highest which [fox-hunting] can offer." The bloody climax reveals the irony of this comment, and Wat's reaction undercuts the much-vaunted thrill of the hunt. Cruel and violent, like other traditional blood sports, fox-hunting has recently been banned in England under the rules of the European Community. Though Conan Doyle was a keen sportsman, and exploits the scarlet coats and the sounds of the hunting horn for all they are worth, it is clear that his sympathies lay with the hunted.

Conan Doyle's stories are economical in style and structure. He uses skillful repetition but never wastes words, and fits all the elements of the tale together in a satisfying whole. On the first page of "The Brazilian Cat" (1898), another story featuring a savage animal, this time in combination with a sadistic human being, the narrator's own voice conveys his naive and foolish character. The spoiled young man about town, Marshall King, in dire financial straits, gets a sudden invitation to visit the country house of his rich cousin Everard, who's returned from Brazil the previous year. Conan Doyle's mysteries often proceed by a cluster of contrasts, and this is true of both main characters. Marshall will inherit a large estate, but is bankrupt; Everard dresses like a South American planter and surrounds himself with exotic fauna, but lives in a solid manor house called "Greylands." Everard's wife is elegant and poised, but viciously rude. The black panther is beautifully chromatic, with "yellow eyes gleaming and his scarlet tongue rippling and quivering over the white line of his jagged teeth," yet he is also a "malignant sight."

As in Poe's horror tale "The Pit and the Pendulum," Conan Doyle's young protagonist has to extricate himself from an apparently hopeless trap, and the pleasure of the story lies in the vivid details of his plight. In a typically domestic image, Conan Doyle describes the cat's "fetid breath . . . like the steam from some foul pot." The ironic plot has some darkly comic moments. Marshall, accustomed to privilege, assumes that his cousin is simply being generous. Even the dogcart driver who carries him up to the house is more circumspect, remarking that Mr. King is so unnaturally generous that he must have "parliamentary ambitions." Everard, showing off his pet, observes: "I think that I have inflicted my hobby upon you long enough," though the ironic remark is lost on Marshall. The whole story is a grisly satire on the hazards of visiting country houses and maniacal hosts.

Conan Doyle loved to play with conventional genres, and "The Brown Hand" (1899) is a ghost story with a comic twist. His tales were much in demand for weekly magazines, and he ingeniously varied the basic plots he used to supply them. Like "The Brazilian Cat," "The Brown Hand" is based on the visit of a poor relation to a rich relative newly returned from an exotic country. The middle-aged, self-satisfied Dr. Hardacre, narrating the story, explains how he ceased to be "a hard-working and impecunious medical man" and came into money and property. Summoned to visit his uncle, a famous surgeon who's retired to England from years of practicing in India, Hardacre approaches Rodenhurst through the weird tumuli that suggest ancient graves. Like Poe's House of Usher, the house is neglected and broken-down. Conan Doyle's description of Sir Dominick Holden stresses the contrast between his craggy strength of character and keen light-blue eyes, and "the look which tells of spirit cowed and crushed, the furtive, expectant look of the dog whose master has taken the whip from the rack." The house is haunted, but Hardacre has dabbled in Psychic Research and feels equal to solving the mystery. He earns his uncle's gratitude by slaying the ghost—but not before making an obvious blunder.

Like his protagonist, Conan Doyle had been interested in the paranormal for many years without taking it very seriously. The ghost story was a popular Victorian genre (the most famous being Dickens's *A Christmas Carol*) and continued to be so through the turn of the century. Rudyard Kipling and Henry James wrote fine examples. The curious tone of this story, in which the calm and objective doctor accepts the ghost's claims on his uncle and solves the problem in a practical way, reflects Conan Doyle's rather ambivalent attitude, at this point, to the supernatural. Later on, Spiritualism would completely fascinate and absorb him.

To his credit Conan Doyle used his skills as a writer to defend those he felt had been wronged. He wrote a short book in defense of British conduct in the Boer War, for which he was knighted in 1902. In 1906 he took up the cause of George Edalji, a strange man unjustly convicted and imprisoned for mutilating animals; and in 1912 he set to work on behalf of Oscar Slater, a German immigrant and petty criminal framed for a murder in Glasgow. Slater escaped execution but served sixteen years in jail before the renewed efforts of Conan Doyle and others secured his freedom. Conan Doyle also worked on reform of the divorce law. He gave an enormous amount of time to all these crusades, often negotiating with obstructive officials and working his connections to reach his goal.

In 1909, in *The Crime of the Congo*, he used his influence in a larger political issue. From 1865 until 1908 the Congo, a vast country in the heart of Africa, was a colonial territory that did not belong to another state, but was the personal property of King Leopold II of Belgium. In "Geography and Some Explorers" (1924) Joseph Conrad, captain of a Congo steamboat in 1890, called the Belgians' ruthless quest for riches "the vilest scramble for loot that ever disfigured the history of human conscience and geographical exploration." In Conan Doyle's polemic, as in Conrad's *Heart of Darkness* (1899), the supposedly civilized Europeans are infinitely more barbaric than the "primitive" Africans.

Conan Doyle's effective method is to give the historical background and offer vivid, stomach-turning descriptions of the brutalities committed in the Congo, based on the eye-witness accounts of European missionaries, traders, travelers and diplomats. One mutilated boy reported that though "wounded at the time he was perfectly sensible of the severing of his wrist, but lay still fearing that if he moved he would be killed." "Women had been killed by thrusting sticks into them from below." In a land where many people were starving, human corpses were efficiently recycled, cut up and eaten.

Conan Doyle places the guilt for these atrocities, for twenty years of uninterrupted slaughter, directly upon King Leopold. "Never before," he thunders in his Preface, "has there been such a mixture of wholesale expropriation and wholesale massacre all done under an odious guise of philanthropy." The State, having flagrantly violated every condition and principle on which it was founded—the introduction of Christianity and the abolition of slavery—must (he argued) be taken "from hands which have proved so unworthy and place[d] in conditions which shall no longer be a disgrace to European civilization." The Congo must, he urged, be returned to the people from whom it was stolen.

Enraged by this cruel injustice and writing at white heat, Conan Doyle completed the entire 45,000-word polemic in only eight days. E. D. Morel, head of the Congo Reform Association, attested to the effectiveness of the pamphlet, which led to radical changes in the way the colony was governed: "It was not his book—excellent as it was—nor his manly eloquence on the platform, nor the influence he wielded in rallying influential men to our cause, which helped us most. It was just the fact that he was—Conan Doyle; and that he was with us."

One of Doyle's main informants was the tall, handsome Roger Casement, an Irishman who had been British consul at Boma. He'd shared a hut with Conrad in the Congo, and was a model for the wandering and elusive "Russian in motley" in *Heart of Darkness*. Casement's 1903 investigation into the treatment of rubber workers in the Upper Congo, which helped put an end to their cruel exploitation, was one of the great humanitarian achievements of its time. It brought him worldwide fame and a knighthood.

After retiring from the Colonial Service because of poor health, Casement became active in the Irish nationalist movement. At the time of the abortive Easter rebellion in 1916, he was landed on the Irish coast from a German submarine and instantly captured. In June 1916 he was convicted of treason and sentenced to hang. Though Conan Doyle—along with Bernard Shaw and other writers—made a public appeal for clemency, there was little sympathy for Casement during the war and he was executed in August.

Conan Doyle is said to have based the appearance and speech of Lord John Roxton, one of the characters in his Professor Challenger stories, on Roger Casement. In 1912 Conan Doyle published *The Lost World*, an early *Jurassic Park* and one of his best adventure novels, featuring a new set of characters. Professor Challenger, the combative zoology professor, throws down challenges to the scientific world. At the beginning of *The Lost World* he maintains that on a previous visit to the Amazon he has seen evidence of the existence of prehistoric animals and people, and persuades three men to go with him on a new expedition: Professor Summerlee, a botanist, Lord John Roxton, a hunter and explorer, and James Malone, a young reporter on the *Gazette*. Malone narrates the story in the form of reports to his Scottish editor, McArdle, back in London.

In *The Lost World* Conan Doyle established the contrasting characters that he drew on for its sequel, *The Poison Belt* (1913). Challenger could not be more different from Sherlock Holmes in appearance—he is short, barrel-chested, red-cheeked and black-haired, with a thick "Assyrian" beard. Arrogant, hot-tempered and willing to come to blows to defend his theories, he has a comically exaggerated self-confidence and sense of superiority, and enrages the members of the Zoological Society. But, like Holmes, he is dedicated to a ruling passion, is master of information unknown to anyone else and has a brilliant knack of finding a way out of an apparently impossible jam. In *The Lost World* Challenger announced his optimistic credo: whatever the problem, he "cannot doubt that the intellect can solve it." Summerlee, his physical opposite, is a sneering and equally contentious botanist. As with Sherlock Holmes, Conan Doyle based these characters on recognizable Edinburgh professors. Throughout *The Lost World* he extracts plenty of fun from the quarrelsome and vain couple. At one point, attacked by a fearsome tribe of ape-men, they continue a heated debate about exactly what species they belong to. Lord John Roxton is a huntin' and fishin' man, and he and young Malone provide the common sense and muscle for the expedition.

The Lost World is a classic adventure story, where our heroes face one problem and joyously overcome it, only to confront another round the corner. It takes place among savages, carnivorous dinosaurs and swamp-dwelling pterodactyls. *The Poison Belt,* a sort of doomsday comedy, is a science fiction set in Conan Doyle's contemporary England. At the *Gazette* in London, Malone hears the disturbing news that whole populations in tropical countries are falling ill and dying for no discernible reason. At the same time Professor Challenger summons him down to his house in the country, and asks him to bring a canister of oxygen. At the shop he meets Summerlee and Roxton on the same errand. There *is* something strange in the air—the cabdriver picks a quarrel when Malone cancels his ride to the station, and people seem to be driving erratically and fighting on street-corners. Once in the train the friends quarrel bitterly and Summerlee is especially rude. Later on, it transpires that all three have been talking nonstop nonsense and have paid no attention to what anyone else is saying. Challenger then tells them the reason. He theorizes that the earth is entering a belt of poisonous ether that will exterminate mankind and that they are suffering its first effects.

Conan Doyle uses the comedy of character to keep the tone light, even when they are destined to be the last people left on earth. Challenger is an irascible employer at the best of times, and has once again fired Austin, his loyal chauffeur and butler. This comic exchange between the gloomy master and imperturbable servant shows why Wodehouse so admired Conan Doyle:

"Austin!" said his master.

"Yes, sir?"

"I thank you for your faithful service."

A smile stole over the servant's gnarled face.

"I've done my duty, sir."

"I'm expecting the end of the world today, Austin."

"Yes, sir. What time, sir?"

"I can't say, Austin. Before evening."

"Very good, sir."

According to Challenger's telegrams, "the less developed races" have already been wiped out, and people in the northern latitudes are slower to succumb. Conan Doyle gets off some witty barbs about the mental excitement that the poison causes: reports from France indicate riots in Paris, "Tumult of vine growers at Nîmes. Socialistic upheaval at Toulon"—as if Socialism were a feverish disorder. There is a fairy-tale element in the novel, as the group (kept alive by their oxygen) look out of the window and see people, like the inhabitants in Sleeping Beauty's castle, who have dropped in their tracks. The conclusion of the novel is equally magical.

Conan Doyle had lost his faith in Christianity in his student days. But in 1893, the year his father died and his wife Louise contracted tuberculosis, he'd joined the Society for Psychical Research. It had many socially prominent members and was keen to use his fame to promote their beliefs. For many years he'd been interested in the possible existence of spirits, and in Southsea he had joined in seances and table-turning, a popular diversion in those days. After he joined the Society he participated in poltergeist investigations, and seems to have convinced himself of the existence of the spirit world.

Challenger's reflections on death and dying in *The Poison Belt* seem to foreshadow the direction of Conan Doyle's views. In response to Summerlee's materialism, Challenger argues: "Nature may build a beautiful door and hang it with many a gauzy and shimmering curtain to make an entrance to the new life for our wondering souls. In all my probings of the actual, I have always found wisdom and kindness at the core; and if ever the frightened mortal needs tenderness, it is surely as he makes the passage perilous from life to life." Death, he claims, cannot destroy that "something" in each of us "which uses matter, but is not of it." Challenger's wife falls into a swoon as she is overcome by the poison, and is revived with oxygen. "Oh, George," she exclaims, "I am so sorry you brought me back. . . . The door of death is indeed, as you said, hung with beautiful, shimmering curtains; for, once the choking feeling had passed, it was all unspeakably soothing and beautiful. Why have you dragged me back?"

Conan Doyle uses the "what if?" suppositions of science fiction to discuss other issues besides the question of life after death. The men wonder if they can rescue anything from the centuries of culture and learning that have apparently come to an end. The idea of the termination of all human life stands in vivid contrast to the perfect summer day outside and the calm, settled, perfect world that is prewar England's green and pleasant land. The young nursemaid who drops dead by the side of the road, along with the baby in the baby carriage, is a poignant image of new life destroyed. H.G. Wells' *In the Days of the Comet* (1906), another science fiction novel about the impact on the population of a natural cataclysm—the collision of the earth with a comet—predates *The Poison Belt* by some years and provides an interesting comparison. Wells, more optimistic about the uses of technology than Conan Doyle, imagines the comet bringing about radical yet benign social change. *The Poison Belt*, however, shows that Conan Doyle wanted the world to stay the same. As different as they are, both writers seemed to be sensing— and fearing—that they were coming to the end of an era.

In "Danger! Being the Log of Captain John Sirius," the fear is no longer vague and is focused on the enemy. Conan Doyle combines the roles of pamphleteer, polemicist and storyteller in a futuristic, technological story about submarine warfare. This effective piece of propaganda, published in the *Strand* in February 1914, was written to show the British public how vulnerable they would be in the coming war. Several naval experts were invited to comment on the story, and their remarks were published alongside it. Most agreed that a food stockpile was an urgent necessity, but doubted that the advanced submarines described in the story could be built in the near future. Two admirals maintained that no civilized nation would attack defenseless merchant ships or neutral vessels, or violate territorial waters. Such ostrich-like responses enraged Conan Doyle. A year later, the Germans announced a plan to blockade England by sinking merchant vessels, and in a propaganda twist of their own, attributed the idea to Conan Doyle.

The boastful and proud Captain Sirius, commander of a fleet of eight submarines belonging to Norland ("one of the smallest powers in Europe," but clearly referring to Germany), tells an exciting David-and-Goliath story, set a year in the future, in 1915. When war is declared the British Navy has easily captured Norland's main ports and disabled her shipping, but Sirius' nimble fleet eludes British planes and ships, effectively blockades the British Isles and starves the nation into submission. With a fleet of small, powerful submarines, carrying a limited crew and an extra number of narrow torpedoes, as well as extra fuel and supplies, Sirius has forced Britain to surrender.

Despite the rumors of war on the continent, England in early 1914 was a complacent country. It had a great source of wealth in its Empire, which provided captive markets for its industries, and had had no experience of major wars for nearly a hundred years. The story was designed to shock—war had not yet been declared—and Conan Doyle used a variety of techniques to construct a convincing sequence of events. He mastered the nautical jargon sufficiently to suggest life on board a submarine, and used specific geographical points and place-names to indicate the attacks. He devised newspaper headlines and reports, sometimes in ironic contrast to the events as seen by Captain Sirius—a technique Orwell imitated in *Nineteen Eighty-Four*. The sinkings are punctuated by the announcements of the price of wheat, maize and barley, which serve to prove the captain's point. The cold, military mind of the narrator sneers at the British notions of fair play and international law. The openness of the press helps him plan his strategy and, because the conventional British defenses can do little to stop him, he sinks neutral ships with impunity.

Conan Doyle's prediction came true. The Germans conducted a deadly campaign against British merchant shipping and even sank ships of neutral nations that brought goods to Britain. Sirius describes the sinking of a magnificent ship which went down "like a broken eggshell." In May 1915, just over a year after the story was published, German submarines sank the *Lusitania*, a British luxury liner, off the Irish coast. Well over a thousand lives, including 124 Americans, were lost, and this disaster influenced the American decision to enter the war. Conan Doyle wrote the story to urge action, and he partly succeeded. By the end of the war the British had developed depth-charges and other methods to counter submarines, and took measures to store supplies and improve food production. One of his key ideas was recently carried out: the building of a tunnel under the English Channel.

It was highly ironic that the German invasion in August 1914 of "gallant little Belgium," which had so recently committed unspeakable atrocities in the Congo, was the immediate cause of Britain's entry into World War I. In May 1916—between the German attack on Verdun and the Second Battle of Ypres—Conan Doyle, rigged out in a specially designed uniform, left for France on a navy destroyer with General Sir William Robertson, the British chief of staff, to visit the British, French and Italian fronts. On his return he published *A Visit to Three Fronts* (1916).

As an important national figure and tremendously persuasive patriot, Conan Doyle was kept well out of danger. He reported glimpses and impressions rather than actual military combat; mixed first-hand accounts and propaganda; and took childish delight in the bloody carnage. He idealized and hero-worshipped the soldiers at the front, and said they had "hard, strong, rugged features, and the eyes of men who have seen strange sights."

Though the soldiers wallowed in mud and were infested with lice and rats, Conan Doyle thought the front trench was "surely the most wonderful spot in the world." The Ypres Salient, at which so many men had been and would be slaughtered, he romanticized as a "marvelous spectacle." The ruined town, pulverized to nothingness, was in Conan Doyle's insistent poetic alliteration, a Poesque "city of a dream, this modern Pompeii, destroyed, deserted and desecrated, but with a sad, proud dignity." Employing a striking image, he described Germany as "a weary and furious bull, tethered fast in place of trespass and waiting for the inevitable pole-axe." Unfortunately, Europe had to endure two and a half more years of war and millions of civilian and military deaths before a doomed Germany would finally succumb to the mortal blow.

Conan Doyle's naive, buoyant and boyish book was effective and no doubt sincere propaganda. Caught up in the jingoistic atmosphere of 1916, he sneered at conscientious objectors, whom he called "neurotic and largely be-spectacled." Though his visit was stage-managed, he lacked the imagination to grasp the true horrors of trench warfare on the Western front, had no idea of where the war was going and what it would achieve. It needed the savage poetry of Edward Thomas and Siegfried Sassoon, Robert Graves and Isaac Rosenberg to bring home the truth—along with all the mutilated bodies, after the war was over—that the sacrifice had been meaningless. In Wilfred Owen's poems, the British soldiers are battered and exhausted:

> Bent double, like old beggars under sacks,
> Knock-kneed, coughing like hags, we cursed through sludge,
> Till on the haunting flares we turned our backs,
> And towards our distant rest began to trudge.

Though it may seem unfair to compare the greatest war poetry with a piece of military propaganda, its grim vision puts Conan Doyle's good cheer in its proper perspective.

The death in October 1918 of his son Kingsley—weakened from his injuries on the Somme and a victim of the influenza epidemic—finally brought home to Conan Doyle the cost of this terrible war. His bereavement served to deepen his commitment to Spiritualism, which allowed him to believe that his son had not only entered a better world, but was also present among the living. Conan Doyle's attitude to religion was typical of a certain type of educated Victorian whose faith was challenged by the new scientific discoveries. Born in the same year that Darwin published *The Origin of Species*, he detested his religious indoctrination at Stonyhurst, his Jesuit boarding school, and rejected his family's Catholicism. For years he'd maintained that it was impossible to believe in something he could not see and could not be proved. Unlike other intellectuals who replaced Christianity with humanism, he paradoxically became fascinated by all aspects of the occult—hypnotism, Theosophy and oriental mysticism. In 1917 he astonished friends and readers by publicly announcing his conversion to Spiritualism. This quasi-religion attempted to communicate through mediums with the spirits of the dead and to make sense of this world through insights from the other-world.

Conan Doyle's *The Wanderings of a Spiritualist* (1921) is a rather rambling account of his lecture tour to Australia and New Zealand. He took his wife Jean (Louise had died in 1906 and he had remarried a year later) and their three young children, as well as the children's nanny, the redoubtable Jakeman, and his secretary, Major Wood. In the first chapter he announces the purpose of his trip: to enlighten as many people as possible about "the overwhelming importance of this subject. . . . All other work which I had ever done, or could ever do, was as nothing compared to this." He wants to "bring consolation to bruised hearts"—to those grieving for sons and husbands lost in World War I.

At Gibraltar, the first stop in his itinerary, Conan Doyle takes the opportunity to urge the English to hand it back to Spain or exchange it for Ceuta, the Spanish city on the coast of Morocco. The ship then goes to Aden and Colombo, and makes its first stop at Fremantle, in Western Australia. Chapter III (included here) covers his visit to Adelaide, where he was respectfully received. He went on to Melbourne, where he met some stormy hecklers and got a hotter reception from the press, and to Sydney. He then traveled to New Zealand by ship, making the short but stormy passage from North to South Island. Conan Doyle acknowledges that his book is an unstructured affair, but his relaxed epistolary style is always readable. It's a mixture of travelogue, political and social commentary, remarks on the recent war (he barely disguises his loathing of the Germans) and accounts of his own lectures and social contacts, especially his meetings with locally famous mediums. In missionary mode, he lectured on the ship when asked to do so.

Upon his arrival in Adelaide he meets Mr. Smythe, the impresario who accompanies them on the trip and constantly expresses his amazement at the huge audiences he's attracted. Conan Doyle made about £750 profit from the tour, even after paying the expenses for his party of seven, and he proudly includes this information. He used the money to set up a Spiritualist foundation in Australia. In Chapter III he also includes some pages of local color, reporting on the Australian drought and the indebtedness and despair of farmers, as well as his meeting with Bellchambers, a rugged immigrant farmer from Sussex. The book is shamelessly padded with quotations from the press and references to Conan Doyle's "world celebrity and his mission." In this chapter he includes a flattering two-page quotation, about his moving speech and rapturous reception, that describes his "big arresting presence," his "kindly strength," his "winning animation when the sun of his rich humour plays on the powerful features."

In Conan Doyle's definition of Spiritualism, the "mere phenomena"—the messages conveyed through mediums, the ghostly movements—were just the spirits' way of getting our attention. The glory of Spiritualism was that the dead could share their "wisdom" with us and urge us to have no fear of death. The dead can "tell us about their own conditions, their present experiences, their outlook upon the secret of the universe." Conan Doyle follows up his lectures with exhibitions of "psychic pictures and photographs" which include "choice samples from the very best collections." According to Conan Doyle, everyone who sees them is "staggered." But they were obviously faked. They consisted of images superimposed upon photographs—as in some infamous "fairies at the bottom of the garden" pictures—or negatives that had been mishandled, so that blotches or mist appeared on the photograph.

The typical seance is attended by people in a highly emotional state, hoping the medium will allow them to speak to a dead beloved. The medium goes into a trance, a "control" (who may be a Chinese or ancient Egyptian) speaks through the medium in a hollow, scary voice; the beloved's voice or even ghostly shape appears and reassures the participants that life persists "on the other side." Conan Doyle constantly argues, in this book and elsewhere, that although some mediums are charlatans (as many of them were proved to be), if even one case of communication with the dead could be proved valid, then the whole doctrine of Spiritualism was proven. Of course, no such case has ever been documented. This is where Conan Doyle made his leap of faith, and convinced himself that his encounters with spirits were genuine.

His wife Jean went in for automatic writing and was a medium herself. Not surprisingly, Conan Doyle was far more hostile to the Catholic and Anglican clergy who opposed him than to "materialists," agnostics or atheists who did not believe in any spiritual dimension to life.

Despite his scientific and medical background, the book makes clear that Conan Doyle was extremely gullible and rarely met a medium he didn't like. He describes clairvoyants who solve crimes, or make successful prophecies; he even accepts that some clairvoyants are "magnetic healers" who can "see" cancers through the flesh. He defends Bailey, an "apport medium," who brought objects like Assyrian tablets, Turkish coins, tortoises and live birds hurtling into the room. He praises Mrs. Roberts, a New Zealand medium who put him in contact with his wife's mother, and with Dr. Russell Wallace, a Spiritualist leader. (Wallace, speaking from the other world, naturally commends Conan Doyle for his work.) A Mrs. Foster Turner sees the spirit of Dr. Wallace standing next to Conan Doyle on the lecture platform, and Conan Doyle is very gratified to hear it.

Conan Doyle was desperate to believe, and he was not alone. Spiritualism—at its lowest level a popular diversion at the turn of the nineteenth century, involving table-turning and seances in darkened rooms—continued to intrigue some of the greatest artists and writers of the twentieth, who at times have expounded the most bizarre and irrational ideas. The painters Kasimir Malevich, Wassily Kandinsky and Piet Mondrian were all followers of Madame Blavatsky's Theosophy. In "An Experience in the Occult" and the "Highly Questionable" chapter of *The Magic Mountain*, Thomas Mann satirized the dubious phenomena of hypnotism and somnambulism, telepathy and second sight, and described the horrific seance in which Hans Castorp begs forgiveness for disturbing his cousin Joachim's post-mortem rest. Yeats, Graves, Huxley, Koestler, Auden and Isherwood all plunged into the mists of the supernatural, the paranormal and the crankish. More recently, the poet James Merrill experimented with and wrote poems about his Ouija board. The Catholic Church has consistently opposed Spiritualism, but has recently felt compelled to conduct a number of exorcisms. Even Saul Bellow, referring to his involvement with the madcap theories of Wilhelm Reich and Rudolf Steiner, admitted: "I'm gullible about spirituality. I have a weakness for it."

The Wanderings of a Spiritualist has some provocative ideas, and is worth reading for its view of Australia and New Zealand in the 1920s. We occasionally see flashes of the old Conan Doyle humor, observation and satiric poise, but all too often these are smothered in the earnestness of his quest. Worst of all is the inescapable conclusion that his success and status had persuaded him to accept, rather than to question, the world as it was and gave him an exaggerated sense of his own importance. His tolerance for the bogus paraphernalia of Spiritualism betrayed him into fuzzy thinking, and led him into an artistic dead end.

Conan Doyle's belief in Spiritualism, commonplace in his day, was remarkable only for its persistence and intensity. It led him away from the work he did best, alarmed his publishers, and hurt his sales and his reputation as a writer. Yet these absurd pursuits were in keeping with his energetic, tender-hearted and essentially innocent nature. He had lived through grinding poverty, his first wife's protracted illness and the death of his son. He had seen the horrors of the Boer War and World War I, which had swept away the certainties of Victorian and Edwardian England. In the face of private and public calamity Conan Doyle retained the confident optimism of his youth. This quality made him a beloved writer in his own time and one who still appeals to readers of all ages. Whatever the obstacle—wild beasts on jungle trails in the Amazon or ruffians in slimy London backstreets—he assures us that we can and will see it through. A master of the detective story and the ripping yarn, he showed in everything he wrote, whether serious or lighthearted, good humor and an almost boyish trust in life.

CHRONOLOGY

1859 Born May 22 in Edinburgh, second child of Charles Doyle and Mary Foley.

1868 Attends Hodder, the prep school for Stonyhurst.

1870–1874 Attends Stonyhurst, a Jesuit school in Lancashire. Excels in cricket and shows first signs of literary talent.

1874 Visits his uncle Richard Doyle, illustrator for *Punch*, in London.

1875 Spends year at Jesuit school in Feldkrich, Austria.

1876 Studies medicine at Edinburgh University. Meets Dr. Joseph Bell, a model for Sherlock Holmes, and the anatomist Professor Rutherford, a model for Professor Challenger.

1878 While still a student, takes summer job assisting doctors in Sheffield and Shropshire.

1879 Father goes into a nursing home. Conan Doyle works as assistant to Dr. Hoare in Birmingham. Publishes his early stories anonymously.

1880 Seven-month voyage as ship's doctor on Arctic whaler. First interest in spiritualism and the paranormal.

1881 Earns medical degree. Second term assisting Dr. Hoare. Second voyage as ship's doctor on cargo steamer to West Africa. Nearly dies of fever.

1882 Loses Catholic faith. Begins medical practice in Southsea, near Portsmouth.

1883 First story in *Cornhill* magazine.

1884 Begins novel, *The Firm of Girdlestone*, published in 1890.

1885 Marries Louise Hawkins, sister of a patient.

1887 First Sherlock Holmes story, *A Study in Scarlet.*

1889 Daughter Mary Louise born. *Micah Clarke.*

1890 Visits Berlin to investigate Robert Koch's claim to having discovered cure for tuberculosis. *The Sign of the Four.*

1891 Gives up Southsea practice. Studies ophthalmology in Vienna for two months. Returns to London and fails to establish practice as eye specialist. Decides to give up medicine and write full time. Six Holmes stories in *Strand* magazine. *The White Company.*

1892 Goes to Norway with writer Jerome K. Jerome and skis for the first time. Son Kingsley born. *The Adventures of Sherlock Holmes.*

1893 Father dies. Louise contracts tuberculosis and given only a few months to live. They move to Davos, Switzerland, where Conan Doyle popularizes skiing as a sport. Kills off Holmes in "The Final Problem." Joins Psychical Research Society.

1894 Successful lecture tour in America. *Round the Red Lamp.*

1895 Builds house in Hindhead, Surrey. Spends winter in Egypt for Louise's health. *The Stark Munro Letters.*

1896 Travels up Nile to Sudan. War correspondent for *Westminster Gazette* when fighting breaks out between British and Dervishes. *The Exploits of Brigadier Gerard* and *Rodney Stone.*

1897 Falls in love with Jean Leckie, later his wife.

1899 Boer War begins. Volunteers for army but is rejected.

1900 Serves as medical officer in South Africa. *The Great Boer War* defends British treatment of the Boers. Defeated in parliamentary election. *The Green Flag.*

1901 Holmes returns in serialization of *The Hound of the Baskervilles*, but story takes place before his death.

1902   *The War in South Africa.* Knighted for defending British role in Boer War.

1903   "The Adventure of the Empty House" brings Holmes back from Reichenbach Falls. *Adventures of Gerard.*

1904   Fine performance in cricket match against Cambridgeshire.

1906   Second defeat in parliamentary election. Takes up cause of George Edalji, unjustly jailed in 1903. Involved in reform of divorce law. Lady Doyle dies after a long illness. *Sir Nigel.*

1907   George Edalji released from prison. Conan Doyle marries Jean Leckie. *Through the Magic Door.*

1908   *Round the Fire Stories.*

1909   *The Crime of the Congo* exposes Belgian cruelties in Africa.

1910   Second son, Adrian, born.

1911   Participates in Anglo-German motor race, won by the British.

1912   Introduces Professor Challenger in *The Lost World.* Daughter Lena Jean born. *The Case of Oscar Slater,* pamphlet defending man convicted of murder. Death sentence commuted to life imprisonment.

1913   *The Poison Belt.*

1914   Joins local volunteer force when Great War breaks out. Patriotic pamphlet *To Arms!*

1915   Begins 6-volume history, *The British Campaign in France and Flanders,* completed in 1920. *The Valley of Fear.*

1916   Observes British, French and Italian fronts. Meets Haig and other generals. *A Visit to Three Fronts.* Appeals for reprieve of Roger Casement, who's executed for treason.

1917   *His Last Bow.* Publicly announces conversion to Spiritualism.

1918   After being wounded on the Somme, son Kingsley dies of pneumonia. First book on Spiritualism, *The New Revelation. Danger! and Other Stories.*

1919   His brother Innes dies of pneumonia.

I

⌒

From *A Study in Scarlet*
(1887)

PART I
BEING A REPRINT FROM THE REMINISCENCES OF
JOHN H. WATSON, M.D.,
LATE OF THE ARMY MEDICAL DEPARTMENT

Chapter 1
Mr. Sherlock Holmes

In the years 1878 I took my degree of Doctor of Medicine of the University of London, and proceeded to Netley to go through the course prescribed for surgeons in the Army. Having completed my studies there, I was duly attached to the Fifth Northumberland Fusiliers as assistant surgeon. The regiment was stationed in India at the time, and before I could join it, the second Afghan war had broken out. On landing at Bombay, I learned that my corps had advanced through the passes, and was already deep in the enemy's country. I followed, however, with many other officers who were in the same situation as myself, and succeeded in reaching Candahar in safety, where I found my regiment, and at once entered upon my new duties.

The campaign brought honours and promotion to many, but for me it had nothing but misfortune and disaster. I was removed from my brigade and attached to the Berkshires, with whom I served at the fatal battle of Maiwand. There I was struck on the shoulder by a Jezail bullet, which shattered the bone and grazed the subclavian artery. I should have fallen into the hands of the murderous Ghazis had it not been for the devotion and courage shown by Murray, my orderly, who threw me across a pack horse, and succeeded in bringing me safely to the British lines.

Worn with pain, and weak from the prolonged hardships which I had undergone, I was removed, with a great train of wounded sufferers, to the base hospital at Peshawar. Here I rallied, and had already improved so far as to be able to walk about the wards, and even to bask a little upon the veranda, when I was struck down by enteric fever, that curse of our Indian possessions. For months my life was despaired of, and when at last I came to myself and became convalescent, I was so weak and emaciated that a medical board determined that not a day should be lost in sending me back to England. I was despatched, accordingly, in the troopship *Orontes*, and landed a month later on Portsmouth jetty, with my health irretrievably ruined, but with permission from a paternal government to spend the next nine months in attempting to improve it.

I had neither kith nor kin in England, and was therefore as free as air—or as free as an income of eleven shillings and sixpence a day will permit a man to be. Under such circumstances I naturally gravitated to London, that great cesspool into which all the loungers and idlers of the Empire are irresistibly drained. There I stayed for some time at a private hotel in the Strand, leading a comfortless, meaningless existence, and spending such money as I had, considerably more freely than I ought. So alarming did the state of my finances become, that I soon realized that I must either leave the metropolis and rusticate somewhere in the country, or that I must make a complete alteration in my style of living. Choosing the latter alternative, I began by making up my mind to leave the hotel, and take up my quarters in some less pretentious and less expensive domicile.

On the very day that I had come to this conclusion, I was standing at the Criterion Bar, when someone tapped me on the shoulder, and turning round I recognized young Stamford, who had been a dresser under me at Bart's. The sight of a friendly face in the great wilderness of London is a pleasant thing indeed to a lonely man. In old days Stamford had never been a particular crony of mine, but now I hailed him with enthusiasm, and he, in his turn, appeared to be delighted to see me. In the exuberance of my joy, I asked him to lunch with me at the Holborn, and we started off together in a hansom.

"Whatever have you been doing with yourself, Watson?" he asked in undisguised wonder, as we rattled through the crowded London streets. "You are as thin as a lath and as brown as a nut."

I gave him a short sketch of my adventures, and had hardly concluded it by the time that we reached our destination.

"Poor devil!" he said, commiseratingly, after he had listened to my misfortunes. "What are you up to now?"

"Looking for lodgings," I answered. "Trying to solve the problem as to whether it is possible to get comfortable rooms at a reasonable price."

"That's a strange thing," remarked my companion; "you are the second man today that has used that expression to me."

"And who was the first?" I asked.

"A fellow who is working at the chemical laboratory up at the hospital. He was bemoaning himself this morning because he could not get someone to go halves with him in some nice rooms which he had found, and which were too much for his purse."

"By Jove!" I cried; "if he really wants someone to share the rooms and the expense, I am the very man for him. I should prefer having a partner to being alone."

Young Stamford looked rather strangely at me over his wine glass. "You don't know Sherlock Holmes yet," he said; "perhaps you would not care for him as a constant companion."

"Why, what is there against him?"

"Oh, I didn't say there was anything against him. He is a little queer in his ideas—an enthusiast in some branches of science. As far as I know he is a decent fellow enough."

"A medical student, I suppose?" said I.

"No—I have no idea what he intends to go in for. I believe he is well up in anatomy, and he is a first-class chemist; but, as far as I know, he has never taken out any systematic medical classes. His studies are very desultory and eccentric, but he has amassed a lot of out-of-the-way knowledge which would astonish his professors."

"Did you never ask him what he was going in for?" I asked.

"No; he is not a man that it is easy to draw out, though he can be communicative enough when the fancy seizes him."

"I should like to meet him," I said. "If I am to lodge with anyone, I should prefer a man of studious and quiet habits. I am not strong enough yet to stand much noise or excitement. I had enough of both in Afghanistan to last me for the remainder of my natural existence. How could I meet this friend of yours?"

"He is sure to be at the laboratory," returned my companion. "He either avoids the place for weeks, or else he works there from morning till night. If you like, we will drive round together after luncheon."

"Certainly," I answered, and the conversation drifted away into other channels.

As we made our way to the hospital after leaving the Holborn, Stamford gave me a few more particulars about the gentleman whom I proposed to take as a fellow-lodger.

"You mustn't blame me if you don't get on with him," he said; "I know nothing more of him than I have learned from meeting him occasionally in the laboratory. You proposed this arrangement, so you must not hold me responsible."

"If we don't get on it will be easy to part company," I answered. "It seems to me, Stamford," I added, looking hard at my companion, "that you have some reason for washing your hands of the matter. Is this fellow's temper so formidable, or what is it? Don't be mealy-mouthed about it."

"It is not easy to express the inexpressible," he answered with a laugh. "Holmes is a little too scientific for my tastes—it approaches to cold-bloodedness. I could imagine his giving a friend a little pinch of the latest vegetable alkaloid, not out of malevolence, you understand, but simply out of a spirit of inquiry in order to have an accurate idea of the effects. To do him justice, I think that he would take it himself with the same readiness. He appears to have a passion for definite and exact knowledge."

"Very right too."

"Yes, but it may be pushed to excess. When it comes to beating the subjects in the dissecting-rooms with a stick, it is certainly taking rather a bizarre shape."

"Beating the subjects!"

"Yes, to verify how far bruises may be produced after death. I saw him at it with my own eyes."

"And yet you say he is not a medical student?"

"No. Heaven knows what the objects of his studies are. But here we are, and you must form your own impressions about him." As he spoke, we turned down a narrow lane and passed through a small side-door, which opened into a wing of the great hospital. It was familiar ground to me, and I needed no guiding as we ascended the bleak stone staircase and made our way down the long corridor with its vista of whitewashed wall and dun-coloured doors. Near the farther end a low arched passage branched away from it and led to the chemical laboratory.

This was a lofty chamber, lined and littered with countless bottles. Broad, low tables were scattered about, which bristled with retorts, test-tubes, and little Bunsen lamps, with their blue flickering flames. There was only one student in the room, who was bending over a distant table absorbed in his work. At the sound of our steps he glanced round and sprang to his feet with a cry of pleasure. "I've found it! I've found it," he shouted to my companion, running towards us with a test-tube in his hand. "I have found a re-agent which is precipitated by hæmoglobin, and by nothing else." Had he discovered a gold mine, greater delight could not have shone upon his features.

"Dr. Watson, Mr. Sherlock Holmes," said Stamford, introducing us.

"How are you?" he said cordially, gripping my hand with a strength for which I should hardly have given him credit. "You have been in Afghanistan, I perceive."

"How on earth did you know that?" I asked in astonishment.

"Never mind," said he, chuckling to himself. "The question now is about hæmoglobin. No doubt you see the significance of this discovery of mine?"

"It is interesting, chemically, no doubt," I answered, "but practically——"

"Why, man, it is the most practical medico-legal discovery for years. Don't you see that it gives us an infallible test for blood stains? Come over here now!" He seized me by the coat-sleeve in his eagerness, and drew me over to the table at which he had been working. "Let us have some fresh blood," he said, digging a long bodkin into his finger, and drawing off the resulting drop of blood in a chemical pipette. "Now, I add this small quantity of blood to a litre of water. You perceive that the resulting mixture has the appearance of pure water. The proportion of blood cannot be more than one in a million. I have no doubt, however, that we shall be able to obtain the characteristic reaction." As he spoke, he threw into the vessel a few white crystals, and then added some drops of a transparent fluid. In an instant the contents assumed a dull mahogany colour, and a brownish dust was precipitated to the bottom of the glass jar.

"Ha! Ha!" he cried, clapping his hands, and looking as delighted as a child with a new toy. "What do you think of that?"

"It seems to be a very delicate test," I remarked.

"Beautiful! beautiful! The old guaiacum test was very clumsy and uncertain. So is the microscopic examination for blood corpuscles. The latter is valueless if the stains are a few hours old. Now, this appears to act as well whether the blood is old or new. Had this test been invented, there are hundreds of men now walking the earth who would long ago have paid the penalty of their crimes."

"Indeed!" I murmured.

"Criminal cases are continually hinging upon that one point. A man is suspected of a crime months perhaps after it has been committed. His linen or clothes are examined and brownish stains discovered upon them. Are they blood stains, or mud stains, or rust stains, or fruit stains, or what are they? That is a question which has puzzled many an expert, and why? Because there was no reliable test. Now we have the Sherlock Holmes's test, and there will no longer be any difficulty."

His eyes fairly glittered as he spoke, and he put his hand over his heart and bowed as if to some applauding crowd conjured up by his imagination.

"You are to be congratulated," I remarked, considerably surprised at his enthusiasm.

"There was the case of Von Bischoff at Frankfort last year. He would certainly have been hung had this test been in existence. Then there was Mason of Bradford, and the notorious Muller, and Lefevre of Montpellier, and Samson of New Orleans. I could name a score of cases in which it would have been decisive."

"You seem to be a walking calendar of crime," said Stamford with a laugh. "You might start a paper on those lines. Call it the 'Police News of the Past.'"

"Very interesting reading it might be made, too," remarked Sherlock Holmes, sticking a small piece of plaster over the prick on his finger. "I have to be careful," he continued, turning to me with a smile, "for I dabble with poisons a good deal." He held out his hand as he spoke, and I noticed that it was all mottled over with similar pieces of plaster, and discoloured with strong acids.

"We came here on business," said Stamford, sitting down on a high three-legged stool, and pushing another one in my direction with his foot. "My friend here wants to take diggings; and as you were complaining that you could get no one to go halves with you, I thought that I had better bring you together."

Sherlock Holmes seemed delighted at the idea of sharing his rooms with me. "I have my eye on a suite in Baker Street," he said, "which would suit us down to the ground. You don't mind the smell of strong tobacco, I hope?"

"I always smoke 'ship's' myself," I answered.

"That's good enough. I generally have chemicals about, and occasionally do experiments. Would that annoy you?"

"By no means."

"Let me see—what are my other shortcomings? I get in the dumps at times, and don't open my mouth for days on end. You must not think I am sulky when I do that. Just let me alone, and I'll soon be right. What have you to confess now? It's just as well for two fellows to know the worst of one another before they begin to live together."

I laughed at this cross-examination. "I keep a bull pup," I said, "and I object to rows because my nerves are shaken, and I get up at all sorts of ungodly hours, and I am extremely lazy. I have another set of vices when I'm well, but those are the principal ones at present."

"Do you include violin playing in your category of rows?" he asked, anxiously.

"It depends on the player," I answered. "A well-played violin is a treat for the gods—a badly played one——"

"Oh, that's all right," he cried, with a merry laugh. "I think we may consider the thing as settled—that is, if the rooms are agreeable to you."

"When shall we see them?"

"Call for me here at noon to-morrow, and we'll go together and settle everything," he answered.

"All right—noon exactly," said I, shaking his hand.

We left him working among his chemicals, and we walked together towards my hotel.

"By the way," I asked suddenly, stopping and turning upon Stamford, "how the deuce did he know that I had come from Afghanistan?"

My companion smiled an enigmatical smile. "That's just his little peculiarity," he said. "A good many people have wanted to know how he finds things out."

"Oh! A mystery is it?" I cried, rubbing my hands. "This is very piquant. I am much obliged to you for bringing us together. 'The proper study of mankind is man,' you know."

"You must study him, then," Stamford said, as he bade me good-bye. "You'll find him a knotty problem, though. I'll wager he learns more about you than you about him. Good-bye."

"Good-bye," I answered, and strolled on to my hotel, considerably interested in my new acquaintance.

Chapter 2
The Science of Deduction

We met next day as he had arranged, and inspected the rooms at No. 221B, Baker Street, of which he had spoken at our meeting. They consisted of a couple of comfortable bedrooms and a single large airy sitting-room, cheerfully furnished, and illuminated by two broad windows. So desirable in every way were the apartments, and so moderate did the terms seem when divided between us, that the bargain was concluded upon the spot, and we at once entered into possession. That very evening I moved my things round from the hotel, and on the following morning Sherlock Holmes followed me with several boxes and portmanteaus. For a day or two we were busily employed in unpacking and laying out our property to the best advantage. That done, we gradually began to settle down and to accommodate ourselves to our new surroundings.

Holmes was certainly not a difficult man to live with. He was quiet in his ways, and his habits were regular. It was rare for him to be up after ten at night, and he had invariably breakfasted and gone out before I rose in the morning. Sometimes he spent his day at the chemical laboratory, sometimes in the dissecting-rooms, and occasionally in long walks, which appeared to take him into the lowest portions of the city. Nothing could exceed his energy when the working fit was upon him; but now and again a reaction would seize him, and for days on end he would lie upon the sofa in the sitting-room, hardly uttering a word or moving a muscle from morning to night. On these occasions I have noticed such a dreamy, vacant expression in his eyes, that I might have suspected him of being addicted to the use of some narcotic, had not the temperance and cleanliness of his whole life forbidden such a notion.

As the weeks went by, my interest in him and my curiosity as to his aims in life gradually deepened and increased. His very person and appearance were such as to strike the attention of the most casual observer. In height he was rather over six feet, and so excessively lean that he seemed to be considerably taller. His eyes were sharp and piercing, save during those intervals of torpor to which I have alluded; and his thin, hawk-like nose gave his whole expression an air of alertness and decision. His chin, too, had the prominence and squareness which mark the man of determination. His hands were invariably blotted with ink and stained with chemicals, yet he was possessed of extraordinary delicacy of touch, as I frequently had occasion to observe when I watched him manipulating his fragile philosophical instruments.

The reader may set me down as a hopeless busybody, when I confess how much this man stimulated my curiosity, and how often I endeavoured to break through the reticence which he showed on all that concerned himself. Before pronouncing judgment, however, be it remembered how objectless was my life, and how little there was to engage my attention. My health forbade me from venturing out unless the weather was exceptionally genial, and I had no friends who would call upon me and break the monotony of my daily existence. Under these circumstances, I eagerly hailed the little mystery which hung around my companion, and spent much of my time in endeavouring to unravel it.

He was not studying medicine. He had himself, in reply to a question, confirmed Stamford's opinion upon that point. Neither did he appear to have pursued any course of reading which might fit him for a degree in science or any other recognized portal which would give him an entrance into the learned world. Yet his zeal for certain studies was remarkable, and within eccentric limits his knowledge was so extraordinarily ample and minute that his observations have fairly astounded me. Surely no man would work so hard or attain such precise information unless he had some definite end in view. Desultory readers are seldom remarkable for the exactness of their learning. No man burdens his mind with small matters unless he has some very good reason for doing so.

His ignorance was as remarkable as his knowledge. Of contemporary literature, philosophy and politics he appeared to know next to nothing. Upon my quoting Thomas Carlyle, he inquired in the naïvest way who he might be and what he had done. My surprise reached a climax, however, when I found incidentally that he was ignorant of the Copernican Theory and of the composition of the Solar System. That any civilized human being in this nineteenth century should not be aware that the earth traveled round the sun appeared to me to be such an extraordinary fact that I could hardly realize it.

"You appear to be astonished," he said, smiling at my expression of surprise. "Now that I do know it I shall do my best to forget it."

"To forget it!"

"You see," he explained, "I consider that a man's brain originally is like a little empty attic, and you have to stock it with such furniture as you choose. A fool takes in all the lumber of every sort that he comes across, so that the knowledge which might be useful to him gets crowded out, or at best is jumbled up with a lot of other things, so that he has a difficulty in laying his hands upon it. Now the skillful workman is very careful indeed as to what he takes into his brain-attic. He will have nothing but the tools which may help him in doing his work, but of these he has a large assortment, and all in the most perfect order. It is a mistake to think that that little room has elastic walls and can distend to any extent. Depend upon it there comes a time when for every addition of knowledge you forget something that you knew before. It is of the highest importance, therefore, not to have useless facts elbowing out the useful ones."

"But the Solar System!" I protested.

"What the deuce is it to me?" he interrupted impatiently: "you say that we go round the sun. If we went round the moon it would not make a pennyworth of difference to me or to my work."

I was on the point of asking him what that work might be, but something in his manner showed me that the question would be an unwelcome one. I pondered over our short conversation, however, and endeavoured to draw my deductions from it. He said that he would acquire no knowledge which did not bear upon his object. Therefore all the knowledge which he possessed was such as would be useful to him. I enumerated in my own mind all the various points upon which he had shown me that he was exceptionally well informed. I even took a pencil and jotted them down. I could not help smiling at the document when I had completed it. It ran in this way:

Sherlock Holmes—his limits
  1. Knowledge of Literature.—Nil.
  2.   "   "   Philosophy.—Nil.
  3.   "   "   Astronomy.—Nil.
  4.   "   "   Politics.—Feeble.
  5.   "   "   Botany.—Variable.
      Well up in belladonna, opium, and poisons generally.
      Knows nothing of practical gardening.
  6. Knowledge of Geology.—Practical, but limited.
      Tells at a glance different soils from each other.
      After walks has shown me splashes upon his trousers, and told me by their colour and consistence in what part of London he had received them.
  7. Knowledge of Chemistry.—Profound.

8.   "   "   Anatomy.—Accurate, but unsystematic.
9.   "   "   Sensational Literature.—Immense.
     He appears to know every detail of every horror perpetrated in
     the century.
10. Plays the violin well.
11. Is an expert singlestick player, boxer, and swordsman.
12. Has a good practical knowledge of British law.

When I had got so far in my list I threw it into the fire in despair.
"If I can only find what the fellow is driving at by reconciling all these
accomplishments, and discovering a calling which needs them all," I said
to myself, "I may as well give up the attempt at once."
     I see that I have alluded above to his powers upon the violin. These
were very remarkable, but as eccentric as all his other accomplishments.
That he could play pieces, and difficult pieces, I knew well, because at
my request he has played me some of Mendelssohn's *Lieder*, and other
favourites. When left to himself, however, he would seldom produce any
music or attempt any recognized air. Leaning back in his armchair of an
evening, he would close his eyes and scrape carelessly at the fiddle which
was thrown across his knee. Sometimes the chords were sonorous and
melancholy. Occasionally they were fantastic and cheerful. Clearly they
reflected the thoughts which possessed him, but whether the music aided
those thoughts, or whether the playing was simply the result of a whim
or fancy, was more than I could determine. I might have rebelled against
these exasperating solos had it not been that he usually terminated them
by playing in quick succession a whole series of my favourite airs as a
slight compensation for the trial upon my patience.
     During the first week or so we had no callers, and I had begun to
think that my companion was as friendless a man as I was myself.
Presently, however, I found that he had many acquaintances, and those
in the most different classes of society. There was one little sallow, rat-
faced, dark-eyed fellow, who was introduced to me as Mr. Lestrade, and
who came three or four times in a single week. One morning a young girl
called, fashionably dressed, and stayed for half an hour or more. The
same afternoon brought a gray-headed, seedy visitor, looking like a Jew
peddler, who appeared to me to be much excited, and who was closely

followed by a slipshod elderly woman. On another occasion an old white-haired gentleman had an interview with my companion; and on another, a railway porter in his velveteen uniform. When any of these nondescript individuals put in an appearance, Sherlock Holmes used to beg for the use of the sitting-room, and I would retire to my bedroom. He always apologized to me for putting me to this inconvenience. "I have to use this room as a place of business," he said, "and these people are my clients." Again I had an opportunity of asking him a point-blank question, and again my delicacy prevented me from forcing another man to confide in me. I imagined at the time that he had some strong reason for not alluding to it, but he soon dispelled the idea by coming round to the subject of his own accord.

It was upon the 4th of March, as I have good reason to remember, that I rose somewhat earlier than usual, and found that Sherlock Holmes had not yet finished his breakfast. The landlady had become so accustomed to my late habits that my place had not been laid nor my coffee prepared. With the unreasonable petulance of mankind I rang the bell and gave a curt intimation that I was ready. Then I picked up a magazine from the table and attempted to while away the time with it, while my companion munched silently at his toast. One of the articles had a pencil mark at the heading, and I naturally began to run my eye through it.

Its somewhat ambitious title was "The Book of Life," and it attempted to show how much an observant man might learn by an accurate and systematic examination of all that came in his way. It struck me as being a remarkable mixture of shrewdness and of absurdity. The reasoning was close and intense, but the deductions appeared to me to be far fetched and exaggerated. The writer claimed by a momentary expression, a twitch of a muscle or a glance of an eye, to fathom a man's inmost thoughts. Deceit, according to him, was an impossibility in the case of one trained to observation and analysis. His conclusions were as infallible as so many propositions of Euclid. So startling would his results appear to the uninitiated that until they learned the processes by which he had arrived at them they might well consider him as a necromancer.

"From a drop of water," said the writer, "a logician could infer the possibility of an Atlantic or a Niagara without having seen or heard of one or the other. So all life is a great chain, the nature of which is known whenever we are shown a single link of it. Like all other arts, the Science of Deduction and Analysis is one which can only be acquired by long and patient study, nor is life long enough to allow any mortal to attain the highest possible perfection in it. Before turning to those moral and mental aspects of the matter which present the greatest difficulties, let the inquirer begin by mastering more elementary problems. Let him, on meeting a fellow-mortal, learn at a glance to distinguish the history of the man, and the trade or profession to which he belongs. Puerile as such an exercise may seem, it sharpens the faculties of observation, and teaches one where to look and what to look for. By a man's finger-nails, by his coat-sleeve, by his boots, by his trouser-knees, by the callosities of his forefinger and thumb, by his expression, by his shirtcuffs—by each of these things a man's calling is plainly revealed. That all united should fail to enlighten the competent inquirer in any case is almost inconceivable."

"What ineffable twaddle!" I cried, slapping the magazine down on the table; "I never read such rubbish in my life."

"What is it?" asked Sherlock Holmes.

"Why, this article," I said, pointing at it with my eggspoon as I sat down to my breakfast. "I see that you have read it since you have marked it. I don't deny that it is smartly written. It irritates me, though. It is evidently the theory of some armchair lounger who evolves all these neat little paradoxes in the seclusion of his own study. It is not practical. I should like to see him clapped down in a third-class carriage on the Underground, and asked to give the trades of all his fellow-travellers. I would lay a thousand to one against him."

"You would lose your money," Holmes remarked calmly. "As for the article, I wrote it myself."

"You!"

"Yes; I have a turn both for observation and for deduction. The theories which I have expressed there, and which appear to you to be so chimerical, are really extremely practical—so practical that I depend upon them for my bread and cheese."

"And how?" I asked involuntarily.

"Well, I have a trade of my own. I suppose I am the only one in the world. I'm a consulting detective, if you can understand what that is.

Here in London we have lots of government detectives and lots of private ones. When these fellows are at fault, they come to me, and I manage to put them on the right scent. They lay all the evidence before me, and I am generally able, by the help of my knowledge of the history of crime, to set them straight. There is a strong family resemblance about misdeeds, and if you have all the details of a thousand at your finger ends, it is odd if you can't unravel the thousand and first. Lestrade is a well-known detective. He got himself into a fog recently over a forgery case, and that was what brought him here."

"And these other people?"

"They are mostly sent on by private inquiry agencies. They are all people who are in trouble about something and want a little enlightening. I listen to their story, they listen to my comments, and then I pocket my fee."

"But do you mean to say," I said, "That without leaving your room you can unravel some knot which other men can make nothing of, although they have seen every detail for themselves?"

"Quite so. I have a kind of intuition that way. Now and again a case turns up which is a little more complex. Then I have to bustle about and see things with my own eyes. You see I have a lot of special knowledge which I apply to the problem, and which facilitates matters wonderfully. Those rules of deduction laid down in that article which aroused your scorn are invaluable to me in practical work. Observation with me is second nature. You appeared to be surprised when I told you, on our first meeting, that you had come from Afghanistan."

"You were told, no doubt."

"Nothing of the sort. I *knew* you came from Afghanistan. From long habit the train of thoughts ran so swiftly through my mind that I arrived at the conclusion without being conscious of intermediate steps. There were such steps, however. The train of reasoning ran, 'Here is a gentleman of a medical type, but with the air of a military man. Clearly an army doctor, then. He has just come from the tropics, for his face is dark, and that is not the natural tint of his skin, for his wrists are fair. He has undergone hardship and sickness, as his haggard face says clearly. His left arm has been injured. He holds it in a stiff and unnatural manner. Where in the tropics could an English army doctor have seen much hardship and got his arm wounded? Clearly in Afghanistan.' The whole train of thought did not occupy a second. I then remarked that you came from Afghanistan, and you were astonished."

"It is simple enough as you explain it," I said, smiling. "You remind me of Edgar Allan Poe's Dupin. I had no idea that such individuals did exist outside of stories."

Sherlock Holmes rose and lit his pipe. "No doubt you think that you are complimenting me in comparing me to Dupin," he observed. "Now, in my opinion, Dupin was a very inferior fellow. That trick of his of breaking in on his friends' thoughts with an apropos remark after a quarter of an hour's silence is really very showy and superficial. He had some analytical genius, no doubt; but he was by no means such a phenomenon as Poe appeared to imagine."

"Have you read Gaboriau's works?" I asked. "Does Lecoq come up to your idea of a detective?"

Sherlock Holmes sniffed sardonically. "Lecoq was a miserable bungler," he said, in an angry voice; "he had only one thing to recommend him, and that was his energy. That book made me positively ill. The question was how to identify an unknown prisoner. I could have done it in twenty-four hours. Lecoq took six months or so. It might be made a textbook for detectives to teach them what to avoid."

I felt rather indignant at having two characters whom I had admired treated in this cavalier style. I walked over to the window and stood looking out into the busy street. "This fellow may be very clever," I said to myself, "but he is certainly very conceited."

"There are no crimes and no criminals in these days," he said, querulously. "What is the use of having brains in our profession? I know well that I have it in me to make my name famous. No man lives or has ever lived who has brought the same amount of study and of natural talent to the detection of crime which I have done. And what is the result? There is no crime to detect, or, at most, some bungling villainy with a motive so transparent that even a Scotland Yard official can see through it."

I was still annoyed at his bumptious style of conversation. I thought it best to change the topic.

"I wonder what that fellow is looking for?" I asked, pointing to a stalwart, plainly dressed individual who was walking slowly down the other side of the street, looking anxiously at the numbers. He had a large blue envelope in his hand, and was evidently the bearer of a message.

"You mean the retired sergeant of Marines," said Sherlock Holmes.

"Brag and bounce!" thought I to myself. "He knows that I cannot verify his guess."

The thought had hardly passed through my mind when the man whom we were watching caught sight of the number on our door, and ran rapidly across the roadway. We heard a loud knock, a deep voice below, and heavy steps ascending the stair.

"For Mr. Sherlock Holmes," he said, stepping into the room and handing my friend the letter.

Here was an opportunity of taking the conceit out of him. He little thought of this when he made that random shot. "May I ask, my lad," I said, in the blandest voice, "what your trade may be?"

"Commissionaire, sir," he said, gruffly. "Uniform away for repairs."

"And you were?" I asked, with a slightly malicious glance at my companion.

"A sergeant, sir, Royal Marine Light Infantry, sir. No answer? Right, sir."

He clicked his heels together, raised his hand in salute, and was gone.

Chapter 3
The Lauriston Garden Mystery

I confess that I was considerably startled by this fresh proof of the practical nature of my companion's theories. My respect for his powers of analysis increased wondrously. There still remained some lurking suspicion in my mind, however, that the whole thing was a prearranged episode, intended to dazzle me, though what earthly object he could have in taking me in was past my comprehension. When I looked at him, he had finished reading the note, and his eyes had assumed the vacant, lack-lustre expression which showed mental abstraction.

"How in the world did you deduce that?" I asked.

"Deduce what?" said he, petulantly.

"Why, that he was a retired sergeant of Marines."

"I have no time for trifles," he answered, brusquely; then with a smile, "Excuse my rudeness. You broke the thread of my thoughts; but perhaps it is as well. So you actually were not able to see that that man was a sergeant of Marines?"

"No, indeed."

"It was easier to know it than to explain why I know it. If you were asked to prove that two and two made four, you might find some difficulty, and yet you are quite sure of the fact. Even across the street I could see a great blue anchor tattooed on the back of the fellow's hand. That smacked of the sea. He had a military carriage, however, and regulation side whiskers. There we have the marine. He was a man with some amount of self-importance and a certain air of command. You must have observed the way in which he held his head and swung his cane. A steady, respectable, middle-aged man, too, on the face of him—all facts which led me to believe that he had been a sergeant."

"Wonderful!" I ejaculated.

"Commonplace," said Holmes, though I thought from his expression that he was pleased at my evident surprise and admiration. "I said just now that there were no criminals. It appears that I am wrong—look at this!" He threw me over the note which the commissionaire had brought.

"Why," I cried, as I cast my eye over it, "this is terrible!"

"It does seem to be a little out of the common," he remarked, calmly. "Would you mind reading it to me aloud?"

This is the letter which I read to him,—

"MY DEAR MR. SHERLOCK HOLMES:

There has been a bad business during the night at 3, Lauriston Gardens, off the Brixton Road. Our man on the beat saw a light there about two in the morning, and as the house was an empty one, suspected that something was amiss. He found the door open, and in the front room, which is bare of furniture, discovered the body of a gentleman, well dressed, and having cards in his pocket bearing the name of 'Enoch J. Drebber, Cleveland, Ohio, U.S.A.' There had been no robbery, nor is there any evidence as to how the man met his death. There are marks of blood in the room, but there is no wound upon his person. We are at a loss as to how he came into the empty house; indeed, the whole affair is a puzzler. If you can come round to the house any time before twelve, you will find me there. I have left everything *in statu quo* until I hear from you. If you are unable to come, I shall give you fuller details, and would esteem it a great kindness if you would favour me with your opinions.

"Yours faithfully.

"TOBIAS GREGSON."

"Gregson is the smartest of the Scotland Yarders," my friend remarked; "he and Lestrade are the pick of a bad lot. They are both quick and energetic, but conventional—shockingly so. They have their knives into one another, too. They are as jealous as a pair of professional beauties. There will be some fun over this case if they are both put upon the scent."

I was amazed at the calm way in which he rippled on. "Surely there is not a moment to be lost," I cried; "shall I go and order you a cab?"

"I'm not sure about whether I shall go. I am the most incurably lazy devil that ever stood in shoe leather—that is, when the fit is on me, for I can be spry enough at times."

"Why, it is just such a chance as you have been longing for."

"My dear fellow, what does it matter to me? Supposing I unravel the whole matter, you may be sure that Gregson, Lestrade, and Co. will pocket all the credit. That comes of being an unofficial personage."

"But he begs you to help him."

"Yes. He knows that I am his superior, and acknowledges it to me; but he would cut his tongue out before he would own it to any third person. However, we may as well go and have a look. I shall work it out on my own hook. I may have a laugh at them, if I have nothing else. Come on!"

He hustled on his overcoat, and bustled about in a way that showed that an energetic fit had superseded the apathetic one.

"Get your hat," he said.

"You wish me to come?"

"Yes, if you have nothing better to do." A minute later we were both in a hansom, driving furiously for the Brixton Road.

It was a foggy, cloudy morning, and a dun-coloured veil hung over the housetops, looking like the reflection of the mud-coloured streets beneath. My companion was in the best of spirits, and prattled away about Cremona fiddles and the difference between a Stradivarius and an Amati. As for myself, I was silent, for the dull weather and the melancholy business upon which we were engaged depressed my spirits.

"You don't seem to give much thought to the matter in hand," I said at last, interrupting Holmes's musical disquisition.

"No data yet," he answered. "It is a capital mistake to theorize before you have all the evidence. It biases the judgment."

"You will have your data soon," I remarked, pointing with my finger; "this is the Brixton Road, and that is the house, if I am not very much mistaken."

"So it is. Stop, driver, stop!" We were still a hundred yards or so from it, but he insisted upon our alighting, and we finished our journey upon foot.

Number 3, Lauriston Gardens wore an ill-omened and minatory look. It was one of four which stood back some little way from the street, two being occupied and two empty. The latter looked out with three tiers of vacant melancholy windows, which were blank and dreary, save that here and there a "To Let" card had developed like a cataract upon the bleared planes. A small garden sprinkled over with a scattered eruption of sickly plants separated each of these houses from the street, and was traversed by a narrow pathway, yellowish in colour, and consisting apparently of a mixture of clay and of gravel. The whole place was very sloppy from the rain which had fallen through the night. The garden was bounded by a three-foot brick wall with a fringe of wood rails upon the top, and against this wall was leaning a stalwart police constable, surrounded by a small knot of loafers, who craned their necks and strained their eyes in the vain hope of catching some glimpse of the proceedings within.

I had imagined that Sherlock Holmes would at once have hurried into the house and plunged into a study of the mystery. Nothing appeared to be further from his intention. With an air of nonchalance which, under the circumstances, seemed to me to border upon affectation, he lounged up and down the pavement, and gazed vacantly at the

ground, the sky, the opposite houses and the line of railings. Having finished his scrutiny, he proceeded slowly down the path, or rather down
the fringe of grass which flanked the path, keeping his eyes riveted upon
the ground. Twice he stopped, and once I saw him smile, and heard him
utter an exclamation of satisfaction. There were many marks of footsteps upon the wet clayey soil; but since the police had been coming and
going over it, I was unable to see how my companion could hope to learn
anything from it. Still I had had such extraordinary evidence of the
quickness of his perceptive faculties, that I had no doubt that he could
see a great deal which was hidden from me.

At the door of the house we were met by a tall, white-faced, flaxen-
haired man, with a notebook in his hand, who rushed forward and
wrung my companion's hand with effusion. "It is indeed kind of you to
come," he said, "I have had everything left untouched."

"Except that!" my friend answered, pointing at the pathway. "If a
herd of buffaloes had passed along, there could not be a greater mess.
No doubt, however, you had drawn your own conclusions, Gregson, before you permitted this."

"I have had so much to do inside the house," the detective said eva-
sively. "My colleague, Mr. Lestrade, is here. I had relied upon him to
look after this."

Holmes glanced at me and raised his eyebrows sardonically. "With
two such men as yourself and Lestrade upon the ground, there will not
be much for a third party to find out," he said.

Gregson rubbed his hands in a self-satisfied way. "I think we have
done all that can be done," he answered; "it's a queer case, though, and I
knew your taste for such things."

"You did not come here in a cab?" asked Sherlock Holmes.

"No, sir."

"Nor Lestrade?"

"No, sir."

"Then let us go and look at the room." With which inconsequent remark he stroke on into the house followed by Gregson, whose features
expressed his astonishment.

A short passage, bare-planked and dusty, led to the kitchen and offices. Two doors opened out of it to the left and to the right. One of

these had obviously been closed for many weeks. The other belonged to the dining-room, which was the apartment in which the mysterious affair had occurred. Holmes walked in, and I followed him with that subdued feeling at my heart which the presence of death inspires.

It was a large square room, looking all the larger from the absence of all furniture. A vulgar flaring paper adorned the walls, but it was blotched in places with mildew, and here and there great strips had become detached and hung down, exposing the yellow plaster beneath. Opposite the door was a showy fireplace, surmounted by a mantelpiece of imitation white marble. On one corner of this was stuck the stump of a red wax candle. The solitary window was so dirty that the light was hazy and uncertain, giving a dull gray tinge to everything, which was intensified by the thick layer of dust which coated the whole apartment.

All these details I observed afterwards. At present my attention was centered upon the single, grim, motionless figure which lay stretched upon the boards, with vacant, sightless eyes staring up at the discoloured ceiling. It was that of a man about forty-three or forty-four years of age, middle-sized, broad-shouldered, with crisp curling black hair, and a short, stubbly beard. He was dressed in a heavy broadcloth frock coat and waistcoat, with light-coloured trousers, and immaculate collar and cuffs. A top hat, well brushed and trim, was placed upon the floor beside him. His hands were clenched and his arms thrown abroad, while his lower limbs were interlocked, as though his death struggle had been a grievous one. On his rigid face there stood an expression of horror, and, as it seemed to me, of hatred, such as I have never seen upon human features. This malignant and terrible contortion, combined with the low forehead, blunt nose, and prognathous jaw, gave the dead man a singularly simious and ape-like appearance, which was increased by his writhing, unnatural posture. I have seen death in many forms, but never has it appeared to me in a more fearsome aspect than in that dark, grimy apartment, which looked out upon one of the main arteries of suburban London.

Lestrade, lean and ferret-like as ever, was standing by the doorway, and greeted my companion and myself.

"This case will make a stir, sir," he remarked. "It beats anything I have seen, and I am no chicken."

"There is no clue?" said Gregson.

"None at all," chimed in Lestrade.

Sherlock Holmes approached the body, and, kneeling down, examined it intently. "You are sure that there is no wound?" he asked, pointing to numerous gouts and splashes of blood which lay all round.

"Positive!" cried both detectives.

"Then, of course, this blood belongs to a second individual—presumably the murderer, if murder has been committed. It reminds me of the circumstances attendant on the death of Van Jansen, in Utrecht, in the year '34. Do you remember the case, Gregson?"

"No, sir."

"Read it up—you really should. There is nothing new under the sun. It has all been done before."

As he spoke, his nimble fingers were flying here, there, and everywhere, feeling, pressing, unbuttoning, examining, while his eyes wore the same far-away expression which I have already remarked upon. So swiftly was the examination made, that one would hardly have guessed the minuteness with which it was conducted. Finally, he sniffed the dead man's lips, and then glanced at the soles of his patent leather boots.

"He has not been moved at all?" he asked.

"No more than was necessary for the purpose of our examination."

"You can take him to the mortuary now," he said. "There is nothing more to be learned."

Gregson had a stretcher and four men at hand. At his call they entered the room, and the stranger was lifted and carried out. As they raised him, a ring tinkled down and rolled across the floor. Lestrade grabbed it up and stared at it with mystified eyes.

"There's been a woman here," he cried. "It's a woman's wedding ring."

He held it out, as he spoke, upon the palm of his hand. We all gathered round him and gazed at it. There could be no doubt that that circlet of plain gold had once adorned the finger of a bride.

"This complicates matters," said Gregson. "Heaven knows, they were complicated enough before."

"You're sure it doesn't simplify them?" observed Holmes. "There's nothing to be learned by staring at it. What did you find in his pockets?"

"We have it all here," said Gregson, pointing to a litter of objects upon one of the bottom steps of the stairs. "A gold watch, No. 97163, by Barraud, of London. Gold Albert chain, very heavy and solid. Gold ring, with masonic device. Gold pin—bull-dog's head, with rubies as eyes. Russian leather cardcase, with cards of Enoch J. Drebber of Cleveland, corresponding with the E. J. D. upon the linen. No purse, but loose money to the extent of seven pounds thirteen. Pocket edition of Boccaccio's 'Decameron,' with name of Joseph Stangerson upon the flyleaf. Two letters—one addressed to E. J. Drebber and one to Joseph Stangerson."

"At what address?"

"American Exchange, Strand—to be left till called for. They are both from the Guion Steamship Company, and refer to the sailing of their boats from Liverpool. It is clear that this unfortunate man was about to return to New York."

"Have you made any inquiries as to this man Stangerson?"

"I did it at once, sir," said Gregson. "I have had advertisements sent to all the newspapers, and one of my men has gone to the American Exchange, but he has not returned yet."

"Have you sent to Cleveland?"

"We telegraphed this morning."

"How did you word your inquiries?"

"We simply detailed the circumstances, and said that we should be glad of any information which could help us."

"You did not ask for particulars on any point which appeared to you to be crucial?"

"I asked about Stangerson."

"Nothing else? Is there no circumstance on which this whole case appears to hinge? Will you not telegraph again?"

"I have said all I have to say," said Gregson, in an offended voice.

Sherlock Holmes chuckled to himself, and appeared to be about to make some remark, when Lestrade, who had been in the front room while we were holding this conversation in the hall, reappeared upon the scene, rubbing his hands in a pompous and self-satisfied manner.

"Mr. Gregson," he said, "I have just made a discovery of the highest importance, and one which would have been overlooked had I not made a careful examination of the walls."

The little man's eyes sparkled as he spoke, and he was evidently in a state of suppressed exultation at having scored a point against his colleague.

"Come here," he said, bustling back into the room, the atmosphere of which felt clearer since the removal of its ghastly inmate. "Now, stand there!"

He struck a match on his boot and held it up against the wall.

"Look at that!" he said, triumphantly.

I have remarked that the paper had fallen away in parts. In this particular corner of the room a large piece had peeled off, leaving a yellow square of coarse plastering. Across this bare space there was scrawled in blood-red letters a single word—

RACHE

"What do you think of that?" cried the detective, with the air of a showman exhibiting his show. "This was overlooked because it was in the darkest corner of the room, and no one thought of looking there. The murderer has written it with his or her own blood. See this smear where it has trickled down the wall! That disposes of the idea of suicide anyhow. Why was that corner chosen to write it on? I will tell you. See that candle on the mantelpiece. It was lit at the time, and if it was lit this corner would be the brightest instead of the darkest portion of the wall."

"And what does it mean now that you *have* found it?" asked Gregson in a depreciatory voice.

"Mean? Why, it means that the writer was going to put the female name Rachel, but was disturbed before he or she had time to finish. You mark my words, when this case comes to be cleared up, you will find that a woman named Rachel has something to do with it. It's all very well for you to laugh, Mr. Sherlock Holmes. You may be very smart and clever, but the old hound is the best, when all is said and done."

"I really beg your pardon!" said my companion, who had ruffled the little man's temper by bursting into an explosion of laughter. "You certainly have the credit of being the first of us to find this out and, as you say, it bears every mark of having been written by the other participant in last night's mystery. I have not had time to examine this room yet, but with your permission I shall do so now."

As he spoke, he whipped a tape measure and a large round magnifying glass from his pocket. With these two implements he trotted noiselessly about the room, sometimes stopping, occasionally kneeling, and once lying flat upon his face. So engrossed was he with his occupation that he appeared to have forgotten our presence, for he chattered away to himself under his breath the whole time, keeping up a running fire of exclamations, groans, whistles, and little cries suggestive of encouragement and of hope. As I watched him I was irresistibly reminded of a pure-blooded, well-trained foxhound, as it dashes backward and forward through the covert, whining in its eagerness, until it comes across the lost scent. For twenty minutes or more he continued his researches, measuring with the most exact care the distance between marks which were entirely invisible to me, and occasionally applying his tape to the walls in an equally incomprehensible manner. In one place he gathered up very carefully a little pile of gray dust from the floor, and packed it away in an envelope. Finally he examined with his glass the word upon the wall, going over every letter of it with the most minute exactness. This done, he appeared to be satisfied, for he replaced his tape and his glass in his pocket.

"They say that genius is an infinite capacity for taking pains," he remarked with a smile. "It's a very bad definition, but it does apply to detective work."

Gregson and Lestrade had watched the manœuvers of their amateur companion with considerable curiosity and some contempt. They evidently failed to appreciate the fact, which I had begun to realize, that Sherlock Holmes's smallest actions were all directed towards some definite and practical end.

"What do you think of it, sir?" they both asked.

"It would be robbing you of the credit of the case if I were to presume to help you," remarked my friend. "You are doing so well now that it would be a pity for anyone to interfere." There was a world of sarcasm in his voice as he spoke. "If you will let me know how your investigations go," he continued, "I shall be happy to give you any help I can. In the meantime I should like to speak to the constable who found the body. Can you give me his name and address?"

Lestrade glanced at his notebook. "John Rance," he said. "He is off duty now. You will find him at 46, Audley Court, Kennington Park Gate."

Holmes took a note of the address.

"Come along, Doctor," he said: "we shall go and look him up. I'll tell you one thing which may help you in the case," he continued, turning to the two detectives. "There has been murder done, and the murderer was a man. He was more than six feet high, was in the prime of life, had small feet for his height, wore coarse, square-toed boots and smoked a Trichinopoly cigar. He came here with his victim in a four-wheeled cab, which was drawn by a horse with three old shoes and one new one on his off fore-leg. In all probability the murderer had a florid face, and the finger-nails of his right hand were remarkably long. These are only a few indications, but they may assist you."

Lestrade and Gregson glanced at each other with an incredulous smile.

"If this man was murdered, how was it done?" asked the former.

"Poison," said Sherlock Holmes curtly, and strode off. "One other thing, Lestrade," he added, turning round at the door: "'Rache,' is the German for 'revenge'; so don't lose your time looking for Miss Rachel."

With which Parthian shot he walked away, leaving the two rivals open mouthed behind him.

Chapter 4
What John Rance Had to Tell

It was one o'clock when we left No. 3, Lauriston Gardens. Sherlock Holmes led me to the nearest telegraph office, whence he dispatched a long telegram. He then hailed a cab, and ordered the driver to take us to the address given us by Lestrade.

"There is nothing like first-hand evidence," he remarked; "as a matter of fact, my mind is entirely made up upon the case, but still we may as well learn all that is to be learned."

"You amaze me, Holmes," said I. "Surely you are not as sure as you pretend to be of all those particulars which you gave."

"There's no room for a mistake," he answered. "The very first thing which I observed on arriving there was that a cab had made two ruts with its wheels close to the curb. Now, up to last night, we have had no rain for a week, so that those wheels which left such a deep impression must have been there during the night. There were the marks of the horse's hoofs, too, the outline of one of which was far more clearly cut than that of the other three, showing that that was a new shoe. Since the cab was there after the rain began, and was not there at any time during the morning—I have Gregson's word for that—it follows that it must have been there during the night, and therefore, that it brought those two individuals to the house."

"That seems simple enough," said I; "but how about the other man's height?"

"Why, the height of a man, in nine cases out of ten, can be told from the length of his stride. It is a simple calculation enough, though there is no use my boring you with figures. I had this fellow's stride both on the clay outside and on the dust within. Then I had a way of checking my calculation. When a man writes on a wall, his instinct leads him to write above the level of his own eyes. Now that writing was just over six feet from the ground. It was child's play."

"And his age?" I asked.

"Well, if a man can stride four and half feet without the smallest effort, he can't be quite in the sere and yellow. That was the breadth of a puddle on the garden walk which he had evidently walked across. Patent-leather boots had gone round, and Square-toes had hopped over. There is no mystery about it at all. I am simply applying to ordinary life a few of those precepts of observation and deduction which I advocated in that article. Is there anything else that puzzles you?"

"The finger-nails and the Trichinopoly," I suggested.

"The writing on the wall was done with a man's forefinger dipped in blood. My glass allowed me to observe that the plaster was slightly scratched in doing it, which would not have been the case if the man's nail had been trimmed. I gathered up some scattered ash from the floor. It was dark in colour and flaky—such an ash is only made by a Trichinopoly. I have made a special study of cigar ashes—in fact, I have written a monograph upon the subject. I flatter myself that I can distinguish at a glance the ash of any known brand either of cigar or of tobacco. It is just in such details that the skilled detective differs from the Gregson and Lestrade type."

"And the florid face?" I asked.

"Ah, that was a more daring shot, though I have no doubt that I was right. You must not ask me that at the present state of the affair."

I passed my hand over my brow. "My head is in a whirl," I remarked; "the more one thinks of it the more mysterious it grows. How came these two men—if there were two men—into an empty house? What has become of the cabman who drove them? How could one man compel another to take poison? Where did the blood come from? What was the object of the murderer, since robbery had no part in it? How came the woman's ring there? Above all, why should the second man write up the German word RACHE before decamping? I confess that I cannot see any possible way of reconciling all these facts."

My companion smiled approvingly.

"You sum up the difficulties of the situation succinctly and well," he said. "There is much that is still obscure, though I have quite made up my mind on the main facts. As to poor Lestrade's discovery, it was simply a blind intended to put the police upon a wrong track, by suggesting Socialism and secret societies. It was not done by a German. The A, if you noticed, was printed somewhat after the German fashion. Now, a real German invariably prints in the Latin character, so that we may safely say that this was not written by one, but by a clumsy imitator who overdid his part. It was simply a ruse to divert inquiry into a wrong channel. I'm not going to tell you much more of the case, Doctor. You know a conjurer gets no credit when once he has explained his trick; and if I show you too much of my method of working, you will come to the conclusion that I am a very ordinary individual after all."

"I shall never do that," I answered; "you have brought detection as near an exact science as it ever will be brought in this world. "

My companion flushed up with pleasure at my words, and the earnest way in which I uttered them. I had already observed that he was as sensitive to flattery on the score of his art as any girl could be of her beauty.

"I'll tell you one other thing," he said. "Patent-leathers and Square-toes came in the same cab, and they walked down the pathway together as friendly as possible—arm-in-arm, in all probability. When they got inside, they walked up and down the room—or rather, Patent-leathers stood still while Square-toes walked up and down. I could read all that in the dust; and I could read that as he walked he grew more and more excited. That is shown by the increased length of his strides. He was talking all the while, and working himself up, no doubt, into a fury. Then the tragedy occurred. I've told you all I know myself now, for the rest is mere surmise and conjecture. We have a good working basis, however, on which to start. We must hurry up, for I want to go to Halle's concert to hear Neruda this afternoon."

This conversation had occurred while our cab had been threading its way through a long succession of dingy streets and dreary byways. In the dingiest and dreariest of them our driver suddenly came to a stand. "That's Audley Court in there," he said, pointing to a narrow slit in the line of dead-coloured brick. "You'll find me here when you come back."

Audley Court was not an attractive locality. The narrow passage led us into a quadrangle paved with flags and lined by sordid dwellings. We picked our way among groups of dirty children, and through lines of discoloured linen, until we came to Number 46, the door of which was decorated with a small slip of brass on which the name Rance was engraved. On inquiry we found that the constable was in bed, and we were shown into a little front parlour to await his coming.

He appeared presently, looking a little irritable at being disturbed in his slumbers. "I made my report at the office," he said.

Holmes took a half-sovereign from his pocket and played with it pensively. "We thought that we should like to hear it all from your own lips," he said.

"I shall be most happy to tell you anything I can," the constable answered, with his eyes upon the little golden disc.

"Just let us hear it all in your own way as it occurred."

Rance sat down on the horsehair sofa, and knitted his brows, as though determined not to omit anything in his narrative.

"I'll tell it ye from the beginning," he said. "My time is from ten at night to six in the morning. At eleven there was a fight at the White Hart; but bar that all was quiet enough on the beat. At one o'clock it began to rain, and I met Harry Murcher—him who has the Holland Grove beat—

and we stood together at the corner of Henrietta Street a-talkin'. Presently—maybe about two or a little after—I thought I would take a look round and see that all was right down the Brixton Road. It was precious dirty and lonely. Not a soul did I meet all the way down, though a cab or two went past me. I was a-strollin' down, thinkin' between ourselves how uncommon handy a four of gin hot would be, when suddenly the glint of a light caught my eye in the window of that same house. Now, I knew that them two houses in Lauriston Gardens was empty on account of him that owns them who won't have the drains seed to, though the very last tenant what lived in one of them died o' typhoid fever. I was knocked all in a heap, therefore, at seeing a light in the window, and I suspected as something was wrong. When I got to the door——"

"You stopped, and then walked back to the garden gate," my companion interrupted. "What did you do that for?"

Rance gave a violent jump, and stared at Sherlock Holmes with the utmost amazement upon his features.

"Why, that's true, sir," he said; "though how you come to know it, Heaven only knows. Ye see when I got up to the door, it was so still and so lonesome, that I thought I'd be none the worse for someone with me. I ain't afeared of anything on this side o' the grave; but I thought that maybe it was him that died o' the typhoid inspecting the drains what killed him. The thought gave me a kind o' turn, and I walked back to the gate to see if I could see Murcher's lantern, but there wasn't no sign of him nor of anyone else."

"There was no one in the street?"

"Not a livin' soul, sir, nor as much as a dog. Then I pulled myself together and went back and pushed the door open. All was quiet inside, so I went into the room where the light was a-burnin'. There was a candle flickerin' on the mantelpiece—a red wax one—and by its light I saw——"

"Yes, I know all that you saw. You walked round the room several times, and you knelt down by the body, and then you walked through and tried the kitchen door, and then——"

John Rance sprang to his feet with a frightened face and suspicion in his eyes. "Where was you hid to see all that?" he cried. "It seems to me that you knows a deal more than you should."

Holmes laughed and threw his card across the table to the constable. "Don't go arresting me for the murder," he said, "I am one of the hounds and not the wolf; Mr. Gregson or Mr. Lestrade will answer for that. Go on, though. What did you do next?"

Rance resumed his seat, without, however, losing his mystified expression. "I went back to the gate and sounded my whistle. That brought Murcher and two more to the spot."

"Was the street empty then?"

"Well, it was, as far as anybody that could be of any good goes."

"What do you mean?"

The constable's features broadened into a grin. "I've seen many a drunk chap in my time," he said, "but never anyone so cryin' drunk as that cove. He was at the gate when I came out, a-leanin' up ag'in the railings, and a-singin' at the pitch o' his lungs about Columbine's New-fangled Banner, or some such stuff. He couldn't stand, far less help."

"What sort of a man was he?" asked Sherlock Holmes.

John Rance appeared to be somewhat irritated at this disgression. "He was an uncommon drunk sort o' man," he said. "He'd ha' found hisself in the station if we hadn't been so took up."

"His face—his dress—didn't you notice them?" Holmes broke in impatiently.

"I should think I did notice them, seeing that I had to prop him up—me and Murcher between us. He was a long chap, with a red face, the lower part muffled round——"

"That will do," cried Holmes. "What became of him?"

"We'd enough to do without lookin' after him," the policeman said, in an aggrieved voice. "I'll wager he found his way home all right."

"How was he dressed?"

"A brown overcoat."

"Had he a whip in his hand?"

"A whip—no."

"He must have left it behind," muttered my companion. "You didn't happen to see or hear a cab after that?"

"No."

"There's a half-sovereign for you," my companion said, standing up and taking his hat. "I am afraid, Rance, that you will never rise in the force. That head of yours should be for use as well as ornament. You might have gained your sergeant's stripes last night. The man whom you held in your hands is the man who holds the clue of this mystery, and whom we are seeking. There is no use of arguing about it now; I tell you that it is so. Come along, Doctor."

We started off for the cab together, leaving our informant incredulous, but obviously uncomfortable.

"The blundering fool!" Holmes said, bitterly, as we drove back to our lodgings. "Just to think of his having such an incomparable bit of good luck, and not taking advantage of it."

"I am rather in the dark still. It is true that the description of this man tallies with your idea of the second party in this mystery. But why should he come back to the house after leaving it? That is not the way of criminals."

"The ring, man, the ring: that was what he came back for. If we have no other way of catching him, we can always bait our line with the ring. I shall have him, Doctor—I'll lay you two to one that I have him. I must thank you for it all. I might not have gone but for you, and so have missed the finest study I ever came across: a study in scarlet, eh? Why shouldn't we use a little art jargon. There's the scarlet thread of murder running through the colourless skein of life, and our duty is to unravel it, and isolate it, and expose every inch of it. And now for lunch, and then for Neruda. Her attack and her bowing are splendid. What's that little thing of Chopin's she plays so magnificently: Tra-la-la-lira-lira-lay."

Leaning back in the cab, this amateur bloodhound carolled away like a lark while I meditated upon the many-sidedness of the human mind.

Chapter 5
Our Advertisement Brings a Visitor

Our morning's exertions had been too much for my weak health, and I was tired out in the afternoon. After Holmes's departure for the concert, I lay down upon the sofa and endeavoured to get a couple of hours' sleep. It was a useless attempt. My mind had been too much excited by all that had occurred, and the strangest fancies and surmises crowded into it. Every time that I closed my eyes I saw before me the distorted, baboon-like countenance of the murdered man. So sinister was the impression which that face had produced upon me that I found it difficult to feel anything but gratitude for him who had removed its owner from the world. If ever human features bespoke vice of the most malignant type, they were certainly those of Enoch J. Drebber, of Cleveland. Still I recognized that justice must be done, and that the depravity of the victim was no condonement in the eyes of the law.

The more I thought of it the more extraordinary did my companion's hypothesis, that the man had been poisoned, appear. I remembered how he had sniffed his lips, and had no doubt that he had detected something which had given rise to the idea. Then, again, if not poison, what had caused the man's death, since there was neither wound nor marks of strangulation? But, on the other hand, whose blood was that which lay so thickly upon the floor? There were no signs of a struggle, nor had the victim any weapon with which he might have wounded an antagonist. As long as all these questions were unsolved, I felt that sleep would be no easy matter, either for Holmes or myself. His quiet, self-confident manner convinced me that he had already formed a theory which explained all the facts, though what it was I could not for an instant conjecture.

He was very late in returning—so late that I knew that the concert could not have detained him all the time. Dinner was on the table before he appeared.

"It was magnificent," he said, as he took his seat. "Do you remember what Darwin says about music? He claims that the power of producing and appreciating it existed among the human race long before the power of speech was arrived at. Perhaps that is why we are so subtly influenced by it. There are vague memories in our souls of those misty centuries when the world was in its childhood."

"That's rather a broad idea," I remarked.

"One's ideas must be as broad as Nature if they are to interpret Nature," he answered. "What's the matter? You're not looking quite yourself. This Brixton Road affair has upset you."

As he spoke there was a sharp ring at the bell. Sherlock Holmes rose softly and moved his chair in the direction of the door. We heard the servant pass along the hall, and the sharp click of the latch as she opened it.

"Does Dr. Watson live here?" asked a clear but rather harsh voice. We could not hear the servant's reply, but the door closed, and someone began to ascend the stairs. The footfall was an uncertain and shuffling one. A look of surprise passed over the face of my companion as he listened to it. It came slowly along the passage, and there was a feeble tap at the door.

"Come in," I cried.

At my summons, instead of the man of violence whom we expected, a very old and wrinkled woman hobbled into the apartment. She appeared to be dazzled by the sudden blaze of light, and after dropping a curtsey, she stood blinking at us with her bleared eyes and fumbling in her pocket with nervous, shaky fingers. I glanced at my companion, and his face had assumed such a disconsolate expression that it was all I could do to keep my countenance.

The old crone drew out an evening paper, and pointed at our advertisement. "It's this as has brought me, good gentlemen," she said, dropping another curtsey; "a gold wedding ring in the Brixton Road. It belongs to my girl Sally, as was married only this time twelvemonth, which her husband is steward aboard a Union boat, and what he'd say if he comes 'ome and found her without her ring is more than I can think, he being short enough at the best o' times, but more especially when he has the drink. If it please you, she went to the circus last night along with——"

"Is that her ring?" I asked.

"The Lord be thanked!" cried the old woman; "Sally will be a glad woman this night. That's the ring."

"And what may your address be?" I inquired, taking up a pencil.

"13, Duncan Street, Houndsditch. A weary way from here."

"The Brixton Road does not lie between any circus and Houndsditch," said Sherlock Holmes sharply.

The old woman faced round and looked keenly at him from her little red-rimmed eyes. "The gentleman asked me for *my* address," she said. "Sally lives in lodgings at 3, Mayfield Place, Peckham."

"And your name is——?"

"My name is Sawyer—hers is Dennis, which Tom Dennis married her—and a smart, clean lad, too, as long as he's at sea, and no steward in the company more thought of; but when on shore, what with the women and what with liquor shops——"

"Here is your ring, Mrs. Sawyer," I interrupted, in obedience to a sign from my companion; "it clearly belongs to your daughter, and I am glad to be able to restore it to the rightful owner."

With many mumbled blessings and protestations of gratitude the old crone packed it away in her pocket, and shuffled off down the stairs. Sherlock Holmes sprang to his feet the moment that she was gone and rushed into his room. He returned in a few seconds enveloped in an ulster and a cravat. "I'll follow her," he said, hurriedly; "she must be an accomplice, and will lead me to him. Wait up for me." The hall door had hardly slammed behind our visitor before Holmes had descended the stair. Looking through the window I could see her walking feebly along the other side, while her pursuer dogged her some little distance behind. "Either his whole theory is incorrect," I thought to myself, "or else he will be led now to the heart of the mystery." There was no need for him to ask me to wait up for him, for I felt that sleep was impossible until I heard the result of his adventure.

It was close upon nine when he set out. I had no idea how long he might be, but I sat stolidly puffing at my pipe and skipping over the pages of Henri Murger's *Vie de Bohème*. Ten o'clock passed, and I heard the footsteps of the maid as she pattered off to bed. Eleven, and the more stately tread of the landlady passed my door, bound for the same destination. It was close upon twelve before I heard the sharp sound of his latchkey. The instant he entered I saw by his face that he had not been successful. Amusement and chagrin seemed to be struggling for the mastery, until the former suddenly carried the day, and he burst into a hearty laugh.

"I wouldn't have the Scotland Yarders know it for the world," he cried, dropping into his chair; "I have chaffed them so much that they would never have let me hear the end of it. I can afford to laugh, because I know that I will be even with them in the long run."

"What is it then?" I asked.

"Oh, I don't mind telling a story against myself. That creature had gone a little way when she began to limp and show every sign of being footsore. Presently she came to a halt, and hailed a four-wheeler which was passing. I managed to be close to her so as to hear the address, but I need not have been so anxious, for she sang it out loud enough to be heard at the other side of the street, 'Drive to 13, Duncan Street, Houndsditch,' she cried. This begins to look genuine, I thought, and having seen her safely inside, I perched myself behind. That's an art which every detective should be an expert at. Well, away we rattled, and never drew rein until we reached the street in question. I hopped off before we came to the door, and strolled down the street in an easy, lounging way. I saw the cab pull up. The driver jumped down, and I saw him open the door and stand expectantly. Nothing came out though. When I reached him, he was groping about frantically in the empty cab, and giving vent to the finest assorted collection of oaths that ever I listened to. There was no sign or trace of his passenger, and I fear it will be some time before he gets his fare. On inquiring at Number 13 we found that the house belonged to a respectable paperhanger, named Keswick, and that no one of the name either of Sawyer or Dennis had ever been heard of there."

"You don't mean to say," I cried, in amazement, "that that tottering, feeble old woman was able to get out of the cab while it was in motion, without either you or the driver seeing her?"

"Old woman be damned!" said Sherlock Holmes, sharply. "We were the old women to be so taken in. It must have been a young man, and an active one, too, besides being an incomparable actor. The get-up was inimitable. He saw that he was followed, no doubt, and used this means of giving me the slip. It shows that the man we are after is not as lonely as I imagined he was, but has friends who are ready to risk something for him. Now, Doctor, you are looking done-up. Take my advice and turn in."

I was certainly feeling very weary, so I obeyed his injunction. I left Holmes seated in front of the smoldering fire, and long into the watches of the night I heard the low melancholy wailings of his violin, and knew that he was still pondering over the strange problem which he had set himself to unravel.

Chapter 6
Tobias Gregson Shows What He Can Do

The papers next day were full of the "Brixton Mystery," as they termed it. Each had a long account of the affair, and some had leaders upon it in addition. There was some information in them which was new to me. I still retain in my scrapbook numerous clippings and extracts bearing upon the case. Here is a condensation of a few of them:

The *Daily Telegraph* remarked that in the history of crime there had seldom been a tragedy which presented stranger features. The German name of the victim, the absence of all other motive, and the sinister inscription on the wall, all pointed to its perpetration by political refugees and revolutionists. The Socialists had many branches in America, and the deceased had, no doubt, infringed their unwritten laws, and been tracked down by them. After alluding airily to the Vehmgericht, aqua tofana, Carbonari, the Marchioness de Brinvilliers, the Darwinian theory, the principles of Malthus, and the Ratcliff Highway murders, the article concluded by admonishing the government and advocating a closer watch over foreigners in England.

The *Standard* commented upon the fact that lawless outrages of the sort usually occurred under a Liberal administration. They arose from the unsettling of the minds of the masses, and the consequent weakening of all authority. The deceased was an American gentleman who had been residing for some weeks in the metropolis. He had stayed at the boarding-house of Madame Charpentier, in Torquay Terrace, Camberwell. He was accompanied in his travels by his private secretary, Mr. Joseph Stangerson. The two bade adieu to their landlady upon Tuesday, the 4th inst., and departed to Euston Station with the avowed intention of catching the Liverpool express. They were afterwards seen together upon the platform. Nothing more is known of them until Mr. Drebber's body was, as recorded, discovered in an empty house in the Brixton

Road, many miles from Euston. How he came there, or how he met his fate, are questions which are still involved in mystery. Nothing is known of the whereabouts of Stangerson. We are glad to learn that Mr. Lestrade and Mr. Gregson, of Scotland Yard, are both engaged upon the case, and it is confidently anticipated that these well-known officers will speedily throw light upon the matter.

The *Daily News* observed that there was no doubt as to the crime being a political one. The despotism and hatred of Liberalism which animated the Continental governments had had the effect of driving to our shores a number of men who might have made excellent citizens were they not soured by the recollection of all that they had undergone. Among these men there was a stringent code of honour, any infringement of which was punished by death. Every effort should be made to find the secretary, Stangerson, and to ascertain some particulars of the habits of the deceased. A great step had been gained by the discovery of the address of the house at which he had boarded—a result which was entirely due to the acuteness and energy of Mr. Gregson of Scotland Yard.

Sherlock Holmes and I read these notices over together at breakfast, and they appeared to afford him considerable amusement.

"I told you that, whatever happened, Lestrade and Gregson would be sure to score."

"That depends on how it turns out."

"Oh, bless you, it doesn't matter in the least. If the man is caught, it will be *on account* of their exertions; if he escapes, it will be *in spite* of their exertions. It's heads I win and tails you lose. Whatever they do, they will have followers. '*Un sot trouve toujours un plus sot qui l' admire.*'"

"What on earth is this?" I cried, for at this moment there came the pattering of many steps in the hall and on the stairs, accompanied by audible expressions of disgust upon the part of our landlady.

"It's the Baker Street division of the detective police force," said my companion gravely; and as he spoke there rushed into the room half a dozen of the dirtiest and most ragged street Arabs that ever I clapped eyes on.

"'Tention!" cried Holmes, in a sharp tone, and the six dirty little scoundrels stood in a line like so many disreputable statuettes. "In future you shall send up Wiggins alone to report, and the rest of you must wait in the street. Have you found it, Wiggins?"

"No, sir, we hain't," said one of the youths.

"I hardly expected you would. You must keep on until you do. Here are your wages." He handed each of them a shilling. "Now, off you go, and come back with a better report next time."

He waved his hand, and they scampered away downstairs like so many rats, and we heard their shrill voices next moment in the street.

"There's more work to be got out of one of those little beggars than out of a dozen of the force," Holmes remarked. "The mere sight of an official-looking person seals men's lips. These youngsters, however, go everywhere and hear everything. They are as sharp as needles, too; all they want is organization."

"Is it on this Brixton case that you are employing them?" I asked.

"Yes; there is a point which I wish to ascertain. It is merely a matter of time. Hullo! we are going to hear some news now with a vengeance! Here is Gregson coming down the road with beatitude written upon every feature of his face. Bound for us, I know. Yes, he is stopping. There he is!"

There was a violent peal at the bell, and in a few seconds the fair-haired detective came up the stairs, three steps at a time, and burst into our sitting-room.

"My dear fellow," he cried, wringing Holmes's unresponsive hand, "congratulate me! I have made the whole thing as clear as day."

A shade of anxiety seemed to me to cross my companion's expressive face.

"Do you mean that you are on the right track?" he asked.

"The right track! Why, sir, we have the man under lock and key."

"And his name is?"

"Arthur Charpentier, sub-lieutenant in Her Majesty's navy," cried Gregson pompously rubbing his fat hands and inflating his chest.

Sherlock Holmes gave a sigh of relief and relaxed into a smile.

"Take a seat, and try one of these cigars," he said. "We are anxious to know how you managed it. Will you have some whisky and water?"

"I don't mind if I do," the detective answered. "The tremendous exertions which I have gone through during the last day or two have worn me out. Not so much bodily exertion, you understand, as the strain upon the mind. You will appreciate that, Mr. Sherlock Holmes, for we are both brain-workers."

"You do me too much honour," said Holmes, gravely. "Let us hear how you arrived at this most gratifying result."

The detective seated himself in the armchair, and puffed complacently at his cigar. Then suddenly he slapped his thigh in a paroxysm of amusement.

"The fun of it is," he cried, "that that fool Lestrade, who thinks himself so smart, has gone off upon the wrong track altogether. He is after the secretary Stangerson, who had no more to do with the crime than the babe unborn. I have no doubt that he has caught him by this time."

The idea tickled Gregson so much that he laughed until he choked.

"And how did you get your clue?"

"Ah, I'll tell you all about it. Of course, Dr. Watson, this is strictly between ourselves. The first difficulty which we had to contend with was the finding of this American's antecedents. Some people would have waited until their advertisements were answered, or until parties came forward and volunteered information. That is not Tobias Gregson's way of going to work. You remember the hat beside the dead man?"

"Yes," said Holmes; "by John Underwood and Sons, 129, Camberwell Road."

Gregson looked quite crestfallen.

"I had no idea that you noticed that," he said. "Have you been there?"

"No."

"Ha!" cried Gregson, in a relieved voice; "you should never neglect a chance, however small it may seem."

"To a great mind, nothing is little," remarked Holmes, sententiously.

"Well, I went to Underwood, and asked him if he had sold a hat of that size and description. He looked over his books, and came on it at once. He had sent the hat to a Mr. Drebber, residing at Charpentier's Boarding Establishment, Torquay Terrace. Thus I got at his address."

"Smart—very smart!" murmured Sherlock Holmes.

"I next called upon Madame Charpentier," continued the detective. "I found her very pale and distressed. Her daughter was in the room, too—an uncommonly fine girl she is, too; she was looking red about the eyes and her lips trembled as I spoke to her. That didn't escape my notice. I began to smell a rat. You know the feeling, Mr. Sherlock Holmes, when you come upon the right scent—a kind of thrill in your nerves. 'Have you heard of the mysterious death of your late boarder Mr. Enoch J. Drebber, of Cleveland?' I asked.

"The mother nodded. She didn't seem able to get out a word. The daughter burst into tears. I felt more than ever that these people knew something of the matter.

"'At what o'clock did Mr. Drebber leave your house for the train?' I asked.

"'At eight o'clock,' she said, gulping in her throat to keep down her agitation. 'His secretary, Mr. Stangerson, said that there were two trains—one at 9:15 and one at 11. He was to catch the first.'

"'And was that the last which you saw of him?'

"A terrible change came over the woman's face as I asked the question. Her features turned perfectly livid. It was some seconds before she could get out the single word 'Yes'—and when it did come it was in a husky, unnatural tone.

"There was silence for a moment, and then the daughter spoke in a calm, clear voice.

"'No good can ever come of falsehood, mother,' she said. 'Let us be frank with this gentleman. We *did* see Mr. Drebber again.'

"'God forgive you!' cried Madame Charpentier, throwing up her hands and sinking back in her chair. 'You have murdered your brother.'

"'Arthur would rather that we spoke the truth,' the girl answered firmly.

"'You had best tell me all about it now,' I said. 'Half-confidences are worse than none. Besides, you do not know how much we know of it.'

"'On your head be it, Alice!' cried her mother; and then, turning to me, 'I will tell you all, sir. Do not imagine that my agitation on behalf of my son arises from any fear lest he should have had a hand in this terrible affair. He is utterly innocent of it. My dread is, however, that in your eyes and in the eyes of others he may appear to be compromised. That, however, is surely impossible. His high character, his profession, his antecedents would all forbid it.'

"'Your best way is to make a clean breast of the facts,' I answered. 'Depend upon it, if your son is innocent he will be none the worse.'

"'Perhaps, Alice, you had better leave us together,' she said, and her daughter withdrew. 'Now, sir,' she continued, 'I had no intention of telling you all this, but since my poor daughter has disclosed it I have no alternative. Having once decided to speak, I will tell you all without omitting any particular.'

"'It is your wisest course,' said I.

"'Mr. Drebber has been with us nearly three weeks. He and his sec-retary, Mr. Stangerson, had been travelling on the Continent. I noticed a Copenhagen label upon each of their trunks, showing that that had been their last stopping place. Stangerson was a quiet, reserved man, but his employer, I am sorry to say, was far otherwise. He was coarse in his habits and brutish in his ways. The very night of his arrival he became very much the worse for drink, and, indeed, after twelve o'clock in the day he could hardly ever be said to be sober. His manners towards the maid-servants were disgustingly free and familiar. Worst of all, he speed-ily assumed the same attitude towards my daughter, Alice, and spoke to her more than once in a way which, fortunately, she is too innocent to understand. On one occasion he actually seized her in his arms and em-braced her—an outrage which caused his own secretary to reproach him for his unmanly conduct.'

"'But why did you stand all this?' I asked. 'I suppose that you can get rid of your boarders when you wish.'

"Mrs. Charpentier blushed at my pertinent question. 'Would to God that I had given him notice on the very day that he came,' she said. 'But it was a sore temptation. They were paying a pound a day each— fourteen pounds a week, and this is the slack season. I am a widow, and my boy in the Navy has cost me much. I grudged to lose the money. I acted for the best. This last was too much, however, and I gave him no-tice to leave on account of it. That was the reason of his going.'

"'Well?'

"'My heart grew light when I saw him drive away. My son is on leave just now, but I did not tell him anything of all this, for his temper is vi-olent, and he is passionately fond of his sister. When I closed the door behind them a load seemed to be lifted from my mind. Alas, in less than an hour there was a ring at the bell, and I learned that Mr. Drebber had returned. He was much excited, and evidently the worse for drink. He forced his way into the room, where I was sitting with my daughter, and made some incoherent remark about having missed his train. He then turned to Alice, and before my very face, proposed to her that she should fly with him. "You are of age," he said, "and there is no law to stop you. I have money enough and to spare. Never mind the old girl here, but come alone with me now straight away. You shall live like a princess." Poor Alice was so frightened that she shrunk away from him, but he caught her by the wrist and endeavoured to draw her towards the door. I screamed, and at that moment my son Arthur came into the room. What happened then I do not know. I heard oaths and the confused sounds of a scuffle. I was too terrified to raise my head. When I did look up I saw Arthur standing in the doorway laughing, with a stick in his hand. "I don't think that fine fellow will trouble us again," he said. "I will just go after him and see what he does with himself." With those words he took his hat and started off down the street. The next morning we heard of Mr. Drebber's mysterious death.'

"This statement came from Mrs. Charpentier's lips with many gasps and pauses. At times she spoke so low that I could hardly catch the words. I made shorthand notes of all that she said, however, so that there should be no possibility of a mistake."

"It's quite exciting," said Sherlock Holmes, with a yawn. "What happened next?"

"When Mrs. Charpentier paused," the detective continued, "I saw that the whole case hung upon one point. Fixing her with my eye in a way which I always found effective with women, I asked her at what hour her son returned.

"'I do not know,' she answered.

"'Not know?'

"'No; he has a latchkey, and he let himself in.'

"'After you went to bed?'

"'Yes.'

"'When did you go to bed?'

"'About eleven.'

"'So your son was gone at least two hours?'

"'Yes.'

"'Possibly four or five?'

"'Yes.'

"'What was he doing during that time?'

"'I do not know,' she answered, turning white to her very lips.

"Of course after that there was nothing more to be done. I found out where Lieutenant Charpentier was, took two officers with me, and arrested him. When I touched him on the shoulder and warned him to come quietly with us, he answered us as bold as brass, 'I suppose you are arresting me for being concerned in the death of that scoundrel Drebber,' he said. We had said nothing to him about it, so that his alluding to it had a most suspicious aspect."

"Very," said Holmes.

"He still carried the heavy stick which the mother described him as having with him when he followed Drebber. It was a stout oak cudgel."

"What is your theory, then?"

"Well, my theory is that he followed Drebber as far as the Brixton Road. When there, a fresh altercation arose between them, in the course of which Drebber received a blow from the stick, in the pit of the stomach perhaps, which killed him without leaving any mark. The night was so wet that no one was about, so Charpentier dragged the body of his victim into the empty house. As to the candle, and the blood, and the writing on the wall, and the ring, they may all be so many tricks to throw the police on to the wrong scent."

"Well done!" said Holmes in an encouraging voice. "Really, Gregson, you are getting along. We shall make something of you yet."

"I flatter myself that I have managed it rather neatly," the detective answered, proudly. "The young man volunteered a statement, in which he said that after following Drebber some time, the latter perceived him, and took a cab in order to get away from him. On his way home he met an old shipmate, and took a long walk with him. On being asked where this old shipmate lived, he was unable to give any satisfactory reply. I think the whole case fits together uncommonly well. What amuses me is to think of Lestrade, who had started off upon the wrong scent. I am afraid he won't make much of it. Why, by Jove, here's the very man himself!"

It was indeed Lestrade, who had ascended the stairs while we were talking, and who now entered the room. The assurance and jauntiness which generally marked his demeanour and dress were, however, wanting. His face was disturbed and troubled, while his clothes were disarranged and untidy. He had evidently come with the intention of consulting with Sherlock Holmes, for on perceiving his colleague he appeared to be embarrassed and put out. He stood in the centre of the room, fumbling nervously with his hat and uncertain what to do. "This is a most extraordinary case," he said at last—"a most incomprehensible affair."

"Ah, you find it so, Mr. Lestrade!" cried Gregson, triumphantly. "I thought you would come to that conclusion. Have you managed to find the secretary, Mr. Joseph Stangerson?"

"The secretary, Mr. Joseph Stangerson," said Lestrade, gravely, "was murdered at Halliday's Private Hotel about six o'clock this morning."

Chapter 7
Light in the Darkness

The intelligence with which Lestrade greeted us was so momentous and so unexpected that we were all three fairly dumfounded. Gregson sprang out of his chair and upset the remainder of his whisky and water. I stared in silence at Sherlock Holmes, whose lips were compressed and his brows drawn down over his eyes.

"Stangerson too!" he muttered. "The plot thickens."

"It was quite thick enough before," grumbled Lestrade, taking a chair, "I seem to have dropped into a sort of council of war."

"Are you—are you sure of this piece of intelligence?" stammered Gregson.

"I have just come from his room," said Lestrade. "I was the first to discover what had occurred."

"We have been hearing Gregson's view of the matter," Holmes observed. "Would you mind letting us know what you have seen and done?"

"I have no objection," Lestrade answered, seating himself. "I freely confess that I was of the opinion that Stangerson was concerned in the death of Drebber. This fresh development has shown me that I was completely mistaken. Full of the one idea, I set myself to find out what had become of the secretary. They had been seen together at Euston Station about half-past eight on the evening of the 3rd. At two in the morning Drebber had been found in the Brixton Road. The question which confronted me was to find out how Stangerson had been employed between 8:30 and the time of the crime, and what had become of him afterwards. I telegraphed to Liverpool, giving a description of the man, and warning them to keep a watch upon the American boats. I then set to work calling upon all the hotels and lodging-houses in the vicinity of Euston. You see, I argued that if Drebber and his companion had become separated, the natural course for the latter would be to put up somewhere in the vicinity for the night, and then to hang about the station again next morning."

"They would be likely to agree on some meeting-place beforehand," remarked Holmes.

"So it proved. I spent the whole of yesterday evening in making inquiries entirely without avail. This morning I began very early, and at eight o'clock I reached Halliday's Private Hotel, in Little George Street. On my inquiry as to whether a Mr. Stangerson was living there, they at once answered me in the affirmative.

"'No doubt you are the gentleman whom he was expecting,' they said. 'He has been waiting for a gentleman for two days.'

"'Where is he now?' I asked.

"'He is upstairs in bed. He wished to be called at nine.'

"'I will go up and see him at once,' I said.

"It seemed to me that my sudden appearance might shake his nerves and lead him to say something unguarded. The boots volunteered to show me the room; it was on the second floor, and there was a small corridor leading up to it. The boots pointed out the door to me, and was about to go downstairs again when I saw something that made me feel sickish, in spite of my twenty years' experience. From under the door there curled a little red ribbon of blood, which had meandered across the passage and formed a little pool along the skirting at the other side. I gave a cry, which brought the boots back. He nearly fainted when he saw it. The door was locked on the inside, but we put our shoulders to it, and knocked it in. The window of the room was open, and beside the window, all huddled up, lay the body of a man in his nightdress. He was quite dead, and had been for some time, for his limbs were rigid and cold. When we turned him over, the boots recognized him at once as being the same gentleman who had engaged the room under the name of Joseph Stangerson. The cause of death was a deep stab in the left side, which must have penetrated the heart. And now comes the strangest part of the affair. What do you suppose was above the murdered man?"

I felt a creeping of the flesh, and a presentiment of coming horror, even before Sherlock Holmes answered.

"The word RACHE, written in letters of blood," he said.

"That was it," said Lestrade, in an awestruck voice, and we were all silent for a while.

There was something so methodical and so incomprehensible about the deeds of this unknown assassin, that it imparted a fresh ghastliness to his crimes. My nerves, which were steady enough on the field of battle, tingled as I thought of it.

"The man was seen," continued Lestrade. "A milk boy, passing on his way to the dairy, happened to walk down the lane which leads from the mews at the back of the hotel. He noticed that a ladder, which usually lay there, was raised against one of the windows of the second floor, which was wide open. After passing, he looked back and saw a man descend the ladder. He came down so quietly and openly that the boy imagined him to be some carpenter or joiner at work in the hotel. He took no particular notice of him, beyond thinking in his own mind that it was early for him to be at work. He has an impression that the man was tall, had a reddish face, and was dressed in a long, brownish coat. He must have stayed in the room some little time after the murder, for we found blood-stained water in the basin, where he had washed his hands, and marks on the sheets where he had deliberately wiped his knife."

I glanced at Holmes on hearing the description of the murder which tallied so exactly with his own. There was, however, no trace of exultation or satisfaction upon his face.

"Did you find nothing in the room which could furnish a clue to the murderer?" he asked.

"Nothing. Stangerson had Drebber's purse in his pocket, but it seems that this was usual, as he did all the paying. There was eighty-odd pounds in it, but nothing had been taken. Whatever the motives of these extraordinary crimes, robbery is certainly not one of them. There were no papers or memoranda in the murdered man's pocket, except a single telegram, dated from Cleveland about a month ago, and containing the words, 'J. H. is in Europe.' There was no name appended to this message."

"And there was nothing else?" Holmes asked.

"Nothing of any importance. The man's novel, with which he had read himself to sleep, was lying upon the bed, and his pipe was on a chair beside him. There was a glass of water on the table, and on the window-sill a small chip ointment box containing a couple of pills."

Sherlock Holmes sprang from his chair with an exclamation of delight.

"The last link," he cried, exultantly. "My case is complete."

The two detectives stared at him in amazement.

"I have now in my hands," my companion said, confidently, "all the threads which have formed such a tangle. There are, of course, details to be filled in, but I am as certain of all the main facts, from the time that Drebber parted from Stangerson at the station, up to the discovery of the body of the latter, as if I had seen them with my own eyes. I will give you a proof of my knowledge. Could you lay your hand upon those pills?"

"I have them," said Lestrade, producing a small white box; "I took them and the purse and the telegram, intending to have them put in a place of safety at the police station. It was the merest chance my taking these pills, for I am bound to say that I do not attach any importance to them."

"Give them here," said Holmes. "Now, Doctor," turning to me, "are those ordinary pills?"

They certainly were not. They were of a pearly gray colour, small, round, and almost transparent against the light. "From their lightness and transparency, I should imagine that they are soluble in water," I remarked.

"Precisely so," answered Holmes. "Now would you mind going down and fetching that poor little devil of a terrier which has been bad so long, and which the landlady wanted you to put out of its pain yesterday?"

I went downstairs and carried the dog upstairs in my arms. Its laboured breathing and glazing eye showed that it was not far from its end. Indeed, its snow-white muzzle proclaimed that it had already exceeded the usual term of canine existence. I placed it upon a cushion on the rug.

"I will now cut one of these pills in two," said Holmes, and drawing his penknife he suited the action to the word. "One half we return into the box for future purposes. The other half I will place in this wineglass, in which is a teaspoonful of water. You perceive that our friend, the doctor, is right, and that it readily dissolves."

"This may be very interesting," said Lestrade, in the injured tone of one who suspects that he is being laughed at; "I cannot see, however, what it has to do with the death of Mr. Joseph Stangerson."

"Patience, my friend, patience! You will find in time that it has everything to do with it. I shall now add a little milk to make the mixture palatable, and on presenting it to the dog we find that he laps it up readily enough."

As he spoke he turned the contents of the wineglass into a saucer and placed it in front of the terrier, who speedily licked it dry. Sherlock Holmes's earnest demeanour had so far convinced us that we all sat in silence, watching the animal intently, and expecting some startling effect. None such appeared, however. The dog continued to lie stretched upon the cushion, breathing in a laboured way, but apparently neither the better nor the worse for its draught.

Holmes had taken out his watch, and as minute followed minute without result, an expression of the utmost chagrin and disappointment appeared upon his features. He gnawed his lip, drummed his fingers upon the table, and showed every other symptom of acute impatience. So great was his emotion that I felt sincerely sorry for him, while the two detectives smiled derisively, by no means displeased at this check which he had met.

"It can't be a coincidence," he cried, at last springing from his chair and pacing wildly up and down the room; "it is impossible that it should be a mere coincidence. The very pills which I suspected in the case of Drebber are actually found after the death of Stangerson. And yet they are inert. What can it mean? Surely my whole chain of reasoning cannot have been false. It is impossible! And yet this wretched dog is none the worse. Ah, I have it! I have it!" With a perfect shriek of delight he rushed to the box, cut the other pill in two, dissolved it, added milk, and presented it to the terrier. The unfortunate creature's tongue seemed hardly to have been moistened in it before it gave a convulsive shiver in every limb, and lay as rigid and lifeless as if it had been struck by lightning.

Sherlock Holmes draw a long breath, and wiped the perspiration from his forehead. "I should have more faith," he said; "I ought to know by this time that when a fact appears to be opposed to a long train of deductions, it invariably proves to be capable of bearing some other interpretation. Of the two pills in that box, one was of the most deadly poison, and the other was entirely harmless. I ought to have known that before ever I saw the box at all."

This last statement appeared to me to be so startling that I could hardly believe that he was in his sober senses. There was the dead dog, however, to prove that his conjecture had been correct. It seemed to me that the mists in my own mind were gradually clearing away, and I began to have a dim, vague perception of the truth.

"All this seems strange to you," continued Holmes, "because you failed at the beginning of the inquiry to grasp the importance of the single real clue which was presented to you. I had the good fortune to seize upon that, and everything which has occurred since then has served to confirm my original supposition, and, indeed, was the logical sequence of it. Hence things which have perplexed you and made the case more obscure have served to enlighten me and to strengthen my conclusions. It is a mistake to confound strangeness with mystery. The most commonplace crime is often the most mysterious, because it presents no new or special features from which deductions may be drawn. This murder would have been infinitely more difficult to unravel had the body of the victim been simply found lying in the roadway without any of those *outré* and sensational accompaniments which have rendered it remarkable. These strange details, far from making the case more difficult, have really had the effect of making it less so."

Mr. Gregson, who had listened to this address with considerable impatience, could contain himself no longer. "Look here, Mr. Sherlock Holmes," he said, "we are all ready to acknowledge that you are a smart man, and that you have your own methods of working. We want something more than mere theory and preaching now, though. It is a case of taking the man. I have made my case out, and it seems I was wrong. Young Charpentier could not have been engaged in this second affair. Lestrade went after his man, Stangerson, and it appears that he was wrong too. You have thrown out hints here, and hints there, and seem to know more than we do, but the time has come when we feel that we have a right to ask you straight how much you do know of the business. Can you name the man who did it?"

"I cannot help feeling that Gregson is right, sir," remarked Lestrade. "We have both tried, and we have both failed. You have remarked more than once since I have been in the room that you had all the evidence which you require. Surely you will not withhold it any longer."

"Any delay in arresting the assassin," I observed, "might give him time to perpetrate some fresh atrocity."

Thus pressed by us all, Holmes showed signs of irresolution. He continued to walk up and down the room with his head sunk on his chest and his brows drawn down, as was his habit when lost in thought.

"There will be no more murders," he said at last, stopping abruptly and facing us. "You can put that consideration out of the question. You have asked me if I know the name of the assassin. I do. The mere knowing of his name is a small thing, however, compared with the power of laying our hands upon him. This I expect very shortly to do. I have good hopes of managing it through my own arrangements; but it is a thing which needs delicate handling, for we have a shrewd and desperate man to deal with, who is supported, as I have had occasion to prove, by another who is as clever as himself. As long as this man has no idea that anyone can have a clue there is some chance of securing him; but if he had the slightest suspicion, he would change his name, and vanish in an instant among the four million inhabitants of this great city. Without meaning to hurt either of your feelings, I am bound to say that I consider these men to be more than a match for the official force, and that is why I have not asked your assistance. If I fail, I shall, of course, incur all the blame due to this omission; but that I am prepared for. At present I am ready to promise that the instant that I can communicate with you without endangering my own combinations, I shall do so."

Gregson and Lestrade seemed to be far from satisfied by this assurance, or by the depreciating allusion to the detective police. The former had flushed up to the roots of his flaxen hair, while the other's beady eyes glistened with curiosity and resentment. Neither of them had time to speak, however, before there was a tap at the door, and the spokesman of the street Arabs, young Wiggins, introduced his insignificant and unsavoury person.

"Please, sir," he said, touching his forelock, "I have the cab downstairs."

"Good boy," said Holmes, blandly. "Why don't you introduce this pattern at Scotland Yard?" he continued, taking a pair of steel handcuffs from a drawer. "See how beautifully the spring works. They fasten in an instant."

"The old pattern is good enough," remarked Lestrade, "if we can only find the man to put them on."

"Very good, very good," said Holmes, smiling. "The cabman may as well help me with my boxes. Just ask him to step up, Wiggins."

I was surprised to find my companion speaking as though he were about to set out on a journey, since he had not said anything to me about it. There was a small portmanteau in the room, and this he pulled out and began to strap. He was busily engaged at it when the cabman entered the room.

"Just give me a help with this buckle, cabman," he said, kneeling over his task, and never turning his head.

The fellow came forward with a somewhat sullen, defiant air, and put down his hands to assist. At that instant there was a sharp click, the jangling of metal, and Sherlock Holmes sprang to his feet again.

"Gentlemen," he cried, with flashing eyes, "let me introduce you to Mr. Jefferson Hope, the murderer of Enoch Drebber and of Joseph Stangerson."

The whole thing occurred in a moment—so quickly that I had no time to realize it. I have a vivid recollection of that instant, of Holmes's triumphant expression and the ring of his voice, of the cabman's dazed, savage face, as he glared at the glittering handcuffs, which had appeared as if by magic upon his wrists. For a second or two we might have been a group of statues. Then with an inarticulate roar of fury, the prisoner wrenched himself free from Holmes's grasp, and hurled himself through the window. Woodwork and glass gave way before him; but before he got quite through, Gregson, Lestrade, and Holmes sprang upon him like so many staghounds. He was dragged back into the room, and then commenced a terrific conflict. So powerful and so fierce was he that the four of us were shaken off again and again. He appeared to have the convulsive strength of a man in a epileptic fit. His face and hands were terribly mangled by his passage through the glass, but loss of blood had no effect in diminishing his resistance. It was not until Lestrade succeeded in getting his hand inside his neckcloth and half-strangling him that we made him realize that his struggles were of no avail; and even then we felt no security until we had pinioned his feet as well as his hands. That done, we rose to our feet breathless and panting.

"We have his cab," said Sherlock Holmes. "It will serve to take him to Scotland Yard. And now, gentlemen," he continued with a pleasant smile, "we have reached the end of our little mystery. You are very welcome to put any questions that you like to me now, and there is no danger that I will refuse to answer them."

2

⌒

"A Scandal in Bohemia"
(1891)

I

To Sherlock Holmes she is always *the* woman. I have seldom heard him mention her under any other name. In his eyes she eclipses and predominates the whole of her sex. It was not that he felt any emotion akin to love for Irene Adler. All emotions, and that one particularly, were abhorrent to his cold, precise but admirably balanced mind. He was, I take it, the most perfect reasoning and observing machine that the world has seen, but as a lover he would have placed himself in a false position. He never spoke of the softer passions, save with a gibe and a sneer. They were admirable things for the observer—excellent for drawing the veil from men's motives and actions. But for the trained reasoner to admit such intrusions into his own delicate and finely adjusted temperament was to introduce a distracting factor which might throw a doubt upon all his mental results. Grit in a sensitive instrument, or a crack in one of his own high-power lenses, would not be more disturbing than a strong emotion in a nature such as his. And yet there was but one woman to him, and that woman was the late Irene Adler, of dubious and questionable memory.

I had seen little of Holmes lately. My marriage had drifted us away from each other. My own complete happiness, and the home-centered interests which rise up around the man who first finds himself master of his own establishment, were sufficient to absorb all my attention, while

Holmes, who loathed every form of society with his whole Bohemian soul, remained in our lodgings in Baker Street, buried among his old books, and alternating from week to week between cocaine and ambition, the drowsiness of the drug, and the fierce energy of his own keen nature. He was still, as ever, deeply attracted by the study of crime, and occupied his immense faculties and extraordinary powers of observation in following out those clues, and clearing up those mysteries which had been abandoned as hopeless by the official police. From time to time I heard some vague account of his doings: of his summons to Odessa in the case of the Trepoff murder, of his clearing up of the singular tragedy of the Atkinson brothers at Trincomalee, and finally of the mission which he had accomplished so delicately and successfully for the reigning family of Holland. Beyond these signs of his activity, however, which I merely shared with all the readers of the daily press, I knew little of my former friend and companion.

One night—it was on the twentieth of March, 1888—I was returning from a journey to a patient (for I had now returned to civil practice), when my way led me through Baker Street. As I passed the well-remembered door, which must always be associated in my mind with my wooing, and with the dark incidents of the *Study in Scarlet,* I was seized with a keen desire to see Holmes again, and to know how he was employing his extraordinary powers. His rooms were brilliantly lit, and, even as I looked up, I saw his tall, spare figure pass twice in a dark silhouette against the blind. He was pacing the room swiftly, eagerly, with his head sunk upon his chest and his hands clasped behind him. To me, who knew his every mood and habit, his attitude and manner told their own story. He was at work again. He had risen out of his drug-created dreams and was hot upon the scent of some new problem. I rang the bell and was shown up to the chamber which had formerly been in part my own.

His manner was not effusive. It seldom was; but he was glad, I think, to see me. With hardly a word spoken, but with a kindly eye, he waved me to an armchair, threw across his case of cigars, and indicated a spirit case and a gasogene in the corner. Then he stood before the fire and looked me over in his singular introspective fashion.

"Wedlock suits you," he remarked. "I think, Watson, that you have put on seven and a half pounds since I saw you."

"Seven!" I answered.

"Indeed, I should have thought a little more. Just a trifle more, I fancy, Watson. And in practice again, I observe. You did not tell me that you intended to go into harness."

"Then, how do you know?"

"I see it, I deduce it. How do I know that you have been getting yourself very wet lately, and that you have a most clumsy and careless servant girl?"

"My dear Holmes," said I, "this is too much. You would certainly have been burned, had you lived a few centuries ago. It is true that I had a country walk on Thursday and came home in a dreadful mess, but as I have changed my clothes I can't imagine how you deduce it. As to Mary Jane, she is incorrigible, and my wife has given her notice; but there, again, I fail to see how you work it out."

He chuckled to himself and rubbed his long, nervous hands together.

"It is simplicity itself," said he; "my eyes tell me that on the inside of your left shoe, just where the firelight strikes it, the leather is scored by six almost parallel cuts. Obviously they have been caused by someone who has very carelessly scraped round the edges of the sole in order to remove crusted mud from it. Hence, you see, my double deduction that you had been out in vile weather, and that you had a particularly malignant boot-slitting specimen of the London slavey. As to your practice, if a gentleman walks into my rooms smelling of iodoform, with a black mark of nitrate of silver upon his right forefinger, and a bulge on the right side of his top-hat to show where he has secreted his stethoscope, I must be dull, indeed, if I do not pronounce him to be an active member of the medical profession."

I could not help laughing at the ease with which he explained his process of deduction. "When I hear you give your reasons," I remarked, "the thing always appears to me to be so ridiculously simple that I could easily do it myself, though at each successive instance of your reasoning I am baffled until you explain your process. And yet I believe that my eyes are as good as yours."

"Quite so," he answered, lighting a cigarette, and throwing himself down into an armchair. "You see, but you do not observe. The distinction is clear. For example, you have frequently seen the steps which lead up from the hall to this room."

"Frequently."

"How often?"

"Well, some hundreds of times."

"Then how many are there?"

"How many? I don't know."

"Quite so! You have not observed. And yet you have seen. That is just my point. Now, I know that there are seventeen steps, because I have both seen and observed. By the way, since you are interested in these little problems, and since you are good enough to chronicle one or two of my trifling experiences, you may be interested in this." He threw over a sheet of thick, pink-tinted note-paper which had been lying open upon the table. "It came by the last post," said he. "Read it aloud."

The note was undated, and without either signature or address.

There will call upon you to-night, at a quarter to eight o'clock [it said], a gentleman who desires to consult you upon a matter of the very deepest moment. Your recent services to one of the royal houses of Europe have shown that you are one who may safely be trusted with matters which are of an importance, which can hardly be exaggerated. This account of you we have from all quarters received. Be in your chamber then at that hour, and do not take it amiss if your visitor wear a mask.

"This is indeed a mystery," I remarked. "What do you imagine that it means?"

"I have no data yet. It is a capital mistake to theorize before one has data. Insensibly one begins to twist facts to suit theories, instead of theories to suit facts. But the note itself. What do you deduce from it?"

I carefully examined the writing, and the paper upon which it was written.

"The man who wrote it was presumably well to do," I remarked, endeavouring to imitate my companion's processes. "Such paper could not be bought under half a crown a packet. It is peculiarly strong and stiff."

"Peculiar—that is the very word," said Holmes. "It is not an English paper at all. Hold it up to the light."

I did so, and saw a large *"E"* with a small *"g,"* a *"P,"* and a large *"G"* with a small *"t"* woven into the texture of the paper.

"What do you make of that?" asked Holmes.

"The name of the maker, no doubt; or his monogram, rather."

"Not at all. The *'G'* with the small *'t'* stands for 'Gesellschaft,' which is the German for 'Company.' It is a customary contraction like our 'Co.' *'P,'* of course, stands for 'Papier.' Now for the *'Eg.'* Let us glance at our Continental Gazetteer." He took down a heavy brown volume from his shelves. "Eglow, Eglonitz—here we are, Egria. It is in a German-speaking country—in Bohemia, not far from Carlsbad. 'Remarkable as being the scene of the death of Wallenstein, and for its numerous glass-factories and paper-mills.' Ha, ha, my boy, what do you make of that?" His eyes sparkled, and he sent up a great blue triumphant cloud from his cigarette.

"The paper was made in Bohemia," I said.

"Precisely. And the man who wrote the note is a German. Do you note the peculiar construction of the sentence—'This account of you we have from all quarters received.' A Frenchman or Russian could not have written that. It is the German who is so uncourteous to his verbs. It only remains, therefore, to discover what is wanted by this German who writes upon Bohemian paper and prefers wearing a mask to showing his face. And here he comes, if I am not mistaken, to resolve all our doubts."

As he spoke there was the sharp sound of horses' hoofs and grating wheels against the curb, followed by a sharp pull at the bell; Holmes whistled.

"A pair, by the sound," said he. "Yes," he continued, glancing out of the window. "A nice little brougham and a pair of beauties. A hundred and fifty guineas apiece. There's money in this case, Watson, if there is nothing else."

"I think that I had better go, Holmes."

"Not a bit, Doctor. Stay where you are. I am lost without my Boswell. And this promises to be interesting. It would be a pity to miss it."

"But your client—"

"Never mind him. I may want your help, and so may he. Here he comes. Sit down in that armchair, Doctor, and give us your best attention."

A slow and heavy step, which had been heard upon the stairs and in the passage, paused immediately outside the door. Then there was a loud and authoritative tap.

"Come in!" said Holmes.

A man entered who could hardly have been less than six feet six inches in height, with the chest and limbs of a Hercules. His dress was rich with a richness which would, in England, be looked upon as akin to bad taste. Heavy bands of astrakhan were slashed across the sleeves and fronts of his double-breasted coat, while the deep blue cloak which was thrown over his shoulders was lined with flame-coloured silk and secured at the neck with a brooch which consisted of a single flaming beryl. Boots which extended halfway up his calves, and which were trimmed at the tops with rich brown fur, completed the impression of barbaric opulence which was suggested by his whole appearance. He carried a broad-brimmed hat in his hand, while he wore across the upper part of his face, extending down past the cheekbones, a black vizard mask, which he had apparently adjusted that very moment, for his hand was still raised to it as he entered. From the lower part of the face he appeared to be a man of strong character, with a thick, hanging lip, and a long, straight chin suggestive of resolution pushed to the length of obstinacy.

"You had my note?" he asked with a deep harsh voice and a strongly marked German accent. "I told you that I would call." He looked from one to the other of us, as if uncertain which to address.

"Pray take a seat," said Holmes. "This is my friend and colleague, Dr. Watson, who is occasionally good enough to help me in my cases. Whom have I the honour to address?"

"You may address me as the Count Von Kramm, a Bohemian nobleman. I understand that this gentleman, your friend, is a man of honour and discretion, whom I may trust with a matter of the most extreme importance. If not, I should much prefer to communicate with you alone."

I rose to go, but Holmes caught me by the wrist and pushed me back into my chair. "It is both, or none," said he. "You may say before this gentleman anything which you may say to me."

The Count shrugged his broad shoulders. "Then I must begin," said he, "by binding you both to absolute secrecy for two years; at the end of that time the matter will be of no importance. At present it is not too much to say that it is of such weight it may have an influence upon European history."

"I promise," said Holmes.

"And I."

"You will excuse this mask," continued our strange visitor. "The august person who employs me wishes his agent to be unknown to you, and I may confess at once that the title by which I have just called myself is not exactly my own."

"I was aware of it," said Holmes drily.

"The circumstances are of great delicacy, and every precaution has to be taken to quench what might grow to be an immense scandal and seriously compromise one of the reigning families of Europe. To speak plainly, the matter implicates the great House of Ormstein, hereditary kings of Bohemia."

"I was also aware of that," murmured Holmes, settling himself down in his armchair and closing his eyes.

Our visitor glanced with some apparent surprise at the languid, lounging figure of the man who had been no doubt depicted to him as the most incisive reasoner and most energetic agent in Europe. Holmes slowly reopened his eyes and looked impatiently at his gigantic client.

"If your Majesty would condescend to state your case," he remarked, "I should be better able to advise you."

The man sprang from his chair and paced up and down the room in uncontrollable agitation. Then, with a gesture of desperation, he tore the mask from his face and hurled it upon the ground. "You are right," he cried; "I am the King. Why should I attempt to conceal it?"

"Why, indeed?" murmured Holmes. "Your Majesty had not spoken before I was aware that I was addressing Wilhelm Gottsreich Sigismond von Ormstein, Grand Duke of Cassel-Felstein, and hereditary King of Bohemia."

"But you can understand," said our strange visitor, sitting down once more and passing his hand over his high white forehead, "you can understand that I am not accustomed to doing such business in my own person. Yet the matter was so delicate that I could not confide it to an agent without putting myself in his power. I have come incognito from Prague for the purpose of consulting you."

"Then, pray consult," said Holmes, shutting his eyes once more.

"The facts are briefly these: Some five years ago, during a lengthy visit to Warsaw, I made the acquaintance of the well-known adventuress, Irene Adler. The name is no doubt familiar to you."

"Kindly look her up in my index, Doctor," murmured Holmes without opening his eyes. For many years he had adopted a system of docketing all paragraphs concerning men and things, so that it was difficult to name a subject or a person on which he could not at once furnish information. In this case I found her biography sandwiched in between that of a Hebrew rabbi and that of a staff-commander who had written a monograph upon the deep-sea fishes.

"Let me see!" said Holmes. "Hum! Born in New Jersey in the year 1858. Contralto—hum! La Scala, hum! Prima donna Imperial Opera of Warsaw—yes! Retired from operatic stage—ha! Living in London—quite so! Your Majesty, as I understand, became entangled with this young person, wrote her some compromising letters, and is now desirous of getting those letters back."

"Precisely so. But how——"

"Was there a secret marriage?"

"None."

"No legal papers or certificates?"

"None."

"Then I fail to follow your Majesty. If this young person should produce her letters for blackmailing or other purposes, how is she to prove their authenticity?"

"There is the writing."

"Pooh, pooh! Forgery."

"My private note-paper."

"Stolen."

"My own seal."

"Imitated."

"My photograph."

"Bought."

"We were both in the photograph."

"Oh, dear! That is very bad! Your Majesty has indeed committed an indiscretion."

"I was mad—insane."

"You have compromised yourself seriously."

"I was only Crown Prince then. I was young. I am but thirty now."

"It must be recovered."

"We have tried and failed."

"Your Majesty must pay. It must be bought."

"She will not sell."

"Stolen, then."

"Five attempts have been made. Twice burglars in my pay ransacked her house. Once we diverted her luggage when she travelled. Twice she has been waylaid. There has been no result."

"No sign of it?"

"Absolutely none."

Holmes laughed. "It is quite a pretty little problem," said he.

"But a very serious one to me," returned the King reproachfully.

"Very, indeed. And what does she propose to do with the photograph?"

"To ruin me."

"But how?"

"I am about to be married."

"So I have heard."

"To Clotilde Lothman von Saxe-Meningen, second daughter of the King of Scandinavia. You may know the strict principles of her family. She is herself the very soul of delicacy. A shadow of a doubt as to my conduct would bring the matter to an end."

"And Irene Adler?"

"Threatens to send them the photograph. And she will do it. I know that she will do it. You do not know her, but she has a soul of steel. She has the face of the most beautiful of women, and the mind of the most resolute of men. Rather than I should marry another woman, there are no lengths to which she would not go—none."

"You are sure that she has not sent it yet?"

"I am sure."

"And why?"

"Because she has said that she would send it on the day when the betrothal was publicly proclaimed. That will be next Monday."

"Oh, then we have three days yet," said Holmes with a yawn. "That is very fortunate, as I have one or two matters of importance to look into just at present. Your Majesty will, of course, stay in London for the present?"

"Certainly. You will find me at the Langham under the name of the Count Von Kramm."

"Then I shall drop you a line to let you know how we progress."

"Pray do so. I shall be all anxiety."

"Then, as to money?"

"You have carte blanche."

"Absolutely?"

"I tell you that I would give one of the provinces of my kingdom to have that photograph."

"And for present expenses?"

The King took a heavy chamois leather bag from under his cloak and laid it on the table.

"There are three hundred pounds in gold and seven hundred in notes," he said.

Holmes scribbled a receipt upon a sheet of his note-book and handed it to him.

"And Mademoiselle's address?" he asked.

"Is Briony Lodge, Serpentine Avenue, St. John's Wood."

Holmes took a note of it. "One other question," said he. "Was the photograph a cabinet?"

"It was."

"Then, good-night, your Majesty, and I trust that we shall soon have some goods news for you. And good-night, Watson," he added, as the wheels of the royal brougham rolled down the street. "If you will be good enough to call to-morrow afternoon at three o'clock I should like to chat this little matter over with you."

2

At three o'clock precisely I was at Baker Street, but Holmes had not yet returned. The landlady informed me that he had left the house shortly after eight o'clock in the morning. I sat down beside the fire, however, with the intention of awaiting him, however long he might be. I was already deeply interested in his inquiry, for, though it was surrounded by none of the grim and strange features which were associated with the two crimes which I have already recorded, still, the nature of the case and the exalted station of his client gave it a character of its own. Indeed, apart from the nature of the investigation which my friend had on hand, there was something in his masterly grasp of a situation, and his keen, incisive reasoning, which made it a pleasure to me to study his system of work, and to follow the quick, subtle methods by which he disentangled the most inextricable mysteries. So accustomed was I to his invariable success that the very possibility of his failing had ceased to enter into my head.

It was close upon four before the door opened, and a drunken-looking groom, ill-kempt and side-whiskered, with an inflamed face and disreputable clothes, walked into the room. Accustomed as I was to my friend's amazing powers in the use of disguises, I had to look three times before I was certain that it was indeed he. With a nod he vanished into the bedroom, whence he emerged in five minutes tweed-suited and respectable, as of old. Putting his hands into his pockets, he stretched out his legs in front of the fire and laughed heartily for some minutes.

"Well, really!" he cried, and then he choked and laughed again until he was obliged to lie back, limp and helpless, in the chair.

"What is it?"

"It's quite too funny. I am sure you could never guess how I employed my morning, or what I ended by doing."

"I can't imagine. I suppose that you have been watching the habits, and perhaps the house, of Miss Irene Adler."

"Quite so; but the sequel was rather unusual. I will tell you, however. I left the house a little after eight o'clock this morning in the character of a groom out of work. There is a wonderful sympathy and freemasonry among horsy men. Be one of them, and you will know all that there is to know. I soon found Briony Lodge. It is a *bijou* villa, with a garden at the back, but built out in front right up to the road, two stories. Chubb lock to the door. Large sitting-room on the right side, well furnished, with long windows almost to the floor, and those preposterous English window fasteners which a child could open. Behind there was nothing remarkable, save that the passage window could be reached from the top of the coach-house. I walked round it and examined it closely from every point of view, but without noting anything else of interest.

"I then lounged down the street and found, as I expected, that there was a mews in a lane which runs down by one wall of the garden. I lent the ostlers a hand in rubbing down their horses, and received in exchange twopence, a glass of half and half, two fills of shag tobacco, and as much information as I could desire about Miss Adler, to say nothing of half a dozen other people in the neighbourhood in whom I was not in the least interested, but whose biographies I was compelled to listen to."

"And what of Irene Adler?" I asked.

"Oh, she has turned all the men's heads down in that part. She is the daintiest thing under a bonnet on this planet. So say the Serpentine-mews, to a man. She lives quietly, sings at concerts, drives out at five every day, and returns at seven sharp for dinner. Seldom goes out at other times, except when she sings. Has only one male visitor, but a good deal of him. He is dark, handsome, and dashing, never calls less than once a day, and often twice. He is a Mr. Godfrey Norton, of the Inner Temple. See the advantages of a cabman as a confidant. They had driven him home a dozen times from Serpentine-mews, and knew all about him. When I had listened to all they had to tell, I began to walk up and down near Briony Lodge once more, and to think over my plan of campaign.

"This Godfrey Norton was evidently an important factor in the matter. He was a lawyer. That sounded ominous. What was the relation between them, and what the object of his repeated visits? Was she his client, his friend, or his mistress? If the former, she had probably transferred the photograph to his keeping. If the latter, it was less likely. On the issue of this question depended whether I should continue my work at Briony Lodge, or turn my attention to the gentleman's chambers in the

Temple. It was a delicate point, and it widened the field of my inquiry. I fear that I bore you with these details, but I have to let you see my little difficulties, if you are to understand the situation."

"I am following you closely," I answered.

"I was still balancing the matter in my mind when a hansom cab drove up to Briony Lodge, and a gentleman sprang out. He was a remarkably handsome man, dark, aquiline, and moustached—evidently the man of whom I had heard. He appeared to be in a great hurry, shouted to the cabman to wait, and brushed past the maid who opened the door with the air of a man who was thoroughly at home.

"He was in the house about half an hour, and I could catch glimpses of him in the windows of the sitting-room, pacing up and down, talking excitedly, and waving his arms. Of her I could see nothing. Presently he emerged, looking even more flurried than before. As he stepped up to the cab, he pulled a gold watch from his pocket and looked at it earnestly, 'Drive like the devil,' he shouted, 'first to Gross & Hankey's in Regent Street, and then to the Church of St. Monica in the Edgware Road. Half a guinea if you do it in twenty minutes!'

"Away they went, and I was just wondering whether I should not do well to follow them when up the lane came a neat little landau, the coachman with his coat only half-buttoned, and his tie under his ear, while all the tags of his harness were sticking out of the buckles. It hadn't pulled up before she shot out of the hall door and into it. I only caught a glimpse of her at the moment, but she was a lovely woman, with a face that a man might die for.

"'The Church of St. Monica, John,' she cried, 'and half a sovereign if you reach it in twenty minutes.'

"This was quite too good to lose, Watson. I was just balancing whether I should run for it, or whether I should perch behind her landau when a cab came through the street. The driver looked twice at such a shabby fare, but I jumped in before he could object. 'The Church of St. Monica,' said I, 'and half a sovereign if you reach it in twenty minutes.' It was twenty-five minutes to twelve, and of course it was clear enough what was in the wind.

"My cabby drove fast. I don't think I ever drove faster, but the others were there before us. The cab and the landau with their steaming horses were in front of the door when I arrived. I paid the man and hurried into the church. There was not a soul there save the two whom I had followed and a surpliced clergyman, who seemed to be expostulating with them. They were all three standing in a knot in front of the altar. I lounged up the side aisle like any other idler who has dropped into a church. Suddenly, to my surprise, the three at the altar faced round to me, and Godfrey Norton came running as hard as he could towards me.

"'Thank God,' he cried. 'You'll do. Come! Come!'

"'What then?' I asked.

"'Come, man, come, only three minutes, or it won't be legal.'

"I was half-dragged up to the altar, and before I knew where I was I found myself mumbling responses which were whispered in my ear, and vouching for things of which I knew nothing, and generally assisting in the secure tying up of Irene Adler, spinster, to Godfrey Norton, bachelor. It was all done in an instant, and there was the gentleman thanking me on the one side and the lady on the other, while the clergyman beamed on me in front. It was the most preposterous position in which I ever found myself in my life, and it was the thought of it that started me laughing just now. It seems that there had been some informality about their license, that the clergyman absolutely refused to marry them without a witness of some sort, and that my lucky appearance saved the bridegroom from having to sally out into the streets in search of a best man. The bride gave me a sovereign, and I mean to wear it on my watch-chain in memory of the occasion."

"This was very unexpected turn of affairs," said I; "and what then?"

"Well, I found my plans very seriously menaced. It looked as if the pair might take an immediate departure, and so necessitate very prompt and energetic measures on my part. At the church door, however, they separated, he driving back to the Temple, and she to her own house. 'I shall drive out in the park at five as usual,' she said as she left him. I heard no more. They drove away in different directions, and I went off to make my own arrangements."

"Which are?"

"Some cold beef and a glass of beer," he answered, ringing the bell. "I have been too busy to think of food, and I am likely to be busier still this evening. By the way, Doctor, I shall want your cooperation."

"I shall be delighted."

"You don't mind breaking the law?"

"Not in the least."

"Nor running a chance of arrest?"

"Not in a good cause."

"Oh, the cause is excellent!"

"Then I am your man."

"I was sure that I might rely on you."

"But what is it you wish?"

"When Mrs. Turner has brought in the tray I will make it clear to you. Now," he said as he turned hungrily on the simple fare that our landlady had provided, "I must discuss it while I eat, for I have not much time. It is nearly five now. In two hours we must be on the scene of action. Miss Irene, or Madame, rather, returns from her drive at seven. We must be at Briony Lodge to meet her."

"And what then?"

"You must leave that to me. I have already arranged what is to occur. There is only one point on which I must insist. You must not interfere, come what may. You understand?"

"I am to be neutral?"

"To do nothing whatever. There will probably be some small unpleasantness. Do not join in it. It will end in my being conveyed into the house. Four or five minutes afterwards the sitting-room window will open. You are to station yourself close to that open window."

"Yes."

"You are to watch me, for I will be visible to you."

"Yes."

"And when I raise my hand—so—you will throw into the room what I give you to throw, and will, at the same time, raise the cry of fire. You quite follow me?"

"Entirely."

"It is nothing very formidable," he said, taking a long cigar-shaped roll from his pocket. "It is an ordinary plumber's smoke-rocket, fitted with a cap at either end to make it self-lighting. Your task is confined to that. When you raise your cry of fire, it will be taken up by quite a number of people. You may then walk to the end of the street, and I will rejoin you in ten minutes. I hope that I have made myself clear?"

"I am to remain neutral, to get near the window, to watch you, and at the signal to throw in this object, then to raise the cry of fire, and to wait you at the corner of the street."

"Precisely."

"Then you may entirely rely on me."

"That is excellent. I think, perhaps, it is almost time that I prepare for the new role I have to play."

He disappeared into his bedroom and returned in a few minutes in the character of an amiable and simple-minded Nonconformist clergyman. His broad black hat, his baggy trousers, his white tie, his sympathetic smile, and general look of peering and benevolent curiosity were such as Mr. John Hare alone could have equalled. It was not merely that Holmes changed his costume. His expression, his manner, his very soul seemed to vary with every fresh part that he assumed. The stage lost a fine actor, even as science lost an acute reasoner, when he became a specialist in crime.

It was a quarter past six when we left Baker Street, and it still wanted ten minutes to the hour when we found ourselves in Serpentine Avenue. It was already dusk, and the lamps were just being lighted as we paced up and down in front of Briony Lodge, waiting for the coming of its occupant. The house was just such as I had pictured it from Sherlock Holmes's succinct description, but the locality appeared to be less private than I expected. On the contrary, for a small street in a quiet neighbourhood, it was remarkably animated. There was a group of shabbily dressed men smoking and laughing in a corner, a scissors-grinder with his wheel, two guardsmen who were flirting with a nurse-girl, and several well-dressed young men who were lounging up and down with cigars in their mouths.

"You see," remarked Holmes, as we paced to and fro in front of the house, "this marriage rather simplifies matters. The photograph becomes a double-edged weapon now. The chances are that she would be as averse to its being seen by Mr. Godfrey Norton, as our client is to its coming to the eyes of his princess. Now the question is, Where are we to find the photograph?"

"Where, indeed?"

"It is most unlikely that she carries it about with her. It is cabinet size. Too large for easy concealment about a woman's dress. She knows that the King is capable of having her waylaid and searched. Two attempts of the sort have already been made. We may take it, then, that she does not carry it about with her."

"Where, then?"

"Her banker or her lawyer. There is that double possibility. But I am inclined to think neither. Women are naturally secretive, and they like to do their own secreting. Why should she hand it over to anyone else? She could trust her own guardianship, but she could not tell what indirect or political influence might be brought to bear upon a business man. Besides, remember that she had resolved to use it within a few days. It must be where she can lay her hands upon it. It must be in her own house."

"But it has twice been burgled."

"Pshaw! They did not know how to look."

"But how will you look?"

"I will not look."

"What then?"

"I will get her to show me."

"But she will refuse."

"She will not be able to. But I hear the rumble of wheels. It is her carriage. Now carry out my orders to the letter."

As he spoke the gleam of the side-lights of a carriage came round the curve of the avenue. It was a smart little landau which rattled up to the door of Briony Lodge. As it pulled up, one of the loafing men at the corner dashed forward to open the door in the hope of earning a copper, but was elbowed away by another loafer, who had rushed up with the same intention. A fierce quarrel broke out, which was increased by the two guardsmen, who took sides with one of the loungers, and by the scissors-grinder, who was equally hot upon the other side. A blow was struck, and in an instant the lady, who had stepped from her carriage, was the center of a little knot of flushed and struggling men, who struck savagely at each other with their fists and sticks. Holmes dashed into the crowd to protect the lady; but just as he reached her he gave a cry and dropped to the ground, with the blood running freely down his face. At his fall the guardsmen took to their heels in one direction and the loungers in the other, while a number of better-dressed people, who had watched the scuffle without taking part in it, crowded in to help the lady and to attend to the injured man. Irene Adler, as I will still call her, had hurried up the steps; but she stood at the top with her superb figure outlined against the lights of the hall, looking back into the street.

"Is the poor gentleman much hurt?" she asked.

"He is dead," cried several voices.

"No, no, there's life in him!" shouted another. "But he'll be gone before you can get him to hospital."

"He's a brave fellow," said a woman. "They would have had the lady's purse and watch if it hadn't been for him. They were a gang, and a rough one, too. Ah, he's breathing now."

"He can't lie in the street. May we bring him in, marm?"

"Surely. Bring him into the sitting room. There is a comfortable sofa. This way, please!"

Slowly and solemnly he was borne into Briony Lodge and laid out in the principal room, while I still observed the proceedings from my post by the window. The lamps had been lit, but the blinds had not been drawn, so that I could see Holmes as he lay upon the couch. I do not know whether he was seized with compunction at that moment for the part he was playing, but I know that I never felt more heartily ashamed of myself in my life than when I saw the beautiful creature against whom I was conspiring, or the grace and kindliness with which she waited upon the injured man. And yet it would be the blackest treachery to Holmes to draw back now from the part which he had intrusted to me. I hardened my heart, and took the smoke-rocket from under my ulster. After all, I thought, we are not injuring her. We are but preventing her from injuring another.

Holmes had sat up upon the couch, and I saw him motion like a man who is in need of air. A maid rushed across and threw open the window. At the same instant I saw him raise his hand, and at the signal I tossed my rocket into the room with a cry of "Fire!" The word was no sooner out of my mouth than the whole crowd of spectators, well dressed and ill—gentlemen, ostlers, and servant-maids—joined in a general shriek of "Fire!" Thick clouds of smoke curled through the room and out at the open window. I caught a glimpse of rushing figures, and a moment later the voice of Holmes from within assuring them that it was a false alarm. Slipping through the shouting crowd I made my way to the corner of the street, and in ten minutes was rejoiced to find my friend's arm in mine, and to get away from the scene of uproar. He walked swiftly and in silence for some few minutes until we had turned down one of the quiet streets which lead towards the Edgware Road.

"You did it very nicely, Doctor," he remarked. "Nothing could have been better. It is all right."

"You have the photograph?"

"I know where it is."

"And how did you find out?"

"She showed me, as I told you she would."

"I am still in the dark."

"I do not wish to make a mystery," said he, laughing. "The matter was perfectly simple. You, of course, saw that everyone in the street was an accomplice. They were all engaged for the evening."

"I guessed as much."

"Then, when the row broke out, I had a little moist red paint in the palm of my hand. I rushed forward, fell down, clapped my hand to my face, and became a piteous spectacle. It is an old trick."

"That also I could fathom."

"Then they carried me in. She was bound to have me in. What else could she do? And into her sitting-room, which was the very room which I suspected. It lay between that and her bedroom, and I was determined to see which. They laid me on a couch, I motioned for air, they were compelled to open the window, and you had your chance."

"How did that help you?"

"It was all-important. When a woman thinks that her house is on fire, her instinct is at once to rush to the thing which she values most. It is a perfectly overpowering impulse, and I have more than once taken advantage of it. In the case of the Darlington substitution scandal it was of use to me, and also in the Arnsworth Castle business. A married woman grabs at her baby; an unmarried one reaches for her jewel-box. Now it was clear to me that our lady of to-day had nothing in the house more precious to her than what we are in quest of. She would rush to

secure it. The alarm of fire was admirably done. The smoke and shouting were enough to shake nerves of steel. She responded beautifully.
The photograph is in a recess behind a sliding panel just above the right
bell-pull. She was there in an instant, and I caught a glimpse of it as she
half-drew it out. When I cried out that it was a false alarm, she replaced
it, glanced at the rocket, rushed from the room, and I have not seen her
since. I rose, and, making my excuses, escaped from the house. I hesitated whether to attempt to secure the photograph at once; but the
coachman had come in, and as he was watching me narrowly it seemed
safer to wait. A little over-precipitance may ruin all."

"And now?" I asked.

"Our quest is practically finished. I shall call with the King to-
morrow, and with you, if you care to come with us. We will be shown
into the sitting-room to wait for the lady; but it is probable that when
she comes she may find neither us nor the photograph. It might be a
satisfaction to his Majesty to regain it with his own hands."

"And when will you call?"

"At eight in the morning. She will not be up, so that we shall have a
clear field. Besides, we must be prompt, for this marriage may mean a complete change in her life and habits. I must wire to the King without delay."

We had reached Baker Street and had stopped at the door. He was
searching his pockets for the key when someone passing said:

"Good-night, Mister Sherlock Holmes."

There were several people on the pavement at the time, but the greeting appeared to come from a slim youth in an ulster who had hurried by.

"I've heard that voice before," said Holmes, staring down the dimly
lit street. "Now, I wonder who the deuce that could have been."

3

I slept at Baker Street that night, and we were engaged upon our
toast and coffee in the morning when the King of Bohemia rushed into
the room.

"You have really got it!" he cried, grasping Sherlock Holmes by either shoulder and looking eagerly into his face.

"Not yet."

"But you have hopes?"

"I have hopes."

"Then, come. I am all impatience to be gone."

"We must have a cab."

"No, my brougham is waiting."

"Then that will simplify matters." We descended and started off once more for Briony Lodge.

"Irene Adler is married," remarked Holmes.

"Married! When?"

"Yesterday."

"But to whom?"

"To an English lawyer named Norton."

"But she could not love him."

"I am in hopes that she does."

"And why in hopes?"

"Because it would spare your Majesty all fear of future annoyance. If the lady loves her husband, she does not love your Majesty. If she does not love your Majesty, there is no reason why she should interfere with your Majesty's plan."

"It is true. And yet——Well! I wish she had been of my own station! What a queen she would have made!" He relapsed into a moody silence, which was not broken until we drew up in Serpentine Avenue.

The door of Briony Lodge was open, and an elderly woman stood upon the steps. She watched us with a sardonic eye as we stepped from the brougham.

"Mr. Sherlock Holmes, I believe?" said she.

"I am Mr. Holmes," answered my companion, looking at her with a questioning and rather startled gaze.

"Indeed! My mistress told me that you were likely to call. She left this morning with her husband by the 5:15 train from Charing Cross for the Continent."

"What!" Sherlock Holmes staggered back, white with chagrin and surprise. "Do you mean that she has left England?"

"Never to return."

"And the papers?" asked the King hoarsely. "All is lost."

"We shall see." He pushed past the servant and rushed into the drawing-room, followed by the King and myself. The furniture was scattered about in every direction, with dismantled shelves and open drawers, as if the lady had hurriedly ransacked them before her flight. Holmes rushed at the bell-pull, tore back a small sliding shutter, and, plunging in his hand, pulled out a photograph and a letter. The photograph was of Irene Adler herself in evening dress, the letter was superscribed to "Sherlock Holmes, Esq. To be left till called for." My friend tore it open, and we all three read it together. It was dated at midnight of the preceding night and ran in this way:

MY DEAR MR. SHERLOCK HOLMES:

You really did it very well. You took me in completely. Until after the alarm of fire, I had not a suspicion. But then, when I found how I had betrayed myself, I began to think. I had been warned against you months ago. I had been told that if the King employed an agent it would certainly be you. And your address had been given me. Yet, with all this, you made me reveal what you wanted to know. Even after I became suspicious, I found it hard to think evil of such a dear, kind old clergyman. But, you know, I have been trained as an actress myself. Male costume is nothing new to me. I often take advantage of the freedom which it gives. I sent John, the coachman, to watch you, ran upstairs, got into my walking-clothes, as I call them, and came down just as you departed.

Well, I followed you to your door, and so made sure that I was really an object of interest to the celebrated Mr. Sherlock Holmes. Then I, rather imprudently, wished you good-night, and started for the Temple to see my husband.

We both thought the best resource was flight, when pursued by so formidable an antagonist; so you will find the nest empty when you call to-morrow. As to the photograph, your client may rest in peace. I love and am loved by a better man than he. The King may do what he will without hindrance from one whom he has cruelly wronged. I keep it only to safeguard myself, and to preserve a weapon which will always secure me from any steps which he might take in the future. I leave a photograph which he might care to possess; and I remain, dear Mr. Sherlock Holmes.

Very truly yours,

Irene Norton, *née* Adler.

"What a woman—oh, what a woman!" cried the King of Bohemia, when we had all three read this epistle. "Did I not tell you how quick and resolute she was? Would she not have made an admirable queen? Is it not a pity that she was not on my level?"

"From what I have seen of the lady she seems indeed to be on a very different level to your Majesty," said Holmes coldly. "I am sorry that I have not been able to bring your Majesty's business to a more successful conclusion."

"On the contrary, my dear sir," cried the King; "nothing could be more successful. I know that her word is inviolate. The photograph is now as safe as if it were in the fire."

"I am glad to hear your Majesty say so."

"I am immensely indebted to you. Pray tell me in what way I can reward you. This ring——" He slipped an emerald snake ring from his finger and held it out upon the palm of his hand.

"Your Majesty has something which I should value even more highly," said Holmes.

"You have but to name it."

"This photograph!"

The King stared at him in amazement.

"Irene's photograph!" he cried. "Certainly, if you wish it."

"I thank your Majesty. Then there is no more to be done in the matter. I have the honour to wish you a very good-morning." He bowed, and, turning away without observing the hand which the King had stretched out to him, he set off in my company for his chambers.

And that was how a great scandal threatened to affect the kingdom of Bohemia, and how the best plans of Mr. Sherlock Holmes were beaten by a woman's wit. He used to make merry over the cleverness of women, but I have not heard him do it of late. And when he speaks of Irene Adler, or when he refers to her photograph, it is always under the honourable title of *the* woman.

3

≈

"The Los Amigos Fiasco"
(1892)

I used to be the leading practitioner of Los Amigos. Of course, everyone has heard of the great electrical generating gear there. The town is widespread and there are dozens of little townlets and villages all around which receive their supply from the same centre, so that the works are on a very large scale. The Los Amigos folk say that they are the largest upon earth, but then we claim that for everything in Los Amigos except the gaol and the death rate. Those are said to be the smallest.

Now, with so fine an electrical supply, it seemed to be a sinful waste of hemp that the Los Amigos criminals should perish in the old-fashioned manner. And then came the news of the electrocutions in the East, and how the results had not after all been so instantaneous as had been hoped. The Western engineers raised their eyebrows when they read of the puny shocks by which these men had perished, and they vowed in Los Amigos that when an irreclaimable came their way he should be dealt handsomely by, and have the run of all the big dynamos. There should be no reserve, said the engineers, but he should have all that they had got. And what the result of that would be none could predict, save that it must be absolutely blasting and deadly. Never before had a man been so charged with electricity as they would charge him. He was to be smitten by the essence of ten thunderbolts. Some prophesied combustion, and some disintegration and disappearance. They were waiting eagerly to settle the question by actual demonstration, and it was just at the moment that Duncan Warner came that way.

Warner had been wanted by the law, and by nobody else, for many years. Desperado, murderer, train robber and road agent, he was a man beyond the pale of human pity. He had deserved a dozen deaths, and the Los Amigos folk grudged him so gaudy a one as that. He seemed to feel himself to be unworthy of it, for he made two frenzied attempts at escape. He was a powerful, muscular man, with a lion head, tangled black locks, and a sweeping beard which covered his broad chest. When he was tried, there was no finer head in all the crowded court. It's no new thing to find the best face looking from the dock. But his good looks could not balance his bad deeds. His advocate did all he knew, but the cards lay against him, and Duncan Warner was handed over to the mercy of the big Los Amigos dynamos.

I was there at the committee meeting when the matter was discussed. The town council had chosen four experts to look after the arrangements. Three of them were admirable. There was Joseph McConnor, the very man who had designed the dynamos, and there was Joshua Westmacott, the chairman of the Los Amigos Electrical Supply Company Limited. Then there was myself, as the chief medical man, and lastly an old German of the name of Peter Stulpnagel. The Germans were a strong body at Los Amigos, and they all voted for their man. That was how he got on the committee. It was said that he had been a wonderful electrician at home, and he was eternally working with wires and insulators and Leyden jars; but, as he never seemed to get any further, or to have any results worth publishing, he came at last to be regarded as a harmless crank who had made science his hobby. We three practical men smiled when we heard that he had been elected as our colleague, and at the meeting we fixed it all up very nicely among ourselves without much thought of the old fellow who sat with his ears scooped forward in his hands, for he was a trifle hard of hearing, taking no more part in the proceedings than the gentlemen of the press who scribbled their notes on the back benches.

We did not take long to settle it all. In New York a strength of some two thousand volts had been used, and death had not been instantaneous. Evidently their shock had been too weak. Los Amigos should not fall into that error. The charge should be six times greater, and therefore, of course, it would be six times more effective. Nothing could possibly be more logical. The whole concentrated force of the great dynamos should be employed on Duncan Warner.

So we three settled it, and had already risen to break up the meeting, when our silent companion opened his mouth for the first time.

'Gentlemen,' said he, 'you appear to me to show an extraordinary ignorance upon the subject of electricity. You have not mastered the first principles of its actions upon a human being.'

The committee was about to break into an angry reply to this brusque comment, but the chairman of the Electrical Company tapped his forehead to claim its indulgence for the crankiness of the speaker.

'Pray tell us, sir,' said he, with an ironical smile, 'what is there in our conclusions with which you find fault?'

'With your assumption that a large dose of electricity will merely increase the effect of a small dose. Do you not think it possible that it might have an entirely different result? Do you know anything, by actual experiment, of the effect of such powerful shocks?'

'We know it by analogy,' said the chairman pompously. 'All drugs increase their effect when they increase their dose; for example—for example—'

'Whisky,' said Joseph McConnor.

'Quite so. Whisky. You see it there.'

Peter Stulpnagel smiled and shook his head. 'Your argument is not very good,' said he. 'When I used to take whisky, I used to find that one glass would excite me, but that six would send me to sleep, which is just the opposite. Now, suppose that electricity were to act in just the opposite way also, what then?'

We three practical men burst out laughing. We had known that our colleague was queer, but we never had thought that he would be as queer as this.

'What then?' repeated Peter Stulpnagel.

'We'll take our chances,' said the chairman.

'Pray consider,' said Peter, 'that workmen who have touched the wires, and who have received shocks of only a few hundred volts, have died instantly. The fact is well known. And yet when a much greater force was used upon a criminal at New York, the man struggled for some little time. Do you not clearly see that the smaller dose is the more deadly?'

'I think, gentlemen, that this discussion has been carried on quite long enough,' said the chairman, rising again. 'The point, I take it, has already been decided by the majority of the committee, and Duncan Warner shall be electrocuted on Tuesday by the full strength of the Los Amigos dynamos. Is it not so?'

'I agree,' said Joseph McConnor.

'I agree,' said I.

'And I protest,' said Peter Stulpnagel.

'Then the motion is carried, and your protest will be duly entered in the minutes,' said the chairman, and so the sitting was dissolved.

The attendance at the electrocution was a very small one. We four members of the committee were, of course, present with the executioner, who was to act under our orders. The others were the United States marshal, the governor of the gaol, the chaplain and three members of the press. The room was a small, brick chamber, forming an out-house to the Central Electrical Station. It had been used as a laundry, and had an oven and copper at one side, but no other furniture save a single chair for the condemned man. A metal plate for his feet was placed in front of it, to which ran a thick, insulated wire. Above, another wire depended from the ceiling, which could be connected with a small, metallic rod projecting from a cap which was to be placed upon his head. When this connection was established Duncan Warner's hour was come.

There was a solemn hush as we waited for the coming of the prisoner. The practical engineers looked a little pale and fidgeted nervously with the wires. Even the hardened marshal was ill at ease, for a mere hanging was one thing and this blasting of flesh and blood a very different one. As to the pressmen, their faces were whiter than the sheets which lay before them. The only man who appeared to feel none of the influence of these preparations was the little German crank, who strolled from one to the other with a smile on his lips and mischief in his eyes. More than once he even went so far as to burst into a shout of laughter, until the chaplain sternly rebuked him for his ill-timed levity.

'How can you so far forget yourself, Mr. Stulpnagel,' said he, 'as to jest in the presence of death?'

But the German was quite unabashed. 'If I were in the presence of death I should not jest,' said he, 'but since I am not I may do what I choose.'

This flippant reply was about to draw another and a sterner reproof from the chaplain when the door was swung open and two warders entered leading Duncan Warner between them. He glanced round him with a set face, stepped resolutely forward and seated himself upon the chair.

'Touch her off!' said he.

It was barbarous to keep him in suspense. The chaplain murmured a few words in his ear, the attendant placed the cap upon his head, and then, while we all held our breath, the wire and the metal were brought in contact.

'Great Scott!' shouted Duncan Warner.

He had bounded in his chair as the frightful shock crashed through his system. But he was not dead. On the contrary, his eyes gleamed far more brightly than they had done before. There was only one change, but it was a singular one. The black had passed from his hair and beard as the shadow passes from a landscape. They were both as white as snow. And yet there was no other sign of decay. His skin was smooth and plump and lustrous as a child's.

The marshal looked at the committee with a reproachful eye. 'There seems to be some hitch here, gentlemen,' said he.

We three practical men looked at each other.

Peter Stulpnagel smiled pensively.

'I think that another one should do it,' said I.

Again the connection was made, and again Duncan Warner sprang in his chair and shouted, but, indeed, were it not that he still remained in the chair, none of us would have recognised him. His hair and his beard had shredded off in an instant, and the room looked like a barber's shop on a Saturday night. There he sat, his eyes still shining, his skin radiant with the glow of perfect health, but with a scalp as bald as a Dutch cheese and a chin without so much as a trace of down. He began to revolve one of his arms, slowly and doubtfully at first, but with more confidence as he went on.

'That jint,' said he, 'has puzzled half the doctors on the Pacific Slope. It's as good as new, and as limber as a hickory twig.'

'You are feeling pretty well?' asked the old German.

'Never better in my life,' said Duncan Warner cheerily.

The situation was a painful one. The marshal glared at the committee. Peter Stulpnagel grinned and rubbed his hands. The engineers scratched their heads. The bald-headed prisoner revolved his arm and looked pleased.

'I think that one more shock—' began the chairman.

'No, sir,' said the marshal; 'we've had foolery enough for one morning. We are here for an execution, and an execution we'll have.'

'What do you propose?'

'There's a hook handy upon the ceiling. Fetch a rope, and we'll soon set this matter straight.'

There was another awkward delay while the warders departed for the cord. Peter Stulpnagel bent over Duncan Warner and whispered something in his ear. The desperado stared in surprise.

'You don't say?' he asked.

The German nodded.

'What! No ways?'

Peter shook his head, and the two began to laugh as though they shared some huge joke between them.

The rope was brought, and the marshal himself slipped the noose over the criminal's neck. Then the two warders, the assistant and he swung their victim into the air. For half an hour he hung—a dreadful sight—from the ceiling. Then in solemn silence they lowered him down, and one of the warders went out to order the shell to be brought round. But as he touched ground again what was our amazement when Duncan Warner put his hands up to his neck, loosened the noose, and took a long, deep breath.

'Paul Jefferson's sale is goin' well,' he remarked. 'I could see the crowd from up yonder,' and he nodded at the hook in the ceiling.

'Up with him again!' shouted the marshal, 'we'll get the life out of him somehow.'

In an instant the victim was up at the hook once more. They kept him there for an hour, but when he came down he was perfectly garrulous.

'Old man Plunket goes too much to the Arcady Saloon,' said he. 'Three times he's been there in an hour; and him with a family. Old man Plunket would do well to swear off.'

It was monstrous and incredible, but there it was. There was no getting round it. The man was there talking when he ought to have been dead. We all sat staring in amazement, but United States Marshal Carpenter was not a man to be euchred so easily. He motioned the others to one side, so that the prisoner was left standing alone.

'Duncan Warner,' said he slowly, 'you are here to play your part and I am here to play mine. Your game is to live if you can, and my game is to carry out the sentence of the law. You've beat us on electricity. I'll give you one there. And you've beat us on hanging, for you seem to thrive on it. But it's my turn to beat you now, for my duty has to be done.'

He pulled a six-shooter from his coat as he spoke and fired all the shots through the body of the prisoner. The room was so filled with smoke that we could see nothing, but when it cleared the prisoner was still standing there, looking down in disgust at the front of his coat.

'Coats must be cheap where you come from,' said he. 'Thirty dollars it cost me, and look at it now. The six holes in front are bad enough, but four of the balls have passed out, and a pretty fine state the back must be in.'

The marshal's revolver fell from his hand, and he dropped his arms to his sides, a beaten man.

'Maybe some of you gentlemen can tell me what this means,' said he, looking helplessly at the committee.

Peter Stulpnagel took a step forward. 'I'll tell you all about it,' said he.

'You seem to be the only person who knows anything.'

'I *am* the only person who knows anything. I should have warned these gentlemen; but, as they would not listen to me, I have allowed them to learn by experience. What you have done with your electricity is that you have increased the man's vitality until he can defy death for centuries.'

'Centuries!'

'Yes, it will take the wear of hundreds of years to exhaust the enormous nervous energy with which you have drenched him. Electricity is life, and you have charged him with it to the utmost. Perhaps in fifty years you might execute him, but I am not sanguine about it.'

'Great Scott! What shall I do with him?' cried the unhappy marshal.

Peter Stulpnagel shrugged his shoulders.

'It seems to me that it does not much matter what you do with him now,' said he.

'Maybe we could drain the electricity out of him again. Suppose we hang him up by the heels?'

'No, no, it's out of the question.'

'Well, well, he shall do no more mischief in Los Amigos, anyhow,' said the marshal, with decision. 'He shall go into the new gaol. The prison will wear him out.'

'On the contrary,' said Peter Stulpnagel, 'I think that it is much more probable that he will wear out the prison.'

It was rather a fiasco, and for years we didn't talk more about it than we could help, but it's no secret now, and I thought you might like to jot down the facts in your case-book.

4

✑

"The Case of Lady Sannox"
(1893)

The relations between Douglas Stone and the notorious Lady Sannox were very well known both among the fashionable circles of which she was a brilliant member, and the scientific bodies which numbered him among their most illustrious *confrères*. There was naturally, therefore, a very widespread interest when it was announced one morning that the lady had absolutely and for ever taken the veil, and that the world would see her no more. When, at the very tail of this rumour, there came the assurance that the celebrated operating surgeon, the man of steel nerves, had been found in the morning by his valet, seated on one side of his bed, smiling pleasantly upon the universe, with both legs jammed into one side of his breeches and his great brain about as valuable as a cap full of porridge, the matter was strong enough to give quite a little thrill of interest to folk who had never hoped that their jaded nerves were capable of such a sensation.

Douglas Stone in his prime was one of the most remarkable men in England. Indeed, he could hardly be said to have ever reached his prime, for he was but nine-and-thirty at the time of this little incident. Those who knew him best were aware that famous as he was as a surgeon, he might have succeeded with even greater rapidity in any of a dozen lines of life. He could have cut his way to fame as a soldier, struggled to it as an explorer, bullied for it in the court or built it out of stone and iron as an engineer. He was born to be great, for he could plan what another man dare not do, and he could do what another man dare not plan. In surgery none could follow him. His nerve, his judgment, his intuition, were things apart. Again and again his knife cut away death, but grazed the very springs of life in doing it, until his assistants were as white as the patient. His energy, his audacity, his full-blooded self-confidence— does not the memory of them still linger in the south of Marylebone Road and the north of Oxford Street?

His vices were as magnificent as his virtues, and infinitely more picturesque. Large as was his income, and it was the third largest of all professional men in London, it was far beneath the luxury of his living. Deep in his complex nature lay a rich vein of sensualism, at the sport of which he placed all the prizes of his life. The eye, the ear, the touch, the palate, all were his masters. The bouquet of old vintages, the scent of rare exotics, the curves and tints of the daintiest potteries of Europe, it was to these that the quick-running stream of gold was transformed. And then there came his sudden mad passion for Lady Sannox, when a single interview with two challenging glances and a whispered word set him ablaze. She was the loveliest woman in London and the only one to him. He was one of the handsomest men in London, but not the only one to her. She had a liking for new experiences, and was gracious to most men who wooed her. It may have been cause or it may have been effect that Lord Sannox looked fifty, though he was but six-and-thirty.

He was a quiet, silent, neutral-tinted man, this lord, with thin lips and heavy eyelids, much given to gardening and full of home-like habits. He had at one time been fond of acting, had even rented a theatre in London, and on its boards had first seen Miss Marion Dawson, to whom he had offered his hand, his title and the third of a county. Since his marriage his early hobby had become distasteful to him. Even in private theatricals it was no longer possible to persuade him to exercise the talent which he had often shown that he possessed. He was happier with a spud and a watering-can among his orchids and chrysanthemums.

It was quite an interesting problem whether he was absolutely devoid of sense or miserably wanting in spirit. Did he know his lady's ways and condone them or was he a mere blind, doting fool? It was a point to be discussed over the teacups in snug little drawing-rooms or with the aid of a cigar in the bow windows of clubs. Bitter and plain were the comments among men upon his conduct. There was but one who had a good word to say for him, and he was the most silent member in the smoking-room. He had seen him break in a horse at the university, and it seemed to have left an impression upon his mind.

But when Douglas Stone became the favourite, all doubts as to Lord Sannox's knowledge or ignorance were set for ever at rest. There was no subterfuge about Stone. In his high-handed, impetuous fashion, he set all caution and discretion at defiance. The scandal became notorious. A learned body intimated that his name had been struck from the list of its vice-presidents. Two friends implored him to consider his professional credit. He cursed them all three, and spent forty guineas on a bangle to take with him to the lady. He was at her house every evening, and she drove in his carriage in the afternoons. There was not an attempt on either side to conceal their relations; but there came at last a little incident to interrupt them.

It was a dismal winter's night, very cold and gusty, with the wind whooping in the chimneys and blustering against the window-panes. A thin spatter of rain tinkled on the glass with each fresh sough of the gale, drowning for the instant the dull gurgle and drip from the eaves. Douglas Stone had finished his dinner, and sat by his fire in the study, a glass of rich port upon the malachite table at his elbow. As he raised it to his lips, he held it up against the lamplight, and watched with the eye of a connoisseur the tiny scales of beeswing which floated in its rich ruby depths. The fire, as it spurted up, threw fitful lights upon his bold, clear-cut face, with its widely opened grey eyes, its thick and yet firm lips, and the deep, square jaw, which had something Roman in its strength and its animalism. He smiled from time to time as he nestled back in his luxurious chair. Indeed, he had a right to feel well pleased, for, against the advice of six colleagues, he had performed an operation that day of which only two cases were on record, and the result had been brilliant beyond all expectation. No other man in London would have had the daring to plan, or the skill to execute, such a heroic measure.

But he had promised Lady Sannox to see her that evening and it was already half-past eight. His hand was outstretched to the bell to order the carriage when he heard the dull thud of the knocker. An instant later there was the shuffling of feet in the hall and the sharp closing of a door.

'A patient to see you, sir, in the consulting room,' said the butler.

'About himself?'

'No, sir; I think he wants you to go out.'

'It is too late,' cried Douglas Stone peevishly. 'I won't go.'

'This is his card, sir.'

The butler presented it upon the gold salver which had been given to his master by the wife of a Prime Minister.

'"Hamil Ali, Smyrna". Hum! The fellow is a Turk, I suppose.'

'Yes, sir. He seems as if he came from abroad, sir. And he's in a terrible way.'

'Tut, tut! I have an engagement. I must go somewhere else. But I'll see him. Show him in here, Pim.'

A few moments later the butler swung open the door and ushered in a small and decrepit man, who walked with a bent back and with the forward push of the face and blink of the eyes which goes with extreme short sight. His face was swarthy, and his hair and beard of the deepest black. In one hand he held a turban of white muslin striped with red, in the other a small chamois-leather bag.

'Good evening,' said Douglas Stone, when the butler had closed the door. 'You speak English, I presume?'

'Yes, sir. I am from Asia Minor, but I speak English when I speak slow.'

'You wanted me to go out, I understand?'

'Yes, sir. I wanted very much that you should see my wife.'

'I could come in the morning, but I have an engagement which prevents me from seeing your wife tonight.'

The Turk's answer was a singular one. He pulled the string which closed the mouth of the chamois-leather bag, and poured a flood of gold on to the table.

'There are one hundred pounds there,' said he, 'and I promise you that it will not take you an hour. I have a cab ready at the door.'

Douglas Stone glanced at his watch. An hour would not make it too late to visit Lady Sannox. He had been there later. And the fee was an extraordinarily high one. He had been pressed by his creditors lately, and he could not afford to let such a chance pass. He would go.

'What is the case?' he asked.

'Oh, it is so sad a one! So sad a one! You have not, perhaps heard of the daggers of the Almohades?'

'Never.'

'Ah, they are Eastern daggers of a great age and of a singular shape, with the hilt like what you call a stirrup. I am a curiosity dealer, you understand, and that is why I have come to England from Smyrna, but next week I go back once more. Many things I brought with me, and I have a few things left, but among them, to my sorrow, is one of these daggers.'

'You will remember that I have an appointment, sir,' said the surgeon, with some irritation; 'pray confine yourself to the necessary details.'

'You will see that it is necessary. Today my wife fell down in a faint in the room in which I keep my wares, and she cut her lower lip upon this cursed dagger of the Almohades.'

'I see,' said Douglas Stone, rising. 'And you wish me to dress the wound?'

'No, no, it is worse than that.'

'What then?'

'These daggers are poisoned.'

'Poisoned!'

'Yes, and there is no man, East or West, who can tell now what is the poison or what the cure. But all that is known I know, for my father was in this trade before me, and we have had much to do with these poisoned weapons.'

'What are the symptoms?'

'Deep sleep, and death in thirty hours.'

'And you say there is no cure. Why then should you pay me this considerable fee?'

'No drug can cure, but the knife may.'

'And how?'

'The poison is slow of absorption. It remains for hours in the wound.'

'Washing, then, might cleanse it?'

'No more than in a snake bite. It is too subtle and too deadly.'

'Excision of the wound, then?'

'That is it. If it be on the finger, take the finger off. So said my father always. But think of where this wound is, and that it is my wife. It is dreadful!'

But familiarity with such grim matters may take the finer edge from a man's sympathy. To Douglas Stone this was already an interesting case, and he brushed aside as irrelevant the feeble objections of the husband.

'It appears to be that or nothing,' said he brusquely. 'It is better to lose a lip than a life.'

'Ah, yes, I know that you are right. Well, well, it is kismet, and it must be faced. I have the cab, and you will come with me and do this thing.'

Douglas Stone took his case of bistouries from a drawer, and placed it with a roll of bandage and a compress of lint in his pocket. He must waste no more time if he was to see Lady Sannox.

'I am ready,' said he, pulling on his overcoat. 'Will you take a glass of wine before you go out into this cold air?'

His visitor shrank away, with a protesting hand upraised. 'You forget that I am a Mussulman, and a true follower of the Prophet,' said he. 'But tell me what is the bottle of green glass which you have placed in your pocket?'

'It is chloroform.'

'Ah, that also is forbidden to us. It is a spirit, and we make no use of such things.'

'What! You would allow your wife to go through an operation without an anesthetic?'

'Ah! She will feel nothing, poor soul. The deep sleep has already come on, which is the first working of the poison. And then I have given her of our Smyrna opium. Come, sir, for already an hour has passed.'

As they stepped out into the darkness, a sheet of rain was driven in upon their faces, and the hall lamp, which dangled from the arm of a marble caryatid, went out with a fluff. Pim, the butler, pushed the heavy door to, straining hard with his shoulder against the wind, while the two men groped their way towards the yellow glare which showed where the cab was waiting. An instant later they were rattling upon their journey.

'Is it far?' asked Douglas Stone.

'Oh, no. We have a very little quiet place off the Euston Road.'

The surgeon pressed the spring of his repeater and listened to the little tings which told him the hour. It was a quarter past nine. He calculated the distances, and the short time which it would take him to perform so trivial an operation. He ought to reach Lady Sannox by ten o'-clock. Through the fogged windows he saw the blurred gas lamps dancing past, with occasionally the broader glare of a shop front. The rain was pelting and rattling upon the leather top of the carriage, and the wheels swashed as they rolled through puddle and mud. Opposite to him the white headgear of his companion gleamed faintly through the obscurity. The surgeon felt in his pockets and arranged his needles, his ligatures and his safety-pins, that no time might be wasted when they arrived. He chafed with impatience and drummed his foot upon the floor.

But the cab slowed down at last and pulled up. In an instant Douglas Stone was out, and the Smyrna merchant's toe was at his very heel.

'You can wait,' said he to the driver.

It was a mean-looking house in a narrow and sordid street. The surgeon, who knew his London well, cast a swift glance into the shadows, but there was nothing distinctive—no shop, no movement, nothing but a double line of dull, flat-faced houses, a double stretch of wet flag-stones which gleamed in the lamplight, and a double rush of water in the gutters which swirled and gurgled towards the sewer gratings. The door which faced them was blotched and discoloured, and a faint light in the fan pane above it served to show the dust and the grime which covered it. Above, in one of the bedroom windows, there was a dull yellow glimmer. The merchant knocked loudly, and, as he turned his dark face towards the light, Douglas Stone could see that it was contracted with anxiety. A bolt was drawn, and an elderly woman with a taper stood in the doorway, shielding the thin flame with her gnarled hand.

'Is all well?' gasped the merchant.

'She is as you left her, sir.'

'She has not spoken?'

'No, she is in a deep sleep.'

The merchant closed the door, and Douglas Stone walked down the narrow passage, glancing about him in some surprise as he did so. There was no oil-cloth, no mat, no hat-rack. Deep grey dust and heavy festoons of cobwebs met his eyes everywhere. Following the old woman up the winding stair, his firm footfall echoed harshly through the silent house. There was no carpet.

The bedroom was on the second landing. Douglas Stone followed the old nurse into it, with the merchant at his heels. Here, at least, there was furniture and to spare. The floor was littered and the corners piled with Turkish cabinets, inlaid tables, coats of chain-mail, strange pipes and grotesque weapons. A single small lamp stood upon a bracket on the wall. Douglas Stone took it down, and picking his way among the lumber, walked over to a couch in the corner on which lay a woman dressed in the Turkish fashion, with yashmak and veil. The lower part of the face was exposed, and the surgeon saw a jagged cut which zigzagged along the border of the underlip.

'You will forgive the yashmak,' said the Turk. 'You know our views about women in the East.'

But the surgeon was not thinking about the yashmak. This was no longer a woman to him. It was a case. He stopped and examined the wound carefully.

'There are no signs of irritation,' said he. 'We might delay the operation until local symptoms develop.'

The husband wrung his hands in uncontrollable agitation.

'Oh! Sir, sir,' he cried. 'Do not trifle. You do not know. It is deadly. I know, and I give you my assurance that an operation is absolutely necessary. Only the knife can save her.'

'And yet I am inclined to wait,' said Douglas Stone.

'That is enough,' the Turk cried, angrily. 'Every minute is of importance, and I cannot stand here and see my wife allowed to sink. It only remains for me to give you my thanks for having come, and to call in some other surgeon before it is too late.'

Douglas Stone hesitated. To refund that hundred pounds was no pleasant matter. But of course if he left the case he must return the money. And if the Turk were right and the woman died, his position before a coroner might be an embarrassing one.

'You have had personal experience of this poison?' he asked.

'I have.'

'And you assure me that an operation is needful?'

'I swear it by all that I hold sacred.'

'The disfigurement will be frightful.'

'I can understand that the mouth will not be a pretty one to kiss.'

Douglas Stone turned fiercely upon the man. The speech was a brutal one. But the Turk has his own fashion of talk and of thought, and there was no time for wrangling. Douglas Stone drew a bistoury from his case, opened it and felt the keen straight edge with his forefinger. Then he held the lamp closer to the bed. Two dark eyes were gazing up at him through the slit in the yashmak. They were all iris, and the pupil was hardly to be seen.

'You have given her a very heavy dose of opium.'

'Yes, she has had a good dose.'

He glanced again at the dark eyes which looked straight at his own. They were dull and lustreless, but, even as he gazed, a little shifting sparkle came into them, and the lips quivered.

'She is not absolutely unconscious,' said he.

'Would it not be well to use the knife while it will be painless?'

The same thought had crossed the surgeon's mind. He grasped the wounded lip with his forceps, and with two swift cuts he took out a broad V-shaped piece. The woman sprang up on the couch with a dreadful gurgling scream. Her covering was torn from her face. It was a face that he knew. In spite of that protruding upper lip and that slobber of blood, it was a face that he knew. She kept on putting her hand up to the gap and screaming. Douglas Stone sat down at the foot of the couch with his knife and his forceps. The room was whirling round, and he had felt something go like a ripping seam behind his ear. A bystander would have said that his face was the more ghastly of the two. As in a dream, or as if he had been looking at something at the play, he was conscious that the Turk's hair and beard lay upon the table, and that Lord Sannox was leaning against the wall with his hand to his side, laughing silently. The screams had died away now, and the dreadful head had dropped back again upon the pillow, but Douglas Stone still sat motionless, and Lord Sannox still chuckled quietly to himself.

'It was really very necessary for Marion, this operation,' said he; 'not physically, but morally, you know, morally.'

Douglas Stone stooped forwards and began to play with the fringe of the coverlet. His knife tinkled down upon the ground, but he still held the forceps and something more.

'I had long intended to make a little example,' said Lord Sannox, suavely. 'Your note of Wednesday miscarried, and I have it here in my pocket-book. I took some pains in carrying out my idea. The wound, by the way, was from nothing more dangerous than my signet ring.'

He glanced keenly at his silent companion, and cocked the small re-volver which he held in his coat pocket. But Douglas Stone was still pick-ing at the coverlet.

'You see you have kept your appointment after all,' said Lord San-nox.

And at that Douglas Stone began to laugh. He laughed long and loudly. But Lord Sannox did not laugh now. Something like fear sharp-ened and hardened his features. He walked from the room, and he walked on tiptoe. The old woman was waiting outside.

'Attend to your mistress when she awakes,' said Lord Sannox. Then he went down to the street. The cab was at the door, and the driver raised his hand to his hat.

'John,' said Lord Sannox, 'you will take the doctor home first. He will want leading downstairs, I think. Tell his butler that he has been taken ill at a case.'

'Very good, sir.'

'Then you can take Lady Sannox home.'

'And how about yourself, sir?'

'Oh, my address for the next few months will be Hotel di Roma, Venice. Just see that the letters are sent on. And tell Stevens to exhibit all the purple chrysanthemums next Monday, and to wire me the result.'

5

⚘

"How the Brigadier
Came to the Castle of Gloom"
(1894)

Y ou do very well, my friends, to treat me with some little reverence, for in honouring me you are honouring both France and yourselves. It is not merely an old, grey-moustached officer whom you see eating his omelet or draining his glass, but it is a fragment of history. In me you see one of the last of those wonderful men, the men who were veterans when they were yet boys, who learned to use a sword earlier than a razor, and who during a hundred battles had never once let the enemy see the colour of their knapsacks. For twenty years we were teaching Europe how to fight, and even when they had learned their lesson it was only the thermometer, and never the bayonet, which could break the Grand Army down. Berlin, Naples, Vienna, Madrid, Lisbon, Moscow—we stabled our horses in them all. Yes, my friends, I say again that you do well to send your children to me with flowers, for these ears have heard the trumpet calls of France, and these eyes have seen her standards in lands where they may never be seen again.

Even now, when I doze in my arm-chair, I can see those great warriors stream before me—the green-jacketed chasseurs, the giant cuirassiers, Poniatowsky's lancers, the white-mantled dragoons, the nodding bearskins of the horse grenadiers. And then there comes the thick,

NOTE.—The term "Brigadier" is used throughout in its English and not in its French significance.

99

low rattle of the drums, and through wreaths of dust and smoke I see the line of high bonnets, the row of brown faces, the swing and toss of the long, red plumes amid the sloping lines of steel. And there rides Ney with his red head, and Lefebvre with his bulldog jaw, and Lannes with his Gascon swagger; and then amidst the gleam of brass and the flaunting feathers I catch a glimpse of *him*, the man with the pale smile, the rounded shoulders, and the far-off eyes. There is an end of my sleep, my friends, for up I spring from my chair, with a cracked voice calling and a silly hand outstretched, so that Madame Titaux has one more laugh at the old fellow who lives among the shadows.

Although I was a full Chief of Brigade when the wars came to an end, and had every hope of soon being made a General of Division, it is still rather to my earlier days that I turn when I wish to talk of the glories and the trials of a soldier's life. For you will understand that when an officer has so many men and horses under him, he has his mind full of recruits and remounts, fodder and farriers, and quarters, so that even when he is not in the face of the enemy, life is a very serious matter for him. But when he is only a lieutenant or a captain, he has nothing heavier than his epaulettes upon his shoulders, so that he can clink his spurs and swing his dolman, drain his glass and kiss his girl, thinking of nothing save of enjoying a gallant life. That is the time when he is likely to have adventures, and it is most often to that time that I shall turn in the stories which I may have for you. So it will be to-night when I tell you of my visit to the Castle of Gloom; of the strange mission of Sub-Lieutenant Duroc, and of the horrible affair of the man who was once known as Jean Carabin, and afterwards as the Baron Straubenthal.

You must know, then, that in the February of 1807, immediately after the taking of Danzig, Major Legendre and I were commissioned to bring four hundred remounts from Prussia into Eastern Poland.

The hard weather, and especially the great battle at Eylau, had killed so many of the horses that there was some danger of our beautiful Tenth of Hussars becoming a battalion of light infantry. We knew, therefore, both the Major and I, that we should be very welcome at the front. We did not advance very rapidly, however, for the snow was deep, the roads detestable, and we had but twenty returning invalids to assist us. Besides, it is impossible, when you have a daily change of forage, and sometimes none at all, to move horses faster than a walk. I am aware that in the story-books the cavalry whirls past at the maddest of gallops; but for my own part, after twelve campaigns, I should be very satisfied to know that my brigade could always walk upon the march and trot in the presence of the enemy. This I say of the hussars and chasseurs, mark you, so that it is far more the case with cuirassiers or dragoons.

For myself I am fond of horses, and to have four hundred of them, of every age and shade and character, all under my own hands, was a very great pleasure to me. They were from Pomerania for the most part, though some were from Normandy and some from Alsace, and it amused us to notice that they differed in character as much as the people of those provinces. We observed also, what I have often proved since, that the nature of a horse can be told by his colour, from the coquettish light bay full of fancies and nerves, to the hardy chestnut, and from the docile roan to the pig-headed rusty-black. All this has nothing in the world to do with my story, but how is an officer of cavalry to get on with his tale when he finds four hundred horses waiting for him at the outset? It is my habit, you see, to talk of that which interests myself, and so I hope that I may interest you.

We crossed the Vistula opposite Marienwerder, and had got as far as Riesenberg, when Major Legendre came into my room in the post-house with an open paper in his hand.

"You are to leave me," said he, with despair upon his face.

It was no very great grief to me to do that, for he was, if I may say so, hardly worthy to have such a subaltern. I saluted, however, in silence.

"It is an order from General Lasalle," he continued; "you are to proceed to Rossel instantly, and to report yourself at the headquarters of the regiment."

No message could have pleased me better. I was already very well thought of by my superior officers, although I may say that none of them had quite done me justice. It was evident to me, therefore, that his sudden order meant that the regiment was about to see service once more, and that Lasalle understood how incomplete my squadron would be without me. It is true that it came at an inconvenient moment, for the keeper of the post-house had a daughter—one of those ivory-skinned, black-haired Polish girls—whom I had hoped to have some further talk with. Still, it is not for the pawn to argue when the fingers of the player move him from the square; so down I went, saddled my big black charger, Rataplan, and set off instantly upon my lonely journey.

My word, it was a treat for those poor Poles and Jews, who have so little to brighten their dull lives to see such a picture as that before their doors. The frosty morning air made Rataplan's great black limbs and the beautiful curves of his back and sides gleam and shimmer with every gambade. As for me, the rattle of hoofs upon a road, and the jingle of bridle chains which comes with every toss of a saucy head, would even now set my blood dancing through my veins. You may think, then, how I carried myself in my five-and-twentieth year—I, Etienne Gerard, the picked horseman and surest blade in the ten regiments of hussars. Blue was our colour in the Tenth—a sky-blue dolman and pelisse with a scarlet front—and it was said of us in the army that we could set a whole population running, the women towards us, and the men away. There were bright eyes in the Riesenberg windows that morning, which seemed to beg me to tarry; but what can a soldier do, save to kiss his hand and shake his bridle as he rides upon his way?

It was a bleak season to ride through the poorest and ugliest country in Europe, but there was a cloudless sky above, and a bright, cold sun, which shimmered on the huge snow-fields. My breath reeked into the frosty air, and Rataplan sent up two feathers of steam from his nostrils, while the icicles drooped from the side-irons of his bit. I let him trot to warm his limbs, while for my own part I had too much to think of to give much heed to the cold. To north and south stretched the great plains, mottled over with dark clumps of fir and lighter patches of larch. A few cottages peeped out here and there, but it was only three months since the Grand Army had passed that way, and you know what that meant to a country. The Poles were our friends, it was true, but out of a hundred thousand men, only the Guard had wagons, and the rest had to live as best they might. It did not surprise me, therefore, to see no signs of cattle and no smoke from the silent houses. A weal had been left across the country where the great host had passed, and it was said that even the rats were starved wherever the Emperor had led his men.

By midday I had got as far as the village of Saalfeldt, but as I was on the direct road for Osterode, where the Emperor was wintering, and also for the main camp of the seven divisions of infantry, the highway was choked with carriages and carts. What with artillery, caissons and wagons and couriers, and the ever-thickening stream of recruits and stragglers, it seemed to me that it would be a very long time before I should join my comrades. The plains, however, were five feet deep in snow, so there was nothing for it but to plod upon our way. It was with joy, therefore, that I found a second road which branched away from the other, trending through a fir-wood towards the north. There was a small auberge at the cross-roads, and a patrol of the third Hussars of Conflans—the very regiment of which I was afterwards colonel—were mounting their horses at the door. On the steps stood their officer, a slight, pale young man, who looked more like a young priest from a seminary than a leader of the devil-may-care rascals before him.

"Good day, sir," said he, seeing that I pulled up my horse.

"Good-day," I answered. "I am Lieutenant Etienne Gerard, of the Tenth."

I could see by his face that he had heard of me. Everybody had heard of me since my duel with the six fencing-masters. My manner, however, served to put him at his ease with me.

"I am Sub-Lieutenant Duroc, of the Third," said he.

"Newly joined?" I asked.

"Last week."

I had thought as much, from his white face and from the way in which he let his men lounge upon their horses. It was not so long, however, since I had learned myself what it was like when a schoolboy has to give orders to veteran troopers. It made me blush, I remember, to shout abrupt commands to men who had seen more battles than I had years, and it would have come more natural for me to say, "With your permission, we shall now wheel into line," or, "If you think it best, we shall trot." I did not think the less of the lad, therefore, when I observed that his men were somewhat out of hand, but I gave them a glance which stiffened them in their saddles.

"May I ask, monsieur, whether you are going by this northern road?" I asked.

"My orders are to patrol it as far as Arensdorf," said he.

"Then I will, with your permission, ride so far with you," said I. "It is very clear that the longer way will be the faster."

So it proved, for this road led away from the army into a country which was given over to Cossacks and marauders, and it was as bare as the other was crowded. Duroc and I rode in front, with our six troopers clattering in the rear. He was a good boy, this Duroc, with his head full of the nonsense that they teach at St. Cyr, knowing more about Alexander and Pompey than how to mix a horse's fodder or care for a horse's feet. Still, he was, as I have said, a good boy, unspoiled as yet by the camp. It pleased me to hear him prattle away about his sister Marie and about his mother in Amiens. Presently we found ourselves at the village of Hayenau. Duroc rode up to the post-house and asked to see the master.

"Can you tell me," said he, "whether the man who calls himself the Baron Straubenthal lives in these parts?"

The postmaster shook his head, and we rode upon our way.

I took no notice of this, but when, at the next village, my comrade repeated the same question, with the same result, I could not help asking him who this Baron Straubenthal might be.

"He is a man," said Duroc, with a sudden flush upon his boyish face, "to whom I have a very important message to convey."

Well, this was not satisfactory, but there was something in my companion's manner which told me that any further questioning would be distasteful to him. I said nothing more, therefore, but Duroc would still ask every peasant whom we met whether he could give him any news of the Baron Straubenthal.

For my own part I was endeavouring, as an officer of light cavalry should, to form an idea of the lay of the country, to note the course of the streams, and to mark the places where there should be fords. Every step was taking us farther from the camp round the flanks of which we were travelling. Far to the south a few plumes of grey smoke in the frosty air marked the position of some of our outposts. To the north, however, there was nothing between ourselves and the Russian winter quarters. Twice on the extreme horizon I caught a glimpse of the glitter of steel, and pointed it out to my companion. It was too distant for us to tell whence it came, but we had little doubt that it was from the lance-heads of marauding Cossacks.

The sun was just setting when we rode over a low hill and saw a small village upon our right, and on our left a high black castle, which jutted out from amongst the pine-woods. A farmer with his cart was approaching us—a matted-haired, downcast fellow, in a sheepskin jacket.

"What village is this?" asked Duroc.

"It is Arensdorf," he answered, in his barbarous German dialect.

"Then here I am to stay the night," said my young companion. Then, turning to the farmer, he asked his eternal question, "Can you tell me where the Baron Straubenthal lives?"

"Why, it is he who owns the Castle of Gloom," said the farmer, pointing to the dark turrets over the distant fir forest.

Duroc gave a shout like the sportsman who sees his game rising in front of him. The lad seemed to have gone off his head—his eyes shining, his face deathly white, and such a grim set about his mouth as made the farmer shrink away from him. I can see him now, leaning forward on his brown horse, with his eager gaze fixed upon the great black tower.

"Why do you call it the Castle of Gloom?" I asked.

"Well, it's the name it bears upon the countryside," said the farmer. "By all accounts there have been some black doings up yonder. It's not for nothing that the wickedest man in Poland has been living there these fourteen years past."

"A Polish nobleman?" I asked.

"Nay, we breed no such men in Poland," he answered.

"A Frenchman, then?" cried Duroc.

"They say that he came from France."

"And with red hair?"

"As red as a fox."

"Yes, yes, it is my man," cried my companion, quivering all over in his excitement. "It is the hand of Providence which has led me here. Who can say that there is not justice in this world? Come, Monsieur Gerard, for I must see the men safely quartered before I can attend to this private matter."

He spurred on his horse, and ten minutes later we were at the door of the inn of Arensdorf, where his men were to find their quarters for the night.

Well, all this was no affair of mine, and I could not imagine what the meaning of it might be. Rossel was still far off, but I determined to ride on for a few hours and take my chance of some wayside barn in which I could find shelter for Rataplan and myself. I had mounted my horse, therefore, after tossing off a cup of wine, when young Duroc came running out of the door and laid his hand upon my knee.

"Monsieur Gerard," he panted, "I beg of you not to abandon me like this!"

"My good sir," said I, "if you would tell me what is the matter and what you would wish me to do, I should be better able to tell you if I could be of any assistance to you."

"You can be of the very greatest," he cried. "Indeed, from all that I have heard of you, Monsieur Gerard, you are the one man whom I should wish to have by my side to-night."

"You forget that I am riding to join my regiment."

"You cannot, in any case, reach it to-night. To-morrow will bring you to Rossel. By staying with me you will confer the very greatest kindness upon me, and you will aid me in a matter which concerns my own honour and the honour of my family. I am compelled, however, to confess to you that some personal danger may possibly be involved."

It was a crafty thing for him to say. Of course, I sprang from Rataplan's back and ordered the groom to lead him back into the stables.

"Come into the inn," said I, "and let me know exactly what it is that you wish me to do."

He led the way into a sitting-room, and fastened the door lest we should be interrupted. He was a well-grown lad, and as he stood in the glare of the lamp, with the light beating upon his earnest face and upon his uniform of silver grey, which suited him to a marvel, I felt my heart warm towards him. Without going so far as to say that he carried himself as I had done at his age, there was at least similarity enough to make me feel in sympathy with him.

"I can explain it all in a few words," said he. "If I have not already satisfied your very natural curiosity, it is because the subject is so painful a one to me that I can hardly bring myself to allude to it. I cannot, however, ask for your assistance without explaining to you exactly how the matter lies.

"You must know, then, that my father was the well-known banker, Christophe Duroc, who was murdered by the people during the September massacres. As you are aware, the mob took possession of the prisons, chose three so-called judges to pass sentence upon the unhappy aristocrats, and then tore them to pieces when they were passed out into the street. My father had been a benefactor of the poor all his life. There were many to plead for him. He had the fever, too, and was carried in, half-dead, upon a blanket. Two of the judges were in favour of acquitting him; the third, a young Jacobin, whose huge body and brutal mind made him a leader among these wretches, dragged him, with his own hands, from the litter, kicked him again and again with his heavy boots, and hurled him out of the door, where in an instant he was torn limb from limb under circumstances which are too horrible for me to describe. This, as you perceive, was murder, even under their own unlawful laws, for two of their own judges had pronounced in my father's favour.

"Well, when the days of order came back again, my elder brother began to make inquiries about this man. I was only a child then, but it was a family matter, and it was discussed in my presence. The fellow's name was Carabin. He was one of Sansterre's Guard, and a noted duellist. A foreign lady named the Baroness Straubenthal having been dragged before the Jacobins, he had gained her liberty for her on the promise that she with her money and estates should be his. He had married her, taken her name and title, and escaped out of France at the time of the fall of Robespierre. What had become of him we had no means of learning.

"You will think, doubtless, that it would be easy for us to find him, since we had both his name and his title. You must remember, however, that the Revolution left us without money, and that without money such a search is very difficult. Then came the Empire, and it became more difficult still, for, as you are aware, the Emperor considered that the 18th Brumaire brought all accounts to a settlement, and that on that day a veil had been drawn across the past. None the less, we kept our own family story and our own family plans.

"My brother joined the army, and passed with it through all Southern Europe, asking everywhere for the Baron Straubenthal. Last October he was killed at Jena, with his mission still unfulfilled. Then it became my turn, and I have the good fortune to hear of the very man of whom I am in search at one of the first Polish villages which I have to visit, and within a fortnight of joining my regiment. And then, to make the matter even better, I find myself in the company of one whose name is never mentioned throughout the army save in connection with some daring and generous deed."

This was all very well, and I listened to it with the greatest interest, but I was none the clearer as to what young Duroc wished me to do.

"How can I be of service to you?" I asked.

"By coming up with me."

"To the Castle?"

"Precisely."

"When?"

"At once."

"But what do you intend to do?"

"I shall know what to do. But I wish you to be with me, all the same."

Well, it was never in my nature to refuse an adventure, and, besides, I had every sympathy with the lad's feelings. It is very well to forgive one's enemies, but one wishes to give them something to forgive also. I held out my hand to him, therefore.

"I must be on my way for Rossel to-morrow morning, but to-night I am yours," said I.

We left our troopers in snug quarters, and, as it was but a mile to the Castle, we did not disturb our horses. To tell the truth, I hate to see a cavalry man walk, and I hold that just as he is the most gallant thing upon earth when he has his saddle-flaps between his knees, so he is the most clumsy when he has to loop up his sabre and his sabre-tasche in one hand and turn in his toes for fear of catching the rowels of his spurs. Still, Duroc and I were of the age when one can carry things off, and I dare swear that no woman at least would have quarrelled with the appearance of the two young hussars, one in blue and one in gray, who set out that night from the Arensdorf post-house. We both carried our swords, and for my own part I slipped a pistol from my holster into the inside of my pelisse, for it seemed to me that there might be some wild work before us.

The track which led to the Castle wound through a pitch-black fir-wood, where we could see nothing save the ragged patch of stars above our head. Presently, however, it opened up, and there was the Castle right in front of us, about as far as a carbine would carry. It was a huge, un-couth place, and bore every mark of being exceedingly old, with turrets at every corner, and a square keep on the side which was nearest to us. In all its great shadow there was no sign of light save for a single win-dow, and no sound came from it. To me there was something awful in its size and its silence, which corresponded so well with its sinister name. My companion pressed on eagerly, and I followed him along the ill-kept path which led to the gate.

There was no bell or knocker upon the great, iron-studded door, and it was only by pounding with the hilts of our sabres that we could attract attention. A thin, hawk-faced man, with a beard up to his tem-ples, opened it at last. He carried a lantern in one hand, and in the other a chain which held an enormous black hound. His manner at the first moment was threatening, but the sight of our uniforms and of our faces turned it into one of sulky reserve.

"The Baron Straubenthal does not receive visitors at so late an hour," said he, speaking in very excellent French.

"You can inform Baron Straubenthal that I have come eight hundred leagues to see him, and that I will not leave until I have done so," said my companion. I could not myself have said it with a better voice and manner.

The fellow took a sidelong look at us, and tugged at his black beard in his perplexity.

"To tell the truth, gentlemen," said he, "the Baron has a cup or two of wine in him at this hour, and you would certainly find him a more entertaining companion if you were to come again in the morning."

He had opened the door a little wider as he spoke, and I saw by the light of the lamp in the hall behind him that three other rough fellows were standing there, one of whom held another of these monstrous hounds. Duroc must have seen it also, but it made no difference to his resolution.

"Enough talk," said he, pushing the man to one side. "It is with your master that I have to deal."

The fellows in the hall made way for him as he strode in among them, so great is the power of one man who knows what he wants over several who are not sure of themselves. My companion tapped one of them upon the shoulder with as much assurance as though he owned him.

"Show me to the Baron," said he.

The man shrugged his shoulders, and answered something in Polish. The fellow with the beard, who had shut and barred the front door, appeared to be the only one among them who could speak French.

"Well, you shall have your way," said he, with a sinister smile. "You shall see the Baron. And perhaps, before you have finished, you will wish that you had taken my advice."

We followed him down the hall, which was stone-flagged and very spacious, with skins scattered upon the floor, and the heads of wild beasts upon the walls. At the farther end he threw open a door, and we entered.

It was a small room, scantily furnished, with the same marks of neglect and decay which met us at every turn. The walls were hung with discoloured tapestry, which had come loose at one corner, so as to expose the rough stonework behind. A second door, hung with a curtain, faced us upon the other side. Between lay a square table, strewn with dirty dishes and the sordid remains of a meal. Several bottles were scattered over it. At the head of it, and facing us, there sat a huge man, with a lion-like head and a great shock of orange-coloured hair. His beard was of the same glaring hue; matted and tangled and coarse as a horse's mane. I have seen some strange faces in my time, but never one more brutal than that, with its small, vicious, blue eyes, its white, crumpled cheeks, and the thick, hanging lip which protruded over his monstrous beard. His head swayed about on his shoulders, and he looked at us with the vague, dim gaze of a drunken man. Yet he was not so drunk but that our uniforms carried their message to him.

"Well, my brave boys," he hiccoughed. "What is the latest news from Paris, eh? You're going to free Poland, I hear, and have meantime all become slaves yourselves—slaves to a little aristocrat with his grey coat and his three-cornered hat. No more citizens either, I am told, and nothing but monsieur and madame. My faith, some more heads will have to roll into the sawdust basket some of these mornings."

Duroc advanced in silence, and stood by the ruffian's side.

"Jean Carabin," said he.

The Baron started, and the film of drunkenness seemed to be clearing from his eyes.

"Jean Carabin," said Duroc, once more.

He sat up and grasped the arms of his chair.

"What do you mean by repeating that name, young man?" he asked.

"Jean Carabin, you are a man whom I have long wished to meet."

"Supposing that I once had such a name, how can it concern you, since you must have been a child when I bore it?"

"My name is Duroc."

"Not the son of ——?"

"The son of the man you murdered."

The Baron tried to laugh, but there was terror in his eyes.

"We must let bygones be bygones, young man," he cried. "It was our life or theirs in those days: the aristocrats or the people. Your father was of the Gironde. He fell. I was of the mountain. Most of my comrades fell. It was all the fortune of war. We must forget all this and learn to know each other better, you and I." He held out a red twitching hand as he spoke.

"Enough," said young Duroc. "If I were to pass my sabre through you as you sit in that chair, I should do what is just and right. I dishonour my blade by crossing it with yours. And yet you are a Frenchman, and have even held a commission under the same flag as myself. Rise, then, and defend yourself!"

"Tut, tut!" cried the Baron. "It is all very well for you young bloods——"

Duroc's patience could stand no more. He swung his open hand into the centre of the great orange beard. I saw a lip fringed with blood, and two glaring blue eyes above it.

"You shall die for that blow."

"That is better," said Duroc.

"My sabre!" cried the other; "I will not keep you waiting, I promise you!" and he hurried from the room.

I have said that there was a second door covered with a curtain. Hardly had the Baron vanished when there ran from behind it a woman, young and beautiful. So swiftly and noiselessly did she move that she was between us in an instant, and it was only the shaking curtains which told us whence she had come.

"I have seen it all," she cried. "Oh, sir, you have carried yourself splendidly." She stooped to my companion's hand, and kissed it again and again ere he could disengage it from her grasp.

"Nay, madame, why should you kiss my hand?" he cried.

"Because it is the hand which struck him on his vile, lying mouth. Because it may be the hand which will avenge my mother. I am his step-daughter. The woman whose heart he broke was my mother. I loathe him, I fear him. Ah, there is his step!" In an instant she had vanished as suddenly as she had come. A moment later, the Baron entered with a drawn sword in his hand, and the fellow who had admitted us at his heels.

"This is my secretary," said he. "He will be my friend in this affair. But we shall need more elbow-room than we can find here. Perhaps you will kindly come with me to a more spacious apartment."

It was evidently impossible to fight in a chamber which was blocked by a great table. We followed him out, therefore, into the dimly-lit hall. At the farther end a light was shining through an open door.

"We shall find what we want in here," said the man with the dark beard. It was a large, empty room, with rows of barrels and cases round the walls. A strong lamp stood upon a shelf in the corner. The floor was level and true, so that no swordsman could ask for more. Duroc drew his sabre and sprang into it. The Baron stood back with a bow and motioned me to follow my companion. Hardly were my heels over the threshold when the heavy door crashed behind us and the key screamed in the lock. We were taken in a trap.

For a moment we could not realize it. Such incredible baseness was outside all our experiences. Then, as we understood how foolish we had been to trust for an instant a man with such a history, a flush of rage came over us, rage against his villainy and against our own stupidity. We rushed at the door together, beating it with our fists and kicking with our heavy boots. The sound of our blows and of our execrations must have resounded through the Castle. We called to this villain, hurling at him every name which might pierce even into his hardened soul. But the door was enormous—such a door as one finds in mediæval castles—made of huge beams clamped together with iron. It was as easy to break as a square of the Old Guard. And our cries appeared to be of as little avail as our blows, for they only brought for answer the clattering echoes from the high roof above us. When you have done some soldiering, you soon learn to put up with what cannot be altered. It was I, then, who first recovered my calmness, and prevailed upon Duroc to join with me in examining the apartment which had become our dungeon.

There was only one window, which had no glass in it and was so narrow that one could not so much as get one's head through. It was high up, and Duroc had to stand upon a barrel in order to see from it.

"What can you see?" I asked.

"Fir-woods, and an avenue of snow between them," said he. "Ah!" he gave a cry of surprise.

I sprang upon the barrel beside him. There was, as he said, a long, clear strip of snow in front. A man was riding down it, flogging his horse and galloping like a madman. As we watched, he grew smaller and smaller, until he was swallowed up by the black shadows of the forest.

"What does that mean?" asked Duroc.

"No good for us," said I. "He may have gone for some brigands to cut our throats. Let us see if we cannot find a way out of this mouse-trap before the cat can arrive."

The one piece of good fortune in our favour was that beautiful lamp. It was nearly full of oil, and would last us until morning. In the dark our situation would have been far more difficult. By its light we proceeded to examine the packages and cases which lined the walls. In some places there was only a single line of them, while in one corner they were piled nearly to the ceiling. It seemed that we were in the storehouse of the Castle, for there were a great number of cheeses, vegetables of various kinds, bins full of dried fruits, and a line of wine barrels. One of these had a spigot in it, and as I had eaten little during the day, I was glad of a cup of claret and some food. As to Duroc, he would take nothing, but paced up and down the room in a fever of anger and impatience. "I'll have him yet!" he cried, every now and then. "The rascal shall not escape me!"

This was all very well, but it seemed to me, as I sat on a great round cheese eating my supper, that this youngster was thinking rather too much of his own family affairs and too little of the fine scrape into which he had got me. After all, his father had been dead fourteen years, and nothing could set that right; but here was Etienne Gerard, the most dashing lieutenant in the whole Grand Army, in imminent danger of being cut off at the very outset of his brilliant career. Who was ever to know the heights to which I might have risen if I were knocked on the head in this hole-and-corner business, which had nothing whatever to do with France or the Emperor? I could not help thinking what a fool I had been, when I had a fine war before me and everything which a man could desire, to go off upon a harebrained expedition of this sort, as if it were not enough to have a quarter of a million Russians to fight against, without plunging into all sorts of private quarrels as well.

"That is all very well," I said at last, as I heard Duroc muttering his threats. "You may do what you like to him when you get the upper hand. At present the question rather is, what is *he* going to do to us?"

"Let him do his worst!" cried the boy. "I owe a duty to my father."

"That is mere foolishness," said I. "If you owe a duty to your father, I owe one to my mother, which is to get out of this business safe and sound."

My remark brought him to his senses.

"I have thought too much of myself!" he cried. "Forgive me, Monsieur Gerard. Give me your advice as to what I should do."

"Well," said I, "it is not for our health that they have shut us up here among the cheeses. They mean to make an end of us if they can. That is certain. They hope that no one knows that we have come here, and that none will trace us if we remain. Do your hussars know where you have gone to?"

"I said nothing."

"Hum! It is clear that we cannot be starved here. They must come to us if they are to kill us. Behind a barricade of barrels we could hold our own against the five rascals whom we have seen. That is, probably, why they have sent that messenger for assistance."

"We must get out before he returns."

"Precisely, if we are to get out at all."

"Could we not burn down this door?" he cried.

"Nothing could be easier," said I. "There are several casks of oil in the corner. My only objection is that we should ourselves be nicely toasted, like two little oyster pâtés."

"Can you not suggest something?" he cried, in despair. "Ah, what is that?"

There had been a low sound at our little window, and a shadow came between the stars and ourselves. A small, white hand was stretched into the lamplight. Something glittered between the fingers.

"Quick! Quick!" cried a woman's voice.

We were on the barrel in an instant.

"They have sent for the Cossacks. Your lives are at stake. Ah, I am lost! I am lost!"

There was the sound of rushing steps, a hoarse oath, a blow, and the stars were once more twinkling through the window. We stood helpless upon our barrel with our blood cold with horror. Half a minute afterwards we heard a smothered scream, ending in a choke. A great door slammed somewhere in the silent night.

"Those ruffians have seized her. They will kill her," I cried.

Duroc sprang down with the inarticulate shouts of one whose reason had left him. He struck the door so frantically with his naked hands that he left a blotch of blood with every blow.

"Here is the key!" I shouted, picking one from the floor. "She must have thrown it in at the instant that she was torn away."

My companion snatched it from me with a shriek of joy. A moment later he dashed it down upon the boards. It was so small that it was lost in the enormous lock. Duroc sank upon one of the boxes with his head between his hands. He sobbed in his despair. I could have sobbed, too, when I thought of the woman and how helpless we were to save her.

But I am not easily baffled. After all, this key must have been sent to us for a purpose. The lady could not bring us that of the door, because this murderous step-father of hers would most certainly have it in his pocket. Yet this other must have a meaning, or why should she risk her life to place it in our hands? It would say little for our wits if we could not find out what that meaning might be.

I set to work moving all the cases out from the wall, and Duroc, gaining new hope from my courage, helped me with all his strength. It was no light task, for many of them were large and heavy. On we went, working like maniacs, slinging barrels, cheeses, and boxes pell-mell into the middle of the room. At last there only remained one huge barrel of vodka, which stood in the corner. With our united strength we rolled it out, and there was a little low wooden door in the wainscot behind it. The key fitted, and with a cry of delight we saw it swing open before us. With the lamp in my hand, I squeezed my way in, followed by my companion.

We were in the powder-magazine of the castle—a rough, walled cellar, with barrels all round it, and one with the top staved in in the centre. The powder from it lay in a black heap upon the floor. Beyond there was another door, but it was locked.

"We are no better off than before," cried Duroc. "We have no key."

"We have a dozen," I cried.

"Where?"

I pointed to the line of powder barrels.

"You would blow this door open?"

"Precisely."

"But you would explode the magazine."

It was true, but I was not at the end of my resources.

"We will blow open the store-room door," I cried.

I ran back and seized a tin box which had been filled with candles. It was about the size of my shako—large enough to hold several pounds of powder. Duroc filled it while I cut off the end of a candle. When we had finished, it would have puzzled a colonel of engineers to make a better petard. I put three cheeses on the top of each other and placed it above them, so as to lean against the lock. Then we lit our candle-end and ran for shelter, shutting the door of the magazine behind us.

It is no joke, my friends, to lie among all those tons of powder, with the knowledge that if the flame of the explosion should penetrate through one thin door our blackened limbs would be shot higher than the Castle keep. Who could have believed that a half-inch of candle could take so long to burn? My ears were straining all the time for the thudding of the hoofs of the Cossacks who were coming to destroy us.

I had almost made up my mind that the candle must have gone out when there was a smack like a bursting bomb, our door flew to bits, and pieces of cheese, with a shower of turnips, apples, and splinters of cases, were shot in among us. As we rushed out we had to stagger through an impenetrable smoke, with all sorts of debris beneath our feet, but there was a glimmering square where the dark door had been. The petard had done its work.

In fact, it had done more for us than we had even ventured to hope. It had shattered gaolers as well as gaol. The first thing that I saw as I came out into the hall was a man with a butcher's axe in his hand, lying flat upon his back, with a gaping wound across his forehead. The second was a huge dog, with two of its legs broken, twisting in agony upon the floor. As it raised itself up I saw the two broken ends flapping like flails. At the same instant I heard a cry, and there was Duroc, thrown against the wall, with the other hound's teeth in his throat. He pushed it off with his left hand, while again and again he passed his sabre through its body, but it was not until I blew out its brains with my pistol that the iron jaws released, and the fierce, bloodshot eyes were glazed in death.

There was no time for us to pause. A woman's scream from in front—a scream of mortal terror—told us that even now we might be too late. There were two other men in the hall, but they cowered away from our drawn swords and furious faces. The blood was streaming from Duroc's neck and dyeing the grey fur of his pelisse. Such was the lad's fire, however, that he shot in front of me, and it was only over his shoulder that I caught a glimpse of the scene as we rushed into the chamber in which we had first seen the master of the Castle of Gloom.

The Baron was standing in the middle of the room, with his tangled mane bristling like an angry lion. He was, as I have said, a huge man, with enormous shoulders; and as he stood there, with his face flushed with rage and his sword advanced, I could not but think that, in spite of all his villainies, he had a proper figure for a grenadier. The lady lay cowering in a chair behind him. A weal across one of her white arms and a dog-whip upon the floor were enough to show that our escape had hardly been in time to save her from his brutality. He gave a howl like a wolf as we broke in, and was upon us in an instant, hacking and driving, with a curse at every blow.

I have already said that the room gave no space for swordsmanship. My young companion was in front of me in the narrow passage between the table and the wall, so that I could only look on without being able to aid him. The lad knew something of his weapon, and was as fierce and active as a wild cat, but in so narrow a space the weight and strength of the giant gave him the advantage. Besides, he was an admirable swordsman. His parade and riposte were as quick as lightning. Twice he touched Duroc upon the shoulder, and then, as the lad slipped up on a lunge, he whirled up his sword to finish him before he could recover his feet. I was quicker than he, however, and took the cut upon the pommel of my sabre.

"Excuse me," said I, "but you have still to deal with Etienne Gerard."

He drew back and leaned against the tapestry-covered wall, breathing in little, hoarse gasps, for his foul living was against him.

"Take your breath," said I. "I will await your convenience."

"You have no cause of quarrel against me," he panted.

"I owe you some little attention," said I, "for having shut me up in your store-room. Besides, if all other were wanting, I see cause enough upon that lady's arm."

"Have your way, then!" he snarled, and leaped at me like a madman. For a minute I saw only the blazing blue eyes, and the red glazed point which stabbed and stabbed, rasping off to right or to left, and yet ever back at my throat and my breast. I have never thought that such good sword-play was to be found at Paris in the days of the Revolution. I do not suppose that in all my little affairs I have met six men who had a better knowledge of their weapon. But he knew that I was his master. He read death in my eyes, and I could see that he read it. The flush died from his face. His breath came in shorter and in thicker gasps. Yet he fought on, even after the final thrust had come, and died still hacking and cursing, with foul cries upon his lips, and his blood clotting upon his orange beard. I who speak to you have seen so many battles, that my old memory can scarce contain their names, and yet of all the terrible sights which these eyes have rested upon, there is none which I care to think of less than of that orange beard with the crimson stain in the centre, from which I had drawn my sword point.

It was only afterwards that I had time to think of all this. His monstrous body had scarcely crashed down upon the floor before the woman in the corner sprang to her feet, clapping her hands together and screaming out in her delight. For my part I was disgusted to see a woman take such delight in a deed of blood, and I gave no thought as to the terrible wrongs which must have befallen her before she could so far forget the gentleness of her sex. It was on my tongue to tell her sharply to be silent, when a strange, choking smell took the breath from my nostrils, and a sudden, yellow glare brought out the figures upon the faded hangings.

"Duroc, Duroc!" I shouted, tugging at his shoulder. "The Castle is on fire!"

The boy lay senseless upon the ground, exhausted by his wounds. I rushed out into the hall to see whence the danger came. It was our explosion which had set a light to the dry framework of the door. Inside the store-room some of the boxes were already blazing. I glanced in, and as I did so my blood was turned to water by the sight of the powder barrels beyond, and of the loose heap upon the floor. It might be seconds, it could not be more than minutes, before the flames would be at the edge of it. These eyes will be closed in death, my friends, before they cease to see those crawling lines of fire and the black heap beyond.

How little I can remember what followed. Vaguely I can recall how I rushed into the chamber of death, how I seized Duroc by one limp hand and dragged him down the hall, the woman keeping pace with me and pulling at the other arm. Out of the gateway we rushed, and on down the snow-covered path until we were on the fringe of the fir forest. It was at that moment that I heard a crash behind me, and, glancing round, saw a great spout of fire shoot up into the wintry sky. An instant later there seemed to come a second crash far louder than the first. I saw the fir trees and the stars whirling round me, and I fell unconscious across the body of my comrade.

It was some weeks before I came to myself in the post-house of Arensdorf, and longer still before I could be told all that had befallen me. It was Duroc, already able to go soldiering, who came to my bedside and gave me an account of it. He it was who told me how a piece of timber had struck me on the head and had laid me almost dead upon the ground. From him, too, I learned how the Polish girl had run to Arensdorf, how she had roused our hussars, and how she had only just brought them back in time to save us from the spears of the Cossacks who had been summoned from their bivouac by that same black-bearded secretary whom we have seen galloping so swiftly over the snow. As to the brave lady who had twice saved our lives, I could not learn very much about her at that moment from Duroc, but when I chanced to meet him in Paris two years later, after the campaign of Wagram, I was not very much surprised to find that I needed no introduction to his bride, and that by the queer turns of fortune he had himself, had he chosen to use it, that very name and title of the Baron Straubenthal, which showed him to be the owner of the blackened ruins of the Castle of Gloom.

6

"How the Brigadier
Slew the Brothers of Ajaccio"
(1895)

When the Emperor needed an agent he was always very ready to do
me the honour of recalling the name of Etienne Gerard, though it occasionally escaped him when rewards were to be distributed. Still, I was
a colonel at twenty-eight, and the chief of a brigade at thirty-one, so that
I have no reason to be dissatisfied with my career. Had the wars lasted
another two or three years I might have grasped my bâton, and the man
who had his hand upon that was only one stride from a throne. Murat
had changed his hussar's cap for a crown, and another light cavalry man
might have done as much. However, all those dreams were driven away
by Waterloo, and, although I was not able to write my name upon history, it is sufficiently well known by all who served with me in the great
wars of the Empire.

What I want to tell you to-night is about the very singular affair
which first started me upon my rapid upward course, and which had the
effect of establishing a secret bond between the Emperor and myself.
There is just one little word of warning which I must give you before I
begin. When you hear me speak, you must always bear in mind that you
are listening to one who has seen history from the inside. I am talking
about what my ears have heard and my eyes have seen, so you must not
try to confute me by quoting the opinions of some student or man of
the pen, who has written a book of history or memoirs. There is much

which is unknown by such people, and much which never will be known by the world. For my own part, I could tell you some very surprising things were it discreet to do so. The facts which I am about to relate to you to-night were kept secret by me during the Emperor's lifetime, because I gave him my promise that it should be so, but I do not think that there can be any harm now in my telling the remarkable part which I played.

You must know, then, that at the time of the Treaty of Tilsit I was a simple lieutenant in the 10th Hussars, without money or interest. It is true that my appearance and my gallantry were in my favour, and that I had already won a reputation as being one of the best swordsmen in the army; but among the host of brave men who surrounded the Emperor it needed more than this to insure a rapid career. I was confident, however, that my chance would come, though I never dreamed that it would take so remarkable a form.

When the Emperor returned to Paris, after the declaration of peace in the year 1807, he spent much of his time with the Empress and the Court at Fontainebleau. It was the time when he was at the pinnacle of his career. He had in three successive campaigns humbled Austria, crushed Prussia, and made the Russians very glad to get upon the right side of the Niemen. The old Bulldog over the Channel was still growling, but he could not get very far from his kennel. If we could have made a perpetual peace at that moment, France would have taken a higher place than any nation since the days of the Romans. So I have heard the wise folk say, though for my part I had other things to think of. All the girls were glad to see the army back after its long absence, and you may be sure that I had my share of any favours that were going. You may judge how far I was a favourite in those days when I say that even now, in my sixtieth year—but why should I dwell upon that which is already sufficiently well known?

Our regiment of hussars was quartered with the horse chasseurs of the guard at Fontainebleau. It is, as you know, but a little place, buried in the heart of the forest, and it was wonderful at this time to see it crowded with Grand Dukes and Electors and Princes, who thronged round Napoleon like puppies round their master, each hoping that some bone might be thrown to him. There was more German than French to be heard in the street, for those who had helped us in the late war had come to beg for a reward, and those who had opposed us had come to try and escape their punishment. And all the time our little man, with his pale face and his cold, grey eyes, was riding to the hunt every morning, silent and brooding, all of them following in his train, in the hope that some word would escape him. And then, when the humour seized him, he would throw a hundred square miles to that man, or tear as much off the other, round off one kingdom by a river, or cut off another by a chain of mountains. That was how he used to do business, this little artilleryman, whom we had raised so high with our sabres and our bayonets. He was very civil to us always, for he knew where his power came from. We knew also, and showed it by the way in which we carried ourselves. We were agreed, you understand, that he was the finest leader in the world, but we did not forget that he had the finest men to lead.

Well, one day I was seated in my quarters playing cards with young Morat, of the horse chasseurs, when the door opened and in walked Lasalle, who was our Colonel. You know what a fine, swaggering fellow he was, and the sky-blue uniform of the Tenth suited him to a marvel. My faith, we youngsters were so taken by him that we all swore and diced and drank and played the deuce whether we liked it or no, just that we might resemble our Colonel! We forgot that it was not because he drank or gambled that the Emperor was going to make him the head of the light cavalry, but because he had the surest eye for the nature of a position or for the strength of a column, and the best judgment as to when infantry could be broken, or whether guns were exposed, of any man in the army. We were too young to understand all that, however, so we waxed our moustaches and clinked our spurs and let the ferrules of our scabbards wear out by trailing them along the pavement in the hope that we should all become Lasalles. When he came clanking into my quarters, both Morat and I sprang to our feet.

"My boy," said he, clapping me on the shoulder, "the Emperor wants to see you at four o'clock."

The room whirled round me at the words, and I had to lean my hands upon the edge of the card-table.

"What?" I cried. "The Emperor!"

"Precisely," said he, smiling at my astonishment.

"But the Emperor does not know of my existence, Colonel," I protested. "Why should he send for me?"

"Well, that's just what puzzles me," cried Lasalle, twirling his moustache. "If he wanted the help of a good sabre, why should he descend to one of my lieutenants when he might have found all that he needed at the head of the regiment? However," he added, clapping me upon the shoulder again in his hearty fashion, "every man has his chance. I have had mine, otherwise I should not be Colonel of the Tenth. I must not grudge you yours. Forwards, my boy, and may it be the first step towards changing your busby for a cocked hat."

It was but two o'clock, so he left me, promising to come back and to accompany me to the palace. My faith, what a time I passed, and how many conjectures did I make as to what it was that the Emperor could want of me! I paced up and down my little room in a fever of anticipation. Sometimes I thought that perhaps he had heard of the guns which we had taken at Austerlitz; but then there were so many who had taken guns at Austerlitz, and two years had passed since the battle. Or it might be that he wished to reward me for my affair with the *aide-de-camp* of the Russian Emperor. But then again a cold fit would seize me, and I would fancy that he had sent for me to reprimand me. There were a few duels which he might have taken in ill part, and there were one or two little jokes in Paris since the peace.

But, no! I considered the words of Lasalle. "If he had need of a brave man," said Lasalle.

It was obvious that my Colonel had some idea of what was in the wind. If he had not known that it was to my advantage, he would not have been so cruel as to congratulate me. My heart glowed with joy as this conviction grew upon me, and I sat down to write to my mother and to tell her that the Emperor was waiting, at that very moment, to have my opinion upon a matter of importance. It made me smile as I wrote it to think that, wonderful as it appeared to me, it would probably only confirm my mother in her opinion of the Emperor's good sense.

At half-past three I heard a sabre come clanking against every step of my wooden stair. It was Lasalle, and with him was a lame gentleman, very neatly dressed in black with dapper ruffles and cuffs. We did not know many civilians, we of the army, but, my word, this was one whom we could not afford to ignore! I had only to glance at those twinkling eyes, the comical, upturned nose, and the straight, precise mouth, to know that I was in the presence of the one man in France whom even the Emperor had to consider.

"This is Monsieur Etienne Gerard, Monsieur de Talleyrand," said Lasalle.

I saluted, and the statesman took me in from the top of my panache to the rowel of my spur, with a glance that played over me like a rapier point.

"Have you explained to the Lieutenant the circumstances under which he is summoned to the Emperor's presence?" he asked, in his dry, creaking voice.

They were such a contrast, these two men, that I could not help glancing from one to the other of them: the little, black, sly politician, and the big, sky-blue hussar, with one fist on his hip and the other on the hilt of his sabre. They both took their seats as I looked, Talleyrand without a sound, and Lasalle with a clash and jingle like a prancing charger.

"It's this way, youngster," said he, in his brusque fashion; "I was with the Emperor in his private cabinet this morning when a note was brought in to him. He opened it, and as he did so he gave such a start that it fluttered down on to the floor. I handed it up to him again, but he was staring at the wall in front of him as if he had seen a ghost. 'Fratelli d'Ajaccio,' he muttered; and then again, 'Fratelli d'Ajaccio.' I don't pretend to know more Italian than a man can pick up in two campaigns, and I could make nothing of this. It seemed to me that he had gone out of his mind; and you would have said so also, Monsieur de Talleyrand, if you had seen the look in his eyes. He read the note, and then he sat for half an hour or more without moving."

"And you?" asked Talleyrand.

"Why, I stood there not knowing what I ought to do. Presently he seemed to come back to his senses.

"'I suppose, Lasalle,' said he, 'that you have some gallant young officers in the Tenth?'

"'They are all that, sire,' I answered.

"'If you had to pick one who was to be depended upon for action, but who would not think too much—you understand me, Lasalle—which would you select?' he asked.

"I saw that he needed an agent who would not penetrate too deeply into his plans.

"'I have one,' said I, 'who is all spurs and moustaches, with never a thought beyond women and horses.'

"'That is the man I want,' said Napoleon. 'Bring him to my private cabinet at four o'clock.'

"So, youngster, I came straight away to you at once, and mind that you do credit to the 10th Hussars."

I was by no means flattered by the reasons which had led to my Colonel's choice, and I must have shown as much in my face, for he roared with laughter and Talleyrand gave a dry chuckle also.

"Just one word of advice before you go, Monsieur Gerard," said he: "you are now coming into troubled waters, and you might find a worse pilot than myself. We have none of us any idea as to what this little affair means, and, between ourselves, it is very important for us, who have the destinies of France upon our shoulders, to keep ourselves in touch with all that goes on. You understand me, Monsieur Gerard?"

I had not the least idea what he was driving at, but I bowed and tried to look as if it was clear to me.

"Act very guardedly, then, and say nothing to anybody," said Talleyrand. "Colonel de Lasalle and I will not show ourselves in public with you, but we will await you here, and we will give you our advice when you have told us what has passed between the Emperor and yourself. It is time that you started now, for the Emperor never forgives unpunctuality."

Off I went on foot to the palace, which was only a hundred paces off. I made my way to the antechamber, where Duroc, with his grand new scarlet and gold coat, was fussing about among the crowd of people who were waiting. I heard him whisper to Monsieur de Caulaincourt that half of them were German Dukes who expected to be made Kings, and the other half German Dukes who expected to be made paupers. Duroc, when he heard my name, showed me straight in, and I found myself in the Emperor's presence.

I had, of course, seen him in camp a hundred times, but I had never been face to face with him before. I have no doubt that if you had met him without knowing in the least who he was, you would simply have said that he was a sallow little fellow with a good forehead and fairly well-turned calves. His tight white cashmere breeches and white stockings showed off his legs to advantage. But even a stranger must have been struck by the singular look of his eyes, which could harden into an expression which would frighten a grenadier. It is said that even Auguereau, who was a man who had never known what fear was, quailed before Napoleon's gaze, at a time, too, when the Emperor was but an unknown soldier. He looked mildly enough at me, however, and motioned me to remain by the door. De Meneval was writing to his dictation, looking up at him between each sentence with his spaniel eyes.

"That will do. You can go," said the Emperor, abruptly. Then, when the secretary had left the room, he strode across with his hands behind his back, and he looked me up and down without a word. Though he was a small man himself, he was very fond of having fine-looking fellows about him, and so I think that my appearance gave him pleasure. For my own part, I raised one hand to the salute and held the other upon the hilt of my sabre, looking straight ahead of me, as a soldier should.

"Well, Monsieur Gerard," said he, at last, tapping his forefinger upon one of the brandebourgs of gold braid upon the front of my pelisse, "I am informed that you are a very deserving young officer. Your Colonel gives me an excellent account of you."

I wished to make a brilliant reply, but I could think of nothing save Lasalle's phrase that I was all spurs and moustaches, so it ended in my saying nothing at all. The Emperor watched the struggle which must have shown itself upon my features, and when, finally, no answer came he did not appear to be displeased.

"I believe that you are the very man that I want," said he. "Brave and clever men surround me upon every side. But a brave man who——" He did not finish his sentence, and for my own part I could not understand what he was driving at. I contented myself with assuring him that he could count upon me to the death.

"You are, as I understand, a good swordsman?" said he.

"Tolerable, sire," I answered.

"You were chosen by your regiment to fight the champion of the Hussars of Chambarant?" said he.

I was not sorry to find that he knew so much of my exploits.

"My comrades, sire, did me that honour," said I.

"And for the sake of practice you insulted six fencing masters in the week before your duel?"

"I had the privilege of being out seven times in as many days, sire," said I.

"And escaped without a scratch?"

"The fencing master of the 23rd Light Infantry touched me on the left elbow, sire."

"Let us have no more child's play of the sort, monsieur," he cried, turning suddenly to that cold rage of his which was so appalling. "Do you imagine that I place veteran soldiers in these positions that you may practise quarte and tierce upon them? How am I to face Europe if my soldiers turn their points upon each other? Another word of your dueling, and I break you between these fingers."

I saw his plump white hands flash before my eyes as he spoke, and his voice had turned to the most discordant hissing and growling. My word, my skin pringled all over as I listened to him, and I would gladly have changed my position for that of the first man in the steepest and narrowest breach that ever swallowed up a storming party. He turned to the table, drank off a cup of coffee, and then when he faced me again every trace of this storm had vanished, and he wore that singular smile which came from his lips but never from his eyes.

"I have need of your services, Monsieur Gerard," said he. "I may be safer with a good sword at my side, and there are reasons why yours should be the one which I select. But first of all I must bind you to secrecy. Whilst I live what passes between us to-day must be known to none but ourselves."

I thought of Talleyrand and of Lasalle, but I promised.

"In the next place, I do not want your opinions or conjectures, and I wish you to do exactly what you are told."

I bowed.

"It is your sword that I need, and not your brains. I will do the thinking. Is that clear to you?"

"Yes, sire."

"You know the Chancellor's Grove, in the forest?"

I bowed.

"You know also the large double fir-tree where the hounds assembled on Tuesday?"

Had he known that I met a girl under it three times a week, he would not have asked me. I bowed once more without remark.

"Very good. You will meet me there at ten o'clock to-night."

I had got past being surprised at anything which might happen. If he had asked me to take his place upon the Imperial throne I could only have nodded my busby.

"We shall then proceed into the wood together," said the Emperor. "You will be armed with a sword, but not with pistols. You must address no remark to me, and I shall say nothing to you. We will advance in silence. You understand?"

"I understand, sire."

"After a time we shall see a man, or more probably two men, under a certain tree. We shall approach them together. If I signal to you to defend me, you will have your sword ready. If, on the other hand, I speak to these men, you will wait and see what happens. If you are called upon to draw, you must see that neither of them, in the event of there being two, escapes from us. I shall myself assist you."

"But, sire," I cried, "I have no doubt that two would not be too many for my sword; but would it not be better that I should bring a comrade than that you should be forced to join in such a struggle?"

"Ta, ta, ta," said he. "I was a soldier before I was an Emperor. Do you think, then, that artillerymen have not swords as well as the hussars? But I ordered you not to argue with me. You will do exactly what I tell you. If swords are once out, neither of these men is to get away alive."

"They shall not, sire," said I.

"Very good. I have no more instructions for you. You can go."

I turned to the door, and then an idea occurring to me I turned.

"I have been thinking, sire——" said I.

He sprang at me with the ferocity of a wild beast. I really thought he would have struck me.

"Thinking!" he cried. "You, *you!* Do you imagine I chose you out because you could think? Let me hear of your doing such a thing again! You, the one man—but, there! You meet me at the fir-tree at ten o'clock."

My faith, I was right glad to get out of the room. If I have a good horse under me, and a sword clanking against my stirrup-iron, I know where I am. And in all that relates to green fodder or dry, barley and oats and rye, and the handling of squadrons upon the march, there is no one who can teach me very much. But when I meet a Chamberlain and a Marshal of the Palace, and have to pick my words with an Emperor, and find that everybody hints instead of talking straight out, I feel like a troop-horse who has been put in a lady's calèche. It is not my trade, all this mincing and pretending. I have learned the manners of a gentleman, but never those of a courtier. I was right glad then to get into the fresh air again, and I ran away up to my quarters like a schoolboy who has just escaped from the seminary master.

But as I opened the door, the very first thing that my eye rested upon was a long pair of sky-blue legs with hussar boots, and a short pair of black ones with knee-breeches and buckles. They both sprang up together to greet me.

"Well, what news?" they cried, the two of them.

"None," I answered.

"The Emperor refused to see you?"

"No, I have seen him."

"And what did he say?"

"Monsieur de Talleyrand," I answered, "I regret to say that it is quite impossible for me to tell you anything about it. I have promised the Emperor."

"Pooh, pooh, my dear young man," said he, sidling up to me, as a cat does when it is about to rub itself against you. "This is all among friends, you understand, and goes no farther than these four walls. Besides, the Emperor never meant to include me in this promise."

"It is but a minute's walk to the palace, Monsieur de Talleyrand," I answered; "if it would not be troubling you too much to ask you to step up to it and bring back the Emperor's written statement that he did not mean to include you in this promise, I shall be happy to tell you every word that passed."

He showed his teeth at me then like the old fox that he was.

"Monsieur Gerard appears to be a little puffed up," said he. "He is too young to see things in their just proportion. As he grows older he may understand that is not always very discreet for a subaltern of cavalry to give such very abrupt refusals."

I did not know what to say to this, but Lasalle came to my aid in his downright fashion.

"The lad is quite right," said he. "If I had known that there was a promise I should not have questioned him. You know very well, Monsieur de Talleyrand, that if he had answered you, you would have laughed in your sleeve and thought as much about him as I think of the bottle when the burgundy is gone. As for me, I promise you that the Tenth would have had no room for him, and that we should have lost our best swordsman if I had heard him give up the Emperor's secret."

But the statesman became only the more bitter when he saw that I had the support of my Colonel.

"I have heard, Colonel de Lasalle," said he, with an icy dignity, "that your opinion is of great weight upon the subject of light cavalry. Should I have occasion to seek information about that branch of the army, I shall be very happy to apply to you. At present, however, the matter concerns diplomacy, and you will permit me to form my own views upon that question. As long as the welfare of France and the safety of the Emperor's person are largely committed to my care, I will use every means in my power to secure them, even if it should be against the Emperor's own temporary wishes. I have the honour, Colonel de Lasalle, to wish you a very good-day!"

He shot a most unamiable glance in my direction, and, turning upon his heel, he walked with little, quick, noiseless steps out of the room.

I could see from Lasalle's face that he did not at all relish finding himself at enmity with the powerful Minister. He rapped out an oath or two, and then, catching up his sabre and his cap, he clattered away down the stairs. As I looked out of the window I saw the two of them, the big blue man and the limping black one, going up the street together. Talleyrand was walking very rigidly, and Lasalle was waving his hands and talking, so I suppose that he was trying to make his peace.

The Emperor had told me not to think, and I endeavoured to obey him. I took up the cards from the table where Morat had left them, and

I tried to work out a few combinations at écarté. But I could not re-member which were trumps, and I threw them under the table in despair. Then I drew my sabre and practised giving point until I was weary, but it was all of no use at all. My mind *would* work, in spite of myself. At ten o'clock I was to meet the Emperor in the forest. Of all extraordinary combinations of events in the whole world, surely this was the last which would have occurred to me when I rose from my couch that morning. But the responsibility—the dreadful responsibility! It was all upon my shoulders. There was no one to halve it with me. It made me cold all over. Often as I have faced death upon the battle-field, I have never known what real fear was until that moment. But then I considered that after all I could but do my best like a brave and honourable gentleman, and above all obey the orders which I had received, to the very letter. And, if all went well, this would surely be the foundation of my for-tunes. Thus, swaying between my fears and my hopes, I spent the long, long evening until it was time for me to keep my appointment.

I put on my military overcoat, as I did not know how much of the night I might have to spend in the woods, and I fastened my sword out-side it. I pulled off my hussar boots also, and wore a pair of shoes and gaiters, that I might be lighter upon my feet. Then I stole out of my quarters and made for the forest, feeling very much easier in my mind, for I am always at my best when the time of thought has passed and the moment for action arrived.

I passed the barracks of the Chasseurs of the Guards, and the line of cafés all filled with uniforms. I caught a glimpse as I went by of the blue and gold of some of my comrades, amid the swarm of dark in-fantry coats and the light green of the Guides. There they sat, sipping their wine and smoking their cigars, little dreaming what their comrade had on hand. One of them, the chief of my squadron, caught sight of me in the lamplight, and came shouting after me into the street. I hur-ried on, however, pretending not to hear him, so he, with a curse at my deafness, went back at last to his wine bottle.

It is not very hard to get into the forest at Fontainebleau. The scat-tered trees steal their way into the very streets, like the tirailleurs in front of a column. I turned into a path, which led to the edge of the woods, and then I pushed rapidly forward towards the old fir-tree. It was a place which, as I have hinted, I had my own reasons for knowing well, and I could only thank the Fates that it was not one of the nights upon which Léonie would be waiting for me. The poor child would have died of terror at sight of the Emperor. He might have been too harsh with her—and worse still, he might have been too kind.

There was a half moon shining, and as I came up to our trysting-place, I saw that I was not the first to arrive. The Emperor was pacing up and down, his hands behind him and his face sunk somewhat forward upon his breast. He wore a grey great-coat with a capote over his head. I had seen him in such a dress in our winter campaign in Poland, and it was said that he used it because the hood was such an excellent disguise. He was always fond, whether in the camp or in Paris, of walking round at night, and overhearing the talk in the cabarets or round the fires. His figure, however, and his way of carrying his head and his hands, were so well known that he was always recognised, and then the talkers would just say whatever they thought would please him best.

My first thought was that he would be angry with me for having kept him waiting, but as I approached him, we heard the big church clock of Fontainebleau clang out the hour of ten. It was evident, therefore, that it was he who was too soon, and not I too late. I remembered his order that I should make no remark, so contented myself with halting within four paces of him, clicking my spurs together, grounding my sabre, and saluting. He glanced at me, and then without a word he turned and walked slowly through the forest, I keeping always about the same distance behind him. Once or twice he seemed to me to look apprehensively to right and to left, as if he feared that someone was observing us. I looked also, but although I have the keenest sight, it was quite impossible to see anything except the ragged patches of moonshine between the great black shadows of the trees. My ears are as quick as my eyes, and once or twice I thought that I heard a twig crack; but you know how many sounds there are in a forest at night, and how difficult it is even to say what direction they come from.

We walked for rather more than a mile, and I knew exactly what our destination was, long before we got there. In the centre of one of the glades there is a shattered stump of what must at some time have been a most gigantic tree. It is called the Abbot's Beech, and there are so many ghostly stories about it, that I know many a brave soldier who would not care about mounting sentinel over it. However, I cared as little for such folly as the Emperor did, so we crossed the glade and made straight for the old broken trunk. As we approached, I saw that two men were waiting for us beneath it.

When I first caught sight of them they were standing rather behind it, as if they were not anxious to be seen, but as we came nearer they emerged from its shadow and walked forward to meet us. The Emperor glanced back at me, and slackened his pace a little, so that I came within arm's length of him. You may think that I had my hilt well to the front, and that I had a very good look at these two people who were approaching us. The one was tall, remarkably so, and of a very spare frame, while the other was rather below the usual height, and had a brisk, determined way of walking. They each wore black cloaks, which were slung right across their figures, and hung down upon one side, like the mantles of Murat's dragoons. They had flat black caps, like those which I have since seen in Spain, which threw their faces into darkness, though I could see the gleam of their eyes from beneath them. With the moon behind them and their long black shadows walking in front, they were such figures as one might expect to meet at night near the Abbot's Beech. I can remember that they had a stealthy way of moving, and that as they approached, the moonshine formed two white diamonds between their legs and the legs of their shadows.

The Emperor had paused, and these two strangers came to a stand also within a few paces of us. I had drawn up close to my companion's elbow, so that the four of us were facing each other without a word spoken. My eyes were particularly fixed upon the taller one, because he was slightly the nearer to me, and I became certain as I watched him that he was in the last state of nervousness. His lean figure was quivering all over, and I heard a quick, thin panting like that of a tired dog. Suddenly one of them gave a short, hissing signal. The tall man bent his back and his knees like a diver about to spring, but before he could move, I had jumped with drawn sabre in front of him. At the same instant the smaller man bounded past me, and buried a long poniard in the Emperor's heart.

My God! the horror of that moment! It is a marvel that I did not drop dead myself. As in a dream, I saw the grey coat whirl convulsively round, and caught a glimpse in the moonlight of three inches of red point which jutted out from between the shoulders. Then down he fell with a dead man's gasp upon the grass, and the assassin, leaving his weapon buried in his victim, threw up both his hands and shrieked with joy. But I—I drove my sword through his midriff with such frantic force, that the mere blow of the hilt against the end of his breast-bone sent him six paces before he fell, and left my reeking blade ready for the other. I sprang round upon him with such a lust for blood upon me as I had never felt, and never have felt, in all my days. As I turned, a dagger flashed before my eyes, and I felt the cold wind of it pass my neck and the villain's wrist jar upon my shoulder. I shortened my sword, but he winced away from me, and an instant afterwards was in full flight, bounding like a deer across the glade in the moonlight.

But he was not to escape me thus. I knew that the murderer's poniard had done its work. Young as I was, I had seen enough of war to know a mortal blow. I paused but for an instant to touch the cold hand.

"Sire! Sire!" I cried, in an agony; and then as no sound came back and nothing moved, save an ever-widening dark circle in the moonlight, I knew that all was indeed over. I sprang madly to my feet, threw off my great-coat, and ran at the top of my speed after the remaining assassin.

Ah, how I blessed the wisdom which had caused me to come in shoes and gaiters! And the happy thought which had thrown off my coat. He could not get rid of his mantle, this wretch, or else he was too frightened to think of it. So it was that I gained upon him from the beginning. He must have been out of his wits, for he never tried to bury himself in the darker parts of the woods, but he flew on from glade to glade, until he came to the heath-land which leads up to the great Fontainebleau quarry. There I had him in full sight, and knew that he could not escape me. He ran well, it is true—ran as a coward runs when his life is the stake. But I ran as Destiny runs when it gets behind a man's heels. Yard by yard I drew in upon him. He was rolling and staggering. I could hear the rasping and crackling of his breath. The great gulf of the quarry suddenly yawned in front of his path, and glancing at me over his shoulder, he gave a shriek of despair. The next instant he had vanished from my sight.

Vanished utterly, you understand. I rushed to the spot, and gazed down into the black abyss. Had he hurled himself over? I had almost made up my mind that he had done so, when a gentle sound rising and falling came out of the darkness beneath me. It was his breathing once more, and it showed me where he must be. He was hiding in the tool-house.

At the edge of the quarry and beneath the summit there is a small platform upon which stands a wooden hut for the use of the labourers. It was into this, then, that he had darted. Perhaps he had thought, the fool, that, in the darkness, I would not venture to follow him. He little knew Etienne Gerard. With a spring I was on the platform, with another I was through the doorway, and then, hearing him in the corner, I hurled myself down upon the top of him.

He fought like a wild cat, but he never had a chance with his shorter weapon. I think that I must have transfixed him with that first mad lunge, for, though he struck and struck, his blows had no power in them, and presently his dagger tinkled down upon the floor. When I was sure that he was dead, I rose up and passed out into the moonlight. I climbed up on the heath again, and wandered across it as nearly out of my mind as a man could be. With the blood singing in my ears, and my naked sword still clutched in my hand, I walked aimlessly on until, looking round me, I found that I had come as far as the glade of the Abbot's Beech, and saw in the distance that gnarled stump which must ever be associated with the most terrible moment of my life. I sat down upon a fallen trunk with my sword across my knees and my head between my hands, and I tried to think about what had happened and what would happen in the future.

The Emperor had committed himself to my care. The Emperor was dead. Those were the two thoughts which clanged in my head, until I had no room for any other ones. He had come with me and he was dead. I had done what he had ordered when living. I had revenged him when dead. But what of all that? The world would look upon me as responsible. They might even look upon me as the assassin. What could I prove? What witnesses had I? Might I not have been the accomplice of these wretches? Yes,

yes, I was eternally dishonoured—the lowest, most despicable creature in all France. This then was the end of my fine military ambitions—of the hopes of my mother. I laughed bitterly at the thought. And what was I to do now? Was I to go into Fontainebleau, to wake up the palace, and to inform them that the great Emperor had been murdered within a pace of me? I could not do it—no, I could not do it! There was but one course for an honourable gentleman whom Fate had placed in so cruel a position. I would fall upon my dishonoured sword, and so share, since I could not avert, the Emperor's fate. I rose with my nerves strung to this last piteous deed, and as I did so, my eyes fell upon something which struck the breath from my lips. The Emperor was standing before me!

He was not more than ten yards off, with the moon shining straight upon his cold, pale face. He wore his grey overcoat, but the hood was turned back, and the front open, so that I could see the green coat of the Guides, and the white breeches. His hands were clasped behind his back, and his chin sunk forward upon his breast, in the way that was usual with him.

"Well," said he, in his hardest and most abrupt voice, "what account do you give of yourself?"

I believe that, if he had stood in silence for another minute, my brain would have given way. But those sharp military accents were exactly what I needed to bring me to myself. Living or dead, here was the Emperor standing before me and asking me questions. I sprang to the salute.

"You have killed one, I see," said he, jerking his head towards the beech.

"Yes, sire."

"And the other escaped?"

"No, sire, I killed him also."

"What!" he cried. "Do I understand that you have killed them both?" He approached me as he spoke with a smile which set his teeth gleaming in the moonlight.

"One body lies there, sire," I answered. "The other is in the tool-house at the quarry."

"Then the Brothers of Ajaccio are no more," he cried, and after a pause, as if speaking to himself: "The shadow has passed me for ever." Then he bent forward and laid his hand upon my shoulder.

"You have done very well, my young friend," said he. "You have lived up to your reputation."

He was flesh and blood, then, this Emperor. I could feel the little, plump palm that rested upon me. And yet I could not get over what I had seen with my own eyes, and so I stared at him in such bewilderment that he broke once more into one of his smiles.

"No, no, Monsieur Gerard," said he, "I am not a ghost, and you have not seen me killed. You will come here, and all will be clear to you."

He turned as he spoke, and led the way towards the great beech stump.

The bodies were still lying upon the ground, and two men were standing beside them. As we approached I saw from the turbans that they were Roustem and Mustafa, the two Mameluke servants. The Emperor paused when he came to the grey figure upon the ground, and turning back the hood which shrouded the features, he showed a face which was very different from his own.

"Here lies a faithful servant who has given up his life for his master," said he. "Monsieur de Goudin resembles me in figure and in manner, as you must admit."

What a delirium of joy came upon me when these few words made everything clear to me. He smiled again as he saw the delight which urged me to throw my arms round him and to embrace him, but he moved a step away, as if he had divined my impulse.

"You are unhurt?" he asked.

"I am unhurt, sire. But in another minute I should in my despair ——"

"Tut, tut!" he interrupted. "You did very well. He should himself have been more on his guard. I saw everything which passed."

"You saw it, sire!"

"You did not hear me follow you through the wood, then? I hardly lost sight of you from the moment that you left your quarters until poor de Goudin fell. The counterfeit Emperor was in front of you and the real one behind. You will now escort me back to the palace."

He whispered an order to his Mamelukes, who saluted in silence and remained where they were standing. For my part, I followed the Emperor with my pelisse bursting with pride. My word, I have always carried myself as a hussar should, but Lasalle himself never strutted and swung his dolman as I did that night! Who should clink his spurs and clatter his sabre if it were not I—I, Etienne Gerard—the confidant of the Emperor, the chosen swordsman of the light cavalry, the man who slew the would-be assassins of Napoleon? But he noticed my bearing and turned upon me like a blight.

"Is that the way to carry yourself on a secret mission?" he hissed, with that cold glare in his eyes. "Is it thus that you will make your comrades believe that nothing remarkable has occurred? Have done with this nonsense, monsieur, or you will find yourself transferred to the sappers, where you would have harder work and duller plumage."

That was the way with the Emperor. If ever he thought that anyone might have a claim upon him, he took the first opportunity to show him the gulf that lay between. I saluted and was silent, but I must confess to you that it hurt me after all that had passed between us. He led on to the palace, where we passed through the side door and up into his own cabinet. There were a couple of grenadiers at the staircase, and their eyes started out from under their fur caps, I promise you, when they saw a young lieutenant of hussars going up to the Emperor's room at midnight. I stood by the door, as I had done in the afternoon, while he flung himself down in an arm-chair, and remained silent so long that it seemed to me that he had forgotten all about me. I ventured at last upon a slight cough to remind him.

"Ah, Monsieur Gerard," said he, "you are very curious, no doubt, as to the meaning of all this?"

"I am quite content, sire, if it is your pleasure not to tell me," I answered.

"Ta, ta, ta," said he impatiently. "These are only words. The moment that you were outside that door you would begin making inquiries about what it means. In two days your brother officers would know about it, in three days it would be all over Fontainebleau, and it would be in Paris on the fourth. Now, if I tell you enough to appease your curiosity, there is some reasonable hope that you may be able to keep the matter to yourself."

He did not understand me, this Emperor, and yet I could only bow and be silent.

"A few words will make it clear to you," said he, speaking very swiftly and pacing up and down the room. "They were Corsicans, these two men. I had known them in my youth. We had belonged to the same society—Brothers of Ajaccio, as we called ourselves. It was founded in the old Paoli days, you understand, and we had some strict rules of our own which were not infringed with impunity."

A very grim look came over his face as he spoke, and it seemed to me that all that was French had gone out of him, and that it was the pure Corsican, the man of strong passions and of strange revenges, who stood before me. His memory had gone back to those early days of his, and for five minutes, wrapped in thought, he paced up and down the room with his quick little tiger steps. Then with an impatient wave of his hands he came back to his palace and to me.

"The rules of such a society," he continued, "are all very well for a private citizen. In the old days there was no more loyal brother than I. But circumstances change, and it would be neither for my welfare nor for that of France that I should now submit myself to them. They wanted to hold me to it, and so brought their fate upon their own heads. These were the two chiefs of the order, and they had come from Corsica to summon me to meet them at the spot which they named. I knew what such a summons meant. No man had ever returned from obeying one. On the other hand, if I did not go, I was sure that disaster would follow. I am a brother myself, you remember, and I know their ways."

Again there came that hardening of his mouth and cold glitter of his eyes.

"You perceive my dilemma, Monsieur Gerard," said he. "How would you have acted yourself, under such circumstances?"

"Given the word to the 10th Hussars, sire," I cried. "Patrols could have swept the woods from end to end, and brought these two rascals to your feet."

He smiled, but he shook his head.

"I had very excellent reasons why I did not wish them taken alive," said he. "You can understand that an assassin's tongue might be as dangerous a weapon as an assassin's dagger. I will not disguise from you that I wished to avoid scandal at all cost. That was why I ordered you to take no pistols with you. That also is why my Mamelukes will remove all traces of the affair, and nothing more will be heard about it. I thought of all possible plans, and I am convinced that I selected the best one. Had I sent more than one guard with de Goudin into the woods, then the brothers would not have appeared. They would not change their plans or miss their chance for the sake of a single man. It was Colonel Lasalle's accidental presence at the moment when I received the summons which led to my choosing one of his hussars for the mission. I selected you, Monsieur Gerard, because I wanted a man who could handle a sword, and who would not pry more deeply into the affair than I desired. I trust that, in this respect, you will justify my choice as well as you have done in your bravery and skill."

"Sire," I answered, "you may rely upon it."

"As long as I live," said he, "you never open your lips upon this subject."

"I dismiss it entirely from my mind, sire. I will efface it from my recollection as if it had never been. I will promise you to go out of your cabinet at this moment exactly as I was when I entered it at four o'clock."

"You cannot do that," said the Emperor, smiling. "You were a lieutenant at that time. You will permit me, Captain, to wish you a very good-night."

7

✍

From *The Stark Munro Letters*
(1895)

BEING A SERIES OF TWELVE LETTERS WRITTEN BY J. STARK
MUNRO, M.B., TO HIS FRIEND & FORMER FELLOW-STUDENT,
HERBERT SWANBOROUGH OF LOWELL, MASSACHUSETTS,
DURING THE YEARS 1881–1884.

VII
1. The Parade, Bradfield, 9th March, 1882.

Well, you see I am as good as my word, Bertie; and here is a full account of this queer little sample gouged out of real life, never to be seen, I should fancy, by any eye save your own. I have written to Horton also, and of course to my mother; but I don't go into detail with them, as I have got into the way of doing with you. You keep on assuring me that you like it; so on your own head be it if you find my experiences gradually developing into a weariness.

When I woke in the morning, and looked round at the bare walls and the basin on the packing case, I hardly knew where I was. Cullingworth came charging into the room in his dressing gown, however, and roused me effectually by putting his hands on the rail at the end of the bed, and throwing a somersault over it which brought his heels on to my pillow with a thud. He was in great spirits, and, squatting on the bed, he held forth about his plans while I dressed.

"I tell you one of the first things I mean to do, Munro," said he. "I mean to have a paper of my own. We'll start a weekly paper here, you and I, and we'll make them sit up all round. We'll have an organ of our own, just like every French politician. If any one crosses us, we'll make them wish they had never been born. Eh, what, laddie? what d'you think? So clever, Munro, that everybody's bound to read it, and so scathing that it will just fetch out blisters every time. Don't you think we could?"

"What politics?" I asked.

"Oh, curse the politics! Red pepper well rubbed in, that's my idea of a paper. Call it the *Scorpion*. Chaff the Mayor and the Council until they call a meeting and hang themselves. I'd do the snappy paragraphs, and you would do the fiction and poetry. I thought about it during the night, and Hetty has written to Murdoch's to get an estimate for the printing. We might get our first number out this day week."

"My dear chap!" I gasped.

"I want you to start a novel this morning. You won't get many patients at first, and you'll have lots of time."

"But I never wrote a line in my life."

"A properly balanced man can do anything he sets his hand to. He's got every possible quality inside him, and all he wants is the will to develop it."

"Could you write a novel yourself?" I asked.

"Of course I could. Such a novel, Munro, that when they'd read the first chapter the folk would just sit groaning until the second came out. They'd wait in rows outside my door in the hope of hearing what was coming next. By Crums, I'll go and begin it now!" And, with another somersault over the end of the bed, he rushed from the room, with the tassels of his dressing gown flying behind him.

I dare say you've quite come to the conclusion by this time that Cullingworth is simply an interesting pathological study—a man in the first stage of lunacy or general paralysis. You might not be so sure about it if you were in close contact with him. He justifies his wildest flights by what he does. It sounds grotesque when put down in black and white; but then it would have sounded equally grotesque a year ago if he had said that he would build up a huge practice in a twelvemonth. Now we see that he has done it. His possibilities are immense. He has such huge energy at the back of his fertility of invention. I am afraid, on thinking over all that I have written to you, that I may have given you a false impression of the man by dwelling too much on those incidents in which he has shown the strange and violent side of his character, and omitting the stretches between where his wisdom and judgment have had a chance. His conversation when he does not fly off at a tangent is full of pitch and idea. "The greatest monument ever erected to Napoleon Buonaparte was the British National debt," said he yesterday. Again, "We must never forget that the principal export of Great Britain to the United States *is* the United States." Again, speaking of Christianity, "What is intellectually unsound cannot be morally sound." He shoots off a whole column of aphorisms in a single evening. I should like to have a man with a note book always beside him to gather up his waste. No; you must not let me give you a false impression of the man's capacity. On the other hand, it would be dishonest to deny that I think him thoroughly unscrupulous, and full of very sinister traits. I am much mistaken, however, if he has not fine strata in his nature. He is capable of rising to heights as well as of sinking to depths.

Well, when we had breakfasted we got into the carriage and drove off to the place of business.

"I suppose you are surprised at Hetty coming with us," said Cullingworth, slapping me on the knee. "Hetty, Munro is wondering what the devil you are here for, only he is too polite to ask."

In fact, it *had* struck me as rather strange that she should, as a matter of course, accompany us to business.

"You'll see when we get there," he cried chuckling. "We run this affair on lines of our own."

It was not very far, and we soon found ourselves outside a square whitewashed building, which had a huge "Dr. Cullingworth" on a great brass plate at the side of the door. Underneath was printed "May be consulted gratis from ten to four." The door was open, and I caught a glimpse of a crowd of people waiting in the hall.

"How many here?" asked Cullingworth of the page boy.

"A hundred and forty, sir."

"All the waiting rooms full?"

"Yes, sir."

"Courtyard full?"

"Yes, sir."

"Stable full?"

"Yes, sir."

"Coach-house full?"

"There's still room in the coach-house, sir."

"Ah, I'm sorry we haven't got a crowded day for you, Munro," said he. "Of course, we can't command these things, and must take them as they come. Now then, now then, make a gangway, can't you?"—this to his patients. "Come here and see the waiting-room. Pooh! What an atmosphere! Why on earth can't you open the windows for yourselves? I never saw such folk! There are thirty people in this room, Munro, and not one with sense enough to open a window to save himself from suffocation."

"I tried, sir, but there's a screw through the sash," cried one fellow.

"Ah, my boy, you'll never get on in the world if you can't open a window without raising a sash," said Cullingworth, slapping him on the shoulder. He took the man's umbrella and stuck it through two of the panes of glass.

"That's the way!" he said. "Boy, see that the screw is taken out. Now then, Munro, come along, and we'll get to work."

We went up a wooden stair, uncarpeted, leaving every room beneath us, as far as I could see, crowded with patients. At the top was a bare passage, which had two rooms opposite to each other at one end, and a single one at the other.

"This is my consulting room," said he, leading the way into one of these. It was a good-sized square chamber, perfectly empty save for two plain wooden chairs and an unpainted table with two books and a stethoscope upon it. "It doesn't look like four or five thousand a year, does it? Now, there is an exactly similar one opposite which you can have for yourself. I'll send across any surgical cases which may turn up. Today, however, I think you had better stay with me, and see how I work things."

"I should very much like to," said I.

"There are one or two elementary rules to be observed in the way of handling patients," he remarked, seating himself on the table and swinging his legs. "The most obvious is that you must never let them see that you want them. It should be pure condescension on your part seeing them at all; and the more difficulties you throw in the way of it, the more they think of it. Break your patients in early, and keep them well to heel. Never make the fatal mistake of being polite to them. Many foolish young men fall into this habit, and are ruined in consequence. Now, this is my form"—he sprang to the door, and putting his two hands to his mouth be bellowed: "Stop your confounded jabbering down there! I might as well be living above a poultry show! There, you see," he added to me, "they will think ever so much more of me for that."

"But don't they get offended?" I asked.

"I'm afraid not. I have a name for this sort of thing now, and they have come to expect it. But an offended patient—I mean a thoroughly insulted one—is the finest advertisement in the world. If it is a woman, she runs clacking about among her friends until your name becomes a household word, and they all pretend to sympathise with her, and agree among themselves that you must be a remarkably discerning man. I quarrelled with one man about the state of his gall duct, and it ended by my throwing him down the stairs. What was the result? He talked so much about it that the whole village from which he came, sick and well, trooped to see me. The little country practitioner who had been buttering them up for a quarter of a century found that he might as well put up his shutters. It's human nature, my boy, and you can't alter it. Eh, what? You make yourself cheap and you become cheap. You put a high price on yourself and they rate you at that price. Suppose I set up in Harley Street to-morrow, and made it all nice and easy, with hours from ten to three, do you think I should get a patient? I might starve first. How would I work it? I should let it be known that I only saw patients from midnight until two in the morning, and that bald-headed people must pay double. That would set people talking, their curiosity would be stimulated, and in four months the street would be blocked all night. Eh, what? laddie, you'd go yourself. That's my principle here. I often come in of a morning and send them all about their business, tell them I'm going off to the country for a day. I turn away forty pounds, and it's worth four hundred as an advertisement!"

"But I understood from the plate that the consultations were gratis."

"So they are, but they have to pay for the medicine. And if a patient wishes to come out of turn he has to pay half-a-guinea for the privilege. There are generally about twenty every day who would rather pay that than wait several hours. But, mind you, Munro, don't you make any mistake about this! All this would go for nothing if you had not something solid behind—I cure them. That's the point. I take cases that others have despaired of, and I cure them right off. All the rest is only to bring them here. But once here I keep them on my merits. It would all be a flash in the pan but for that. Now, come along and see Hetty's department."

We walked down the passage to the other room. It was elaborately fitted up as a dispensary, and there with a chic little apron Mrs. Cullingworth was busy making up pills. With her sleeves turned up and a litter of glasses and bottles all round her, she was laughing away like a little child among its toys.

"The best dispenser in the world!" cried Cullingworth, patting her on the shoulder. "You see how I do it, Munro. I write on a label what the prescription is, and make a sign which shows how much is to be charged. The man comes along the passage and passes the label through the pigeon hole. Hetty makes it up, passes out the bottle, and takes the money. Now, come on and clear some of these folk out of the house."

It is impossible for me to give you any idea of that long line of patients, filing hour after hour through the unfurnished room, and departing, some amused, and some frightened, with their labels in their hands. Cullingworth's antics are beyond belief. I laughed until I thought the wooden chair under me would have come to pieces. He roared, he raved, he swore, he pushed them about, slapped them on the back, shoved them against the wall, and occasionally rushed out to the head of the stair to address them *en masse*. At the same time, behind all this tomfoolery, I, watching his prescriptions, could see a quickness of diagnosis, a scientific insight, and a daring and unconventional use of drugs, which satisfied me that he was right in saying that, under all this charlatanism, there lay solid reasons for his success. Indeed, "charlatanism" is a misapplied word in this connection; for it would describe the doctor who puts on an artificial and conventional manner with his patients, rather than one who is absolutely frank and true to his own extraordinary nature.

To some of his patients he neither said one word nor did he allow them to say one. With a loud "hush" he would rush at them, thump them on the chests, listen to their hearts, write their labels, and then run them out of the room by their shoulders. One poor old lady he greeted with a perfect scream. "You've been drinking too much tea!" he cried. "You are suffering from tea poisoning!" Then, without allowing her to get a word in, he clutched her by her crackling black mantle, dragged her up to the table, and held out a copy of "Taylor's Medical Jurisprudence" which was lying there. "Put your hand on the book," he thundered, "and swear that for fourteen days you will drink nothing but cocoa." She swore with upturned eyes, and was instantly whirled off with her label in her hand, to the dispensary. I could imagine that to the last day of her life, the old lady would talk of her interview with Cullingworth; and I could well understand how the village from which she came would send fresh recruits to block up his waiting rooms.

Another portly person was seized by the two armholes of his waistcoat, just as he was opening his mouth to explain his symptoms, and was rushed backward down the passage, down the stairs, and finally into the street, to the immense delight of the assembled patients, "You eat too much, drink too much, and sleep too much," Cullingworth roared after him. "Knock down a policeman, and come again when they let you out." Another patient complained of a "sinking feeling." "My dear," said he, "take your medicine; and if that does no good, swallow the cork, for there is nothing better when you are sinking."

As far as I could judge, the bulk of the patients looked upon a morning at Cullingworth's as a most enthralling public entertainment, tempered only by a thrill lest it should be their turn next to be made an exhibition of.

Well, with half-an-hour for lunch, this extraordinary business went on till a quarter to four in the afternoon. When the last patient had departed, Cullingworth led the way into the dispensary, where all the fees had been arranged upon the counter in the order of their value. There were seventeen half-sovereigns, seventy-three shillings, and forty-six florins; or thirty-two pounds eight and sixpence in all. Cullingworth counted it up, and then mixing the gold and silver into one heap, he sat running his fingers through it and playing with it. Finally, he raked it into the canvas bag which I had seen the night before, and lashed the neck up with a boot-lace.

We walked home, and that walk struck me as the most extraordinary part of all that extraordinary day. Cullingworth paraded slowly through the principal streets with his canvas bag, full of money, outstretched at the full length of his arm. His wife and I walked on either side, like two acolytes supporting a priest, and so we made our way solemnly homewards, the people stopping to see us pass.

"I always make a point of walking through the doctors' quarter," said Cullingworth. "We are passing through it now. They all come to their windows and gnash their teeth and dance until I am out of sight."

"Why should you quarrel with them? What is the matter with them?" I asked.

"Pooh! what's the use of being mealy-mouthed about it?" said he. "We are all trying to cut each other's throats, and why should we be hypocritical over it? They haven't got a good word for me, any one of them; so I like to take a rise out of them."

"I must say that I can see no sense in that. They are your brothers in the profession, with the same education and the same knowledge. Why should you take an offensive attitude towards them?"

"That's what I say, Dr. Munro," cried his wife. "It is so very unpleasant to feel that one is surrounded by enemies on every side."

"Hetty's riled because their wives wouldn't call upon her," he cried. "Look at that, my dear," jingling his bag. "That is better than having a lot of brainless women drinking tea and cackling in your drawing-room. I've had a big card printed, Munro, saying that we don't desire to increase the circle of our acquaintance. The maid has orders to show it to every suspicious person who calls."

"Why should you not make money at your practice, and yet remain on good terms with your professional brethren?" said I. "You speak as if the two things were incompatible."

"So they are. What's the good of beating about the bush, laddie? My methods are all unprofessional, and I break every law of medical etiquette as often as I can think of it. You know very well that the British Medical Association would hold up their hands in horror if it could see what you have seen to-day."

"But why not conform to professional etiquette?"

"Because I know better. My boy, I'm a doctor's son, and I've seen too much of it. I was born inside the machine, and I've seen all the wires. All this etiquette is a dodge for keeping the business in the hands of the older men. It's to hold the young men back, and to stop the holes by which they might slip through to the front. I've heard my father say so a score of times. He had the largest practice in Scotland, and yet he was absolutely devoid of brains. He slipped into it through seniority and decorum. No pushing, but take your turn. Very well, laddie, when you're at the top of the line, but how about it when you've just taken your place at the tail? When I'm on the top rung I shall look down and say, 'Now, you youngsters, we are going to have a very strict etiquette, and I beg that you will come up very quietly and not disarrange me from my comfortable position.' At the same time, if they do what I tell them, I shall look upon them as a lot of infernal blockheads. Eh, Munro, what?"

I could only say again that I thought he took a very low view of the profession, and that I disagreed with every word he said.

"Well, my boy, you may disagree as much as you like, but if you are going to work with me you must throw etiquette to the devil!"

"I can't do that."

"Well, if you are too clean handed for the job you can clear out. We can't keep you here against your will."

I said nothing; but when we got back, I went upstairs and packed up my trunk, with every intention of going back to Yorkshire by the night train. He came up to my room, and finding what I was at, he burst into apologies which would have satisfied a more exacting man than I am.

"You shall do just exactly what you like, my dear chap. If you don't like my way, you may try some way of your own."

"That's fair enough," said I. "But it's a little trying to a man's self-respect if he is told to clear out every time there is a difference of opinion."

"Well, well, there was no harm meant, and it shan't occur again. I can't possibly say more than that; so come along down and have a cup of tea."

And so the matter blew over; but I very much fear, Bertie, that this is the first row of a series. I have a presentiment that sooner or later my position here will become untenable. Still, I shall give it a fair trial as long as he will let me. Cullingworth is a fellow who likes to have nothing but inferiors and dependents round him. Now, I like to stand on my own legs, and think with my own mind. If he'll let me do this we'll get along very well; but if I know the man he will claim submission, which is more than I am inclined to give. He has a right to my gratitude, which I freely admit. He has found an opening for me when I badly needed one and had no immediate prospects. But still, one may pay too high a price even for that, and I should feel that I was doing so if I had to give up my individuality and my manhood.

We had an incident that evening which was so characteristic that I must tell you of it. Cullingworth has an air gun which fires little steel darts. With this he makes excellent practice at about twenty feet, the length of the back room. We were shooting at a mark after dinner, when he asked me whether I would hold a halfpenny between my finger and thumb, and allow him to shoot it out. A halfpenny not being forthcoming, he took a bronze medal out of his waistcoat pocket, and I held that up as a mark. "Kling!" went the air gun, and the medal rolled upon the floor.

"Plumb in the centre," said he.

"On the contrary," I answered, "you never hit it at all!"

"Never hit it! I must have hit it!"

"I am confident you didn't."

"Where's the dart, then?"

"Here," said I, holding up a bleeding forefinger, from which the tail end of the fluff with which the dart was winged was protruding.

I never saw a man so abjectly sorry for anything in my life. He used language of self-reproach which would have been extravagant if he had shot off one of my limbs. Our positions were absurdly reversed; and it was he who sat collapsed in a chair, while it was I, with the dart still in my finger, who leaned over him and laughed the matter off. Mrs. Cullingworth had run for hot water, and presently with a tweezer we got the intruder out. There was very little pain (more to-day than yesterday), but if ever you are called upon to identify my body you may look for a star at the end of my right forefinger.

When the surgery was completed (Cullingworth writhing and groaning all the time) my eyes happened to catch the medal which I had dropped, lying upon the carpet. I lifted it up and looked at it, eager to find some topic which would be more agreeable. Printed upon it was— "Presented to James Cullingworth for gallantry in saving life. Jan. 1879."

"Hullo, Cullingworth," said I. "You never told me about this!"

He was off in an instant in his most extravagant style.

"What! The medal? Haven't you got one? I thought every one had. You prefer to be select, I suppose. It was a little boy. You've no idea the trouble I had to get him in."

"Get him out, you mean."

"My dear chap, you don't understand! Any one could get a child out. It's getting one in that's the bother. One deserves a medal for it. Then there are the witnesses, four shillings a day I had to pay them, and a quart of beer in the evenings. You see you can't pick up a child and carry it to the edge of a pier and throw it in. You'd have all sorts of complications with the parents. You must be patient and wait until you get a legitimate chance. I caught a quinsy walking up and down Avonmouth pier before I saw my opportunity. He was rather a stolid fat boy, and he was sitting on the very edge, fishing. I got the sole of my foot on to the small of his back, and shot him an incredible distance. I had some little difficulty in getting him out, for his fishing line got twice round my legs, but it all ended well, and the witnesses were as staunch as possible. The boy came up to thank me next day, and said that he was quite uninjured save for a bruise on the back. His parents always send me a brace of fowls every Christmas."

I was sitting with my finger in the hot water listening to this rigmarole. When he had finished he ran off to get his tobacco box, and we could hear the bellowing of his laughter dwindling up the stair. I was still looking at the medal, which, from the dents all over it, had evidently been often used as a target, when I felt a timid touch upon my sleeve; it was Mrs. Cullingworth, who was looking earnestly at me with a very distressed expression upon her face.

"You believe far too much what James says," said she. "You don't know him in the least, Mr. Munro. You don't look at a thing from his point of view, and you will never understand him until you do. It is not, of course, that he means to say anything that is untrue; but his fancy is excited, and he is quite carried away by the humour of any idea, whether it tells against himself or not. It hurts me, Mr. Munro, to see the only man in the world towards whom he has any feeling of friendship, misunderstanding him so completely, for very often when you say nothing your face shows very clearly what you think."

I could only answer lamely that I was very sorry if I had misjudged her husband in any way, and that no one had a keener appreciation of some of his qualities than I had.

"I saw how gravely you looked when he told you that absurd story about pushing a little boy into the water," she continued; and, as she spoke, she drew from somewhere in the front of her dress a much creased slip of paper. "Just glance at that, please, Dr. Munro."

It was a newspaper cutting, which gave the true account of the incident. Suffice it that it was an ice accident, and that Cullingworth had really behaved in a heroic way and had been drawn out himself insensible, with the child so clasped in his arms that it was not until he had recovered his senses that they were able to separate them. I had hardly finished reading it when we heard his step on the stairs; and she, thrusting the paper back into her bosom, became in an instant the same silently watchful woman as ever.

Is he not a conundrum? If he interests you at a distance (and I take for granted that what you say in your letters is not merely conventional compliment) you can think how piquant he is in actual life. I must confess, however, that I can never shake off the feeling that I am living with some capricious creature who frequently growls and may possibly bite. Well, it won't be very long before I write again, and by that time I shall probably know whether I am likely to find any permanent billet here or not. I am so sorry to hear about Mrs. Swanborough's indisposition. You know that I take the deepest interest in everything that affects you. They tell me here that I am looking very fit, though I think they ought to spell it with an "a."

IX
I. The Parade, Bradfield, 23rd April, 1882.

I have some recollection, my dear Bertie, that when I wrote you a rambling disconnected sort of letter about three weeks ago, I wound up by saying that I might have something more interesting to tell you next time. Well, so it has turned out! The whole game is up here, and I am off upon a fresh line of rails altogether. Cullingworth is to go one way and I another; and yet I am glad to say that there has not been any quarrel between us. As usual, I have begun my letter at the end, but I'll work up to it more deliberately now, and let you know exactly how it came about.

And first of all, a thousand thanks for your two long letters, which lie before me as I write. There is little enough personal news in them, but I can quite understand that the quiet happy routine of your life reels off very smoothly from week to week. On the other hand, you give me plenty of proof of that inner life which is to me so very much more interesting. After all, we may very well agree to differ. You think some things are proved which I don't believe in. You think some things edifying which do not appear to me to be so. Well, I know that you are perfectly honest in your belief. I am sure you give me credit for being the same. The future will decide which of us is right. The survival of the truest is a constant law, I fancy, though it must be acknowledged that it is very slow in action.

You make a mistake, however, in assuming that those who think as I do are such a miserable minority. The whole essence of our thought is independence and individual judgment; so that we don't get welded into single bodies as the churches do, and have no opportunity of testing our own strength. There are, no doubt, all shades of opinion among us; but if you merely include those who in their private hearts disbelieve the doctrines usually accepted, and think that sectarian churches tend to evil rather than good, I fancy that the figures would be rather surprising. When I read your letter, I made a list of all those men with whom I ever had intimate talk upon such matters. I got seventeen names, with four orthodox. Cullingworth tried and got twelve names, with one orthodox. From all sides, one hears that every church complains of the absence of men in the congregations. The women predominate three to one. Is it that women are more earnest than men? I think it is quite the other way. But the men are following their reason, and the women their emotion. It is the women only who keep orthodoxy alive.

No, you mustn't be too sure of that majority of yours. Taking the scientific, the medical, the professional classes, I question whether it exists at all. The clergy, busy in their own limited circles, and coming in contact only with those who agree with them, have not realised how largely the rising generation has outgrown them. And (with exceptions like yourself) it is not the most lax, but the *best* of the younger men, and larger-brained and the larger-hearted, who have shaken themselves most clear of the old theology. They cannot abide its want of charity, its limitations of God's favours, its claims for a special Providence, its dogmatism about what seems to be false, its conflict with what we know to be true. We *know* that man has ascended, not descended; so what is the value of a scheme of thought which depends upon the supposition of his fall? We *know* that the world was not made in six days, that the sun could never be stopped since it was never moving, and that no man ever lived three days in a fish; so what becomes of the inspiration of a book which contains such statements? "Truth, though it crush me!"

There, now, you see what comes of waving the red rag! Let me make a concession to appease you. I do believe that Christianity in its different forms has been the very best thing for the world during all this long barbarous epoch. Of course, it has been the best thing, else Providence would not have permitted it. The engineer knows best what tools to use in strengthening his own machine. But when you say that this is the best and last tool which will be used, you are laying down the law a little too much.

Now, first of all, I want to tell you about how the practice has been going on. The week after I wrote last showed a slight relapse. I only took two pounds. But on the next I took a sudden jump up to three pounds seven shillings, and this last week I took three pounds ten. So it was steadily creeping up; and I really thought that I saw my road clear in front of me, when the bolt suddenly fell from the blue. There were reasons, however, which prevented my being very disappointed when it did come down; and these I must make clear to you.

I think that I mentioned, when I gave you a short sketch of my dear old mother, that she has a very high standard of family honour. She really tries to live up to the Percy-Plantagenet blend which is said to flow in our veins; and it is only our empty pockets which prevent her from sailing through life, like the *grande dame* that she is, throwing *largesse* to right and left, with her head in the air and her soul in the clouds. I have often heard her say (and I am quite convinced that she meant it) that she would far rather see any one of us in our graves than know that we had committed a dishonourable action. Yes; for all her softness and femininity, she could freeze iron-hard at the suspicion of baseness; and I have seen the blood flush from her white cap to her lace collar when she has heard of an act of meanness.

Well, she had heard some details about the Cullingworths which displeased her when I first knew them. Then came the smash-up at Avonmouth, and my mother liked them less and less. She was averse to my joining them in Bradfield, and it was only by my sudden movement at the end that I escaped a regular prohibition. When I got there, the very first question she asked (when I told her of their prosperity) was whether they had paid their Avonmouth creditors. I was compelled to answer that they had not. In reply she wrote imploring me to come away, and saying that, poor as our family was, none of them had ever fallen so low as to enter into a business partnership with a man of unscrupulous character and doubtful antecedents. I answered that Cullingworth spoke sometimes of paying his creditors, that Mrs. Cullingworth was in favour of it also, and that it seemed to me to be unreasonable to expect that I should sacrifice a good opening on account of things with which I had no connection. I assured her that if Cullingworth did anything from then onwards which seemed to me dishonourable, I would disassociate myself from him, and I mentioned that I had already refused to adopt some of his professional methods. Well, in reply to this, my mother wrote a pretty violent letter about what she thought of Cullingworth, which led to another from me defending him, and showing that there were some deep and noble traits in his character. That produced another still more outspoken letter from her; and so the correspondence went on, she attacking and I defending, until a serious breach seemed to be opening between us. I refrained from writing at last, not out of ill temper, but because I thought that if she were given time she would cool down, and take, perhaps, a more reasonable view of the situation. My father, from the short note which he sent me, seemed to think the whole business absolutely irregular, and to refuse to believe my accounts of Cullingworth's practice and receipts. This double opposition, from the very people whose interests had really been nearest my heart in the whole affair, caused me to be less disappointed than I should otherwise have been when it all came to an end. In fact, I was quite in the humour to finish it myself when fate did it for me.

Now about the Cullingworths. Madam is as amiable as ever; and yet somehow, unless I am deceiving myself, she has changed somewhat of late in her feelings towards me. I have turned upon her suddenly more than once, and caught the skirt of a glance which was little less than malignant. In one or two small matters I have also detected a hardness in her which I had never observed before. Is it that I have intruded too much into their family life? Have I come between the husband and the wife? Goodness knows I have striven with all my little stock of tact to avoid doing so. And yet I have often felt that my position was a false one. Perhaps a young man attaches too much importance to a woman's glances and gestures. He wishes to assign a definite meaning to each, when they may be only the passing caprice of the moment. Ah, well, I have nothing to blame myself with; and in any case it will soon be all over now.

And then I have seen something of the same sort in Cullingworth; but he is so strange a being that I never attach much importance to his variations. He glares at me like an angry bull occasionally; and then when I ask him what is the matter, he growls out, "Oh, nothing!" and turns on his heel. Then at other times he is so cordial and friendly that he almost overdoes it, and I find myself wondering whether he is not acting. It must seem ungracious to you that I should speak so of a man who has been my benefactor; and it seems so to me also, but still that *is* the impression which he leaves upon me sometimes. It's an absurd idea, too; for what possible object could his wife and he have in pretending to be amiable, if they did not really feel so? And yet you know the feeling that you get when a man smiles with his lips and not with his eyes.

One day we went to the Central Hotel billiard-room in the evening to play a match. Our form is just about the same, and we should have had an enjoyable game if it had not been for that queer temper of his. He had been in a sullen humour the whole day, pretending not to hear what I said to him, or else giving snappy answers, and looking like a thunder-cloud. I was determined not to have a row, so I took no notice at all of his continual provocations, which, instead of pacifying him, seemed to encourage him to become more offensive. At the end of the match, wanting two to win, I put down the white which was in the jaws of the pocket. He cried out that this was bad form. I contended that it was folly to refrain from doing it when one was only two off game, and, on his continuing to make remarks, I appealed to the marker, who took the same view as I did. This opposition only increased his anger, and he suddenly broke out into most violent language, abusing me in unmeasured terms. I said to him, "If you have anything to say to me, Cullingworth, come out into the street and say it there. It's a caddish thing to speak like that before the marker." He lifted his cue, and I thought he was going to strike me with it; but he flung it clattering on the floor, and chucked half a crown to the man. When we got out in the street, he began at once in as offensive a tone as ever.

"That's enough, Cullingworth," I said. "I've stood already rather more than I can carry."

We were in the bright light of a shop window at that moment. He looked at me, and looked a second time, uncertain what to do. At any moment I might have found myself in a desperate street row with a man who was my medical partner. I gave no provocation, but kept myself keenly on the alert. Suddenly, to my relief, he burst out laughing (such a roar as made the people stop on the other side of the road), and passing his arm through mine, he hurried me down the street.

"Devil of a temper you've got, Munro," said he. "By Crums, it's hardly safe to go out with you. I never know what you're going to do next. Eh, what? You mustn't be peppery with me, though; for I mean well towards you, as you'll see before you get finished with me."

I have told you this trivial little scene, Bertie, to show the strange way in which Cullingworth springs quarrels upon me; suddenly, without the slightest possible provocation, taking a most offensive tone, and then when he sees he has goaded me to the edge of my endurance, turning the whole thing to chaff. This has occurred again and again recently; and, when coupled with the change in Mrs. Cullingworth's demeanour, makes one feel that something has happened to change one's relations. What that something may be, I give you my word that I have no more idea than you have. Between their coldness, however, and my unpleasant correspondence with my mother, I was often very sorry that I had not taken the South American liner.

Cullingworth is preparing for the issue of our new paper. He has carried the matter through with his usual energy, but he doesn't know enough about local affairs to be able to write about them, and it is a question whether he can interest the people here in anything else. At present we are prepared to run the paper single-handed; we are working seven hours a day at the practice; we are building a stable; and in our odd hours we are practising at our magnetic ship-protector, with which Cullingworth is still well pleased, though he wants to get it more perfect before submitting it to the Admiralty.

His mind runs rather on naval architecture at present, and he has been devising an ingenious method of preventing wooden-sided vessels from being crippled by artillery fire. I did not think much of his magnetic attractor, because it seemed to me that even if it had all the success that he claimed for it, it would merely have the effect of substituting some other metal for steel in the manufacture of shells. This new project has, however, more to recommend it. This is the idea, as put in his own words; and, as he has been speaking of little else for the last two days, I ought to remember them.

"If you've got your armour there, laddie, it will be pierced," says he. "Put up forty feet thick of steel; and I'll build a gun that will knock it into tooth-powder. It would blow away, and set the folk coughing after I had one shot at it. But you can't pierce armour which only drops after the shot has passed through. What's the good of it? Why it keeps out the water. That's the main thing, after all. I call it the Cullingworth spring-shutter screen. Eh, what, Munro? I wouldn't take a quarter of a million for the idea. You see how it would work. Spring shutters are furled all along the top of the bulwarks where the hammocks used to be. They are in sections, three feet broad, we will say, and capable when let down of reaching the keel. Very well! Enemy sends a shot through Section A of the side. Section A shutter is lowered. Only a thin film, you see, but enough to form a temporary plug. Enemy's ram knocks in sections B, C, D of the side. What do you do? Founder? Not a bit; you lower sections B, C, and D of Cullingworth's spring-shutter screen. Or you knock a hole on a rock. The same thing again. It's a ludicrous sight to see a big ship founder when so simple a precaution would absolutely save her. And it's equally good for ironclads also. A shot often starts their plates and admits water without breaking them. Down go your shutters, and all is well."

That's his idea, and he is busy on a model made out of the steels of his wife's stays. It sounds plausible, but he has the knack of making anything plausible when he is allowed to slap his hands and bellow.

We are both writing novels, but I fear that the results don't bear out his theory that a man may do anything which he sets his will to. I thought mine was not so bad (I have done nine chapters), but Cullingworth says he has read it all before, and that it is much too conventional. We must rivet the attention of the public from the start, he says. Certainly, his own is calculated to do so, for it seems to me to be wild rubbish. The end of his first chapter is the only tolerable point that he has made. A fraudulent old baronet is running race-horses on the cross. His son, who is just coming of age, is an innocent youth. The news of the great race of the year has just been received.

"Sir Robert tottered into the room with dry lips and a ghastly face.

"'My poor boy!' he cried. 'Prepare for the worst!'

"'Our horse has lost!' cried the young heir, springing from his chair.

"The old man threw himself in agony upon the rug. 'No, no!' he screamed. '*It has won!*'"

Most of it, however, is poor stuff, and we are each agreed that the other was never meant for a novelist.

So much for our domestic proceedings, and all these little details which you say you like to hear of. Now I must tell you of the great big change in my affairs, and how it came about.

I have told you about the strange, sulky behaviour of Cullingworth, which has been deepening from day to day. Well, it seemed to reach a climax this morning, and on our way to the rooms I could hardly get a word out of him. The place was fairly crowded with patients, but my own share was rather below the average. When I had finished I added a chapter to my novel, and waited until he and his wife were ready for the daily bag-carrying homewards.

It was half-past three before he had done. I heard him stamp out into the passage, and a moment later he came banging into my room. I saw in an instant that some sort of a crisis had come.

"Munro," he cried, "this practice is going to the devil!"

"Ah!" said I. "How's that?"

"It's going to little pieces, Munro. I've been taking figures, and I know what I am talking about. A month ago I was seeing six hundred a week. Then I dropped to five hundred and eighty; then to five-seventy-five; and now to five-sixty. What do you think of that?"

"To be honest, I don't think much of it," I answered. "The summer is coming on. You are losing all your coughs and colds and sore throats. Every practice must dwindle at this time of year."

"That's all very well," said he, pacing up and down the room, with his hands thrust into his pockets, and his great shaggy eyebrows knotted together. "You may put it down to that, but I think quite differently about it."

"What do you put it down to, then?"

"To you."

"How's that?" I asked.

"Well," said he, "you must allow that it is a very queer coincidence—if it is a coincidence—that from the day when your plate was put up my practice has taken a turn for the worse."

"I should be very sorry to think it was cause and effect," I answered. "How do you think that my presence could have hurt you?"

"I'll tell you frankly, old chap," said he, putting on suddenly that sort of forced smile which always seems to me to have a touch of a sneer in it. "You see, many of my patients are simple country folk, half imbecile for the most part, but then the half-crown of an imbecile is as good as any other half-crown. They come to my door, and they see two names, and their silly jaws begin to drop, and they say to each other, 'There's two of 'em here. It's Dr. Cullingworth we want to see, but if we go in we'll be shown as likely as not to Dr. Munro.' So it ends in some cases in their not coming at all. Then there are the women. Women don't care a toss whether you are a Solomon, or whether you are hot from an asylum. It's all personal with them. You fetch them, or you don't fetch them. I know how to work them, but they won't come if they think they are going to be turned over to anybody else. That's what I put the falling away down to."

"Well," said I, "that easily set right." I marched out of the room and downstairs, with both Cullingworth and his wife behind me. Into the yard I went, and, picking up a big hammer, I started for the front door, with the pair still at my heels. I got the forked end of the hammer under my plate, and with a good wrench I brought the whole thing clattering on to the pavement.

"That won't interfere with you any more," said I.

"What do you intend to do now?" he asked.

"Oh, I shall find plenty to do. Don't you worry about that," I answered.

"Oh, but this is all rot," said he, picking up the plate. "Come along upstairs and let us see where we stand."

We filed off once more, he leading with the huge brass "Dr. Munro" under his arm; then the little woman, and then this rather perturbed and bemuddled young man. He and his wife sat on the deal table in the consulting room, like a hawk and a turtle-dove on the same perch, while I leaned against the mantelpiece with my hands in my pockets. Nothing could be more prosaic and informal; but I knew very well that I was at a crisis of my life. Before, it was only a choosing between two roads. Now my main track had run suddenly to nothing, and I must go back or find a bye-path.

"It's this way, Cullingworth," said I. "I am very much obliged to you, and to you, Mrs. Cullingworth, for all your kindness and good wishes, but I did not come here to spoil your practice; and, after what you have told me, it is quite impossible for me to work with you any more."

"Well, my boy," said he, "I am inclined myself to think that we should do better apart; and that's Hetty's idea also, only she is too polite to say so."

"It is a time for plain speaking," I answered, "and we may as well thoroughly understand each other. If I have done your practice any harm, I assure you that I am heartily sorry, and I shall do all I can to repair it. I cannot say more."

"What are you going to do, then?" asked Cullingworth.

"I shall either go to sea or else start a practice on my own account."

"But you have no money."

"Neither had you when you started."

"Ah, that was different. Still, it may be that you are right. You'll find it a stiff pull at first."

"Oh, I am quite prepared for that."

"Well, you know, Munro, I feel that I am responsible to you to some extent, since I persuaded you not to take that ship the other day."

"It was a pity, but it can't be helped."

"We must do what we can to make up. Now, I tell you what I am prepared to do. I was talking about it with Hetty this morning, and she thought as I did. If we were to allow you one pound a week until you got your legs under you, it would encourage you to start for yourself, and you could pay it back as soon as you were able."

"It is very kind of you," said I. "If you would let the matter stand just now, I should like just to take a short walk by myself, and to think it all over."

So the Cullingworths did their bag-procession through the doctors' quarter alone to-day, and I walked to the park, where I sat down on one of the seats, lit a cigar, and thought the whole matter over. I was down on my luck at first; but the balmy air and the smell of spring and the budding flowers soon set me right again. I began my last letter among the stars, and I am inclined to finish this one among the flowers, for they are rare companions when one's mind is troubled. Most things on this earth, from a woman's beauty to the taste of a nectarine, seem to be the various baits with which Nature lures her silly gudgeons. They shall eat, they shall propagate, and for the sake of pleasing themselves they shall hurry down the road which has been laid out for them. But there lurks no bribe in the smell and beauty of the flower. Its charm has no ulterior motive.

Well, I sat down there and brooded. In my heart I did not believe that Cullingworth had taken alarm at so trifling a decrease. That could not have been his real reason for driving me from the practice. He had found me in the way in his domestic life, no doubt, and he had devised this excuse for getting rid of me. Whatever the reason was, it was suffi-

ciently plain that all my hopes of building up a surgical practice, which
should keep parallel with his medical one, were for ever at an end. On
the whole, bearing in mind my mother's opposition, and the continual
janglings which we had had during the last few weeks, I was not very
sorry. On the contrary, a sudden curious little thrill of happiness took
me somewhere about the back of the midriff, and, as a drift of rooks
passed cawing over my head, I began cawing also in the overflow of my
spirits.

And then as I walked back I considered how far I could avail myself of this money from Cullingworth. It was not much, but it would
be madness to start without it, for I had sent home the little which I
had saved at Horton's. I had not more than six pounds in the whole
world. I reflected that the money could make no difference to
Cullingworth, with his large income, while it made a vast one to me.
I should repay him in a year or two at the latest. Perhaps I might get
on so well as to be able to dispense with it almost at once. There
could be no doubt that it was the representations of Cullingworth as
to my future prospects in Bradfield which had made me refuse the excellent appointment in the *Decia*. I need not therefore have any scru-
ples at accepting some temporary assistance from his hands. On my
return, I told him that I had decided to do so, and thanked him at the
same time for his generosity.

"That's all right," said he. "Hetty, my dear, get a bottle of fez in, and
we shall drink success to Munro's new venture."

It seemed only the other day that he had been drinking my entrance
into partnership; and here we were, the same three, sipping good luck to
my exit from it! I'm afraid our second ceremony was on both sides the
heartier of the two.

"I must decide now where I am to start," I remarked. "What I want
is some nice little town where all the people are rich and ill."

"I suppose you wouldn't care to settle here in Bradfield?" asked
Cullingworth.

"Well, I cannot see much point in that. If I harmed you as a partner, I might do so more as a rival. If I succeeded it might be at your expense."

"Well," said he, "choose your town, and my offer still holds good."

We hunted out an atlas, and laid the map of England before us on the table. Cities and villages lay beneath me as thick as freckles, and yet there was nothing to lead me to choose one rather than another.

"I think it should be some place large enough to give you plenty of room for expansion," said he.

"Not too near London," added Mrs. Cullingworth.

"And, above all, a place where I know nobody," said I. "I can rough it by myself, but I can't keep up appearances before visitors."

"What do you say to Stockwell?" said Cullingworth, putting the amber of his pipe upon a town within thirty miles of Bradfield.

I had hardly heard of the place, but I raised my glass. "Well, here's to Stockwell!" I cried; "I shall go there to-morrow morning and prospect." We all drank the toast (as you will do at Lowell when you read this); and so it is arranged, and you may rely upon it that I shall give you a full and particular account of the result.

8

&

"The King of the Foxes"
(1898)

It was after a hunting dinner, and there were as many scarlet coats as black ones round the table. The conversation over the cigars had turned, therefore, in the direction of horses and horsemen, with reminiscences of phenomenal runs where foxes had led the pack from end to end of a county, and been overtaken at last by two or three limping hounds and a huntsman on foot, while every rider in the field had been pounded. As the port circulated the runs became longer and more apocryphal, until we had the whips inquiring their way and failing to understand the dialect of the people who answered them. The foxes, too, became more eccentric, and we had foxes up pollard willows, foxes which were dragged by the tail out of horses', mangers, and foxes which had raced through an open front door and gone to ground in a lady's bonnet-box. The master had told one or two tall reminiscences, and when he cleared his throat for another we were all curious, for he was a bit of an artist in his way and produced his effects in a crescendo fashion. His face wore the earnest, practical, severely accurate expression which heralded some of his finest efforts.

"It was before I was master," said he. "Sir Charles Adair had the hounds at that time, and then afterwards they passed to old Lathom, and then to me. It may possibly have been just after Lathom took them over, but my strong impression is that it was in Adair's time. That would be early in the seventies—about seventy-two, I should say."

"The man I mean has moved to another part of the country, but I dare say that some of you can remember him. Danbury was the name—Walter Danbury, or Wat Danbury, as the people used to call him. He was the son of old Joe Danbury, of High Ascombe, and when his father died he came into a very good thing, for his only brother was drowned when the *Magna Charta* foundered, so he inherited the whole estate. It was but a few hundred acres, but it was good arable land, and those were the great days of farming. Besides, it was freehold, and a yeoman farmer without a mortgage was a warmish man before the great fall in wheat came. Foreign wheat and barbed wire—those are the two curses of this country, for the one spoils the farmer's work and the other spoils his play.

"This young Wat Danbury was a very fine fellow, a keen rider, and thorough sportsman, but his head was a little turned at having come, when so young, into a comfortable fortune, and he went the pace for a year or two. The lad had no vice in him, but there was a hard-drinking set in the neighbourhood at that time, and Danbury got drawn in among them; and, being an amiable fellow who liked to do what his friends were doing, he very soon took to drinking a great deal more than was good for him. As a rule, a man who takes his exercise may drink as much as he likes in the evening, and do himself no very great harm, if he will leave it alone during the day. Danbury had too many friends for that, however, and it really looked as if the poor chap was going to the bad, when a very curious thing happened which pulled him up with such a sudden jerk that he never put his hand upon the neck of a whisky bottle again.

"He had a peculiarity which I have noticed in a good many other men, that though he was always playing tricks with his own health, he was none the less very anxious about it, and was extremely fidgety if ever he had any trivial symptom. Being a tough, open-air fellow, who was always as hard as a nail, it was seldom that there was anything amiss with him; but at last the drink began to tell, and he woke one morning with his hands shaking and all his nerves tingling like overstretched fiddle-strings. He had been dining at some very wet house the night before, and the wine had, perhaps, been more plentiful than choice; at any rate, there he was, with a tongue like a bath-towel and a head that ticked like an eight-day clock. He was very alarmed at his own condition, and he sent for Doctor Middleton, of Ascombe, the father of the man who practises there now.

"Middleton had been a great friend of old Danbury's, and he was very sorry to see his son going to the devil; so he improved the occasion by taking his case very seriously, and lecturing him upon the danger of his ways. He shook his head and talked about the possibility of *delirium tremens,* or even of mania, if he continued to lead such a life. Wat Danbury was horribly frightened.

"'Do you think I am going to get anything of the sort?' he wailed.

"'Well, really, I don't know,' said the doctor, gravely. 'I cannot undertake to say that you are out of danger. Your system is very much out of order. At any time during the day you might have those grave symptoms of which I warn you.'

"'You think I shall be safe by evening?'

"'If you drink nothing during the day, and have no nervous symptoms before evening, I think you may consider yourself safe,' the doctor answered. A little fright would, he thought, do his patient good, so he made the most of the matter.

"'What symptoms may I expect?' asked Danbury.

"'It generally takes the form of optical delusions.'

"'I see specks floating all about.'

"'That is mere biliousness,' said the doctor soothingly, for he saw that the lad was highly strung and he did not wish to overdo it. 'I dare say that you will have no symptoms of the kind, but when they do come they usually take the shape of insects, or reptiles, or curious animals.'

"'And if I see anything of the kind?'

"'If you do, you will at once send for me;' and so, with a promise of medicine, the doctor departed.

"Young Wat Danbury rose and dressed and moped about the room feeling very miserable and unstrung, with a vision of the County Asylum for ever in his mind. He had the doctor's word for it that if he could get through to evening in safety he would be all right; but it is not very exhilarating to be waiting for symptoms, and to keep on glancing at your bootjack to see whether it is still a bootjack or whether it has begun to develop antennæ and legs. At last he could stand it no longer, and an overpowering longing for the fresh air and the green grass came over him.

Why should he stay indoors when the Ascombe Hunt was meeting within half a mile of him? If he was going to have these delusions which the doctor talked of, he would not have them the sooner nor the worse because he was on horseback in the open. He was sure, too, it would ease his aching head. And so it came about that in ten minutes he was in his hunting-kit, and in ten more he was riding out of his stable-yard with his roan mare Matilda between his knees. He was a little unsteady in his saddle just at first, but the farther he went the better he felt, until by the time he reached the meet his head was almost clear, and there was nothing troubling him except those haunting words of the doctor's about the possibility of delusions any time before nightfall.

"But soon he forgot that also, for as he came up the hounds were thrown off, and they drew the Gravel Hanger and afterwards the Hickory Copse. It was just the morning for a scent—no wind to blow it away, no water to wash it out, and just damp enough to make it cling. There was a field of forty, all keen men and good riders, so when they came to the Black Hanger they knew that there would be some sport, for that's a cover which never draws blank. The woods were thicker in those days than now, and the foxes were thicker also, and that great dark oak-grove was swarming with them. The only difficulty was to make them break, for it is, as you know, a very close country, and you must coax them out into the open before you can hope for a run.

"When they came to the Black Hanger the field took their positions along the cover-side wherever they thought that they were most likely to get a good start. Some went in with the hounds, some clustered at the ends of the drives, and some kept outside in the hope of the fox breaking in that direction. Young Wat Danbury knew the country like the palm of his hand, so he made for a place where several drives intersected, and there he waited. He had a feeling that the faster and the farther he galloped the better he should be, and so he was chafing to be off. His mare, too, was in the height of fettle and one of the fastest goers in the country. Wat was a splendid light-weight rider—under ten stone with his saddle—and the mare was a powerful creature, all quarters and shoulders, fit to carry a lifeguardsman; and so it was no wonder that there was hardly a man in the field who could hope to stay with him. There he waited and listened to the shouting of the huntsman and the whips, catching a glimpse now and then in the darkness of the wood of a whisking tail, or the gleam of a white-and-tan side amongst the underwood. It was a well-trained pack, and there was not so much as a whine to tell you that forty hounds were working all round you.

"And then suddenly there came one long-drawn yell from one of them, and it was taken up by another, and another, until within a few seconds the whole pack was giving tongue together and running on a hot scent. Danbury saw them stream across one of the drives and disappear upon the other side, and an instant later the three red coats of the hunt-servants flashed after them upon the same line. He might have made a shorter cut down one of the other drives, but he was afraid of heading the fox, so he followed the lead of the huntsman. Right through the wood they went in a bee-line, galloping with their faces brushed by their horses' manes as they stooped under the branches. It's ugly going, as you know, with the roots all wriggling about in the darkness, but you can take a risk when you catch an occasional glimpse of the pack running with a breast-high scent; so in and out they dodged, until the wood began to thin at the edges, and they found themselves in the long bottom where the river runs. It is clear going there upon grassland, and the hounds were running very strong about two hundred yards ahead, keeping parallel with the stream. The field, who had come round the wood instead of going through, were coming hard over the fields upon the left; but Danbury, with the hunt-servants, had a clear lead, and they never lost it. Two of the field got on terms with them: Parson Geddes on a big seventeen-hand bay which he used to ride in those days, and Squire Foley, who rode as a feather-weight, and made his hunters out of cast thoroughbreds from the Newmarket sales; but the others never had a look-in from start to finish, for there was no check and no pulling, and it was clear cross-country racing from start to finish. If you had drawn a line right across the map with a pencil you couldn't go straighter than that fox ran, heading for the South Downs and the sea; and the hounds ran as surely as if they were running to view, and yet from the beginning no one ever saw the fox, and there was never a hallo forrard to tell them that he had been spied. This, however, is not so surprising, for if you've been over that line of country you will know that there are not very many people about.

"There were six of them then in the front row: Parson Geddes, Squire Foley, the huntsman, two whips, and Wat Danbury, who had forgotten all about his head and the doctor by this time, and had not a thought for anything but the run. All six were galloping just as hard as they could lay hoofs to the ground. One of the whips dropped back, however, as some of the hounds were tailing off, and that brought them down to five. Then Foley's thoroughbred strained herself, as these slim-legged, dainty-fetlocked thoroughbreds will do when the going is rough, and he had to take a back seat. But the other four were still going strong, and they did four or five miles down the river flat at a rasping pace. It had been a wet winter, and the waters had been out a little time before, so there was a deal of sliding and splashing; but by the time they came to the bridge the whole field was out of sight, and these four had the hunt to themselves.

"The fox had crossed the bridge—for foxes do not care to swim a chilly river any more than humans do—and from that point he had streaked away southward as hard as he could tear. It is broken country, rolling heaths, down one slope and up another, and it's hard to say whether the up or the down is the more trying for the horses. This sort of switchback work is all right for a cobby, short-backed, short-legged little horse, but it is killing work for a big, long-striding hunter such as one wants in the Midlands. Anyhow, it was too much for Parson Geddes's seventeen-hand bay, and, though he tried the Irish trick—for he was a rare keen sportsman—of running up the hills by his horse's head, it was all to no use, and he had to give it up. So then there was only the huntsman, the whip, and Wat Danbury—all going strong.

"But the country got worse and worse, and the hills were steeper and more thickly covered in heather and bracken. The horses were over their hocks all the time, and the place was pitted with rabbit-holes; but the hounds were still streaming along, and the riders could not afford to pick their steps. As they raced down one slope, the hounds were always flowing up the opposite one, until it looked like that game where the one figure in falling makes the other one rise. But never a glimpse did they get of the fox, although they knew very well that he must be only a very short way ahead for the scent to lie so strong. And then Wat Danbury heard a crash and a thud at his elbow, and looking round he saw a pair of white cords and top-boots kicking out of a tussock of brambles. The whip's horse had stumbled, and the whip was out of the running. Danbury and the huntsman eased down for an instant; and then, seeing the man staggering to his feet all right, they turned and settled into their saddles once more.

"Joe Clarke, the huntsman, was a famous old rider, known for five counties round; but he reckoned upon his second horse, and the second horses had all been left many miles behind. However, the one he was riding was good enough for anything with such a horseman upon his back, and he was going as well as when he started. As to Wat Danbury, he was going better. With every stride his own feelings improved, and the mind of the rider has its influence upon the mind of the horse. The stout little roan was gathering its muscular limbs under it and stretching to the gallop as if it were steel and whalebone instead of flesh and blood. Wat had never come to the end of its powers yet, and to-day he had such a chance of testing them as he had never had before.

"There was a pasture country beyond the heather slopes, and for several miles the two riders were either losing ground as they fumbled with their crop-handles at the bars of gates, or gaining it again as they galloped over the fields. Those were the days before this accursed wire came into the country, and you could generally break a hedge where you could not fly it, so they did not trouble the gates more than they could help. Then they were down in a hard lane, where they had to slacken their pace, and through a farm where a man came shouting excitedly after them; but they had no time to stop and listen to him, for the hounds were on some ploughland, only two fields ahead. It was sloping upwards, that ploughland, and the horses were over their fetlocks in the red, soft soil. When they reached the top they were blowing badly, but a grand valley sloped before them, leading up to the open country of the South Downs. Between, there lay a belt of pinewoods, into which the hounds were streaming, running now in a long, straggling line and shedding one here and one there as they ran. You could see the white-and-tan dots here and there where the limpers were tailing away. But half the pack were still going well, though the pace and distance had both been tremendous—two clear hours now without a check.

"There was a drive through the pinewood—one of those green, slightly-rutted drives where a horse can get the last yard out of itself, for the ground is hard enough to give him clean going and yet springy enough to help him. Wat Danbury got alongside of the huntsman and they galloped together with their stirrup-irons touching, and the hounds within a hundred yards of them.

"'We have it all to ourselves,' said he.

"'Yes, sir, we've shook off the lot of 'em this time,' said old Joe Clarke. 'If we get this fox it's worth while 'aving 'im skinned an' stuffed, for 'e's a curiosity 'e is.'

"'It's the fastest run I ever had in my life!' cried Danbury.

"'And the fastest that ever I 'ad, an' that means more,' said the old huntsman. 'But what licks me is that we've never 'ad a look at the beast. 'E must leave an amazin' scent be'ind 'im when these 'ounds can follow 'im like this, and yet none of us have seen 'im when we've 'ad a clear 'alf mile view in front of us.'

"'I expect we'll have a view of him presently,' said Danbury; and in his mind he added, 'at least, I shall,' for the huntsman's horse was gasping as it ran, and the white foam was pouring down it like the side of a washing-tub.

"They had followed the hounds on to one of the side tracks which led out of the main drive, and that divided into a smaller track still, where the branches switched across their faces as they went and there was barely room for one horse at a time. Wat Danbury took the lead, and he heard the huntsman's horse clumping along heavily behind him, while his own mare was going with less spring than when she had started. She answered to a touch of his crop or spur, however, and he felt that there was something still left to draw upon. And then he looked up, and there was a heavy wooden stile at the end of the narrow track, with a lane of stiff young saplings leading down to it, which was far too thick to break through. The hounds were running clear upon the grassland on the other side, and you were bound either to get over that stile or lose sight of them, for the pace was too hot to let you go round.

"Well, Wat Danbury was not the lad to flinch, and at it he went full split, like a man who means what he is doing. She rose gallantly to it, rapped it hard with her front hoof, shook him on to her withers, recovered herself, and was over. Wat had hardly got back into his saddle when there was a clatter behind him like the fall of a woodstack, and there was the top bar in splinters, the horse on its belly, and the huntsman on hands and knees half a dozen yards in front of him. Wat pulled up for an instant, for the fall was a smasher; but he saw old Joe spring to his feet and get to his horse's bridle. The horse staggered up, but the moment it put one foot in front of the other Wat saw that it was hopelessly lame—a slipped shoulder and a six weeks' job. There was nothing he could do, and Joe was shouting to him not to lose the hounds, so off he went again, the one solitary survivor of the whole hunt. When a man finds himself there, he can retire from fox-hunting, for he has tasted the highest which it has to offer. I remember once when I was out with the Royal Surrey—but I'll tell you that story afterwards.

"The pack, or what was left of them, had got a bit ahead during this time; but he had a clear view of them on the downland, and the mare seemed full of pride at being the only one left, for she was stepping out rarely and tossing her head as she went. There were two miles over the green shoulder of a hill, a rattle down a stony, deep-rutted country lane, where the mare stumbled and nearly came down, a jump over a five-foot brook, a cut through a hazel copse, another dose of heavy ploughland, a couple of gates to open, and then the green, unbroken Downs beyond. 'Well,' said Wat Danbury to himself, 'I'll see this fox run into or I shall see it drowned, for it's all clear going now between this and the chalk cliffs which line the sea.'

"But he was wrong in that, as he speedily discovered. In all the little hollows of the Downs at that part there are plantations of fir-woods, some of which have grown to a good size. You do not see them until you come upon the edge of the valleys in which they lie. Danbury was galloping hard over the short, springy turf when he came over the lip of one of these depressions, and there was the dark clump of wood lying in front of and beneath him. There were only a dozen hounds still running, and they were just disappearing among the trees. The sunlight was shining straight upon the long, olive-green slopes which curved down towards this wood, and Danbury, who had the eyes of a hawk, swept them over this great expanse; but there was nothing moving upon it. A few sheep were grazing far up on the right, but there was no other sight of any living creature. He was certain then that he was very near to the end, for either the fox must have gone to ground in the wood or the hounds' noses must be at his very brush. The mare seemed to know also what that great empty sweep of countryside meant, for she quickened her stride, and a few minutes afterwards Danbury was galloping into the fir-wood.

"He had come from bright sunshine, but the wood was very closely planted, and so dim that he could hardly see to right or to left out of the narrow path down which he was riding. You know what a solemn, churchyard sort of place a fir-wood is. I suppose it is the absence of any undergrowth, and the fact that the trees never move at all. At any rate a kind of chill suddenly struck Wat Danbury, and it flashed through his mind that there had been some very singular points about this run—its length and its straightness, and the fact that from the first find no one had ever caught a glimpse of the creature. Some silly talk which had been going round the country about the king of the foxes—a sort of demon fox, so fast that it could outrun any pack, and so fierce that they could do nothing with it if they overtook it—suddenly came back into his mind, and it did not seem so laughable now in the dim fir-wood as it had done when the story had been told over the wine and cigars. The nervousness which had been on him in the morning, and which he had hoped that he had shaken off, swept over him again in an overpowering wave. He had been so proud of being alone, and yet he would have given ten pounds now to have had Joe Clarke's homely face beside him. And then, just at that moment, there broke out from the thickest part of the wood the most frantic hullaballoo that ever he had heard in his life. The hounds had run into their fox.

"Well, you know, or you ought to know, what your duty is in such a case. You have to be whip, huntsman, and everything else if you are the first man up. You get in among the hounds, lash them off, and keep the brush and pads from being destroyed. Of course, Wat Danbury knew all about that, and he tried to force his mare through the trees to the place where all this hideous screaming and howling came from, but the wood was so thick that it was impossible to ride it. He sprang off, therefore, left the mare standing, and broke his way through as best he could with his hunting-lash ready over his shoulder. But as he ran forward he felt his flesh go cold and creepy all over. He had heard hounds run into foxes many times before, but he had never heard such sounds as these. They were not the cries of triumph, but of fear. Every now and then came a shrill yelp of mortal agony. Holding his breath, he ran on until he broke through the interlacing branches and found himself in a little clearing with the hounds all crowding round a patch of tangled bramble at the further end.

"When he first caught sight of them the hounds were standing in a half-circle round this bramble-patch with their backs bristling and their jaws gaping. In front of the brambles lay one of them with his throat torn out, all crimson and white-and-tan. Wat came running out into the clearing, and at the sight of him the hounds took heart again, and one of them sprang with a growl into the bushes. At the same instant, a creature the size of a donkey jumped on to its feet, a huge grey head, with monstrous glistening fangs and tapering fox jaws, shot out from among the branches, and the hound was thrown several feet into the air, and fell howling among the cover. Then there was a clashing snap like a rat-trap closing, and the howls sharpened into a scream and then were still.

"Danbury had been on the look-out for symptoms all day, and now he had found them. He looked once more at the thicket, saw a pair of savage red eyes fixed upon him, and fairly took to his heels. It might only be a passing delusion, or it might be the permanent mania of which the doctor had spoken, but, anyhow, the thing to do was to get back to bed and to quiet, and to hope for the best. He forgot the hounds, the hunt, and everything else in his desperate fears for his own reason. He sprang upon his mare, galloped her madly over the downs, and only stopped when he found himself at a country station. There he left his mare at the inn, and made back for home as quickly as steam would take him. It was evening before he got there, shivering with apprehension and seeing those red eyes and savage teeth at every turn. He went straight to bed and sent for Dr. Middleton.

"'I've got 'em, doctor,' said he. 'It came about exactly as you said—strange creatures, optical delusions, and everything. All I ask you now is to save my reason.'

"The doctor listened to his story and was shocked as he heard it.

"'It appears to be a very clear case,' said he. 'This must be a lesson to you for life.'

"'Never a drop again if I only come safely through this,' cried Wat Danbury.

"'Well, my dear boy, if you will stick to that it may prove a blessing in disguise. But the difficulty in this case is to know where fact ends and fancy begins. You see, it is not as if there was only one delusion. There have been several. The dead dogs, for example, must have been one as well as the creature in the bush.'

"'I saw it all as clearly as I see you.'

"'One of the characteristics of this form of delirium is that what you see is even clearer than reality. I was wondering whether the whole run was not a delusion also.'

"Wat Danbury pointed to his hunting-boots still lying upon the floor, flecked with the splashings of two counties.

"'Hum! That looks very real, certainly. No doubt, in your weak state, you over-exerted yourself and so brought this attack upon yourself. Well, whatever the cause, our treatment is clear. You will take the soothing mixture which I will send to you, and we shall put two leeches upon your temples to-night to relieve any congestion of the brain.'

"So Wat Danbury spent the night in tossing about and reflecting what a sensitive thing this machinery of ours is, and how very foolish it is to play tricks with what is so easily put out of gear and so difficult to mend. And so he repeated and repeated his oath that this first lesson should be his last, and that from that time forward he would be a sober, hard-working yeoman as his father had been before him. So he lay, tossing and still repentant, when his door flew open in the morning and in rushed the doctor with a newspaper crumpled up in his hand.

"'My dear boy,' he cried. 'I owe you a thousand apologies. You're the most ill-used lad and I the greatest numskull in the county. Listen to this!" And he sat down upon the side of the bed, flattened out his paper upon his knee, and began to read.

"The paragraph was headed, 'Disaster to the Ascombe Hounds,' and it went on to say that four of the hounds, shockingly torn and mangled, had been found in Winton Fir Wood upon the South Downs. The run had been so severe that half the pack were lamed; but the four found in the wood were actually dead, although the cause of their extraordinary injuries was still unknown. 'So you see,' said the doctor, looking up, 'that I was wrong when I put the dead hounds among the delusions.'

"'But the cause?' cried Wat.

"'Well, I think we may guess the cause from an item which has been inserted just as the paper went to press. "Late last night, Mr. Brown, of Smither's Farm, to the east of Hastings, perceived what he imagined to be an enormous dog worrying one of his sheep. He shot the creature, which proves to be a grey Siberian wolf of the variety known as *Lupus Giganticus*. It is supposed to have escaped from some traveling menagerie.'"

"That's the story, gentlemen, and Wat Danbury stuck to his good resolutions, for the fright which he had, cured him of all wish to run such a risk again; and he never touches anything stronger than lime-juice—at least, he hadn't before he left this part of the country, five years ago next Lady Day."

9

"The Brazilian Cat"

(1898)

It is hard luck on a young fellow to have expensive tastes, great expectations, aristocratic connections, but no actual money in his pocket and no profession by which he may earn any. The fact was that my father, a good, sanguine, easy-going man, had such confidence in the wealth and benevolence of his bachelor elder brother, Lord Southerton, that he took it for granted that I, his only son, would never be called upon to earn a living for myself. He imagined that if there were not a vacancy for me on the great Southerton Estates, at least there would be found some post in that diplomatic service which still remains the special preserve of our privileged classes. He died too early to realise how false his calculations had been. Neither my uncle nor the state took the slightest notice of me or showed any interest in my career. An occasional brace of pheasants, or basket of hares, was all that ever reached me to remind me that I was heir to Otwell House and one of the richest estates in the country. In the meantime, I found myself a bachelor and man about town, living in a suite of apartments in Grosvenor Mansions, with no occupation save that of pigeon-shooting and polo playing at Hurlingham. Month by month, I realised that it was more and more difficult to get the brokers to renew my bills or to cash any further post-obits upon an unentailed property. Ruin lay right across my path, and every day I saw it clearer, nearer and more absolutely unavoidable.

What made me feel my own poverty the more was that, apart from the great wealth of Lord Southerton, all my other relations were fairly well-to-do. The nearest of these was Everard King, my father's nephew and my own first cousin, who had spent an adventurous life in Brazil and had now returned to this country to settle down on his fortune. We never knew how he made his money, but he appeared to have plenty of it, for he bought the estate of Greylands, near Clipton-on-the-Marsh, in Suffolk. For the first year of his residence in England he took no more notice of me than my miserly uncle; but at last one summer morning, to my very great relief and joy, I received a letter asking me to come down that very day and spend a short visit at Greylands Court. I was expecting a rather long visit to Bankruptcy Court at the time, and this interruption seemed almost providential. If I could only get on terms with this unknown relative of mine, I might pull through yet. For the family credit, he could not let me go entirely to the wall. I ordered my valet to pack my valise, and I set off the same evening for Clipton-on-the-Marsh.

After changing at Ipswich, a little local train deposited me at a small, deserted station lying amidst a rolling grassy country, with a sluggish and winding river curving in and out amidst the valleys, between high, silted banks, which showed that we were within reach of the tide. No carriage was awaiting me (I found afterwards that my telegram had been delayed), so I hired a dogcart at the local inn. The driver, an excellent fellow, was full of my relative's praises, and I learned from him that Mr Everard King was already a name to conjure with in that part of the country. He had entertained the schoolchildren, he had thrown his grounds open to visitors, he had subscribed to charities—in short, his benevolence had been so universal that my driver could only account for it on the supposition that he had parliamentary ambitions.

My attention was drawn away from my driver's panegyric by the appearance of a very beautiful bird which settled on a telegraph-post beside the road. At first I thought that it was a jay, but it was larger, with brighter plumage. The driver accounted for its presence at once by saying that it belonged to the very man whom we were about to visit. It seems that the acclimatisation of foreign creatures was one of his hobbies, and that he had brought with him from Brazil a number of birds and beasts which he was endeavouring to rear in England. When once we had passed the gates of Greylands Park we had ample evidence of this taste of his. Some small spotted deer, a curious wild pig known, I believe, as a peccary, a gorgeously feathered oriole, some sort of armadillo and a singular lumbering in-toed beast like a very fat badger were among the creatures which I observed as we drove along the winding avenue.

Mr Everard King, my unknown cousin, was standing in person upon the steps of his house, for he had seen us in the distance and guessed that it was I. His appearance was very homely and benevolent, short and stout, forty-five years old, perhaps, with a round, good-humoured face, burned with the tropical sun and shot with a thousand wrinkles. He wore white linen clothes, in true planter style, with a cigar between his lips and a large panama hat upon the back of his head. It was such a figure as one associates with a verandahed bungalow, and it looked curiously out of place in front of this broad, stone English mansion, with its solid wings and its Palladio pillars before the doorway.

'My dear!' he cried, glancing over his shoulder; 'my dear, here is our guest! Welcome, welcome to Greylands! I am delighted to make your acquaintance, Cousin Marshall, and I take it as a great compliment that you should honour this sleepy little country place with your presence.'

Nothing could be more hearty than his manner, and he set me at my ease in an instant. But it needed all his cordiality to atone for the frigidity and even rudeness of his wife, a tall, haggard woman, who came forward at his summons. She was, I believe, of Brazilian extraction, though she spoke excellent English, and I excused her manners on the score of her ignorance of our customs. She did not attempt to conceal, however, either then or afterwards, that I was no very welcome visitor at Greylands Court. Her actual words were, as a rule, courteous, but she was the possessor of a pair of particularly expressive dark eyes, and I read in them very clearly from the first that she heartily wished me back in London once more.

However, my debts were too pressing and my designs upon my wealthy relative were too vital for me to allow them to be upset by the ill-temper of his wife, so I disregarded her coldness and reciprocated the extreme cordiality of his welcome. No pains had been spared by him to make me comfortable. My room was a charming one. He implored me to tell him anything which could add to my happiness. It was on the tip of my tongue to inform him that a blank cheque would materially help towards that end, but I felt that it might be premature in the present state of our acquaintance. The dinner was excellent, and as we sat together afterwards over his Havanas and coffee, which later he told me was specially prepared upon his own plantation, it seemed to me that all my driver's eulogies were justified, and that I had never met a more large-hearted and hospitable man.

But, in spite of his cheery good nature, he was a man with a strong will and a fiery temper of his own. Of this I had an example upon the following morning. The curious aversion which Mrs Everard King had conceived towards me was so strong that her manner at breakfast was almost offensive. But her meaning became unmistakable when her husband had quitted the room.

'The best train in the day is at twelve fifteen,' said she.

'But I was not thinking of going today,' I answered, frankly—perhaps even defiantly, for I was determined not to be driven out by this woman.

'Oh, if it rests with you—' said she, and stopped with a most insolent expression in her eyes.

'I am sure,' I answered, 'that Mr Everard King would tell me if I were outstaying my welcome.'

'What's this? What's this?' said a voice, and there he was in the room. He had overheard my last words, and a glance at our faces had told him the rest. In an instant his chubby, cheery face set into an expression of absolute ferocity.

'Might I trouble you to walk outside, Marshall?' said he. (I may mention that my own name is Marshall King.)

He closed the door behind me, and then, for an instant, I heard him talking in a low voice of concentrated passion to his wife. This gross breach of hospitality had evidently hit upon his tenderest point. I am no eavesdropper, so I walked out on to the lawn. Presently I heard a hurried step behind me, and there was the lady, her face pale with excitement and her eyes red with tears.

'My husband has asked me to apologise to you, Mr Marshall King,' said she, standing with downcast eyes before me.

'Please do not say another word, Mrs King.'

Her dark eyes suddenly blazed out at me.

'You fool!' she hissed, with frantic vehemence, and turning on her heel swept back to the house.

The insult was so outrageous, so insufferable, that I could only stand staring after her in bewilderment. I was still there when my host joined me. He was his cheery, chubby self once more.

'I hope that my wife has apologised for her foolish remarks,' said he.

'Oh, yes—yes, certainly!'

He put his hand through my arm and walked with me up and down the lawn.

'You must not take it seriously,' said he. 'It would grieve me inexpressibly if you curtailed your visit by one hour. The fact is—there is no reason why there should be any concealment between relatives—that my poor dear wife is incredibly jealous. She hates that anyone—male or female—should for an instant come between us. Her ideal is a desert island and an eternal tête-à-tête. That gives you the clue to her actions, which are, I confess, upon the particular point, not very far removed from mania. Tell me that you will think no more of it.'

"No, no; certainly not.'

'Then light this cigar and come round with me and see my little menagerie.'

The whole afternoon was occupied by this inspection, which included all the birds, beasts and even reptiles which he had imported. Some were free, some in cages, a few actually in the house. He spoke with enthusiasm of his successes and his failures, his births and his deaths, and he would cry out in his delight, like a schoolboy, when, as we walked, some gaudy bird would flutter up from the grass, or some curious beast slink into the cover. Finally he led me down a corridor which extended from one wing of the house. At the end of this there was a heavy door with a sliding shutter in it, and beside it there projected from the wall an iron handle attached to a wheel and a drum. A line of stout bars extended across the passage.

'I am about to show you the jewel of my collection,' said he. 'There is only one other specimen in Europe, now that the Rotterdam cub is dead. It is a Brazilian cat.'

'But how does that differ from any other cat?'

'You will soon see that,' said he, laughing. 'Will you kindly draw that shutter and look through?'

I did so, and found that I was gazing into a large, empty room, with stone flags, and small, barred windows upon the farther wall. In the centre of this room, lying in the middle of a golden patch of sunlight, there was stretched a huge creature, as large as a tiger, but as black and sleek as ebony. It was simply a very enormous and very well-kept black cat, and it cuddled up and basked in that yellow pool of light exactly as a cat would do. It was so graceful, so sinewy, and so gently and smoothly diabolical, that I could not take my eyes from the opening.

'Isn't he splendid?' said my host, enthusiastically.

'Glorious! I never saw such a noble creature.'

'Some people call it a black puma, but really it is not a puma at all. That fellow is nearly eleven feet from tail to tip. Four years ago he was a little ball of black fluff, with two yellow eyes staring out of it. He was sold me as a new-born cub up in the wild country at the head-waters of the Rio Negro. They speared his mother to death after she had killed a dozen of them.'

'They are ferocious, then?'

'The most absolutely treacherous and bloodthirsty creatures upon earth. You talk about a Brazilian cat to an up-country Indian, and see him get the jumps. They prefer humans to game. This fellow has never tasted living blood yet, but when he does he will be a terror. At present he won't stand anyone but me in his den. Even Baldwin, the groom, dare not go near him. As to me, I am his mother and father in one.'

As he spoke he suddenly, to my astonishment, opened the door and slipped in, closing it instantly behind him. At the sound of his voice the huge, lithe creature rose, yawned and rubbed its round, black head affectionately against his side, while he patted and fondled it.

'Now, Tommy, into your cage!' said he.

The monstrous cat walked over to one side of the room and coiled itself up under a grating. Everard King came out, and taking the iron handle which I have mentioned, he began to turn it. As he did so the line of bars in the corridor began to pass through a slot in the wall and closed up the front of this grating, so as to make an effective cage. When it was in position, he opened the door once more and invited me into the room, which was heavy with the pungent, musty smell peculiar to the great carnivora.

'That's how we work it,' said he. 'We give him the run of the room for exercise, and then at night we put him in his cage. You can let him out by turning the handle from the passage, or you can, as you have seen, coop him up in the same way. No, no, you should not do that!'

I had put my hand between the bars to pat the glossy, heaving flank. He pulled it back, with a serious face.

'I assure you that he is not safe. Don't imagine that because I can take liberties with him anyone else can. He is very exclusive in his friends— aren't you, Tommy? Ah, he hears his lunch coming to him! Don't you, boy?'

A step had sounded in the stone-flagged passage and the creature had sprung to his feet and was pacing up and down the narrow cage, his yellow eyes gleaming and his scarlet tongue rippling and quivering over the white line of his jagged teeth. A groom entered with a coarse joint upon a tray, and thrust it through the bars to him. He pounced lightly upon it, carried it off to the corner, and there, holding it between his paws, tore and wrenched at it, raising his bloody muzzle every now and then to look at us. It was a malignant and yet fascinating sight.

'You can't wonder that I am fond of him, can you?' said my host, as we left the room, 'especially when you consider that I have had the rearing of him. It was no joke bringing him over from the centre of South America; but here he is safe and sound—and, as I have said, far the most perfect specimen in Europe. The people at the Zoo are dying to have him, but I really can't part with him. Now, I think that I have inflicted my hobby upon you long enough, so we cannot do better than follow Tommy's example, and go to our lunch.'

My South American relative was so engrossed by his grounds and their curious occupants, that I hardly gave him credit at first for having any interests outside them. That he had some, and pressing ones, was soon borne in upon me by the number of telegrams which he received. They arrived at all hours, and were always opened by him with the utmost eagerness and anxiety upon his face. Sometimes I imagined that it must be the Turf, and sometimes the Stock Exchange, but certainly he had some very urgent business going forward which was not transacted upon the downs of Suffolk. During the six days of my visit he had never fewer than three or four telegrams a day, and sometimes as many as seven or eight.

I had occupied these six days so well, that by the end of them I had succeeded in getting upon the most cordial terms with my cousin. Every night we had sat up late in the billiard-room, he telling me the most extraordinary stories of his adventures in America—stories so desperate and reckless, that I could hardly associate them with the brown little chubby man before me. In return, I ventured upon some of my own reminiscences of London life, which interested him so much that he vowed he would come up to Grosvenor Mansions and stay with me. He was anxious to see the faster side of city life, and certainly, though I say it, he could not have chosen a more competent guide. It was not until the last day of my visit that I ventured to approach that which was on my mind. I told him frankly about my pecuniary difficulties and my impending ruin, and I asked his advice—though I hoped for something more solid. He listened attentively, puffing hard at his cigar.

'But surely,' said he, 'you are the heir of our relative, Lord Southerton?'

'I have every reason to believe so, but he would never make me any allowance.'

'No, no, I have heard of his miserly ways. My poor Marshall, your position has been a very hard one. By the way, have you heard any news of Lord Southerton's health lately?'

'He has always been in a critical condition ever since my childhood.'

'Exactly—a creaking hinge, if ever there was one. Your inheritance may be a long way off. Dear me, how awkwardly situated you are!'

'I had some hopes, sire, that you, knowing all the facts, might be inclined to advance—'

'Don't say another word, my dear boy,' he cried, with the utmost cordiality; 'we shall talk it over tonight, and I give you my word that whatever is in my power shall be done.'

I was not sorry that my visit was drawing to a close, for it is unpleasant to feel that there is one person in the house who eagerly desires your departure. Mrs King's sallow face and forbidding eyes had become more and more hateful to me. She was no longer actively rude—her fear of her husband prevented her—but she pushed her insane jealousy to the extent of ignoring me, never addressing me, and in every way making my stay at Greylands as uncomfortable as she could. So offensive was her manner during the last day, that I should certainly have left had it not been for that interview with my host in the evening which would, I hoped, retrieve my broken fortunes.

It was very late when it occurred, for my relative, who had been receiving even more telegrams than usual during the day, went off to his study after dinner and only emerged when the household had retired to bed. I heard him go round locking the doors, as his custom was of a night, and finally he joined me in the billiard-room. His stout figure was wrapped in a dressing-gown and he wore a pair of red turkish slippers without any heels. Settling down into an armchair, he brewed himself a glass of grog, in which I could not help noticing that the whisky considerably predominated over the water.

'My word!' said he, 'what a night!'

It was, indeed. The wind was howling and screaming round the house, and the latticed windows rattled and shook as if they were coming in. The glow of the yellow lamps and the flavour of our cigars seemed the brighter and more fragrant for the contrast.

'Now, my boy,' said my host, 'we have the house and the night to ourselves. Let me have an idea of how your affairs stand, and I will see what can be done to set them in order. I wish to hear every detail.'

Thus encouraged, I entered into a long exposition, in which all my tradesmen and creditors, from my landlord to my valet, figured in turn. I had notes in my pocket-book and I marshalled my facts and gave, I flatter myself, a very businesslike statement of my own unbusinesslike ways and lamentable position. I was depressed, however, to notice that my companion's eyes were vacant and his attention elsewhere. When he did occasionally throw out a remark it was so entirely perfunctory and pointless, that I was sure he had not in the least followed my remarks. Every now and then he roused himself and put on some show of interest, asking me to repeat or to explain more fully, but it was always to sink once more into the same brown study. At last he rose and threw the end of his cigar into the grate.

'I'll tell you what, my boy,' said he. 'I never had a head for figures, so you will excuse me. You must jot it all down upon paper, and let me have a note of the amount. I'll understand it when I see it in black and white.'

The proposal was encouraging. I promised to do so.

'And now it's time we were in bed. By Jove, there's one o'clock striking in the hall.'

The tingling of the chiming clock broke through the deep roar of the gale. The wind was sweeping past with the rush of a great river.

'I must see my cat before I go to bed,' said my host. 'A high wind excites him. Will you come?'

'Certainly,' said I.

'Then tread softly and don't speak, for everyone is asleep.'

We passed quietly down the lamp-lit Persian-rugged hall, and through the door at the farther end. All was dark in the stone corridor, but a stable lantern hung on a hook, and my host took it down and lit it. There was no grating visible in the passage, so I knew that the beast was in its cage.

'Come in!' said my relative, and opened the door.

A deep growling as we entered showed that the storm had really excited the creature. In the flickering light of the lantern, we saw it, a huge black mass coiled in the corner of its den and throwing a squat, uncouth shadow upon the whitewashed wall. Its tail switched angrily among the straw.

'Poor Tommy is not in the best of tempers,' said Everard King, holding up the lantern and looking in at him. 'What a black devil he looks, doesn't he? I must give him a little supper to put him in a better humour. Would you mind holding the lantern for a moment?'

I took it from his hand and he stepped to the door.

'His larder is just outside here,' said he. 'You will excuse me for an instant, won't you?' He passed out, and the door shut with a sharp metallic click behind him.

That hard crisp sound made my heart stand still. A sudden wave of terror passed over me. A vague perception of some monstrous treachery turned me cold. I sprang to the door, but there was no handle upon the inner side.

'Here!' I cried. 'Let me out!'

'All right! Don't make a row!' said my host from the passage. 'You've got the light all right.'

'Yes, but I don't care about being locked in alone like this.'

'Don't you?' I heard his hearty, chuckling laugh. 'You won't be alone long.'

'Let me out, sir!' I repeated angrily. 'I tell you I don't allow practical jokes of this sort.'

'Practical is the word,' said he, with another hateful chuckle. And then suddenly I heard, amidst the roar of the storm, the creak and whine of the winch-handle turning and the rattle of the grating as it passed through the slot. Great God, he was letting loose the Brazilian cat!

In the light of the lantern I saw the bars sliding slowly before me. Already there was an opening a foot wide at the farther end. With a scream I seized the last bar with my hands and pulled with the strength of a madman. I was a madman with rage and horror. For a minute or more I held the thing motionless. I knew that he was straining with all his force upon the handle and that the leverage was sure to overcome me. I gave inch by inch, my feet sliding along the stones, and all the time I begged and prayed this inhuman monster to save me from this horrible death. I conjured him by his kinship. I reminded him that I was his guest; I begged to know what harm I had ever done him. His only answers were the tugs and jerks upon the handle, each of which, in spite of all my struggles, pulled another bar through the opening. Clinging and clutching, I was dragged across the whole front of the cage, until at last, with aching wrists and lacerated fingers, I gave up the hopeless struggle. The grating clanged back as I released it, and an instant later I heard the shuffle of the Turkish slippers in the passage, and the slam of the distant door. Then everything was silent.

The creature had never moved during this time. He lay still in the corner, and his tail had ceased switching. This apparition of a man adhering to his bars and dragged screaming across him had apparently filled him with amazement. I saw his great eyes staring steadily at me. I had dropped the lantern when I seized the bars, but it still burned upon the floor, and I made a movement to grasp it, with some idea that its light might protect me. But the instant I moved, the beast gave a deep and menacing growl. I stopped and stood still, quivering with fear in every limb. The cat (if one may call so fearful a creature by so homely a name) was not more than ten feet from me. The eyes glimmered like two disks of phosphorus in the darkness. They appalled and yet fascinated me. I could not take my own eyes from them. Nature plays strange tricks with us at such moments of intensity, and those glimmering lights waxed and waned with a steady rise and fall. Sometimes they seemed to be tiny points of extreme brilliancy—little electric sparks in the black obscurity—then they would widen and widen until all that corner of the room was filled with their shifting and sinister light. And then suddenly they went out altogether.

The beast had closed its eyes. I do not know whether there may be any truth in the old idea of the dominance of the human gaze, or whether the huge cat was simply drowsy, but the fact remains that, far from showing any symptom of attacking me, it simply rested its sleek, black head upon its huge forepaws and seemed to sleep. I stood, fearing to move lest I should rouse it into malignant life once more. But at least I was able to think clearly now that the baleful eyes were off me. Here I was shut up for the night with the ferocious beast. My own instincts, to say nothing of the words of the plausible villain who laid this trap for me, warned me that the animal was as savage as its master. How could I stave it off until morning? The door was hopeless, and so were the narrow, barred windows. There was no shelter anywhere in the bare, stone-flagged room. To cry for assistance was absurd. I knew that this den was an outhouse, and that the corridor which connected it with the house was at least a hundred feet long. Besides, with that gale thundering outside, my cries were not likely to be heard. I had only my own courage and my own wits to trust to.

And then, with a fresh wave of horror, my eyes fell upon the lantern. The candle had burned low, and was already beginning to gutter. In ten minutes it would be out. I had only ten minutes then in which to do something, for I felt that if I were once left in the dark with that fearful beast I should be incapable of action. The very thought of it paralysed me. I cast my despairing eyes round this chamber of death, and they rested upon one spot which seemed to promise I will not say safety, but less immediate and imminent danger than the open floor.

I have said that the cage had a top as well as a front, and this top was left standing when the front was wound through the slot in the wall. It consisted of bars at a few inches' interval, with stout wire netting between, and it rested upon a strong stanchion at each end. It stood now as a great barred canopy over the crouching figure in the corner. The space between this iron shelf and the roof may have been from two to three feet. If I could only get up there, squeezed in between bars and ceiling, I should have only one vulnerable side. I should be safe from below, from behind, and from each side. Only on the open face of it could I be attacked. There, it is true, I had no protection whatever; but at least I should be out of the brute's path when he began to pace about his den. He would have to come out of his way to reach me. It was now or never, for once the light were out it would be impossible. With a gulp in my throat I sprang up, seized the iron edge of the top, and swung myself on to it. I writhed in, face downwards, and found myself looking straight into the terrible eyes and yawning jaws of the cat. Its fetid breath came up into my face like the steam from some foul pot.

It appeared, however, to be rather curious than angry. With a sleek ripple of its long black back it rose, stretched itself, and then rearing itself on its hind legs, with one forepaw against the wall, it raised the other and drew its claws across the wire meshes beneath me. One sharp, white hook tore through my trousers—for I may mention that I was still in evening dress—and dug a furrow in my knee. It was not meant as an attack, but rather as an experiment, for upon my giving a sharp cry of pain he dropped down again, and springing lightly into the room, he began walking swiftly round it, looking up every now and again in my direction. For my part I shuffled backwards until I lay with my back against the wall, screwing myself into the smallest space possible. The farther I got the more difficult it was for him to attack me.

He seemed more excited now that he had begun to move about, and he ran swiftly and noiselessly round and round the den, passing continually underneath the iron couch upon which I lay. It was wonderful to see so great a bulk passing like a shadow, with hardly the softest thudding of velvety pads. The candle was burning low—so low that I could hardly see the creature. And then, with a last flare and splutter, it went out altogether. I was alone with the cat in the dark!

It helps one to face a danger when one knows that one has done all that possibly can be done. There is nothing for it then but to quietly await the result. In this case, there was no chance of safety anywhere except the precise spot where I was. I stretched myself out, therefore, and lay silently, almost breathlessly, hoping that the beast might forget my presence if I did nothing to remind him. I reckoned that it must already be two o'clock. At four it would be full dawn. I had not more than two hours to wait for daylight.

Outside, the storm was still raging, and the rain lashed continually against the little windows. Inside, the poisonous and fetid air was over-powering. I could neither hear nor see the cat. I tried to think about other things—but only one had power enough to draw my mind from my terrible position. That was the contemplation of my cousin's villainy, his unparalleled hypocrisy, his malignant hatred of me. Beneath that cheerful face there lurked the spirit of a medieval assassin. And as I thought of it I saw more clearly how cunningly the thing had been arranged. He had apparently gone to bed with the others. No doubt he had his witnesses to prove it. Then, unknown to them, he had slipped down, had lured me into this den and abandoned me. His story would be so simple. He had left me to finish my cigar in the billiard-room. I had gone down on my own account to have a last look at the cat. I had entered the room without observing that the cage was opened, and I had been caught. How could such a crime be brought home to him? Suspicion, perhaps—but proof, never!

How slowly those dreadful two hours went by! Once I heard a low, rasping sound, which I took to be the creature licking its own fur. Several times those greenish eyes gleamed at me through the darkness, but never in a fixed stare, and my hopes grew stronger that my presence had been forgotten or ignored. At last the least faint glimmer of light came through the windows—I first dimly saw them as two grey squares upon the black wall, then grey turned to white, and I could see my terrible companion once more. And he, alas, could see me!

It was evident to me at once that he was in a much more dangerous and aggressive mood than when I had seen him last. The cold of the morning had irritated him, and he was hungry as well. With a continual growl he paced swiftly up and down the side of the room which was farthest from my refuge, his whiskers bristling angrily and his tail switching and lashing. As he turned at the corners his savage eyes always looked upwards at me with a dreadful menace. I knew then that he meant to kill me. Yet I found myself even at that moment admiring the sinuous grace of the devilish thing, its long, undulating, rippling movements, the gloss of its beautiful flanks, the vivid, palpitating scarlet of the glistening tongue which hung from the jet-black muzzle. And all the time that deep, threatening growl was rising and rising in an unbroken crescendo. I knew that the crisis was at hand.

It was a miserable hour to meet such a death—so cold, so comfortless, shivering in my light dress clothes upon this gridiron of torment upon which I was stretched. I tried to brace myself to it, to raise my soul above it, and at the same time, with the lucidity which comes to a perfectly desperate man, I cast round for some possible means of escape. One thing was clear to me. If that front of the cage was only back in its position once more, I could find a sure refuge behind it. Could I possibly pull it back? I hardly dared to move for fear of bringing the creature upon me. Slowly, very slowly, I put my hand forward until it grasped the edge of the front, the final bar, which protruded through the wall. To my surprise it came quite easily to my jerk. Of course the difficulty of drawing it out arose from the fact that I was clinging to it. I pulled again, and three inches of it came through. It ran apparently on wheels. I pulled again . . . and then the cat sprang!

It was so quick, so sudden that I never saw it happen. I simply heard the savage snarl and in an instant afterwards the blazing yellow eyes, the flattened black head with its red tongue and flashing teeth, were within reach of me. The impact of the creature shook the bars upon which I lay, until I thought (as far as I could think of anything at such a moment) that they were coming down. The cat swayed there for an instant, the head and front paws quite close to me, the hind paws clawing to find a grip upon the edge of the grating. I heard the claws rasping as they clung to the wire-netting and the breath of the beast made me sick. But its bound had been miscalculated. It could not retain its position. Slowly, grinning with rage, and scratching madly at the bars, it swung backwards and dropped heavily upon the floor. With a growl it instantly faced round to me and crouched for another spring.

I knew that the next few moments would decide my fate. The creature had learned by experience. It would not miscalculate again. I must act promptly, fearlessly, if I were to have a chance of life. In an instant I had formed my plan. Pulling off my dress-coat, I threw it down over the head of the beast. At the same moment I dropped over the edge, seized the end of the front grating, and pulled it frantically out of the wall.

It came more easily than I could have expected. I rushed across the room, bearing it with me; but, as I rushed, the accident of my position put me upon the outer side. Had it been the other way, I might have come off scathless. As it was, there was a moment's pause as I stopped it and tried to pass it through the opening which I had left. That moment was enough to give time to the creature to toss off the coat with which I had blinded him and to spring upon me. I hurled myself through the gap and pulled the rails to behind me, but he seized my leg before I could entirely withdraw it. One stroke of that huge paw tore off my calf as a shaving of wood curls off before a plane. The next moment, bleeding and fainting, I was lying among the foul straw with a line of friendly bars between me and the creature which ramped so frantically against them.

Too wounded to move and too faint to be conscious of fear, I could only lie, more dead than alive, and watch it. It pressed its broad, black chest against the bars and angled for me with its crooked paws as I have seen a kitten do before a mousetrap. It ripped my clothes, but, stretch as it would, it could not quite reach me. I have heard of the curious numbing effect produced by wounds from the great carnivora, and now I was destined to experience it, for I had lost all sense of personality and was as interested in the cat's failure or success as if it were some game which I was watching. And then, gradually my mind drifted away into strange vague dreams, always with that black face and red tongue coming back into them, and so I lost myself in the nirvana of delirium, the blessed relief of those who are too sorely tried.

Tracing the course of events afterwards, I conclude that I must have been insensible for about two hours. What roused me to consciousness once more was that sharp metallic click which had been the precursor of my terrible experience. It was the shooting back of the spring lock. Then, before my senses were clear enough entirely to apprehend what they saw, I was aware of the round, benevolent face of my cousin peering in through the open door. What he saw evidently amazed him. There was the cat crouching on the floor. I was stretched upon my back in my shirt-sleeves within the cage, my trousers torn to ribbons and a great pool of blood all around me. I can see his amazed face now, with the morning sunlight upon it. He peered at me, and peered again. Then he closed the door behind him, and advanced to the cage to see if I were really dead.

I cannot undertake to say what happened. I was not in a fit state to witness or to chronicle such events. I can only say that I was suddenly conscious that his face was away from me—that he was looking towards the animal.

'Good old Tommy!' he cried. 'Good old Tommy!'

Then he came near the bars, with his back still towards me.

'Down, you stupid beast!' he roared. 'Down, sir! Don't you know your master?'

Suddenly even in my bemuddled brain a remembrance came of those words of his when he had said that the taste of blood would turn the cat into a fiend. My blood had done it, but he was to pay the price.

'Get away!' he screamed. 'Get away, you devil! Baldwin! Baldwin! Oh, my God!'

And then I heard him fall, and rise, and fall again, with a sound like the ripping of sacking. His screams grew fainter until they were lost in the worrying snarl. And then, after I thought that he was dead, I saw, as in a nightmare, a blinded, tattered, blood-soaked figure running wildly round the room—and that was the last glimpse I had of him before I fainted once again.

I was many months in my recovery—in fact, I cannot say that I have ever recovered, for to the end of my days I shall carry a stick as a sign of my night with the Brazilian cat. Baldwin, the groom, and the other servants could not tell what had occurred, when, drawn by the death-cries of their master, they found me behind the bars, and his remains—or what they afterwards discovered to be his remains—in the clutch of the creature which he had reared. They stalled him off with hot irons, and afterwards shot him through the loophole of the door before they could finally extricate me. I was carried to my bedroom, and there, under the roof of my would-be murderer, I remained between life and death for several weeks. They had sent for a surgeon from Clipton and a nurse from London, and in a month I was able to be carried to the station, and so conveyed back once more to Grosvenor Mansions.

I have one remembrance of that illness, which might have been part of the ever-changing panorama conjured up by a delirious brain were it not so definitely fixed in my memory. One night, when the nurse was absent, the door of my chamber opened and a tall woman in blackest mourning slipped into the room. She came across to me and as she bent her sallow face I saw by the faint gleam of the nightlight that it was the Brazilian woman whom my cousin had married. She stared intently into my face, and her expression was more kindly than I had ever seen it.

'Are you conscious?' she asked.

I feebly nodded—for I was still very weak.

'Well, then, I only wished to say to you that you have yourself to blame. Did I not do all I could for you? From the beginning I tried to drive you from the house. By every means, short of betraying my husband, I tried to save you from him. I knew that he had a reason for bringing you here. I knew that he would never let you get away again. No one knew him as I knew him, who had suffered from him so often. I did not dare to tell you all this. He would have killed me. But I did my best for you. As things have turned out, you have been the best friend that I ever had. You have set me free, and I fancied that nothing but death would do that. I am sorry if you are hurt, but I cannot reproach myself. I told you that you were a fool—and a fool you have been.' She crept out of the room, the bitter, singular woman, and I was never destined to see her again. With what remained from her husband's property she went back to her native land, and I have heard that she afterwards took the veil at Pernambuco.

It was not until I had been back in London for some time that the doctors pronounced me to be well enough to do business. It was not a very welcome permission to me, for I feared that it would be the signal for an inrush of creditors; but it was Summers, my lawyer, who first took advantage of it.

'I am very glad to see that your lordship is so much better,' said he. 'I have been waiting a long time to offer my congratulations.'

'What do you mean, Summers? This is no time for joking.'

"I mean what I say,' he answered. 'You have been Lord Southerton for the last six weeks, but we feared that it would retard your recovery if you were to learn it.'

Lord Southerton! One of the richest peers in England! I could not believe my ears. And then suddenly I thought of the time which had elapsed, and how it coincided with my injuries.

'Then Lord Southerton must have died about the same time that I was hurt?'

'His death occurred upon that very day.' Summers looked hard at me as I spoke, and I am convinced—for he was a very shrewd fellow—that he had guessed the true state of the case. He paused for a moment as if awaiting a confidence from me, but I could not see what was to be gained by exposing such a family scandal.

'Yes, a very curious coincidence,' he continued, with the same knowing look. 'Of course, you are aware that your cousin Everard King was the next heir to the estates. Now, if it had been you instead of him who had been torn to pieces by this tiger, or whatever it was, then of course he would have been Lord Southerton at the present moment.'

'No doubt,' said I.

'And he took such an interest in it,' said Summers. 'I happen to know that the late Lord Southerton's valet was in his pay, and that he used to have telegrams from him every few hours to tell him how he was getting on. That would be about the time when you were down there. Was it not strange that he should wish to be so well informed, since he knew that he was not the direct heir?'

'Very strange,' said I. 'And now, Summers, if you will bring me my bills and a new chequebook, we will begin to get things into order.'

10

⟋

"The Brown Hand"
(1899)

Everyone knows that Sir Dominick Holden, the famous Indian surgeon, made me his heir, and that his death changed me in an hour from
a hard-working and impecunious medical man to a well-to-do landed
proprietor. Many know also that there were at least five people between
the inheritance and me, and that Sir Dominick's selection appeared to be
altogether arbitrary and whimsical. I can assure them, however, that they
are quite mistaken, and that, although I only knew Sir Dominick in the
closing years of his life, there were, none the less, very real reasons why
he should show his goodwill towards me. As a matter of fact, though I
say it myself, no man ever did more for another than I did for my Indian
uncle. I cannot expect the story to be believed, but it is so singular that
I should feel that it was a breach of duty if I did not put it upon
record—so here it is, and your belief or incredulity is your own affair.

Sir Dominick Holden, CB, KCSL, and I don't know what besides, was
the most distinguished Indian surgeon of his day. In the army originally,
he afterwards settled down into civil practice in Bombay, and visited, as
a consultant, every part of India. His name is best remembered in connection with the Oriental Hospital, which he founded and supported.
The time came, however, when his iron constitution began to show signs
of the long strain to which he had subjected it, and his brother practi-
tioners (who were not, perhaps, entirely disinterested upon the point)

were unanimous in recommending him to return to England. He held on so long as he could, but at last, he developed nervous symptoms of a very pronounced character, and so came back, a broken man, to his native county of Wiltshire. He bought a considerable estate with an ancient manor house upon the edge of Salisbury Plain, and devoted his old age to the study of comparative pathology, which has been his learned hobby all his life and in which he was a foremost authority.

We of the family were, as may be imagined, much excited by the news of the return of this rich and childless uncle to England. On his part, although by no means exuberant in his hospitality, he showed some sense of his duty to his relations, and each of us in turn had an invitation to visit him. From the accounts of my cousins it appeared to be a melancholy business, and it was with mixed feelings that I at last received my own summons to appear at Rodenhurst. My wife was so carefully excluded from the invitation that my first impulse was to refuse it, but the interests of the children had to be considered, and so, with her consent, I set out one October afternoon upon my visit to Wiltshire, with little thought of what that visit was to entail.

My uncle's estate was situated where the arable land of the plains begins to swell upwards into the rounded chalk hills which are characteristic of the county. As I drove from Dinton Station in the waning light of that autumn day, I was impressed by the weird nature of the scenery. The few scattered cottages of the peasants were so dwarfed by the huge evidences of prehistoric life, that the present appeared to be a dream and the past to be the obtrusive and masterful reality. The road wound through the valleys, formed by a succession of grassy hills, and the summit of each was cut and carved into the most elaborate fortifications, some circular and some square but all on a scale which has defied the winds and the rains of many centuries. Some call them Roman and some British, but their true origin and the reasons for this particular tract of country being so interlaced with entrenchments have never been finally made clear. Here and there on the long, smooth, olive-coloured slopes there rose small, rounded barrows or tumuli. Beneath them lie the cremated ashes of the race which cut so deeply into the hills, but their graves tell us nothing save that a jar full of dust represents the man who once laboured under the sun.

It was through this weird country that I approached my uncle's residence of Rodenhurst, and the house was, as I found, in due keeping with its surroundings. Two broken and weather-stained pillars, each surmounted by a mutilated heraldic emblem, flanked the entrance to a neglected drive. A cold wind whistled though the elms which lined it and the air was full of the drifting leaves. As the far end, under the gloomy arch of trees, a single yellow lamp burned steadily. In the dim half-light of the coming night I saw a long, low building stretching out two irregular wings, with deep eaves, a sloping gambrel roof and walls which were criss-crossed with timber balks in the fashion of the Tudors. The cheery light of a fire flickered in the broad, latticed window to the left of the low-porched door, and this, as it proved, marked the study of my uncle, for it was thither that I was led by his butler in order to make my host's acquaintance.

He was cowering over his fire, for the moist chill of an English autumn had set him shivering. His lamp was unlit, and I only saw the red glow of the embers beating upon a huge, craggy face, with a Red Indian nose and cheek, and deep furrows and seams from eye to chin, the sinister marks of hidden volcanic fires. He sprang up at my entrance with something of an old-world courtesy and welcomed me warmly to Rodenhurst. At the same time I was conscious, as the lamp was carried in, that it was a very critical pair of light-blue eyes which looked out at me from under shaggy eyebrows, like scouts beneath a bush, and that this outlandish uncle of mine was carefully reading off my character with all the ease of a practised observer and an experienced man of the world.

For my part I looked at him, and looked again, for I had never seen a man whose appearance was more fitted to hold one's attention. His figure was the framework of a giant, but he had fallen away until his coat dangled straight down in a shocking fashion from a pair of broad and bony shoulders. All his limbs were huge and yet emaciated, and I could not take my gaze from his knobby wrists and long, gnarled hands. But his eyes—those peering, light-blue eyes—they were the most arrestive of any of his peculiarities. It was not their colour alone, nor was it the ambush of hair in which they lurked; but it was the expression which I read in them. For the appearance and bearing of the man were masterful, and one expected a certain corresponding arrogance in his eyes, but instead of that I read the look which tells of a spirit cowed and crushed, the furtive, expectant look of the dog whose master has taken the whip from the rack. I formed my own medical diagnosis upon one glance at those critical and yet appealing eyes. I believed that he was stricken with some mortal ailment, that he knew himself to be exposed to sudden death and that he lived in terror of it. Such was my judgement—a false one, as the event showed; but I mention it that it may help you to realise the look which I read in his eyes.

My uncle's welcome was, as I have said, a courteous one, and in an hour or so I found myself seated between him and his wife at a comfortable dinner, with curious, pungent delicacies upon the table and a stealthy, quick-eyed Oriental waiter behind his chair. The old couple had come round to that tragic imitation of the dawn of life when husband and wife, having lost or scattered all those who were their intimates, find themselves face to face and alone once more, their work done, and the end nearing fast. Those who have reached that stage in sweetness and love, who can change their winter into a gentle, Indian summer, have come as victors through the ordeal of life. Lady Holden was a small, alert woman with a kindly eye, and her expression as she glanced at him was a certificate of character to her husband. And yet, though I read a mutual love in their glances, I read also mutual horror, and recognised in her face some reflection of that stealthy fear which I had detected in his. Their talk was sometimes merry and sometimes sad, but there was a forced note in their merriment and a naturalness in their sadness which told me that a heavy heart beat upon either side of me.

We were sitting over our first glass of wine, and the servants had left the room, when the conversation took a turn which produced a remarkable effect upon my host and hostess. I cannot recall what it was which started the topic of the supernatural, but it ended in my showing them that the abnormal in psychical experiences was a subject to which I had, like many neurologists, devoted a great deal of attention. I concluded by narrating my experiences when, as a member of the Psychical Research Society, I had formed one of a committee of three who spent the night in a haunted house. Our adventures were neither exciting nor convincing, but, such as it was, the story appeared to interest my auditors in a remarkable degree. They listened with an eager silence, and I caught a look of intelligence between them which I could not understand. Lady Holden immediately afterwards rose and left the room.

Sir Dominick pushed the cigar-box over to me, and we smoked for some little time in silence. That huge, bony hand of his was twitching as he raised it with his cheroot to his lips, and I felt that the man's nerves were vibrating like fiddle-strings. My instincts told me that he was on the verge of some intimate confidence, and I feared to speak lest I should interrupt it. At last he turned towards me with a spasmodic gesture, like a man who throws his last scruple to the winds.

'From the little that I have seen of you it appears to me, Dr. Hardacre,' said he, 'that you are the very man I have wanted to meet.'

'I am delighted to hear it, sir.'

'Your head seems to be cool and steady. You will acquit me of any desire to flatter you, for the circumstances are too serious to permit of insincerities. You have some special knowledge upon these subjects, and you evidently view them from that philosophical standpoint which robs them of all vulgar terror. I presume that the sight of an apparition would not seriously discompose you?'

'I think not, sir.'

'Would even interest you, perhaps?'

'Most intensely.'

'As a psychical observer, you would probably investigate it in as impersonal a fashion as an astronomer investigates a wandering comet?'

'Precisely.'

He gave a heavy sigh.

'Believe me, Dr. Hardacre, there was a time when I could have spoken as you do now. My nerve was a byword in India. Even the Mutiny never shook it for an instant. And yet you see what I am reduced to— the most timorous man, perhaps, in all this county of Wiltshire. Do not speak too bravely upon this subject, or you may find yourself subjected to as long-drawn a test as I am—a test which can only end in the madhouse or the grave.'

I waited patiently until he should see fit to go further in his confidence. His preamble had, I need not say, filled me with interest and expectation.

'For some years, Dr. Hardacre,' he continued, 'my life and that of my wife have been made miserable by a cause which is so grotesque that it borders upon the ludicrous. And yet familiarity has never made it more easy to bear—on the contrary, as time passes my nerves become more worn and shattered by the constant attrition. If you have no physical fears, Dr. Hardacre, I should very much value your opinion upon this phenomenon which troubles us so.'

'For what it is worth my opinion is entirely at your service. May I ask the nature of the phenomenon?'

'I think that your experiences will have a higher evidential value if you are not told in advance what you may expect to encounter. You are yourself aware of the quibbles of unconscious cerebration and subjective impressions with which a scientific sceptic may throw a doubt upon your statement. It would be as well to guard against them in advance.'

'What shall I do, then?'

'I will tell you. Would you mind following me this way?' He led me out of the dining-room and down a long passage until we came to a terminal door. Inside there was a large, bare room fitted as a laboratory, with numerous scientific instruments and bottles. A shelf ran along one side, upon which there stood a long line of glass jars containing pathological and anatomical specimens.

'You see that I still dabble in some of my old studies,' said Sir Dominick. 'These jars are the remains of what was once a most excellent collection, but unfortunately I lost the greater part of them when my house was burned down in Bombay in '92. It was a most unfortunate affair for me—in more ways than one. I had examples of many rare conditions, and my splenic collection was probably unique. These are the survivors.'

I glanced over them and saw that they really were of a very great value and rarity from a pathological point of view: bloated organs, gaping cysts, distorted bones, odious parasites—a singular exhibition of the products of India.

'There is, as you see, a small settee here,' said my host. 'It was far from our intention to offer a guest so meagre an accommodation, but since affairs have taken this turn, it would be a great kindness upon your part if you would consent to spend the night in this apartment. I beg that you will not hesitate to let me know if the idea should be at all repugnant to you.'

'On the contrary,' I said, 'it is most acceptable.'

'My own room is the second on the left, so that if you should feel that you are in need of company a call would always bring me to your side.'

'I trust that I shall not be compelled to disturb you.'

'It is unlikely that I shall be asleep. I do not sleep much. Do not hesitate to summon me.'

And so with this agreement we joined Lady Holden in the drawing-room and talked of lighter things.

It was no affectation upon my part to say that the prospect of my night's adventure was an agreeable one. I have no pretence to greater physical courage than my neighbours, but familiarity with a subject robs it of those vague and undefined terrors which are the most appalling to the imaginative mind. The human brain is capable of only one strong emotion at a time, and if it be filled with curiosity or scientific enthusiasm, there is no room for fear. It is true that I had my uncle's assurance that he had himself originally taken this point of view, but I reflected that the breakdown of his nervous system might be due to his forty years in India as much as to any psychical experiences which had befallen him. I at least was sound in nerve and brain, and it was with something of the pleasurable thrill of anticipation with which the sportsman takes his position beside the haunt of his game that I shut the laboratory door behind me, and partially undressing, lay down upon the rug-covered settee.

It was not an ideal atmosphere for a bedroom. The air was heavy with many chemical odours, that of methylated spirit predominating. Nor were the decorations of my chamber very sedative. The odious line of glass jars with their relics of disease and suffering stretched in front of my very eyes. There was no blind to the window, and a three-quarter moon streamed its white light into the room, tracing a silver square with filigree lattices upon the opposite wall. When I had extinguished my candle this one bright patch in the midst of the general gloom had certainly an eerie and discomposing aspect. A rigid and absolute silence reigned throughout the old house, so that the low swish of the branches in the garden came softly and smoothly to my ears. It may have been the hypnotic lullaby of this gentle susurrus, or it may have been the result of my tiring day, but after many dozings and many efforts to regain my clearness of perception, I fell at last into a deep and dreamless sleep.

I was awakened by some sound in the room, and I instantly raised myself upon my elbow on the couch. Some hours had passed, for the square patch upon the wall had slid downwards and sideways until it lay obliquely at the end of my bed. The rest of the room was in deep shadow. At first I could see nothing; presently, as my eyes became accustomed to the faint light, I was aware, with a thrill which all my scientific absorption could not entirely prevent, that something was moving slowly along the line of the wall. A gentle, shuffling sound, as of soft slippers, came to my ears, and I dimly discerned a human figure walking stealthily from the direction of the door. As it emerged into the patch of moonlight I saw very clearly what it was and how it was employed. It was a man, short and squat, dressed in some sort of dark-grey gown, which hung straight from his shoulders to his feet. The moon shone upon the side of his face, and I saw that it was chocolate-brown in colour, with a ball of black hair like a woman's at the back of his head. He walked slowly, and his eyes were cast upwards towards the line of bottles which contained those gruesome remnants of humanity. He seemed to examine each jar with attention, and then to pass on to the next. When he had come to the end of the line, immediately opposite my bed, he stopped, faced me, threw up his hands with a gesture of despair, and vanished from my sight.

I have said that he threw up his hands, but I should have said his arms, for as he assumed that attitude of despair I observed a singular peculiarity about his appearance. He had only one hand! As the sleeves drooped down from the upflung arms I saw the left plainly, but the right ended in a knobby and unsightly stump. In every other way his appearance was so normal, and I had both seen and heard him so clearly, that I could easily have believed that he was an Indian servant of Sir Dominick's who had come into my room in search of something. It was only his sudden disappearance which suggested anything more sinister to me. As it was I sprang from my couch, lit a candle, and examined the whole room carefully. There were no signs of my visitor, and I was forced to conclude that there had really been something outside the normal laws of nature in his appearance. I lay awake for the remainder of the night, but nothing else occurred to disturb me.

I am an early riser, but my uncle was an even earlier one, for I found him pacing up and down the lawn at the side of the house. He ran towards me in his eagerness when he saw me come out from the door.

'Well, well!' he cried. 'Did you see him?'

'An Indian with one hand?'

'Precisely.'

'Yes, I saw him'—and I told him all that occurred. When I had finished, he led the way into his study.

'We have a little time before breakfast,' said he. 'It will suffice to give you an explanation of this extraordinary affair—so far as I can explain that which is essentially inexplicable. In the first place, when I tell you that for four years I have never passed one single night, either in Bombay, aboard ship or here in England, without my sleep being broken by this fellow, you will understand why it is that I am a wreck of my former self. His programme is always the same. He appears by my bedside, shakes me roughly by the shoulder, passes from my room into the laboratory, walks slowly along the line of my bottles and then vanishes. For more than a thousand times he has gone through the same routine.'

'What does he want?'

'He wants his hand.'

'His hand?'

'Yes, it came about in this way. I was summoned to Peshawar for a consultation some ten years ago, and while there I was asked to look at the hand of a native who was passing through with an Afghan caravan. The fellow came from some mountain tribe living away at the back of beyond somewhere on the other side of Kaffiristan. He talked a bastard Pushtu, and it was all I could do to understand him. He was suffering from a soft sarcomatous swelling of one of the metacarpal joints, and I made him realise that it was only by losing his hand that he could hope to save his life. After much persuasion he consented to the operation, and he asked me, when it was over, what fee I demanded. The poor fellow was almost a beggar, so that the idea of a fee was absurd, but I answered in jest that my fee should be his hand and that I proposed to add it to my pathological collection.

'To my surprise he demurred very much to the suggestion, and he explained that according to his religion it was an all-important matter that the body should be reunited after death and so make a perfect dwelling for the spirit. The belief is, of course, an old one, and the mummies of the Egyptians arose from an analogous superstition. I answered him that his hand was already off, and asked him how he intended to preserve it. He replied that he would pickle it in salt and carry it about with him. I suggested that it might be safer in my keeping than his, and that I had better means than salt for preserving it. On realising that I really intended to keep it carefully, his opposition vanished instantly. "But remember, sahib," he said, "I shall want it back when I am dead." I laughed at the remark, and so the matter ended. I returned to my practice, and he no doubt in the course of time was able to continue his journey to Afghanistan.

'Well, as I told you last night, I had a bad fire in my house at Bombay. Half of it was burned down and, among other things, my pathological collection was largely destroyed. What you see are the poor remains of it. The hand of the human went with the rest, but I gave the matter no particular thought at the time. That was six years ago.

'Four years ago—two years after the fire—I was awakened one night by a furious tugging at my sleeve. I sat up under the impression that my favourite mastiff was trying to arouse me. Instead of this, I saw my Indian patient of long ago, dressed in the long, grey gown which was the badge of his people. He was holding up his stump and looking reproachfully at me. He then went over to my bottles, which at that time I kept in my room, and he examined them carefully, after which he gave a gesture of anger and vanished. I realised that he had just died, and that he had come to claim my promise that I should keep his limb in safety for him.

'Well, there you have it all, Dr. Hardacre. Every night at the same hour for four years this performance has been repeated. It is a simple thing in itself, but it has worn me out like water dropping on a stone. It has brought a vile insomnia with it, for I cannot sleep now for the expectation of his coming. It has poisoned my old age and that of my wife, who has been the sharer in this great trouble. But there is the breakfast gong, and she will be waiting impatiently to know how it fared with you last night. We are both much indebted to you for your gallantry, for it takes something from the weight of our misfortune when we share it, even for a single night, with a friend, and it reassures us as to our sanity, which we are sometimes driven to question.'

This was the curious narrative which Sir Dominick confided to me—a story which to many would have appeared to be a grotesque impossibility, but which, after my experience of the night before and my previous knowledge of such things, I was prepared to accept as an absolute fact. I thought deeply over the matter, and brought the whole range of my reading and experience to bear upon it. After breakfast, I surprised my host and hostess by announcing that I was returning to London by the next train.

'My dear doctor,' cried Sir Dominick in great distress, 'you make me feel that I have been guilty of a gross breach of hospitality in intruding this unfortunate matter upon you. I should have borne my own burden.'

'It is, indeed, that matter which is taking me to London,' I answered; 'but you are mistaken, I assure you, if you think that my experience of last night was an unpleasant one to me. On the contrary, I am about to ask your permission to return in the evening and spend one more night in your laboratory. I am very eager to see this visitor once again.'

My uncle was exceedingly anxious to know what I was about to do, but fears of raising false hopes prevented me from telling him. I was back in my own consulting room a little after luncheon, and was confirming my memory of a passage in a recent book upon occultism which had arrested my attention when I read it.

In the case of earth-bound spirits [said my authority], some one dominant idea obsessing them at the hour of death is sufficient to hold them in this material world. They are the amphibia of this life and of the next, capable of passing from one to the other as the turtle passes from land to water. The causes which may bind a soul so strongly to a life which its body has abandoned are any violent emotion. Avarice, revenge, anxiety, love and pity have all been known to have this effect. As a rule it springs from some unfulfilled wish, and when the wish has been fulfilled the material bond relaxes. There are many cases upon record which show the singular persistence of these visitors, and also their disappearance when wishes have been fulfilled, or in some cases when a reasonable compromise has been effected.

'A *reasonable compromise effected*'—those were the words which I had brooded over all the morning, and which I now verified in the original. No actual atonement could be made here—but a reasonable compromise! I made my way as fast as a train could take me to the Shadwell Seamen's Hospital, where my old friend Jack Hewett was house-surgeon. Without explaining the situation I made him understand what it was that I wanted.

'A brown man's hand!' said he, in amazement. 'What in the world do you want that for?'

'Never mind. I'll tell you some day. I know that your wards are full of Indians.'

'I should think so. But a hand—' He thought a little and then struck a bell.

"Travers,' said he to a student-dresser 'what became of the hands of the Lascar which we took off yesterday? I mean the fellow from the East India Dock who got caught in the steam winch.'

'They are in the post-mortem room, sir.'

'Just pack one of them in antiseptics and give it to Dr. Hardacre.'

And so I found myself back at Rodenhurst before dinner with this curious outcome of my day in town. I still said nothing to Sir Dominick, but I slept that night in the laboratory, and I placed the Lascar's hand in one of the glass jars at the end of my couch.

So interested was I in the result of my experiment that sleep was out of the question. I sat with a shaded lamp beside me and waited patiently for my visitor. This time I saw him clearly from the first. He appeared beside the door, nebulous for an instant, and then hardening into as distinct an outline as any living man. The slippers beneath his grey gown were red and heelless, which accounted for the low shuffling sound which he made as he walked. As on the previous night he passed slowly along the line of bottles until he paused before that which contained the hand. He reached up to it, his whole figure quivering with expectation, took it down, examined it eagerly, and then, with a face which was convulsed with fury and disappointment, he hurled it down on the floor. There was a crash which resounded through the house, and when I looked up the mutilated Indian had disappeared. A moment later my door flew open and Sir Dominick rushed in.

'You are not hurt?' he cried.

'No—but deeply disappointed.'

He looked in astonishment at the splinters of glass and the brown hand lying upon the floor.

'Good God!' he cried. 'What is this?'

I told him my idea and its wretched sequel. He listened intently, but shook his head.

'It was well thought of,' said he, 'but I fear that there is no such easy end to my sufferings. But one thing I now insist upon. It is that you shall never again upon any pretext occupy this room. My fears that something might have happened to you—when I heard that crash—have been the most acute of all the agonies which I have undergone. I will not expose myself to a repetition of it.'

He allowed me, however, to spend the remainder of that night where I was, and I lay there worrying over the problem and lamenting my own failure. With the first light of morning there was the Lascar's hand still lying upon the floor to remind me of my fiasco. I lay looking at it—and as I lay suddenly an idea flew like a bullet through my head and brought me quivering with excitement out of my couch. I raised the grim relic from where it had fallen. Yes, it was indeed so. The hand was the left hand of the Lascar.

By the first train I was on my way to town, and hurried at once to the Seamen's Hospital. I remembered that both hands of the Lascar had been amputated, but I was terrified lest the precious organ which I was in search of might have been already consumed in the crematory. My suspense was soon ended. It had still been preserved in the post-mortem room. And so I returned to Rodenhurst in the evening with my mission accomplished and the material for a fresh experiment.

But Sir Dominick Holden would not hear of my occupying the laboratory again. To all my entreaties he turned a deaf ear. It offended his sense of hospitality, and he could no longer permit it. I left the hand, therefore, as I had done its fellow the night before, and I occupied a comfortable bedroom in another portion of the house, some distance from the scene of my adventures.

But in spite of that my sleep was not destined to be uninterrupted. In the dead of night my host burst into my room, a lamp in his hand. His huge, gaunt figure was enveloped in a loose dressing-gown, and his whole appearance might certainly have seemed more formidable to a weak-nerved man than that of the Indian of the night before. But it was not his entrance so much as his expression which amazed me. He had turned suddenly younger by twenty years at the least. His eyes were shining, his features radiant, and he waved one hand in triumph over his head. I sat up astounded, staring sleepily at this extraordinary visitor. But his words soon drove the sleep from my eyes.

'We have done it! We have succeeded!' he shouted. 'My dear Hardacre, how can I ever in this world repay you?'

'You don't mean to say that it is all right?'

'Indeed I do. I was sure that you would not mind being awakened to hear such blessed news.'

'Mind! I should think not indeed. But is it really certain?'

'I have no doubt whatever upon the point. I owe you such a debt, my dear nephew, as I have never owed a man before, and never expected to. What can I possibly do for you that is commensurate? Providence must have sent you to my rescue. You have saved both my reason and my life, for another six months of this must have seen me either in a cell or a coffin. And my wife—it was wearing her out before my eyes. Never could I have believed that any human being could have lifted this burden off me.' He seized my hand and wrung it in his bony grip.

'It was only an experiment—a forlorn hope—but I am delighted from my heart that it has succeeded. But how do you know that it is all right? Have you seen something?'

He seated himself at the foot of my bed.

'I have seen enough,' said he. 'It satisfies me that I shall be troubled no more. What has passed is easily told. You know that at a certain hour this creature always comes to me. Tonight he arrived at the usual time, and aroused me with even more violence than is his custom. I can only surmise that his disappointment of last night increased the bitterness of his anger against me. He looked angrily at me, and then went on his usual round. But in a few minutes I saw him, for the first time since this persecution began, return to my chamber. He was smiling, I saw the gleam of his white teeth through the dim light. He stood facing me at the end of my bed and three times he made the low, Eastern salaam which is their solemn leave-taking. And the third time that he bowed he raised his arms over his head, and I saw his *two* hands outstretched in the air. So he vanished—as I believe, for ever.'

So that is the curious experience which won me the affection and the gratitude of my celebrated uncle, the famous Indian surgeon. His anticipations were realised, and never again was he disturbed by the visits of the restless hillman in search of his lost member. Sir Dominick and Lady Holden spent a very happy old age, unclouded, so far as I know, by any trouble, and they finally died during the great influenza epidemic within a few weeks of each other. In his lifetime he always turned to me for advice in everything which concerned that English life of which he knew so little; and I aided him also in the purchase and development of his estates. It was no great surprise to me, therefore, that I found myself eventually promoted over the heads of five exasperated cousins, and changed in a single day from a hard-working country doctor into the head of an important Wiltshire family. I, at least, have reason to bless the memory of the man with the brown hand, and the day when I was fortunate enough to relieve Rodenhurst of his unwelcome presence.

II

&

"The Adventure of the Empty House"
(1903)

I
t was in the spring of the year 1894 that all London was interested,
and the fashionable world dismayed, by the murder of the Honourable
Ronald Adair under most unusual and inexplicable circumstances. The
public has already learned those particulars of the crime which came
out in the police investigation, but a good deal was suppressed upon
that occasion, since the case for the prosecution was so overwhelmingly
strong that it was not necessary to bring forward all the facts. Only now,
at the end of nearly ten years, am I allowed to supply those missing
links which make up the whole of that remarkable chain. The crime was
of interest in itself, but that interest was as nothing to me compared to
the inconceivable sequel, which afforded me the greatest shock and surprise of any event in my adventurous life. Even now, after this long interval, I find myself thrilling as I think of it, and feeling once more that
sudden flood of joy, amazement, and incredulity which utterly submerged my mind. Let me say to that public, which has shown some interest in those glimpses which I have occasionally given them of the
thoughts and actions of a very remarkable man, that they are not to
blame me if I have not shared my knowledge with them, for I should
have considered it my first duty to do so, had I not been barred by a
positive prohibition from his own lips, which was only withdrawn upon
the third of last month.

It can be imagined that my close intimacy with Sherlock Holmes had interested me deeply in crime, and that after his disappearance I never failed to read with care the various problems which came before the public. And I even attempted, more than once, for my own private satisfaction, to employ his methods in their solution, though with indifferent success. There was none, however, which appealed to me like this tragedy of Ronald Adair. As I read the evidence at the inquest, which led up to a verdict of willful murder against some person or persons unknown, I realized more clearly than I had ever done the loss which the community had sustained by the death of Sherlock Holmes. There were points about this strange business which would, I was sure, have specially appealed to him, and the efforts of the police would have been supplemented, or more probably anticipated, by the trained observation and the alert mind of the first criminal agent in Europe. All day, as I drove upon my round, I turned over the case in my mind and found no explanation which appeared to me to be adequate. At the risk of telling a twice-told tale, I will recapitulate the facts as they were known to the public at the conclusion of the inquest.

The Honourable Ronald Adair was second son of the Earl of Maynooth, at that time governor of one of the Australian colonies. Adair's mother had returned from Australia to undergo the operation for cataract, and she, her son Ronald, and her daughter Hilda were living together at 427 Park Lane. The youth moved in the best society—had, so far as was known, no enemies and no particular vices. He had been engaged to Miss Edith Woodley, of Carstairs, but the engagement had been broken off by mutual consent some months before, and there was no sign that it had left any very profound feeling behind it. For the rest of the man's life moved in a narrow and conventional circle, for his habits were quiet and his nature unemotional. Yet it was upon this easy-going young aristocrat that death came, in most strange and unexpected form, between the hours of ten and eleven-twenty on the night of March 30, 1894.

Ronald Adair was fond of cards—playing continually but never for such stakes as would hurt him. He was a member of the Baldwin, the Cavendish, and the Bagatelle card clubs. It was shown that, after dinner on the day of his death, he had played a rubber of whist at the latter club. He had also played there in the afternoon. The evidence of those who had played with him—Mr. Murray, Sir John Hardy, and Colonel Moran—showed that the game was whist, and that there was a fairly equal fall of the cards. Adair might have lost five pounds, but not more. His fortune was a considerable one, and such a loss could not in any way affect him. He had played nearly every day at one club or other, but he was a cautious player, and usually rose a winner. It came out in evidence that, in partnership with Colonel Moran, he had actually won as much as four hundred and twenty pounds in a sitting, some weeks before, from Godfrey Milner and Lord Balmoral. So much for his recent history as it came out at the inquest.

On the evening of the crime, he returned from the club exactly at ten. His mother and sister were out spending the evening with a relation. The servant deposed that she heard him enter the front room on the second floor, generally used as his sitting-room. She had lit a fire there, and as it smoked she had opened the window. No sound was heard from the room until eleven-twenty, the hour of the return of Lady Maynooth and her daughter. Desiring to say good-night, she attempted to enter her son's room. The door was locked on the inside, and no answer could be got to their cries and knocking. Help was obtained, and the door forced. The unfortunate young man was found lying near the table. His head had been horribly mutilated by an expanding revolver bullet, but no weapon of any sort was to be found in the room. On the table lay two banknotes for ten pounds each and seventeen pounds ten in silver and gold, the money arranged in little piles of varying amount. There were some figures also upon a sheet of paper, with the names of some club friends opposite to them, from which it was conjectured that before his death he was endeavoring to make out his losses or winnings at cards.

A minute examination of the circumstances served only to make the case more complex. In the first place, no reason could be given why the young man should have fastened the door upon the inside. There was the possibility that the murderer had done this, and had afterwards escaped by the window. The drop was at least twenty feet, however, and a bed of crocuses in full bloom lay beneath. Neither the flowers nor the earth showed any sign of having been disturbed, nor were there any marks upon the narrow strip of grass which separated the house from the road. Apparently, therefore, it was the young man himself who had fastened the door. But how did he come by his death? No one could have climbed up to the window without leaving traces. Suppose a man had fired through the window, he would indeed be a remarkable shot who could with a revolver inflict so deadly a wound. Again, Park Lane is a frequented thoroughfare; there is a cab stand within a hundred yards of the house. No one had heard a shot. And yet there was a dead man, and there the revolver bullet, which had mushroomed out, as soft-nosed bullets will, and so inflicted a wound which must have caused instantaneous death. Such were the circumstances of the Park Lane Mystery, which were further complicated by entire absence of motive, since, as I have said, young Adair was not known to have any enemy, and no attempt had been made to remove the money or valuables in the room.

All day I turned these facts over in my mind, endeavouring to hit upon some theory which would reconcile them all, and to find that line of least resistance which my poor friend had declared to be the starting-point of every investigation. I confess that I made little progress. In the evening I strolled across the Park, and found myself about six o'clock at the Oxford Street end of Park Lane. A group of loafers upon the pavements, all staring up at a particular window, directed me to the house which I had come to see. A tall, thin man with coloured glasses, whom I strongly suspected of being a plain-clothes detective, was pointing out some theory of his own, while the others crowded round to listen to what he said. I got as near him as I could, but his observations seemed to me to be absurd, so I withdrew again in some disgust. As I did so I struck against an elderly, deformed man, who had been behind me, and I knocked down several books which he was carrying. I remember that as I picked them up, I observed the title of one of them, *The Origin of Tree Worship*, and it struck me that the fellow must be some poor bibliophile, who, either as a trade or as a hobby, was a collector of obscure volumes. I endeavoured to apologize for the accident, but it was evident that these books which I had so unfortunately maltreated were very precious objects in the eyes of their owner. With a snarl of contempt he turned upon his heel, and I saw his curved back and white side-whiskers disappear among the throng.

My observations of No. 427 Park Lane did little to clear up the problem in which I was interested. The house was separated from the street by a low wall and railing, the whole not more than five feet high. It was perfectly easy, therefore, for anyone to get into the garden, but the window was entirely inaccessible, since there was no waterpipe or anything which could help the most active man to climb it. More puzzled than ever, I retraced my steps to Kensington. I had not been in my study five minutes when the maid entered to say that a person desired to see me. To my astonishment it was none other than my strange old book collector, his sharp, wizened face peering out from a frame of white hair, and his precious volumes, a dozen of them at least, wedged under his right arm.

"You're surprised to see me, sir," said he, in a strange, croaking voice.

I acknowledged that I was.

"Well, I've a conscience, sir, and when I chanced to see you go into this house, as I came hobbling after you, I thought to myself, I'll just step in and see that kind gentleman, and tell him that if I was a bit gruff in my manner there was not any harm meant, and that I am much obliged to him for picking up my books."

"You make too much of a trifle," said I. "May I ask how you knew who I was?"

"Well, sir, if it isn't too great a liberty, I am a neighbour of yours, for you'll find my little bookshop at the corner of Church Street, and very happy to see you, I am sure. Maybe you collect yourself, sir. Here's British Birds, and Catullus, and The Holy War—a bargain, every one of them. With five volumes you could just fill that gap on that second shelf. It looks untidy, does it not, sir?"

I moved my head to look at the cabinet behind me. When I turned again, Sherlock Holmes was standing smiling at me across my study table. I rose to my feet, stared at him for some seconds in utter amazement, and then it appears that I must have fainted for the first and the last time in my life. Certainly a gray mist swirled before my eyes, and when it cleared I found my collar-ends undone and the tingling aftertaste of brandy upon my lips. Holmes was bending over my chair, his flask in his hand.

"My dear Watson," said the well-remembered voice. "I owe you a thousand apologies. I had no idea that you would be so affected."

I gripped him by the arms.

"Holmes!" I cried. "Is it really you? Can it indeed be that you are alive? Is it possible that you succeeded in climbing out of that awful abyss?"

"Wait a moment," said he. "Are you sure that you are really fit to discuss things? I have given you a serious shock by my unnecessarily dramatic reappearance."

"I am all right, but indeed, Holmes, I can hardly believe my eyes. Good heavens! To think that you—you of all men—should be standing in my study." Again I gripped him by the sleeve, and felt the thin, sinewy arm beneath it. "Well, you're not a spirit, anyhow," said I. "My dear chap, I'm overjoyed to see you. Sit down, and tell me how you came alive out of that dreadful chasm."

He sat opposite to me, and lit a cigarette in his old, nonchalant manner. He was dressed in the seedy frockcoat of the book merchant, but the rest of that individual lay in a pile of white hair and old books upon the table. Holmes looked even thinner and keener than of old, but there was a dead-white tinge in his aquiline face which told me that his life recently had not been a healthy one.

"I am glad to stretch myself, Watson," said he. "It is no joke when a tall man has to take a foot off his stature for several hours on end. Now, my dear fellow, in the matter of these explanations, we have, if I may ask for your coöperation, a hard and dangerous night's work in front of us. Perhaps it would be better if I gave you an account of the whole situation when that work is finished."

"I am full of curiosity. I should much prefer to hear now."

"You'll come with me to-night?"

"When you like and where you like."

"This is, indeed, like the old days. We shall have time for a mouthful of dinner before we need go. Well, then, about that chasm. I had no serious difficulty in getting out of it. For the very simple reason that I never was in it."

"You never were in it?"

"No, Watson I never was in it. My note to you was absolutely genuine. I had little doubt that I had come to the end of my career when I perceived the somewhat sinister figure of the late Professor Moriarty standing upon the narrow pathway which led to safety. I read an inexorable purpose in his gray eyes. I exchanged some remarks with him, therefore, and obtained his courteous permission to write the short note which you afterwards received. I left it with my cigarette-box and my stick, and I walked along the pathway, Moriarty still at my heels. When I reached the end I stood at bay. He drew no weapon, but he rushed at me and threw his long arms around me. He knew that his own game was up, and was only anxious to revenge himself upon me. We tottered together upon the brink of the fall. I have some knowledge, however, of baritsu, or the Japanese system of wrestling, which has more than once been very useful to me. I slipped through his grip, and he with a horrible scream kicked madly for a few seconds, and clawed the air with both his hands. But for all his efforts he could not get his balance, and over he went. With my face over the brink, I saw him fall for a long way. Then he struck a rock, bounded off, and splashed into the water."

I listened with amazement to this explanation, which Holmes delivered between the puffs of his cigarette.

"But the tracks!" I cried. "I saw, with my own eyes, that two went down the path and none returned."

"It came about in this way. The instant that the Professor had disappeared, it struck me what a really extraordinary lucky chance Fate had placed in my way. I knew that Moriarty was not the only man who had sworn my death. There were at least three others whose desire for vengeance upon me would only be increased by the death of their leader. They were all most dangerous men. One or other would certainly get me. On the other hand, if all the world was convinced that I was dead they would take liberties, these men, they would soon lay themselves open, and sooner or later I could destroy them. Then it would be time for me to announce that I was still in the land of the living. So rapidly does the brain act that I believe I had thought this all out before Professor Moriarty had reached the bottom of the Reichenbach Fall.

"I stood up and examined the rocky wall behind me. In your picturesque account of the matter, which I read with great interest some months later, you assert that the wall was sheer. That was not literally true. A few small footholds presented themselves, and there was some indication of a ledge. The cliff is so high that to climb it all was an obvious impossibility, and it was equally impossible to make my way along the wet path without leaving some tracks. I might, it is true, have reversed my boots, as I have done on similar occasions, but the sight of three sets of tracks in one direction would certainly have suggested a deception. On the whole, then, it was best that I should risk the climb. It was not a pleasant business, Watson. The fall roared beneath me. I am not a fanciful person, but I give you my word that I seemed to hear Moriarty's voice screaming to me out of the abyss. A mistake would have been fatal. More than once, as tufts of grass came out in my hand or my foot slipped in the wet notches of the rock, I thought that I was gone. But I struggled upward, and at last I reached a ledge several feet deep and covered with soft green moss, where I could lie unseen, in the most perfect comfort. There I was stretched, when you, my dear Watson, and all your following were investigating in the most sympathetic and inefficient manner the circumstances of my death.

"At last, when you had all formed your inevitable and totally erroneous conclusions, you departed for the hotel, and I was left alone. I had imagined that I had reached the end of my adventures, but a very unexpected occurrence showed me that there were surprises still in store for me. A huge rock, falling from above, boomed past me, struck the path, and bounded over into the chasm. For an instant I thought that it was an accident, but a moment later, looking up, I saw a man's head against the darkening sky, and another stone struck the very ledge upon which I was stretched, within a foot of my head. Of course, the meaning of this was obvious. Moriarty had not been alone. A confederate—and even that one glance had told me how dangerous a man that confederate—had kept guard while the Professor had attacked me. From a distance, unseen by me, he had been a witness of his friend's death and of my escape. He had waited, and then making his way round to the top of the cliff, he had endeavoured to succeed where his comrade had failed.

"I did not take long to think about it, Watson. Again I saw that grim face look over the cliff, and I knew that it was the precursor of another stone. I scrambled down on to the path. I don't think I could have done it in cold blood. It was a hundred times more difficult than getting up. But I had no time to think of the danger, for another stone sang past me as I hung by my hands from the edge. Halfway down I slipped, but, by the blessing of God, I landed, torn and bleeding, upon the path. I took to my heels, did ten miles over the mountains in the darkness, and a week later I found myself in Florence, with the certainty that no one in the world knew what had become of me.

"I had only one confidant—my brother Mycroft. I owe you many apologies, my dear Watson, but it was all-important that it should be thought I was dead, and it is quite certain that you would not have written so convincing an account of my unhappy end had you not yourself thought that it was true. Several times during the last three years I have taken up my pen to write to you, but always I feared lest your affectionate regard for me should tempt you to some indiscretion which would betray my secret. For that reason I turned away from you this evening when you upset my books, for I was in danger at the time, and any show of surprise and emotion upon your part might have drawn attention to my identity and led to the most deplorable and irreparable results. As to Mycroft, I had to confide in him in order to obtain the money which I needed. The course of events in London did not run so well as I hoped, for the trial of the Moriarty gang left two of its most dangerous members, my own most vindictive enemies, at liberty. I travelled for two years in Tibet, therefore, and amused myself by visiting Lhassa, and spending some days with the head lama. You may have read of the remarkable explorations of a Norwegian named Sigerson, but I am sure that it never occurred to you that you were receiving news of your friend. I then passed through Persia, looked in at Mecca, and paid a short but interesting visit to the Khalifa at Khartoum, the results of which I have communicated to the Foreign Office. Returning to France, I spent some months in a research into the coal-tar derivatives, which I conducted in a laboratory at Montpellier, in the south of France. Having concluded this to my satisfaction and learning that only one of my enemies was now left in London, I was about to return when my movements were hastened by the news of this very remarkable Park Lane Mystery, which not only appealed to me by its own merits, but which seemed to offer some most peculiar personal opportunities. I came over at once to London, called in my own person at Baker Street, threw Mrs. Hudson into violent hysterics, and found that Mycroft had preserved my rooms and my papers exactly as they had always been. So it was, my dear Watson, that at two o'clock to-day I found myself in my old armchair in my own old room, and only wishing that I could have seen my old friend Watson in the other chair which he has so often adorned."

Such was the remarkable narrative to which I listened on that April evening—a narrative which would have been utterly incredible to me had it not been confirmed by the actual sight of the tall, spare figure and the keen, eager face, which I had never thought to see again. In some manner he had learned of my own sad bereavement, and his sympathy was shown in his manner rather than in his words. "Work is the best antidote to sorrow, my dear Watson," said he; "and I have a piece of work for us both to-night which, if we can bring it to a successful conclusion, will in itself justify a man's life on this planet." In vain I begged him to tell me more. "You will hear and see enough before morning," he answered. "We have three years of the past to discuss. Let that suffice until half-past nine, when we start upon the notable adventure of the empty house."

It was indeed like old times when, at that hour, I found myself seated beside him in a hansom, my revolver in my pocket, and the thrill of adventure in my heart. Holmes was cold and stern and silent. As the gleam of the streetlamps flashed upon his austere features, I saw that his brows were drawn down in thought and his thin lips compressed. I knew not what wild beast we were about to hunt down in the dark jungle of criminal London, but I was well assured, from the bearing of this master huntsman, that the adventure was a most grave one—while the sardonic smile which occasionally broke through his ascetic gloom boded little good for the object of our quest.

I had imagined that we were bound for Baker Street, but Holmes stopped the cab at the corner of Cavendish Square. I observed that as he stepped out he gave a most searching glance to right and left, and at every subsequent street corner he took the utmost pains to assure that he was not followed. Our route was certainly a singular one. Holmes's knowledge of the byways of London was extraordinary, and on this occasion he passed rapidly and with an assured step through a network of mews and stables, the very existence of which I had never known. We emerged at last into a small road, lined with old, gloomy houses, which led us into Manchester Street, and so to Blandford Street. Here he turned swiftly down a narrow passage, passed though a wooden gate into a deserted yard, and then opened with a key the back door of a house. We entered together, and he closed it behind us.

The place was pitch dark, but it was evident to me that it was an empty house. Our feet creaked and crackled over the bare planking, and my outstretched hand touched a wall from which the paper was hanging in ribbons. Holmes's cold, thin fingers closed round my wrist and led me forward down a long hall, until I dimly saw the murky fanlight over the door. Here Holmes turned suddenly to the right, and we found ourselves in a large, square, empty room, heavily shadowed in the corners, but faintly lit in the centre from the lights of the street beyond. There was no lamp near, and the window was thick with dust, so that we could only just discern each other's figures within. My companion put his hand upon my shoulder and his lips close to my ear.

"Do you know where we are?" he whispered.

"Surely that is Baker Street," I answered, staring through the dim window.

"Exactly. We are in Camden House, which stands opposite to our own old quarters."

"But why are we here?"

"Because it commands so excellent a view of that picturesque pile. Might I trouble you, my dear Watson, to draw a little nearer to the window, taking every precaution not to show yourself, and then to look up at our old rooms—the starting-point of so many of your little fairy-tales? We will see if my three years of absence have entirely taken away my power to surprise you."

I crept forward and looked across at the familiar window. As my eyes fell upon it, I gave a gasp and a cry of amazement. The blind was down, and a strong light was burning in the room. The shadow of a man who was seated in a chair within was thrown in hard, black outline upon the luminous screen of the window. There was no mistaking the poise of the head, the squareness of the shoulders, the sharpness of the features. The face was turned half-round, and the effect was that of one of those black silhouettes which our grandparents loved to frame. It was a perfect reproduction of Holmes. So amazed was I that I threw out my hand to make sure that the man himself was standing beside me. He was quivering with silent laughter.

"Well?" said he.

"Good heavens!" I cried. "It is marvellous."

"I trust that age doth not wither nor custom stale my infinite variety," said he, and I recognized in his voice the joy and pride which the artist takes in his own creation. "It really is rather like me, is it not?"

"I should be prepared to swear that it was you."

"The credit of the execution is due to Monsieur Oscar Meunier, of Grenoble, who spent some days in doing the moulding. It is a bust in wax. The rest I arranged myself during my visit to Baker Street this afternoon."

"But why?"

"Because, my dear Watson, I had the strongest possible reason for wishing certain people to think that I was there when I was really elsewhere."

"And you thought the rooms were watched?"

"I *knew* that they were watched."

"By whom?"

"By my old enemies, Watson. By the charming society whose leader lies in the Reichenbach Fall. You must remember that they knew, and only they knew, that I was still alive. Sooner or later they believed that I should come back to my rooms. They watched them continuously, and this morning they saw me arrive."

"How do you know?"

"Because I recognized their sentinel when I glanced out of my window. He is a harmless enough fellow, Parker by name, a garroter by trade, and a remarkable performer upon the jew's-harp. I cared nothing for him. But I cared a great deal for the much more formidable person who was behind him, the bosom friend of Moriarty, the man who dropped the rocks over the cliff, the most cunning and dangerous criminal in London. That is the man who is after me to-night, Watson, and that is the man who is quite unaware that we are after *him!*"

My friend's plans were gradually revealing themselves. From this convenient retreat, the watchers were being watched and the trackers tracked. That angular shadow up yonder was the bait, and we were the hunters. In silence we stood together in the darkness and watched the hurrying figures who passed and repassed in front of us. Holmes was silent and motionless; but I could tell that he was keenly alert, and that his eyes were fixed intently upon the stream of passers-by. It was a bleak and boisterous night, and the wind whistled shrilly down the long street. Many people were moving to and fro, most of them muffled in their coats and cravats. Once or twice it seemed to me that I had seen the same figure before, and I especially noticed two men who appeared to be sheltering themselves from the wind in the doorway of a house some distance up the street. I tried to draw my companion's attention to them; but he gave a little ejaculation of impatience, and continued to stare into the street. More than once he fidgeted with his feet and tapped rapidly with his fingers upon the wall. It was evident to me that he was becoming uneasy, and that his plans were not working out altogether as he had hoped. At last, as midnight approached and the street gradually cleared, he paced up and down the room in uncontrollable agitation. I was about to make some remark to him, when I raised my eyes to the lighted window, and again experienced almost as great a surprise as before. I clutched Holmes's arm, and pointed upward.

"The shadow has moved!" I cried.

It was indeed no longer the profile, but the back, which was turned towards us.

Three years had certainly not smoothed the asperities of his temper or his impatience with a less active intelligence than his own.

"Of course it has moved," said he. "Am I such a farcical bungler, Watson, that I should erect an obvious dummy, and expect that some of the sharpest men in Europe would be deceived by it? We have been in this room two hours, and Mrs. Hudson has made some change in that figure eight times, or once in every quarter of an hour. She works it from the front, so that her shadow may never be seen. Ah!" He drew in his breath with a shrill, excited intake. In the dim light I saw his head thrown forward, his whole attitude rigid with attention. Outside the street was absolutely deserted. Those two men might still be crouching in the doorway, but I could no longer see them. All was still and dark, save only that brilliant yellow screen in front of us with the black figure outlined upon its centre. Again in the utter silence I heard that thin, sibilant note which spoke of intense suppressed excitement. An instant later he pulled me back into the blackest corner of the room and I felt his warning hand upon my lips. The fingers which clutched me were quivering. Never had I known my friend more moved, and yet the dark street still stretched lonely and motionless before us.

But suddenly I was aware of that which his keener senses had already distinguished. A low, stealthy sound came to my ear, not from the direction of Baker Street, but from the back of the very house in which we lay concealed. A door opened and shut. An instant later steps crept down the passage—steps which were meant to be silent, but which reverberated harshly through the empty house. Holmes crouched back against the wall, and I did the same, my hand closing upon the handle of my revolver. Peering through the gloom, I saw the vague outline of a man, a shade blacker than the blackness of the open door. He stood for an instant, and then he crept forward, crouching, menacing, into the room. He was within three yards of us, this sinister figure, and I had braced myself to meet his spring, before I realized that he had no idea of our presence. He passed close beside us, stole over to the window, and very softly and noiselessly raised it for half a foot. As he sank to the level of this opening, the light of the street, no longer dimmed by the dusty glass, fell full upon his face. The man seemed to be beside himself with excitement. His two eyes shone like stars, and his features were working convulsively. He was an elderly man, with a thin, projecting nose, a high, bald forehead, and a huge grizzled moustache. An opera hat was pushed to the back of his head, and an evening dress shirt-front gleamed out through his open overcoat. His face was gaunt and swarthy, scored with deep, savage lines. In his hand he carried what appeared to be a stick, but as he laid it down upon the floor it gave a metallic clang. Then from the pocket of his overcoat he drew a bulky object, and he busied himself in some task which ended with a loud, sharp click, as if a spring or bolt had fallen into its place. Still kneeling upon the floor he bent forward and threw all his weight and strength upon some lever, with the result that there came a long, whirling, grinding noise, ending once more in a powerful click. He straightened himself then, and I saw that what he held in his hand was a sort of gun, with a curiously misshapen butt. He opened it at the breech, put something in, and snapped the breech-lock. Then, crouching down, he rested the end of the barrel upon the ledge of the open window, and I saw his long moustache droop over the stock and his eye gleam as it peered along the sights. I heard a little sigh of satisfaction as he cuddled the butt into his shoulder, and saw that amazing target, the black man on the yellow ground, standing clear at the end of his foresight. For an instant he was rigid and motionless. Then his finger tightened on the trigger. There was a strange, loud whiz, and a long, silvery tinkle of broken glass. At that instant Holmes sprang like a tiger on to the marksman's back, and hurled him flat upon his face. He was up again in a moment, and with convulsive strength he seized Holmes by the throat, but I struck him on the head with the butt of my revolver, and he dropped again upon the floor. I fell upon him, and as I held him my comrade blew a shrill call upon a whistle. There was the clatter of running feet upon the pavement, and two policemen in uniform, with one plain-clothes detective, rushed through the front entrance and into the room.

"That you, Lestrade?" said Holmes.

"Yes, Mr. Holmes. I took the job myself. It's good to see you back in London, sir."

"I think you want a little unofficial help. Three undetected murders in one year won't do, Lestrade. But you handled the Molesey Mystery with less than your usual—that's to say, you handled it fairly well."

We had all risen to our feet, our prisoner breathing hard, with a stalwart constable on each side of him. Already a few loiterers had begun to collect in the street. Holmes stepped up to the window, closed it, and dropped the blinds. Lestrade had produced two candles, and the policemen had uncovered their lanterns. I was able at last to have a good look at our prisoner.

It was a tremendously virile and yet sinister face which was turned towards us. With the brow of a philosopher above and the jaw of a sensualist below, the man must have started with great capacities for good or for evil. But one could not look upon his cruel blue eyes, with their drooping, cynical lids, or upon the fierce, aggressive nose and the threatening, deep-lined brow, without reading Nature's plainest danger-signals. He took no heed of any of us, but his eyes were fixed upon Holmes's face with an expression in which hatred and amazement were equally blended. "You fiend!" he kept on muttering. "You clever, clever fiend!"

"Ah, Colonel!" said Holmes, arranging his rumpled collar. "'Journeys end in lovers' meetings,' as the old play says. I don't think I have had the pleasure of seeing you since you favoured me with those attentions as I lay on the ledge above the Reichenbach Fall."

The colonel still stared at my friend like a man in a trance. "You cunning, cunning fiend!" was all that he could say.

"I have not introduced you yet," said Holmes. "This, gentlemen, is Colonel Sebastian Moran, once of Her Majesty's Indian Army, and the best heavy-game shot that our Eastern Empire has ever produced. I believe I am correct, Colonel, in saying that your bag of tigers still remains unrivalled?"

The fierce old man said nothing, but still glared at my companion. With his savage eyes and bristling moustache he was wonderfully like a tiger himself.

"I wonder that my very simple stratagem could deceive so old a *shikari*," said Holmes. "It must be very familiar to you. Have you not tethered a young kid under a tree, lain above it with your rifle, and waited for the bait to bring up your tiger? This empty house is my tree, and you are my tiger. You have possibly had other guns in reserve in case there should be several tigers, or in the unlikely supposition of your own aim failing you. There," he pointed around, "are my other guns. The parallel is exact."

Colonel Moran sprang forward with a snarl of rage, but the constables dragged him back. The fury upon his face was terrible to look at.

"I confess that you had one small surprise for me," said Holmes. "I did not anticipate that you would yourself make use of this empty house and this convenient front window. I had imagined you as operating from the street, where my friend Lestrade and his merry men were awaiting you. With that exception, all has gone as I expected."

Colonel Moran turned to the official detective.

"You may or may not have just cause for arresting me," said he, "but at least there can be no reason why I should submit to the gibes of this person. If I am in the hands of the law, let things be done in a legal way."

"Well, that's reasonable enough," said Lestrade. "Nothing further you have to say, Mr. Holmes, before we go?"

Holmes had picked up the powerful air-gun from the floor, and was examining its mechanism.

"An admirable and unique weapon," said he, "noiseless and of tremendous power: I knew Von Herder, the blind German mechanic, who constructed it to the order of the late Professor Moriarty. For years I have been aware of its existence, though I have never before had the opportunity of handling it. I commend it very specially to your attention, Lestrade, and also the bullets which fit it."

"You can trust us to look after that, Mr. Holmes," said Lestrade, as the whole party moved towards the door. "Anything further to say?"

"Only to ask what charge you intend to prefer?"

"What charge, sir? Why, of course, the attempted murder of Mr. Sherlock Holmes."

"Not so, Lestrade. I do not propose to appear in the matter at all. To you, and to you only, belongs the credit of the remarkable arrest which you have effected. Yes, Lestrade, I congratulate you! With your usual happy mixture of cunning and audacity, you have got him."

"Got him! Got whom, Mr. Holmes?"

"The man that the whole force has been seeking in vain—Colonel Sebastian Moran, who shot the Honourable Ronald Adair with an expanding bullet from an air-gun through the open window of the second-floor front of No. 427 Park Lane, upon the thirtieth of last month. That's the charge, Lestrade. And now, Watson, if you can endure the draught from a broken window, I think that half an hour in my study over a cigar may afford you some profitable amusement."

Our old chambers had been left unchanged through the supervision of Mycroft Holmes and the immediate care of Mrs. Hudson. As I entered I saw, it is true, an unwonted tidiness, but the old landmarks were all in their place. There were the chemical corner and the acid-stained, deal-topped table. There upon a shelf was the row of formidable scrap-books and books of reference which many of our fellow-citizens would have been so glad to burn. The diagrams, the violin-case, and the pipe-rack—even the Persian slipper which contained the tobacco—all met my eyes as I glanced round me. There were two occupants of the room—one, Mrs. Hudson, who beamed upon us both as we entered—the other, the strange dummy which had played so important a part in the evening's adventures. It was a wax-coloured model of my friend, so admirably done that it was a perfect facsimile. It stood on a small pedestal table with an old dressing-gown of Holmes's so draped round it that the illusion from the street was absolutely perfect.

"I hope you observed all precautions, Mrs. Hudson?" said Holmes.

"I went to it on my knees, sir, just as you told me."

"Excellent. You carried the thing out very well. Did you observe where the bullet went?"

"Yes, sir. I'm afraid it has spoilt your beautiful bust, for it passed right through the head and flattened itself on the wall. I picked it up from the carpet. Here it is!"

Holmes held it out to me. "A soft revolver bullet, as you perceive, Watson. There's genius in that, for who would expect to find such a thing fired from an air-gun? All right, Mrs. Hudson. I am much obliged for your assistance. And now, Watson, let me see you in your old seat once more, for there are several points which I should like to discuss with you."

He had thrown off the seedy frockcoat, and now he was the Holmes of old in the mouse-coloured dressing-gown which he took from his effigy.

"The old *shikari*'s nerves have not lost their steadiness, nor his eyes their keenness," said he, with a laugh, as he inspected the shattered forehead of his bust.

"Plumb in the middle of the back of the head and smack through the brain. He was the best shot in India, and I expected that there are few better in London. Have you heard the name?"

"No, I have not."

"Well, well, such is fame! But then, if I remember right, you had not heard the name of Professor James Moriarty, who had one of the great brains of the century. Just give me down my index of biographies from the shelf."

He turned over the pages lazily, leaning back in his chair and blowing great clouds from his cigar.

"My collection of M's is a fine one," said he. "Moriarty himself is enough to make any letter illustrious, and here is Morgan the poisoner, and Merridew of abominable memory, and Mathews, who knocked out my left canine in the waiting-room at Charing Cross, and finally, here is our friend of to-night."

He handed over the book, and I read:

Moran, Sebastian, Colonel. Unemployed, Formerly 1st Bangalore Pioneers. Born London, 1840. Son of Sir Augustus Morgan, D.B., once British Minister to Persia. Educated Eton and Oxford. Served in Jowaki Campaign, Afghan Campaign, Charasiab (despatches), Sherpur, and Cabul. Author of *Heavy Game of the Western Himalayas* (1881); *Three Months in the Jungle* (1884). Address: Conduit Street. Clubs: The Anglo-Indian, the Tankerville, the Bagatelle Card Club.

On the margin was written, in Holmes's precise hand:

The second most dangerous man in London.

"This is astonishing," said I, and I handed back the volume. "This man's career is that of an honourable soldier."

"It is true," Holmes answered. "Up to a certain point he did well. He was always a man of iron nerve, and the story is still told in India how he crawled down a drain after a wounded man-eating tiger. There are some trees, Watson, which grow to a certain height, and then suddenly develop some unsightly eccentricity. You will see it often in humans. I have a theory that the individual represents in his development the whole procession of his ancestors, and that such a sudden turn to good or evil stands for some strong influence which came into the line of his pedigree. The person becomes, as it were, the epitome of the history of his own family."

"It is surely rather fanciful."

"Well, I don't insist upon it. Whatever the cause, Colonel Moran began to go wrong. Without any open scandal, he still made India too hot to hold him. He retired, came to London, and again acquired an evil name. It was at this time that he was sought out by Professor Moriarty, to whom for a time he was chief of the staff. Moriarty supplied him liberally with money, and used him only in one or two very high-class jobs, which no ordinary criminal could have undertaken. You may have some recollection of the death of Mrs. Steward, of Lauder, in 1887. Not? Well, I am sure Moran was at the bottom of it, but nothing could be proved. So cleverly was the colonel concealed that, even when the Moriarty gang was broken up, we could not incriminate him. You remember at that date, when I called upon you in your rooms, how I put up the shutters for fear of air-guns? No doubt you thought me fanciful. I knew exactly what I was doing, for I knew of the existence of this remarkable gun, and I knew also that one of the best shots in the world would be behind it. When we were in Switzerland he followed us with Moriarty, and it was undoubtedly he who gave me that evil five minutes on the Reichenbach ledge.

"You may think that I read the papers with some attention during my sojourn in France, on the look-out for any chance of laying him by the heels. So long as he was free in London, my life would really not have been worth living. Night and day the shadow would have been over me, and sooner or later his chance must have come. What could I do? I could not shoot him at sight, or I should myself be in the dock. There was no use appealing to a magistrate. They cannot interfere on the strength of what would appear to them to be a wild suspicion. So I could do nothing. But I watched the criminal news, knowing that sooner or later I should get him. Then came the death of this Ronald Adair. My chance had come at last. Knowing what I did, was it not certain that Colonel Moran had done it? He had played cards with the lad, he had followed him home from the club, he had shot him through the open window. There was not a doubt of it. The bullets alone are enough to put his head in a noose. I came over at once. I was seen by the sentinel, who would, I knew, direct the colonel's attention to my presence. He could not fail to connect my sudden return with his crime, and to be terribly alarmed. I was sure that he would make an attempt to get me out of the way *at once*, and would bring round his murderous weapon for that purpose. I left him an excellent mark in the window, and, having warned the police that they might be needed—by the way, Watson, you spotted their presence in that doorway with unerring accuracy—I took up what seemed to me to be a judicious post for observation, never dreaming that he would choose the same spot for his attack. Now, my dear Watson, does anything remain for me to explain?"

"Yes," said I. "You have not made it clear what was Colonel Moran's motive in murdering the Honourable Ronald Adair?"

"Ah! my dear Watson, there we come into those realms of conjecture, where the most logical mind may be at fault. Each may form his own hypothesis upon the present evidence, and yours is as likely to be correct as mine."

"You have formed one, then?"

"I think that it is not difficult to explain the facts. It came out in evidence that Colonel Moran and young Adair had, between them, won a considerable amount of money. Now, Moran undoubtedly played foul—of that I have long been aware. I believe that on the day of the murder Adair had discovered that Moran was cheating. Very likely he had spoken to him privately, and had threatened to expose him unless he voluntarily resigned his membership of the club, and promised not to play cards again. It is unlikely that a youngster like Adair would at once make a hideous scandal by exposing a well-known man so much older than himself. Probably he acted as I suggest. The exclusion from his clubs would mean ruin to Moran, who lived by his ill-gotten card-gains. He therefore murdered Adair, who at the time was endeavouring to work out how much money he should himself return, since he could not profit by his partner's foul play. He locked the door lest the ladies should surprise him and insist upon knowing what he was doing with these names and coins. Will it pass?"

"I have no doubt that you have hit upon the truth."

"It will be verified or disproved at the trial. Meanwhile, come what may, Colonel Moran will trouble us no more. The famous air-gun of Von Herder will embellish the Scotland Yard Museum, and once again Mr. Sherlock Holmes is free to devote his life to examining those interesting little problems which the complex life of London so plentifully presents."

12

&

"The Adventure of the Dancing Men" (1903)

Holmes had been seated for some hours in silence with his long, thin back curved over a chemical vessel in which he was brewing a particularly malodorous product. His head was sunk upon his breast, and he looked from my point of view like a strange, lank bird, with dull gray plumage and a black top-knot.

"So, Watson," said he, suddenly, "you do not propose to invest in South African securities?"

I gave a start of astonishment. Accustomed as I was to Holmes's curious faculties, this sudden intrusion into my most intimate thoughts was utterly inexplicable.

"How on earth do you know that?" I asked.

He wheeled round upon his stool, with a steaming test-tube in his hand, and a gleam of amusement in his deep-set eyes.

"Now, Watson, confess yourself utterly taken aback," said he.

"I am."

"I ought to make you sign a paper to that effect."

"Why?"

"Because in five minutes you will say that it is all so absurdly simple."

"I am sure that I shall say nothing of the kind."

"You see, my dear Watson"—he propped his test-tube in the rack, and began to lecture with the air of a professor addressing his class—"it is not really difficult to construct a series of inferences, each dependent upon its predecessor and each simple in itself. If, after doing so, one simply knocks out all the central inferences and presents one's audience with the starting-point and the conclusion, one may produce a startling, though possibly a meretricious, effect. Now, it was not really difficult, by an inspection of the groove between your left forefinger and thumb, to feel sure that you did *not* propose to invest your small capital in the gold fields."

"I see no connection."

"Very likely not; but I can quickly show you a close connection. Here are the missing links of the very simple chain: 1. You had chalk be-tween you left finger and thumb when you returned from the club last night. 2. You put chalk there when you play billiards, to steady the cue. 3. You never play billiards except with Thurston. 4. You told me, four weeks ago, that Thurston had an option on some South African prop-erty which would expire in a month, and which he desired you to share with him. 5. Your check book is located in my drawer, and you have not asked for the key. 6. You do not propose to invest your money in this manner."

"How absurdly simple!" I cried.

"Quite so!" said he, a little nettled. "Every problem becomes very childish when once it is explained to you. Here is an unexplained one. See what you can make of that, friend Watson." He tossed a sheet of pa-per upon the table, and turned once more to his chemical analysis.

I looked with amazement at the absurd hieroglyphics upon the paper.

"Why Holmes, it is a child's drawing," I cried.

"Oh, that's your idea!"

"What else could it be?"

"That is what Mr. Hilton Cubitt, of Ridling Thorpe Manor, Nor-folk, is very anxious to know. This little conundrum came by the first post, and he was to follow by the next train. There's a ring at the bell, Watson. I should not be very much surprised if this were he."

A heavy step was heard upon the stairs, and an instant later there en-tered a tall, ruddy, clean-shaven gentleman, whose clear eyes and florid cheeks told of a life led far from the fogs of Baker Street. He seemed to bring a whiff of his strong, fresh, bracing, east-coast air with him as he entered. Having shaken hands with each of us, he was about to sit down, when his eyes rested upon the paper with the curious marking, which I had just examined and left upon the table.

"Well, Mr. Holmes, what do you make of these?" he cried. "They told me that you were fond of queer mysteries, and I don't think you can find a queerer one than that. I sent the paper on ahead, so that you might have time to study it before I came."

"It is certainly rather a curious production," said Holmes. "At first sight it would appear to be some childish prank. It consists of a number of absurd little figures dancing across the paper upon which they are drawn. Why should you attribute any importance to so grotesque an object?"

"I never should, Mr. Holmes. But my wife does. It is frightening her to death. She says nothing, but I can see terror in her eyes. That's why I want to sift the matter to the bottom."

Holmes held up the paper so that the sunlight shone full upon it. It was a page torn from a notebook. The markings were done in pencil, and ran in this way:

Holmes examined it for some time, and then, folding it carefully up, he placed it in his pocketbook.

"This promises to be a most interesting and unusual case," said he. "You gave me a few particulars in your letter, Mr. Hilton Cubitt, but I should be very much obliged if you would kindly go over it all again for the benefit of my friend, Dr. Watson."

"I'm not much of a story-teller," said our visitor, nervously clasping and unclasping his great, strong hands. "You'll just ask me anything that I don't make clear. I'll begin at the time of my marriage last year, but I want to say first of all that, though I'm not a rich man, my people have been at Ridling Thorpe for a matter of five centuries, and there is no better known family in the County of Norfolk. Last year I came up to

London for the Jubilee, and I stopped at a boardinghouse in Russell Square, because Parker, the vicar of our parish, was staying in it. There was an American young lady there—Patrick was the name—Elsie Patrick. In some way we became friends, until before my month was up I was as much in love as a man could be. We were quietly married at a registry office, and we returned to Norfolk a wedded couple. You'll think it very mad, Mr. Holmes, that a man of a good old family should marry a wife in this fashion, knowing nothing of her past or of her people, but if you saw her and knew her, it would help you to understand.

"She was very straight about it, was Elsie. I can't say that she did not give me every chance of getting out of it if I wished to do so. 'I have had some very disagreeable associations in my life,' said she. 'I wish to forget all about them. I would rather never allude to the past, for it is very painful to me. If you take me, Hilton, you will take a woman who has nothing that she need be personally ashamed of; but you will have to be content with my word for it, and to allow me to be silent as to all that passed up to the time when I became yours. If these conditions are too hard, then go back to Norfolk, and leave me to the lonely life in which you found me.' It was only the day before our wedding that she said those very words to me. I told her that I was content to take her on her own terms, and I have been as good as my word.

"Well, we have been married now for a year, and very happy we have been. But about a month ago, at the end of June, I saw for the first time signs of trouble. One day my wife received a letter from America. I saw the American stamp. She turned deadly white, read the letter, and threw it into the fire. She made no allusion to it afterwards, and I made none, for a promise is a promise, but she has never known an easy hour from that moment. There is always a look of fear upon her face—a look as if she were waiting and expecting. She would do better to trust me. She would find that I was her best friend. But until she speaks, I can say nothing. Mind you, she is a truthful woman, Mr. Holmes, and whatever trouble there may have been in her past life it has been no fault of hers. I am only a simple Norfolk squire, but there is not a man in England who ranks his family honour more highly than I do. She knows it well, and she knew it well before she married me. She would never bring any stain upon it—of that I am sure.

"Well, now I come to the queer part of my story. About a week ago—it was the Tuesday of last week—I found on one of the window-sills a number of absurd little dancing figures like these upon the paper. They were scrawled with chalk. I thought that it was the stable-boy who had drawn them, but the lad swore he knew nothing about it. Anyhow, they had come there during the night. I had them washed out, and I only mentioned the matter to my wife afterwards. To my surprise, she took it very seriously, and begged me if any more came to let her see them. None did come for a week, and then yesterday morning I found this paper lying on the sundial in the garden. I showed it to Elsie, and down she dropped in a dead faint. Since then she has looked like a woman in a dream, half dazed, and with terror always lurking in her eyes. It was then that I wrote and sent the paper to you, Mr. Holmes. It was not a thing that I could take to the police, for they would have laughed at me, but you will tell me what to do. I am not a rich man, but if there is any danger threatening my little woman, I would spend my last copper to shield her."

He was a fine creature, this man of the old English soil—simple, straight, and gentle, with his great, earnest blue eyes and broad, comely face. His love for his wife and his trust in her shone in his features. Holmes had listened to his story with the utmost attention, and now he sat for some time in silent thought.

"Don't you think, Mr. Cubitt," said he, at last, "that your best plan would be to make a direct appeal to your wife, and to ask her to share her secret with you?"

Hilton Cubitt shook his massive head.

"A promise is a promise, Mr. Holmes. If Elsie wished to tell me she would. If not, it is not for me to force her confidence. But I am justified in taking my own line—and I will."

"Then I will help you with all my heart. In the first place, have you heard of any strangers being seen in your neighbourhood?"

"No."

"I presume that it is very quiet place. Any fresh face would cause comment?"

"In the immediate neighbourhood, yes. But we have several small watering-places not very far away. And the farmers take in lodgers."

"These hieroglyphics have evidently a meaning. If it is a purely arbitrary one, it may be impossible for us to solve it. If, on the other hand, it is systematic, I have no doubt that we shall get to the bottom of it. But this particular sample is so short that I can do nothing, and the facts which you have brought me are so indefinite that we have no basis for an investigation. I would suggest that you return to Norfolk, that you keep a keen lookout, and that you take an exact copy of any fresh dancing men which may appear. It is a thousand pities that we have not a reproduction of those which were done in chalk upon the window-sill. Make a discreet inquiry also as to any strangers in the neighbourhood. When you have collected some fresh evidence, come to me again. That is the best advice which I can give you, Mr. Hilton Cubitt. If there are any pressing fresh developments, I shall be always ready to run down and see you in your Norfolk home."

The interview left Sherlock Holmes very thoughtful, and several times in the next few days I saw him take his slip of paper from his notebook and look long and earnestly at the curious figures inscribed upon it. He made no allusion to the affair, however, until one afternoon a fortnight or so later. I was going out when he called me back.

"You had better stay here, Watson."

"Why?"

"Because I had a wire from Hilton Cubitt this morning. You remember Hilton Cubitt, of the dancing men? He was to reach Liverpool Street at one-twenty. He may be here at any moment. I gather from his wire that there have been some new incidents of importance."

We had not long to wait, for our Norfolk squire came straight from the station as fast as a hansom could bring him. He was looking worried and depressed, with tired eyes and a lined forehead.

"It's getting on my nerves, this business, Mr. Holmes," said he, as he sank, like a wearied man, into an armchair. "It's bad enough to feel that you are surrounded by unseen, unknown folk, who have some kind of design upon you, but when, in addition to that, you know that it is just killing your wife by inches, then it becomes as much as flesh and blood can endure. She's wearing away under it—just wearing away before my eyes."

"Has she said anything yet?"

"No, Mr. Holmes, she has not. And yet there have been times when the poor girl has wanted to speak, and yet could not quite bring herself to take the plunge. I have tried to help her, but I daresay I did it clumsily, and scared her from it. She has spoken about my old family, and our reputation in the county, and our pride in our unsullied honour, and I always felt it was leading to the point, but somehow it turned off before we got there."

"But you have found out something for yourself?"

"A good deal, Mr. Holmes. I have several fresh dancing men pictures for you to examine, and what is more important, I have seen the fellow."

"What, the man who draws them?"

"Yes, I saw him at his work. But I will tell you everything in order. When I got back from my visit to you, the very first thing I saw next morning was a fresh crop of dancing men. They had been drawn in chalk upon the black wooden door of the tool-house, which stands beside the lawn in full view of the front windows. I took an exact copy, and here it is." He unfolded a paper and laid it upon the table. Here is a copy of the hieroglyphics:

"Excellent!" said Holmes. "Excellent! Pray continue."

"When I had taken the copy, I rubbed out the marks, but two mornings later, a fresh inscription had appeared. I have a copy of it here":

Holmes rubbed his hands and chuckled with delight.

"Our material is rapidly accumulating," said he.

"Three days later a message was left scrawled upon paper, and placed under a pebble upon the sundial. Here it is. The characters are, as you see, exactly the same as the last one. After that I determined to lie in wait, so I got out my revolver and I sat up in my study, which overlooks the lawn and garden. About two in the morning I was seated by the window, all being dark save for the moonlight outside, when I heard steps behind me, and there was my wife in her dressing-gown. She implored me to come to bed. I told her frankly that I wished to see who it was who played such absurd tricks upon us. She answered that it was some senseless practical joke, and that I should not take any notice of it.

"'If it really annoys you, Hilton, we might go and travel, you and I, and so avoid the nuisance.'

"'What, be driven out of our own house by a practical joker?' said I. 'Why, we should have the whole county laughing at us.'

"'Well, come to bed,' said she, 'and we can discuss it in the morning.'

"Suddenly, as she spoke, I saw her white face grow whiter yet in the moonlight, and her hand tightened upon my shoulder. Something was moving in the shadow of the toolhouse. I saw a dark, creeping figure which crawled round the corner and squatted in front of the door. Seizing my pistol, I was rushing out, when my wife threw her arms round me and held me with convulsive strength. I tried to throw her off, but she clung to me most desperately. At last I got clear, but by the time I had opened the door and reached the house the creature was gone. He had left the trace of his presence, however, for there on the door was the very same arrangement of dancing men which had already twice appeared, and which I have copied on that paper. There was no other sign of the fellow anywhere, though I ran all over the grounds. And yet the amazing thing is that he must have been there all the time, for when I examined the door again in the morning, he had scrawled some more of his pictures under the line which I had already seen."

"Have you that fresh drawing?"

"Yes, it is very short, but I made a copy of it, and here it is."

Again he produced a paper. The new dance was in this form:

"Tell me," said Holmes—and I could see by his eyes that he was much excited—"was this a mere addition to the first or did it appear to be entirely separate?"

"It was on a different panel of the door."

"Excellent! This is far the most important of all for our purpose. It fills me with hopes. Now, Mr. Hilton Cubitt, please continue your most interesting statement."

"I have nothing more to say, Mr. Holmes, except that I was angry with my wife that night for having held me back when I might have caught the skulking rascal. She said that she feared that I might have come to harm. For an instant it had crossed my mind that perhaps what she really feared was that *he* might come to harm, for I could not doubt that she knew who this man was, and what he meant by these strange signals. But there is a tone in my wife's voice, Mr. Holmes, and a look in her eyes which forbid doubt, and I am sure that it was indeed my own safety that was in her mind. There's the whole case, and now I want your advice as to what I ought to do. My own inclination is to put half a dozen of my farm lads in the shrubbery, and when this fellow comes again to give him such a hiding that he will leave us in peace for the future."

"I fear that it is too deep a case for such simple remedies," said Holmes. "How long can you stay in London?"

"I must go back to-day. I would not leave my wife alone all night for anything. She is very nervous, and begged me to come back."

"I daresay you are right. But if you could have stopped, I might possibly have been able to return with you in a day or two. Meanwhile you will leave me these papers, and I think that it is very likely that I shall be able to pay you a visit shortly and to throw some light upon your case."

Sherlock Holmes preserved his calm professional manner until our visitor had left us, although it was easy for me, who knew him so well, to see that he was profoundly excited. The moment that Hilton Cubitt's broad back had disappeared through the door my comrade rushed to the table, laid out all the slips of paper containing dancing men in front of him, and threw himself into an intricate and elaborate calculation. For two hours I watched him as he covered sheet after sheet of paper with figures and letters, so completely absorbed in his task that he had evidently forgotten my presence. Sometimes he was making progress and whistled and sang at his work; sometimes he was puzzled, and would sit for long spells with a furrowed brow and a vacant eye. Finally he sprang from his chair with a cry of satisfaction, and walked up and down the room rubbing his hands together. Then he wrote a long telegram upon a cable form. "If my answer to this is as I hope, you will have a very pretty case to add to your collection, Watson," said he. "I expect that we shall be able to go down to Norfolk to-morrow, and to take our friend some very definite news as to the secret of his annoyance."

I confess that I was filled with curiosity, but I was aware that Holmes liked to make his disclosures at his own time and in his own way, so I waited until it should suit him to take me into his confidence.

But there was a delay in that answering telegram, and two days of impatience followed, during which Holmes pricked up his ears at every ring of the bell. On the evening of the second there came a letter from Hilton Cubitt. All was quiet with him, save that a long inscription had appeared that morning upon the pedestal of the sundial. He inclosed a copy of it, which is here reproduced:

Holmes bent over this grotesque frieze for some minutes, and then suddenly sprang to his feet with an exclamation of surprise and dismay. His face was haggard with anxiety.

"We have let this affair go far enough," said he. "Is there a train to North Walsham to-night?"

I turned up the time-table. The last had just gone.

"Then we shall breakfast early and take the very first in the morning," said Holmes. "Our presence is most urgently needed. Ah! here is our expected cablegram. One moment, Mrs. Hudson, there may be an answer. No, that is quite as I expected. This message makes it even more essential that we should not lose an hour in letting Hilton Cubitt know how matters stand, for it is a singular and dangerous web in which our simple Norfolk squire is entangled."

So, indeed, it proved, and as I come to the dark conclusion of a story which had seemed to me to be only childish and bizarre, I experience once again the dismay and horror with which I was filled. Would that I had some brighter ending to communicate to my reader, but these are the chronicles of fact, and I must follow to their dark crisis the strange chain of events which for some days made Ridling Thorpe Manor a household word the length and breadth of England.

We had hardly alighted at North Walsham, and mentioned the name of our destination, when the stationmaster hurried towards us. "I suppose that you are the detectives from London?" said he.

A look of annoyance passed over Holmes's face.

"What makes you think such a thing?"

"Because Inspector Martin from Norwich has just passed through. But maybe you are the surgeons. She's not dead—or wasn't by last account. You may be in time to save her yet—though it be for the gallows."

Holmes's brow was dark with anxiety.

"We are going to Ridling Thorpe Manor," said he, "but we have heard nothing of what has passed there."

"It's a terrible business," said the stationmaster. "They are shot, both Mr. Hilton Cubitt and his wife. She shot him and then herself—so the servants say. He's dead and her life is despaired of. Dear, dear, one of the oldest families in the county of Norfolk, and one of the most honoured."

Without a word Holmes hurried to a carriage, and during the long seven miles' drive he never opened his mouth. Seldom have I seen him so utterly despondent. He had been uneasy during all our journey from town, and I had observed that he had turned over the morning papers with anxious attention, but now this sudden realization of his worst fears left him in a blank melancholy. He leaned back in his seat, lost in gloomy speculation. Yet there was much around to interest us, for we were passing through as singular a countryside as any in England, where a few scattered cottages represented the population of to-day, while on every hand enormous square-towered churches bristled up from the flat green landscape and told of the glory and prosperity of old East Anglia. At last the violet rim of the German Ocean appeared over the green edge of the Norfolk coast, and the driver pointed with his whip to two old brick and timber gables which projected from a grove of trees. "That's Ridling Thorpe Manor," said he.

As we drove up to the porticoed front door, I observed in the front of it, beside the tennis lawn, the black toolhouse and the pedestalled sundial with which we had such strange associations. A dapper little man, with a quick, alert manner and a waxed moustache, had just descended from a high dogcart. He introduced himself as Inspector Martin, of the Norfolk Constabulary, and he was considerably astonished when he heard the name of my companion.

"Why, Mr. Holmes, the crime was only committed at three this morning. How could you hear of it in London and get to the spot as soon as I?"

"I anticipated it. I came in the hope of preventing it."

"Then you must have important evidence, of which we are ignorant, for they were said to be a most united couple."

"I have only the evidence of the dancing men," said Holmes. "I will explain the matter to you later. Meanwhile, since it is too late to prevent this tragedy, I am very anxious that I should use the knowledge which I possess in order to insure that justice be done. Will you associate me in your investigation, or will you prefer that I should act independently?"

"I should be proud to feel that we were acting together, Mr. Holmes," said the inspector, earnestly.

"In that case I should be glad to hear the evidence and to examine the premises without an instant of unnecessary delay."

Inspector Martin had the good sense to allow my friend to do things in his own fashion, and contented himself with carefully noting the results. The local surgeon, an old, white-haired man, had just come down from Mrs. Hilton Cubitt's room, and he reported that her injuries were serious, but not necessarily fatal. The bullet had passed through the front of her brain, and it would probably be some time before she could regain consciousness. On the question of whether she had been shot or had shot herself, he would not venture to express any decided opinion. Certainly the bullet had been discharged at very close quarters. There was only the one pistol found in the room, two barrels of which had been emptied. Mr. Hilton Cubitt had been shot through the heart. It was equally conceivable that he had shot her and then himself, or that she had been the criminal, for the revolver lay upon the floor midway between them.

"Has he been moved?" asked Holmes.

"We have moved nothing except the lady. We could not leave her lying wounded upon the floor."

"How long have you been here, Doctor?"

"Since four o'clock."

"Anyone else?"

"Yes, the constable here."

"And you have touched nothing?"

"Nothing."

"You have acted with great discretion. Who sent for you?"

"The housemaid, Saunders."

"Was it she who gave the alarm?"

"She and Mrs. King, the cook."

"Where are they now?"

"In the kitchen, I believe."

"Then I think we had better hear their story at once."

The old hall, oak-panelled and high-windowed, had been turned into a court of investigation. Holmes sat in a great, old-fashioned chair, his inexorable eyes gleaming out of his haggard face. I could read in them a set purpose to devote his life to this quest until the client whom he had failed to save should at last be avenged. The trim Inspector Martin, the old, gray-headed country doctor, myself, and a stolid village policeman made up the rest of that strange company.

The two women told their story clearly enough. They had been aroused from their sleep by the sound of an explosion, which had been followed a minute later by a second one. They slept in adjoining rooms, and Mrs. King had rushed in to Saunders. Together they had descended the stairs. The door of the study was open, and a candle was burning upon the table. Their master lay upon his face in the centre of the room. He was quite dead. Near the window his wife was crouching, her head leaning against the wall. She was horribly wounded, and the side of her face was red with blood. She breathed heavily, but was incapable of saying anything. The passage, as well as the room, was full of smoke and the smell of powder. The window was certainly shut and fastened upon the inside. Both women were positive upon the point. They had at once sent for the doctor and for the constable. Then, with the aid of the groom and the stable-boy, they had conveyed their injured mistress to her room. Both she and her husband had occupied the bed. She was clad in her dress—he in his dressing-gown, over his night-clothes. Nothing had been moved in the study. So far as they knew, there had never been any quarrel between husband and wife. They had always looked upon them as a very united couple.

These were the main points of the servants' evidence. In answer to Inspector Martin, they were clear that every door was fastened upon the inside, and that no one could have escaped from the house. In answer to Holmes, they both remembered that they were conscious of the smell of powder from the moment that they ran out of their rooms upon the top floor. "I commend that fact very carefully to your attention," said Holmes to his professional colleague. "And now I think that we are in a position to undertake a thorough examination of the room."

The study proved to be a small chamber, lined on three sides with books, and with a writing-table facing an ordinary window, which looked out upon the garden. Our first attention was given to the body of the unfortunate squire, whose huge frame lay stretched across the room. His disordered dress showed that he had been hastily aroused from sleep. The bullet had been fired at him from the front, and had remained in his body, after penetrating the heart. His death had certainly been instantaneous and painless. There was no powder-marking either upon his dressing-gown or on his hands. According to the country surgeon, the lady had stains upon her face, but none upon her hand.

"The absence of the latter means nothing, though its presence may mean everything," said Holmes. "Unless the powder from a badly fitting cartridge happens to spurt backward, one may fire many shots without leaving a sign. I would suggest that Mr. Cubitt's body may now be removed. I suppose, Doctor, you have not recovered the bullet which wounded the lady?"

"A serious operation will be necessary before that can be done. But there are still four cartridges in the revolver. Two have been fired and two wounds inflicted, so that each bullet can be accounted for."

"So it would seem," said Holmes. "Perhaps you can account also for the bullet which has so obviously struck the edge of the window?"

He had turned suddenly, and his long, thin finger was pointing to a hole which had been drilled right through the lower window-sash, about an inch above the bottom.

"By George!" cried the inspector. "How ever did you see that?"

"Because I looked for it."

"Wonderful!" said the country doctor. "You are certainly right, sir. Then a third shot has been fired, and therefore a third person must have been present. But who could that have been, and how could he have got away?"

"That is the problem which we are now about to solve," said Sherlock Holmes. "You remember, Inspector Martin, when the servants said that on leaving their room they were at once conscious of a smell of powder, I remarked that the point was an extremely important one?"

"Yes, sir; but I confess I did not quite follow you."

"It suggested that at the time of the firing, the window as well as the door of the room had been open. Otherwise the fumes of powder could not have been blown so rapidly through the house. A draught in the room was necessary for that. Both door and window were only open for a very short time, however."

"How do you prove that?"

"Because the candle was not guttered."

"Capital!" cried the inspector. "Capital!"

"Feeling sure that the window had been open at the time of the tragedy, I conceived that there might have been a third person in the affair, who stood outside this opening and fired through it. Any shot directed at this person might hit the sash. I looked, and there, sure enough, was the bullet mark!"

"But how came the window to be shut and fastened?"

"The woman's first instinct would be to shut and fasten the window. But, halloa! what is this?"

It was a lady's hand-bag which stood upon the study table—a trim little hand-bag of crocodile-skin and silver. Holmes opened it and turned the contents out. There were twenty fifty-pound notes of the Bank of England, held together by an india-rubber band—nothing else.

"This must be preserved, for it will figure in the trial," said Holmes, as he handed the bag with its contents to the inspector. "It is now necessary that we should try to throw some light upon this third bullet, which has clearly, from the splintering of the wood, been fired from inside the room. I should like to see Mrs. King, the cook again. You said, Mrs. King, that you were awakened by a *loud* explosion. When you said that, did you mean that it seemed to you to be louder than the second one?"

"Well, sir, it wakened me from my sleep, so it is hard to judge. But it did seem very loud."

"You don't think that it might have been two shots fired almost at the same instant?"

"I am sure I couldn't say, sir."

"I believe that it was undoubtedly so. I rather think, Inspector Martin, that we have now exhausted all that this room can teach us. If you will kindly step round with me, we shall see what fresh evidence the garden has to offer."

A flower-bed extended up to the study window, and we all broke into an exclamation as we approached it. The flowers were trampled down, and the soft soil was imprinted all over with footmarks. Large, masculine feet they were, with peculiarly long, sharp toes. Holmes hunted about among the grass and leaves like a retriever after a wounded bird. Then, with a cry of satisfaction, he bent forward and picked up a little brazen cylinder.

"I thought so," said he; "the revolver had an ejector, and here is the third cartridge. I really think, Inspector Martin, that our case is almost complete."

The country inspector's face had shown his intense amazement at the rapid and masterful progress of Holmes's investigation. At first he had shown some disposition to assert his own position, but now he was overcome with admiration, and ready to follow without question wherever Holmes led.

"Whom do you suspect?" he asked.

"I'll go into that later. There are several points in this problem which I have not been able to explain to you yet. Now that I have got so far, I had best proceed on my own lines, and then clear the whole matter up once and for all."

"Just as you wish, Mr. Holmes, so long as we get our man."

"I have no desire to make mysteries, but it is impossible at the moment of action to enter into long and complex explanations. I have the threads of the affair all in my hand. Even if this lady should never recover consciousness, we can still reconstruct the events of last night, and insure that justice be done. First of all, I wish to know whether there is any inn in this neighbourhood known as 'Elrige's'?"

The servants were cross-questioned, but none of them had heard of such a place. The stable-boy threw a light upon the matter by remembering that a farmer of that name lived some miles off, in the direction of East Ruston.

"Is it a lonely farm?"

"Very lonely, sir."

"Perhaps they have not heard yet of all that happened here during the night?"

"Maybe not, sir."

Holmes thought for a little, and then a curious smile played over his face.

"Saddle a horse, my lad," said he. "I shall wish you to take a note to Elrige's Farm."

He took from his pocket the various slips of the dancing men. With these in front of him, we worked for some time at the study-table. Finally he handed a note to the boy, with directions to put it into the hands of the person to whom it was addressed, and especially to answer no questions of any sort which might be put to him. I saw the outside of the note, addressed in straggling, irregular characters, very unlike Holmes's usual precise hand. It was consigned to Mr. Abe Slaney, Elrige's Farm, East Ruston, Norfolk.

"I think, Inspector," Holmes remarked, "that you would do well to telegraph for an escort, as, if my calculations prove to be correct, you may have a particularly dangerous prisoner to convey to the county jail. The boy who takes this note could no doubt forward your telegram. If there is an afternoon train to town, Watson, I think we should do well to take it, as I have a chemical analysis of some interest to finish, and this investigation draws rapidly to a close."

When the youth had been dispatched with the note, Sherlock Holmes gave his instructions to the servants. If any visitor were to call asking for Mrs. Hilton Cubitt, no information should be given as to her condition, but he was to be shown at once into the drawing-room. He impressed these points upon them with the utmost earnestness. Finally he led the way into the drawing-room, with the remark that the business was now out of our hands, and that we must while away the time as best we might until we could see what was in store for us. The doctor had departed to his patients, and only the inspector and myself remained.

"I think that I can help you to pass an hour in an interesting and profitable manner," said Holmes, drawing his chair up to the table, and spreading out in front of him the various papers upon which were recorded the antics of the dancing men. "As to you, friend Watson, I owe you every atonement for having allowed your natural curiosity to remain so long unsatisfied. To you, Inspector, the whole incident may appeal as a remarkable professional study. I must tell you, first of all, the interesting circumstances connected with the previous consultations which Mr. Hilton Cubitt has had with me in Baker Street." He then shortly recapitulated the facts which have already been recorded. "I have here in front of me these singular productions, at which one might smile, had they not proved themselves to be the forerunners of so terrible a tragedy. I am fairly familiar with all forms of secret writings, and am myself the author of a trifling monograph upon the subject, in which I analyze one hundred and sixty separate ciphers, but I confess that this is entirely new to me. The object of those who invented the system has apparently been to conceal that these characters convey a message, and to give the idea that they are the mere random sketches of children.

"Having once recognized, however, that the symbols stood for letters, and having applied the rules which guide us in all forms of secret writings, the solution was easy enough. The first message submitted to me was so short that it was impossible for me to do more than to say, with some confidence, that the symbol ⚡ stood for E. As you are aware, E is the most common letter in the English alphabet, and it predominates to so marked an extent that even in a short sentence one would expect to find it most often. Out of fifteen symbols in the first message, four were the same, so it was reasonable to set this down as E. It is true that in some cases the figure was bearing a flag, and in some cases not, but it was probable, from the way in which the flags were distributed, that they were used to break the sentence up into words. I accepted this as a hypothesis, and noted that E was represented by ⚡ .

"But now came the real difficulty of the inquiry. The order of the English letters after E is by no means well marked, and any preponderance which may be shown in an average of a printed sheet may be reversed in a single short sentence. Speaking roughly, T, A, O, I, N, S, H,

R, D, and L are the numerical order in which letters occur; but T, A, O, and I are very nearly abreast of each other, and it would be an endless task to try each combination until a meaning was arrived at. I therefore waited for fresh material. In my second interview with Mr. Hilton Cubitt he was able to give me two other short sentences and one message, which appeared—since there was no flag—to be a single word. Here are the symbols. Now, in the single word I have already got the two E's coming second and fourth in a word of five letters. It might be 'sever', or 'lever', or 'never'. There can be no question that the latter as a reply to an appeal is far the most probable, and the circumstances pointed to its being a reply written by the lady. Accepting it as correct, we are now able to say that the symbols stand respectively for N, V, and R.

"Even now I was in considerable difficulty, but a happy thought put me in possession of several other letters. It occurred to me that if these appeals came, as I expected, from someone who had been intimate with the lady in her early life, a combination which contained two E's with three letters between might very well stand for the name 'ELSIE.' On examination I found that such a combination formed the termination of the message which was three times repeated. It was certainly some appeal to 'Elsie.' In this way I had got my L, S, and I. But what appeal could it be? There were only four letters in the word which preceded 'Elsie,' and it ended in E. Surely the word must be 'COME.' I tried all other four letters ending in E, but could find none to fit the case. So now I was in possession of C, O, and M, and I was in a position to attack the first message, once more, dividing it into words and putting dots for each symbol which was still unknown. So treated, it worked out in this fashion:

. M . ERE . . E SL . NE.

"Now the first letter *can* only be A, which is a most useful discovery, since it occurs no fewer than three times in this short sentence, and the H is also apparent in the second word. Now it becomes:

AM HERE A . E SLANE.

Or, filling in the obvious vacancies in the name:

AM HERE ABE SLANEY.

I had so many letters now that I could proceed with considerable confidence to the second message, which worked out in this fashion:

A . ELRI . ES.

Here I could only make sense by putting T and G for the missing letters, and supposing that the name was that of some house or inn at which the writer was staying."

Inspector Martin and I had listened with the utmost interest to the full and clear account of how my friend had produced results which had led to so complete a command over our difficulties.

"What did you do then, sir?" asked the inspector.

"I had every reason to suppose that this Abe Slaney was an American, since Abe is an American contraction, and since a letter from America had been the starting-point of all the trouble. I had also every cause to think that there was some criminal secret in the matter. The lady's allusions to her past, and her refusal to take her husband into her confidence, both pointed in that direction. I therefore cabled to my friend Wilson Hargreave, of the New York Police Bureau, who has more than once made use of my knowledge of London crime. I asked him whether the name Abe Slaney was known to him. Here is his reply: 'The most dangerous crook in Chicago.' On the very evening upon which I had his answer, Hilton Cubitt sent me the last message from Slaney. Working with known letters, it took this form:

ELSIE . RE . ARE TO MEET THY GO.

The addition of a P and a D completed a message which showed me that the rascal was proceeding from persuasion to threats, and my knowledge of the crooks of Chicago prepared me to find that he might very rapidly put his words into action. I at once came to Norfolk with my friend and colleague, Dr. Watson, but, unhappily, only in time to find that the worst had already occurred."

"It is a privilege to be associated with you in the handling of a case," said the inspector, warmly. "You will excuse me, however, if I speak frankly to you. You are only answerable to yourself, but I have to answer to my superiors. If this Abe Slaney, living at Elrige's, is indeed the murderer, and if he has made his escape while I am seated here, I should certainly get into serious trouble."

"You need not be uneasy. He will not try to escape."

"How do you know?"

"To fly would be a confession of guilt."

"Then let us go to arrest him."

"I expect him here every instant."

"But why should he come?"

"Because I have written and asked him."

"But this is incredible, Mr. Holmes! Why should he come because you have asked him? Would not such a request rather rouse his suspicious and cause him to fly?"

"I think I have known how to frame the letter," said Sherlock Holmes. "In fact if I am not very much mistaken, here is the gentleman himself coming up the drive."

A man was striding up the path which led to the door. He was a tall, handsome, swarthy fellow, clad in a suit of gray flannel, with a Panama hat, a bristling black beard, and a great, aggressive hooked nose, and flourishing a cane as he walked. He swaggered up the path as if the place belonged to him, and we heard his loud, confident peal at the bell.

"I think, gentlemen," said Holmes, quietly, "that we had best take up our position behind the door. Every precaution is necessary when dealing with such a fellow. You will need your handcuffs, Inspector. You can leave the talking to me."

We waited in silence for a minute—one of those minutes which one can never forget. Then the door opened and the man stepped in. In an instant Holmes clapped a pistol to his head, and Martin slipped the handcuffs over his wrists. It was all done so swiftly and deftly that the fellow was helpless before he knew that he was attacked. He glared from one to the other of us with a pair of blazing black eyes. Then he burst into a bitter laugh.

"Well, gentlemen, you have the drop on me this time. I seem to have knocked up against something hard. But I came here in answer to a letter from Mrs. Hilton Cubitt. Don't tell me that she is in this? Don't tell me that she helped to set a trap for me?"

"Mrs Hilton Cubitt was seriously injured, and is at death's door."

The man gave a hoarse cry of grief, which rang through the house.

"You're crazy!" he cried, fiercely. "It was he that was hurt, not she. Who would have hurt little Elsie? I may have threatened her—God forgive me!—but I would not have touched a hair of her pretty head. Take it back—you! Say that she is not hurt!"

"She was found, badly wounded, by the side of her dead husband."

He sank with a deep groan on to the settee, and buried his face in his manacled hands. For five minutes he was silent. Then he raised his face once more, and spoke with the cold composure of despair.

"I have nothing to hide from you, gentlemen," said he. "If I shot the man he had his shot at me, and there's no murder in that. But if you think I could have hurt that woman, then you don't know either me or her. I tell you, there was never a man in this world loved a woman more than I loved her. I had a right to her. She was pledged to me years ago. Who was this Englishman that he should come between us? I tell you that I had the first right to her, and I was only claiming my own."

"She broke away from your influence when she found the man that you are," said Holmes, sternly. "She fled from America to avoid you, and she married an honourable gentleman in England. You dogged her and followed her and made her life a misery to her, in order to induce her to abandon the husband whom she loved and respected in order to fly with you, whom she feared and hated. You have ended by bringing about the death of a noble man and driving his wife to suicide. That is your record in this business, Mr. Abe Slaney, and you will answer for it to the law."

"If Elsie dies, I care nothing what becomes of me," said the American. He opened one of his hands, and looked at the note crumpled up in his palm. "See here, mister," he cried, with a gleam of suspicion in his eyes, "you're not trying to scare me over this, are you? If the lady is hurt as bad as you say, who was it that wrote this note?" He tossed it forward on to the table.

"I wrote it, to bring you here."

"You wrote it? There was no one on earth outside the Joint who knew the secret of the dancing men. How came you to write it?"

"What one man can invent another can discover," said Holmes. "There is a cab coming to convey you to Norwich, Mr. Slaney. But, meanwhile, you have time to make some small reparation for the injury you have wrought. Are you aware that Mrs. Hilton Cubitt has herself lain under grave suspicion of the murder of her husband, and that it was only my presence here, and the knowledge which I happened to possess, which has saved her from the accusation? The least that you owe her is to make it clear to the whole world that she was in no way, directly or indirectly, responsible for his tragic end."

"I ask nothing better," said the American. "I guess the very best case I can make for myself is the absolute naked truth."

"It is my duty to warn you that it will be used against you," cried the inspector, with the magnificent fair play of the British criminal law.

Slaney shrugged his shoulders.

"I'll chance that," said he. "First of all, I want you gentlemen to understand that I have known this lady since she was a child. There were seven of us in a gang in Chicago, and Elsie's father was the boss of the Joint. He was a clever man, was old Patrick. It was he who invented that writing, which would pass as a child's scrawl unless you just happened to have the key to it. Well, Elsie learned some of our ways, but she couldn't stand the business, and she had a bit of honest money of her own, so she gave us all the slip and got away to London. She had been engaged to me, and she would have married me, I believe, if I had taken over another profession, but she would have nothing to do with anything on the cross. It was only after her marriage to this Englishman that I was able to find out where she was. I wrote to her, but got no answer. After that I came over, and as letters were no use, I put my messages where she could read them.

"Well, I have been here a month now. I lived in that farm, where I had a room down below, and could get in and out every night, and no one the wiser. I tried all I could to coax Elsie away. I knew that she read the messages, for once she wrote an answer under one of them. Then my temper got the better of me, and I began to threaten her. She sent me a letter then, imploring me to go away, and saying that it would break her heart if any scandal should come upon her husband. She said that she would come down when her husband was asleep at three in the morning, and speak with me through the end window, if I would go away afterwards and leave her in peace. She came down and brought money with her, trying to bribe me to go. This made me mad, and I caught her arm and tried to pull her through the window. At that moment in rushed the husband with his revolver in his hand. Elsie had sunk down upon the floor, and we were face to face. I was heeled also, and I held up my gun to scare him off and let me get away. He fired and missed me. I pulled off almost at the same instant, and down he dropped. I made away across the garden, and as I went I heard the window shut behind me. That's God's truth, gentlemen, every word of it; and I heard no more about it until that lad came riding up with a note which made me walk in here, like a jay, and give myself into your hands."

A cab had driven up whilst the American had been talking. Two uniformed policemen sat inside. Inspector Martin rose and touched his prisoner on the shoulder.

"It is time for us to go."

"Can I see her first?"

"No, she is not conscious. Mr. Sherlock Holmes, I only hope that, if ever again I have an important case, I shall have the good fortune to have you by my side."

We stood at the window and watched the cab drive away. As I turned back, my eye caught the pellet of paper which the prisoner had tossed upon the table. It was the note with which Holmes had decoyed him.

"See if you can read it, Watson," said he, with a smile.

It contained no word, but this little line of dancing men:

"If you use the code which I have explained," said Holmes, "you will find that it simply means 'Come here at once.' I was convinced that it was an invitation which he would not refuse, since he could never imagine that it could come from anyone but the lady. And so, my dear Watson, we have ended by turning the dancing men to good when they have so often been the agents of evil, and I think that I have fulfilled my promise of giving you something unusual for your notebook. Three-forty is our train, and I fancy we should be back in Baker Street for dinner."

Only one word of epilogue. The American, Abe Slaney, was condemned to death at the winter assizes at Norwich, but this penalty was
changed to penal servitude in consideration of mitigating circumstances,
and the certainty that Hilton Cubitt had fired the first shot. Of Mrs.
Hilton Cubitt I only know that I have heard she recovered entirely, and
that she still remains a widow, devoting her whole life to the care of the
poor and to the administration of her husband's estate.

13

From *The Crime of the Congo*
(1909)

Preface

There are many of us in England who consider the crime which has been wrought in the Congo lands by King Leopold of Belgium and his followers to be the greatest which has ever been known in human annals. Personally I am strongly of that opinion. There have been great expropriations like that of the Normans in England or of the English in Ireland. There have been massacres of populations like that of the South Americans by the Spaniards or of subject nations by the Turks. But never before has there been such a mixture of wholesale expropriation and wholesale massacre all done under an odious guise of philanthropy and with the lowest commercial motives as a reason. It is this sordid cause and the unctuous hypocrisy which makes this crime unparalleled in its horror.

The witnesses of the crime are of all nations, and there is no possibility of error concerning facts. There are British consuls like Casement,

Thesiger, Mitchell and Armstrong, all writing in their official capacity with every detail of fact and date. There are Frenchmen like Pierre Mille and Félicien Challaye, both of whom have written books upon the subject. There are missionaries of many races—Harris, Weeks and Stannard (British); Morrison, Clarke and Shepherd (American); Sjoblom (Swedish) and Father Vermeersch, the Jesuit. There is the eloquent action of the Italian Government, who refused to allow Italian officers to be employed any longer in such hangman's work, and there is the report of the Belgian commission, the evidence before which was suppressed because it was too dreadful for publication; finally, there is the incorruptible evidence of the kodak. Any American citizen who will glance at Mark Twain's "King Leopold's Soliloquy" will see some samples of that. A perusal of all of these sources of information will show that there is not a grotesque, obscene or ferocious torture which human ingenuity could invent which has not been used against these harmless and helpless people.

This would, to my mind, warrant our intervention in any case. Turkey has several times been interfered with simply on the general ground of humanity. There is in this instance a very special reason why America and England should not stand by and see these people done to death. They are, in a sense, their wards. America was the first to give official recognition to King Leopold's enterprise in 1884, and so has the responsibility of having actually put him into that position which he has so dreadfully abused. She has been the indirect and innocent cause of the whole tragedy. Surely some reparation is due. On the other hand England has, with the other European Powers, signed the treaty of 1885, by which each and all of them make it responsible for the condition of the native races. The other Powers have so far shown no desire to live up to this pledge. But the conscience of England is uneasy and she is slowly rousing herself to act. Will America be behind?

At this moment two American citizens, Shepherd and that noble Virginian, Morrison, are about to be tried at Boma for telling the truth about the scoundrels. Morrison in the dock makes a finer Statue of Liberty than Bartholdi's in New York harbour.

Attempts will be made in America (for the Congo has its paid apologists everywhere) to pretend that England wants to oust Belgium from

her colony and take it herself. Such accusations are folly. To run a tropical colony honestly without enslaving the natives is an expensive process.
For example Nigeria, the nearest English colony, has to be subsidized to
the extent of $2,000,000 a year. Whoever takes over the Congo will,
considering its present demoralized condition, have a certain expense of
$10,000,000 a year for twenty years. Belgium has not run the colony. It
has simply sacked it, forcing the inhabitants without pay to ship everything of value to Antwerp. No decent European Power could do this.
For many years to come the Congo will be a heavy expense and it will
truly be a philanthropic call upon the next owner. I trust it will not fall
to England.

Attempts have been made too (for there is considerable ingenuity
and unlimited money on the other side) to pretend that it is a question
of Protestant missions against Catholic. Any one who thinks this should
read the book, "La Question Kongolaise, " of the eloquent and holy Jesuit, Father Vermeersch. He lived in the country and, as he says, it was
the sight of the "immeasurable misery, " which drove him to write.

We English who are earnest over this matter look eagerly to the
westward to see some sign of moral support of material leading. It
would be a grand sight to see the banner of humanity and civilization
carried forward in such a cause by the two great English-speaking nations.

I
How the Congo Free State Came to Be Founded

In the earlier years of his reign King Leopold of Belgium began to display that interest in Central Africa which for a long time was ascribed to
nobility and philanthropy, until the contrast between such motives, and
the actual unscrupulous commercialism, became too glaring to be sustained. As far back as the year 1876 he called a conference of humani-
tarians and travellers, who met at Brussels for the purpose of debating
various plans by which the Dark Continent might be opened up. From
this conference sprang the so-called International African Association,

which, in spite of its name, was almost entirely a Belgian body with the Belgian King as President. Its professed object was the exploration of the country and the founding of stations which should be rest-houses for travellers and centres of civilization.

On the return of Stanley from his great journey in 1878, he was met at Marseilles by a representative from the King of Belgium, who enrolled the famous traveller as an agent for his Association. The immediate task given to Stanley was to open up the Congo for trade, and to make such terms with the natives as would enable stations to be built and depôts established. In 1879 Stanley was at work with characteristic energy. His own intentions were admirable. "We shall require but mere contact, " he wrote, "to satisfy the natives that our intentions are pure and honourable, seeking their own good, materially and socially, more than our own interests. We go to spread what blessings arise from amiable and just intercourse with people who have been strangers to them." Stanley was a hard man, but he was no hypocrite. What he said he undoubtedly meant. It is worth remarking, in view of the accounts of the laziness or stupidity of the natives given by King Leopold's apologists in order to justify their conduct toward them, that Stanley had the very highest opinion of their industry and commercial ability. The following extracts from his writings set this matter beyond all doubt:

"Bolobo is a great centre for the ivory and camwood powder trade, principally because its people are so enterprising."

Of Irebu—"a Venice of the Congo"—he says:

"These people were really acquainted with many lands and tribes on the Upper Congo. From Stanley Pool to Upoto, a distance of 6,000 miles, they knew every landing-place on the river banks. All the ups and downs of savage life, all the profits and losses derived from barter, all the diplomatic arts used by tactful savages, were as well known to them as the Roman alphabet to us. . . . No wonder that all this commercial knowledge had left its traces on their faces; indeed, it is the same as in your own cities in Europe. Know you not the military man among you, the lawyer and the merchant, the banker, the artist, or the poet? It is the same in Africa, MORE ESPECIALLY ON THE CONGO, WHERE THE PEOPLE ARE SO DEVOTED TO TRADE."

"During the few days of our mutual intercourse they gave us a high idea of their qualities—industry, after their own style, not being the least conspicuous."

"As in the old time, Umangi, from the right bank, and Mpa, from the left bank, despatched their representatives with ivory tusks, large and small, goats and sheep, and vegetable food, clamorously demanding that we should buy from them. Such urgent entreaties, accompanied with blandishments to purchase their stock, were difficult to resist."

"I speak of eager native traders following us for miles for the smallest piece of cloth. I mention that after travelling many miles to obtain cloth for ivory and redwood powder, the despairing natives asked: 'Well, what is it you do want? Tell us, and we will get it for you.'"

Speaking of English scepticism as to King Leopold's intentions, he says:

"Though they understand the satisfaction of a sentiment when applied to England, they are slow to understand that it may be a sentiment that induced King Leopold II to father this International Association. He is a dreamer, like his *confrères* in the work, because the sentiment is applied to the neglected millions of the Dark Continent. They cannot appreciate rightly, because there are no dividends attaching to it, this ardent, vivifying and expansive sentiment, which seeks to extend civilizing influences among the dark races, and to brighten up with the glow of civilization the dark places of sad-browed Africa."

One cannot let these extracts pass without noting that Bolobo, the first place named by Stanley, has sunk in population from 40,000 to 7,000; that Irebu, called by Stanley the populous Venice of the Congo, had in 1903 a population of fifty; that the natives who used to follow Stanley, beseeching him to trade, now, according to Consul Casement, fly into the bush at the approach of a steamer, and that the unselfish sentiment of King Leopold II has developed into dividends of 300 per cent per annum. Such is the difference between Stanley's anticipation and the actual fulfilment.

Untroubled, however, with any vision as to the destructive effects of his own work, Stanley laboured hard among the native chiefs and returned to his employer with no less than 450 alleged treaties which transferred land to the Association. We have no record of the exact payment made in order to obtain these treaties, but we have the terms of a similar transaction carried out by a Belgian officer in 1883 at Palabala. In this case the payment made to the Chief consisted of "one coat of red cloth with gold facings, one red cap, one white tunic, one piece of white baft, one piece of red points, one box of liqueurs, four demijohns of rum, two boxes of gin, 128 bottles of gin, twenty red handkerchiefs, forty singlets and forty old cotton caps." It is clear that in making such treaties the Chief thought that he was giving permission for the establishment of a station. The idea that he was actually bartering away the land was never even in his mind, for it was held by a communal tenure for the whole tribe, and it was not his to barter. And yet it is on the strength of such treaties as these that twenty millions of people have been expropriated, and the whole wealth and land of the country proclaimed to belong, not to the inhabitants, but to the State—that is, to King Leopold.

With this sheaf of treaties in his portfolio the King of the Belgians now approached the Powers with high sentiments of humanitarianism, and with a definite request that the State which he was forming should receive some recognized status among the nations. Was he at that time consciously hypocritical? Did he already foresee how widely his future actions would differ from his present professions? It is a problem which will interest the historian of the future, who may have more materials than we upon which to form a judgment. On the one hand, there was a furtive secrecy about the evolution of his plans and the despatch of his expeditions which should have no place in a philanthropic enterprise. On the other hand, there are limits to human powers of deception, and it is almost inconceivable that a man who was acting a part could so completely deceive the whole civilized world. It is more probable, as it seems to me, that his ambitious mind discerned that it was possible for him to acquire a field of action which his small kingdom could not give, in mixing himself with the affairs of Africa. He chose the obvious path, that of a civilizing and elevating mission, taking the line of least resistance without any definite idea whither it might lead him. Once faced with the facts, his astute brain perceived the great material possibilities of this country; his early dreams faded away to be replaced by unscrupulous cupidity, and step by step he was led downward until he, the man of holy aspirations in 1885, stands now in 1909 with such a cloud of terrible direct personal responsibility resting upon him as no man in modern European history has had to bear.

It is, indeed, ludicrous, with our knowledge of the outcome, to read the declarations of the King and of his representatives at that time. They were actually forming the strictest of commercial monopolies—an organization which was destined to crush out all general private trade in a country as large as the whole of Europe with Russia omitted. That was the admitted outcome of their enterprise. Now listen to M. Beernaert, the Belgian Premier, speaking in the year 1885:

"The State, of which our King will be the Sovereign, will be a sort of international Colony. There will be no monopolies, no privileges. . . . Quite the contrary: absolute freedom of commerce, freedom of property, freedom of navigation."

Here, too, are the words of Baron Lambermont, the Belgian Plenipotentiary at the Berlin Conference:

"The temptation to impose abusive taxes will find its corrective, if need be, in the freedom of commerce. . . . No doubt exists as to the strict and literal meaning of the term 'in commercial matters.' It means . . . the unlimited right for every one to buy and to sell."

The question of humanity is so pressing that it obscures that of the broken pledges about trade, but on the latter alone there is ample reason to say that every condition upon which this State was founded has been openly and notoriously violated, and that, therefore, its title-deeds are vitiated from the beginning.

At the time the professions of the King made the whole world his enthusiastic allies. The United States was the first to hasten to give formal recognition to the new State. May it be the first, also, to realize the truth and to take public steps to retract what it has done. The churches and the Chambers of Commerce of Great Britain were all for Leopold, the one attracted by the prospect of pushing their missions into the heart of Africa, the others delighted at the offer of an open market for their produce. At the Congress of Berlin, which was called to regulate the situation, the nations vied with each other in furthering the plans of the King of the Belgians and in extolling his high aims. The Congo Free State was created amid general rejoicings. The veteran Bismarck, as credulous as the others, pronounced its baptismal blessing. "The New Congo State is called upon," said he, "to become one of the chief promoters of the work" (of civilization) "which we have in view, and I pray for its prosperous development and for the fulfilment of the noble aspirations of its illustrious founder." Such was the birth of the Congo Free State. Had the nations gathered round been able to perceive its future, the betrayal of religion and civilization of which it would be guilty, the immense series of crimes which it would perpetrate throughout Central Africa, the lowering of the prestige of all the white races, they would surely have strangled the monster in its cradle.

It is not necessary to record in this statement the whole of the provisions of the Berlin Congress. Two only will suffice, as they are at the same time the most important and the most flagrantly abused. The first of these (which forms the fifth article of the agreement) proclaims that "No Power which exercises sovereign rights in the said regions shall be allowed to grant therein either monopoly or privilege of any kind in commercial matters." No words could be clearer than that, but the Belgian representatives, conscious that such a clause must disarm all opposition, went out of their way to accentuate it. "No privileged situation can be created in this respect, " they said. "The way remains open without any restriction to free competition in the sphere of commerce." It would be interesting now to send a British or German trading expedition up the Congo in search of that free competition which has been so explicitly promised, and to see how it would fare between the monopolist companies who have divided the land between them. We have travelled some distance since Prince Bismarck at the last sitting of the Conference declared that the result was "to secure to the commerce of all nations free access to the centre of the African Continent."

More important, however, is Article IV, both on account of the issues at stake, and because the signatories of the treaty bound themselves solemnly, "in the name of Almighty God," to watch over its enforcement. It ran: "All the Powers exercising sovereign rights or influence in these territories pledge themselves to watch over the preservation of the native populations and the improvement of their moral and material conditions of existence, and to work together for the suppression of slavery and of the slave trade." That was the pledge of the united nations of Europe. It is a disgrace to each of them, including ourselves, the way in which they have fulfilled that oath. Before their eyes, as I shall show in the sequel, they have had enacted one long, horrible tragedy, vouched for by priests and missionaries, traders, travellers and consuls, all corroborated, but in no way reformed, by a Belgium commission of inquiry. They have seen these unhappy people, who were their wards, robbed of all they possessed, debauched, degraded, mutilated, tortured, murdered, all on such a scale as has never, to my knowledge, occurred before in the whole course of history, and now, after all these years, with all the facts notorious, we are still at the stage of polite diplomatic expostulations. It is no answer to say that France and Germany have shown even less regard for the pledge they took at Berlin. An individual does not condone the fact that he has broken his word by pointing out that his neighbour has done the same.

III
The Working of the System

Having claimed, as I have shown, the whole of the land, and therefore the whole of its products, the State—that is, the King—proceeded to construct a system by which these products could be gathered most rapidly and at least cost. The essence of this system was that the people who had been dispossessed (ironically called "citizens") were to be forced to gather, for the profit of the State, those very products which had been taken from them. This was to be effected by two means; the one, taxation, by which an arbitrary amount, ever growing larger until it consumed almost their whole lives in the gathering, should be claimed for nothing. The other, so-called barter by which the natives were paid for the stuff exactly what the State chose to give, and in the form the State chose to give it, there being no competition allowed from any other purchase. This remuneration, ridiculous in value, took the most absurd shape, the natives being compelled to take it, whatever the amount, and however little they might desire it. Consul Thesiger, in 1908, describing their so-called barter, says: "The goods he proceeds to distribute, giving a hat to one man, or an iron hoe-head to another, and so on. Each recipient is then at the end of a month responsible for so many balls of rubber. No choice of the objects is given, no refusal is allowed. If any one makes any objection, the stuff is thrown down at his door, and whether it is taken or left, the man is responsible for so many balls at the end of the month. The total amounts are fixed by the agents at the maximum which the inhabitants are capable of producing."

But is it not clear that no natives, especially tribes who, as Stanley has recorded, had remarkable aptitude for trade, would do business at all upon such terms? That is just where the system came in.

By this system some two thousand white agents were scattered over the Free State to collect the produce. These whites were placed in ones and twos in the more central points, and each was given a tract of country containing a certain number of villages. By the help of the inmates he was to gather the rubber, which was the most valuable asset. These whites, many of whom were men of low *morale* before they left Europe, were wretchedly paid, the scale running from 150 to 300 francs a month. This pay they might supplement by a commission or bonus on the amount of rubber collected. If their returns were large it meant increased pay, official praise, a more speedy return to Europe, and a better chance of promotion. If, on the other hand, the returns were small, it meant poverty, harsh reproof and degradation. No system could be devised by which a body of men could be so driven to attain results at any cost. It is not to the absolute discredit of Belgians that such an existence should have demoralized them, and, indeed, there were other nationalities besides Belgians in the ranks of the agents. I doubt if Englishmen,

Americans, or Germans could have escaped the same result had they been exposed in a tropical country to similar temptations.

And now, the two thousand agents being in place, and eager to enforce the collection of rubber upon very unwilling natives, how did the system intend that they should set about it? The method was as efficient as it was absolutely diabolical. Each agent was given control over a certain number of savages, drawn from the wild tribes, but armed with firearms. One or more of these was placed in each village to ensure that the villagers should do their task. These are the men who are called "capitas," or head-men in the accounts, and who are the actual, though not the moral, perpetrators of so many horrible deeds. Imagine the nightmare which lay upon each village while this barbarian squatted in the midst of it. Day or night they could never get away from him. He called for palm wine. He called for women. He beat them, mutilated them, and shot them down at his pleasure. He enforced public incest in order to amuse himself by the sight. Sometimes they plucked up spirit and killed him. The Belgian Commission records that 142 capitas had been killed in seven months in a single district. Then came the punitive expedition, and the destruction of the whole community. The more terror the capita inspired, the more useful he was, the more eagerly the villagers obeyed him, and the more rubber yielded its commission to the agent. When the amount fell off, then the capita was himself made to feel some of those physical pains which he had inflicted upon others. Often the white agent far exceeded in cruelty the barbarian who carried out his commissions. Often, too, the white man pushed the black aside, and acted himself as torturer and executioner. As a rule, however, the relationship was as I have stated, the outrages being actually committed by the capitas, but with the approval of, and often in the presence of, their white employers.

It would be absurd to suppose that the agents were all equally merciless, and that there were not some who were torn in two by the desire for wealth and promotion on the one side and the horror of their daily task upon the other. Here are two illustrative extracts from the letters of Lieutenant Tilkens, as quoted by Mr. Vandervelde in the debate in the Belgian Chamber: "The steamer *v. d. Kerkhove* is coming up the Nile. It will require the colossal number of fifteen hundred porters—unhappy blacks! I cannot think of them. I ask myself how I shall find such a number. If the roads were passable it would make some difference, but they are hardly cleared of morasses where many will meet their death. Hunger and weariness will make an end of many more in the eight days' march. How much blood will the transport make to flow? Already I have had to make war three times against the chieftains who will not take part in this work. The people prefer to die in the forest instead of doing this work. If a chieftain refuses, it is war, and this horrible war—perfect firearms against spear and lance. A chieftain has just left me with the complaint: 'My village is in ruins, my women are killed.' But what can I do? I am often compelled to put these unhappy chieftains into chains until they collect one or two hundred porters. Very often my soldiers find the villages empty, then they seize the women and children."

To his mother he writes:

"Com. Verstraeten visited my station and highly congratulated me. He said the attitude of his report hung upon the quantity of rubber I would bring. My quantity rose from 360 kilos in September to 1,500 in October, and from January it will be 4,000 per month, which gives me 500 francs over my pay. Am I not a lucky fellow? And if I continue, in two years I shall have reached an additional 12,000 francs."

But a year later he writes in a different tone to Major Leussens:

"I look forward to a general rising. I warned you before, I think; already in my last letter. The cause is always the same. The natives are weary of the hitherto *régime*—transport labour, collection of rubber, preparation of food stores for blacks and whites. Again for three months I have had to fight with only ten days' rest. I have 152 prisoners. For two years now I have been carrying on war in this neighbourhood. But I cannot say I have subjected the people. They prefer to die. What can I do? I am paid to do my work, I am a tool in the hands of my superiors, and I follow orders as discipline requires."

Let us consider now for an instant the chain of events which render such a situation not only possible, but inevitable. The State is run with the one object of producing revenue. For this end all land and its produce are appropriated. How, then, is this produce to be gathered? It can only be by the natives. But if the natives gather it they must be paid their price, which will diminish profits, or else they will refuse to work. Then they must be made to work. But the agents are too few to make them work. Then they must employ such sub-agents as will strike most terror into the people. But if these sub-agents are to make the people work all the time, then they must themselves reside in the villages. So a capita must be sent as a constant terror to each village. Is it not clear that these steps are not accidental, but are absolutely essential to the original idea? Given the confiscation of the land, all the rest must logically follow. It is utterly futile, therefore, to imagine that any reform can set matters right. Such a thing is impossible. Until unfettered trade is unconditionally restored, as it now exists in every German and English colony, it is absolutely out of the question that any specious promises or written decrees can modify the situation. But, on the other hand, if trade be put upon this natural basis, then for many years the present owners of the Congo land, instead of sharing dividends, must pay out at least a million a year to administer the country, exactly as England pays half a million a year to administer the neighbouring land of Nigeria. To grasp that fact is to understand the root of the whole question.

And one more point before we proceed to the dark catalogue of the facts. Where did the responsibility for these deeds of blood, these thousands of cold-blooded murders lie? Was it with the capita?

He was a cannibal and a ruffian, but if he did not inspire terror in the village he was himself punished by the agent. Was it, then, with the agent? He was a degraded man, and yet, as I have already said, no men could serve on such terms in a tropical country without degradation. He was goaded and driven to crime by the constant clamour from those above him. Was it, then, with the District Commissary? He had reached a responsible and well-paid post, which he would lose if his particular district fell behind in the race of production. Was it, then, with the Governor-General at Boma? He was a man of a hardened conscience, but for him also there was mitigation. He was there for a purpose with definite orders from home which it was his duty to carry through. It would take a man of exceptional character to throw up his high position, sacrifice his career, and refuse to carry out the evil system which had been planned before he was allotted a place in it.

Where, then, was the guilt? There were half a dozen officials in Brussels who were, as shown already, so many bailiffs paid to manage a property upon lines laid down for them. Trace back the chain from the red-handed savage, through the worried, bilious agent, the pompous Commissary, the dignified Governor-General, the smooth diplomatist, and you come finally, without a break, and without a possibility of mitigation or excuse, up to the cold, scheming brain which framed and drove the whole machine. It is upon the King, always the King, that the guilt must lie. He planned it, knowing the results which must follow. They did follow. He was well informed of it. Again and again, and yet again, his attention was drawn to it. A word from him would have altered the system. The word was never said. There is no possible subterfuge by which the moral guilt can be deflected from the head of the State, the man who went to Africa for the freedom of commerce and the regeneration of the native.

V
Further Fruits of the System

For a moment I must interrupt the narrative of the long, dismal succession of atrocities in order to explain certain new factors in the situation.

It has already been shown that the Congo State, unable to handle the whole of its vast domain, had sublet large tracts of it to monopolist companies, in absolute contradiction to Article V of the Berlin Treaty. Up to the year 1897, these companies were registered in Belgium, and had some pretence to being international in scope. The State had no open or direct control over them. This was now altered. The State drew closer the bonds which united it to these commercial undertakings. They were, for the most part, dissolved, and then reconstructed under Congo law. In most cases, in return for the monopoly, the State was given control, sometimes to the extent of appointing all managers and agents. Half the shares of the company or half the profits were usually made over to the State. Thus one must bear in mind in the future that whether one talks of the Abir Company, of the Kasai, the Katanga, the Anversoise, or any other, it is really with the State—that is, with King

Leopold—that one has to do. He owned the companies, but paid them fifty per cent commission for doing all the work. As their profits were such as might be expected where nothing was paid either for produce or for labour (varying from fifty to seven hundred per cent per annum), all parties to the bargain were the gainers.

Another new factor in the situation was the completion, in 1898, of the Lower Congo Railway, which connects Boma with Stanley Pool, and so outflanks the cataracts. The enterprise itself was beneficent and splendid. The means by which it was carried out were unscrupulous and inhuman. Had civilization no complaint against the Congo State save the history of its railway construction with its forced labour, so different to the tradition of the tropical procedure of other European colonies, it would be a heavy indictment. Now it sinks to insignificance when compared with the enslavement of a whole people and the twenty years of uninterrupted massacre. As a sketch of the condition of the railway district here is a little pen picture by M. Edouard Picard, of the Belgian Senate, who saw it in the building:

"The cruel impression conveyed by the mutilated forests, " he wrote, "is heightened in the places where, till lately, native villages nestled, hidden and protected by thick and lofty foliage. The inhabitants have fled. They have fled in spite of encouraging palavers and promises of peace and kind treatment. They have burnt their huts, and great heaps of cinders mark the sites, amid deserted palm-groves and trampled-down banana fields. The terrors caused by the memory of inhuman floggings, of massacres, of rapes and abductions, haunt their poor brains, and they go as fugitives to seek shelter in the recesses of the hospitable bush, or, across the frontiers, to find it in French or Portuguese Congo, not yet afflicted with so many labours and alarms, far from the roads traversed by white men, those baneful intruders, and their train of strange and disquieting habits." The outlook was as gloomy when he wandered along the path trodden by the caravans to the Pool and back again. "We are constantly meeting these carriers, either isolated or in Indian file; blacks, blacks, miserable blacks, with horribly filthy loin-clothes for their only garments; their bare and frizzled heads supporting their loads—chest, bale, ivory-tusk, hamper of rubber, or barrel; for the most part broken down, sinking under the burdens made heavier by their weariness and insufficiency of food, consisting of a handful of rice and tainted dried fish; pitiful walking caryatids; beasts of burden with the lank limbs of monkeys, pinched-up features, eyes fixed and round with the strain of keeping their balance in the dulness of exhaustion. Thus they come and go by thousands, organized in a system of human transport, requisitioned by the State armed with its irresistible *force publique*, supplied by the chiefs whose slaves they are and who pounce on their wages; jogging on, with knees bent and stomach protruding, one arm raised up and the other resting on a long stick, dusty and malodorous; covered with insects as their huge procession passes over mountains and through valleys; dying on the tramp, or, when the tramp is over, going to their villages to die of exhaustion."

It will be remembered that Captain Lothaire, having been acquitted of the murder of Mr. Stokes, was sent out by King Leopold to act as managing-director of the Anversoise Trust. In 1898, he arrived in the Mongalla District, and from then onward there came to Europe vague rumours of native attacks and bloody reprisals, with those other symptoms of violence and unrest which might be expected where a large population accustomed to freedom is suddenly reduced to slavery. How huge were the rubber operations which were carried through under the ferocious rule of Captain Lothaire, may be guessed from the fact that the profits of the company, which had been 120,000 francs in 1897, rose to 3,968,000 in 1899—a sum which is considerably more than twice the total capital. M. Mille tells of a Belgian agent who showed 25,000 cartridges and remarked, "I can turn those into 25,000 pounds of rubber." Captain Lothaire believed in the same trade methods, for his fighting and his output increased together. It is worth while to slaughter one-fourth of the population if the effect is to drive the others to frenzied and unceasing work.

No definite details might ever have reached Europe of those doings had not Lothaire made the capital mistake of quarrelling with his subordinates. One of these, named Lacroix, sent a communication to the *Nieuw Gazet*, of Antwerp, which, with the *Petit Bleu*, acted an honourable and independent part at this epoch. The Congo Press Bureau, which has stifled the voice of the more venal portion of the Belgian and Parisian Press, had not at that time attained the efficiency which it afterward reached. This letter from Lacroix was published on April 10th, 1900, and shed a lurid light upon what had been going on in the Mongalla District. It was a confession, but a confession which involved his superiors as well as himself. He told how he had been instructed by his chief to massacre all the natives of a certain village which had been slow in bringing its rubber. He had carried out the order. Later, his chief had put sixty women in irons, and allowed nearly all of them to die of hunger because the village—Mummumbula—had not brought enough rubber. "I am going to be tried, " he wrote, "for having murdered one hundred and fifty men, for having crucified women and children, and for having mutilated many men and hung the remains on the village fence." At the same moment as this confession of Lacroix, *Le Petit Bleu* published sworn affidavits of soldiers employed by the Trust, telling how they had put to death whole villages for being short with their rubber. Moray, another agent, published a confession in *Le Petit Bleu*, from which this is an extract:

"At Ambas we were a party of thirty, under Van Eycken, who sent us into a village to ascertain if the natives were collecting rubber, and in the contrary case to murder all, including men, women and children. We found the natives sitting peaceably. We asked them what they were doing. They were unable to reply, thereupon we fell upon them all, and killed them without mercy. An hour later we were joined by Van Eycken, and told him what had been done. He answered: 'It is well, but you have not done enough!' Thereupon he ordered us to cut off the heads of the men and hang them on the village palisades, also their sexual members, and to hang the women and children on the palisades in the form of a cross."

In the face of these fresh revelations there was an outburst of feeling in Belgium, showing that it is only their ignorance of the true facts which prevents the inhabitants of that country from showing the same humanity as any other civilized nation would do. They have not yet realized the foul things which have been done in their name. Surely when they do realize it there will be a terrible reckoning! Some were already very alive to the question. MM. Vandervelde and Lorand fought bravely in the Chamber. The officials, with MM. Liebrichts and De Cuvelier at their head, made the usual vague professions and general denials. "Ah, you can rest assured light will be forthcoming, complete, striking!" cried the former. Light was indeed forthcoming, though not so complete as might be wished, for some, at least, of the scoundrels implicated were tried and condemned. In any other European colony they would have been hanged offhand, as the villainous murderers that they were. But they do not hang white men in the Congoland, even with the blood of a hundred murders on their hands. The only white man ever hanged there was the Englishman Stokes for competing in trade.

What is to be remarked, however, is that only subordinates were punished. Van Eycken was acquitted; Lacroix had imprisonment; Mattheys, another agent accused of horrible practices, got twelve years—which sounded well at the time, but he was liberated at the end of three. In the sentence upon this man the Judge used the words, "Seeing that it is just to take into account the example which his superiors gave him in showing no respect for the lives or rights of the natives." Brave words, but how helpless is justice when such words can be said, and no result follow! They referred, of course, to Captain Lothaire, who had, in the meanwhile, fled aboard a steamer at Matadi, and made his escape to Europe. His flight was common knowledge, but who would dare to lay his hand upon the favourite of the King. Lothaire has had occasion several times since to visit the Congo, but Justice has indeed sat with bandaged eyes where that man was concerned!

There is one incident which should be marked in the story of this trial. Moray, whose testimony would have been of great importance, was found dead in his bed just before the proceedings. There have been several such happenings in Congo history. Commandant Dooms, having threatened to expose the misdeeds of Lieutenant Massard before Europe, was shortly afterward declared to have been mysteriously drowned by a hippopotamus. Dr. Barotti, returning hot with anger after an inspection of the State, declares vehemently that he was poisoned. There is much that is of the sixteenth century in this State, besides its views of its duties to the natives.

Before passing these revelations with the attendant burst of candour in the Belgian Press, it may be well to transcribe the following remark in an interview from a returned Congo official which appears in the *Antwerp Nieuw Gazet* (April 10th, 1900). He says:

"When first commissioned to establish a fort, I was given some native soldiers and a prodigious stock of ammunition. My chief gave me the following instructions: 'Crush every obstacle!' I obeyed and cut through my district by fire and sword. I had left Antwerp thinking I was simply to gather rubber. Great was my stupefaction when the truth dawned on me."

This, with the letter of Lieutenant Tilken, as quoted before, gives some insight into the position of the agent.

Indeed, there is something to be said for these unfortunate men, for it is a more awful thing to be driven to crime than to endure it. Consider the sequence of events! The man sees an advertisement offering a commercial situation in the tropics. He applies to a bureau. He is told that the salary is some seventy-five pounds a year, with a bonus on results. He knows nothing of the country or conditions. He accepts. He is then asked if he has any money. He has not. One hundred pounds is advanced to him for expenses and outfit, and he is pledged to work it off. He goes out and finds the terrible nature of the task before him. He must condone crime to get his results. Suppose he resigns? "Certainly, " say the authorities; "but you must remain there until you have worked off your debt!" He cannot possibly get down the river, for the steamers are all under Government control. What can he do then? There is one thing which he very frequently does, and that is to blow out his brains. The statistics of suicide are higher than in any service in the world. But suppose he takes the line: "Very well, I will stay if you make me do so, but I will expose these misdeeds to Europe." What then? The routine is a simple one. An official charge is preferred against him of ill-treating the natives. Ill-treating of some sort is always going forward, and there is no difficulty with the help of the sentries in proving that something for which the agent is responsible does not tally with the written law, however much it might be the recognized custom. He is taken to Boma, tried and condemned. Thus it comes about that the prison of Boma may at the same time contain the best men and the worst—the men whose ideas were too humane for the authorities as well as those whose crimes could not be overlooked even by a Congolese administration. Take warning, you who seek service in this dark country, for suicide, the Boma prison, or such deeds as will poison your memory forever are the only choice which will lie before you.

Here is the sort of official circular which descends in its thousands upon the agent. This particular one was from the Commissioner in the Wille district:

"I give you *carte blanche* to procure 4,000 kilos of rubber a month. You have two months in which to work your people. Employ gentleness at first, and if they persist in resisting the demands of the State, employ force of arms."

And this State was formed for the "moral and material advantage of the native."

While dealing with trials of Boma I will give some short account of the Caudron case, which occurred in 1904. This case was remarkable as establishing judicially what was always clear enough: the complicity between the State and the criminal. Caudron was a man against whom 120 cold-blooded murders were charged. He was, in fact, a zealous and efficient agent of the Anversoise Society, that same company whose red-edged securities rose to such a height when Manager Lothaire taught the natives what a minister in the Belgian House described as the Christian law of work. He did his best for the company, and he did his best for himself, for he had a three per cent commission upon the rubber. Why he should be chosen among all his fellow-murderers is hard to explain, but it was so, and he found himself at Boma with a sentence of twenty years. On appealing, this was reduced to fifteen years, which experience has shown to mean in practice two or three. The interesting point of his trial, however, is that his appeal, and the consequent decrease of sentence which justified that appeal, were based upon the claim that the Government was cognisant of the murderous raids, and that the Government soldiers were used to effect them. The points brought out by the trial were:

1. The existence of a system of organized oppression, plunder and massacre, in order to increase the output of india-rubber for the benefit of a "company, " which is only a covering name for the Government itself.

2. That the local authorities of the Government are cognisant, and participatory in this system.

3. That local officials of the Government engage in these rubber raids, and that Government troops are regularly employed there on.

4. That the Judicature is powerless to place the real responsibility on the proper shoulders.

5. That, consequently, these atrocities will continue until the system itself is extirpated.

Caudron's counsel called for the production of official documents to show how the chain of responsibility went, but the President of the Appeal Court refused it, knowing as clearly as we do, that it could only conduct to the Throne itself.

One might ask how the details of this trial came to Europe when it is so seldom that anything leaks out from the Courts of Boma. The reason was that there lived in Boma a British coloured subject named Shanir, who was at pains to attend the court day by day in order to preserve some record of the procedure. This he dispatched to Europe. The sequel is interesting. The man's trade, which was a very large one, was boycotted, he lost his all, brooded over his misfortunes, and finally took his own life—another martyr in the cause of Congo.

VII
Consul Roger Casement's Report

Up to this time the published reports as to the black doings of King Leopold and his men were, with the exception of a guarded document from Consul Pickersgill, in 1898, entirely from private individuals. No doubt there were official reports but the Government withheld them. In 1904, this policy of reticence was abandoned, and the historic report of Consul Roger Casement confirmed, and in some ways amplified, all that had reached Europe from other sources.

A word or two as to Mr. Casement's own personality and qualifications may not be amiss, since both were attacked by his Belgian detractors. He is a tried and experienced public servant, who has had exceptional opportunities of knowing Africa and the natives. He entered the Consular Service in 1892, served on the Niger till 1895, was Consul at Delagoa Bay to 1898, and was finally transferred to the Congo. Personally, he is a man of the highest character, truthful, unselfish—one who is deeply respected by all who know him. His experience, which deals with the Crown Domain districts in the year 1903, covers some sixty-two pages, to be read in full in "White Book, Africa, No. I, 1904." I will not apologize for the length of the extracts, as this, the first official exposure, was an historical document and from its publication we mark the first step in that train of events which is surely destined to remove the Congo State from hands which have proved so unworthy, and to place it in conditions which shall no longer be a disgrace to European civilization. It may be remarked before beginning that at some of these conversations with the natives Mr. Scrivener was present, and that he corroborates the account given by the Consul.

The beginning of Mr. Casement's report shows how willing he was to give praise where praise was possible, and to say all that could be said for the Administration. He talks of "energetic European intervention, " and adds, "that very much of the intervention has been called for no one who formerly knew the Upper Congo could doubt." "Admirably built and admirably kept stations greet the traveller at many points." "To-day the railway works most efficiently." He attributes sleeping sickness as "one cause of the seemingly wholesale diminution of human life which I everywhere observed in the regions re-visited; a prominent place must be assigned to this malady. The natives certainly attribute their alarming death-rate to this as one of the inducing causes, although they attribute, and I think principally, their rapid decrease in numbers to other causes as well."

The Government work shop "was brightness, care, order, and activity, and it was impossible not to admire and commend the industry which had created and maintained in constant working order this useful establishment."

These are not the words of a critic who has started with a prejudiced mind or the desire to make out a case.

In the lower reaches of the river above Stanley Pool Casement found no gross ill-usage. The natives were hopeless and listless, being debarred from trade and heavily taxed in food, fish and other produce. It was not until he began to approach the cursed rubber zones that terrible things began to dawn upon him. Casement had travelled in 1887 in the Congo, and was surprised to note the timidity of the natives. Soon he had his explanation:

"At one of these villages, S———, after confidence had been restored and the fugitives had been induced to come in from the surrounding forest, where they had hidden themselves, I saw women coming back, carrying their babies, their household utensils, and even the food they had hastily snatched up, up to a late hour of the evening. Meeting some of these returning women in one of the fields I asked them why they had run away at my approach, and they said, smiling, 'We thought you were Bula Matadi' (*i.e.*, 'men of the Government'). Fear of this kind was formerly unknown on the Upper Congo; and in much more out-of-the-way places visited many years ago the people flocked from all sides to greet a white stranger. But to-day the apparition of a white man's steamer evidently gave the signal for instant flight."

". . . Men, he said, still came to him whose hands had been cut off by the Government soldiers during those evil days, and he said there were still many victims of these species of mutilation in the surrounding country. Two cases of the kind came to my actual notice while I was in the lake. One, a young man, both of whose hands had been beaten off with the butt-ends of rifles against a tree, the other a young lad of eleven or twelve years of age, whose right hand was cut off at the wrist. This boy described the circumstances of his mutilation, and, in answer to my inquiry, said that although wounded at the time he was perfectly sensible of the severing of his wrist, but lay still fearing that if he moved he would be killed. In both these cases the Government soldiers had been accompanied by white officers whose names were given to me. Of six natives (one a girl, three little boys, one youth, and one old woman) who had been mutilated in this way during the rubber *régime*, all except one were dead at the date of my visit. The old woman had died at the beginning of this year, and her niece described to me how the act of mutilation in her case had been accomplished."

The fines inflicted upon villages for trifling offences were such as to produce the results here described:

"The officer had then imposed as further punishment a fine of 55,000 brass rods (2,750 fr.)—£110. This sum they had been forced to pay, and as they had no other means of raising so large a sum they had, many of them, been compelled to sell their children and their wives. I saw no live-stock of any kind in W—— save a very few fowls—possibly under a dozen—and it seemed, indeed, not unlikely that, as these people asserted, they had great difficulty in always getting their supplies ready. A father and mother stepped out and said that they had been forced to sell their son, a little boy called F, for 1,000 rods to meet their share of the fine. A widow came and declared that she had been forced, in order to meet her share of the fine, to sell her daughter G, a little girl whom I judged from her description to be about ten years of age. She had been sold to a man in Y——, who was named, for 1,000 rods, which had then gone to make up the fine."

The natives were broken in spirit by the treatment:

"One of them—a strong, indeed, a splendid-looking man—broke down and wept, saying that their lives were useless to them, and that they knew of no means of escape from the troubles which were gathering around them. I could only assure these people that their obvious course to obtain relief was by appeal to their own constituted authorities, and that if their circumstances were clearly understood by those responsible for these fines I trusted and believed some satisfaction would be forthcoming."

These fines, it may be added, were absolutely illegal. It was the officer, not the poor, harried natives, who had broken the law.

"These fines, it should be borne in mind, are illegally imposed; they are not 'fines of Court'; are not pronounced after any judicial hearing, or for any proved offence against the law, but are quite arbitrarily levied according to the whim or ill-will of the executive officers of the district, and their collection, as well as their imposition, involves continuous breaches of the Congolese laws. They do not, moreover, figure in the account of public revenues in the Congo 'Budgets'; they are not paid into the public purse of the country, but are spent on the needs of the station or military camp of the officer imposing them, just as seems good to this official."

Here is an illustrative anecdote:

"One of the largest Congo Concession Companies had, when I was on the Upper River, addressed a request to its Directors in Europe for a further supply of ball-cartridge. The Directors had met this demand by asking what had become of the 72,000 cartridges shipped some three years ago, to which a reply was sent to the effect that these had all been used in the production of india-rubber. I did not see this correspondence, and cannot vouch for the truth of the statement; but the officer who informed me that it had passed before his own eyes was one of the highest standing in the interior."

Another witness showed the exact ratio between cartridges and rubber:

"'The S. A. B. on the Bussira, with 150 guns, get only ten tons (rubber) a month; we, the State at Momboyo, with 130 guns, get thirteen tons per month.' 'So you count by guns?' I asked him. 'Partout, ' M. P. said. 'Each time the corporal goes out to get rubber cartridges are given to him. He must bring back all not used; and for every one used, he must bring back a right hand.' M. P. told me that sometimes they shot a cartridge at an animal in hunting; they then cut off a hand from a living man. As to the extent to which this is carried on, he informed me that in six months they, the State, on the Momboyo River, had used 6,000 cartridges, which means that 6,000 people are killed or mutilated. It means more than 6,000 for the people have told me repeatedly that the soldiers kill children with the butt of their guns."

That the statement about the cutting off of living hands is correct is amply proved by the Kodak. I have photographs of at least twenty such mutilated Negroes in my own possession.

Here is a copy of a dispatch from an official quoted in its naked frankness:

"Le Chef Ngulu de Wangata est envoyé dans la Maringa, pour m'y acheter des esclaves. Prière a MM. les agents de l'A.B.I.R. de bien vouloir me signaler les méfaits que celui-ci pourrait commettre en route.

"Le Capitaine-Commandant,
(Signé) "SARRAZZYN."
"*Colquilhatville, le* Ier *Mai,* 1896."

Pretty good for the State which boasts that it has put down the slave trade.

There is a passage showing the working of the rubber system which is so clear and authoritative that I transcribe it in full:

"I went to the homes of these men some miles away and found out their circumstances. To get the rubber they had first to go fully a two days' journey from their homes, leaving their wives, and being absent for from five to six days. They were seen to the forest limits under guard, and if not back by the sixth day trouble was likely to ensue. To get the rubber in the forests—which, generally speaking, are very swampy—involves much fatigue and often fruitless searching for a well-flowing vine. As the area of supply diminishes, moreover, the demand for rubber constantly increases. Some little time back I learned the Bongandanga district supplied seven tons of rubber a month, a quantity which it was hoped would shortly be increased to ten tons. The quantity of rubber brought by the three men in question would have represented, probably, for the three of them certainly not less than seven kilog. of pure rubber. That would be a very safe estimate, and at an average of 7fr. per kilog. they might be said to have brought in £2 worth of rubber. In return for this labour, or imposition, they have received goods which cost certainly under 1s., and whose local valuation came to 45 rods (1s. 10d.). As this process repeats itself twenty-six times year, it will be seen that they would have yielded £52 in kind at the end of the year to the local factory, and would have received in return some 24s. or 25s. worth of goods, which had a market value on the spot of £2 7s. 8d. In addition to these formal payments they were liable at times to be dealt with in another manner, for should their work, which might have been just as hard, have proved less profitable in its yield of rubber, the local prison would have seen them. The people everywhere assured me that they were not happy under this system, and it was apparent to a callous eye that in this they spoke the strict truth."

Again I insert a passage to show that Casement was by no means an ill-natured critic:

"It is only right to say that the present agent of the A.B.I.R. Society I met at Bongandanga seemed to me to try, in very difficult and embarrassing circumstances, to minimize as far as possible, and within the limits of his duties, the evils of the system I there observed at work."

Speaking of the Mongalla massacres—those in which Lothaire was implicated—he quotes from the judgment of the Court of Appeal:

"That it is just to take into account that, by the correspondence produced in the case, the chiefs of the Concession Company have, if not by formal orders, at least by their example and their tolerance, induced their agents to take no account whatever of the rights, property, and lives of the natives; to use the arms and the soldiers which should have served for their defence and the maintenance of order to force the natives to furnish them with produce and to work for the Company, as also to pursue as rebels and outlaws those who sought to escape from the requisitions imposed upon them. . . . That, above all, the fact that the arrest of women and their detention to compel the villages to furnish both produce and workmen, was tolerated and admitted even by certain of the administrative authorities of the region."

Yet another example of the workings of the system:

"In the morning, when about to start for K——, many people from the surrounding country came in to see me. They brought with them three individuals who had been shockingly wounded by gun fire, two men and a very small boy, not more than six years of age, and a fourth— a boy child of six or seven—whose right hand was cut off at the wrist. One of the men, who had been shot through the arm, declared that he was Y of L——, a village situated some miles away. He declared that he had been shot as I saw under the following circumstances: the soldiers had entered his town, he alleged, to enforce the due fulfilment of the rubber tax due by the community. These men had tied him up and said that unless he paid 1,000 brass rods to them they would shoot him. Having no rods to give them they had shot him through the arm and had left him."

I may say that among my photographs are several with shattered arms who have been treated in this fashion.

This is how the natives were treated when they complained to the white man:

"In addition, fifty women are required each morning to go to the factory and work there all day. They complained that the remuneration given for these services was most inadequate, and that they were continually beaten. When I asked the Chief W why he had not gone to D F to complain if the sentries beat him or his people, opening his mouth he pointed to one of the teeth which was just dropping out, and said 'That is what I got from the D F four days ago when I went to tell him what I now say to you.' He added that he was frequently beaten, along with others of his people, by the white man."

One sentry was taken almost red-handed by Mr. Casement:

"After some little delay a boy of about fifteen years of age appeared, whose left arm was wrapped up in a dirty rag. Removing this, I found the left hand had been hacked off by the wrist, and that a shot hole appeared in the fleshy part of the forearm. The boy, who gave his name as I I, in answer to my inquiry, said that a sentry of the La Lulanga Company now in the town had cut off his hand. I proceeded to look for this man, who at first could not be found, the natives to a considerable number gathering behind me as I walked through the town. After some delay the sentry appeared, carrying a cap-gun. The boy, whom I placed before him, then accused him to his face of having mutilated him. The men of the town, who were questioned in succession, corroborated the boy's statement. The sentry, who gave his name as K K, could make no answer to the charge. He met it by vaguely saying some other sentry of the Company had mutilated I I; his predecessor, he said, had cut off several hands, and probably this was one of the victims. The natives around said that there were two other sentries at present in the town, who were not so bad as K K, but that he was a villain. As the evidence against him was perfectly clear, man after man standing out and declaring he had seen the act committed, I informed him and the people present that I should appeal to the local authorities for his immediate arrest and trial."

The following extract must be my final quotation from Consul Casement's report:

"I asked then how this tax was imposed. One of them, who had been hammering out an iron neck-collar on my arrival, spoke first. He said:
"'I am N N. These other two beside me are O O and P P, all of us Y——. From our country each village had to take twenty loads of rubber. These loads were big: they were as big as this. . . .' (Producing an empty basket which came nearly to the handle of my walking-stick.) 'That was the first size. We had to fill that up, but as rubber got scarcer the white man reduced the amount. We had to take these loads in four times a month.'
"Q. 'How much pay did you get for this?'
"A. (Entire audience.) 'We got no pay! We got nothing!'

"And then N N, whom I asked again, said:

"'Our village got cloth and a little salt, but not the people who did the work. Our chiefs eat up the cloth; the workers got nothing. The pay was a fathom of cloth and a little salt for every big basketful, but it was given to the chief, never to the men. It used to take ten days to get the twenty baskets of rubber—we were always in the forest and then when we were late we were killed. We had to go further and further into the forest to find the rubber vines, to go without food, and our women had to give up cultivating the fields and gardens. Then we starved. Wild beasts—the leopards—killed some of us when we were working away in the forest, and others got lost or died from exposure and starvation, and we begged the white man to leave us alone, saying we could get no more rubber, but the white men and their soldiers said: "Go! You are only beasts yourselves; you are nyama (meat)." We tried, always going further into the forest, and when we failed and our rubber was short, the soldiers came to our towns and killed us. Many were shot, some had their ears cut off: others were tied up with ropes around their necks and bodies and taken away. The white men sometimes at the posts did not know of the bad things the soldiers did to us, but it was the white men who sent the soldiers to punish us for not bringing in enough rubber.'

"Here P P took up the tale from N N:

"'We said to the white men, "We are not enough people now to do what you want us. Our country has not many people in it and we are dying fast. We are killed by the work you make us do, by the stoppage of our plantations, and the breaking up of our homes." The white man looked at us and said: "There are lots of people in Mputu"' (Europe, the white man's country). "If there are lots of people in the white man's country there must also be many people in the black man's country." The white man who said this was the chief white man at F F——; his name was A B; he was a very bad man. Other white men of Bula Matadi who had been bad and wicked were B C, C D, and D E.' These had killed us often, and killed us by their own hands as well as by their soldiers. Some white men were good. These were E F, F G, G H, H I, I K, K L.'

"These ones told them to stay in their homes and did not hunt and chase them as the others had done, but after what they had suffered they did not trust more any one's word, and they had fled from their country and were now going to stay here, far from their homes, in this country where there was no rubber.

"Q. 'How long is it since you left your homes, since the big trouble you speak of?'

"A. 'It lasted for three full seasons, and it is now four seasons since we fled and came into the K—— country.'

"Q. 'How many days is it from N—— to your own country?'

"A. 'Six days of quick marching. We fled because we could not endure the things done to us. Our chiefs were hanged, and we were killed and starved and worked beyond endurance to get rubber.'

"Q. 'How do you know it was the white men themselves who ordered these cruel things to be done to you? These things must have been done without the white man's knowledge by the black soldiers.'

"A. (P P): 'The white men told their soldiers: "You kill only women; you cannot kill men. You must prove that you kill men." So then the soldiers when they killed us' (here he stopped and hesitated, and then pointing to the private parts of my bulldog—it was lying asleep at my feet), he said: 'then they cut off those things and took them to the white men, who said: "It is true, you have killed men."'

"Q. 'You mean to tell me that any white man ordered your bodies to be mutilated like that, and those parts of you carried to him?'

"P P, O O, and all (shouting): 'Yes! many white men. D E did it.'

"Q. 'You say this is true? Were many of you so treated after being shot?'

"All (shouting out): 'Nkoto! Nkoto!' (Very many! Very many!)

"There was no doubt that these people were not inventing. Their vehemence, their flashing eyes, their excitement, was not simulated. Doubtless they exaggerated the numbers, but they were clearly telling what they knew and loathed. I was told that they often became so furious at the recollection of what had been done to them that they lost control over themselves. One of the men before me was getting into this state now."

Such is the story—or a very small portion of it—which His Majesty's Consul conveyed to His Majesty's Government as to the condition of those natives, who, "in the name of Almighty God, " we had pledged ourselves to defend!

The same damning White Book contained a brief account of Lord Cromer's experience upon the Upper Nile in the Lado district. He notes that for eighty miles the side of the river which is British territory was crowded with native villages, the inhabitants of which ran along the bank calling to the steamer. The other bank (Congolese territory), was a deserted wilderness. The "Tu quoque" argument which King Leopold's henchmen are so fond of advancing will find it hard to reconcile the difference. Lord Cromer ends his report:

"It appears to me that the facts which I have stated above afford amply sufficient evidence of the spirit which animates the Belgian Administration, if, indeed, Administration it can be called. The Government, so far as I could judge, is conducted almost exclusively on commercial principles, and, even judged by that standard, it would appear that those principles are somewhat short-sighted."

In the same White Book which contains these documents there is printed the Congolese defence drawn up by M. de Cuvelier. The defence consists in simply ignoring all the definite facts laid before the public, and in making such statements as that the British have themselves made war upon natives, as if there were no distinction between war and massacre, and that the British have put a poll-tax upon natives, which, if it be reasonable in amount, is a perfectly just proceeding adopted by all Colonial nations. Let the possessors of the Free State use this system, and at the same time restore the freedom of trade by throwing open the country to all, and returning to the natives that land and produce which has been taken from them. When they have done this—and punished the guilty—there will be an end of anti-Congo agitation. Beyond this, a large part (nearly half) of the Congo Reply (*notes sur le rapport de Mr. Casement, de Dec.* 11, 1903), is taken up by trying to show that in one case of mutilation the injuries were, in truth, inflicted by a wild boar. There must be many wild boars in Congo land, and their habits are of a singular nature. It is not in the Congo that these boars are bred.

IX
The Congo after the Commission

The high hopes which the advent of the Commission raised among the natives and the few Europeans who had acted as their champions, were soon turned to bitter disappointment. The indefatigable Mr. Harris had sent on after the Commission a number of fresh cases which had come to his notice. In one of these a chief deposed that he had been held back in his village (Boendo) in order to prevent him from reaching the Commission. He succeeded in breaking away from his guards, but was punished for his enterprise by having his wife clubbed to death by a sentry. He brought with him, in hope that he might lay them before the judges, one hundred and eighty-two long twigs and seventy-six smaller ones, to represent so many adults and children who had been murdered by the A.B.I.R. Company in his district during the last few years. His account of the methods by which these unfortunate people met their deaths will not bear printing. The wildest dreams of the Inquisition were outdone. Women had been killed by thrusting stakes into them from below. When the horrified mission asked the chief if this was personally known to him, his answer was, "They killed my daughter, Nsinga, in this manner; I found the stake in her." And a reputable Belgian statesman can write in this year of grace that they are carrying on the beneficent and philanthropic mission which has been handed down to them.

In a later communication Mr. Harris gives the names of men, women and children killed by the sentries of a M. Pilaet.

"Last year, " he says, "or the year before, the young woman, Imenega, was tied to a forked tree and chopped in half with a hatchet beginning at the left shoulder, chopping down through the chest and abdomen and out at the side." Again, with every detail of name and place, he dwelt upon the horrible fact that public incest had been enforced by the sentries—brother with sister, and father with daughter. "Oh, Inglesia," cried the chief in conclusion, "don't stay away long; if you do, they will come, I am sure they will come, and then these enfeebled legs will not support me, I cannot run away. I am near my end; try and see to it that they let me die in peace; don't stay away."

"I was so moved, your Excellency, at these people's story that I took the liberty of promising them, in the name of the Congo Free State, that you will only kill them in future for crimes. I told them the Inspector Royal was, I hoped, on his way, and that I was sure he would listen to their story, and give them time to recover themselves."

It is terrible to think that such a promise, through no fault of Mr. Harris, has not been fulfilled. Are the dreams of the Commissioners never haunted by the thought of those who put such trust in them, but whose only reward has been that they have been punished for the evidence they gave and that their condition has been more miserable than ever. The final practical result of the Commission was that upon the natives, and not upon their murderers, came the punishment.

M. Malfeyt, a Royal High Commissioner, had been sent out on pretence of reform. How hollow was this pretence may be seen from the fact that at the same time M. Wahis had been despatched as Governor-General in place of that Constermann who had committed suicide after his interview with the judges of the Commission. Wahis had already served two terms as Governor, and it was under his administration that all the abuses the Commission had condemned had actually grown up. Could King Leopold have shown more clearly how far any real reform was from his mind?

M. Malfeyt's visit had been held up as a step toward improvement. The British Government had been assured that his visit would be of a nature to effect all necessary reforms. On arriving in the country, however, he announced that he had no power to act, and only came to see and hear. Thus a few more months were gained before any change could be effected. The only small consolation which we can draw from all this succession of impotent ambassadors and reforming committees, which do not, and were never intended to, reform, is that the game has been played and exposed, and surely cannot be played again. A Government would deservedly be the laughing-stock of the world which again accepted assurances from the same source.

What, in the meanwhile, was the attitude of that A.B.I.R. Company, whose iniquities had been thoroughly exposed before the Commission, and whose manager M. Le Jeune, had fled to Europe? Was it ashamed of its bloodthirsty deeds? Was it prepared in any way to modify its policy after the revelations which its representatives had admitted to be true? Read the following interview which Mr. Stannard had with M. Delvaux, who had visited the stations of his disgraced colleague:

"He spoke of the Commission of Inquiry in a contemptuous manner, and showed considerable annoyance about the things we had said to the Commission. He declared the A.B.I.R. had full authority and power to send out armed sentries, and force the people to bring in rubber, and to imprison those who did not. A short time ago, the natives of a town brought in some rubber to the agent here, but he refused it because it was not enough, and the men were thrashed by the A.B.I.R. employees, and driven away. The director justified the agent in refusing the rubber because the quantity was too small. The Commissioners had declared that the A.B.I.R. had no power to send armed sentries into the towns in order to flog the people and drive them into the forests to seek rubber; they were 'guards of the forest,' and that was their work. When we pointed this out to M. Delvaux, he pooh-poohed the idea, and said the name had no significance; some called the sentries by one name, some by another. We pointed out that the people were not compelled to pay their taxes in rubber only, but could bring in other things, or even currency. He denied this, and said that the alternative tax only meant that an agent could impose whatever tax he thought fit. It had no reference whatever to the natives. The A.B.I.R. preferred the taxes to be paid in rubber. This is what the A.B.I.R. says, in spite of the interpretation by Baron Nisco, the highest judicial authority in the State, that the natives could pay their taxes in what they were best able. All these things were said in the presence of the Royal High Commissioner, who, whether he approved or not, certainly did not contradict or protest against them."

Within a week or two of the departure of the Commission the state of the country was as bad as ever. It cannot be too often repeated that it was not local in its origin, but that it occurred there, as elsewhere, on account of pressure from the central officials. If further proof were needed of this it is to be found in the Van Caelchen trial. This agent, having been arrested, succeeded in showing (as was done in the Caudron case) that the real guilt lay with his superior officers. In his defence he

"Bases his power on a letter of the Commissaire-Général de Bauw (the Supreme Executive Officer in the District), and in a circular transmitted to him by his director, and signed 'Constermann' (Governor-General), which he read to the Court, deploring the diminished output in rubber, and saying that the agents of the A.B.I.R. should not forget that they had the same powers of '*contrainte par corps*' (bodily detention) as were delegated to the agent of the Société Commerciale Anversoise au Congo for the increase of rubber production; that if the Governor-General or his Commissaire-Général did not know what they were writing and what they signed, he knows what orders he had to obey; it was not for him to question the legality or illegality of these orders; his superiors ought to have known and have weighed what they wrote before giving him orders to execute; that bodily detention of natives for rubber was no secret, seeing that at the end of every month a statement of '*contrainte par corps*' (bodily detention) during the month has to be furnished in duplicate, the book signed, and one of the copies transmitted to the Government."

Whilst these organized outrages were continuing in the Congo, King Leopold, at Belgium, had taken a fresh step, which, in its cynical disregard for any attempt at consistency, surpassed any of his previous performances. Feeling that something must be done in the face of the finding of his own delegates, he appointed a fresh Commission, whose terms of reference were "to study the conclusions of the Commission of Inquiry, to formulate the proposals they call for, and to seek for practical means for realizing them." It is worth while to enumerate the names of the men chosen for this work. Had a European Areopagus called before it the head criminals of this terrible business, all of these men, with the exception of two or three, would have been standing in the dock. Take their names in turn: Van Maldeghem, the President—a jurist, who had written on Congo law, but had no direct complicity in the crimes; Janssens, the President of the former Commission, a man of integrity; M. Davignon, a Belgian politician—so far the selection is a possible one—now listen to the others! De Cuvelier, creature of the King, and responsible for the Congo horrors; Droogmans, creature of the King, administrator of the secret funds derived from his African estates, and himself President of a Rubber Trust; Arnold, creature of the King;

Liebrechts, the same; Gohr, the same; Chenot, a Congo Commissioner; Tombeur, the same; Fivé, a Congo inspector; Nys, the chief legal upholder of the King's system; De Hemptinne, President of the Kasai Rubber Trust; Mobs, an Administrator of the A.B.I.R. Is it not evident that, save the first three, these were the very men who were on their trial? The whole appointment is an example of that cynical humour which gives a grotesque touch to this inconceivable story. It need not be added that no result making for reform ever came from such an assembly. One can but rejoice that the presence of the small humane minority may have prevented the others from devising some fresh methods of oppression.

It cannot be said, however, that no judicial proceedings and no condemnation arose from the actions of the Congo Commission. But who could ever guess who the man was who was dragged to the bar. On the evidence of natives and missionaries, the whole white hierarchy, from Governor-General to subsidized cannibal, had been shown to be bloodguilty. Which of them was punished? None of them, but Mr. Stannard, one of the accusing witnesses. He had shown that the soldiers of a certain M. Hagstrom had behaved brutally to the natives. This was the account of Lontulu the chief:

"Lontulu, the senior chief of Bolima, came with twenty witnesses, which was all the canoe would hold. He brought with him one hundred and ten twigs, each of which represented a life sacrificed for rubber. The twigs were of different lengths and represented chiefs, men, women and children, according to their length. It was a horrible story of massacre, mutilation and cannibalism that he had to tell, and it was perfectly clear that he was telling the truth. He was further supported by other eyewitnesses. These crimes were committed by those who were acting under the instructions and with the knowledge of white men. On one occasion the sentries were flogged because they had not killed enough people. At one time, after they had killed a number of people, including Isekifasu, the principal chief, his wives and children, the bodies, except that of Isekifasu, were cut up, and the cannibalistic fighters attached to the A.B.I.R. force were rationed on the meat thus supplied. The intestines, etc., were hung up in and about the house, and a little child who had been cut in halves was impaled. After one attack,

Lontulu, the chief, was shown the dead bodies of his people, and asked by the rubber agent if he would bring in rubber now. He replied that he would. Although a chief of considerable standing, he has been flogged, imprisoned, tied by the neck with men who were regarded as slaves, made to do the most menial work, and his beard, which was of many years' growth, and reached almost to the ground, was cut off by the rubber agent because he visited another town."

Longulu was cross-examined by the Commission and his evidence was not shaken. Here are some of the questions and answers:

"President Janssens: 'M. Hagstrom leur a fait la guerre. Il a tué beaucoup d'hommes avec ses soldats.'

"To Lontulu: 'Were the people of Monji, etc., given the corpses to eat?'

"Lontulu: 'Yes, they cut them up and ate them.'

"Baron Nisco: 'Did they flog you?'

"Lontulu: 'Repeatedly.'

"Baron Nisco: 'Who cut your beard off?'

"Lontulu: 'M. Hannotte.'

"President Janssens: 'Did you see sentries kill your people? Did they kill many?'

"Lontulu: 'Yes, all my family is finished.'

"President: 'Give us names.'

"Lontulu: 'Chiefs Bokomo, Isekifasu, Botamba, Longeva, Bosangi, Booifa, Eongo, Lomboto, Loma, Bayolo.'

"Then followed names of women and children and ordinary men (not chiefs).

"Lontulu: 'May I call my son lest I make a mistake?'

"President: 'It is unnecessary; go on.'

"Lontulu: 'Bomposa, Beanda, Ekila.'

"President: 'Are you sure that each of your twigs (110) represents one person killed?'

"Lontulu: 'Yes.'

"President: 'Was Isekifasu killed at this time?'

"Reply not recorded.

"President: 'Did you see his entrails hanging on his house?'

"Lontulu: 'Yes.'

"*Question:* 'Were the sentries and people who helped given the dead bodies to eat?'

"*Answer:* 'Yes, they ate them. Those who took part in the fight cut them up and ate them. . . . He was *chicotted* (flogged), and said, "Why do you do this? Is it right to flog a chief?" Gave a very full account of his harsh treatment and sufferings."

The action was taken for criminal libel by M. Hagstrom against Mr. Stannard, for saying that this evidence had been given before the Commission. Of course, the only way to establish the fact was a reference to the evidence itself which lay at Brussels. But as Hagstrom was only a puppet of the higher Government of the Congo (which means the King himself), in their attempt to revenge themselves upon the missionaries it was not very likely that official documents would be produced for the mere purpose of serving the end of Justice. The minutes then were not forthcoming. How, then, was Mr. Stannard to produce evidence that his account was correct? Obviously by producing Lontulu, the chief. But the wretched Lontulu, beaten and tortured, with his beard plucked off and his spirit broken, had been cast into gaol before the trial, and knew well what would be his fate if he testified against his masters. He withdrew all that he had said at the Commission—and who can blame him? So M. Hagstrom obtained his verdict and the Belgian reptile Press proclaimed that Mr. Stannard had been proved to be a liar. He was sentenced to three months' imprisonment, with the alternative of a £40 fine. Even as I write, two more of these lion-hearted missionaries, Americans this time—Mr. Morrison and Mr. Shepherd—are undergoing a similar prosecution on the Congo. This time it is the Kasai Company which is the injured innocent. But the eyes of Europe and America are on the transaction, and M. Vandervelde, the fearless Belgian advocate of liberty, has set forth to act for the accused. What M. Labori was to Dreyfus, M. Vandervelde has been to the Congo, save that it is a whole nation who are his clients. He and his noble comrade, Mr. Lorand, are the two men who redeem the record of infamy which must long darken the good name of Belgium.

I will now deal swiftly with the records of evil deeds which have occurred since the time which I have already treated. I say "swiftly" not because there is not much material from which to choose, but because I feel that my reader must be as sated with horrors as I who have to write them. Here are some notes of a journey undertaken by W. Cassie Murdoch, as recently as July and September, 1907. This time we are concerned with the Crown Domain, King Leopold's private estate, of which we have such accounts from Mr. Clark and Mr. Scrivener dating as far back as 1894. Thirteen years had elapsed and no change! What do these thirteen represent in torture and murder? Could all these screams be united, what a vast cry would have reached the heavens. In the Congo hell the most lurid glow is to be found in the Royal Domain. And the money dragged from these tortured people is used in turn to corrupt newspapers and public men—that it may be possible to continue the system. So the devil's wheel goes round and round! Here are some extracts from Mr. Murdoch's report:

"I remarked to the old chief of the largest town I came across that his people seemed to be numerous. 'Ah, ' said he, 'my people are all dead. These you see are only a very few of what I once had.' And, indeed, it was evident enough that his town had once been a place of great size and importance. There cannot be the least doubt that this depopulation is directly due to the State. Everywhere I went I heard stories of the raids made by the State soldiers. The number of people they shot, or otherwise tortured to death, must have been enormous. Perhaps as many more of those who escaped the rifle died from starvation and exposure. More than one of my carriers could tell of how their villages had been raided, and of their own narrow escapes. They are not a warlike people, and I could hear of no single attempt at resistance. They are the kind of people the State soldiers are most successful with. They would rather any day run away than fight. And in fact, they have nothing to fight with except a few bows and arrows. I have been trying to reckon the probable number of people I met with. I should say that five thousand is, if anything, beyond the mark. A few years ago the population of the district I passed through must have been four times that number. On my return march I was desirous of visiting Mbelo, the place where Lieutenant Massard had been stationed, and in which he committed his unspeakable outrages. On making inquiries, however, I was told that there were no people there now, and that the roads were all 'dead.' On reaching one of the roads that led there, it was evident enough that it had not been used for a long time. Later on, I was able to confirm the statement that what had once been a district with numerous large towns, was now completely empty. . . .

"With the exception of a few people living near the one State post now existing on this side of the Lake, who supply the State with *kwanga* and large mats, all the people I saw are taxed with rubber. The rubber tax is an intolerable burden—how intolerable I should have found it almost impossible to believe had I not seen it. It is DIFFICULT TO DESCRIBE IT CALMLY. What I found was simply this: The *'tax' demands from twenty to twenty-five days' labour every month*. There never was a 'forty hours per month labour law' in the Crown Domain, and so long as the tax is demanded in rubber, there never will be—at least in the section of it I visited. If that law were applied, no rubber would, or could possibly, be produced for the simple reason that *there is no rubber left in this section of the Domain*.

"It was some time before I made the discovery that in the Domaine de la Couronne west of Lake Leopold there is no rubber. On my way through I was continually meeting numbers of men going out on the hunt for rubber, and heard with amazement the distance they had to walk. It seemed so impossible that I was somewhat sceptical of the truth of what I was told. But I heard the same story so often, and in so many different places, that I was at last obliged to accept it. On my return I followed up this track, and found that it was all true. And I found also that the rubber is collected from the Domaine Privé in forests from ten to forty miles beyond the boundary of the Crown Domain.

"Once the vines had been found the working of the rubber is a small part of the labour. I have made a careful calculation of the distance the people I met have to walk, and I find that the average *cannot be less than 300 miles there and back*. But walking to the forest and back does not occupy from twenty to twenty-five days per month. They will cover the 300 miles in ten or twelve days. The rest of the time is used in hunting for the vines, and in tapping them when found. I met a party returning with their rubber who had been six nights in the forest. This was the lowest number. *Most of them have to spend ten, some as many as fifteen, nights in the forest.* Two days after I left the Domain on my way back I saw some men returning empty-handed. They had been hunting for over eight days and had found nothing. What the poor wretches would do I cannot imagine. If they failed to produce the usual amount of rubber on the appointed day they would be put in '*bloc*' (imprisoned).

"The workmen of the *chef de poste* at Mbongo described a concoction which is sometimes administered to capitas when their tale of rubber is short. The white man chops up green tobacco leaves and soaks them in water. Red peppers are added, and a dose of the liquid is administered to defaulting capitas. This wily official manages to get thirteen monthly 'taxes' in the year. At one village I bought a contrivance by which the natives reckon when the tax falls due. Pieces of wood are strung on a piece of cane. One piece is moved up every day. On counting them I found there were only twenty-eight. I asked why, and was told that originally there were thirty pieces, but the white man had so often sent on the twenty-eighth day to say the time was up, that at last they took off two.

"Individual acts of atrocity here have for the most part ceased. The State agents seem to have come to the conclusion that it is a waste of cartridges to shoot down these people. BUT THE WHOLE SYSTEM IS A VAST ATROCITY INVOLVING THE PEOPLE IN A STATE OF UNIMAGINABLE MISERY. One man said to me, 'Slaves are happy compared with us. Slaves are protected by their masters, they are fed and clothed. As for us—the capitas do with us what they like. Our wives have to plant the cassava gardens and fish in the stream to feed us while we spend our days working for Bula Matadi. No, we are not even slaves.' And he is right. *It is not slavery as slavery was generally understood: it is not even the uncivilized African's idea of slavery. There never was a slavery more absolute in its despotism or more fiendish in its tyranny.*"

It will be seen that, so far as the people are concerned, the problem is largely solved, the bitterness of death is past. No European intervention can save them. In many places they have been utterly destroyed. But they were the wards of Europe, and surely Europe, if she is not utterly lost to shame, will have something to say to their fate.

XIII
Some Congolese Apologies

It only remains to examine some of the Congolese attempts to answer the unanswerable. It is but fair to hear the other side, and I will set down such points as they advance as clearly as I can:

1.—*That the Congo State is independent and that it is no one else's business what occurs within its borders.*

I have, I trust, clearly shown that by the Berlin Treaty of 1885 the State was formed on certain conditions, and that these conditions as affecting both trade and the natives have not been fulfilled. Therefore, we have the right to interfere. Apart from the Treaty this right might be claimed on the general grounds of humanity, as has been done more than once with Turkey.

2.—*That the French Congo is as bad, and that we do not interfere.*

The French Colonial system has usually been excellent, and there is, therefore, every reason to believe that this one result of evil example will soon be amended. There, at least, we have no Treaty obligation to interfere.

3.—*That the English agitation is due to jealousy of Belgian success.*

We do not look upon it as success, but the most stupendous failure in history. What is there to be jealous of? Is it the making of money? But we could do the same at once in any tropical Colony if we stooped to the same methods.

4.—*That it is a plot of the Liverpool merchants.*

This legend had its origin in the fact that Mr. Morel, the leader and hero of the cause, was in business in Liverpool, and was afterward elected to be a member of the Liverpool Chamber of Commerce. There is, indeed, a connection between Liverpool and the movement, because it was while engaged in the shipping trade there that Mr. Morel was brought into connection with the persons and the facts which moved him to generous indignation, and started him upon the long struggle which he has so splendidly and unselfishly maintained. As a matter of fact, all business men in England have very good reason to take action against a system which has kept their commerce out of a country which was declared to be open to international trade. But of all towns Liverpool has the least reason to complain, as it is the centre of that shipping line which (alas! that any English line should do so) conveys the Congo rubber from Boma to Antwerp.

5.—*That it is a Protestant scheme in order to gain an advantage over the Catholic missions.*

In all British Colonies Catholic missions may be founded and developed without any hindrance. If the Congo were British to-morrow, no Catholic church or school would be disturbed. What advantage, then, would the Protestants gain by any change? These charges are, as a matter of fact, borne out by Catholics as well as by Protestants. Father Vermeersch is as fervid as any English or American pastor.

6.—*That travellers who have passed through the country, and others who reside in the country, have seen no trace of outrages.*

Such a defence reminds one of the ancient pleasantry of the man who, being accused on the word of three men who were present and saw him do the crime, declared that the balance of evidence was in his favour, since he was prepared to produce ten men who were not present and did not see it. Of the white people who live in the country the great majority are in the Lower Congo, which is not affected by the murderous rubber traffic. Their evidence is beside the question. When a traveller passes up the main river his advent is known and all is ready for him. Captain Boyd Alexander passed, as I understand, along the frontier, where naturally one would expect the best conditions, since a discontented tribe has only to cross the line. To show the fallacy of such reasoning I would instance the case of the Reverend John Howell, who for many years travelled on one of the mission boats upon the main river and during that time never saw an outrage. No doubt he had formed the opinion that his brethren had been exaggerating. Then one day he heard an outburst of firing, and turned his little steamer to the spot. This is what he saw: "They were horrified to find the native soldiers of the Government under the eyes of their white officers engaged in mutilating the dead bodies of the natives who had just been killed. Three native bodies were lying near the river's edge and human limbs were lying within a few yards from the steamer. A State soldier was seen drawing away the legs and other portions of a human body. Another soldier was seen standing by a large basket in which were the viscera of a human body. The missionaries were promptly ordered off the beach by the two officers presiding over this human shambles." And this was on the main river, twenty years after the European occupation.

7.—*That land has been claimed by Government in Uganda and other British Colonies.*

Where land has been so claimed, it has been worked by free labour for the benefit of the African community itself, and not for the purpose of sending the proceeds to Europe.

8.—*That odious incidents occur in all Colonies.*

It is true that no Colonial system is always free from such reproach.

But the object of the normal European system is to discourage and to punish such abuses, especially if they occur in high places. I have already given the instance of Eyre, Governor of Jamaica, who was tried for his life in England because he had executed a half-caste at a time when there was actual revolt among the black population, of which he was the leader. Germany also has not hesitated to bring to the bar of Justice any of her officers who have lowered her prestige by their conduct in the tropics. But in the Congo, after twenty years of unexampled horror and brutality, not one single officer above the rank of a simple clerk has ever been condemned, or even, so far as I can learn, tried for conduct which, had they been British, would assuredly have earned them the gallows. What chance would Lothaire or Le Jeune have before a Middlesex jury? There lies the difference between the systems.

9.—*That the British charges did not begin until the Congo became a flourishing State.*

Since the Congo's wealth sprang from this barbarous system, it is natural that they both attracted attention at the same time. Rising wealth meant a more rigidly enforced system.

10.—*That the Congo State deserves great credit for having prohibited the sale of alcohol to the natives.*

It is true that the sale of alcohol to natives should be forbidden in all parts of Africa. It is caused by the competition of trade. If a chief desires gin for his ivory, it is clear that the nation which supplies that gin will get the trade, and that which refuses will lose it. This by way of explanation, not of apology. But as there is no trade competition in the Congo, they have no reason to introduce alcohol, which would simply detract from the quality and value of their slave population. When compared with the absolute immorality of other Congo proceedings, it is clear that the prohibition of alcohol springs from no high motive, but is purely dictated by self-interest.

11.—*That the depopulation is due to sleeping sickness.*

Sleeping sickness is one of the contributory causes, but all the evidence in this book will tend to show that the great wastage of the people has occurred where the Congo rule has pressed heavily upon them.

So I bring my task to an end.

I look at my statement of the facts and I wince at its many faults of omission. How many specific examples have I left out, how many deductions have I missed, how many fresh sides to the matter have I neglected. It is hurried and broken, as a man's speech may be hurried and broken when he is driven to it by a sense of burning injustice and intolerable wrong. But it is true—and I defy any man to read it without rising with the conviction of its truth. Consider the cloud of witnesses. Consider the minute and specific detail in the evidence. Consider the undenied system which must *prima facie* produce such results. Consider the admissions of the Belgian Commission. Not one shadow of doubt can remain in the most sceptical mind that the accusations of the Reformers have been absolutely proved. It is not a thing of the past. It is going on at this hour. The Belgian annexation has made no difference. The machinery and the men who work it are the same. There are fewer outrages it is true. The spirit of the unhappy people is so broken that it is a waste of labour to destroy them further. That their conditions have not improved is shown by the unanswerable fact that the export of rubber has not decreased. That export is the exact measure of the terrorism employed. Many of the old districts are worked out, but the new ones must be exploited with greater energy to atone. The problem, I say, remains as ever. But surely the answer is at hand. Surely there is some limit to the silent complicity of the civilized world?

XIV
Solutions

But what can be done? What course should we pursue? Let us consider a few possible solutions and the reasons which bear upon them.

There is one cardinal fact which dominates everything. It is that *any* change must be for the better. Under their old savage *régime* as Stanley found them the tribes were infinitely happier, richer and more advanced than they are to-day. If they should return undisturbed to such an existence, the situation would, at least, be free from all that lowering of the ideals of the white race which is implied by a Belgian occupation. We may start with a good heart, therefore, since whatever happens must be for the better.

Can a solution be found through Belgium?

No, it is impossible, and that should be recognized from the outset. The Belgians have been given their chance. They have had nearly twenty-five years of undisturbed possession, and they have made it a hell upon earth. They cannot disassociate themselves from this work or pretend that it was done by a separate State. It was done by a Belgian King, Belgian soldiers, Belgian financiers, Belgian lawyers, Belgian capital, and was endorsed and defended by Belgian governments. It is out of the question that Belgium should remain on the Congo.

Nor, in face of reform, would Belgium wish to be there. She could not carry the burden. When the country is restored to its inhabitants together with their freedom, it will be in the same position as those German and English colonies which entail heavy annual expenditure from the mother country. It is a proof of the honesty of German colonial policy, and the fitness of Germany to be a great land-owning Power, that nearly all her tropical colonies, like our own, show, or have shown, a deficit. It is easy to show a profit if a land be exploited as Spain exploited Central America, or Belgium the Congo. It would always be more profitable to sack a business than to run it. Now, if the forced revenue of the Congo State disappeared, it would, at a moderate estimate, take a minimum of a million a year for twenty years to bring the demoralized State back to the normal condition of a tropical colony. Would Belgium pay this £20,000,000? It is certain that she would not. Reform, then, is an absolute impossibility so long as Belgium holds the Congo.

What, then, should be done?

That is for the statesmen of Europe and America to determine. America hastened before all the rest of the world in 1884 to recognize this new State, and her recognition caused the rest of the world to follow suit. But since then she has done nothing to control what she created. American citizens have suffered as much as British, and American commerce has met with the same impediments, in spite of the shrewd attempt of King Leopold to bribe American complicity by allowing some of her citizens to form a Concessionnaire Company and so to share in the unholy spoils. But America has a high moral sense, and when the true facts are known to her, and when she learns to distinguish the outcome of King Leopold's dollars from the work of honest publicists, she will surely be ready to move in the matter. It was in crushing pirates that America made her first international appearance upon the world's stage. May it be a precedent.

But to bring the matter to a head the British Government should surely act with no further delay. The obvious course would appear to be that having prepared the ground by sounding each of the Great Powers, they should then lay before each of them the whole evidence, and ask that a European Congress should meet to discuss the situation. Such a Congress would surely result in the partition of the Congo lands—a partition in which Great Britain, whose responsibilities of empire are already too vast, might well play the most self-denying part. If France, having given a pledge to rule her Congo lands in the same excellent fashion as she does the rest of her African Empire, were to extend her borders to the northern bank of the river along its whole course until it turns to the south, then an orderly government might be hoped for in those regions. Germany, too, might well extend her East African Protectorate, so as to bring it up to the eastern bank of the Congo, where it runs to the south. With these large sections removed it would not be difficult to arrange some great native reservation in the centre, which should be under some international guarantee which would be less of a fiasco than the last one. The Lower Congo and the Boma railway would, no doubt, present difficulties, but surely they are not above solution. And always one may repeat that any change is a change for good.

Such a partition would form one solution. Another, less permanent and stable—and to that extent, as it seems to me, less good—is that which is advanced by Mr. Morel and others. It is an international control of the river, some provision for which is, as I understand, already in existence. The trouble is that what belongs to all nations belongs to no nation, and that when the native risings and general turmoil come, which will surely succeed the withdrawal of Belgian pressure, something stronger and richer than an International Riverine Board will be needed to meet them. I am convinced that partition affords the only chance of solid, lasting amendment.

Let us suppose, however, that the Powers refuse to convene a meeting, and that we are deserted even by America. Then it is our duty, as it has often been in the world's history, to grapple single-handed with that which should be a common task. We have often done so before, and if we are worthy of our fathers, we will do it again. A warning and a date must be fixed, and then we must decide our course of action.

And what shall that action be? War with Belgium? On them must rest the responsibility for that. Our measures must be directed against the Congo State, which has not yet been recognized by us as being a possession of Belgium. If Belgium take up the quarrel then so be it. There are many ways in which we can bring the Congo State to her knees. A blockade of the Congo is one, but it has the objection of the international complications which might ensue. An easier way would be to proclaim this guilty land as an outlaw State. Such a proclamation means that to no British subject does the law of that land apply. If British traders enter it, they shall be stopped at the peril of those who stop them. If British subjects are indicted, they shall be tried in our own Consular Courts. If complications ensue, as is likely, then Boma shall be occupied. This would surely lead to that European Conference which we are supposing to have been denied us.

Yet another solution. Let a large trading caravan start into the Congoland from Northern Rhodesia. We claim that we have a right to free trade by the Berlin Treaty. We will enforce our claim. To do so would cut at the very roots of the Congo system. If the caravan be opposed, then again Boma and a conference.

Many solutions could be devised, but there is one which will come of itself, and may bring about a very sudden end of the Congo Power. Northern Rhodesia is slowly filling up. The railhead is advancing. The nomad South African population, half Boers, half English, adventurers and lion hunters, are trekking toward the Katanga border. They are not men who will take less than those rights of free entry and free commerce which are, in fact, guaranteed them. Only last year twelve Boer wagons appeared upon the Katanga border and were, contrary to all international law, warned off. They are the pioneers of many more. No one has the right, and no one, save their own Government, has the force to keep them out. Let the Powers of Europe hasten to regulate the situation, or some day they may find themselves in the presence of a *fait accompli*. Better an orderly partition conducted from Paris or Berlin, than the intrusion of some Piet Joubert, with his swarthy followers, who will see no favour in taking that which they believe to be their right.

But whatever solution is adopted, the conscience of Europe should not be content merely with the safeguarding of the future. Surely there should be some punishment for those who by their injustice and violence have dragged Christianity and civilization in the dirt. Surely, also, there should be compulsory compensation out of the swollen moneybags of the three hundred per cent concessionnaires for the widows and the orphans, the maimed and the incapacitated. Justice cannot be satisfied with less. An International Commission, with punitive powers, may be exceptional, but the whole circumstances are exceptional, and Europe must rise to them. The fear is, however, that it is the wretched agents on the spot, the poor driven bonus-hunters who will be offered up as victims, whereas the real criminals will escape. The curse of blood and the scorn of every honest man rest upon them already. Would that they were within the reach of human justice also! They have been guilty of the sack of a country, the spoliation of a nation, the greatest crime in all history, the greater for having been carried out under an odious pretence of philanthropy. Surely somehow, somewhere, they will have their reward!

14

✏

From *The Lost World*
(1912)

9
Who Could Have Foreseen It?

A dreadful thing has happened to us. Who could have foreseen it? I cannot foresee any end to our troubles. It may be that we are condemned to spend our whole lives in this strange, inaccessible place. I am still so confused that I can hardly think clearly of the facts of the present or of the chances of the future. To my astounded senses the one seems most terrible and the other as black as night.

No men have ever found themselves in a worse position; nor is there any use in disclosing to you our exact geographical si tuation and asking our friends for a relief party. Even if they could send one, our fate will in all human probability be decided long before it could arrive in South America.

We are, in truth, as far from any human aid as if we were on the moon. If we are to win through, it is only our own qualities which can save us. I have as companions three remarkable men, men of great brain-power and of unshaken courage. There lies our one and only hope. It is only when I look upon the untroubled faces of my comrades that I see some glimmer through the darkness. Outwardly I trust that I appear as unconcerned as they. Inwardly I am filled with apprehension.

Let me give you, with as much detail as I can, the sequence of events which have led us to this catastrophe.

When I finished my last letter I stated that we were within seven miles from an enormous line of ruddy cliffs which encircled, beyond all doubt, the plateau of which Professor Challenger spoke. Their height, as we approached them, seemed to me in some places to be greater than he had stated—running up in parts to at least a thousand feet—and they were curiously striated, in a manner which is, I believe, characteristic of basaltic upheavals. Something of the sort is to be seen in Salisbury Crags at Edinburgh. The summit showed every sign of a luxuriant vegetation, with bushes near the edge, and farther back many high trees. There was no indication of any life that we could see.

That night we pitched our camp immediately under the cliff—a most wild and desolate spot. The crags above us were not merely perpendicular, but curved outwards at the top, so that ascent was out of the question. Close to us was the high, thin pinnacle of rock which I believe I mentioned earlier in this narrative. It is like a broad red church spire, the top of it being level with the plateau, but a great chasm gaping between. On the summit of it there grew one high tree. Both pinnacle and cliff were comparatively low—some five or six hundred feet, I should think.

"It was on that," said Professor Challenger, pointing to this tree, "that the pterodactyl was perched. I climbed halfway up the rock before I shot him. I am inclined to think that a good mountaineer like myself could ascend the rock to the top, though he would, of course, be no nearer to the plateau when he had done so."

As Challenger spoke of his pterodactyl I glanced at Professor Summerlee, and for the first time I seemed to see some signs of a dawning credulity and repentance. There was no sneer upon his thin lips, but, on the contrary, a grey, drawn look of excitement and amazement. Challenger saw it, too, and revelled in the first taste of victory.

"Of course," said he, with his clumsy and ponderous sarcasm, "Professor Summerlee will understand that when I speak of a pterodactyl I mean a stork—only it is the kind of stork which has no feathers, a leathery skin, membranous wings, and teeth in its jaws." He grinned and blinked and bowed until his colleague turned and walked away.

In the morning, after a frugal breakfast of coffee and manioc—we had to be economical of our stores—we held a council of war as to the best method of ascending to the plateau above us.

Challenger presided with a solemnity as if he were the Lord Chief Justice on the Bench. Picture him seated upon a rock, his absurd boyish straw hat tilted on the back of his head, his supercilious eyes dominating us from under his drooping lids, his great black beard wagging as he slowly defined our present situation and our future movements.

Beneath him you might have seen the three of us—myself, sunburnt, young, and vigorous after our open-air tramp; Summerlee, solemn, but still critical, behind his eternal pipe; Lord John, as keen as a razor-edge, with his supple, alert figure leaning upon his rifle, and his eagle eyes fixed eagerly upon the speaker. Behind us were grouped the two swarthy half-breeds and the little knot of Indians, while in front and above us towered those huge, ruddy ribs of rocks which kept us from our goal.

"I need not say," said our leader, "that on the occasion of my last visit I exhausted every means of climbing the cliff, and where I failed I do not think that anyone else is likely to succeed, for I am something of a mountaineer. I had none of the appliances of a rock-climber with me, but I have taken the precaution to bring them now. With their aid I am positive I could climb that detached pinnacle to the summit; but so long as the main cliff overhangs, it is vain to attempt ascending that. I was hurried upon my last visit by the approach of the rainy season and by the exhaustion of my supplies. These considerations limited my time, and I can only claim that I have surveyed about six miles of the cliff to the east of us, finding no possible way up. What, then, shall we now do?"

"There seems to be only one reasonable course," said Professor Summerlee. "If you have explored the east, we should travel along the base of the cliff to the west, and seek for a practicable point for our ascent."

"That's it," said Lord John. "The odds are that this plateau is of no great size, and we shall travel round it until we either find an easy way up it, or come back to the point from which we started."

"I have already explained to our young friend here," said Challenger (he has a way of alluding to me as if I were a school child ten years old), "that it is quite impossible that there should be an easy way up anywhere, for the simple reason that if there were the summit would not be isolated, and those conditions would not obtain which have effected so singular an interference with the general laws of survival. Yet I admit that there may very well be places where an expert human climber may reach the summit, and yet a cumbrous and heavy animal be unable to descend. It is certain that there *is* a point where an ascent is possible."

"How do you know that, sir?" asked Summerlee sharply.

"Because my predecessor, the American Maple White actually made such an ascent. How otherwise could he have seen the monster which he sketched in his notebook?"

"There you reason somewhat ahead of the proved facts," said the stubborn Summerlee. "I admit your plateau, because I have seen it; but I have not as yet satisfied myself that it contains any form of life whatever."

"What you admit, sir, or what you do not admit, is really of inconceivably small importance. I am glad to perceive that the plateau itself has actually obtruded itself upon your intelligence." He glanced up at it, and then, to our amazement, he sprang from his rock, and, seizing Summerlee by the neck, he tilted his face into the air. "Now, sir!" he shouted hoarse with excitement. "Do I help you to realize that the plateau contains some animal life?"

I have said that a thick fringe of green overhung the edge of the cliff. Out of this there had emerged a black, glistening object. As it came slowly forth and overhung the chasm, we saw that it was a very large snake with a peculiar flat spade-like head. It wavered and quivered above us for a minute, the morning sun gleaming upon its sleek, sinuous coils. Then it slowly drew inwards and disappeared.

Summerlee had been so interested that he had stood unresisting while Challenger tilted his head into the air. Now he shook his colleague off and came back to his dignity.

"I should be glad, Professor Challenger," said he, "if you could see your way to make any remarks which may occur to you without seizing me by the chin. Even the appearance of a very ordinary rock python does not appear to justify such a liberty."

"But there is life upon the plateau all the same," his colleague replied in triumph. "And now, having demonstrated this important conclusion so that it is clear to anyone, however prejudiced or obtuse, I am of opinion that we cannot do better than break up our camp and travel westward until we find some means of ascent."

The ground at the foot of the cliff was rocky and broken, so that the going was slow and difficult. Suddenly we came, however, upon something which cheered our hearts. It was the site of an old encampment, with several empty Chicago meat tins, a bottle labelled "Brandy," a broken tin-opener, and a quantity of other travellers' debris. A crumpled, disintegrated newspaper revealed itself as the *Chicago Democrat*, though the date had been obliterated.

"Not mine," said Challenger. "It must be Maple White's."

Lord John had been gazing curiously at a great tree-fern which overshadowed the encampment. "I say, look at this," said he. "I believe it is meant for a sign-post."

A slip of hard wood had been nailed to the tree in such a way as to point to the westward.

"Most certainly a sign-post," said Challenger. "What else? Finding himself upon a dangerous errand, our pioneer has left this sign so that any party which follows him may know the way he has taken. Perhaps we shall come upon some other indications as we proceed."

We did indeed, but they were of a terrible and most unexpected nature. Immediately beneath the cliff there grew a considerable patch of high bamboo, like that which we had traversed in our journey. Many of these stems were twenty feet high, with sharp, strong tops, so that even as they stood they made formidable spears. We were passing along the edge of this cover when my eye was caught by the gleam of something white within it. Thrusting in my head between the stems, I found myself gazing at a fleshless skull. The whole skeleton was there, but the skull had detached itself and lay some feet nearer to the open.

With a few blows from the machetes of our Indians we cleared the spot and were able to study the details of this old tragedy. Only a few shreds of clothes could still be distinguished, but there were the remains of boots upon the bony feet, and it was very clear that the dead man was a European. A gold watch by Hudson, of New York, and a chain which held a stylographic pen, lay among the bones. There was also a silver cigarette-case, with "J. C., from A. E. S.," upon the lid. The state of the metal seemed to show that the catastrophe had occurred no great time before.

"Who can he be?" asked Lord John. "Poor devil! every bone in his body seems to be broken."

"And the bamboo grows through his smashed ribs," said Summerlee. "It is a fast-growing plant, but it is surely inconceivable that this body could have been here while the canes grew to be twenty feet in length."

"As to the man's identity," said Professor Challenger, "I have no doubt whatever upon that point. As I made my way up the river before I reached you at the fazenda I instituted very particular inquiries about Maple White. At Para they knew nothing. Fortunately, I had a definite clue, for there was a particular picture in his sketch-book which showed him taking lunch with a certain ecclesiastic at Rosario. This priest I was able to find, and though he proved a very argumentative fellow, who took it absurdly amiss that I should point out to him the corrosive effect which modern science must have upon his beliefs, he none the less gave me some positive information. Maple White passed Rosario four years ago, or two years before I saw his dead body. He was not alone at the time, but there was a friend, an American named James Colver, who remained in the boat and did not meet this ecclesiastic. I think, therefore, that there can be no doubt that we are now looking upon the remains of this James Colver."

"Nor," said Lord John, "is there much doubt as to how he met his death. He has fallen or been chucked from the top, and so been impaled. How else could he come by his broken bones, and how could he have been stuck through by these canes with their points so high above our heads?"

A hush came over us as we stood round these shattered remains and realized the truth of Lord John Roxton's words. The beetling head of the cliff projected over the cane-brake. Undoubtedly he had fallen from above. But *had* he fallen? Had it been an accident? Or—— Already ominous and terrible possibilities began to form round that unknown land.

We moved off in silence, and continued to coast round the line of cliffs, which were as even and unbroken as some of those monstrous Antarctic ice-fields which I have seen depicted as stretching from horizon to horizon and towering high above the mast-heads of the exploring vessel. In five miles we saw no rift or break. And then suddenly we perceived something which filled us with new hope. In a hollow of the rock, protected from rain, there was drawn a rough arrow in chalk, pointing still to the westward.

"Maple White again," said Professor Challenger. "He had some presentiment that worthy footsteps would follow close behind him."

"He had chalk, then?"

"A box of coloured chalks was among the effects I found in his knapsack. I remember that the white one was worn to a stump."

"That is certainly good evidence," said Summerlee. "We can only accept his guidance and follow on to the westward."

We had proceeded some five more miles when again we saw a white arrow upon the rocks. It was at a point where the face of the cliff was for the first time split into a narrow cleft. Inside the cleft was a second guidance mark, which pointed right up it with the tip somewhat elevated, as if the spot indicated were above the level of the ground.

It was a solemn place, for the walls were so gigantic and the slit of blue sky so narrow and so obscured by a double fringe of verdure that only a dim and shadowy light penetrated to the bottom. We had had no food for many hours, we were very weary with the stony and irregular journey, but our nerves were too strung to allow us to halt. We ordered the camp to be pitched however, and, leaving the Indians to arrange it, we four, with the two half-breeds, proceeded up the narrow gorge.

It was not more than forty feet across at the mouth, but it rapidly closed until it ended in an acute angle, too straight and smooth for an ascent. Certainly it was not this which our pioneer had attempted to indicate. We made our way back—the whole gorge was not more than a quarter of a mile deep—and then suddenly the quick eyes of Lord John fell upon what we were seeking. High up above our heads, amid the dark shadows, there was one circle of deeper gloom. Surely it could only be the opening of a cave.

The base of the cliff was heaped with loose stones at the spot, and it was not difficult to clamber up. When we reached it, all doubt was removed. Not only was it an opening into the rock, but on the side of it was marked once again the sign of the arrow. Here was the point, and this the means by which Maple White and his ill-fated comrade had made their ascent.

We were too excited to return to the camp, but must make our first exploration at once. Lord John had an electric torch in his knapsack, and this had to serve us as light. He advanced, throwing his little clear circlet of yellow radiance before him, while in single file we followed at his heels.

The cave had evidently been water-worn, the sides being smooth and the floor covered with rounded stones. It was of such a size that a single man could just fit through by stooping. For fifty yards it ran almost straight into the rock, and then it ascended at an angle of forty-five. Presently this incline became even steeper, and we found ourselves climbing upon hands and knees among loose rubble which slid from beneath us. Suddenly an exclamation broke from Lord Roxton.

"It's blocked!" said he.

Clustering behind him we saw in the yellow field of light a wall of broken basalt which extended to the ceiling.

"The roof has fallen in!"

In vain we dragged out some of the pieces. The only effect was that the larger ones became detached and threatened to roll down the gradient and crush us. It was evident that the obstacle was far beyond any efforts which we could make to remove it. The road by which Maple White had ascended was no longer available.

Too much cast down to speak, we stumbled down the dark tunnel and made our way back to the camp.

One incident occurred, however, before we left the gorge, which is of importance in view of what came afterwards. We had gathered in a little group at the bottom of the chasm, some forty feet beneath the mouth of the cave, when a huge rock rolled suddenly downwards and shot past us with tremendous force. It was the narrowest escape for one or all of us. We could not ourselves see whence the rock had come, but our half-breed servants, who were still at the opening of the cave, said that it had flown past them, and must therefore have fallen from the summit. Looking upwards, we could see no sign of movement above us amidst the green jungle which topped the cliff. There could be little doubt, however, that the stone was aimed at us, so the incident surely pointed to humanity—and malevolent humanity—upon the plateau!

We withdrew hurriedly from the chasm, our minds full of this new development and its bearing upon our plans. The situation was difficult enough before, but if the obstructions of Nature were increased by the deliberate opposition of man, then our case was indeed a hopeless one. And yet, as we looked up at that beautiful fringe of verdure only a few hundreds of feet above our heads, there was not one of us who could conceive the idea of returning to London until we had explored it to its depths.

On discussing the situation, we determined that our best course was to continue to coast round the plateau in the hope of finding some other means of reaching the top. The line of cliffs, which had decreased considerably in height, had already begun to trend from west to north, and if we could take this as representing the arc of a circle, the whole circumference could not be very great. At the worst, then, we should be back in a few days at our starting-point.

We made a march that day which totalled some two-and-twenty miles, without any change in our prospects. I may mention that our aneroid shows us that in the continual incline which we have ascended since we abandoned our canoes we have risen to no less than three thousand feet above sea-level. Hence there is a considerable change both in the temperature and in the vegetation. We have shaken off some of that horrible insect life which is the bane of tropical travel. A few palms still survive, and many tree-ferns, but the Amazonian trees have been all left behind. It was pleasant to see the convolvulus, the passion-flower, and the begonia, all reminding me of home, here among these inhospitable rocks. There was a red begonia just the same colour as one that is kept in a pot in the window of a certain villa in Streatham—but I am drifting into private reminiscence.

That night—I am still speaking of the first day of our circumnavigation of the plateau—a great experience awaited us, and one which for ever set at rest any doubt which we could have had as to the wonders so near us.

You will realize as you read it, my dear Mr. McArdle, and possibly for the first time, that the paper has not sent me on a wild-goose chase, and that there is conceivably fine copy waiting for the world whenever we have the Professor's leave to make use of it. I shall not dare to publish these articles unless I can bring back my proofs to England, or I shall be hailed as the journalistic Munchausen of all time. I have no doubt that you feel the same way yourself, and that you would not care to stake the whole credit of the *Gazette* upon this adventure until we can meet the chorus of criticism and scepticism which such articles must of necessity elicit. So this wonderful incident, which would make such a headline for the old paper, must still wait its turn in the editorial drawer.

And yet it was all over in a flash, and there was no sequel to it, save in our own convictions.

What occurred was this. Lord John had shot an ajouti—which is a small, pig-like animal—and, half of it having been given to the Indians, we were cooking the other half upon our fire. There is a chill in the air after dark, and we had all drawn close to the blaze. The night was moonless, but there were some stars, and one could see for a little distance across the plain. Well, suddenly out of the darkness, out of the night, there swooped something with a swish like an aeroplane. The whole group of us were covered for an instant by a canopy of leathery wings, and I had a momentary vision of a long, snake-like neck, a fierce, red, greedy eye, and a great snapping beak, filled, to my amazement, with little, gleaming teeth. The next instant it was gone—and so was our dinner. A huge black shadow, twenty feet across, skimmed up into the air; for an instant the monster wings blotted out the stars, and then it vanished over the brow of the cliff above us. We all sat in amazed silence round the fire, like the heroes of Virgil when the Harpies came down upon them. It was Summerlee who was the first to speak.

"Professor Challenger," said he, in a solemn voice, which quavered with emotion, "I owe you an apology. Sir, I am very much in the wrong, and I beg that you will forget what is past."

It was handsomely said, and the two men for the first time shook hands. So much we have gained by this clear vision of our first pterodactyl. It was worth a stolen supper to bring two such men together.

But if prehistoric life existed upon the plateau, it was not superabundant, for we had no further glimpse of it during the next three days. During this time we traversed a barren and forbidding country, which alternated between stony desert and desolate marshes full of many wildfowl, upon the north and east of the cliffs. From that direction the place is really inaccessible, and, were it not for a hardish ledge which runs at the very base of the precipice, we should have had to turn back. Many times we were up to our waists in the slime and blubber of an old, semi-tropical swamp. To make matters worse, the place seemed to be a favourite breeding-place of the Jaracaca snake, the most venomous and aggressive in South America. Again and again these horrible creatures came writhing and springing towards us across the surface of this putrid bog, and it was only by keeping our shot guns for ever ready that we could feel safe from them. One funnel-shaped depression in the morass, of a livid green in colour from some lichen which festered in it, will always remain as a nightmare memory in my mind. It seems to have been a special nest of these vermin, and the slopes were alive with them, all writhing in our direction, for it is a peculiarity of the Jaracaca that it will always attack man at first sight. There were too many for us to shoot, so we fairly took to our heels and ran until we were exhausted. I shall always remember as we looked back how far behind we could see the heads and necks of our horrible pursuers rising and falling amid the reeds. Jaracaca Swamp we named it in the map which we are constructing.

The cliffs upon the farther side had lost their ruddy tint, being chocolate-brown in colour; the vegetation was more scattered along the top of them, and they had sunk to three or four hundred feet in height, but in no place did we find any point where they could be ascended. If anything, they were more impossible than at the first point where we had met them. Their absolute steepness is indicated in the photograph which I took over the stony desert.

"Surely," said I, as we discussed the situation, "the rain must find its way down somehow. There are bound to be water-channels in the rocks."

"Our young friend has glimpses of lucidity," said Professor Challenger patting me upon the shoulder.

"The rain must go somewhere," I repeated.

"He keeps a firm grip upon actuality. The only drawback is that we have conclusively proved by ocular demonstration that there are *no* water channels down the rocks."

"Where, then, does it go?" I persisted.

"I think it may be fairly assumed that if it does not come outwards it must run inwards."

"Then there is a lake in the centre."

"So I should suppose."

"It is more than likely that the lake may be an old crater," said Summerlee. "The whole formation is, of course, highly volcanic. But however that may be, I should expect to find the surface of the plateau slope inwards with a considerable sheet of water in the centre, which may drain off, by some subterranean channel, into the marshes of the Jaracaca Swamp."

"Or evaporation might preserve an equilibrium," remarked Challenger, and the two learned men wandered off into one of their usual scientific arguments, which were as comprehensible as Chinese to the layman.

On the sixth day we completed our circuit of the cliffs, and found ourselves back at the first camp, beside the isolated pinnacle of rock. We were a disconsolate party, for nothing could have been more minute than our investigation, and it was absolutely certain that there was no single point where the most active human being could possibly hope to scale the cliff. The place which Maple White's chalk-marks had indicated as his own means of access was now entirely impassable.

What were we to do now? Our stores of provisions, supplemented by our guns, were holding out well, but the day must come when they would need replenishment. In a couple of months the rains might be expected, and we should be washed out of our camp. The rock was harder than marble, and any attempt at cutting a path for so great a height was more than our time or resources would admit. No wonder that we looked gloomily at each other that night, and sought our blankets without hardly a word exchanged. I remember that as I dropped off to sleep my last recollection was that Challenger was squatting, like a monstrous bull-frog, by the fire, his huge head in his hands, sunk apparently in the deepest thought, and entirely oblivious to the good-night which I wished him.

But it was a very different Challenger who greeted us in the morning—a Challenger with contentment and self-congratulation shining from his whole person. He faced us as we assembled for breakfast with a deprecating false modesty in his eyes, as who should say, "I know that I deserve all that you can say, but I pray you to spare my blushes by not saying it." His beard bristled exultantly, his chest was thrown out, and his hand was thrust into the front of his jacket. So, in his fancy, may he see himself sometimes, gracing the vacant pedestal in Trafalgar Square, and adding one more to the horrors of the London streets.

"Eureka!" he cried, his teeth shining through his beard. "Gentlemen, you may congratulate me and we may congratulate each other. The problem is solved."

"You have found a way up?"

"I venture to think so."

"And where?"

For answer he pointed to the spire-like pinnacle upon our right.

Our faces—or mine, at least—fell as we surveyed it. That it could be climbed we had our companion's assurance. But a horrible abyss lay between it and the plateau.

"We can never get across," I gasped.

"We can at least all reach the summit," said he. "When we are up I may be able to show you that the resources of an inventive mind are not yet exhausted."

After breakfast we unpacked the bundle in which our leader had brought his climbing accessories. From it he took a coil of the strongest and lightest rope, a hundred and fifty feet in length, and climbing irons, clamps, and other devices. Lord John was an experienced mountaineer, and Summerlee had done some rough climbing at various times, so that I was really the novice at rock-work of the party; but my strength and activity may have made up for my want of experience.

It was not in reality a very stiff task, though there were moments which made my hair bristle upon my head. The first half was perfectly easy, but from there upwards it became continually steeper, until, for the last fifty feet, we were literally clinging with our fingers and toes to tiny ledges and crevices in the rock. I could not have accomplished it, nor could Summerlee, if Challenger had not gained the summit (it was extraordinary to see such activity in so unwieldy a creature) and there fixed the rope round the trunk of the considerable tree which grew there. With this as our support, we were soon able to scramble up the jagged wall until we found ourselves upon the small grassy platform, some twenty-five feet each way, which formed the summit.

The first impression which I received when I had recovered my breath was the extraordinary view over the country which we traversed.

The whole Brazilian plain seemed to lie beneath us, extending away and away until it ended in dim blue mists upon the farthest sky-line. In the foreground was the long slope, strewn with rocks and dotted with tree-ferns; farther off in the middle distance, looking over the saddle-back hill, I could just see the yellow and green mass of bamboos through which we had passed; and then, gradually, the vegetation increased until it formed the huge forest which extended as far as the eyes could reach, and for a good two thousand miles beyond.

I was still drinking in this wonderful panorama when the heavy hand of the Professor fell upon my shoulder.

"This way, my young friend," said he; "*vestigia nulla restrorsum*. Never look rearwards, but always to our glorious goal."

The level of the plateau, when I turned, was exactly that on which we stood, and the green bank of bushes, with occasional trees, was so near that it was difficult to realize how inaccessible it remained. At a rough guess the gulf was forty feet across, but, so far as I could see, it might as well have been forty miles. I placed one arm round the trunk of the tree and leaned over the abyss. Far down were the small dark figures of our servants, looking up at us. The wall was absolutely precipitous, as was that which faced me.

"This is indeed curious," said the creaking voice of Professor Summerlee.

I turned, and found that he was examining with great interest the tree to which I clung. That smooth bark and those small, ribbed leaves seemed familiar to my eyes. "Why," I cried, "it's a beech!"

"Exactly," said Summerlee. "A fellow-countryman in a far land."

"Not only a fellow-countryman, my good sir," said Challenger, "but also, if I may be allowed to enlarge your simile, an ally of the first value. This beech tree will be our saviour."

"By George!" cried Lord John, "a bridge!"

"Exactly, my friends, a bridge! It is not for nothing that I expended an hour last night in focusing my mind upon the situation. I have some recollection of once remarking to our young friend here that G. E. C. is at his best when his back is to the wall. Last night you will admit that all our backs were to the wall. But where will-power and intellect go together, there is always a way out. A drawbridge had to be found which could be dropped across the abyss. Behold it!"

It was certainly a brilliant idea. The tree was a good sixty feet in height, and if it only fell the right way it would easily cross the chasm. Challenger had slung the camp axe over his shoulder when he ascended. Now he handed it to me.

"Our young friend has the thews and sinews," said he. "I think he will be the most useful at this task. I must beg, however, that you will kindly refrain from thinking for yourself, and that you will do exactly what you are told."

Under his direction I cut such gashes in the sides of the tree as would ensure that it should fall as we desired. It had already a strong, natural tilt in the direction of the plateau, so that the matter was not difficult. Finally I set to work in earnest upon the trunk, taking turn and turn with Lord John. In a little over an hour there was a loud crack, the tree swayed forward, and then crashed over, burying its branches among the bushes on the farther side. The severed trunk rolled to the very edge of our platform, and for one terrible second we all thought that it was over. It balanced itself, however, a few inches from the edge, and there was our bridge to the unknown.

All of us, without a word, shook hands with Professor Challenger, who raised his straw hat and bowed deeply to each in turn.

"I claim the honour," said he, "to be the first to cross to the unknown land—a fitting subject, no doubt, for some future historical painting."

He had approached the bridge when Lord John laid his hand upon his coat.

"My dear chap," said he, "I really cannot allow it."

"Cannot allow it, sir!" The head went back and the beard forward.

"When it is a matter of science, don't you know, I follow your lead because you are by way of bein' a man of science. But it's up to you to follow me when you come into my department."

"Your department, sir?"

"We all have our professions, and soldierin' is mine. We are, accordin' to my ideas, invadin' a new country, which may or may not be chock-full of enemies of sorts. To barge blindly into it for want of a little common sense and patience isn't my notion of management."

The remonstrance was too reasonable to be disregarded. Challenger tossed his head and shrugged his heavy shoulders.

"Well, sir, what do you propose?"

"For all I know there may be a tribe of cannibals waitin' for lunch-time among those very bushes," said Lord John, looking across the bridge. "It's better to learn wisdom before you get into a cookin'-pot; so we will content ourselves with hopin' that there is no trouble waitin' for us, and at the same time we will act as if there were. Malone and I will go down again, therefore, and we will fetch up the four rifles, together with Gomez and the other. One man can then go across and the rest will cover him with guns, until he sees that it is safe for the whole crowd to come along."

Challenger sat down upon the cut stump and groaned his impatience; but Summerlee and I were of one mind that Lord John was our leader when such practical details were in question. The climb was a more simple thing now that the rope dangled down the face of the worst part of the ascent. Within an hour we had brought up the rifles and a shot-gun. The half-breeds had ascended also, and under Lord John's orders they had carried up a bale of provisions in case our first exploration should be a long one. We had each bandoliers of cartridges.

"Now, Challenger, if you really insist upon being the first man in," said Lord John, when every preparation was complete.

"I am much indebted to you for your gracious permission," said the angry Professor; for never was a man so intolerant of every form of authority. "Since you are good enough to allow it, I shall most certainly take it upon myself to act as pioneer upon this occasion."

Seating himself with a leg overhanging the abyss on each side, and his hatchet slung upon his back, Challenger hopped his way across the trunk and was soon at the other side. He clambered up and waved his arms in the air.

"At last!" he cried, "at last!"

I gazed anxiously at him, with a vague expectation that some terrible fate would dart at him from the curtain of green behind him. But all was quiet, save that a strange, many-coloured bird flew up from under his feet and vanished among the trees.

Summerlee was the second. His wiry energy is wonderful in so frail a frame. He insisted upon having two rifles slung upon his back, so that both Professors were armed when he had made his transit. I came next, and tried not to look down into the horrible gulf over which I was pass-ing. Summerlee held out the butt-end of his rifle, and an instant later I was able to grasp his hand. As to Lord John, he walked across—actually walked, without support! He must have nerves of iron.

And there we were, the four of us, upon the dreamland, the lost world, of Maple White. To all of us it seemed the moment of our supreme triumph. Who could have guessed that it was the prelude to our supreme disaster? Let me say in a few words how the crushing blow fell upon us.

We had turned away from the edge, and had penetrated about fifty yards of close brushwood, when there came a frightful rending crash from behind us. With one impulse we rushed back the way we had come. The bridge was gone!

Far down at the base of the cliff I saw, as I looked over, a tangled mass of branches and splintered trunk. It was our beech tree. Had the edge of the platform crumbled and let it through? For a moment this explanation was in all our minds. The next, from the farther side of the rocky pinnacle before us a swarthy face, the face of Gomez the half-breed, was slowly protruded. Yes, it was Gomez, but no longer the Gomez of the demure smile and the mask-like expression. Here was a face with flashing eyes and distorted features, a face convulsed with ha-tred and with the mad joy of gratified revenge.

"Lord Roxton!" he shouted. "Lord John Roxton!"

"Well," said our companion, "here I am."

A shriek of laughter came across the abyss.

"Yes, there you are, you English dog, and there you will remain! I have waited and waited, and now has come my chance. You found it hard to get up; you will find it harder to get down. You cursed fools, you are trapped, every one of you!"

We were too astounded to speak. We could only stand there staring in amazement. A great broken bough upon the grass showed whence he had gained his leverage to tilt over our bridge. The face had vanished, but presently it was up again, more frantic than before.

"We nearly killed you with a stone at the cave," he cried, "but this is better. It is slower and more terrible. Your bones will whiten up there, and none will know where you lie or come to cover them. As you lie dying, think of Lopez, whom you shot five years ago on the Putomayo River. I am his brother, and, come what will I die happy now, for his memory has been avenged." A furious hand was shaken at us, and then all was quiet.

Had the half-breed simply wrought his vengeance and then escaped, all might have been well with him. It was that foolish irresistible Latin impulse to be dramatic which brought his own downfall. Roxton, the man who had earned himself the name of the Flail of the Lord through three countries, was not one who could be safely taunted. The half-breed was descending on the farther side of the pinnacle; but before he could reach the ground Lord John had run along the edge of the plateau and gained a point from which he could see his man. There was a single crack of his rifle, and, though we saw nothing, we heard the scream and then the distant thud of the falling body. Roxton came back to us with a face of granite.

"I have been a blind simpleton," said he, bitterly. "It's my folly that has brought you all into this trouble. I should have remembered that these people have long memories for blood-feuds, and have been more upon my guard."

"What about the other one? It took two of them to lever that tree over the edge."

"I could have shot him, but I let him go. He may have had no part in it. Perhaps it would have been better if I had killed him, for he must, as you say, have lent a hand."

Now that we had the clue to his action, each of us could cast back and remember some sinister act upon the part of the half-breed—his constant desire to know our plans, his arrest outside our tent when he was over-hearing them, the furtive looks of hatred which from time to time one or other of us had surprised. We were still discussing it, endeavouring to adjust our minds to these new conditions, when a singular scene in the plain below arrested our attention.

A man in white clothes, who could only be the surviving half-breed, was running as one does run when Death is the pacemaker. Behind him, only a few yards in his rear, bounded the huge ebony figure of Zambo, our devoted negro. Even as we looked, he sprang upon the back of the fugitive and flung his arms round his neck. They rolled on the ground together. An instant afterwards Zambo rose, looked at the prostrate man, and then, waving his hand joyously to us, came running in our direction. The white figure lay motionless in the middle of the great plain.

Our two traitors had been destroyed, but the mischief that they had done lived after them. By no possible means could we get back to the pinnacle. We had been natives of the world, now we were natives of the plateau. The two things were separate and apart. There was the plain which led to the canoes. Yonder, beyond the violet, hazy horizon, was the stream which led back to civilization. But the link between was missing. No human ingenuity could suggest a means of bridging the chasm which yawned between ourselves and our past lives. One instant had altered the whole condition of our existence.

It was at such a moment that I learned the stuff of which my three comrades were composed. They were grave, it is true, and thoughtful, but of an invincible serenity. For the moment we could only sit among the bushes in patience and wait the coming of Zambo. Presently his honest black face topped the rocks and his Herculean figure emerged upon the top of the pinnacle.

"What I do now?" he cried. "You tell me and I do it."

It was a question which it was easier to ask than to answer. One thing only was clear. He was our one trusty link with the outside world. On no account must he leave us.

"No, no!" he cried. "I not leave you. Whatever come, you always find me here. But no able to keep Indians. Already they say too much, Curupuri live on this place, and they go home. Now you leave them me no able to keep them."

"Make them wait till to-morrow, Zambo," I shouted, "then I can send letter back by them."

"Very good, sarr! I promise they wait till to-morrow," said the negro. "But what I do for you now?"

There was plenty for him to do, and admirably the faithful fellow did it. First of all, under our directions, he undid the rope from the tree-stump and threw one end of it across to us. It was not thicker than a clothes-line, but it was of great strength, and though we could not make a bridge of it, we might well find it invaluable if we had any climbing to do. He then fastened his end of the rope to the package of supplies which had been carried up, and we were able to drag it across. This gave us the means of life for at least a week, even if we found nothing else. Finally he descended and carried up two other packets of mixed goods—a box of ammunition and a number of other things, all of which we got across by throwing our rope to him and hauling it back. It was evening when he at last climbed down, with a final assurance that he would keep the Indians till next morning.

And so it is that I have spent nearly the whole of this our first night upon the plateau writing up our experiences by the light of a single candle-lantern.

We supped and camped at the very edge of the cliff, quenching our thirst with two bottles of Apollinaris which were in one of the cases. It is vital to us to find water, but I think even Lord John himself had had adventures enough for one day, and none of us felt inclined to make the first push into the unknown. We forbore to light a fire or to make any unnecessary sound.

To-morrow (or to-day, rather, for it is already dawn as I write) we shall make our first venture into this strange land. When I shall be able to write again—or if I ever shall write again—I know not. Meanwhile, I can see that the Indians are still in their place, and I am sure that the faithful Zambo will be here presently to get my letter. I only trust that it will come to hand.

P.S.—The more I think the more desperate does our position seem. I see no possible hope of our return. If there were a high tree near the edge of the plateau we might drop a return bridge across, but there is none within fifty yards. Our united strength could not carry a trunk which would serve our purpose. The rope, of course, is far too short that we could descend by it. No, our position is hopeless—hopeless!

10
The Most Wonderful Things Have Happened

The most wonderful things have happened and are continually happening to us. All the paper that I possess consists of five old note-books and a lot of scraps, and I have only the one stylographic pencil; but so long as I can move my hand I will continue to set down our experiences and impressions, for, since we are the only men of the whole human race to see such things, it is of enormous importance that I should record them whilst they are fresh in my memory and before that fate which seems to be constantly impending does actually overtake us. Whether Zambo can at last take these letters to the river, or whether I shall myself in some miraculous way carry them back with me, or, finally, whether some daring explorer, coming upon our tracks, with the advantage, perhaps, of a perfected monoplane, should find this bundle of manuscript, in any case I can see that what I am writing is destined to immortality as a classic of true adventure.

On the morning after our being trapped upon the plateau by the villainous Gomez we began a new stage in our experiences. The first incident in it was not such as to give me a very favourable opinion of the place to which we had wandered. As I roused myself from a short nap after day had dawned, my eyes fell upon a most singular appearance upon my own leg. My trouser had slipped up, exposing a few inches of skin above my sock. On this there rested a large, purplish grape. Astonished at the sight, I leaned forward to pick it off, when, to my horror, it burst between my finger and thumb, squirting blood in every direction. My cry of disgust had brought the two Professors to my side.

"Most interesting," said Summerlee, bending over my skin. "An enormous blood-tick, as yet I believe, unclassified."

"The first-fruits of our labours," said Challenger in his booming, pedantic fashion. "We cannot do less than call it *Ixodes Maloni*. The very small inconvenience of being bitten, my young friend, cannot, I am sure, weigh with you as against the glorious privilege of having your name inscribed in the deathless roll of zoology. Unhappily you have crushed this fine specimen at the moment of satiation."

"Filthy vermin!" I cried.

Professor Challenger raised his great eyebrows in protest, and placed a soothing paw upon my shoulder.

"You should cultivate the scientific eye and the detached scientific mind," said he. "To a man of philosophic temperament like myself the blood-tick, with its lancet-like proboscis and its distending stomach, is as beautiful a work of Nature as the peacock, or, for that matter, the aurora borealis. It pains me to hear you speak of it in so unappreciative a fashion. No doubt, with due diligence, we can secure some other specimen."

"There can be no doubt of that," said Summerlee, grimly, "for one has just disappeared behind your shirt-collar."

Challenger sprang into the air bellowing like a bull, and tore frantically at his coat and shirt to get them off. Summerlee and I laughed so that we could hardly help him. At last we exposed that monstrous torso (fifty-four inches, by the tailor's tape). His body was all matted with black hair, out of which jungle we picked the wandering tick before it had bitten him. But the bushes round were full of the horrible pests, and it was clear that we must shift our camp,

But first of all it was necessary to make our arrangements with the faithful negro, who appeared presently on the pinnacle with a number of tins of cocoa and biscuits, which he tossed over to us. Of the stores which remained below he was ordered to retain as much as would keep him for two months. The Indians were to have the remainder as a reward for their services and as payment for taking our letters back to the Amazon. Some hours later we saw them in a single file far out upon the plain, each with a bundle on his head, making their way back along the path we had come. Zambo occupied our little tent at the base of the pinnacle, and there he remained, our one link with the world below.

And now we had to decide upon our immediate movements. We shifted our position from among the tick-laden bushes until we came to a small clearing thickly surrounded by trees upon all sides. There were some flat slabs of rock in the centre, with an excellent well close by, and there we sat in cleanly comfort while we made our first plans for the invasion of this new country. Birds were calling among the foliage—especially one with a peculiar whooping cry which was new to us—but beyond these sounds there were no signs of life.

Our first care was to make some sort of list of our own stores, so that we might know what we had to rely upon. What with the things we had ourselves brought up and those which Zambo had sent across on the rope, we were fairly well supplied. Most important of all, in view of the dangers which might surround us, we had our four rifles and one thousand three hundred rounds, also a shot-gun, but not more than a hundred and fifty medium pellet cartridges. In the matter of provisions we had enough to last for several weeks, with a sufficiency of tobacco and a few scientific implements, including a large telescope and a good field-glass. All these things we collected together in the clearing, and as a first precaution, we cut down with our hatchet and knives a number of thorny bushes, which we piled round in a circle some fifteen yards in diameter. This was to be our headquarters for the time—our place of refuge against sudden danger and the guard-house for our stores. Fort Challenger, we called it.

It was midday before we had made ourselves secure, but the heat was not oppressive, and the general character of the plateau, both in its temperature and in its vegetation, was almost temperate. The beech, the oak, and even the birch were to be found among the tangle of trees which girt us in. One huge gingko tree, topping all the others, shot its great limbs and maidenhair foliage over the fort which we had constructed. In its shade we continued our discussion, while Lord John, who had quickly taken command in the hour of action, gave us his views.

"So long as neither man nor beast has seen or heard us, we are safe," said he. "From the time they know we are here our troubles begin. There are no signs that they have found us out as yet. So our game surely is to lie low for time and spy out the land. We want to have a good look at our neighbours before we get on visitin' terms."

"But we must advance," I ventured to remark.

"By all means, sonny my boy! We will advance. But with common sense. We must never go so far that we can't get back to our base. Above all, we must never, unless it is life or death, fire off our guns."

"But *you* fired yesterday," said Summerlee.

"Well, it couldn't be helped. However, the wind was strong and blew outwards. It is not likely that the sound could have travelled far into the plateau. By the way, what shall we call this place? I suppose it is up to us to give it a name?"

There were several suggestions, more or less happy, but Challenger's was final.

"It can only have one name," said he. "It is called after the pioneer who discovered it. It is Maple White Land."

Maple White Land it became, and so it is named in that chart which has become my special task. So it will, I trust, appear in the atlas of the future.

The peaceful penetration of Maple White Land was the pressing subject before us. We had the evidence of our own eyes that the place was inhabited by some unknown creatures, and there was that of Maple White's sketch-book to show that more dreadful and more dangerous monsters might still appear. That there might also prove to be human occupants and that they were of a malevolent character was suggested by the skeleton impaled upon the bamboos, which could not have got there had it not been dropped from above. Our situation, stranded without possibility of escape in such a land, was clearly full of danger, and our reason endorsed every measure of caution which Lord John's experience could suggest. Yet it was surely impossible that we should halt on the edge of this world of mystery when our very souls were tingling with impatience to push forward and to pluck the heart from it.

We therefore blocked the entrance to our zareba by filling it up with several thorny bushes, and left our camp with the stores entirely surrounded by this protecting hedge. We then slowly and cautiously set forth into the unknown, following the course of the little stream which flowed from our spring, as it should always serve us as a guide on our return.

Hardly had we started when we came across signs that there were indeed wonders awaiting us. After a few hundred yards of thick forest, containing many trees which were quite unknown to me, but which Summerlee, who was the botanist of the party, recognized as forms of conifera and of cycadaceous plants which have long passed away in the world below, we entered a region where the stream widened out and formed a considerable bog. High reeds of a peculiar type grew thickly before us, which were pronounced to be equisetacea, or mare's-tails, with tree-ferns scattered amongst them, all of them swaying in a brisk wind. Suddenly Lord John, who was walking first, halted with uplifted hand.

"Look at this!" said he. "By George, this must be the trail of the father of all birds!"

An enormous three-toed track was imprinted in the soft mud before us. The creature, whatever it was, had crossed the swamp and had passed on into the forest. We all stopped to examine that monstrous spoor. If it were indeed a bird—and what animal could leave such a mark?—its foot was so much larger than an ostrich's that its height upon the same scale must be enormous. Lord John looked eagerly round him and slipped two cartridges into his elephant-gun.

"I'll stake my good name as a shikaree," said he, "that the track is a fresh one. The creature has not passed ten minutes. Look how the water is still oozing into that deeper print! By Jove! See, here is the mark of a little one!"

Sure enough, smaller tracks of the same general form were running parallel to the large ones.

"But what do you make of this?" cried Professor Summerlee, triumphantly, pointing to what looked like the huge print of a five-fingered human hand appearing among the three-toed marks.

"Wealden!" cried Challenger, in an ecstasy. "I've seen them in the Wealden clay. It is a creature walking erect upon three-toed feet, and occasionally putting one of its five-fingered fore-paws upon the ground. Not a bird, my dear Roxton—not a bird."

"A beast?"

"No; a reptile—a dinosaur. Nothing else could have left such a track. They puzzled a worthy Sussex doctor some ninety years ago; but who in the world could have hoped—hoped—to have seen a sight like that?"

His words died away into a whisper, and we all stood in motionless amazement. Following the tracks, we had left the morass and passed through a screen of brushwood and trees. Beyond was an open glade, and in this were five of the most extraordinary creatures that I have ever seen. Crouching down among the bushes, we observed them at our leisure.

There were, as I say, five of them, two being adults and three young ones. In size they were enormous. Even the babies were as big as elephants, while the two large ones were far beyond all creatures I have ever seen. They had slate-coloured skin, which was scaled like a lizard's and shimmered where the sun shone upon it. All five were sitting up, balancing themselves upon their broad, powerful tails and their huge three-toed hind-feet, while with their small five-fingered front-feet they pulled down the branches upon which they browsed. I do not know that I can bring their appearance home to you better than by saying that they looked like monstrous kangaroos, twenty feet in length, and with skins like black crocodiles.

I do not know how long we stayed motionless gazing at this marvellous spectacle. A strong wind blew towards us and we were well concealed, so there was no chance of discovery. From time to time the little ones played round their parents in unwieldy gambols, the great beasts bounding into the air and falling with dull thuds upon the earth. The strength of the parents seemed to be limitless, for one of them, having some difficulty in reaching a bunch of foliage which grew upon a considerable-sized tree, put his fore-legs round the trunk and tore it down as if it had been a sapling. The action seemed, as I thought, to show not only the great development of its muscles, but also the small one of its brain, for the whole weight came crashing down upon the top of it, and it uttered a series of shrill yelps to show that, big as it was, there was a limit to what it could endure. The incident made it think, apparently, that the neighbourhood was dangerous, for it slowly lurched off through the wood, followed by its mate and its three enormous infants. We saw the shimmering slatey gleam of their skins between the tree-trunks, and their heads undulating high above the brushwood. Then they vanished from our sight.

I looked at my comrades. Lord John was standing at gaze with his finger on the trigger of his elephant-gun, his eager hunter's soul shining from his fierce eyes. What would he not give for one such head to place between the two crossed oars above the mantelpiece in his snuggery at the Albany! And yet his reason held him in, for all our exploration of the wonders of this unknown land depended upon our presence being concealed from its inhabitants. The two professors were in silent ecstasy. In their excitement they had unconsciously seized each other by the hand, and stood like two little children in the presence of a marvel, Challenger's cheeks bunched up into a seraphic smile, and Summerlee's sardonic face softening for the moment into wonder and reverence.

"*Nunc dimittis!*" he cried at last. "What will they say in England of this?"

"My dear Summerlee, I will tell you with great confidence exactly what they will say in England," said Challenger. "They will say that you are an infernal liar and a scientific charlatan, exactly as you and others said of me."

"In the face of photographs?"

"Faked, Summerlee! Clumsily faked!"

"In the face of specimens?"

"Ah, there we may have them! Malone and his filthy Fleet Street crew may be all yelping our praises yet. August the twenty-eighth—the day we saw five live iguanodons in a glade of Maple White Land. Put it down in your diary, my young friend, and send it to your rag."

"And be ready to get the toe-end of the editorial boot in return," said Lord John. "Things look a bit different from the latitude of London, young fellah-my-lad. There's many a man who never tells his adventures for he can't hope to be believed. Who's to blame them? For this will seem a bit of a dream to ourselves in a month or two. *What* did you say they were?"

"Iguanodons," said Summerlee. "You'll find their foot-marks all over the Hastings sands, in Kent, and in Sussex. The South of England was alive with them when there was plenty of good lush green-stuff to keep them going. Conditions have changed, and the beasts died. Here it seems that the conditions have not changed, and the beasts have lived."

"If ever we get out of this alive, I must have a head with me," said Lord John. "Lord, how some of that Somaliland-Uganda crowd would turn a beautiful pea-green if they saw it! I don't know what you chaps think, but it strikes me that we are on mighty thin ice all this time."

I had the same feeling of mystery and danger around us. In the gloom of the trees there seemed a constant menace, and as we looked up into their shadowy foliage vague terrors crept into one's heart. It is true that these monstrous creatures which we had seen were lumbering, inoffensive brutes which were unlikely to hurt anyone, but in this world of wonders what other survivals might there not be—what fierce, active horrors ready to pounce upon us from their lair among the rocks or brushwood? I knew little of prehistoric life, but I had a clear remembrance of one book which I had read in which it spoke of creatures who would live upon our lions and tigers as a cat lives upon mice. What if these also were to be found in the woods of Maple White Land!

It was destined that on this very morning—our first in the new country—we were to find out what strange hazards lay around us. It was a loathsome adventure, and one of which I hate to think. If, as Lord John said, the glade of the iguanodons will remain with us as a dream, then surely the swamp of the pterodactyls will for ever be our nightmare. Let me set down exactly what occurred.

We passed very slowly through the woods, partly because Lord John acted as scout before he would let us advance, and partly because at every second step one or other of our professors would fall, with a cry of wonder, before some flower or insect which presented him with a new type. We may have travelled two or three miles in all, keeping to the right of the line of the stream, when we came upon a considerable opening in the trees. A belt of brushwood led up to a tangle of rocks—the whole plateau was strewn with boulders. We were walking slowly towards these rocks, among bushes which reached over our waists, when we became aware of a strange low gabbling and whistling sound, which filled the air with a constant clamour and appeared to come from some spot immediately before us. Lord John held up his hand as a signal for us to stop, and he made his way swiftly, stooping and running, to the line of rocks. We saw him peep over them and give a gesture of amazement. Then he stood staring as if forgetting us, so utterly entranced was he by what he saw. Finally he waved us to come on, holding up his hand as a signal for caution. His whole bearing made me feel that something wonderful but dangerous lay before us.

Creeping to his side, we looked over the rocks. The place into which we gazed was a pit, and may, in the early days, have been one of the smaller volcanic blow-holes of the plateau. It was bowl-shaped, and at the bottom, some hundreds of yards from where we lay, were pools of green-scummed stagnant water, fringed with bulrushes. It was a weird place in itself, but its occupants made it seem like a scene from the Seven Circles of Dante. The place was a rookery of pterodactyls. There were hundreds of them congregated within view. All the bottom area round the water-edge was alive with their young ones, and with hideous mothers brooding upon their leathery, yellowish eggs. From this crawling flapping mass of obscene reptilian life came the shocking clamour which filled the air and the mephitic, horrible, musty odour which turned us sick. But above, perched each upon its own stone, tall, grey, and withered, more like dead and dried specimens than actual living creatures, sat the horrible males, absolutely motionless save for the rolling of their red eyes or an occasional snap of their rat-trap beaks as a dragonfly went past them. Their huge, membranous wings were closed by folding their fore-arms, so that they sat like gigantic old women, wrapped in hideous web-coloured shawls, and with their ferocious heads protruding above them. Large and small, not less than a thousand of these filthy creatures lay in the hollow before us.

Our professors would gladly have stayed there all day, so entranced were they by this opportunity of studying the life of a prehistoric age. They pointed out the fish and dead birds lying about among the rocks as proving the nature of the food of these creatures, and I heard them congratulating each other on having cleared up the point why the bones of this flying dragon are found in such great numbers in certain well-defined areas, as in the Cambridge Green-sand, since it was now seen that, like penguins, they lived in gregarious fashion.

Finally, however, Challenger, bent upon proving some point which Summerlee had contested, thrust his head over the rock and nearly brought destruction upon us all. In an instant the nearest male gave a shrill, whistling cry, and flapped its twenty-foot span of leathery wings as it soared up into the air. The females and young ones huddled together beside the water, while the whole circle of sentinels rose one after the other and sailed off into the sky. It was a wonderful sight to see at least a hundred creatures of such enormous size and hideous appearance all swooping like swallows with swift, shearing wing-strokes above us; but soon we realized that it was not one on which we could afford to linger. At first the great brutes flew round in a huge ring, as if to make sure what the exact extent of the danger might be. Then, the flight grew lower and the circle narrower, until they were whizzing round and round us, the dry, rustling flap of their huge slate-coloured wings filling the air with a volume of sound that made me think of Hendon aerodrome upon a race day.

"Make for the wood and keep together," cried Lord John, clubbing his rifle. "The brutes mean mischief."

The moment we attempted to retreat the circle closed in upon us, until the tips of the wings of those nearest to us nearly touched our faces. We beat at them with the stocks of our guns, but there was nothing solid or vulnerable to strike. Then suddenly out of the whizzing, slate-coloured circle a long neck shot out, and a fierce beak made a thrust at us. Another and another followed. Summerlee gave a cry and put his hand to his face, from which the blood was streaming. I felt a prod at the back of my neck, and turned dizzy with the shock. Challenger fell, and as I stooped to pick him up I was again struck from behind and dropped on the top of him. At the same instant I heard the crash of Lord John's elephant-gun, and, looking up, saw one of the creatures with a broken wing struggling upon the ground, spitting and gurgling at us with a wide-opened beak and blood-shot, goggled eyes, like some devil in a mediaeval picture. Its comrades had flown higher at the sudden sound, and were circling above our heads.

"Now," cried Lord John, "now for our lives!"

We staggered through the brushwood, and even as we reached the trees the harpies were on us again. Summerlee was knocked down, but we tore him up and rushed among the trunks. Once there we were safe, for those huge wings had no space for their sweep beneath the branches. As we limped homewards, sadly mauled and discomfited, we saw them for a long time flying at a great height against the deep blue sky above our heads, soaring round and round, no bigger than wood-pigeons, with their eyes no doubt still following our progress. At last, however, as we reached the thicker woods they gave up the chase, and we saw them no more.

"A most interesting and convincing experience," said Challenger, as we halted beside the brook and he bathed a swollen knee. "We are exceptionally well informed, Summerlee, as to the habits of the enraged pterodactyl."

Summerlee was wiping the blood from a cut in his forehead, while I was tying up a nasty stab in the muscle of the neck. Lord John had the shoulder of his coat torn away, but the creature's teeth had only grazed the flesh.

"It is worth noting," Challenger continued, "that our young friend has received an undoubted stab, while Lord John's coat could only have been torn by a bite. In my own case, I was beaten about the head by their wings, so we have had a remarkable exhibition of their various methods of offence."

"It has been touch and go for our lives," said Lord John gravely, "and I could not think of a more rotten sort of death than to be outed by such filthy vermin. I was sorry to fire my rifle, but, by Jove! there was no great choice."

"We should not be here if you hadn't," said I, with conviction.

"It may do no harm," said he. "Among these woods there must be many loud cracks from splitting or falling trees which would be just like the sound of a gun. But now, if you are of my opinion, we have had thrills enough for one day, and had best get back to the surgical box at the camp for some carbolic. Who knows what venom these beasts may have in their hideous jaws?"

But surely no men ever had just such a day since the world began. Some fresh surprise was ever in store for us. When, following the course of our brook, we at last reached our glade and saw the thorny barricade of our camp, we thought that our adventures were at an end. But we had something more to think of before we could rest. The gate of Fort Challenger had been untouched, the walls were unbroken, and yet it had been visited by some strange and powerful creature in our absence. No foot-mark showed a trace of its nature, and only the overhanging branch of the enormous gingko tree suggested how it might have come and gone; but of its malevolent strength there was ample evidence in the condition of our stores. They were strewn at random all over the ground, and one tin of meat had been crushed into pieces so as to extract the contents. A case of cartridges had been shattered into matchwood, and one of the brass shells lay shredded into pieces beside it. Again the feeling of vague horror came upon our souls, and we gazed round with frightened eyes at the dark shadows which lay around us, in all of which some fearsome shape might be lurking. How good it was when we were hailed by the voice of Zambo, and, going to the edge of the plateau, saw him sitting grinning at us upon the top of the opposite pinnacle.

"All well, Massa Challenger, all well!" he cried. "Me stay here. No fear. You always find me when you want."

His honest black face, and the immense view before us, which carried us half-way back to the affluent of the Amazon, helped us to remember that we really were upon this earth in the twentieth century, and had not by some magic been conveyed to some raw planet in its earliest and wildest state. How difficult it was to realise that the violet line upon the far horizon was well advanced to that great river upon which huge

steamers ran, and folk talked of the small affairs of life, while we, marooned among the creatures of a bygone age, could but gaze towards it
and yearn for all that it meant!

One other memory remains with me of this wonderful day, and with
it I will close this letter. The two professors, their tempers aggravated no
doubt by their injuries, had fallen out as to whether our assailants were
of the genus pterodactylus or dimorphodon, and high words had en-
sued. To avoid their wrangling I moved some little way apart, and was
seated smoking upon the trunk of a fallen tree, when Lord John strolled
over in my direction.

"I say, Malone," said he, "do you remember that place where those
beasts were?"

"Very clearly."

"A sort of volcanic pit, was it not?"

"Exactly," said I.

"Did you notice the soil?"

"Rocks."

"But round the water—where the reeds were?"

"It was a bluish soil. It looked like clay."

"Exactly. A volcanic tube full of blue clay."

"What of that?" I asked.

"Oh, nothing, nothing," said he, and strolled back to where the
voices of the contending men of science rose in a prolonged duet, the
high, strident note of Summerlee rising and falling to the sonorous bass
of Challenger. I should have thought no more of Lord John's remark
were it not that once again that night I heard him mutter to himself;
"Blue clay—clay in a volcanic tube!" They were the last words I heard
before I dropped into an exhausted sleep.

11

For Once I Was the Hero

Lord John Roxton was right when he thought that some specially toxic
quality might lie in the bite of the horrible creatures which had attacked

us. On the morning after our first adventure upon the plateau, both Summerlee and I were in great pain and fever, while Challenger's knee was so bruised that he could hardly limp. We kept to our camp all day, therefore, Lord John busying himself, with such help as we could give him, in raising the height and thickness of the thorny walls which were our only defence. I remember that during the whole long day I was haunted by the feeling that we were closely observed, though by whom or whence I could give no guess.

So strong was the impression that I told Professor Challenger of it, who put it down to the cerebral excitement caused by my fever. Again and again I glanced round swiftly, with the conviction that I was about to see something, but only to meet the dark tangle of our hedge or the solemn and cavernous gloom of the great trees which arched above our heads. And yet the feeling grew ever stronger in my own mind that something observant and something malevolent was at our very elbow. I thought of the Indian superstition of the Curupuri—the dreadful, lurking spirit of the woods—and I could have imagined that his terrible presence haunted those who have invaded his most remote and sacred retreat.

That night (our third in Maple White Land) we had an experience which left a fearful impression upon our minds, and made us thankful that Lord John had worked so hard in making our retreat impregnable. We were all sleeping round our dying fire when we were aroused—or, rather, I should say, shot out of our slumbers—by a succession of the most frightful cries and screams to which I have ever listened. I know no sound to which I could compare this amazing tumult, which seemed to come from some spot within a few hundred yards of our camp. It was as ear-splitting as any whistle of a railway-engine; but whereas the whistle is a clear, mechanical, sharp-edged sound, this was far deeper in volume and vibrant with the uttermost strain of agony and horror. We clapped our hands to our ears to shut out that never-shaking appeal. A cold sweat broke out over my body, and my heart turned sick at the misery of it. All the woes of tortured life, all its stupendous indictment of high heaven, its innumerable sorrows, seemed to be centred and condensed into that one dreadful, agonized cry. And then, under this high-pitched, ringing sound there was another, more intermittent, a low, deep-chested laugh, a growling, throaty gurgle of merriment which formed a grotesque accompaniment to the shriek with which it was blended. For three or four minutes on end the fearsome duet continued, while all the foliage rustled with the rising of startled birds. Then it shut off as suddenly as it began. For a long time we sat in horrified silence. Then Lord John threw a bundle of twigs upon the fire, and their red glare lit up the intent faces of my companions and flickered over the great boughs above our heads.

"What was it?" I whispered.

"We shall know in the morning," said Lord John. "It was close to us—not farther than the glade."

"We have been privileged to overhear a prehistoric tragedy, the sort of drama which occurred among the reeds upon the border of some Jurassic lagoon, when the greater dragon pinned the lesser among the slime," said Challenger, with more solemnity than I had ever heard in his voice. "It was surely well for man that he came late in the order of creation. There were powers abroad in earlier days which no courage and no mechanism of his could have met. What could his sling, his throwing-stick, or his arrow avail him against such forces as have been loose tonight? Even with a modern rifle it would be all odds on the monster."

"I think I should back my little friend," said Lord John, caressing his Express. "But the beast would certainly have a good sporting chance."

Summerlee raised his hand.

"Hush!" he cried. "Surely I hear something?"

From the utter silence there emerged a deep, regular pat-pat. It was the tread of some animal—the rhythm of soft but heavy pads placed cautiously upon the ground. It stole slowly round the camp, and then halted near our gateway. There was a low, sibilant rise and fall—the breathing of the creature. Only our feeble hedge separated us from this horror of the night. Each of us had seized his rifle, and Lord John had pulled out a small bush to make an embrasure in the hedge.

"By George!" he whispered. "I think I can see it!"

I stooped and peered over his shoulder through the gap. Yes, I could see it, too. In the deep shadow of the tree there was a deeper shadow yet, black, inchoate, vague—a crouching form full of savage vigour and menace. It was no higher than a horse but the dim outline suggested vast bulk and strength. That hissing pant, as regular and full-volumed as the exhaust of an engine, spoke of a monstrous organism. Once, as it moved, I thought I saw the glint of two terrible, greenish eyes. There was an uneasy rustling, as if it were crawling slowly forward.

"I believe it is going to spring!" said I, cocking my rifle.

"Don't fire! Don't fire!" whispered Lord John. "The crash of a gun in this silent night would be heard for miles. Keep it as a last card."

"If it gets over the hedge we're done," said Summerlee, and his voice crackled into a nervous laugh as he spoke.

"No, it must not get over," cried Lord John; "but hold your fire to the last. Perhaps I can make something of the fellow. I'll chance it, anyhow."

It was as brave an act as ever I saw a man do. He stooped to the fire, picked up a blazing branch, and slipped in an instant through a sallyport which he had made in our gateway. The thing moved forward with a dreadful snarl. Lord John never hesitated, but, running towards it with a quick, light step, he dashed the flaming wood into the brute's face. For one moment I had a vision of a horrible mask like a giant toad's, of a warty, leprous skin, and of a loose mouth all beslobbered with fresh blood. The next, there was a crash in the underwood and our dreadful visitor was gone.

"I thought he wouldn't face the fire," said Lord John, laughing, as he came back and threw his branch among the faggots.

"You should not have taken such a risk!" we all cried.

"There was nothing else to be done. If he had got among us we should have shot each other in tryin' to down him. On the other hand, if we had fired through the hedge and wounded him he would soon have been on the top of us—to say nothin' of giving ourselves away. On the whole, I think that we are jolly well out of it. What was he, then?"

Our learned men looked at each other with some hesitation.

"Personally, I am unable to classify the creature with any certainty," said Summerlee, lighting his pipe from the fire.

"In refusing to commit yourself you are but showing a proper scientific reserve," said Challenger, with massive condescension. "I am not myself prepared to go farther than to say in general terms that we have almost certainly been in contact to-night with some form of carnivorous dinosaur. I have already expressed my anticipation that something of the sort might exist upon this plateau."

"We have to bear in mind," remarked Summerlee, "that there are many prehistoric forms which have never come down to us. It would be rash to suppose that we can give a name to all that we are likely to meet."

"Exactly. A rough classification may be the best that we can attempt. To-morrow some further evidence may help us to an identification. Meantime we can only renew our interrupted slumbers."

"But not without a sentinel," said Lord John, with decision. "We can't afford to take chances in a country like this. Two-hour spells in the future, for each of us."

"Then I'll just finish my pipe in starting the first one," said Professor Summerlee; and from that time onwards we never trusted ourselves again without a watchman.

In the morning it was not long before we discovered the source of the hideous uproar which had aroused us in the night. The iguanodon glade was the scene of a horrible butchery. From the pools of blood and the enormous lumps of flesh scattered in every direction over the green sward we imagined at first that a number of animals had been killed, but on examining the remains more closely we discovered that all this carnage came from one of these unwieldy monsters, which had been literally torn to pieces by some creature not larger, perhaps, but far more ferocious, than itself.

Our two professors sat in absorbed argument, examining piece after piece, which showed the marks of savage teeth and of enormous claws.

"Our judgment must still be in abeyance," said Professor Challenger, with a huge slab of whitish-coloured flesh across his knee. "The indications would be consistent with the presence of a sabre-toothed tiger, such as are still found among the breccia of our caverns; but the creature actually seen was undoubtedly of a larger and more reptilian character. Personally, I should pronounce for allosaurus."

"Or megalosaurus," said Summerlee.

"Exactly. Any one of the larger carnivorous dinosaurs would meet the case. Among them are to be found all the most terrible types of animal-life that have ever cursed the earth or blessed a museum." He laughed sonorously at his own conceit, for, though he had little sense of humour, the crudest pleasantry from his own lips moved him always to roars of appreciation.

"The less noise the better," said Lord John, curtly. "We don't know who or what may be near us. If this fellah comes back for his breakfast and catches us here we won't have so much to laugh at. By the way, what is this mark upon the iguanodon's hide?"

On the dull, scaly, slate-coloured skin, somewhere above the shoulder, there was a singular black circle of some substance which looked like asphalt. None of us could suggest what it meant, though Summerlee was of opinion that he had seen something similar upon one of the young ones two days before. Challenger said nothing, but looked pompous and puffy, as if he could if he would, so that finally Lord John asked his opinion direct.

"If your lordship will graciously permit me to open my mouth, I shall be happy to express my sentiments," said he, with elaborate sarcasm. "I am not in the habit of being taken to task in the fashion which seems to be customary with your lordship. I was not aware that it was necessary to ask your permission before smiling at a harmless pleasantry."

It was not until he had received his apology that our touchy friend would suffer himself to be appeased. When at last his ruffled feelings were at ease, he addressed us at some length from his seat upon a fallen tree, speaking, as his habit was, as if he were imparting most precious information to a class of a thousand.

"With regard to the marking," said he, "I am inclined to agree with my friend and colleague, Professor Summerlee, that the stains are from asphalt. As this plateau is, in its very nature, highly volcanic, and as asphalt is a substance which one associates with Plutonic forces, I cannot doubt that it exists in the free liquid state, and that the creatures may have come in contact with it. A much more important problem is the question as to the existence of the carnivorous monster which has left its traces in this glade. We know roughly that this plateau is not larger than an average English county. Within this confined space a certain number of creatures, mostly types which have passed away in the world below, have lived together for innumerable years. Now, it is very clear to me that in so long a period one would have expected that the carnivorous creatures, multiplying unchecked, would have exhausted their food supply and have been compelled to either modify their flesh-eating habits or die of hunger. This we see has not been so. We can only imagine therefore that the balance of Nature is preserved by some check which limits the numbers of these ferocious creatures. One of the many interesting problems, therefore, which await our solution is to discover what that check may be and how it operates. I venture to trust that we may have some future opportunity for the closer study of the carnivorous dinosaurs."

"And I venture to trust that we may not," I observed.

The Professor only raised his great eyebrows, as the schoolmaster meets the irrelevant observation of the naughty boy.

"Perhaps Professor Summerlee may have an observation to make," he said, and the two *savants* ascended together into some rarified scientific atmosphere, where the possibilities of a modification of the birth-rate were weighed against the decline of the food supply as a check in the struggle for existence.

That morning we mapped out a small portion of the plateau, avoiding the swamp of the pterodactyls, and keeping to the east of our brook instead of to the west. In that direction the country was still thickly wooded, with so much undergrowth that our progress was very slow.

I have dwelt up to now upon the terrors of Maple White Land; but there was another side to the subject, for all that morning we wandered among lovely flowers—mostly, as I observed, white or yellow in colour, these being, as our professors explained, the primitive flower-shades. In many places the ground was absolutely covered with them, and as we walked ankle-deep on that wonderful yielding carpet, the scent was almost intoxicating in its sweetness and intensity. The homely English bee buzzed everywhere around us. Many of the trees under which we passed had their branches bowed down with fruit, some of which were of familiar sorts, while other varieties were new. By observing which of them were pecked by the birds we avoided all danger of poison and added a delicious variety to our food reserve. In the jungle which we traversed were numerous hard-trodden paths made by the wild-beasts, and in the more marshy places we saw a profusion of strange foot-marks, including many of the iguanodon. Once in a grove we observed several of these great creatures grazing, and Lord John, with his glass, was able to report that they also were spotted with asphalt, though in a different place to the one which we had examined in the morning. What this phenomenon meant we could not imagine.

We saw many small animals, such as porcupines, a scaly ant-eater, and a wild pig, piebald in colour and with long curved tusks. Once, through a break in the trees, we saw a clear shoulder of green hill some distance away, and across this a large dun-coloured animal was travelling at a considerable pace. It passed so swiftly that we were unable to say what it was; but if it were a deer, as was claimed by Lord John, it must have been as large as those monstrous Irish elks which are still dug up from time to time in the bogs of my native land.

Ever since the mysterious visit which had been paid to our camp we always returned to it with some misgivings. However, on this occasion we found everything in order. That evening we had a grand discussion upon our present situation and future plans, which I must describe at some length, as it led to a new departure by which we were enabled to gain a more complete knowledge of Maple White Land than might have come in many weeks of exploring. It was Summerlee who opened the debate. All day he had been querulous in manner, and now some remark of Lord John's as to what we should do on the morrow brought all his bitterness to a head.

"What we ought to be doing to-day, to-morrow, and all the time," said he, "is finding some way out of the trap into which we have fallen. You are all turning your brains towards getting into this country. I say that we should be scheming how to get out of it."

"I am surprised, sir," boomed Challenger, stroking his majestic beard, "that any man of science should commit himself to so ignoble a sentiment. You are in a land which offers such an inducement to the ambitious naturalist as none ever has since the world began, and you suggest leaving it before we have acquired more than the most superficial knowledge of it or of its contents. I expected better things of you, Professor Summerlee."

"You must remember," said Summerlee, sourly, "that I have a large class in London who are at present at the mercy of an extremely inefficient *locum tenens*. This makes my situation different from yours, Professor Challenger, since, so far as I know, you have never been entrusted with any responsible educational work."

"Quite so," said Challenger. "I have felt it to be a sacrilege to divert a brain which is capable of the highest original research to any lesser object. That is why I have sternly set my face against any proffered scholastic appointment."

"For example?" asked Summerlee, with a sneer; but Lord John hastened to change the conversation.

"I must say," said he, "that I think it would be a mighty poor thing to go back to London before I know a great deal more of this place than I do at present."

"I could never dare to walk into the back office of my paper and face old McArdle," said I. (You will excuse the frankness of this report, will you not, sir?) "He'd never forgive me for leaving such unexhausted copy behind me. Besides, so far as I can see, it is not worth discussing, since we can't get down, even if we wanted."

"Our young friend makes up for many obvious mental lacunæ by some measure of primitive common sense," remarked Challenger. "The interests of his deplorable profession are immaterial to us; but, as he observes, we cannot get down in any case, so it is a waste of energy to discuss it."

"It is a waste of energy to do anything else," growled Summerlee from behind his pipe. "Let me remind you that we came here upon a perfectly definite mission, entrusted to us at the meeting of the Zoological Institute in London. That mission was to test the truth of Professor Challenger's statements. Those statements, as I am bound to admit, we are now in a position to endorse. Our ostensible work is therefore done. As to the detail which remains to be worked out upon this plateau, it is so enormous that only a large expedition, with a very special equipment, could hope to cope with it. Should we attempt to do so ourselves, the only possible result must be that we shall never return with the important contribution to science which we have already gained. Professor Challenger has devised a means for getting us on to this plateau when it appeared to be inaccessible; I think that we should now call upon him to use the same ingenuity in getting us back to the world from which we came."

I confess that as Summerlee stated his view it struck me as altogether reasonable. Even Challenger was affected by the consideration that his

enemies would never stand confuted if the confirmation of his statements should never reach those who had doubted them.

"The problem of the descent is at first sight a formidable one," said
he, "and yet I cannot doubt that the intellect can solve it. I am prepared
to agree with our colleague that a protracted stay in Maple White Land
is at present inadvisable, and that the question of our return will soon
have to be faced. I absolutely refuse to leave however, until we have made
at least a superficial examination of this country, and are able to take
back with us something in the nature of a chart."

Professor Summerlee gave a snort of impatience.

"We have spent two long days in exploration," said he, "and we are
no wiser as to the actual geography of the place than when we started.
It is clear that it is all thickly wooded, and it would take months to penetrate it and to learn the relations of one part to another. If there were
some central peak it would be different, but it all slopes downwards, so
far as we can see. The farther we go the less likely it is that we will get
any general view."

It was at that moment that I had an inspiration. My eyes chanced to
light upon the enormous gnarled trunk of the gingko tree which cast its
huge branches over us. Surely, if its bole exceeded that of all the others,
its height must do the same. If the rim of the plateau was indeed the
highest point, then why should this mighty tree not prove to be a watch-
tower which commanded the whole country? Now, ever since I ran wild
as a lad in Ireland I have been a bold and skilled tree-climber. My comrades might be masters on the rocks, but I knew that I would be supreme
among those branches. Could I only get my legs on to the lowest of the
giant off-shoots, then it would be strange indeed if I could not make my
way to the top. My comrades were delighted at my idea.

"Our young friend," said Challenger, bunching up the red apples of
his cheeks, "is capable of acrobatic exertions which would be impossible
to a man of a more solid, though possibly of a more commanding, appearance. I applaud his resolution."

"By George, young fellah, you've put your hand on it!" said Lord
John, clapping me on the back. "How we never came to think of it before I can't imagine! There's not more than an hour of daylight left, but
if you take your notebook you may be able to get some rough sketch of

the place. If we put these three ammunition cases under the branch, I will soon hoist you on to it."

He stood on the boxes while I faced the trunk, and was gently raising me when Challenger sprang forward and gave me such a thrust with his huge hand that he fairly shot me into the tree. With both arms clasping the branch, I scrambled hard with my feet until I had worked, first my body, and then my knees, on to it. There were three excellent offshoots, like huge rungs of a ladder, above my head, and a tangle of convenient branches beyond, so that I clambered onwards with such speed that I soon lost sight of the ground and had nothing but foliage beneath me. Now and then I encountered a check, and once I had to shin up a creeper for eight or ten feet, but I made excellent progress, and the booming of Challenger's voice seemed to be a great distance beneath me. The tree was, however, enormous, and, looking upwards, I could see no thinning of the leaves above my head. There was some thick, bush-like clump which seemed to be a parasite upon a branch up which I was swarming. I leaned my head round it in order to see what was beyond, and I nearly fell out of the tree in my surprise and horror at what I saw.

A face was gazing into mine—at the distance of only a foot or two. The creature that owned it had been crouching behind the parasite, and had looked round it at the same instant that I did. It was a human face— or at least it was far more human than any monkey's that I have ever seen. It was long, whitish, and blotched with pimples, the nose flattened, and the lower jaw projecting, with a bristle of coarse whiskers round the chin. The eyes, which were under thick and heavy brows, were bestial and ferocious, and as it opened its mouth to snarl what sounded like a curse at me I observed that it had curved, sharp canine teeth. For an instant I read hatred and menace in the evil eyes. Then, as quick as a flash, came an expression of overpowering fear. There was a crash of broken boughs as it dived wildly down into the tangle of green. I caught a glimpse of a hairy body like that of a reddish pig, and then it was gone amid a swirl of leaves and branches.

"What's the matter?" shouted Roxton from below. "Anything wrong with you?"

"Did you see it?" I cried with my arms round the branch and all my nerves tingling.

"We heard a row, as if your foot had slipped. What was it?"

I was so shocked at the sudden and strange appearance of this ape-man that I hesitated whether I should not climb down again and tell my experience to my companions. But I was already so far up the great tree that it seemed a humiliation to return without having carried out my mission.

After a long pause therefore, to recover my breath and my courage, I continued my ascent. Once I put my weight upon a rotten branch and swung for a few seconds by my hands, but in the main it was all easy climbing. Gradually the leaves thinned around me, and I was aware, from the wind upon my face, that I had topped all the trees of the forest. I was determined, however, not to look about me before I had reached the very highest point, so I scrambled on until I had got so far that the topmost branch was bending beneath my weight. There I settled into a convenient fork, and, balancing myself securely, I found myself looking down at a most wonderful panorama of this strange country in which we found ourselves.

The sun was just above the western sky-line, and the evening was a particularly bright and clear one, so that the whole extent of the plateau was visible beneath me. It was, as seen from this height, of an oval contour, with a breadth of about thirty miles and a width of twenty. Its general shape was that of a shallow funnel, all the sides sloping down to a considerable lake in the centre. This lake may have been ten miles in circumference, and lay very green and beautiful in the evening light, with a thick fringe of reeds at its edges, and with its surface broken by several yellow sandbanks, which gleamed golden in the mellow sunshine. A number of long dark objects, which were too large for alligators and too long for canoes, lay upon the edges of these patches of sand. With my glass I could clearly see that they were alive, but what their nature might be I could not imagine.

From the side of the plateau on which we were, slopes of woodland, with occasional glades, stretched down for five or six miles to the central lake. I could see at my very feet the glade of the iguanodons, and farther off was a round opening in the trees which marked the swamp of the pterodactyls. On the side facing me, however, the plateau presented a very different aspect. There the basalt cliffs of the outside were reproduced upon the inside, forming an escarpment about two hundred feet high, with a woody slope beneath it. Along the base of these red cliffs, some distance above the ground, I could see a number of dark holes through the glass, which I conjectured to be the mouths of caves. At the opening of one of these something white was shimmering but I was unable to make out what it was. I sat charting the country until the sun had set and it was so dark that I could no longer distinguish details. Then I climbed down to my companions waiting for me so eagerly at the bottom of the great tree. For once I was the hero of the expedition. Alone I had thought of it, and alone I had done it; and here was the chart which would save us a month's blind groping among unknown dangers. Each of them shook me solemnly by the hand. But before they discussed the details of my map I had to tell them of my encounter with the ape-man among the branches.

"He has been there all the time," said I.

"How do you know that?" asked Lord John.

"Because I have never been without that feeling that something malevolent was watching us. I mentioned it to you, Professor Challenger."

"Our young friend certainly said something of the kind. He is also the one among us who is endowed with that Celtic temperament which would make him sensitive to such impressions."

"The whole theory of telepathy—" began Summerlee filling his pipe.

"Is too vast to be now discussed," said Challenger, with decision. "Tell me, now," he added, with the air of a bishop addressing a Sunday-school, "did you happen to observe whether the creature could cross its thumb over its palm?"

"No, indeed."

"Had it a tail?"

"No."

"Was the foot prehensile?"

"I do not think it could have made off so fast among the branches if it could not get a grip with its feet."

"In South America there are, if my memory serves me—you will check the observation, Professor Summerlee—some thirty-six species of monkeys, but the anthropoid ape is unknown. It is clear, however, that he exists in this country, and that he is not the hairy, gorilla-like variety, which is never seen out of Africa or the East." (I was inclined to interpolate, as I looked at him, that I had seen his first cousin in Kensington.) "This is a whiskered and colourless type, the latter characteristic pointing to the fact that he spends his days in arboreal seclusion. The question which we have to face is whether he approaches more closely to the ape or the man. In the latter case, he may well approximate to what the vulgar have called the 'missing link.' The solution of this problem is our immediate duty."

"It is nothing of the sort," said Summerlee, abruptly. "Now that, through the intelligence and activity of Mr. Malone" (I cannot help quoting the words), "we have got our chart, our one and only immediate duty is to get ourselves safe and sound out of this awful place."

"The flesh-pots of civilization," groaned Challenger.

"The ink-pots of civilization, sir. It is our task to put on record what we have seen, and to leave the further exploration to others. You all agreed as much before Mr. Malone got us the chart."

"Well," said Challenger, "I admit that my mind will be more at ease when I am assured that the result of our expedition has been conveyed to our friends. How we are to get down from this place I have not as yet an idea. I have never yet encountered any problem, however, which my inventive brain was unable to solve, and I promise you that to-morrow I will turn my attention to the question of our descent."

And so the matter was allowed to rest. But that evening, by the light of the fire and of a single candle, the first map of the lost world was elaborated. Every detail which I had roughly noted from my watch-tower was drawn out in its relative place. Challenger's pencil hovered over the great blank which marked the lake.

"What shall we call it?" he asked.

"Why should you not take the chance of perpetuating your own name?" said Summerlee, with his usual touch of acidity.

"I trust, sir, that my name will have other and more personal claims upon posterity," said Challenger, severely. "Any ignoramus can hand down his worthless memory by imposing a mountain or a river. I need no such monument."

Summerlee, with a twisted smile, was about to make some fresh assault when Lord John hastened to intervene.

"It's up to you, young fellah, to name the lake," said he. "You saw it first, and, by George, if you choose to put 'Lake Malone' on it, no one has a better right."

"By all means. Let our young friend give it a name," said Challenger.

"Then," said I, blushing, I dare say, as I said it, "let it be named Lake Gladys."

"Don't you think the Central Lake would be more descriptive?" remarked Summerlee.

"I should prefer Lake Gladys."

Challenger looked at me sympathetically, and shook his great head in mock disapproval. "Boys will be boys," said he. "Lake Gladys let it be."

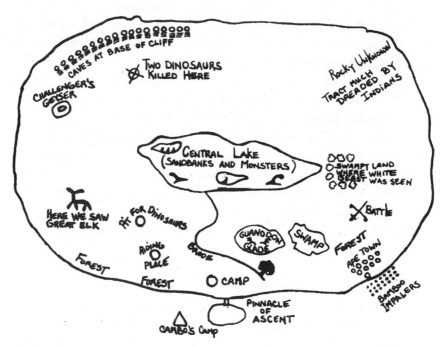

Rough Chart of Maple-White Land

15

The Poison Belt
(1913)

ONE
THE BLURRING OF THE LINES

It is imperative that now at once, while these stupendous events are still clear in my mind, I should set them down with that exactness of detail which time may blur. But even as I do so, I am overwhelmed by the wonder of the fact that it should be our little group of the "Lost World"— Professor Challenger, Professor Summerlee, Lord John Roxton, and myself—who have passed through this amazing experience.

When, some years ago, I chronicled in the *Daily Gazette* our epoch-making journey in South America, I little thought that it should ever fall to my lot to tell an even stranger personal experience, one which is unique in all human annals and must stand out in the records of history as a great peak among the humble foothills which surround it. The event itself will always be marvelous, but the circumstances that we four were together at the time of this extraordinary episode came about in a most natural and, indeed, inevitable fashion. I will explain the events which led up to it as shortly and as clearly as I can, though I am well aware that the fuller the detail upon such a subject the more welcome it will be to the reader, for the public curiosity has been and still is insatiable.

It was upon Friday, the twenty-seventh of August—a date forever memorable in the history of the world—that I went down to the office of my paper and asked for three days' leave of absence from Mr. McArdle, who still presided over our news department. The good old Scotchman shook his head, scratched his dwindling fringe of ruddy fluff, and finally put his reluctance into words.

"I was thinking, Mr. Malone, that we could employ you to advantage these days. I was thinking there was a story that you are the only man that could handle as it should be handled."

"I am sorry for that," said I, trying to hide my disappointment. "Of course if I am needed, there is an end of the matter. But the engagement was important and intimate. If I could be spared—"

"Well, I don't see that you can."

It was bitter, but I had to put the best face I could upon it. After all, it was my own fault, for I should have known by this time that a journalist has no right to make plans of his own. "Then I'll think no more of it," said I with as much cheerfulness as I could assume at so short a notice. "What was it that you wanted me to do?"

"Well, it was just to interview that deevil of a man down at Rotherfield."

"You don't mean Professor Challenger?" I cried.

"Aye, it's just him that I do mean. He ran young Alec Simpson of the *Courier* a mile down the high road last week by the collar of his coat and the slack of his breeches. You'll have read of it, likely, in the police report. Our boys would as soon interview a loose alligator in the zoo. But you could do it, I'm thinking—an old friend like you."

"Why," said I, greatly relieved, "this makes it all easy. It so happens that it was to visit Professor Challenger at Rotherfield that I was asking for leave of absence. The fact is, that it is the anniversary of our main adventure on the plateau three years ago, and he has asked our whole party down to his house to see him and celebrate the occasion."

"Capital!" cried McArdle, rubbing his hands and beaming through his glasses. "Then you will be able to get his opeenions out of him. In any other man I would say it was all moonshine, but the fellow has made good once, and who knows but he may again!"

"Get what out of him?" I asked. "What has he been doing?"

"Haven't you seen his letter on 'Scientific Possibeelities' in today's *Times?*"

"No."

McArdle dived down and picked a copy from the floor. "Read it aloud," said he, indicating a column with his finger. "I'd be glad to hear it again, for I am not sure now that I have the man's meaning clear in my head."

This was the letter which I read to the news editor of the *Gazette*:

SCIENTIFIC POSSIBILITIES

"Sir, I have read with amusement, not wholly unmixed with some less complimentary emotion, the complacent and wholly fatuous letter of James Wilson MacPhail which has lately appeared in your columns upon the subject of the blurring of Fraunhofer's lines in the spectra both of the planets and of the fixed stars. He dismisses the matter as of no significance. To a wider intelligence it may well seem of very great possible importance—so great as to involve the ultimate welfare of every man, woman, and child upon this planet. I can hardly hope, by the use of scientific language, to convey any sense of my meaning to those ineffectual people who gather their ideas from the columns of a daily newspaper. I will endeavor, therefore, to condescend to their limitation and to indicate the situation by the use of a homely analogy which will be within the limits of the intelligence of your readers."

"Man, he's a wonder—a living wonder!" said McArdle, shaking his head reflectively. "He'd put up the feathers of a sucking dove and set up a riot in a Quaker's meeting. No wonder he has made London too hot for him. It's a peety, Mr. Malone, for it's a grand brain! Well, let's have the analogy."

We will suppose [I read] that a small bundle of connected corks was launched in a sluggish current upon a voyage across the Atlantic. The corks drift slowly on from day to day with the same conditions all round them. If the corks were sentient we could imagine that they would consider these conditions to be permanent and assured. But we, with our superior knowledge, know that many things might happen to surprise the corks. They might possibly float up against a ship, or a sleeping whale, or become entangled in seaweed. In any case, their voyage would probably end by their being thrown up on the rocky coast of Labrador. But what could they know of all this while they drifted so gently day by day in what they thought was a limitless and homogeneous ocean?

Your readers will possibly comprehend that the Atlantic, in this parable, stands for the mighty ocean of ether through which we drift and that the bunch of corks represents the little and obscure planetary system to which we belong. A third-rate sun, with its rag tag and bobtail of insignificant satellites, we float under the same daily conditions towards some unknown end, some squalid catastrophe which will overwhelm us at the ultimate confines of space, where we are swept over an etheric Niagara or dashed upon some unthinkable Labrador. I see no room here for the shallow and ignorant optimism of your correspondent, Mr. James Wilson MacPhail, but many reasons why we should watch with a very close and interested attention every indication of change in those cosmic surroundings upon which our own ultimate fate may depend."

"Man, he'd have made a grand meenister," said McArdle. "It just booms like an organ. Let's get doun to what it is that's troubling him."

The general blurring and shifting of Fraunhofer's lines of the spectrum point, in my opinion, to a widespread cosmic change of a subtle and singular character. Light from a planet is the reflected light of the sun. Light from a star is a self-produced light. But the spectra both from planets and stars have, in this instance, all undergone the same change. Is it, then, a change in those planets and stars? To me such an idea is inconceivable. What common change could simultaneously come upon them all? Is it a change in our own atmosphere? It is possible, but in the highest degree improbable, since we see no signs of it around us, and chemical analysis has failed to reveal it. What, then, is the third possibility? That it may be a change in the conducting medium, in that infinitely fine ether which extends from star to star and pervades the whole universe. Deep in that ocean we are floating upon a slow current. Might that current not drift us into belts of ether which are novel and have properties of which we have never conceived? There is a change somewhere. This cosmic disturbance of the spectrum proves it. It may be a good change. It may be an evil one. It may be a neutral one. We do not know.

Shallow observers may treat the matter as one which can be disregarded, but one who like myself is possessed of the deeper intelligence of the true philosopher will understand that the possibilities of the universe are incalculable and that the wisest man is he who holds himself ready for the unexpected. To take an obvious example, who would undertake to say that the mysterious and universal outbreak of illness, recorded in your columns this very morning as having broken out among the indigenous races of Sumatra, has no connection with some cosmic change to which they may respond more quickly than the more complex peoples of Europe? I throw out the idea for what it is worth. To assert it is, in the present stage, as unprofitable as to deny it, but it is an unimaginative numskull who is too dense to perceive that it is well within the bounds of scientific possibility.

> Yours faithfully,
> GEORGE EDWARD CHALLENGER.

THE BRIARS, ROTHERFIELD.

"It's a fine, steemulating letter," said McArdle thoughtfully, fitting a cigarette into the long glass tube which he used as a holder. "What's your opeenion of it, Mr. Malone?"

I had to confess my total and humiliating ignorance of the subject at issue. What, for example, were Fraunhofer's lines? McArdle had just been studying the matter with the aid of our tame scientist at the office, and he picked from his desk two of those many-colored spectral bands which bear a general resemblance to the hat ribbons of some young and ambitious cricket club. He pointed out to me that there were certain black lines which formed crossbars upon the series of brilliant colors extending from the red at one end through gradations of orange, yellow, green, blue, and indigo to the violet at the other.

"Those dark bands are Fraunhofer's lines," said he. "The colors are just light itself. Every light, if you can split it up with a prism, gives the same colors. They tell us nothing. It is the lines that count, because they vary according to what it may be that produces the light. It is these lines that have been blurred instead of clear this last week, and all the astronomers have been quarreling over the reason. Here's a photograph of the blurred lines for our issue tomorrow. The public have taken no interest in the matter up to now, but this letter of Challenger's in *The Times* will make them wake up, I'm thinking."

"And this about Sumatra?"

"Well, it's a long cry from a blurred line in a spectrum to a sick native in Sumatra. And yet the chiel has shown us once before that he knows what he's talking about. There is some queer illness down yonder, that's beyond all doubt, and today there's a cable just come in from Singapore that the lighthouses are out of action in the Straits of Sunda, and two ships on the beach in consequence. Anyhow, it's good enough for you to interview Challenger about. If you get anything definite, let us have a column by Monday."

I was coming out from the news editor's room, turning over my new mission in my mind, when I heard my name called from the waiting room below. It was a telegraph boy with a wire which had been forwarded from my lodgings at Streatham. The message was from the very man we had been discussing, and ran thus:

"Malone, 17 Hill Street, Streatham.—Bring oxygen.—Challenger."

"Bring oxygen!" The Professor, as I remembered him, had an elephantine sense of humor capable of the most clumsy and unwieldy gambolings. Was this one of those jokes which used to reduce him to uproarious laughter, when his eyes would disappear and he was all gaping mouth and wagging beard, supremely indifferent to the gravity of all around him? I turned the words over, but could make nothing even remotely jocose out of them. Then surely it was a concise order—though a very strange one. He was the last man in the world whose deliberate command I should care to disobey. Possibly some chemical experiment was afoot; possibly—Well, it was no business of mine to speculate upon why he wanted it. I must get it. There was nearly an hour before I should catch the train at Victoria. I took a taxi, and having ascertained the address from the telephone book, I made for the Oxygen Tube Supply Company in Oxford Street.

As I alighted on the pavement at my destination, two youths emerged from the door of the establishment carrying an iron cylinder, which, with some trouble, they hoisted into a waiting motorcar. An elderly man was at their heels scolding and directing in a creaky, sardonic voice. He turned towards me. There was no mistaking those austere features and that goatee heard. It was my old cross-grained companion, Professor Summerlee.

"What!" he cried. "Don't tell me that *you* have had one of these preposterous telegrams for oxygen?"

I exhibited it.

"Well, well! I have had one too, and, as you see, very much against the grain, I have acted upon it. Our good friend is as impossible as ever. The need for oxygen could not have been so urgent that he must desert the usual means of supply and encroach upon the time of those who are really busier than himself. Why could he not order it direct?"

I could only suggest that he probably wanted it at once.

"Or thought he did, which is quite another matter. But it is superfluous now for you to purchase any, since I have this considerable supply."

"Still, for some reason he seems to wish that I should bring oxygen too. It will be safer to do exactly what he tells me."

Accordingly, in spite of many grumbles and remonstrances from Summerlee, I ordered an additional tube, which was placed with the other in his motorcar, for he had offered me a lift to Victoria.

I turned away to pay off my taxi, the driver of which was very cantankerous and abusive over his fare. As I came back to Professor Summerlee, he was having a furious altercation with the men who had carried down the oxygen, his little white goat's beard jerking with indignation. One of the fellows called him, I remember, "a silly old bleached cockatoo," which so enraged his chauffeur that he bounded out of his seat to take the part of his insulted master, and it was all we could do to prevent a riot in the street.

These little things may seem trivial to relate, and passed as mere incidents at the time. It is only now, as I look back, that I see their relation to the whole story which I have to unfold.

The chauffeur must, as it seemed to me, have been a novice or else have lost his nerve in this disturbance, for he drove vilely on the way to the station. Twice we nearly had collisions with other equally erratic vehicles, and I remember remarking to Summerlee that the standard of driving in London had very much declined. Once we brushed the very edge of a great crowd which was watching a fight at the corner of the Mall. The people, who were much excited, raised cries of anger at the clumsy driving, and one fellow sprang upon the step and waved a stick above our heads. I pushed him off, but we were glad when we had got clear of them and safe out of the park. These little events, coming one after the other, left me very jangled in my nerves, and I could see from my companion's petulant manner that his own patience had got to a low ebb.

But our good humor was restored when we saw Lord John Roxton waiting for us upon the platform, his tall thin figure clad in a yellow tweed shooting suit. His keen face, with those unforgettable eyes, so fierce and yet so humorous, flushed with pleasure at the sight of us. His ruddy hair was shot with gray, and the furrows upon his brow had been cut a little deeper by Time's chisel, but in all else he was the Lord John who had been our good comrade in the past.

"Hullo, Herr Professor! Hullo, young fella!" he shouted as he came toward us.

He roared with amusement when he saw the oxygen cylinders upon the porter's trolley behind us. "So you've got them too!" he cried. "Mine is in the van. Whatever can the old dear be after?"

"Have you seen his letter in *The Times*?" I asked.

"What was it?"

"Stuff and nonsense!" said Summerlee harshly.

"Well, it's at the bottom of this oxygen business, or I am mistaken," said I.

"Stuff and nonsense!" cried Summerlee again with quite unnecessary violence. We had all got into a first-class smoker, and he had already lit the short and charred old briar pipe which seemed to singe the end of his long, aggressive nose.

"Friend Challenger is a clever man," said he with great vehemence. "No one can deny it. It's a fool that denies it. Look at his hat. There's a sixty-ounce brain inside it—a big engine, running smooth, and turning out clean work. Show me the engine house and I'll tell you the size of the engine. But he is a born charlatan—you've heard me tell him so to his face—a born charlatan, with a kind of dramatic trick of jumping into the limelight. Things are quiet, so friend Challenger sees a chance to set the public talking about him. You don't imagine that he seriously believes all this nonsense about a change in the ether and a danger to the human race? Was ever such a cock-and-bull story in this life?"

He sat like an old white raven, croaking and shaking with sardonic laughter.

A wave of anger passed through me as I listened to Summerlee. It was disgraceful that he should speak thus of the leader who had been the source of all our fame and given us such an experience as no men have ever enjoyed.

I had opened my mouth to utter some hot retort, when Lord John got before me.

"You had a scrap once before with old man Challenger," said he sternly, "and you were down and out inside ten seconds. It seems to me, Professor Summerlee, he's beyond your class, and the best you can do with him is to walk wide and leave him alone."

"Besides," said I, "he has been a good friend to every one of us. Whatever his faults may be, he is as straight as a line, and I don't believe he ever speaks evil of his comrades behind their backs."

"Well said, young fella-my-lad," said Lord John Roxton. Then, with a kindly smile, he slapped Professor Summerlee upon his shoulder. "Come, Herr Professor, we're not going to quarrel at this time of day. We've seen too much together. But keep off the grass when you get near Challenger, for this young fella and I have a bit of a weakness for the old dear."

But Summerlee was in no humor for compromise. His face was screwed up in rigid disapproval, and thick curls of angry smoke rolled up from his pipe.

"As to you, Lord John Roxton," he creaked, "your opinion upon a matter of science is of as much value in my eyes as my views upon a new type of shot gun would be in yours. I have my own judgment, sir, and I use it in my own way. Because it has misled me once, is that any reason why I should accept without criticism anything, however farfetched, which this man may care to put forward? Are we to have a pope of science, with infallible decrees laid down ex cathedra, and accepted without question by the poor humble public? I tell you, sir, that I have a brain of my own and that I should feel myself to be a snob and a slave if I did not use it. If it pleases you to believe this rigmarole about ether and Fraunhofer's lines upon the spectrum, do so by all means, but do not ask one who is older and wiser than yourself to share in your folly. Is it not evident that if the ether were affected to the degree which he maintains, and if it were obnoxious to human health, the result of it would already be apparent upon ourselves?" Here he laughed with uproarious triumph over his own argument. "Yes, sir, we should already be very far from our normal selves, and instead of sitting quietly discussing scientific problems in a railway train we should be showing actual symptoms of the poison which was working within us. Where do we see any signs of this poisonous cosmic disturbance? Answer me that, sir! Answer me that! Come, come, no evasion! I pin you to an answer!"

I felt more and more angry. There was something very irritating and aggressive in Summerlee's demeanor.

"I think that if you knew more about the facts you might be less positive in your opinion," said I.

Summerlee took his pipe from his mouth and fixed me with a stony stare. "Pray what do you mean, sir, by that somewhat impertinent observation?"

"I mean that when I was leaving the office the news editor told me that a telegram had come in confirming the general illness of the Sumatra natives, and adding that the lights had not been lit in the Straits of Sunda."

"Really, there should be some limits to human folly!" cried Summerlee in a positive fury. "Is it possible that you do not realize that ether, if for a moment we adopt Challenger's preposterous supposition, is a universal substance which is the same here as at the other side of the world? Do you for an instant suppose that there is an English ether and a Sumatran ether? Perhaps you imagine that the ether of Kent is in some way superior to the ether of Surrey, through which this train is now bearing us. There really are no bounds to the credulity and ignorance of the average layman. Is it conceivable that the ether in Sumatra should be so deadly as to cause total insensibility at the very time when the ether here has had no appreciable effect upon us whatever? Personally, I can truly say that I never felt stronger in body or better balanced in mind in my life."

"That may be. I don't profess to be a scientific man," said I, "though I have heard somewhere that the science of one generation is usually the fallacy of the next. But it does not take much common sense to see that, as we seem to know so little about ether, it might be affected by some local conditions in various parts of the world and might show an effect over there which would only develop later with us."

"With 'might' and 'may' you can prove anything," cried Summerlee furiously. "Pigs may fly. Yes, sir, pigs *may* fly—but they don't. It is not worth arguing with you. Challenger has filled you with his nonsense and you are both incapable of reason. I had as soon lay arguments before those railway cushions."

"I must say, Professor Summerlee, that your manners do not seem to have improved since I last had the pleasure of meeting you," said Lord John severely.

"You lordlings are not accustomed to hear the truth," Summerlee answered with a bitter smile. "It comes as a bit of a shock, does it not, when someone makes you realize that your title leaves you none the less a very ignorant man?"

"Upon my word, sir," said Lord John, very stern and rigid, "if you were a younger man you would not dare to speak to me in so offensive a fashion."

Summerlee thrust out his chin, with its little wagging tuft of goatee beard. "I would have you know, sir, that, young or old, there has never been a time in my life when I was afraid to speak my mind to an ignorant coxcomb—yes, sir, an ignorant coxcomb, if you had as many titles as slaves could invent and fools could adopt."

For a moment Lord John's eyes blazed, and then, with a tremendous effort, he mastered his anger and leaned back in his seat with arms folded and a bitter smile upon his face. To me all this was dreadful and deplorable. Like a wave, the memory of the past swept over me, the good comradeship, the happy, adventurous days—all that we had suffered and worked for and won. That it should have come to this—to insults and abuse! Suddenly I was sobbing—sobbing in loud, gulping, uncontrollable sobs which refused to be concealed. My companions looked at me in surprise. I covered my face with my hands.

"It's all right," said I. "Only—only it *is* such a pity!"

"You're ill, young fella, that's what's amiss with you," said Lord John. "I thought you were queer from the first."

"Your habits, sir, have not mended in these three years," said Summerlee, shaking his head. "I also did not fail to observe your strange manner the moment we met. You need not waste your sympathy, Lord John. These tears are purely alcoholic. The man has been drinking. By the way, Lord John, I called you a coxcomb just now, which was perhaps unduly severe. But the word reminds me of a small accomplishment, trivial but amusing, which I used to possess. You know me as the austere man of science. Can you believe that I once had a well-deserved reputation in several nurseries as a farmyard imitator? Perhaps I can help you to pass the time in a pleasant way. Would it amuse you to hear me crow like a cock?"

"No, sir," said Lord John, who was still greatly offended, "it would *not* amuse me."

"My imitation of the clucking hen who had just laid an egg was also considered rather above the average. Might I venture?"

"No, sir, no—certainly not."

But in spite of this earnest prohibition, Professor Summerlee laid down his pipe and for the rest of our journey he entertained—or failed to entertain—us by a succession of bird and animal cries which seemed so absurd that my tears were suddenly changed into boisterous laughter, which must have become quite hysterical as I sat opposite this grave Professor and saw him—or rather heard him—in the character of the uproarious rooster or the puppy whose tail had been trodden upon. Once Lord John passed across his newspaper, upon the margin of which he had written in pencil, "Poor devil! Mad as a hatter." No doubt it was very eccentric, and yet the performance struck me as extraordinarily clever and amusing.

While this was going on, Lord John leaned forward and told me some interminable story about a buffalo and an Indian rajah which seemed to me to have neither beginning nor end. Professor Summerlee had just begun to chirrup like a canary, and Lord John to get to the climax of his story, when the train drew up at Jarvis Brook, which had been given us as the station for Rotherfield.

And there was Challenger to meet us. His appearance was glorious. Not all the turkey cocks in creation could match the slow, high-stepping dignity with which he paraded his own railway station and the benignant smile of condescending encouragement with which he regarded every-body around him. If he had changed in anything since the days of old, it was that his points had become accentuated. The huge head and broad sweep of forehead, with its plastered lock of black hair, seemed even greater than before. His black beard poured forward in a more impres-sive cascade, and his clear gray eyes, with their insolent and sardonic eye-lids, were even more masterful than of yore.

He gave me the amused handshake and encouraging smile which the headmaster bestows upon the small boy, and, having greeted the others and helped to collect their bags and their cylinders of oxygen, he stowed us and them away in a large motorcar which was driven by the same im-passive Austin, the man of few words, whom I had seen in the character of butler upon the occasion of my first eventful visit to the Professor. Our journey led us up a winding hill through beautiful country. I sat in front with the chauffeur, but behind me my three comrades seemed to me to be all talking together. Lord John was still struggling with his buf-falo story, so far as I could make out, while once again I heard, as of old, the deep rumble of Challenger and the insistent accents of Summerlee as their brains locked in high and fierce scientific debate. Suddenly Austin slanted his mahogany face toward me without taking his eyes from his steering wheel.

"I'm under notice," said he.

"Dear me!" said I.

Everything seemed strange today. Everyone said queer, unexpected things. It was like a dream.

"It's forty-seven times," said Austin reflectively.

"When do you go?" I asked, for want of some better observation.

"I don't go," said Austin.

The conversation seemed to have ended there, but presently he came back to it.

"If I was to go, who would look after 'im?" He jerked his head to-ward his master. "Who would 'e get to serve 'im?"

"Someone else," I suggested lamely.

"Not 'e. No one would stay a week. If I was to go, that 'ouse would run down like a watch with the mainspring out. I'm telling you because you're 'is friend, and you ought to know. If I was to take 'im at 'is word—but there, I wouldn't have the 'eart. 'E and the missus would be like two babes left out in a bundle. I'm just everything. And then 'e goes and gives me notice."

"Why would no one stay?" I asked.

"Well, they wouldn't make allowances, same as I do. 'E's a very clever man, the master—so clever that 'e's clean balmy sometimes. I've seen 'im right off 'is onion, and no error. Well, look what 'e did this morning."

"What did he do?"

Austin bent over to me. "'E bit the 'ousekeeper," said he in a hoarse whisper.

"Bit her?"

"Yes, sir. Bit 'er on the leg. I saw 'er with my own eyes startin' a marathon from the 'all door."

"Good gracious!"

"So you'd say, sir, if you could see some of the goings on. 'E don't make friends with the neighbors. There's some of them thinks that when 'e was up among those monsters you wrote about, it was just "Ome, Sweet 'Ome' for the master, and 'e was never in fitter company. That's what *they* say. But I've served 'im ten years, and I'm fond of 'im, and, mind you, 'e's a great man, when all's said an' done, and it's an honor to serve 'im. But 'e does try one cruel at times. Now look at that, sir. That ain't what you might call old-fashioned 'ospitality, is it now? Just you read it for yourself."

The car on its lowest speed had ground its way up a steep, curving ascent. At the corner a notice board peered over a well-clipped hedge. As Austin said, it was not difficult to read, for the words were few and arresting.

WARNING.

Visitors, Pressmen, and Mendicants
are not encouraged.

G. E. CHALLENGER.

"No, it's not what you might call 'earty," said Austin shaking his head and glancing up at the deplorable placard. "It wouldn't look well in

a Christmas card. I beg your pardon, sir, for I haven't spoke as much as
this for many a long year, but today my feelings seem to 'ave got the better of me. 'E can sack me till 'e's blue in the face, but I ain't going, and
that's flat. I'm 'is man and 'e's my master and so it will be, I expect, to
the end of the chapter."

We had passed between the white posts of a gate and up a curving
drive, lined with rhododendron bushes. Beyond stood a low brick house,
picked out with white woodwork, very comfortable and pretty. Mrs.
Challenger, a small, dainty, smiling figure, stood in the open doorway to
welcome us.

"Well, my dear," said Challenger, bustling out of the car, "here are
our visitors. It is something new for us to have visitors, is it not? No love
lost between us and our neighbors, is there? If they could get rat poison
into our baker's cart, I expect it would be there."

"It's dreadful-dreadful!" cried the lady, between laughter and tears.
"George is always quarreling with every one. We haven't a friend in the
countryside."

"It enables me to concentrate my attention upon my incomparable
wife," said Challenger, passing his short thick arm round her waist. Picture a gorilla and a gazelle and you have the pair of them. "Come, come,
these gentlemen are tired from the journey, and luncheon should be
ready. Has Sarah returned?"

The lady shook her head ruefully, and the Professor laughed loudly
and stroked his beard in his masterful fashion.

"Austin," he cried, "when you have put up the car you will kindly
help your mistress to lay the lunch. Now, gentlemen, will you please step
into my study, for there are one or two very urgent things which I am
anxious to say to you."

TWO

THE TIDE OF DEATH

As we crossed the hall the telephone bell rang, and we were the in-
voluntary auditors of Professor Challenger's end of the ensuing dialogue. I say "we," but no one within a hundred yards could have failed

to hear the booming of that monstrous voice, which reverberated through the house. His answers lingered in my mind: "Yes, yes, of course, it is I. . . . Yes, certainly, *the* Professor Challenger, the famous Professor, who else? . . . Of course, every word of it, otherwise I should not have written it. . . . I shouldn't be surprised. . . . There is every indication of it. . . . Within a day or so at the furthest. . . . Well, I can't help that, can I? . . . Very unpleasant, no doubt, but I rather fancy it will affect more important people than you. There is no use whining about it. . . . No, I couldn't possibly. You must take your chance. . . . That's enough, sir. Nonsense! I have something more important to do than to listen to such twaddle."

He shut off with a crash and led us upstairs into a large airy apartment which formed his study. On the great mahogany desk seven or eight unopened telegrams were lying. "Really," he said as he gathered them up. "I begin to think that it would save my correspondents' money if I were to adopt a telegraphic address. Possibly 'Noah, Rotherfield,' would be the most appropriate."

As usual when he made an obscure joke, he leaned against the desk and bellowed in a paroxysm of laughter, his hands shaking so that he could hardly open the envelopes. "Noah! Noah!" he gasped, with a face of beet-root, while Lord John and I smiled in sympathy and Summerlee, like a dyspeptic goat, wagged his head in sardonic disagreement. Finally Challenger, still rumbling and exploding, began to open his telegrams. The three of us stood in the bow window and occupied ourselves in admiring the magnificent view.

It was certainly worth looking at. The road in its gentle curves had really brought us to a considerable elevation—seven hundred feet, as we afterwards discovered. Challenger's house was on the very edge of the hill, and from its southern face, in which was the study window, one looked across the vast stretch of the Weald to where the gentle curves of the South Downs formed an undulating horizon. In a cleft of the hills a haze of smoke marked the position of Lewes. Immediately at our feet there lay a rolling plain of heather, with the long, vivid green stretches of the Crowborough golf course, all dotted with the players. A little to the south, through an opening in the woods, we could see a section of the main line from London to Brighton. In the immediate foreground, under our very noses, was a small enclosed yard, in which stood the car which had brought us from the station.

An ejaculation from Challenger caused us to turn. He had read his telegrams and had arranged them in a little methodical pile upon his desk. His broad, rugged face, or as much of it as was visible over the matted beard, was still deeply flushed, and he seemed to be under the influence of some strong excitement.

"Well, gentlemen," he said, in a voice as if he was addressing a public meeting, "this is indeed an interesting reunion, and it takes place under extraordinary—I may say unprecedented—circumstances. May I ask if you have observed anything upon your journey from town?"

"The only thing which I observed," said Summerlee with a sour smile, "was that our young friend here has not improved in his manners during the years that have passed. I am sorry to state that I have had to seriously complain of his conduct in the train, and I should be wanting in frankness if I did not say that it has left a most unpleasant impression in my mind."

"Well, well, we all get a bit prosy sometimes," said Lord John. "The young fella meant no real harm. After all, he's an International, so if he takes half an hour to describe a game of football he has more right to do it than most folk."

"Half an hour to describe a game!" I cried indignantly. "Why, it was you that took half an hour with some long-winded story about a buffalo. Professor Summerlee will be my witness."

"I can hardly judge which of you was the most utterly wearisome," said Summerlee. "I declare to you, Challenger, that I never wish to hear of football or of buffaloes so long as I live."

"I have never said one word today about football," I protested.

Lord John gave a shrill whistle, and Summerlee shook his head sadly. "So early in the day too," said he. "It is indeed deplorable. As I sat there in sad but thoughtful silence—"

"In silence!" cried Lord John. "Why, you were doin' a music-hall turn of imitations all the way—more like a runaway gramophone than a man."

Summerlee drew himself up in bitter protest. "You are pleased to be facetious, Lord John," said he with a face of vinegar.

"Why, dash it all, this is clear madness," cried Lord John. "Each of us seems to know what the others did and none of us knows what he did himself. Let's put it all together from the first. We got into a first-class smoker, that's clear, ain't it? Then we began to quarrel over friend Challenger's letter in *The Times*."

"Oh, you did, did you?" rumbled our host, his eyelids beginning to droop.

"You said, Summerlee, that there was no possible truth in his contention."

"Dear me!" said Challenger, puffing out his chest and stroking his beard. "No possible truth! I seem to have heard the words before. And may I ask with what arguments the great and famous Professor Summerlee proceeded to demolish the humble individual who had ventured to express an opinion upon a matter of scientific possibility? Perhaps before he exterminates that unfortunate nonentity he will condescend to give some reasons for the adverse views which he has formed."

He bowed and shrugged and spread open his hands as he spoke with his elaborate and elephantine sarcasm.

"The reason was simple enough," said the dogged Summerlee. "I contended that if the ether surrounding the earth was so toxic in one quarter that it produced dangerous symptoms, it was hardly likely that we three in the railway carriage should be entirely unaffected."

The explanation only brought uproarious merriment from Challenger. He laughed until everything in the room seemed to rattle and quiver.

"Our worthy Summerlee is, not for the first time, somewhat out of touch with the facts of the situation," said he at last, mopping his heated brow. "Now, gentlemen, I cannot make my point better than by detailing to you what I have myself done this morning. You will the more easily condone any mental aberration upon your own part when you realize that even I have had moments when my balance has been disturbed. We have had for some years in this household a housekeeper—one Sarah, with whose second name I have never attempted to burden my memory. She is a woman of a severe and forbidding aspect, prim and demure in her bearing, very impassive in her nature, and never known within our experience to show signs of any emotion. As I sat alone at my breakfast—Mrs. Challenger is in the habit of keeping her room of a morning—it suddenly entered my head that it would be entertaining and instructive to see whether I could find any limits to this woman's imperturbability. I devised a simple but effective experiment. Having upset a small vase of flowers which stood in the center of the cloth, I rang the bell and slipped under the table. She entered and, seeing the room empty, imagined that I had withdrawn to the study. As I had expected, she approached and leaned over the table to replace the vase. I had a vision of a cotton stocking and an elastic-sided boot. Protruding my head, I sank my teeth into the calf of her leg. The experiment was successful beyond belief. For some moments she stood paralyzed, staring down at my head. Then with a shriek she tore herself free and rushed from the room. I pursued her with some thoughts of an explanation, but she flew down the drive, and some minutes afterwards I was able to pick her out with my fieldglasses traveling very rapidly in a southwesterly direction. I tell you the anecdote for what it is worth. I drop it into your brains and await its germination. Is it illuminative? Has it conveyed anything to your minds? What do *you* think of it, Lord John?"

Lord John shook his head gravely. "You'll be gettin' into serious trouble some of these days if you don't put a brake on," said he.

"Perhaps you have some observation to make, Summerlee?"

"You should drop all work instantly, Challenger, and take three months in a German watering place," said he.

"Profound! Profound!" cried Challenger. "Now, my young friend, is it possible that wisdom may come from you where your seniors have so signally failed?"

And it did. I say it with all modesty, but it did. Of course, it all seems obvious to you who know what occurred, but it was not so very clear when everything was new. But it came on me suddenly with the full force of absolute conviction. "Poison!" I cried.

Then, even as I said the word, my mind flashed back over the whole morning's experiences, past Lord John with his buffalo, past my own hysterical tears, past the outrageous conduct of Professor Summerlee, to the queer happenings in London, the row in the park, the driving of the chauffeur, the quarrel at the oxygen warehouse. Everything fitted suddenly into its place.

"Of course," I cried again. "It is poison. We are all poisoned."

"Exactly," said Challenger, rubbing his hands, "we are all poisoned. Our planet has swum into the poison belt of ether, and is now flying deeper into it at the rate of some millions of miles a minute. Our young friend has expressed the cause of all our troubles and perplexities in a single word, 'poison.'"

We looked at each other in amazed silence. No comment seemed to meet the situation.

"There is a mental inhibition by which such symptoms can be checked and controlled," said Challenger. "I cannot expect to find it developed in all of you to the same point which it has reached in me, for I suppose that the strength of our different mental processes bears some proportion to each other. But no doubt it is appreciable even in our young friend here. After the little outburst of high spirits which so alarmed my domestic I sat down and reasoned with myself. I put it to myself that I had never before felt impelled to bite any of my household. The impulse had then been an abnormal one. In an instant I perceived the truth. My pulse upon examination was ten beats above the usual, and my reflexes were increased. I called upon my higher and saner self, the real G. E. C., seated serene and impregnable behind all mere molecular disturbance. I summoned him, I say, to watch the foolish and mental tricks which the poison would play. I found that I was indeed the master. I could recognize and control a disordered mind. It was a remarkable exhibition of the victory of mind over matter, for it was a victory over that particular form of matter which is most intimately connected with mind. I might almost say that mind was at fault and that personality controlled it. Thus, when my wife came downstairs and I was impelled to slip behind the door and alarm her by some wild cry as she entered, I was able to stifle the impulse and to greet her with dignity and restraint. An overpowering desire to quack like a duck was met and mastered in the same fashion. Later, when I descended to order the car and found Austin bending over it absorbed in repairs, I controlled my open hand even after I had lifted it and refrained from giving him an experience which would possibly have caused him to follow in the steps of the housekeeper. On the contrary, I touched him on the shoulder and ordered the car to be at the door in time to meet your train. At the present instant I am most forcibly tempted to take Professor Summerlee by that silly old beard of his and to shake his head violently backwards and forwards. And yet, as you see, I am perfectly restrained. Let me commend my example to you."

"I'll look out for that buffalo," said Lord John.

"And I for the football match."

"It may be that you are right, Challenger," said Summerlee in a chastened voice. "I am willing to admit that my turn of mind is critical rather than constructive and that I am not a ready convert to any new theory, especially when it happens to be so unusual and fantastic as this one. However, as I cast my mind back over the events of the morning, and as I reconsider the fatuous conduct of my companions, I find it easy to believe that some poison of an exciting kind was responsible for their symptoms."

Challenger slapped his colleague good-humoredly upon the shoulder. "We progress," said he. "Decidedly we progress."

"And pray, sir," asked Summerlee humbly, "what is your opinion as to the present outlook?"

"With your permission I will say a few words upon that subject." He seated himself upon his desk, his short, stumpy legs swinging in front of him. "We are assisting at a tremendous and awful function. It is, in my opinion, the end of the world."

The end of the world! Our eyes turned to the great bow window and we looked out at the summer beauty of the countryside, the long slopes of heather, the great country houses, the cozy farms, the pleasure seekers upon the links. The end of the world! One had often heard the words, but the idea that they could ever have an immediate practical significance, that it should not be at some vague date, but now, today, that was a tremendous, a staggering thought. We were all struck solemn and waited in silence for Challenger to continue. His overpowering presence and appearance lent such force to the solemnity of his words that for a moment all the crudities and absurdities of the man vanished, and he loomed before us as something majestic and beyond the range of ordinary humanity. Then to me, at least, there came back the cheering recollection of how twice since we had entered the room he had roared with laughter. Surely, I thought, there are limits to mental detachment. The crisis cannot be so great or so pressing after all.

"You will conceive a bunch of grapes," said he, "which are covered by some infinitesimal but noxious bacillus. The gardener passes it through a disinfecting medium. It may be that he desires his grapes to be cleaner. It may be that he needs space to breed some fresh bacillus less noxious than the last. He dips it into the poison and they are gone. Our Gardener is, in my opinion, about to dip the solar system, and the human bacillus, the little mortal vibrio which twisted and wriggled upon the outer rind of the earth, will in an instant be sterilized out of existence."

Again there was silence. It was broken by the high trill of the telephone bell.

"There is one of our bacilli squeaking for help," said he with a grim smile. "They are beginning to realize that their continued existence is not really one of the necessities of the universe."

He was gone from the room for a minute or two. I remember that none of us spoke in his absence. The situation seemed beyond all words or comments.

"The medical officer of health for Brighton," said he when he returned. "The symptoms are for some reason developing more rapidly upon the sea level. Our seven hundred feet of elevation give us an advantage. Folk seem to have learned that I am the first authority upon the question. No doubt it comes from my letter in *The Times*. That was the mayor of a provincial town with whom I talked when we first arrived. You may have heard me upon the telephone. He seemed to put an entirely inflated value upon his own life. I helped him to readjust his ideas."

Summerlee had risen and was standing by the window. His thin, bony hands were trembling with his emotion.

"Challenger," said he earnestly, "this thing is too serious for mere futile argument. Do not suppose that I desire to irritate you by any question I may ask. But I put it to you whether there may not be some fallacy in your information or in your reasoning. There is the sun shining as brightly as ever in the blue sky. There are the heather and the flowers and the birds. There are the folk enjoying themselves upon the golf links and the laborers yonder cutting the corn. You tell us that they and we may be upon the very brink of destruction—that this sunlit day may be that day of doom which the human race has so long awaited. So far as we know, you found this tremendous judgment upon what? Upon some abnormal lines in a spectrum—upon rumors from Sumatra—upon some curious personal excitement which we have discerned in each other. This latter symptom is not so marked but that you and we could, by a deliberate effort, control it. You need not stand on ceremony with us, Challenger. We have all faced death together before now. Speak out, and let us know exactly where we stand, and what, in your opinion, are our prospects for our future."

It was a brave, good speech, a speech from that stanch and strong spirit which lay behind all the acidities and angularities of the old zoologist. Lord John rose and shook him by the hand.

"My sentiment to a tick," said he. "Now, Challenger, it's up to you to tell us where we are. We ain't nervous folk, as you know well; but when it comes to makin' a weekend visit and finding you've run full butt into the Day of Judgment, it wants a bit of explainin'. What's the danger, and how much of it is there, and what are we goin' to do to meet it?"

He stood, tall and strong, in the sunshine at the window, with his brown hand upon the shoulder of Summerlee. I was lying back in an armchair, an extinguished cigarette between my lips, in that sort of half-dazed state in which impressions become exceedingly distinct. It may have been a new phase of the poisoning, but the delirious promptings had all passed away and were succeeded by an exceedingly languid and, at the same time, perceptive state of mind. I was a spectator. It did not seem to be any personal concern of mine. But here were three strong men at a great crisis, and it was fascinating to observe them.

Challenger bent his heavy brows and stroked his beard before he answered. One could see that he was very carefully weighing his words. "What was the last news when you left London?" he asked.

"I was at the *Gazette* office about ten," said I. "There was a Reuter just come in from Singapore to the effect that the sickness seemed to be universal in Sumatra and that the lighthouses had not been lit in consequence."

"Events have been moving somewhat rapidly since then," said Challenger, picking up his pile of telegrams. "I am in close touch both with the authorities and with the press, so that news is converging upon me from all parts. There is, in fact, a general and very insistent demand that

I should come to London; but I see no good end to be served. From the accounts the poisonous effect begins with mental excitement; the rioting in Paris this morning is said to have been very violent, and the Welsh colliers are in a state of uproar. So far as the evidence to hand can be trusted, this stimulative stage, which varies much in races and in individuals, is succeeded by a certain exaltation and mental lucidity—I seem to discern some signs of it in our young friend here—which, after an appreciable interval, turns to coma, deepening rapidly into death. I fancy, so far as my toxicology carries me, that there are some vegetable nerve poisons—"

"Datura," suggested Summerlee.

"Excellent!" cried Challenger. "It would make for scientific precision if we named our toxic agent. Let it be daturon. To you, my dear Summerlee, belongs the honor—posthumous, alas, but none the less unique—of having given a name to the universal destroyer, the Great Gardener's disinfectant. The symptoms of daturon, then, may be taken to be such as I indicate. That it will involve the whole world and that no life can possibly remain behind seems to me to be certain, since ether is a universal medium. Up to now it has been capricious in the places which it has attacked, but the difference is only a matter of a few hours, and it is like an advancing tide which covers one strip of sand and then another, running hither and thither in irregular streams, until at last it has submerged it all. There are laws at work in connection with the action and distribution of daturon which would have been of deep interest had the time at our disposal permitted us to study them. So far as I can trace them"—here he glanced over his telegrams—"the less developed races have been the first to respond to its influence. There are deplorable accounts from Africa, and the Australian aborigines appear to have been already exterminated. The Northern races have as yet shown greater resisting power than the Southern. This, you see, is dated from Marseilles at nine-forty-five this morning. I give it to you verbatim:

"'All night delirious excitement throughout Provence. Tumult of vine growers at Nîmes. Socialistic upheaval at Toulon. Sudden illness attended by coma attacked population this morning. *Peste foudroyante.* Great numbers of dead in the streets. Paralysis of business and universal chaos.'

"An hour later came the following, from the same source:

"'We are threatened with utter extermination. Cathedrals and churches full to overflowing. The dead outnumber the living. It is inconceivable and horrible. Decease seems to be painless, but swift and inevitable.'

"There is a similar telegram from Paris, where the development is not yet as acute. India and Persia appear to be utterly wiped out. The Slavonic population of Austria is down, while the Teutonic has hardly been affected. Speaking generally, the dwellers upon the plains and upon the seashore seem, so far as my limited information goes, to have felt the effects more rapidly than those inland or on the heights. Even a little elevation makes a considerable difference, and perhaps if there be a survivor of the human race, he will again be found upon the summit of some Ararat. Even our own little hill may presently prove to be a temporary island amid a sea of disaster. But at the present rate of advance a few short hours will submerge us all."

Lord John Roxton wiped his brow, "What beats me," said he, "is how you could sit there laughin' with that stack of telegrams under your hand. I've seen death as often as most folk, but universal death—it's awful!"

"As to the laughter," said Challenger, "you will bear in mind that, like yourselves, I have not been exempt from the stimulating cerebral effects of the etheric poison. But as to the horror with which universal death appears to inspire you, I would put it to you that it is somewhat exaggerated. If you were sent to sea alone in an open boat to some unknown destination, your heart might well sink within you. The isolation, the uncertainty, would oppress you. But if your voyage were made in a goodly ship, which bore within it all your relations and your friends, you would feel that, however uncertain your destination might still remain, you would at least have one common and simultaneous experience which would hold you to the end in the same close communion. A lonely death may be terrible, but a universal one, as painless as this would appear to be, is not, in my judgment, a matter for apprehension. Indeed, I could sympathize with the person who took the view that the horror lay in the idea of surviving when all that is learned, famous, and exalted had passed away."

"What, then, do you propose to do?" asked Summerlee, who had for once nodded his assent to the reasoning of his brother scientist.

"To take our lunch," said Challenger as the boom of a gong sounded through the house. "We have a cook whose omelets are only excelled by her cutlets. We can but trust that no cosmic disturbance has dulled her excellent abilities. My Scharzberger of '96 must also be rescued, so far as our earnest and united efforts can do it, from what would be a deplorable waste of a great vintage." He levered his great bulk off the desk, upon which he had sat while he announced the doom of the planet. "Come," said he. "If there is little time left, there is the more need that we should spend it in sober and reasonable enjoyment."

And, indeed, it proved to be a very merry meal. It is true that we could not forget our awful situation. The full solemnity of the event loomed ever at the back of our minds and tempered our thoughts. But surely it is the soul which has never faced death which shies strongly from it at the end. To each of us men it had, for one great epoch in our lives, been a familiar presence. As to the lady, she leaned upon the strong guidance of her mighty husband and was well content to go whither his path might lead. The future was our fate. The present was our own. We passed it in goodly comradeship and gentle merriment. Our minds were, as I have said, singularly lucid. Even I struck sparks at times. As to Challenger, he was wonderful! Never have I so realized the elemental greatness of the man, the sweep and power of his understanding. Summerlee drew him on with his chorus of subacid criticism, while Lord John and I laughed at the contest and the lady, her hand upon his sleeve, controlled the bellowings of the philosopher. Life, death, fate, the destiny of man—these were the stupendous subjects of that memorable hour, made vital by the fact that as the meal progressed strange, sudden exaltations in my mind and tinglings in my limbs proclaimed that the invisible tide of death was slowly and gently rising around us. Once I saw Lord John put his hand suddenly to his eyes, and once Summerlee dropped back for an instant in his chair. Each breath we breathed was charged with strange forces. And yet our minds were happy and at ease. Presently Austin laid the cigarettes upon the table and was about to withdraw.

"Austin!" said his master.

"Yes, sir?"

"I thank you for your faithful service."

A smile stole over the servant's gnarled face.

"I've done my duty, sir."

"I'm expecting the end of the world today, Austin."

"Yes, sir. What time, sir?"

"I can't say, Austin. Before evening."

"Very good, sir." The taciturn Austin saluted and withdrew.

Challenger lit a cigarette, and, drawing his chair to his wife's, he took her hand in his. "You know how matters stand, dear," said he. "I have explained it also to our friends here. You're not afraid are you?"

"It won't be painful, George?"

"No more than laughing gas at the dentist's. Every time you have had it you have practically died."

"But that is a pleasant sensation."

"So may death be. The worn-out bodily machine can't record its impression, but we know the mental pleasure which lies in a dream or a trance. Nature may build a beautiful door and hang it with many a gauzy and shimmering curtain to make an entrance to the new life for our wondering souls. In all my probings of the actual, I have always found wisdom and kindness at the core; and if ever the frightened mortal needs tenderness, it is surely as he makes the passage perilous from life to life. No, Summerlee, I will have none of your materialism, for I, at least, am too great a thing to end in mere physical constituents, a packet of salts and three bucketfuls of water. Here—here"—and he beat his great head with his huge, hairy fist—"there is something which uses matter, but is not of it—something which might destroy death, but which death can never destroy."

"Talkin' of death," said Lord John. "I'm a Christian of sorts, but it seems to me there was somethin' mighty natural in those ancestors of ours who were buried with their axes and bows and arrows and the like, same as if they were livin' on just the same as they used to. I don't know," he added, looking round the table in a shamefaced way, "that I wouldn't feel more homely myself if I was put away with my old .450 Express and the fowlin' piece, the shorter one with the rubbered stock, and a clip or two of cartridges—just a fool's fancy, of course, but there it is. How does it strike you, Herr Professor?"

"Well," said Summerlee, "since you ask my opinion, it strikes me as an indefensible throwback to the Stone Age or before it. I'm of the twentieth century myself, and would wish to die like a reasonable civilized man. I don't know that I am more afraid of death than the rest of you, for I am an oldish man, and, come what may, I can't have very much longer to live; but it is all against my nature to sit waiting without a struggle like a sheep for the butcher. Is it quite certain, Challenger, that there is nothing we can do?"

"To save us—nothing," said Challenger. "To prolong our lives a few hours and thus to see the evolution of this mighty tragedy before we are actually involved in it—that may prove to be within my powers. I have taken certain steps—"

"The oxygen?"

"Exactly. The oxygen."

"But what can oxygen effect in the fact of a poisoning of the ether? There is not a greater difference in quality between a brickbat and a gas than there is between oxygen and ether. They are different planes of matter. They cannot impinge upon one another. Come, Challenger, you could not defend such a proposition."

"My good Summerlee, this etheric poison is most certainly influenced by material agents. We see it in the methods and distribution of the outbreak. We should not a priori have expected it, but it is undoubtedly a fact. Hence I am strongly of opinion that a gas like oxygen, which increases the vitality and the resisting power of the body, would be extremely likely to delay the action of what you have so happily named the daturon. It may be that I am mistaken, but I have every confidence in the correctness of my reasoning."

"Well," said Lord John, "if we've got to sit suckin' at those tubes like so many babies with their bottles, I'm not takin' any."

"There will be no need for that," Challenger answered. "We have made arrangements—it is to my wife that you chiefly owe it—that her boudoir shall be made as airtight as is practicable. With matting and varnished paper."

"Good heavens, Challenger, you don't suppose you can keep out ether with varnished paper?"

"Really, my friend, you are a trifle perverse in missing the point. It is not to keep out the ether that we have gone to such trouble. It is to keep in the oxygen. I trust that if we can ensure an atmosphere hyperox-ygenated to a certain point, we may be able to retain our senses. I had two tubes of the gas and you have brought me three more. It is not much, but it is something."

"How long will they last?"

"I have not an idea. We will not turn them on until our symptoms become unbearable. Then we shall dole the gas out as it is urgently needed. It may give us some hours, possibly even some days, on which we may look out upon a blasted world. Our own fate is delayed to that extent, and we will have the very singular experience, we five, of being, in all probability, the absolute rear guard of the human race upon its march into the unknown. Perhaps you will be kind enough now to give me a hand with the cylinders. It seems to me that the atmosphere already grows somewhat more oppressive."

THREE

SUBMERGED

The chamber which was destined to be the scene of our unforget-table experience was a charmingly feminine sitting room, some fourteen or sixteen feet square. At the end of it, divided by a curtain of red vel-vet, was a small apartment which formed the Professor's dressing room. This in turn opened into a large bedroom. The curtain was still hanging, but the boudoir and dressing room could be taken as one chamber for the purposes of our experiment. One door and the window frame had been plastered round with varnished paper so as to be practically sealed. Above the other door, which opened on to the landing, there hung a fan-light which could be drawn by a cord when some ventilation became ab-solutely necessary. A large shrub in a tub stood in each corner.

"How to get rid of our excessive carbon dioxide without unduly wasting our oxygen is a delicate and vital question," said Challenger, looking round him after the five iron tubes had been laid side by side against the wall. "With longer time for preparation I could have brought the whole concentrated force of my intelligence to bear more fully upon the problem, but as it is we must do what we can. The shrubs will be of some small service. Two of the oxygen tubes are ready to be turned on at an instant's notice, so that we cannot be taken unawares. At the same time, it would be well not to go far from the room, as the crisis may be a sudden and urgent one."

There was a broad, low window opening out upon a balcony. The view beyond was the same as that which we had already admired from the study. Looking out, I could see no sign of disorder anywhere. There was a road curving down the side of the hill, under my very eyes. A cab from the station, one of those prehistoric survivals which are only to be found in our country villages, was toiling slowly up the hill. Lower down was a nurse girl wheeling a perambulator and leading a second child by the hand. The blue reeks of smoke from the cottages gave the whole widespread landscape an air of settled order and homely comfort. Nowhere in the blue heaven or on the sunlit earth was there any fore-shadowing of a catastrophe. The harvesters were back in the fields once more and the golfers, in pairs and fours, were still streaming round the links. There was so strange a turmoil within my own head, and such a jangling of my overstrung nerves, that the indifference of those people was amazing.

"Those fellows don't seem to feel any ill effects," said I, pointing down at the links.

"Have you played golf?" asked Lord John.

"No, I have not."

"Well, young fella, when you do you'll learn that once fairly out on a round, it would take the crack of doom to stop a true golfer. Halloa! There's that telephone bell again."

From time to time during and after lunch the high insistent ring had summoned the Professor. He gave us the news as it came through to him in a few curt sentences. Such terrific items had never been registered in the world's history before. The great shadow was creeping up from the south like a rising tide of death. Egypt had gone through its delirium and was now comatose. Spain and Portugal, after a wild frenzy in which the Clericals and the Anarchists had fought most desperately, were now fallen silent. No cable messages were received any longer from South America. In North America the southern states, after some terrible racial rioting, had succumbed to the poison. North of Maryland the effect was not yet marked, and in Canada it was hardly perceptible. Belgium, Holland, and Denmark had each in turn been affected. Despairing messages were flashing from every quarter to the great centers of learning, to the chemists and the doctors of world-wide repute, imploring their advice. The astronomers too were deluged with inquiries. Nothing could be done. The thing was universal and beyond our human knowledge or control. It was death—painless but inevitable—death for young and old, for weak and strong, for rich and poor, without hope or possibility of escape. Such was the news which, in scattered, distracted messages, the telephone had brought us. The great cities already knew their fate and so far as we could gather were preparing to meet it with dignity and resignation. Yet here were our golfers and laborers like the lambs who gambol under the shadow of the knife. It seemed amazing. And yet how could they know? It had all come upon us in one giant stride. What was there in the morning paper to alarm them? And now it was but three in the afternoon. Even as we looked some rumor seemed to have spread, for we saw the reapers hurrying from the fields. Some of the golfers were returning to the clubhouse. They were running as if taking refuge from a shower. Their little caddies trailed behind them. Others were continuing their game. The nurse had turned and was pushing her perambulator hurriedly up the hill again. I noticed that she had her hand to her brow. The cab had stopped and the tired horse, with his head sunk to his knees, was resting. Above there was a perfect summer sky—one huge vault of unbroken blue, save for a few fleecy white clouds over the distant downs. If the human race must die today, it was at least upon a glorious deathbed. And yet all that gentle loveliness of nature made this terrific and wholesale destruction the more pitiable and awful. Surely it was too goodly a residence that we should be so swiftly, so ruthlessly, evicted from it!

But I have said that the telephone bell had rung once more. Suddenly I heard Challenger's tremendous voice from the hall. "Malone!" he cried. "You are wanted."

I rushed down to the instrument. It was McArdle speaking from London.

"That you, Mr. Malone?" cried his familiar voice. "Mr. Malone, there are terrible goings on in London. For God's sake, see if Professor Challenger can suggest anything that can be done."

"He can suggest nothing, sir," I answered. "He regards the crisis as universal and inevitable. We have some oxygen here, but it can only defer our fate for a few hours."

"Oxygen!" cried the agonized voice. "There is no time to get any. The office has been a perfect pandemonium ever since you left in the morning. Now half of the staff are insensible. I am weighed down with heaviness myself. From my window I can see the people lying thick in Fleet Street. The traffic is all held up. Judging by the last telegrams, the whole world—"

His voice had been sinking, and suddenly stopped. An instant later I heard through the telephone a muffled thud, as if his head had fallen forward on the desk.

"Mr. McArdle!" I cried. "Mr. McArdle!"

There was no answer. I knew as I replaced the receiver that I should never hear his voice again.

At that instant, just as I took a step backwards from the telephone, the thing was on us. It was as if we were bathers, up to our shoulders in water, who suddenly are submerged by a rolling wave. An invisible hand seemed to have quietly closed round my throat and to be gently pressing the life from me. I was conscious of immense oppression upon my chest, great tightness within my head, a loud singing in my ears, and bright flashes before my eyes. I staggered to the balustrades of the stair. At the same moment, rushing and snorting like a wounded buffalo, Challenger dashed past me, a terrible vision, with red-purple face, engorged eyes, and bristling hair. His little wife, insensible to all appearance, was slung over his great shoulder, and he blundered and thundered up the stair, scrambling and tripping, but carrying himself and her through sheer will force through that mephitic atmosphere to the haven of temporary safety. At the sight of his effort I too rushed up the steps, clambering, falling, clutching at the rail, until I tumbled half senseless upon my face on the upper landing. Lord John's fingers of steel were in the collar of my coat, and a moment later I was stretched upon my back, unable to speak or move, on the boudoir carpet. The woman lay beside me, and Summerlee was bunched in a chair by the window, his head nearly touching his knees. As in a dream I saw Challenger, like a monstrous beetle, crawling slowly across the floor, and a moment later I heard the gentle hissing of the escaping oxygen. Challenger breathed two or three times with enormous gulps, his lungs roaring as he drew in the vital gas.

"It works!" he cried exultantly. "My reasoning has been justified!" He was up on his feet again, alert and strong. With a tube in his hand he rushed over to his wife and held it to her face. In a few seconds she moaned, stirred, and sat up. He turned to me, and I felt the tide of life stealing warmly through my arteries. My reason told me that it was but a little respite, and yet, carelessly as we talk of its value, every hour of existence now seemed an inestimable thing. Never have I known such a thrill of sensuous joy as came with that freshet of life. The weight fell away from my lungs, the band loosened from my brow, a sweet feeling of peace and gentle, languid comfort stole over me. I lay watching Summerlee revive under the same remedy, and finally Lord John took his turn. He sprang to his feet and gave me a hand to rise, while Challenger picked up his wife and laid her on the settee.

"Oh, George, I am so sorry you brought me back," she said, holding him by the hand. "The door of death is indeed, as you said, hung with beautiful, shimmering curtains; for, once the choking feeling had passed, it was all unspeakably soothing and beautiful. Why have you dragged me back?"

"Because I wish that we make the passage together. We have been together so many years. It would be sad to fall apart at the supreme moment."

For a moment in his tender voice I caught a glimpse of a new Challenger, something very far from the bullying, ranting, arrogant man who had alternately amazed and offended his generation. Here in the shadow of death was the innermost Challenger, the man who had won and held a woman's love. Suddenly his mood changed and he was our strong captain once again. "Alone of all mankind I saw and foretold this catastrophe," said he with a ring of exultation and scientific triumph in his voice. "As to you, my good Summerlee, I trust your last doubts have been resolved as to the meaning of the blurring of the lines in the spectrum and that you will no longer contend that my letter in *The Times* was based upon a delusion."

For once our pugnacious colleague was deaf to a challenge. He could but sit gasping and stretching his long, thin limbs, as if to assure himself that he was still really upon this planet. Challenger walked across to the oxygen tube, and the sound of the loud hissing fell away till it was the most gentle sibilation. "We must husband our supply of the gas," said he. "The atmosphere of the room is now strongly hyperoxygenated, and I take it that none of us feel any distressing symptoms. We can only determine by actual experiments what amount added to the air will serve to neutralize the poison. Let us see how that will do."

We sat in silent nervous tension for five minutes or more, observing our own sensations. I had just began to fancy that I felt the constriction round my temples again when Mrs. Challenger called out from the sofa that she was fainting. Her husband turned on more gas. "In prescientific days," said he, "they used to keep a white mouse in every submarine, as its more delicate organization gave signs of a vicious atmosphere before it was perceived by the sailors. You, my dear, will be our white mouse. I have now increased the supply and you are better."

"Yes, I am better."

"Possibly we have hit upon the correct mixture. When we have ascertained exactly how little will serve we shall be able to compute how long we shall be able to exist. Unfortunately, in resuscitating ourselves we have already consumed a considerable proportion of this first tube."

"Does it matter?" asked Lord John, who was standing with his hands in his pockets close to the window. "If we have to go, what is the use of holdin' on? You don't suppose there's any chance for us?"

Challenger smiled and shook his head.

"Well, then, don't you think there is more dignity in takin' the jump and not waitin' to be pushed in? If it must be so, I'm for sayin' our prayers, turnin' off the gas, and openin' the window."

"Why not?" said the lady bravely. "Surely, George, Lord John is right and it is better so."

"I most strongly object," cried Summerlee in a querulous voice. "When we must die let us by all means die, but to deliberately anticipate death seems to me to be a foolish and unjustifiable action."

"What does our young friend say to it?" asked Challenger.

"I think we should see it to the end."

"And I am strongly of the same opinion," said he.

"Then, George, if you say so, I think so too," cried the lady.

"Well, well, I'm only puttin' it as an argument," said Lord John. "If you all want to see it through I am with you. It's dooced interestin', and no mistake about that. I've had my share of adventures in my life, and as many thrills as most folk, but I'm endin' on my top note."

"Granting the continuity of life," said Challenger.

"A large assumption!" cried Summerlee.

Challenger stared at him in silent reproof. "Granting the continuity of life," said he, in his most didactic manner, "none of us can predicate what opportunities of observation one may have from what we may call the spirit plane to the plane of matter. It surely must be evident to the most obtuse person" (here he glared at Summerlee) "that it is while we are ourselves material that we are most fitted to watch and form a judgment upon material phenomena. Therefore it is only by keeping alive for these few extra hours that we can hope to carry on with us to some future existence a clear conception of the most stupendous event that the world, or the universe so far as we know it, has ever encountered. To me it would seem a deplorable thing that we should in any way curtail by so much as a minute so wonderful an experience."

"I am strongly of the same opinion," cried Summerlee,

"Carried without a division," said Lord John. "By George, that poor devil of a chauffeur of yours down in the yard has made his last journey. No use makin' a sally and bringin' him in?"

"It would be absolute madness," cried Summerlee.

"Well, I suppose it would," said Lord John. "It couldn't help him and would scatter our gas all over the house, even if we ever got back alive. My word, look at the little birds under the trees!"

We drew four chairs up to the long, low window, the lady still resting with closed eyes upon the settee. I remember that the monstrous and grotesque idea crossed my mind—the illusion may have been heightened by the heavy stuffiness of the air which we were breathing—that we were in four front seats of the stalls at the last act of the drama of the world.

In the immediate foreground, beneath our very eyes, was the small yard with the half-cleaned motorcar standing in it. Austin, the chauffeur, had received his final notice at last, for he was sprawling beside the wheel, with a great black bruise upon his forehead where it had struck the step or mudguard in falling. He still held in his hand the nozzle of the hose with which he had been washing down his machine. A couple of small plane trees stood in the corner of the yard, and underneath them lay several pathetic little balls of fluffy feathers, with tiny feet uplifted. The sweep of death's scythe had included everything, great and small, within its swath.

Over the wall of the yard we looked down upon the winding road, which led to the station. A group of the reapers whom we had seen running from the fields were lying all pell-mell, their bodies crossing each other, at the bottom of it. Farther up, the nursegirl lay with her head and shoulders propped against the slope of the grassy bank. She had taken the baby from the perambulator, and it was a motionless bundle of wraps in her arms. Close behind her a tiny patch upon the roadside showed where the little boy was stretched. Still nearer to us was the dead cab horse, kneeling between the shafts. The old driver was hanging over the splashboard like some grotesque scarecrow, his arms dangling absurdly in front of him. Through the window we could dimly discern that a young man was seated. The door was swinging open and his hand was grasping the handle, as if he had attempted to leap forth at the last instant. In the middle distance lay the golf links, dotted as they had been in the morning with the dark figures of the golfers, lying motionless upon the grass of the course or among the heather which skirted it. On one particular green there were eight bodies stretched where a foursome with its caddies had held to their game to the last. No bird flew in the blue vault of heaven, no man or beast moved upon the vast countryside which lay before us. The evening sun shone its peaceful radiance across it, but there brooded over it all the stillness and the silence of universal death—a death in which we were so soon to join. At the present instant that one frail sheet of glass, by holding in the extra oxygen which counteracted the poisoned ether, shut us off from the fate of all our kind. For a few short hours the knowledge and foresight of one man could preserve our little oasis of life in the vast desert of death and save us from participation in the common catastrophe. Then the gas would run low, we too should lie gasping upon that cherry-colored boudoir carpet, and the fate of the human race and of all earthly life would be complete. For a long time, in a mood which was too solemn for speech, we looked out at the tragic world.

"There is a house on fire," said Challenger at last, pointing to a column of smoke which rose above the trees. "There will, I expect, be many such—possibly whole cities in flames—when we consider how many folk may have dropped with lights in their hands. The fact of combustion is in itself enough to show that the proportion of oxygen in the atmosphere is normal and that it is the ether which is at fault. Ah, there you see another blaze on the top of Crowborough Hill. It is the golf clubhouse, or I am mistaken. There is the church clock chiming the hour. It would interest our philosophers to know that man-made mechanism has survived the race who made it."

"By George!" cried Lord John, rising excitedly from his chair. "What's that puff of smoke? It's a train."

We heard the roar of it, and presently it came flying into sight, going at what seemed to me to be a prodigious speed. Whence it had come, or how far, we had no means of knowing. Only by some miracle of luck could it have gone any distance. But now we were to see the terrific end of its career. A train of coal trucks stood motionless upon the line. We held our breath as the express roared along the same track. The crash was horrible. Engine and carriages piled themselves into a hill of splintered wood and twisted iron. Red spurts of flame flickered up from the wreckage until it was all ablaze. For half an hour we sat with hardly a word, stunned by the stupendous sight.

"Poor, poor people!" cried Mrs. Challenger at last, clinging with a whimper to her husband's arm.

"My dear, the passengers on that train were no more animate than the coals into which they crashed or the carbon which they have now become," said Challenger, stroking her hand soothingly. "It was a train of the living when it left Victoria, but it was driven and freighted by the dead long before it reached its fate."

"All over the world the same thing must be going on," said I, as a vision of strange happenings rose before me. "Think of the ships at sea— how they will steam on and on, until the furnaces die down or until they run full tilt upon some beach. The sailing ships too—how they will back and fill with their cargoes of dead sailors, while their timbers rot and their joints leak, till one by one they sink below the surface. Perhaps a century hence the Atlantic may still be dotted with the old drifting derelicts."

"And the folk in the coal mines," said Summerlee with a dismal chuckle. "If ever geologists should by any chance live upon earth again they will have some strange theories of the existence of man in carboniferous strata."

"I don't profess to know about such things," remarked Lord John, "but it seems to me the earth will be 'To let, empty' after this. When once our human crowd is wiped off it, how will it ever get on again?"

"The world was empty before," Challenger answered gravely. "Under laws which in their inception are beyond and above us, it became peopled. Why may the same process not happen again?"

"My dear Challenger, you can't mean that?"

"I am not in the habit, Professor Summerlee, of saying things which I do not mean. The observation is trivial." Out went the beard and down came the eyelids.

"Well, you lived an obstinate dogmatist, and you mean to die one," said Summerlee sourly.

"And you, sir, have lived an unimaginative obstructionist and never can hope now to emerge from it."

"Your worst critics will never accuse you of lacking imagination," Summerlee retorted.

"Upon my word!" said Lord John. "It would be like you if you used up our last gasp of oxygen in abusing each other. What can it matter whether folk come back or not? It surely won't be in our time."

"In that remark, sir, you betray your own very pronounced limitations," said Challenger severely. "The true scientific mind is not to be tied down by its own conditions of time and space. It builds itself an observatory erected upon the border line of present, which separates the infinite past from the infinite future. From this sure post it makes its sallies even to the beginning and to the end of all things. As to death, the scientific mind dies at its post working in normal and methodic fashion to the end. It disregards so petty a thing as its own physical dissolution as completely as it does all other limitations upon the plane of matter. Am I right, Professor Summerlee?"

Summerlee grumbled an ungracious assent. "With certain reservations, I agree," said he.

"The ideal scientific mind," continued Challenger—"I put it in the third person rather than appear to be too self-complacent—the ideal scientific mind should be capable of thinking out a point of abstract knowledge in the interval between its owner falling from a balloon and reaching the earth. Men of this strong fiber are needed to form the conquerors of nature and the bodyguard of truth."

"It strikes me nature's on top this time," said Lord John, looking out of the window. "I've read some leadin' articles about you gentlemen controllin' her, but she's gettin' a bit of her own back."

"It is but a temporary setback" said Challenger with conviction. "A few million years, what are they in the great cycle of time? The vegetable world has, as you can see, survived. Look at the leaves of that plane tree. The birds are dead, but the plant flourishes. From this vegetable life in pond and in marsh will come, in time, the tiny crawling microscopic slugs which are the pioneers of that great army of life in which for the instant we five have the extraordinary duty of serving as rear guard. Once the lowest form of life has established itself, the final advent of man is as certain as the growth of the oak from the acorn. The old circle will swing round once more."

"But the poison?" I asked. "Will that not nip life in the bud?"

"The poison may be a mere stratum or layer in the ether—a mephitic Gulf Stream across that mighty ocean in which we float. Or tolerance may be established and life accommodate itself to a new condition. The mere fact that with a comparatively small hyperoxygenation of our blood we can hold out against it is surely a proof in itself that no very great change would be needed to enable animal life to endure it."

The smoking house beyond the trees had burst into flames. We could see the high tongues of fire shooting up into the air.

"It's pretty awful," muttered Lord John, more impressed than I had ever seen him.

"Well, after all, what does it matter?" I remarked. "The world is dead. Cremation is surely the best burial."

"It would shorten us up if this house went ablaze."

"I foresaw the danger," said Challenger, "and asked my wife to guard against it."

"Everything is quite safe, dear. But my head begins to throb again. What a dreadful atmosphere!"

"We must change it," said Challenger. He bent over his cylinder of oxygen. "It's nearly empty," said he. "It has lasted us some three hours. It is now close on eight o'clock. We shall get through the night comfortably. I should expect the end about nine o'clock tomorrow morning. We shall see one sunrise, which shall be our own."

He turned on his second tube and opened for half a minute the fanlight over the door. Then as the air became perceptibly better, but our own symptoms more acute, he closed it once again.

"By the way," said he, "man does not live upon oxygen alone. It's dinner time and over. I assure you, gentlemen, that when I invited you to my home and to what I had hoped would be an interesting reunion, I had intended that my kitchen should justify itself. However, we must do what we can. I am sure that you will agree with me that it would be folly to consume our air too rapidly by lighting an oilstove. I have some small provision of cold meats, bread, and pickles which, with a couple of bottles of claret, may serve our turn. Thank you, my dear—now as ever you are the queen of managers."

It was indeed wonderful how, with the self-respect and sense of propriety of the British housekeeper, the lady had within a few minutes adorned the central table with a snow-white cloth, laid the napkins upon it, and set forth the simple meal with all the elegance of civilization, including an electric torch lamp in the center. Wonderful also was it to find that our appetites were ravenous.

"It is the measure of our emotion," said Challenger with that air of condescension with which he brought his scientific mind to the explanation of humble facts. "We have gone through a great crisis. That means molecular disturbance. That in turn means the need for repair. Great sorrow or great joy should bring intense hunger—not abstinence from food, as our novelists will have it."

"That's why the country folk have great feasts at funerals," I hazarded.

"Exactly. Our young friend has hit upon an excellent illustration. Let me give you another slice of tongue."

"The same with savages," said Lord John, cutting away at the beef. "I've seen them buryin' a chief up the Aruwimi River, and they ate a hippo that must have weighed as much as a tribe. There are some of them down New Guinea way that eat the late-lamented himself, just by way of a last tidy up. Well, of all the funeral feasts on this earth, I suppose the one we are takin' is the queerest."

"The strange thing is," said Mrs. Challenger, "that I find it impossible to feel grief for those who are gone. There are my father and mother at Bedford. I know that they are dead, and yet in this tremendous universal tragedy I can feel no sharp sorrow for any individuals, even for them."

"And my old mother in her cottage in Ireland," said I. "I can see her in my mind's eye, with her shawl and her lace cap, lying back with closed eyes in the old high-backed chair near the window, her glasses and her book beside her. Why should I mourn her? She has passed and I am passing, and I may be nearer her in some other life than England is to Ireland. Yet I grieve to think that that dear body is no more."

"As to the body," remarked Challenger, "we do not mourn over the parings of our nails nor the cut locks of our hair, though they were once part of ourselves. Neither does a one-legged man yearn sentimentally over his missing member. The physical body has rather been a source of pain and fatigue to us. It is the constant index of our limitations. Why then should we worry about its detachment from our psychical selves?"

"If they can indeed be detached," Summerlee grumbled. "But, anyhow, universal death is dreadful."

"As I have already explained," said Challenger, "a universal death must in its nature be far less terrible than an isolated one."

"Same in a battle," remarked Lord John. "If you saw a single man lying on that floor with his chest knocked in and a hole in his face it would turn you sick. But I've seen ten thousand on their backs in the Sudan, and it gave me no such feelin', for when you are makin' history the life of any man is too small a thing to worry over. When a thousand million pass over together, same as happened today, you can't pick your own partic'lar out of the crowd."

"I wish it were well over with us," said the lady wistfully. "Oh, George, I am so frightened."

"You'll be the bravest of us all, little lady, when the time comes. I've been a blusterous old husband to you, dear, but you'll just bear in mind that G. E. C. is as he was made and couldn't help himself. After all, you wouldn't have had anyone else?"

"No one in the whole wide world, dear," said she, and put her arms round his bull neck. We three walked to the window and stood amazed at the sight which met our eyes.

Darkness had fallen and the dead world was shrouded in gloom. But right across the southern horizon was one long vivid scarlet streak, waxing and waning in vivid pulses of life, leaping suddenly to a crimson zenith and then dying down to a glowing line of fire.

"Lewes is ablaze!"

"No, it is Brighton which is burning," said Challenger, stepping across to join us. "You can see the curved back of the downs against the glow. That fire is miles on the farther side of it. The whole town must be alight."

There were several red glares at different points, and the pile of debris upon the railway line was still smoldering darkly, but they all seemed mere pin points of light compared to that monstrous conflagration throbbing beyond the hills. What copy it would have made for the *Gazette!* Had ever a journalist such an opening and so little chance of using it—the scoop of scoops, and no one to appreciate it? And then, suddenly, the old instinct of recording came over me. If these men of science could be so true to their life's work to the very end, why should not I, in my humble way, be as constant? No human eye might ever rest upon what I had done. But the long night had to be passed somehow, and for me at least, sleep seemed to be out of the question. My notes would help to pass the weary hours and to occupy my thoughts. Thus it is that now I have before me the notebook with its scribbled pages, written confusedly upon my knee in the dim, waning light of our one electric torch. Had I the literary touch, they might have been worthy of the occasion. As it is, they may still serve to bring to other minds the long-drawn emotions and tremors of that awful night.

FOUR

A DIARY OF THE DYING

How strange the words look scribbled at the top of the empty page of my book! How stranger still that it is I, Edward Malone, who have written them—I who started only some twelve hours ago from my rooms in Streatham without one thought of the marvels which the day was to bring forth! I look back at the chain of incidents, my interview with McArdle, Challenger's first note of alarm in *The Times*, the absurd journey in the train, the pleasant luncheon, the catastrophe, and now it has come to this—that we linger alone upon an empty planet, and so sure is our fate that I can regard these lines, written from mechanical professional habit and never to be seen by human eyes, as the words of one who is already dead, so closely does he stand to the shadowed borderland over which all outside this one little circle of friends have already gone. I feel how wise and true were the words of Challenger when he said that the real tragedy would be if we were left behind when all that is noble and good and beautiful had passed. But of that there can surely be no danger. Already our second tube of oxygen is drawing to an end. We can count the poor dregs of our lives almost to a minute.

We have just been treated to a lecture, a good quarter of an hour long, from Challenger, who was so excited that he roared and bellowed as if he were addressing his old rows of scientific sceptics in the Queen's Hall. He had certainly a strange audience to harangue: his wife perfectly acquiescent and absolutely ignorant of his meaning, Summerlee seated in the shadow, querulous and critical but interested, Lord John lounging in a corner somewhat bored by the whole proceeding, and myself beside the window watching the scene with a kind of detached attention, as if it were all a dream or something in which I had no personal interest whatever. Challenger sat at the center table with the electric light illuminating the slide under the microscope which he had brought from his dressing room. The small vivid circle of white light from the mirror left half of his rugged, bearded face in brilliant radiance and half in deepest shadow. He had, it seems, been working of late upon the lowest forms of life, and what excited him at the present moment was that in the microscopic slide made up the day before he found the amoeba to be still alive.

"You can see it for yourselves," he kept repeating in great excitement. "Summerlee, will you step across and satisfy yourself upon the point? Malone, will you kindly verify what I say? The little spindle-shaped things in the center are diatoms and may be disregarded since they are probably vegetable rather than animal. But the right-hand side you will see an undoubted amoeba, moving sluggishly across the field. The upper screw is the fine adjustment. Look at it for yourselves."

Summerlee did so and acquiesced. So did I and perceived a little creature which looked as if it were made of ground grass flowing in a sticky way across the lighted circle. Lord John was prepared to take him on trust. "I'm not troublin' my head whether he's alive or dead," said he. "We don't so much as know each other by sight, so why should I take it to heart? I don't suppose he's worryin' himself over the state of *our* health."

I laughed at this, and Challenger looked in my direction with his coldest and most supercilious stare. It was a most petrifying experience. "The flippancy of the half-educated is more obstructive to science than the obtuseness of the ignorant," said he. "If Lord John Roxton would condescend—"

"My dear George, don't be so peppery," said his wife, with her hand on the black mane that drooped over the microscope. "What can it matter whether the amoeba is alive or not?"

"It matters a great deal," said Challenger gruffly.

"Well, let's hear about it," said Lord John with a good-humored smile. "'We may as well talk about that as anything else. If you think I've been too offhand with the thing, or hurt its feelin's in any way, I'll apologize."

"For my part," remarked Summerlee in his creaky, argumentative voice, "I can't see why you should attach such importance to the creature being alive. It is in the same atmosphere as ourselves, so naturally the poison does not act upon it. If it were outside of this room it would be dead, like all other animal life."

"Your remarks, my good Summerlee," said Challenger with enormous condescension (oh, if I could paint that overbearing, arrogant face in the vivid circle of reflection from the microscope mirror!), "your remarks show that you imperfectly appreciate the situation. This specimen was mounted yesterday and was hermetically sealed. None of our oxygen can reach it. But the ether, of course, has penetrated to it, as to every other point upon the universe. Therefore, it has survived the poison. Hence, we may argue that every amoeba outside this room, instead of being dead, as you have erroneously stated, has really survived the catastrophe."

"Well, even now I don't feel inclined to hip-hurrah about it," said Lord John. "What does it matter?"

"It just matters this, that the world is a living instead of a dead one. If you had the scientific imagination, you would cast your mind forward from this one fact, and you would see some few millions of years hence—a mere passing moment in the enormous flux of the ages—the whole world teeming once more with the animal and human life which will spring from this tiny root. You have seen a prairie fire where the flames have swept every trace of grass or plant from the surface of the earth and left only a blackened waste. You would think that it must be forever desert. Yet the roots of growth have been left behind, and when you pass the place a few years hence you can no longer tell where the black scars used to be. Here in this tiny creature are the roots of growth of the animal world, and by its inherent development, and evolution, it will surely in time remove every trace of this incomparable crisis in which we are now involved."

"Dooced interestin'!" said Lord John, lounging across and looking through the microscope. "Funny little chap to hang number one among the family portraits. Got a fine big shirt stud on him!"

"The dark object is his nucleus," said Challenger with the air of a nurse teaching letters to a baby.

"Well, we needn't feel lonely," said Lord John laughing. "There's somebody livin' besides us on the earth."

"You seem to take it for granted, Challenger," said Summerlee, "that the object for which this world was created was that it should produce and sustain human life."

"Well, sir, and what object do you suggest?" asked Challenger, bristling at the least hint of contradiction.

"Sometimes I think that it is only the monstrous conceit of mankind which makes him think that all this stage was erected for him to strut upon."

"We cannot be dogmatic about it, but at least without what you have ventured to call monstrous conceit we can surely say that we are the highest thing in nature."

"The highest of which we have cognizance."

"That, sir, goes without saying."

"Think of all the millions and possibly billions of years that the earth swung empty through space—or, if not empty, at least without a sign or thought of the human race. Think of it, washed by the rain and scorched by the sun and swept by the wind for those unnumbered ages. Man only came into being yesterday so far as geological time goes. Why, then, should it be taken for granted that all this stupendous preparation was for his benefit?"

"For whose then—or for what?"

Summerlee shrugged his shoulders. "How can we tell? For some reason altogether beyond our conception—and man may have been a mere accident, a by-product evolved in the process. It is as if the scum upon the surface of the ocean imagined that the ocean was created in order to produce and sustain it or a mouse in a cathedral thought that the building was its own proper ordained residence."

I have jotted down the very words of their argument, but now it degenerates into a mere noisy wrangle with much polysyllabic scientific jargon upon each side. It is no doubt a privilege to hear two such brains discuss the highest questions; but as they are in perpetual disagreement, plain folk like Lord John and me get little that is positive from the exhibition. They neutralize each other and we are left as they found us. Now the hubbub has ceased, and Summerlee is coiled up in his chair, while Challenger, still fingering the screws of his microscope, is keeping up a continual low, deep, inarticulate growl like the sea after a storm. Lord John comes over to me, and we look out together into the night.

There is a pale new moon—the last moon that human eyes will ever rest upon—and the stars are most brilliant. Even in the clear plateau air of South America I have never seen them brighter. Possibly this etheric change has some effect upon light. The funeral pyre of Brighton is still blazing, and there is a very distant patch of scarlet in the western sky, which may mean trouble at Arundel or Chichester, possibly even at Portsmouth. I sit and muse and make an occasional note. There is a sweet melancholy in the air. Youth and beauty and chivalry and love—is this to be the end of it all? The starlit earth looks a dreamland of gentle peace. Who would imagine it as the terrible Golgotha strewn with the bodies of the human race? Suddenly, I find myself laughing.

"Halloa, young fella!" says Lord John, staring at me in surprise. "We could do with a joke in these hard times. What was it, then?"

"I was thinking of all the great unsolved questions," I answer, "the questions that we spent so much labor and thought over. Think of Anglo-German competition, for example—or the Persian Gulf that my old chief was so keen about. Whoever would have guessed, when we fumed and fretted so, how they were to be eventually solved?"

We fall into silence again. I fancy that each of us is thinking of friends that have gone before. Mrs. Challenger is sobbing quietly, and her husband is whispering to her. My mind turns to all the most unlikely people, and I see each of them lying white and rigid as poor Austin does in the yard. There is McArdle, for example, I know exactly where he is, with his face upon his writing desk and his hand on his own telephone, just as I heard him fall. Beaumont, the editor, too—I suppose he is lying upon the blue-and-red Turkey carpet which adorned his sanctum. And the fellows in the reporters' room—Macdona and Murray and Bond. They had certainly died hard at work on their job, with note books full of vivid impressions and strange happenings in their hands. I could just imagine how this one would have been packed off to the doctors, and that other to Westminster, and yet a third to St. Paul's. What glorious rows of headlines they must have seen as a last vision beautiful, never destined to materialize in printer's ink! I could see Macdona among the doctors—"Hope in Harley Street"—Mac had always a weakness for alliteration. "Interview with Mr. Soley Wilson." "Famous Specialist says 'Never despair!'" "Our Special Correspondent found the eminent scientist seated upon the roof, whither he had retreated to avoid the crowd of terrified patients who had stormed his dwelling. With a manner which plainly showed his appreciation of the immense gravity of the occasion, the celebrated physician refused to admit that every avenue of hope had been closed." That's how Mac would start. Then there was Bond; he would probably do St. Paul's. He fancied his own literary touch. My word, what a theme for him! "Standing in the little gallery under the dome and looking down upon that packed mass of despairing humanity, groveling at this last instant before a Power which they had so persistently ignored, there rose to my ears from the swaying crowd such a low moan of entreaty and terror, such a shuddering cry for help to the Unknown, that—" and so forth.

Yes, it would be a great end for a reporter, though, like myself, he would die with the treasures still unused. What would Bond not give, poor chap, to see "J. H. B." at the foot of a column like that?

But what drivel I am writing! It is just an attempt to pass the weary time. Mrs. Challenger has gone to the inner dressing room, and the Professor says that she is asleep. He is making notes and consulting books at the central table, as calmly as if years of placid work lay before him. He writes with a very noisy quill pen which seems to be screeching scorn at all who disagree with him.

Summerlee has dropped off in his chair and gives from time to time a peculiarly exasperating snore. Lord John lies back with his hands in his pockets and his eyes closed. How people can sleep under such conditions is more than I can imagine.

Three-thirty a.m. I have just awakened with a start. It was five minutes past eleven when I made my last entry. I remember winding up my watch and noting the time. So I have wasted some five hours of the little span still left to us. Who would have believed it possible? But I feel very much fresher, and ready for my fate—or try to persuade myself that I am. And yet, the fitter a man is, and the higher his tide of life, the more must he shrink from death. How wise and how merciful is that provision of nature by which his earthly anchor is usually loosened by many little imperceptible tugs, until his consciousness has drifted out of its untenable earthly harbor into the great sea beyond!

Mrs. Challenger is still in the dressing room. Challenger has fallen asleep in his chair. What a picture! His enormous frame leans back, his huge, hairy hands are clasped across his waistcoat, and his head is so tilted that I can see nothing above his collar save a tangled bristle of luxuriant beard. He shakes with the vibration of his own snoring. Summerlee adds his occasional high tenor to Challenger's sonorous bass. Lord John is sleeping also, his long body doubled up sideways in a basket chair. The first cold light of dawn is just stealing into the room, and everything is gray and mournful.

I look out at the sunrise—that fateful sunrise which will shine upon an unpeopled world. The human race is gone, extinguished in a day, but the planets swing round and the tides rise or fall, and the wind whispers, and all nature goes her way, down, as it would seem, to the very amoeba, with never a sign that he who styled himself the lord of creation had ever blessed or cursed the universe with his presence. Down in the yard lies Austin with sprawling limbs, his face glimmering white in the dawn, and the hose nozzle still projecting from his dead hand. The whole of human kind is typified in that one half-ludicrous and half-pathetic figure, lying so helpless beside the machine which it used to control.

Here end the notes which I made at the time. Henceforward events were too swift and too poignant to allow me to write, but they are too clearly outlined in my memory that any detail could escape me.

Some chokiness in my throat made me look at the oxygen cylinders, and I was startled at what I saw. The sands of our lives were running very low. At some period in the night Challenger had switched the tube from the third to the fourth cylinder. Now it was clear that this also was nearly exhausted. That horrible feeling of constriction was closing in upon me. I ran across and, unscrewing the nozzle, I changed it to our last supply. Even as I did so my conscience pricked me, for I felt that perhaps if I had held my hand all of them might have passed in their sleep. The thought was banished, however, by the voice of the lady from the inner room crying: "George, George, I am stifling!"

"It is all right, Mrs Challenger," I answered as the others started to their feet. "I have just turned on a fresh supply."

Even at such a moment I could not help smiling at Challenger, who with a great hairy fist in each eye was like a huge, bearded baby, new wakened out of sleep. Summerlee was shivering like a man with the ague, human fears, as he realized his position, rising for an instant above the stoicism of the man of science.

Lord John, however, was as cool and alert as if he had just been roused on a hunting morning. "Fifthly and lastly," said he, glancing at the tube. "Say, young fella, don't tell me you've been writin' up your impressions in that paper on your knee."

"Just a few notes to pass the time."

"Well, I don't believe anyone but an Irishman would have done that. I expect you'll have to wait till little brother amoeba gets grown up before you'll find a reader. He don't seem to take much stock of things just at present. Well, Herr Professor, what are the prospects?"

Challenger was looking out at the great drifts of morning mist which lay over the landscape. Here and there the wooded hills rose like conical islands out of this woolly sea.

"It might be a winding sheet," said Mrs. Challenger, who had entered in her dressing gown. "There's that song of yours, George, 'Ring out the old, ring in the new.' It was prophetic. But you are shivering, my poor dear friends. I have been warm under a coverlet all night, and you cold in your chairs. But I'll soon set you right."

The brave little creature hurried away, and presently we heard the sizzling of a kettle. She was back soon with five steaming cups of cocoa upon a tray. "Drink these," said she. "You will feel so much better."

And we did. Summerlee asked if he might light his pipe, and we all had cigarettes. It steadied our nerves, I think, but it was a mistake, for it made a dreadful atmosphere in that stuffy room. Challenger had to open the ventilator.

"How long, Challenger?" asked Lord John.

"Possibly three hours," he answered with a shrug.

"I used to be frightened," said his wife. "But the nearer I get to it, the easier it seems. Don't you think we ought to pray, George?"

"You will pray, dear, if you wish," the big man answered, very gently. "We all have our own ways of praying. Mine is a complete acquiescence in whatever fate may send me—a cheerful acquiescence. The highest religion and the highest science seem to unite on that."

"I cannot truthfully describe my mental attitude as acquiescence and far less cheerful acquiescence," grumbled Summerlee over his pipe. "I submit because I have to. I confess that I should have liked another year of life to finish my classification of the chalk fossils."

"Your unfinished work is a small thing," said Challenger pompously, "when weighed against the fact that my own magnum opus, 'The Ladder of Life,' is still in the first stages. My brain, my reading, my experience—in fact, my whole unique equipment—were to be condensed into that epoch-making volume. And yet, as I say, I acquiesce."

"I expect we've all left some loose ends stickin' out," said Lord John. "What are yours, young fella?"

"I was working at a book of verses," I answered.

"Well, the world has escaped that, anyhow," said Lord John. "There's always compensation somewhere if you grope around."

"What about you?" I asked.

"Well, it just so happens that I was tidied up and ready. I'd promised Merivale to go to Tibet for a snow leopard in the spring. But it's hard on you, Mrs. Challenger, when you have just built up this pretty home."

"Where George is, there is my home. But, oh, what would I not give for one last walk together in the fresh morning air upon those beautiful downs!"

Our hearts re-echoed her words. The sun had burst through the gauzy mists which veiled it, and the whole broad Weald was washed in golden light. Sitting in our dark and poisonous atmosphere that glorious, clean, wind-swept countryside seemed a very dream of beauty. Mrs Challenger held her hand stretched out to it in her longing. We drew up chairs and sat in a semicircle in the window. The atmosphere was already very close. It seemed to me that the shadows of death were drawing in upon us—the last of our race. It was like an invisible curtain closing down upon every side.

"That cylinder is not lastin' too well," said Lord John with a long gasp for breath.

"The amount contained is variable," said Challenger, "depending upon the pressure and care with which it has been bottled. I am inclined to agree with you, Roxton, that this one is defective."

"So we are to be cheated out of the last hour of our lives," Summerlee remarked bitterly. "An excellent final illustration of the sordid age in which we have lived. Well, Challenger, now is your time if you wish to study the subjective phenomena of physical dissolution."

"Sit on the stool at my knee and give me your hand," said Challenger to his wife. "I think, my friends, that a further delay in this insufferable atmosphere is hardly advisable. You would not desire it dear, would you?"

His wife gave a little groan and sank her face against his leg.

"I've seen the folk bathin' in the Serpentine in winter," said Lord John. "When the rest are in, you see one or two shiverin' on the bank, envyin' the others that have taken the plunge. It's the last that have the worst of it. I'm all for a header and have done with it."

"You would open the window and face the ether?"

"Better be poisoned than stifled."

Summerlee nodded his reluctant acquiescence and held out his thin hand to Challenger. "We've had our quarrels in our time, but that's all over," said he. "We were good friends and had a respect for each other under the surface. Good-by!"

"Good-by, young fella!" said Lord John. "The window's plastered up. You can't open it."

Challenger stooped and raised his wife, pressing her to his breast, while she threw her arms round his neck. "Give me that field glass, Malone," said he gravely.

I handed it to him.

"Into the hands of the Power that made us we render ourselves again!" he shouted in his voice of thunder, and at the words he hurled the field glass through the window.

Full in our flushed faces, before the last tinkle of falling fragments had died away, there came the wholesome breath of the wind, blowing strong and sweet.

I don't know how long we sat in amazed silence. Then as in a dream, I heard Challenger's voice once more. "We are back in normal conditions," he cried. "The world has cleared the poison belt, but we alone of all mankind are saved."

FIVE

THE DEAD WORLD

I remember that we all sat gasping in our chairs, with that sweet, wet southwestern breeze, fresh from the sea, flapping the muslin curtains and cooling our flushed faces. I wonder how long we sat! None of us afterwards could agree at all on that point. We were bewildered, stunned, semiconscious. We had all braced our courage for death, but this fearful and sudden new fact—that we must continue to live after we had survived the race to which we belonged—struck us with the shock of a physical blow and left us prostrate. Then gradually the suspended mechanism began to move once more; the shuttles of memory worked; ideas weaved themselves together in our minds. We saw, with vivid, merciless clearness, the relations between the past, the present, and the future—the lives that we had led and the lives which we would have to live. Our eyes turned in silent horror upon those of our companions and found the same answering look in theirs. Instead of the joy which men might have been expected to feel who had so narrowly escaped an imminent death, a terrible wave of darkest depression submerged us. Everything on earth that we loved had been washed away into the great, infinite, unknown ocean, and here were we marooned upon this desert island of a world, without companions, hopes, or aspirations. A few years' skulking like jackals among the graves of the human race and then our belated and lonely end would come.

"It's dreadful, George, dreadful!" the lady cried in an agony of sobs. "If we had only passed with the others! Oh, why did you save us? I feel as if it is we that are dead and everyone else alive."

Challenger's great eyebrows were drawn down in concentrated thought, while his huge, hairy paw closed upon the outstretched hand of his wife. I had observed that she always held out her arms to him in trouble as a child would to its mother. "Without being a fatalist to the point of nonresistance," said he, "I have always found that the highest wisdom lies in an acquiescence with the actual." He spoke slowly, and there was a vibration of feeling in his sonorous voice.

"I do *not* acquiesce," said Summerlee firmly.

"I don't see that it matters a row of pins whether you acquiesce or whether you don't," remarked Lord John. "You've got to take it, whether you take it fightin' or take it lyin' down, so what's the odds whether you acquiesce or not? I can't remember that anyone asked our permission before the thing began, and nobody's likely to ask it now. So what difference can it make what we may think of it?"

"It is just all the difference between happiness and misery," said Challenger with an abstracted face, still patting his wife's hand. "You can swim with the tide and have peace in mind and soul, or you can thrust against it and be bruised and weary. This business is beyond us, so let us accept it as it stands and say no more."

"But what in the world are we to do with our lives?" I asked, appealing in desperation to the blue, empty heaven. "What am I to do, for example? There are no newspapers, so there's an end of my vocation."

"And there's nothin' left to shoot, and no more soldierin', so there's an end of mine," said Lord John.

"And there are no students, so there's an end of mine," cried Summerlee.

"But I have my husband and my house, so I can thank heaven that there is no end of mine," said the lady.

"Nor is there an end of mine," remarked Challenger, "for science is not dead, and this catastrophe in itself will offer us many more absorbing problems for investigation." He had now flung open the windows and we were gazing out upon the silent and motionless landscape. "Let me consider," he continued. "It was about three, or a little after, yesterday afternoon that the world finally entered the poison belt to the extent of being completely submerged. It is now nine o'clock. The question is, at what hour did we pass out from it?"

"The air was very bad at daybreak," said I.

"Later than that," said Mrs. Challenger. "As late as eight o'clock I distinctly felt the same choking at my throat which came at the outset."

"Then we shall say that it passed just after eight o'clock. For seventeen hours the world has been soaked in the poisonous ether. For that length of time the Great Gardener has sterilized the human mold which had grown over the surface of His fruit. Is it possible that the work is incompletely done—that others may have survived besides ourselves?"

"That's what I was wonderin'," said Lord John. "Why should we be the only pebbles on the beach?"

"It is absurd to suppose that anyone besides ourselves can possibly have survived," said Summerlee with conviction. "Consider that the poison was so virulent that even a man who is as strong as an ox and has not a nerve in his body, like Malone here, could hardly get up the stairs before he fell unconscious. Is it likely that anyone could stand seventeen minutes of it, far less hours?"

"Unless someone saw it coming and made preparation, same as old friend Challenger did."

"That, I think, is hardly probable," said Challenger, projecting his beard and sinking his eyelids. "The combination of observation, inference, and anticipatory imagination which enabled me to foresee the danger is what one can hardly expect twice in the same generation."

"Then your conclusion is that everyone is certainly dead?"

"There can be little doubt of that. We have to remember, however, that the poison worked from below upwards and would possibly be less virulent in the higher strata of the atmosphere. It is strange, indeed, that it should be so; but it presents one of those features which will afford us in the future a fascinating field for study. One could imagine, therefore, that if one had to search for survivors one would turn one's eyes with best hopes of success to some Tibetan village or some Alpine farm, many thousand of feet above the sea level."

"Well, considerin' that there are no railroads and no steamers you might as well talk about survivors in the moon," said Lord John. "But what I'm askin' myself is whether it's really over or whether it's only half time."

Summerlee craned his neck to look round the horizon. "It seems clear and fine," said he in a dubious voice, "but so it did yesterday. I am by no means assured that it is all over."

Challenger shrugged his shoulders. "We must come back once more to our fatalism," said he. "If the world has undergone this experience before, which is not outside the range of possibility, it was certainly a very long time ago. Therefore, we may reasonably hope that it will be very long before it occurs again."

"That's all very well," said Lord John, "but if you get an earthquake shock you are mighty likely to have a second one right on the top of it. I think we'd be wise to stretch our legs and have a breath of air while we have the chance. Since our oxygen is exhausted we may just as well be caught outside as in."

It was strange the absolute lethargy which had come upon us as a reaction after our tremendous emotions of the last twenty-four hours. It was both mental and physical, a deep-lying feeling that nothing mattered and that everything was a weariness and a profitless exertion. Even Challenger had succumbed to it, and sat in his chair, with his great head leaning upon his hands and his thoughts far away, until Lord John and I, catching him by each arm, fairly lifted him on to his feet, receiving only the glare and growl of an angry mastiff for our trouble. However, once we had got out of our narrow haven of refuge into the wider atmosphere of everyday life, our normal energy came gradually back to us once more.

But what were we to begin to do in that graveyard of a world? Could ever men have been faced with such a question since the dawn of time? It is true that our own physical needs, and even our luxuries, were assured for the future. All the stores of food, all the vintages of wine, all the treasures of art were ours for the taking. But what were we to *do?* Some few tasks appealed to us at once, since they lay ready to our hands. We descended into the kitchen and laid the two domestics upon their respective beds. They seemed to have died without suffering, one in the chair by the fire, the other upon the scullery floor. Then we carried in poor Austin from the yard. His muscles were set as hard as a board in the most exaggerated rigor mortis, while the contraction of the fibers had drawn his mouth into a hard sardonic grin. This symptom was prevalent among all who had died from the poison. Wherever we went we were confronted by those grinning faces, which seemed to mock at our dreadful position, smiling silently and grimly at the ill-fated survivors of their race. "Look here," said Lord John, who had paced restlessly about the dining room whilst we partook of some food, "I don't know how you fellows feel about it, but for my part, I simply *can't* sit here and do nothin'."

"Perhaps," Challenger answered, "you would have the kindness to suggest what you think we ought to do."

"Get a move on us and see all that has happened."

"That is what I should myself propose."

"But not in this little country village. We can see from the window all that this place can teach us."

"Where should we go, then?"

"To London!"

"That's all very well," grumbled Summerlee. "You may be equal to a forty-mile walk, but I'm not so sure about Challenger, with his stumpy legs, and I am perfectly sure about myself."

Challenger was very much annoyed. "If you could see your way, sir, to confining your remarks to your own physical peculiarities, you would find that you had an ample field for comment," he cried.

"I had no intention to offend you, my dear Challenger," cried our tactless friend. "You can't be held responsible for your own physique. If nature has given you a short, heavy body you cannot possibly help having stumpy legs."

Challenger was too furious to answer. He could only growl and blink and bristle.

Lord John hastened to intervene before the dispute became more violent. "You talk of walking. Why should we walk?" said he.

"Do you suggest taking a train?" asked Challenger, still simmering.

"What's the matter with the motor car? Why should we not go in that?"

"I am not an expert," said Challenger, pulling at his beard reflectively. "At the same time, you are right in supposing that the human intellect in its higher manifestations should be sufficiently flexible to turn itself to anything. Your idea is an excellent one, Lord John. I myself will drive you all to London."

"You will do nothing of the kind," said Summerlee with decision.

"No, indeed, George!" cried his wife. "You only tried once, and you remember how you crashed through the gate of the garage."

"It was a momentary want of concentration," said Challenger complacently. "You can consider the matter settled. I will certainly drive you all to London."

The situation was relieved by Lord John. "What's the car?" he asked.

"A twenty horsepower Humber."

"Why, I've driven one for years," said he. "By George!" he added. "I never thought I'd live to take the whole human race in one load. There's just room for five, as I remember it. Get your things on, and I'll be ready at the door by ten o'clock."

Sure enough, at the hour named, the car came purring and crackling from the yard with Lord John at the wheel. I took my seat beside him, while the lady, a useful buffer state, was squeezed in between the two men of wrath at the back. Then Lord John released his brakes, slid his lever rapidly from first to third, and we sped off upon the strangest drive that ever human beings have taken since man first came upon the earth.

You are to picture the loveliness of nature upon that August day, the freshness of the morning air, the golden glare of the summer sunshine, the cloudless sky, the luxuriant green of the Sussex woods, and the deep purple of heather-clad downs. As you looked round upon the many-colored beauty of the scene all thought of a vast catastrophe would have passed from your mind had it not been for one sinister sign—the solemn, all-embracing silence. There is a gentle hum of life which pervades a closely settled country, so deep and constant that one ceases to observe it, as the dweller by the sea loses all sense of the constant murmur of the waves. The twitter of birds, the buzz of insects, the far-off echo of voices, the lowing of cattle, the distant barking of dogs, roar of trains, and rattle of carts—all these form one low, unremitting note, striking unheeded upon the ear. We missed it now. This deadly silence was appalling. So solemn was it, so impressive, that the buzz and rattle of our motor car seemed an unwarrantable intrusion, an indecent disregard of this reverent stillness which lay like a pall over and round the ruins of humanity. It was this grim hush, and the tall clouds of smoke which rose here and there over the countryside from smoldering buildings, which cast a chill into our hearts as we gazed round at the glorious panorama of the Weald.

And then there were the dead! At first those endless groups of drawn and grinning faces filled us with a shuddering horror. So vivid and mordant was the impression that I can live over again that slow descent of the station hill, the passing by the nursegirl with the two babes, the sight of the old horse on his knees between the shafts, the cabman twisted across his seat, and the young man inside with his hand upon the open door in the very act of springing out. Lower down were six reapers all in a litter, their limbs crossing, their dead, unwinking eyes gazing upwards at the glare of heaven. These things I see as in a photograph. But soon, by the merciful provision of nature, the overexcited nerve ceased to respond. The very vastness of the horror took away from its personal appeal. Individuals merged into groups, groups into crowds, crowds into a universal phenomenon which one soon accepted as the inevitable detail of every scene. Only here and there, where some particularly brutal or grotesque incident caught the attention, did the mind come back with a sudden shock to the personal and human meaning of it all.

Above all, there was the fate of the children. That, I remember, filled us with the strongest sense of intolerable injustice. We could have wept—Mrs. Challenger did weep—when we passed a great council school and saw the long trail of tiny figures scattered down the road which led from it. They had been dismissed by their terrified teachers and were speeding for their homes when the poison caught them in its net. Great numbers of people were at the open windows of the houses. In Tunbridge Wells there was hardly one which had not its staring, smiling face. At the last instant the need of air, that very craving for oxygen which we alone had been able to satisfy, had sent them flying to the window. The sidewalks too were littered with men and women, hatless and bonnetless, who had rushed out of the houses. Many of them had fallen in the roadway. It was a lucky thing that in Lord John we had found an expert driver, for it was no easy matter to pick one's way. Passing through the villages or towns we could only go at a walking pace, and once, I remember, opposite the school at Tonbridge, we had to halt some time while we carried aside the bodies which blocked our path.

A few small, definite pictures stand out in my memory from amid that long panorama of death upon the Sussex and Kentish high roads. One was that of a great, glittering motorcar standing outside the inn at the village of Southborough. It bore, as I should guess, some pleasure party upon their return from Brighton or from Eastbourne. There were three gaily dressed women, all young and beautiful, one of them with a Peking spaniel upon her lap. With them were a rakish-looking elderly man and a young aristocrat, his eyeglass still in his eye, his cigarette burned down to the stub between the fingers of his begloved hand. Death must have come on them in an instant and fixed them as they sat. Save that the elderly man had at the last moment torn out his collar in an effort to breathe, they might all have been asleep. On one side of the car a waiter with some broken glasses beside a tray was huddled near the step. On the other, two very ragged tramps, a man and a woman, lay where they had fallen, the man with his long, thin arm still outstretched, even as he had asked for alms in his lifetime. One instant of time had put aristocrat, waiter, tramp, and dog upon one common footing of inert and dissolving protoplasm.

I remember another singular picture, some miles on the London side of Sevenoaks. There is a large convent upon the left, with a long, green slope in front of it. Upon this slope were assembled a great number of school children, all kneeling at prayer. In front of them was a fringe of nuns, and higher up the slope, facing towards them, a single figure whom we took to be the mother superior. Unlike the pleasure seekers in the motor car, these people seemed to have had warning of their danger and to have died beautifully together, the teachers and the taught, assembled for their last common lesson.

My mind is still stunned by that terrific experience, and I grope vainly for means of expression by which I can reproduce the emotions which we felt. Perhaps it is best and wisest not to try, but merely to indicate the facts. Even Summerlee and Challenger were crushed, and we heard nothing of our companions behind us save an occasional whimper from the lady. As to Lord John, he was too intent upon his wheel and the difficult task of threading his way along such roads to have time or inclination for conversation. One phrase he used with such wearisome iteration that it stuck in my memory and at last almost made me laugh as a comment upon the day of doom: "Pretty doin's! What!"

That was his ejaculation as each fresh tremendous combination of death and disaster displayed itself before us. "Pretty doin's! What!" he cried, as we descended the station hill at Rotherfield, and it was still "Pretty doin's! What!" as we picked our way through a wilderness of death in the High Street of Lewisham and the Old Kent Road.

It was here that we received a sudden and amazing shock. Out of the window of a humble corner house there appeared a fluttering handkerchief waving at the end of a long, thin human arm. Never had the sight of unexpected death caused our hearts to stop and then throb so wildly as did this amazing indication of life. Lord John ran the motor to the curb, and in an instant we had rushed through the open door of the house and up the staircase to the second-floor front room from which the signal proceeded.

A very old lady sat in a chair by the open window, and close to her, laid across a second chair, was a cylinder of oxygen, smaller but of the same shape as those which had saved our own lives. She turned her thin, drawn, bespectacled face toward us as we crowded in at the doorway. "I feared that I was abandoned here forever," said she, "for I am an invalid and cannot stir."

"Well, madam," Challenger answered, "it is a lucky chance that we happened to pass."

"I have one all-important question to ask you," said she. "Gentlemen, I beg that you will be frank with me. What effect will these events have upon London and North-Western Railway shares?"

We should have laughed had it not been for the tragic eagerness with which she listened for our answer. Mrs. Burston, for that was her name, was an aged widow, whose whole income depended upon a small holding of this stock. Her life had been regulated by the rise and fall of the dividend, and she could form no conception of existence save as it was affected by the quotation of her shares. In vain we pointed out to her that all the money in the world was hers for the taking and was useless when taken. Her old mind would not adapt itself to the new idea, and she wept loudly over her vanished stock. "It was all I had," she wailed. "If that is gone I may as well go too."

Amid her lamentations we found out how this frail old plant had lived where the whole great forest had fallen. She was a confirmed invalid and an asthmatic. Oxygen had been prescribed for her malady, and a tube was in her room at the moment of the crisis. She had naturally inhaled some as had been her habit when there was a difficulty with her breathing. It had given her relief, and by doling out her supply she had managed to survive the night. Finally she had fallen asleep and been awakened by the buzz of our motorcar. As it was impossible to take her on with us, we saw that she had all necessaries of life and promised to communicate with her in a couple of days at the latest. So we left her, still weeping bitterly over her vanished stock.

As we approached the Thames the block in the streets became thicker and the obstacles more bewildering. It was with difficulty that we made our way across London Bridge. The approaches to it upon the Middlesex side were choked from end to end with frozen traffic which made all further advance in that direction impossible. A ship was blazing brightly alongside one of the wharves near the bridge, and the air was full of drifting smuts and of a heavy acrid smell of burning. There was a cloud of dense smoke somewhere near the Houses of Parliament, but it was impossible from where we were to see what was on fire.

"I don't know how it strikes you," Lord John remarked as he brought his engine to a standstill, "but it seems to me the country is more cheerful

than the town. Dead London is gettin' on my nerves. I'm for a cast round
and then gettin' back to Rotherfield."

"I confess that I do not see what we can hope for here," said Professor Summerlee.

"At the same time," said Challenger, his great voice booming
strangely amid the silence, "it is difficult for us to conceive that out of
seven millions of people there is only this one old woman who by some
peculiarity of constitution or some accident of occupation has managed
to survive this catastrophe."

"If there should be others, how can we hope to find them, George?"
asked the lady. "And yet I agree with you that we cannot go back until
we have tried."

Getting out of the car and leaving it by the curb, we walked with
some difficulty along the crowded pavement of King William Street
and entered the open door of a large insurance office. It was a corner
house, and we chose it as commanding a view in every direction. Ascending the stair, we passed through what I suppose to have been the
board room, for eight elderly men were seated round a long table in
the center of it. The high window was open and we all stepped out
upon the balcony. From it we could see the crowded city streets radiating in every direction, while below us the road was black from side
to side with the tops of the motionless taxis. All, or nearly all, had
their heads pointed outwards, showing how the terrified men of the
city had at the last moment made a vain endeavor to rejoin their families in the suburbs or the country. Here and there amid the humbler
cabs towered the great brass-spangled motorcar of some wealthy mag-
nate, wedged hopelessly among the dammed stream of arrested traffic. Just beneath us there was such a one of great size and luxurious
appearance, with its owner, a fat old man, leaning out, half his gross
body through the window, and his podgy hand, gleaming with diamonds, outstretched as he urged his chauffeur to make a last effort to
break through the press.

A dozen motorbuses towered up like islands in this flood, the passengers who crowded the roofs lying all huddled together and across each
others' laps like a child's toys in a nursery. On a broad lamp pedestal in
the center of the roadway, a burly policeman was standing, leaning his

back against the post in so natural an attitude that it was hard to realize that he was not alive, while at his feet there lay a ragged newsboy with his bundle of papers on the ground beside him. A paper cart had got blocked in the crowd, and we could read in large letters, black upon yellow, "Scene at Lord's. County Match Interrupted." This must have been the earliest edition, for there were other placards bearing the legend, "Is It the End? Great Scientist's Warning." And another, "Is Challenger Justified? Ominous Rumors."

Challenger pointed the latter placard out to his wife, as it thrust itself like a banner above the throng. I could see him throw out his chest and stroke his beard as he looked at it. It pleased and flattered that complex mind to think that London had died with his name and his words still present in their thoughts. His feelings were so evident that they aroused the sardonic comment of his colleague.

"In the limelight to the last, Challenger," he remarked.

"So it would appear," he answered complacently. "Well," he added as he looked down the long vista of the radiating streets, all silent and all choked up with death, "I really see no purpose to be served by our staying any longer in London. I suggest that we return at once to Rotherfield and then take counsel as to how we shall most profitably employ the years which lie before us."

Only one other picture shall I give of the scenes which we carried back in our memories from the dead city. It is a glimpse which we had of the interior of the old church of St. Mary's, which is at the very point where our car was awaiting us. Picking our way among the prostrate figures upon the steps, we pushed open the swing door and entered. It was a wonderful sight. The church was crammed from end to end with kneeling figures in every posture of supplication and abasement. At the last dreadful moment, brought suddenly face to face with the realities of life, those terrific realities which hang over us even while we follow the shadows, the terrified people had rushed into those old city churches which for generations had hardly ever held a congregation. There they huddled as close as they could kneel, many of them in their agitation still wearing their hats, while above them in the pulpit a young man in lay dress had apparently been addressing them when he and they had been overwhelmed by the same fate. He lay now, like Punch in his booth, with his head and two limp arms hanging over the ledge of the pulpit. It was a nightmare, the gray, dusty church, the rows of agonized figures, the dimness and silence of it all. We moved about with hushed whispers, walking upon our tiptoes.

And then suddenly I had an idea At one corner of the church near the door, stood the ancient font, and behind it a deep recess in which there hung the ropes for the bell-ringers. Why should we not send a message out over London which would attract to us anyone who might still be alive? I ran across, and pulling at the list-covered rope, I was surprised to find how difficult it was to swing the bell.

Lord John had followed me. "By George, young fella!" said he, pulling off his coat. "You've hit on a dooced good notion. Give me a grip and we'll soon have a move on it."

But, even then, so heavy was the bell that it was not until Challenger and Summerlee had added their weight to ours that we heard the roaring and clanging above our heads which told us that the great clapper was ringing out its music. Far over dead London resounded our message of comradeship and hope to any fellow man surviving. It cheered our own hearts, that strong, metallic call, and we turned the more earnestly to our work, dragged two feet off the earth with each upward jerk of the rope, but all straining together on the downward heave, Challenger the lowest of all, bending all his great strength to the task and flopping up and down like a monstrous bull frog, croaking with every pull. It was at that moment that an artist might have taken a picture of the four adventurers, the comrades of many strange perils in the past, whom fate had now chosen for so supreme an experience. For half an hour we worked, the sweat dropping from our faces, our arms and backs aching with the exertion. Then we went out into the portico of the church and looked eagerly up and down the silent, crowded streets. Not a sound, not a motion, in answer to our summons.

"It's no use. No one is left," I cried.

"We can do nothing more," said Mrs. Challenger. "For God's sake, George, let us get back to Rotherfield. Another hour of this dreadful, silent city would drive me mad."

We got into the car without another word. Lord John backed her round and turned her to the south. To us the chapter seemed closed. Little did we foresee the strange new chapter which was to open.

SIX
THE GREAT AWAKENING

And now I come to the end of this extraordinary incident, so overshadowing in its importance, not only in our own small, individual lives, but in the general history of the human race. As I said when I began my narrative, when that history comes to be written, this occurrence will surely stand out among all other events like a mountain towering among its foothills. Our generation has been reserved for a very special fate since it has been chosen to experience so wonderful a thing. How long its effect may last—how long mankind may preserve the humility and reverence which this great shock has taught it—can only be shown by the future. I think it is safe to say that things can never be quite the same again. Never can one realize how powerless and ignorant one is, and how one is upheld by an unseen hand, until for an instant that hand has seemed to close and to crush. Death has been imminent upon us. We know that at any moment it may be again. That grim presence shadows our lives, but who can deny that in that shadow the sense of duty, the feeling of sobriety and responsibility, the appreciation of the gravity and of the objects of life, the earnest desire to develop and improve, have grown and become real with us to a degree that has leavened our whole society from end to end? It is something beyond sects and beyond dogmas. It is rather an alteration of perspective, a shifting of our sense of proportion, a vivid realization that we are insignificant and evanescent creatures, existing on sufferance and at the mercy of the first chill wind from the unknown. But if the world has grown graver with this knowledge it is not, I think, a sadder place in consequence. Surely we are agreed that the more sober and restrained pleasures of the present are deeper as well as wiser than the noisy, foolish hustle which passed so often for enjoyment in the days of old—days so recent and yet already so inconceivable. Those empty lives which were wasted in aimless visiting and being visited, in the worry of great and unnecessary households, in the arranging and eating of elaborate and tedious meals, have now found rest and health in the reading, the music, the gentle family communion which comes from a simpler and saner division of their time. With greater health and greater pleasure they are richer than before, even after they have paid those increased contributions to the common fund which have so raised the standard of life in these islands.

There is some clash of opinion as to the exact hour of the great awakening. It is generally agreed that, apart from the difference of clocks, there may have been local causes which influenced the action of the poison. Certainly, in each separate district the resurrection was practically simultaneous. There are numerous witnesses that Big Ben pointed to ten minutes past six at the moment. The Astronomer Royal has fixed the Greenwich time at twelve past six. On the other hand, Laird Johnson, a very capable East Anglia observer, has recorded six-twenty as the hour. In the Hebrides it was as late as seven. In our own case there can be no doubt whatever, for I was seated in Challenger's study with his carefully tested chronometer in front of me at the moment. The hour was a quarter-past six.

An enormous depression was weighing upon my spirits. The cumulative effect of all the dreadful sights which we had seen upon our journey was heavy upon my soul. With my abounding animal health and great physical energy any kind of mental clouding was a rare event. I had the Irish faculty of seeing some gleam of humor in every darkness. But now the obscurity was appalling and unrelieved. The others were downstairs making their plans for the future. I sat by the open window, my chin resting upon my hand and my mind absorbed in the misery of our situation. Could we continue to live? That was the question which I had begun to ask myself. Was it possible to exist upon a dead world? Just as in physics the greater body draws to itself the lesser, would we not feel an overpowering attraction from that vast body of humanity which had passed into the unknown? How would the end come? Would it be from a return of the poison? Or would the earth be uninhabitable from the mephitic products of universal decay? Or, finally, might our awful situation prey upon and unbalance our minds? A group of insane folk upon a dead world! My mind was brooding upon this last dreadful idea when some slight noise caused me to look down upon the road beneath me. The old cab horse was coming up the hill!

I was conscious at the same instant of the twittering of birds, of someone coughing in the yard below, and of a background of movement in the landscape. And yet I remember that it was that absurd, emaciated, superannuated cab horse which held my gaze. Slowly and wheezily it was climbing the slope. Then my eye traveled to the driver sitting hunched up upon the box and finally to the young man who was leaning out of the window in some excitement and shouting a direction. They were all indubitably, aggressively alive!

Everybody was alive once more! Had it all been a delusion? Was it conceivable that this whole poison belt incident had been an elaborate dream? For an instant my startled brain was really ready to believe it. Then I looked down, and there was the rising blister on my hand where it was frayed by the rope of the city bell. It had really been so, then. And yet here was the world resuscitated—here was life come back in an instant full tide to the planet. Now, as my eyes wandered all over the great landscape, I saw it in every direction—and moving, to my amazement, in the same groove in which it had halted. There were the golfers. Was it possible that they were going on with their game? Yes, there was a fellow driving off from a tee, and that other group upon the green were surely putting for the hole. The reapers were slowly trooping back to their work. The nursegirl slapped one of her charges and then began to push the perambulator up the hill. Everyone had unconcernedly taken up the thread at the very point where they had dropped it.

I rushed downstairs, but the hall door was open, and I heard the voices of my companions, loud in astonishment and congratulation, in the yard. How we all shook hands and laughed as we came together, and how Mrs. Challenger kissed us all in her emotion, before she finally threw herself into the bear hug of her husband.

"But they could not have been asleep!" cried Lord John. "Dash it all, Challenger, you don't mean to believe that those folk were asleep with their staring eyes and stiff limbs and that awful death grin on their faces!"

"It can only have been the condition that is called catalepsy," said Challenger. "It has been a rare phenomenon in the past and has constantly been mistaken for death. While it endures, the temperature falls, the respiration disappears, the heartbeat is indistinguishable—in fact, it *is* death, save that it is evanescent. Even the most comprehensive mind"—here he closed his eyes and simpered—"could hardly conceive a universal outbreak of it in this fashion."

"You may label it catalepsy," remarked Summerlee, "but, after all, that is only a name, and we know as little of the result as we do of the poison which has caused it. The most we can say is that the vitiated ether has produced a temporary death."

Austin was seated all in a heap on the step of the car. It was his coughing which I had heard from above. He had been holding his head in silence, but now he was muttering to himself and running his eyes over the car. "Young fathead!" he grumbled. "Can't leave things alone!"

"What's the matter, Austin?"

"Lubricators left running, sir. Someone has been fooling with the car. I expect it's that young garden boy, sir."

Lord John looked guilty.

"I don't know what's amiss with me," continued Austin, staggering to his feet. "I expect I came over queer when I was hosing her down. I seem to remember flopping over by the step. But I'll swear I never left those lubricator taps on."

In a condensed narrative the astonished Austin was told what had happened to himself and the world. The mystery of the dripping lubricators was also explained to him. He listened with an air of deep distrust when told how an amateur had driven his car and with absorbed interest to the few sentences in which our experiences of the sleeping city were recorded. I can remember his comment when the story was concluded. "Was you outside the Bank of England, sir?"

"Yes, Austin."

"With all them millions inside and everybody asleep?"

"That was so."

"And I not there!" he groaned, and turned dismally once more to the hosing of his car.

There was a sudden grinding of wheels upon gravel. The old cab had actually pulled up at Challenger's door. I saw the young occupant step out from it. An instant later the maid, who looked as tousled and bewildered as if she had that instant been aroused from the deepest sleep, appeared with a card upon a tray. Challenger snorted ferociously as he looked at it, and his thick black hair seemed to bristle up in his wrath. "A pressman!" he growled. Then with a deprecating smile: "After all, it is natural that the whole world should hasten to know what I think of such an episode."

"That can hardly be his errand," said Summerlee, "for he was on the road in his cab before ever the crisis came."

I looked at the card: "James Baxter, London Correspondent, *New York Monitor*."

"You'll see him?" said I.

"Not I."

"Oh, George! You should be kinder and more considerate to others. Surely you have learned something from what we have undergone."

He tut-tutted and shook his big, obstinate head. "A poisonous breed! Eh, Malone? The worst breed in modern civilization, the ready tool of the quack and the hindrance of the self-respecting man! When did they ever say a good word for me?"

"When did you ever say a good word to them?" I answered. "Come, sir, this is a stranger who has made a journey to see you. I am sure that you won't be rude to him."

"Well, well," he grumbled, "you come with me and do the talking. I protest in advance against any such outrageous invasion of my private life." Muttering and mumbling, he came rolling after me like an angry and rather ill-conditioned mastiff.

The dapper young American pulled out his notebook and plunged instantly into his subject. "I came down, sir," said he, "because our people in America would very much like to hear more about this danger which is, in your opinion, pressing upon the world."

"I know of no danger which is now pressing upon the world," Challenger answered gruffly.

The pressman looked at him in mild surprise. "I meant, sir, the chances that the world might run into a belt of poisonous ether."

"I do not now apprehend any such danger," said Challenger.

The pressman looked even more perplexed. "You are Professor Challenger, are you not?" he asked.

"Yes, sir, that is my name."

"I cannot understand, then, how you can say that there is no such danger. I am alluding to your own letter, published above your name in the London *Times* of this morning."

It was Challenger's turn to look surprised. "This morning?" said he. "No London *Times* was published this morning."

"Surely, sir," said the American in mild remonstrance, "you must admit that the London *Times* is a daily paper." He drew out a copy from his inside pocket. "Here is the letter to which I refer."

Challenger chuckled and rubbed his hands. "I begin to understand," said he. "So you read this letter this morning?"

"Yes, sir."

"And came at once to interview me?"

"Yes, sir."

"Did you observe anything unusual upon the journey down?"

"Well, to tell the truth, your people seemed more lively and generally human than I have ever seen them. The baggage man set out to tell me a funny story, and that's a new experience for me in this country."

"Nothing else?"

"Why, no, sir, not that I can recall."

"Well, now, what hour did you leave Victoria?"

The American smiled. "I came here to interview you, Professor, but it seems to be a case of 'Is this nigger fishing, or is this fish niggering?' You're doing most of the work."

"It happens to interest me. Do you recall the hour?"

"Sure. It was half-past twelve."

"And you arrived?"

"At a quarter-past two."

"And you hired a cab?"

"That was so."

"How far do you suppose it is to the station?"

"Well, I should reckon the best part of two miles."

"So how long do you think it took you?"

"Well, half an hour, maybe, with that asthmatic in front."

"So it should be three o'clock?"

"Yes, or a trifle after it."

"Look at your watch."

The American did so and then stared at us in astonishment. "Say!" he cried. "It's run down. That horse has broken every record, sure. The sun is pretty low, now that I come to look at it. Well, there's something here I don't understand."

"Have you no remembrance of anything remarkable as you came up the hill?"

"Well, I seem to recollect that I was mighty sleepy once. It comes back to me that I wanted to say something to the driver and that I couldn't make him heed me. I guess it was the heat, but I felt swimmy for a moment. That's all."

"So it is with the whole human race," said Challenger to me. "They have all felt swimmy for a moment. None of them has as yet any comprehension of what has occurred. Each will go on with his interrupted job as Austin has snatched up his hose pipe or the golfer continued his game. Your editor, Malone, will continue the issue of his papers, and very much amazed he will be at finding that an issue is missing. Yes, my young friend," he added to the American reporter, with a sudden mood of amused geniality, "it may interest you to know that the world has swum through the poisonous current which swirls like the Gulf Stream through the ocean of ether. You will also kindly note for your own future convenience that today is not Friday, August the twenty-seventh, but Saturday, August the twenty-eighth, and that you sat senseless in your cab for twenty-eight hours upon the Rotherfield hill."

And "right here," as my American colleague would say, I may bring this narrative to an end. It is, as you are probably aware, only a fuller and more detailed version of the account which appeared in the Monday edition of the *Daily Gazette*—an account which has been universally admitted to be the greatest journalistic scoop of all time, which sold no fewer than three and a half million copies of the paper. Framed upon the wall of my sanctum I retain those magnificent headlines:

TWENTY-EIGHT HOURS' WORLD COMA
UNPRECEDENTED EXPERIENCE
CHALLENGER JUSTIFIED
OUR CORRESPONDENT ESCAPES
ENTHRALLING NARRATIVE
THE OXYGEN ROOM
WEIRD MOTOR DRIVE
DEAD LONDON
REPLACING THE MISSING PAGE
GREAT FIRES AND LOSS OF LIFE
WILL IT RECUR?

Underneath this glorious scroll came nine and a half columns of narrative, in which appeared the first, last, and only account of the history of the planet, so far as one observer could draw it, during one long day of its existence. Challenger and Summerlee have treated the matter in a joint scientific paper, but to me alone was left the popular account. Surely I can sing "Nunc dimittis." What is left but anticlimax in the life of a journalist after that!

But let me not end on sensational headlines and a merely personal triumph. Rather let me quote the sonorous passages in which the greatest of daily papers ended its admirable leader upon the subject—a leader which might well be filed for reference by every thoughtful man.

"It has been a well-worn truism," said *The Times*, "that our human race are a feeble folk before the infinite latent forces which surround us. From the prophets of old and from the philosophers of our own time the same message and warning have reached us. But, like all oft-repeated truths, it has in time lost something of its actuality and cogency. A lesson, an actual experience, was needed to bring it home. It is from that salutary but terrible ordeal that we have just emerged, with minds which are still stunned by the suddenness of the blow and with spirits which are chastened by the realization of our own limitations and impotence. The world has paid a fearful price for its schooling.

Hardly yet have we learned the full rate of disaster, but the destruction by fire of New York, of Orleans, and of Brighton constitutes in itself one of the greatest tragedies in the history of our race. When the account of the railway and shipping accidents has been completed, it will furnish grim reading, although there is evidence to show that in the vast majority of cases the drivers of trains and engineers of steamers succeeded in shutting off their motive power before succumbing to the poison. But the material damage, enormous as it is both in life and in property, is not the consideration which will be uppermost in our minds today. All this may in time be forgotten. But what will not be forgotten, and what will and should continue to obsess our imaginations, is this revelation of the possibilities of the universe, this destruction of our ignorant self-complacency, and this demonstration of how narrow is the path of our material existence and what abysses may 'lie upon either side of it. Solemnity and humility are at the base of our emotions today. May they be the foundations upon which a more earnest and reverent race may build a more worthy temple."

16

"Danger!"
(1914)

Being the Log of Captain John Sirius

It is an amazing thing that the English, who have the reputation of being a practical nation, never saw the danger to which they were exposed. For many years they had been spending nearly a hundred millions a year upon their army and their fleet. Squadrons of Dreadnoughts costing two millions each had been launched. They had spent enormous sums upon cruisers, and both their torpedo and their submarine squadrons were exceptionally strong. They were also by no means weak in their aerial power, especially in the matter of hydroplanes. Besides all this, their army was very efficient, in spite of its limited numbers, and it was the most expensive in Europe. Yet when the day of trial came, all this imposing force was of no use whatever, and might as well have not existed. Their ruin could not have been more complete or more rapid if they had not possessed an ironclad or a regiment. And all this was accomplished by me, Captain John Sirius, belonging to the navy of one of the smallest Powers in Europe, and having under my command a flotilla of eight vessels, the collective cost of which was eighteen hundred thousand pounds. No one has a better right to tell the story than I.

I will not trouble you about the dispute concerning the Colonial frontier, embittered, as it was, by the subsequent death of the two missionaries. A naval officer has nothing to do with politics. I only came

435

upon the scene after the ultimatum had been actually received. Admiral Horli had been summoned to the Presence, and he asked that I should be allowed to accompany him, because he happened to know that I had some clear ideas as to the weak points of England, and also some schemes as to how to take advantage of them. There were only four of us present at this meeting—the King, the Foreign Secretary, Admiral Horli, and myself. The time allowed by the ultimatum expired in forty-eight hours.

I am not breaking any confidence when I say that both the King and the Minister were in favour of a surrender. They saw no possibility of standing up against the colossal power of Great Britain. The Minister had drawn up an acceptance of the British terms, and the King sat with it before him on the table. I saw the tears of anger and humiliation run down his cheeks as he looked at it.

"I fear that there is no possible alternative, Sire," said the Minister. "Our envoy in London has just sent this report, which shows that the public and the Press are more united than he has ever known them. The feeling is intense, especially since the rash act of Malort in desecrating the flag. We must give way."

The King looked sadly at Admiral Horli.

"What is your effective fleet, Admiral?" he asked.

"Two battleships, four cruisers, twenty torpedo-boats, and eight submarines," said the Admiral.

The King shook his head.

"It would be madness to resist," said he.

"And yet, Sire," said the Admiral, "before you come to a decision I should wish you to hear Captain Sirius, who has a very definite plan of campaign against the English."

"Absurd!" said the King, impatiently. "What is the use? Do you imagine that you could defeat their vast armada?"

"Sire," I answered, "I will stake my life that if you will follow my advice you will, within a month or six weeks at the utmost, bring proud England to her knees."

There was an assurance in my voice which arrested the attention of the King.

"You seem self-confident, Captain Sirius."

"I have no doubt at all, Sire."

"What then would you advise?"

"I would advise, Sire, that the whole fleet be gathered under the forts of Blankenberg and be protected from attack by booms and piles. There they can stay till the war is over. The eight submarines, however, you will leave in my charge to use as I think fit."

"Ah, you would attack the English battleships with submarines?"

"Sire, I would never go near an English battleship."

"And why not?"

"Because they might injure me, Sire."

"What, a sailor and afraid?"

"My life belongs to the country, Sire. It is nothing. But these eight ships—everything depends upon them. I could not risk them. Nothing would induce me to fight."

"Then what will you do?"

"I will tell you, Sire." And I did so. For half an hour I spoke. I was clear and strong and definite, for many an hour on a lonely watch I had spent in thinking out every detail. I held them enthralled. The King never took his eyes from my face. The Minister sat as if turned to stone.

"Are you sure of all this?"

"Perfectly, Sire."

The King rose from the table.

"Send no answer to the ultimatum," said he. "Announce in both houses that we stand firm in the face of menace. Admiral Horli, you will in all respects carry out that which Captain Sirius may demand in furtherance of his plan. Captain Sirius, the field is clear. Go forth and do as you have said. A grateful King will know how to reward you."

I need not trouble you by telling you the measures which were taken at Blankenberg, since, as you are aware, the fortress and the entire fleet were destroyed by the British within a week of the declaration of war. I will confine myself to my own plans, which had so glorious and final a result.

The fame of my eight submarines, *Alpha, Beta, Gamma, Theta, Delta, Epsilon, Iota,* and *Kappa*, have spread through the world to such an extent that people have begun to think that there was something peculiar in their form and capabilities. This is not so. Four of them, the *Delta, Epsilon, Iota,* and *Kappa*, were, it is true, of the very latest model, but had their equals (though not their superiors) in the navies of all the great Powers. As to *Alpha, Beta, Gamma*, and *Theta*, they were by no means modern vessels, and found their prototypes in the old F class of British boats, having a submerged displacement of eight hundred tons, with heavy oil engines of sixteen hundred horse-power, giving them a speed of eighteen knots on the surface and of twelve knots submerged. Their length was one hundred and eighty-six and their breadth twenty-four feet. They had a radius of action of four thousand miles and a submerged endurance of nine hours. These were considered the latest word in 1915, but the four new boats exceeded them in all respects. Without troubling you with precise figures, I may say that they represented roughly a twenty-five per cent advance upon the older boats, and were fitted with several auxiliary engines which were wanting in the others. At my suggestion, instead of carrying eight of the very large Bakdorf torpedoes, which are nineteen feet long, weigh half a ton, and are charged with two hundred pounds of wet gun-cotton, we had tubes designed for eighteen of less than half the size. It was my design to make myself independent of my base.

And yet it was clear that I must have a base, so I made arrangements at once with that object. Blankenberg was the last place I would have chosen. Why should I have a port of any kind? Ports would be watched or occupied. Any place would do for me. I finally chose a small villa standing alone nearly five miles from any village and thirty miles from any port. To this I ordered them to convey, secretly by night, oil, spare parts, extra torpedoes, storage batteries, reserve periscopes, and everything that I could need for refitting. The little whitewashed villa of a retired confectioner—that was the base from which I operated against England.

The boats lay at Blankenberg, and thither I went. They were working frantically at the defences, and they had only to look seawards to be spurred to fresh exertions. The British fleet was assembling. The ultimatum had not yet expired, but it was evident that a blow would be struck the instant that it did. Four of their aeroplanes, circling at an immense height, were surveying our defences. From the top of the lighthouse I counted thirty battleships and cruisers in the offing, with a number of the trawlers with which in the British service they break through the minefields. The approaches were actually sown with two hundred mines, half contact and half observation, but the result showed that they were insufficient to hold off the enemy, since three days later both town and fleet were speedily destroyed.

However, I am not here to tell you the incidents of the war, but to explain my own part in it, which had such a decisive effect upon the result. My first action was to send my four second-class boats away instantly to the point which I had chosen for my base. There they were to wait submerged, lying with negative buoyancy upon the sands in twenty foot of water, and rising only at night. My strict orders were that they were to attempt nothing upon the enemy, however tempting the opportunity. All they had to do was to remain intact and unseen, until they received further orders. Having made this clear to Commander Panza, who had charge of this reserve flotilla, I shook him by the hand and bade him farewell, leaving with him a sheet of notepaper upon which I had explained the tactics to be used and given him certain general principles which he could apply as circumstances demanded.

My whole attention was now given to my own flotilla, which I divided into two divisions, keeping *Iota* and *Kappa* under my own command, while Captain Miriam had *Delta* and *Epsilon*. He was to operate separately in the British Channel, while my station was the Straits of Dover. I made the whole plan of campaign clear to him. Then I saw that each ship was provided with all it could carry. Each had forty tons of heavy oil for surface propulsion and charging the dynamo which supplied the electric engines under water. Each had also eighteen torpedoes as explained and five hundred rounds for the collapsible quick-firing twelve-pounder which we carried on deck, and which, of course, disappeared into a water-tight tank when we were submerged. We carried spare periscopes and a wireless mast, which could be elevated above the conning-tower when necessary. There were provisions for sixteen days for the ten men who manned each craft. Such was the equipment of the four boats which were destined to bring to naught all the navies and armies of Britain. At sundown that day—it was April 10th—we set forth upon our historic voyage.

Miriam had got away in the afternoon, since he had so much farther to go to reach his station. Stephan, of the *Kappa*, started with me; but, of course, we realised that we must work independently, and that from that moment when we shut the sliding hatches of our conning-towers on the still waters of Blankenberg Harbour it was unlikely that we should ever see each other again, though consorts in the same waters. I waved to Stephan from the side of my conning-tower, and he to me. Then I called through the tube to my engineer (our water-tanks were already filled and all kingstons and vents closed) to put her full speed ahead.

Just as we came abreast of the end of the pier and saw the white-capped waves rolling in upon us, I put the horizontal rudder hard down and she slid under water. Through my glass portholes I saw its light green change to a dark blue, while the manometer in front of me indicated twenty feet. I let her go to forty, because I should then be under the warships of the English, though I took the chance of fouling the moorings of our own floating contact mines. Then I brought her on an even keel, and it was music to my ear to hear the gentle, even ticking of my electric engines and to know that I was speeding at twelve miles an hour on my great task.

At that moment, as I stood controlling my levers in my tower, I could have seen, had my cupola been of glass, the vast shadows of the British blockaders hovering above me. I held my course due westward for ninety minutes, and then, by shutting off the electric engine without blowing out the water-tanks, I brought her to the surface. There was a rolling sea and the wind was freshening, so I did not think it safe to keep my hatch open long, for so small is the margin of buoyancy that one must run no risks. But from the crests of the rollers I had a look back-wards at Blankenberg, and saw the black funnels and upper works of the enemy's fleet with the lighthouse and the castle behind them, all flushed with the pink glow of the setting sun. Even as I looked there was the boom of a great gun, and then another. I glanced at my watch. It was six o'clock. The time of the ultimatum had expired. We were at war.

There was no craft near us, and our surface speed is nearly twice that of our submerged, so I blew out the tanks and our whale-back came over the surface. All night we were steering south-west, making an average of eighteen knots. At about five in the morning, as I stood alone upon my tiny bridge, I saw, low down in the west, the scattered lights of the Nor-folk coast. "Ah, Johnny, Johnny Bull," I said, as I looked at them, "you are going to have your lesson, and I am to be your master. It is I who have been chosen to teach you that one cannot live under artificial conditions and yet act as if they were natural ones. More foresight, Johnny, and less party politics—that is my lesson to you." And then I had a wave of pity, too, when I thought of those vast droves of helpless people, Yorkshire miners, Lancashire spinners, Birmingham metal-workers, the dockers and workers of London, over whose little homes I would bring the shadow of starvation. I seemed to see all those wasted eager hands held out for food, and I, John Sirius, dashing it aside. Ah, well! war is war, and if one is foolish one must pay the price.

Just before daybreak I saw the lights of a considerable town, which must have been Yarmouth, bearing about ten miles west-south-west on our starboard bow. I took her farther out, for it is a sandy, dangerous coast, with many shoals. At five-thirty we were abreast of the Lowestoft lightship. A coastguard was sending up flash signals which faded into a pale twinkle as the white dawn crept over the water. There was a good deal of shipping about, mostly fishing-boats and small coasting craft, with one large steamer hull-down to the west, and a torpedo destroyer between us and the land. It could not harm us, and yet I thought it as well that there should be no word of our presence, so I filled my tanks again and went down to ten feet. I was pleased to find that we got under in one hundred and fifty seconds. The life of one's boat may depend on this when a swift craft comes suddenly upon you.

We were now within a few hours of our cruising ground, so I determined to snatch a rest, leaving Vornal in charge. When he woke me at ten o'clock we were running on the surface, and had reached the Essex coast off the Maplin Sands. With that charming frankness which is one of their characteristics, our friends of England had informed us by their Press that they had put a cordon of torpedo-boats across the Straits of Dover to prevent the passage of submarines, which is about as sensible as to lay a wooden plank across a stream to keep the eels from passing. I knew that Stephan, whose station lay at the western end of the Solent, would have no difficulty in reaching it. My own cruising ground was to be at the mouth of the Thames, and here I was at the very spot with my tiny *Iota*, my eighteen torpedoes, my quick-firing gun, and, above all, a brain that knew what should be done and how to do it.

When I resumed my place in the conning-tower I saw in the periscope (for we had dived) that a lightship was within a few hundred yards of us upon the port bow. Two men were sitting on her bulwarks, but neither of them cast an eye upon the little rod that clove the water so close to them. It was an ideal day for submarine action, with enough ripple upon the surface to make us difficult to detect, and yet smooth enough to give me a clear view. Each of my three periscopes had an angle of sixty degrees so that between them I commanded a complete semi-circle of the horizon. Two British cruisers were steaming north from the Thames within half a mile of me. I could easily have cut them off and attacked them had I allowed myself to be diverted from my great plan. Farther south a destroyer was passing westwards to Sheerness. A dozen small steamers were moving about. None of these were worthy of my notice. Great countries are not provisioned by small steamers. I kept the engines running at the lowest pace which would hold our position under water, and, moving slowly across the estuary, I waited for what must assuredly come.

I had not long to wait. Shortly after one o'clock I perceived in the periscope a cloud of smoke to the south. Half an hour later a large steamer raised her hull, making for the mouth of the Thames. I ordered Vornal to stand by the starboard torpedo-tube, having the other also loaded in case of a miss. Then I advanced slowly, for though the steamer was going very swiftly we could easily cut her off. Presently I laid the *Iota* in a position near which she must pass, and would very gladly have lain to, but could not for fear of rising to the surface. I therefore steered out in the direction from which she was coming. She was a very large ship, fifteen thousand tons at the least, painted black above and red below, with two cream-coloured funnels. She lay so low in the water that it was clear she had a full cargo. At her bows were a cluster of men, some of them looking, I dare say, for the first time at the mother country. How little could they have guessed the welcome that was awaiting them!

On she came with the great plumes of smoke floating from her funnels, and two white waves foaming from her cut-water. She was within a quarter of a mile. My moment had arrived. I signalled full speed ahead and steered straight for her course. My timing was exact. At a hundred yards I gave the signal, and heard the clank and swish of the discharge.

At the same instant I put the helm hard down and flew off at an angle. There was a terrific lurch, which came from the distant explosion. For a moment we were almost upon our side. Then, after staggering and trembling, the *Iota* came on an even keel. I stopped the engines, brought her to the surface, and opened the conning-tower, while all my excited crew came crowding to the hatch to know what had happened.

The ship lay within two hundred yards of us, and it was easy to see that she had her death-blow. She was already settling down by the stern. There was a sound of shouting and people were running wildly about her decks. Her name was visible, the *Adela*, of London, bound, as we afterwards learned, from New Zealand with frozen mutton. Strange as it may seem to you, the notion of a submarine had never even now occurred to her people, and all were convinced that they had struck a floating mine. The starboard quarter had been blown in by the explosion, and the ship was sinking rapidly. Their discipline was admirable. We saw boat after boat slip down crowded with people as swiftly and quietly as if it were part of their daily drill. And suddenly, as one of the boats lay off waiting for the others, they caught a glimpse for the first time of my conning-tower so close to them. I saw them shouting and pointing, while the men in the other boats got up to have a better look at us. For my part, I cared nothing, for I took it for granted that they already knew that a submarine had destroyed them. One of them clambered back into the sinking ship. I was sure that he was about to send a wireless message as to our presence. It mattered nothing, since, in any case, it must be known; otherwise I could easily have brought him down with a rifle. As it was, I waved my hand to them, and they waved back to me. War is too big a thing to leave room for personal ill-feeling, but it must be remorseless all the same.

I was still looking at the sinking *Adela* when Vornal, who was beside me, gave a sudden cry of warning and surprise, gripping me by the shoulder and turning my head. There behind us, coming up the fairway, was a huge black vessel with black funnels, flying the well-known house-flag of the P. and O. Company. She was not a mile distant, and I calculated in an instant that even if she had seen us she would not have time to turn and get away before we could reach her. We went straight for her, therefore, keeping awash just as we were. They saw the sinking vessel in front of them and that little dark speck moving over the surface, and they suddenly understood their danger. I saw a number of men rush to the bows, and there was a rattle of rifle-fire. Two bullets were flattened upon our four-inch armour. You might as well try to stop a charging bull with paper pellets as the *Iota* with rifle-fire. I had learned my lesson from the *Adela*, and this time I had the torpedo discharged at a safer distance—two hundred and fifty yards. We caught her amidships and the explosion was tremendous, but we were well outside its area. She sank almost instantaneously. I am sorry for her people, of whom I hear that more than two hundred, including seventy Lascars and forty passengers, were drowned. Yes, I am sorry for them. But when I think of the huge floating granary that went to the bottom, I rejoice as a man does who has carried out that which he plans.

It was a bad afternoon that for the P. and O. Company. The second ship which we destroyed was, as we have since learned, the *Moldavia*, of fifteen thousand tons, one of their finest vessels; but about half-past three we blew up the *Cusco*, of eight thousand, of the same line, also from Eastern ports, and laden with corn. Why she came on in face of the wireless messages which must have warned her of danger, I cannot imagine. The other two steamers which we blew up that day, the *Maid of Athens* (Robson Line) and the *Cormorant*, were neither of them provided with apparatus, and came blindly to their destruction. Both were small boats of from five thousand to seven thousand tons. In the case of the second, I had to rise to the surface and fire six twelve-pound shells under her water-line before she would sink. In each case the crew took to the boats, and so far as I know no casualties occurred.

After that no more steamers came along, nor did I expect them. Warnings must by this time have been flying in all directions. But we had no reason to be dissatisfied with our first day. Between the Maplin Sands and the Nore we had sunk five ships of a total tonnage of about fifty thousand tons. Already the London markets would begin to feel the pinch. And Lloyd's—poor old Lloyd's—what a demented state it would be in! I could imagine the London evening papers and the howling in Fleet Street. We saw the result of our actions, for it was quite laughable to see the torpedo-boats buzzing like angry wasps out of Sheerness in the evening. They were darting in every direction across the estuary, and the aeroplanes and hydroplanes were like flights of crows, black dots against the red western sky. They quartered the whole river mouth, until they discovered us at last. Some sharp-sighted fellow with a telescope on board of a destroyer got a sight of our periscope, and came for us full speed. No doubt he would very gladly have rammed us, even if it had meant his own destruction, but that was not part of our programme at all. I sank her and ran her east-southeast with an occasional rise. Finally we brought her to, not very far from the Kentish coast, and the search-lights of our pursuers were far on the western skyline. There we lay quietly all night, for a submarine at night is nothing more than a very third-rate surface torpedo-boat. Besides, we were all weary and needed rest. Do not forget, you captains of men, when you grease and trim your pumps and compressors and rotators, that the human machine needs some tending also.

I had put up the wireless mast above the conning-tower, and had no difficulty in calling up Captain Stephan. He was lying, he said, off Ventnor and had been unable to reach his station, on account of engine trouble, which he had now set right. Next morning he proposed to block the Southampton approach. He had destroyed one large Indian boat on his way down Channel. We exchanged good wishes. Like myself, he needed rest. I was up at four in the morning, however, and called all hands to overhaul the boat. She was somewhat up by the head, owing to the forward torpedoes having been used, so we trimmed her by opening the forward compensating tank, admitting as much water as the torpedoes had weighed. We also overhauled the starboard air-compressor and one of the periscope motors which had been jarred by the shock of the first explosion. We had hardly got ourselves shipshape when the morning dawned.

I have no doubt that a good many ships which had taken refuge in the French ports at the first alarm had run across and got safely up the river in the night. Of course I could have attacked them, but I do not care to take risks—and there are always risks for a submarine at night. But one had miscalculated his time, and there she was, just abreast of Warden Point, when the daylight disclosed her to us. In an instant we were after her. It was a near thing, for she was a flier, and could do two miles to our one; but we just reached her as she went swashing by. She saw us at the last moment, for I attacked her awash, since otherwise we could not have had the pace to reach her. She swung away and the first torpedo missed, but the second took her full under the counter. Heavens, what a smash! The whole stern seemed to go aloft. I drew off and watched her sink. She went down in seven minutes, leaving her masts and funnels over the water and a cluster of her people holding on to them. She was the *Virginia*, of the Bibby Line—twelve thousand tons—and laden, like the others, with foodstuffs from the East. The whole surface of the sea was covered with the floating grain. "John Bull will have to take up a hole or two of his belt if this goes on," said Vornal, as we watched the scene.

And it was at that moment that the very worst danger occurred that could befall us. I tremble now when I think how our glorious voyage might have been nipped in the bud. I had freed the hatch of my tower, and was looking at the boats of the *Virginia* with Vornal near me, when there was a swish and a terrific splash in the water beside us, which covered us both with spray. We looked up, and you can imagine our feelings when we saw an aeroplane hovering a few hundred feet above us like a hawk. With its silencer, it was perfectly noiseless, and had its bomb not fallen into the sea we should never have known what had destroyed us. She was circling round in the hope of dropping a second one, but we shoved on all speed ahead, crammed down the rudders, and vanished into the side of a roller. I kept the deflection indicator falling until I had put fifty good feet of water between the aeroplane and ourselves, for I knew well how deeply they can see under the surface. However, we soon threw her off our track, and when we came to the surface near Margate there was no sign of her, unless she was one of several which we saw hovering over Herne Bay.

There was not a ship in the offing save a few small coasters and little thousand-ton steamers, which were beneath my notice. For several hours I lay submerged with a blank periscope. Then I had an inspiration. Orders had been marconied to every foodship to lie in French waters and dash across after dark. I was as sure of it as if they had been recorded in our own receiver. Well, if they were there, that was where I should be also. I blew out the tanks and rose, for there was no sign of any warship near. They had some good system of signalling from the shore, however, for I had not got to the North Foreland before three destroyers came foaming after me, all converging from different directions. They had about as good a chance of catching me as three spaniels would have of overtaking a porpoise. Out of pure bravado—I know it was very wrong—I waited until they were actually within gunshot. Then I sank and we saw each other no more.

It is, as I have said, a shallow sandy coast, and submarine navigation is very difficult. The worst mishap that can befall a boat is to bury its nose in the side of a sand-drift and be held there. Such an accident might have been the end of our boat, though with our Fleuss cylinders and electric lamps we should have found no difficulty in getting out at the air-lock and in walking ashore across the bed of the ocean. As it was, however, I was able, thanks to our excellent charts, to keep the channel and so to gain the open straits. There we rose about midday, but, observing a hydroplane at no great distance, we sank again for half an hour. When we came up for the second time, all was peaceful around us, and the English coast was lining the whole western horizon. We kept outside the Goodwins and straight down Channel until we saw a line of black dots in front of us, which I knew to be the Dover-Calais torpedo-boat cordon. When two miles distant we dived and came up again seven miles to the southwest, without one of them dreaming that we had been within thirty feet of their keels.

When we rose, a large steamer flying the German flag was within half a mile of us. It was the North German Lloyd *Altona*, from New York to Bremen. I raised our whole hull and dipped our flag to her. It was amusing to see the amazement of her people at what they must have regarded as our unparalleled impudence in those English-swept waters. They cheered us heartily, and the tricolour flag was dipped in greeting as they went roaring past us. Then I stood in to the French coast.

It was exactly as I had expected. There were three great British steamers lying at anchor in Boulogne outer harbour. They were the *Caesar*, the *King of the East*, and the *Pathfinder*, none less than ten thousand tons. I suppose they thought they were safe in French waters, but what did I care about three-mile limits and international law! The view of my

Government was that England was blockaded, food contraband, and vessels carrying it to be destroyed. The lawyers could argue about it afterwards. My business was to starve the enemy any way I could. Within an hour the three ships were under the waves and the *Iota* was steaming down the Picardy coast, looking for fresh victims. The Channel was covered with English torpedo-boats buzzing and whirling like a cloud of midges. How they thought they could hurt me I cannot imagine, unless by accident I were to come up underneath one of them. More dangerous were the aeroplanes which circled here and there.

The water being calm, I had several times to descend as deep as a hundred feet before I was sure that I was out of their sight. After I had blown up the three ships at Boulogne I saw two aeroplanes flying down Channel, and I knew that they would head off any vessels which were coming up. There was one very large white steamer lying off Havre, but she steamed west before I could reach her. I dare say Stephan or one of the others would get her before long. But those infernal aeroplanes spoiled our sport for that day. Not another steamer did I see, save the never-ending torpedo-boats. I consoled myself with the reflection, however, that no food was passing me on its way to London. That was what I was there for, after all. If I could do it without spending my torpedoes, all the better. Up to date I had fired ten of them and sunk nine steamers, so I had not wasted my weapons. That night I came back to the Kent coast and lay upon the bottom in shallow water near Dungeness.

We were all trimmed and ready at the first break of day, for I expected to catch some ships which had tried to make the Thames in the darkness and had miscalculated their time. Sure enough, there was a great steamer coming up Channel and flying the American flag. It was all the same to me what flag she flew so long as she was engaged in conveying contraband of war to the British Isles. There were no torpedo-boats about at the moment, so I ran out on the surface and fired a shot across her bows. She seemed inclined to go on so I put a second one just above her water-line on her port bow. She stopped then and a very angry man began to gesticulate from the bridge. I ran the *Iota* almost alongside.

"Are you the captain?" I asked.

"What the ——" I won't attempt to reproduce his language.

"You have food-stuffs on board?" I said.

"It's an American ship, you blind beetle!" he cried. "Can't you see the flag? It's the *Vermondia*, of Boston."

"Sorry, Captain," I answered. "I have really no time for words. Those shots of mine will bring the torpedo-boats, and I dare say at this very moment your wireless is making trouble for me. Get your people into the boats."

I had to show him I was not bluffing, so I drew off and began putting shells into him just on the waterline. When I had knocked six holes in it he was very busy on his boats. I fired twenty shots altogether, and no torpedo was needed, for she was lying over with a terrible list to port, and presently came right on to her side. There she lay for two or three minutes before she foundered. There were eight boats crammed with people lying round her when she went down. I believe everybody was saved, but I could not wait to inquire. From all quarters the poor old panting, useless war-vessels were hurrying. I filled my tanks, ran her bows under, and came up fifteen miles to the south. Of course, I knew there would be a big row afterwards—as there was—but that did not help the starving crowds round the London bakers, who only saved their skins, poor devils, by explaining to the mob that they had nothing to bake.

By this time I was becoming rather anxious, as you can imagine, to know what was going on in the world and what England was thinking about it all. I ran alongside a fishing-boat, therefore, and ordered them to give up their papers. Unfortunately they had none, except a rag of an evening paper, which was full of nothing but betting news. In a second attempt I came alongside a small yachting party from Eastbourne, who were frightened to death at our sudden appearance out of the depths. From them we were lucky enough to get the London *Courier* of that very morning.

It was interesting reading—so interesting that I had to announce it all to the crew. Of course, you know the British style of headline, which gives you all the news at a glance. It seemed to me that the whole paper was headlines, it was in such a state of excitement. Hardly a word about me and my flotilla. We were on the second page. The first one began something like this:—

CAPTURE OF BLANKENBERG!

DESTRUCTION OF ENEMY'S FLEET

BURNING OF TOWN

TRAWLERS DESTROY MINE FIELD
LOSS OF TWO BATTLESHIPS

IS IT THE END?

Of course, what I had foreseen had occurred. The town was actually occupied by the British. And they thought it was the end! We would see about that.

On the round-the-corner page, at the back of the glorious resonant leaders, there was a little column which read like this:—

HOSTILE SUBMARINES

Several of the enemy's submarines are at sea, and have inflicted some appreciable damage upon our merchant ships. The danger-spots upon Monday and the greater part of Tuesday appear to have been the mouth of the Thames and the western entrance to the Solent. On Monday, between the Nore and Margate, there were sunk five large steamers, the *Adela, Moldavia, Cusco, Cormorant,* and *Maid of Athens,* particulars of which will be found below. Near Ventnor, on the same day, was sunk the *Verulam,* from Bombay. On Tuesday the *Virginia, Caesar, King of the East,* and *Pathfinder* were de-stroyed between the foreland and Boulogne. The latter three were actually lying in French waters, and the most energetic representa-tions have been made by the Government of the Republic. On the same day *The Queen of Sheba, Orontes, Diana,* and *Atalanta* were destroyed near the Needles. Wireless messages have stopped all ingoing cargo-ships from coming up Channel, but unfortunately there is evidence that at least two of the enemy's submarines are in the West. Four cattle-ships from Dublin to Liverpool were sunk yesterday evening, while three Bristol-bound steamers, *The Hilda, Mercury,* and *Maria Toser,* were blown up in the neighbourhood of Lundy Island. Commerce has, so far as possible, been diverted into safer channels, but in the meantime, however vexatious these incidents may be, and however grievous the loss both to the owners and to Lloyd's, we may console ourselves by the reflection that since a submarine cannot keep the sea for more than ten days without refitting, and since the base has been captured, there must come a speedy term to these depredations.

So much for the *Courier's* account of our proceedings. Another small paragraph was, however, more eloquent:—

The price of wheat, which stood at thirty-five shillings a week before the declaration of war, was quoted yesterday on the Baltic at fifty-two. Maize has gone from twenty-one to thirty-seven, barley from nineteen to thirty-five, sugar (foreign granulated) from eleven shillings and threepence to nineteen shillings and sixpence.

"Good, my lads!" said I, when I read it to the crew. "I can assure you that those few lines will prove to mean more than the whole page about the Fall of Blankenberg. Now let us get down Channel and send those prices up a little higher."

All traffic had stopped for London—not so bad for the little *Iota*—and we did not see a steamer that was worth a torpedo between Dungeness and the Isle of Wight. There I called Stephan up by wireless, and by seven o'clock we were actually lying side by side in a smooth rolling sea—Hengistbury Head bearing N.N.W. and about five miles distant. The two crews clustered on the whale-backs and shouted their joy at seeing friendly faces once more. Stephan had done extraordinarily well. I had, of course, read in the London paper of his four ships on Tuesday, but he had sunk no fewer than seven since, for many of those which should have come to the Thames had tried to make Southampton. Of the seven, one was of twenty thousand tons, a grain-ship from America, a second was a grain-ship from the Black Sea, and two others were great liners from South Africa. I congratulated Stephan with all my heart upon his splendid achievement. Then as we had been seen by a destroyer which was approaching at a great pace, we both dived, coming up again off the Needles, where we spent the night in company. We could not visit each other, since we had no boat, but we lay so nearly alongside that we were able, Stephan and I, to talk from hatch to hatch and so make our plans.

He had shot away more than half his torpedoes, and so had I, and yet we were very averse to returning to our base so long as our oil held out. I told him of my experience with the Boston steamer, and we mutually agreed to sink the ships by gun-fire in future so far as possible. I remember old Horli saying, "What use is a gun aboard a submarine?" We were about to show. I read the English paper to Stephan by the light of my electric torch, and we both agreed that few ships would now come up the Channel. That sentence about diverting commerce to safer routes could only mean that the ships would go round the North of Ireland and unload at Glasgow. Oh, for two more ships to stop that entrance! Heavens, what *would* England have done against a foe with thirty or forty submarines, since we only needed six instead of four to complete her destruction! After much talk we decided that the best plan would be that I should despatch a cipher telegram next morning from a French port to tell them to send the four second-rate boats to cruise off the North of Ireland and West of Scotland. Then when I had done this I should move down Channel with Stephan and operate at the mouth, while the other two boats could work in the Irish Sea. Having made these plans, I set off across the Channel in the early morning, reaching the small village of Etretat, in Normandy. There I got off my telegram and then laid my course for Falmouth, passing under the keels of two British cruisers which were making eagerly for Etretat, having heard by wireless that we were there.

Half-way down Channel we had trouble with a short circuit in our electric engines, and were compelled to run on the surface for several hours while we replaced one of the cam-shafts and renewed some washers. It was a ticklish time, for had a torpedo-boat come upon us we could not have dived. The perfect submarine of the future will surely have some alternative engines for such an emergency. However by the skill of Engineer Morro, we got things going once more. All the time we lay there I saw a hydroplane floating between us and the British coast. I can understand how a mouse feels when it is in a tuft of grass and sees a hawk high up in the heavens. However, all went well; the mouse became a water-rat, it wagged its tail in derision at the poor blind old hawk, and it dived down into a nice safe green, quiet world where there was nothing to injure it.

It was on the Wednesday night that the *Iota* crossed to Etretat. It was Friday afternoon before we had reached our new cruising ground. Only one large steamer did I see upon our way. The terror we had caused had cleared the Channel. This big boat had a clever captain on board. His tactics were excellent and took him in safety to the Thames. He came zigzagging up Channel at twenty-five knots, shooting off from his course at all sorts of unexpected angles. With our slow pace we could not catch him, nor could we calculate his line so as to cut him off. Of course, he had never seen us, but he judged, and judged rightly, that wherever we were those were the tactics by which he had the best chance of getting past. He deserved his success.

But, of course, it is only in a wide Channel that such things can be done. Had I met him in the mouth of the Thames there would have been a different story to tell. As I approached Falmouth I destroyed a three-thousand-ton boat from Cork, laden with butter and cheese. It was my only success for three days.

That night (Friday, April 16th) I called up Stephan, but received no reply. As I was within a few miles of our rendezvous, and as he would not be cruising after dark, I was puzzled to account for his silence. I could only imagine that his wireless was deranged. But, alas! I was soon to find the true reason from a copy of the *Western Morning News*, which I obtained from a Brixham trawler. The *Kappa*, with her gallant commander and crew, were at the bottom of the English Channel.

It appeared from this account that after I had parted from him he had met and sunk no fewer than five vessels. I gathered these to be his work, since all of them were by gun fire, and all were on the south coast of Dorset or Devon. How he met his fate was stated in a short telegram which was headed "Sinking of a Hostile Submarine." It was marked "Falmouth," and ran thus:—

> The P. and O. mail steamer *Macedonia* came into this port last night with five shell holes between wind and water. She reports having been attacked by a hostile submarine ten miles to the southeast of the Lizard. Instead of using her torpedoes, the submarine for some reason approached from the surface and fired five shots from a semi-automatic twelve-pounder gun. She was evidently under the impression that the *Macedonia* was unarmed. As a matter of fact, being warned of the presence of submarines in the Channel, the *Macedonia* had mounted her armament as an auxiliary cruiser. She opened fire with two quick-firers and blew away the conning-tower of the submarine. It is probable that the shells went right through her, as she sank at once with her hatches open. The *Macedonia* was only kept afloat by her pumps.

Such was the end of the *Kappa*, and my gallant friend, Commander Stephan. His best epitaph was in a corner of the same paper, and was headed "Mark Lane." It ran:—

Wheat (average) 66, maize 48, barley 50.

Well, if Stephan was gone there was the more need for me to show energy. My plans were quickly taken, but they were comprehensive. All that day (Saturday) I passed down the Cornish coast and round Land's End, getting two steamers on the way. I had learned from Stephan's fate that it was better to torpedo the large craft, but I was aware that the auxiliary cruisers of the British Government were all over ten thousand tons, so that for all ships under that size it was safe to use my gun. Both these craft, the *Yelland* and the *Playboy*—the latter an American ship—were perfectly harmless, so I came up within a hundred yards of them and speedily sank them, after allowing their people to get into boats. Some other steamers lay farther out, but I was so eager to make my new arrangements that I did not go out of my course to molest them. Just before sunset, however, so magnificent a prey came within my radius of action that I could not possibly refuse her. No sailor could fail to recognise that glorious monarch of the sea, with her four cream funnels tipped with black, her huge black sides, her red bilges, and her high white top-hamper, roaring up Channel at twenty-three knots, and carrying her forty-five thousand tons as lightly as if she were a five-ton motor-boat. It was the queenly *Olympic*, of the White Star—once the largest and still the comeliest of liners. What a picture she made, with the blue Cornish sea creaming round her giant forefoot, and the pink western sky with one evening star forming the background to her noble lines.

She was about five miles off when we dived to cut her off. My calculation was exact. As we came abreast we loosed our torpedo and struck her fair. We swirled round with the concussion of the water. I saw her in my periscope list over on her side, and I knew that she had her death-blow. She settled down slowly, and there was plenty of time to save her people. The sea was dotted with her boats. When I got about three miles off I rose to the surface, and the whole crew clustered up to see the wonderful sight. She dived bows foremost, and there was a terrific explosion, which sent one of the funnels into the air. I suppose we should have cheered—somehow, none of us felt like cheering. We were all keen sailors, and it went to our hearts to see such a ship go down like a broken egg-shell. I gave a gruff order, and all were at their posts again while we headed north-west. Once round Land's End I called up my two consorts, and we met next day at Hartland Point, the south end of Bideford Bay. For the moment the Channel was clear, but the English could not know it, and I reckoned that the loss of the *Olympic* would stop all ships for a day or two at least.

Having assembled the *Delta* and *Epsilon*, one on each side of me, I received the report from Miriam and Var, the respective commanders. Each had expended twelve torpedoes, and between them they had sunk twenty-two steamers. One man had been killed by the machinery on board of the *Delta*, and two had been burned by the ignition of some oil on the *Epsilon*. I took these injured men on board, and I gave each of the boats one of my crew. I also divided my spare oil, my provisions, and my torpedoes among them, though we had the greatest possible difficulty in those crank vessels in transferring them from one to the other. However, by ten o'clock it was done, and the two vessels were in condition to keep the sea for another ten days. For my part, with only two torpedoes left, I headed north up the Irish Sea. One of my torpedoes I expended that evening upon a cattle-ship making for Milford Haven. Late at night, being abreast of Holyhead, I called upon my four northern boats, but without reply. Their Marconi range is very limited. About three in the afternoon of the next day I had a feeble answer. It was a great relief to me to find that my telegraphic instructions had reached them and that they were on their station. Before evening we all assembled in the lee of Sanda Island, in the Mull of Kintyre. I felt an admiral indeed when I saw my five whalebacks all in a row. Panza's report was excellent. They had come round by the Pentland Firth and reached their cruising ground on the fourth day. Already they had destroyed twenty vessels without any mishap. I ordered the *Beta* to divide her oil and torpedoes among the other three, so that they were in good condition to continue their cruise. Then the *Beta* and I headed for home, reaching our base upon Sunday, April 25th. Off Cape Wrath I picked up a paper from a small schooner.

"Wheat, 84; Maize, 60; Barley, 62." What were battles and bombardments compared to that!

The whole coast of Norland was closely blockaded by cordon within cordon, and every port, even the smallest, held by the British. But why should they suspect my modest confectioner's villa more than any other of the ten thousand houses that face the sea? I was glad when I picked up its homely white front in my periscope. That night I landed and found my stores intact. Before morning the *Beta* reported itself, for we had the windows lit as a guide.

It is not for me to recount the messages which I found waiting for me at my humble headquarters. They shall ever remain as the patents of nobility of my family. Among others was that never-to-be-forgotten salutation from my King. He desired me to present myself at Hauptville, but for once I took it upon myself to disobey his commands. It took me two days—or rather two nights, for we sank ourselves during the daylight hours—to get all our stores on board, but my presence was needful every minute of the time. On the third morning, at four o'clock, the *Beta* and my own little flagship were at sea once more, bound for our original station off the mouth of the Thames.

I had no time to read our papers whilst I was refitting, but I gathered the news after we got under way. The British occupied all our ports, but otherwise we had not suffered at all, since we have excellent railway communications with Europe. Prices had altered little, and our industries continued as before. There was talk of a British invasion, but this I knew to be absolute nonsense, for the British must have learned by this time that it would be sheer murder to send transports full of soldiers to sea in the face of submarines. When they have a tunnel they can use their fine expeditionary force upon the Continent, but until then it might just as well not exist so far as Europe is concerned. My own country, therefore, was in good case and had nothing to fear. Great Britain, however, was already feeling my grip upon her throat. As in normal times four-fifths of her food is imported, prices were rising by leaps and bounds. The supplies in the country were beginning to show signs of depletion, while little was coming in to replace it. The insurances at Lloyd's had risen to a figure which made the price of the food prohibitive to the mass of the people by the time it had reached the market. The loaf, which under ordinary circumstances stood at fivepence, was already at one and twopence. Beef was three shillings and fourpence a pound, and mutton two shillings and ninepence. Everything else was in proportion. The Government had acted with energy and offered a big bounty for corn to be planted at once. It could only be reaped five months hence, however, and long before then, as the papers pointed out, half the island would be dead from starvation. Strong appeals had been made to the patriotism of the people, and they were assured that the interference with trade was temporary, and that with a little patience all would be well. But already there was a marked rise in the death-rate, especially among children, who suffered from want of milk, the cattle being slaughtered for food. There was serious rioting in the Lanarkshire coal-fields and in the Midlands, together with a Socialistic upheaval in the East of London, which had assumed the proportions of a civil war. Already there were responsible papers which declared that England was in an impossible position, and that an immediate peace was necessary to prevent one of the greatest tragedies in history. It was my task now to prove to them that they were right.

It was May 2nd when I found myself back at the Maplin Sands to the north of the estuary of the Thames. The *Beta* was sent on to the Solent to block it and take the place of the lamented *Kappa*. And now I was throttling Britain indeed—London, Southampton, the Bristol Channel, Liverpool, the North Channel, the Glasgow approaches, each was guarded by my boats. Great liners were, as we learned afterwards, pouring their supplies into Galway and the West of Ireland, where provisions were cheaper than has ever been known. Tens of thousands were embarking from Britain for Ireland in order to save themselves from starvation. But you cannot transplant a whole dense population. The main body of the people, by the middle of May, were actually starving. At that date wheat was at a hundred, maize and barley at eighty. Even the most obstinate had begun to see that the situation could not possibly continue.

In the great towns starving crowds clamoured for bread before the municipal offices, and public officials everywhere were attacked and often murdered by frantic mobs, composed largely of desperate women who had seen their infants perish before their eyes. In the country, roots, bark, and weeds of every sort were used as food. In London the private mansions of Ministers were guarded by strong pickets of soldiers, while a battalion of Guards was camped permanently round the Houses of Parliament. The lives of the Prime Minister and of the Foreign Secretary were continually threatened and occasionally attempted. Yet the Government had entered upon the war with the full assent of every party in the State. The true culprits were those, be they politicians or journalists, who had not the foresight to understand that unless Britain grew her own supplies, or unless by means of a tunnel she had some way of conveying them into the island, all her mighty expenditure upon her army and her fleet was a mere waste of money so long as her antagonists had a few submarines and men who could use them. England has often been stupid, but has got off scot-free. This time she was stupid and had to pay the price. You can't expect Luck to be your saviour always.

It would be a mere repetition of what I have already described if I were to recount all our proceedings during that first ten days after I resumed my station. During my absence the ships had taken heart and had begun to come up again. In the first day I got four. After that I had to go farther afield, and again I picked up several in French waters. Once I had a narrow escape through one of my kingston valves getting some grit into it and refusing to act when I was below the surface. Our margin of buoyancy just carried us through. By the end of that week the Channel was clear again, and both *Beta* and my own boat were down West once more. There we had encouraging messages from our Bristol consort, who in turn had heard from *Delta* at Liverpool. Our task was completely done. We could not prevent all food from passing into the British Islands, but at least we had raised what did get in to a price which put it far beyond the means of the penniless, workless multitudes. In vain Government commandeered it all and doled it out as a general feeds the garrison of a fortress. The task was too great—the responsibility too horrible. Even the proud and stubborn English could not face it any longer.

I remember well how the news came to me. I was lying at the time off Selsey Bill when I saw a small war-vessel coming down Channel. It had never been my policy to attack any vessel coming *down*. My torpedoes and even my shells were too precious for that. I could not help being attracted, however, by the movements of this ship, which came slowly zigzagging in my direction.

"Looking for me," thought I. "What on earth does the foolish thing hope to do if she could find me?"

I was lying awash at the time and got ready to go below in case she should come for me. But at that moment—she was about half a mile away—she turned her quarter, and there to my amazement was the red flag with the blue circle, our own beloved flag, flying from her peak. For a moment I thought that this was some clever dodge of the enemy to tempt me within range. I snatched up my glasses and called on Vornal. Then we both recognised the vessel. It was the *Juno*, the only one left intact of our own cruisers. What could she be doing flying the flag in the enemy's waters? Then I understood it, and turning to Vornal, we threw ourselves into each other's arms. It could only mean an armistice—or peace!

And it was peace. We learned the glad news when we had risen alongside the *Juno*, and the ringing cheers which greeted us had at last died away. Our orders were to report ourselves at once at Blankenberg. Then she passed on down Channel to collect the others. We returned to port upon the surface, steaming through the whole British fleet as we passed up the North Sea. The crews clustered thick along the sides of the vessels to watch us. I can see now their sullen, angry faces. Many shook their fists and cursed us as we went by. It was not that we had damaged them—I will do them the justice to say that the English, as the old Boer War has proved, bear no resentment against a brave enemy—but that they thought us cowardly to attack merchant ships and avoid the warships. It is like the Arabs who think that a flank attack is a mean, unmanly device. War is not a big game, my English friends. It is a desperate business to gain the upper hand, and one must use one's brain in order to find the weak spot of one's enemy. It is not fair to blame me if I have found yours. It was my duty.

Perhaps those officers and sailors who scowled at the little *Iota* that May morning have by this time done me justice when the first bitterness of undeserved defeat was passed.

Let others describe my entrance into Blankenberg; the mad enthusiasm of the crowds, and the magnificent public reception of each successive boat as it arrived. Surely the men deserved the grant made them by the State which has enabled each of them to be independent for life. As a feat of endurance, that long residence in such a state of mental tension in cramped quarters, breathing an unnatural atmosphere, will long remain as a record. The country may well be proud of such sailors.

The terms of peace were not made onerous, for we were in no condition to make Great Britain our permanent enemy. We knew well that we had won the war by circumstances which would never be allowed to occur again, and that in a few years the Island Power would be as strong as ever—stronger, perhaps—for the lesson that she had learned. It would be madness to provoke such an antagonist. A mutual salute of flags was arranged, the Colonial boundary was adjusted by arbitration, and we claimed no indemnity beyond an undertaking on the part of Britain that she would pay any damages which an International Court might award to France or to the United States for injury received through the operations of our submarines. So ended the war!

Of course, England will not be caught napping in such a fashion again! Her foolish blindness is partly explained by her delusion that her enemy would not torpedo merchant vessels. Common sense should have told her that her enemy will play the game that suits them best—that they will not inquire what they may do, but they will do it first and talk about it afterwards. The opinion of the whole world now is that if a blockade were proclaimed one may do what one can with those who try to break it, and that it was as reasonable to prevent food from reaching England in war time as it is for a besieger to prevent the victualling of a beleaguered fortress.

I cannot end this account better than by quoting the first few paragraphs of a leader in the *Times*, which appeared shortly after the declaration of peace. It may be taken to epitomise the saner public opinion of England upon the meaning and lessons of the episode.

"In all this miserable business," said the writer, "which has cost us the loss of a considerable portion of our merchant fleet and more than fifty thousand civilian lives, there is just one consolation to be found. It lies in the fact that our temporary conqueror is a Power which is not strong enough to reap the fruits of her victory. Had we endured this humiliation at the hands of any of the first-class Powers it would certainly have entailed the loss of all our Crown Colonies and tropical possessions, besides the payment of a huge indemnity. We were absolutely at the feet of our conqueror and had no possible alternative but to submit to her terms, however onerous. Norland has had the good sense to understand that she must not abuse her temporary advantage, and has been generous in her dealings. In the grip of any other Power we should have ceased to exist as an Empire.

"Even now we are not out of the wood. Some one may maliciously pick a quarrel with us before we get our house in order, and use the easy weapon which has been demonstrated. It is to meet such a contingency that the Government has rushed enormous stores of food at the public expense into the country. In a very few months the new harvest will have appeared. On the whole we can face the immediate future without undue depression, though there remain some causes for anxiety. These will no doubt be energetically handled by this new and efficient Government, which has taken the place of those discredited politicians who led us into a war without having foreseen how helpless we were against an obvious form of attack.

"Already the lines of our reconstruction are evident. The first and most important is that our Party men realise that there is something more vital than their academic disputes about Free Trade or Protection, and that all theory must give way to the fact that a country is in an artificial and dangerous condition if she does not produce within her own borders sufficient food to at least keep life in her population. Whether this should be brought about by a tax upon foreign foodstuffs, or by a bounty upon home products, or by a combination of the two, is now under discussion. But all Parties are combined upon the principle, and, though it will undoubtedly entail either a rise in prices or a deterioration in quality in the food of the working-classes, they will at least be insured against so terrible a visitation as that which is fresh in our memories. At any rate, we have got past the stage of argument. It *must* be so. The increased prosperity of the farming interest, and, as we will hope, the cessation of agricultural emigration, will be benefits to be counted against the obvious disadvantages.

"The second lesson is the immediate construction of not one but two double-lined railways under the Channel. We stand in a white sheet over the matter, since the project has always been discouraged in these columns, but we are prepared to admit that had such railway communication been combined with adequate arrangements for forwarding supplies from Marseilles, we should have avoided our recent surrender. We still insist that we cannot trust entirely to a tunnel, since our enemy might have allies in the Mediterranean; but in a single contest with any Power of the North of Europe it would certainly be of inestimable benefit. There may be dangers attendant upon the existence of a tunnel, but it must now be admitted that they are trivial compared to those which come from its absence. As to the building of large fleets of merchant submarines for the carriage of food, that is a new departure which will be an additional insurance against the danger which has left so dark a page in the history of our country."

17

❧

From *A Visit to Three Fronts* (1916)

A Glimpse of the British Army

I

It is not an easy matter to write from the front. You know that there are several courteous but inexorable gentlemen who may have a word in the matter, and their presence "imparts but small ease to the style." But above all you have the twin censors of your own conscience and common sense, which assure you that, if all other readers fail you, you will certainly find a most attentive one in the neighbourhood of the Haupt-Quartier. An instructive story is still told of how a certain well-meaning traveller recorded his satisfaction with the appearance of the big guns at the retiring and peaceful village of Jamais, and how three days later, by an interesting coincidence, the village of Jamais passed suddenly off the map and dematerialised into brickdust and splinters.

I have been with soldiers on the warpath before, but never have I had a day so crammed with experiences and impressions as yesterday. Some of them at least I can faintly convey to the reader, and if they ever reach the eye of that gentleman at the Haupt-Quartier they will give him little joy. For the crowning impression of all is the enormous imperturbable confidence of the Army and its extraordinary efficiency in organisation, administration, material, and personnel. I met in one day a sample of many types, an Army commander, a corps commander, two divisional commanders, staff officers of many grades, and, above all, I met repeatedly the two very great men whom Britain has produced, the private soldier and the regimental officer. Everywhere and on every face one read the same spirit of cheerful bravery. Even the half-mad cranks whose absurd consciences prevent them from barring the way to the devil seemed to me to be turning into men under the prevailing influence. I saw a batch of them, neurotic and largely be-spectacled, but working with a will by the roadside. They will volunteer for the trenches yet.

*   *   *   *   *

If there are pessimists among us they are not to be found among the men who are doing the work. There is no foolish bravado, no under-rating of a dour opponent, but there is a quick, alert, confident attention to the job in hand which is an inspiration to the observer. These brave lads are guarding Britain in the present. See to it that Britain guards them in the future! We have a bad record in this matter. It must be changed. They are the wards of the nation, both officers and men. Socialism has never had an attraction for me, but I should be a Socialist to-morrow if I thought that to ease a tax on wealth these men should ever suffer for the time or health that they gave to the public cause.

"Get out of the car. Don't let it stay here. It may be hit." These words from a staff officer give you the first idea that things are going to happen. Up to then you might have been driving through the black country in the Walsall district with the population of Aldershot let loose upon its dingy roads. "Put on this shrapnel helmet. That hat of yours would infuriate the Boche"—this was an unkind allusion to the only uniform which I have a right to wear. "Take this gas helmet. You won't need it, but it is a standing order. Now come on!"

We cross a meadow and enter a trench. Here and there it comes to the surface again where there is dead ground. At one such point an old church stands, with an unexploded shell sticking out of the wall. A century hence folk will journey to see that shell. Then on again through an endless cutting. It is slippery clay below. I have no nails in my boots, an iron pot on my head, and the sun above me. I will remember that walk. Ten telephone wires run down the side. Here and there large thistles and other plants grow from the clay walls, so immobile have been our lines. Occasionally there are patches of untidiness. "Shells," says the officer la-

conically. There is a racket of guns before us and behind, especially behind, but danger seems remote with all these Bairnfather groups of cheerful Tommies at work around us. I pass one group of grimy, tattered boys.
A glance at their shoulders shows me that they are of a public school battalion. "I thought you fellows were all officers now," I remarked. "No, sir,
we like it better so." "Well, it will be a great memory for you. We are all
in your debt." They salute, and we squeeze past them. They had the fresh,
brown faces of boy cricketers. But their comrades were men of a different type, with hard, strong, rugged features, and the eyes of men who have
seen strange sights. These are veterans, men of Mons, and their young
pals of the public schools have something to live up to.

*　*　*　*　*

Up to this we have only had two clay walls to look at. But now our
interminable and tropical walk is lightened by the sight of a British aeroplane sailing overhead. Numerous shrapnel bursts are all round it, but
she floats on serenely, a thing of delicate beauty against the blue background. Now another passes—and yet another. All morning we saw
them circling and swooping, and never a sign of a Boche. They tell me it
is nearly always so—that we hold the air, and that the Boche intruder,
save at early morning, is a rare bird. A visit to the line would reassure Mr.
Pemberton-Billing. "We have never met a British aeroplane which was
not ready to fight," said a captured German aviator the other day. There
is a fine stern courtesy between the airmen on either side, each dropping
notes into the other's aerodromes to tell the fate of missing officers. Had
the whole war been fought by the Germans as their airmen have conducted it (I do not speak of course of the Zeppelin murderers), a peace
would eventually have been more easily arranged. As it is, if every frontier could be settled, it would be a hard thing to stop until all that is associated with the words Cavell, Zeppelin, Wittenberg, Lusitania, and
Louvain has been brought to the bar of the world's Justice.

And now we are there—in what is, surely the most wonderful spot
in the world, the front firing trench, the outer breakwater which holds
back the German tide. How strange that this monstrous oscillation of
giant forces, setting in from east to west, should find their equilibrium
here across this particular meadow of Flanders. "How far?" I ask. "180

yards," says my guide. "Pop!" remarks a third person just in front. "A sniper," says my guide. "Take a look through the periscope." I do so. There is some rusty wire before me, then a field sloping slightly upwards with knee-deep grass, then rusty wire again, and a red line of broken earth. There is not a sign of movement, but sharp eyes are always watching us, even as these crouching soldiers around me are watching them. There are dead Germans in the grass before us. You need not see them to know that they are there. A wounded soldier sits in a corner nursing his leg. Here and there men pop out like rabbits from dug-outs and mine-shafts. Others sit on the fire-step or lean smoking against the clay wall. Who would dream to look at their bold, careless faces that this is a front line, and that at any moment it is possible that a grey wave may submerge them? With all their careless bearing I notice that every man has his gas helmet and his rifle within easy reach.

A mile of front trenches and then we are on our way back down that weary walk. Then I am whisked off upon a ten mile drive. There is a pause for lunch at Corps Headquarters, and after it we are taken to a medal presentation in a market square. Generals Munro, Haking and Landon, famous fighting soldiers all three, are the British representatives. Munro with a ruddy face, all brain above all bulldog below; Haking, pale, distinguished, intellectual; Landon a pleasant, genial country squire. An elderly French General stands beside them. British infantry keep the ground. In front are about fifty Frenchmen in civil dress of every grade of life, workmen and gentlemen, in a double rank. They are all so wounded that they are back in civil life, but to-day they are to have some solace for their wounds. They lean heavily on sticks, their bodies are twisted and maimed, but their faces are shining with pride and joy. The French General draws his sword and addresses them. One catches words like "honneur" and "patrie." They lean forward on their crutches, hanging on every syllable which comes hissing and rasping from under that heavy white moustache. Then the medals are pinned on. One poor lad is terribly wounded and needs two sticks. A little girl runs out with some flowers. He leans forward and tries to kiss her, but the crutches slip and he nearly falls upon her. It was a pitiful but beautiful little scene.

Now the British candidates march up one by one for their medals, hale, hearty men, brown and fit. There is a smart young officer of Scottish Rifles; and then a selection of Worcesters, Welsh Fusiliers and Scots Fusiliers, with one funny little Highlander, a tiny figure with a soup-bowl helmet, a grinning boy's face beneath it, and a bedraggled uniform. "Many acts of great bravery," such was the record for which he was decorated. Even the French wounded smiled at his quaint appearance, as they did at another Briton who had acquired the chewing-gum habit, and came up for his medal as if he had been called suddenly in the middle of his dinner, which he was still endeavouring to bolt. Then came the end, with the National Anthem. The British regiment formed fours and went past. To me that was the most impressive sight of any. They were the Queen's West Surreys, a veteran regiment of the great Ypres battle. What grand fellows! As the order came "Eyes right," and all those fierce, dark faces flashed round about us, I felt the might of the British infantry, the intense individuality which is not incompatible with the highest discipline. Much they had endured, but a great spirit shone from their faces. I confess that as I looked at those brave English lads, and thought of what we owe to them and to their like who have passed on, I felt more emotional than befits a Briton in foreign parts.

✻   ✻   ✻   ✻   ✻

Now the ceremony was ended, and once again we set out for the front. It was to an artillery observation post that we were bound, and once again my description must be bounded by discretion. Suffice it, that in an hour I found myself, together with a razor-keen young artillery observer and an excellent old sportsman of a Russian prince, jammed into a very small space, and staring through a slit at the German lines. In front of us lay a vast plain, scarred and slashed, with bare places at intervals, such as you see where gravel pits break a green common. Not a sign of life or movement, save some wheeling crows. And yet down there, within a mile or so, is the population of a city. Far away a single train is puffing at the back of the German lines. We are here on a definite errand. Away to the right, nearly three miles off, is a small red house, dim to the eye but clear in the glasses, which is suspected as a German post. It is to go up this afternoon. The gun is some distance away, but I hear the telephone directions. "'Mother' will soon do her in," remarks the gunner boy cheerfully. "Mother" is the name of the gun. "Give her

five six three four," he cries through the 'phone. "Mother" utters a horrible bellow from somewhere on our right. An enormous spout of smoke
rises ten seconds later from near the house. "A little short," says our gunner. "Two and a half minutes left," adds a little small voice, which represents another observer at a different angle. "Raise her seven five," says
our boy encouragingly. "Mother" roars more angrily than ever. "How
will that do?" she seems to say. "One and a half right," says our invisible
gossip. I wonder how the folk in the house are feeling as the shells creep
ever nearer. "Gun laid, sir," says the telephone. "Fire!" I am looking
through my glass. A flash of fire on the house, a huge pillar of dust and
smoke—then it settles and an unbroken field is there. The German post
has gone up. "It's a dear little gun," says the officer boy. "And her shells
are reliable," remarked a senior behind us. "They vary with different cal-
ibres, but 'Mother' never goes wrong." The German line was very quiet.
"Pourquoi ils ne repondent pas?" asked the Russian prince. "Yes, they
are quiet to-day," answered the senior. "But we get it in the neck sometimes." We are all led off to be introduced to "Mother," who sits, squat
and black, amid twenty of her grimy children who wait upon and feed
her. She is an important person is "Mother," and her importance grows.
It gets clearer with every month that it is she, and only she, who can lead
us to the Rhine. She can and she will if the factories of Britain can beat
those of the Hun. See to it, you working men and women of Britain.
Work now if you rest for ever after, for the fate of Europe and of all
that is dear to us is in your hands. For "Mother" is a dainty eater, and
needs good food and plenty. She is fond of strange lodgings, too, in
which she prefers safety to dignity. But that is a dangerous subject.

✳   ✳   ✳   ✳   ✳

One more experience of this wonderful day—the most crowded with
impressions of my whole life. At night we take a car and drive north, and
ever north, until at a late hour we halt and climb a hill in the darkness.
Below is a wonderful sight. Down on the flats, in a huge semi-circle, lights
are rising and falling. They are very brilliant, going up for a few seconds
and then dying down. Sometimes a dozen are in the air at one time. There
are the dull thuds of explosions and an occasional rat-tat-tat. I have seen
nothing like it, but the nearest comparison would be an enormous ten-

mile railway station in full swing at night, with signals winking, lamps waving, engines hissing and carriages bumping. It is a terrible place down yonder, a place which will live as long as military history is written, for it is the Ypres Salient. What a salient it is, too! A huge curve, as outlined by the lights, needing only a little more to be an encirclement. Something caught the rope as it closed, and that something was the British soldier. But it is a perilous place still by day and by night. Never shall I forget the impression of ceaseless, malignant activity which was borne in upon me by the white, winking lights, the red sudden glares, and the horrible thudding noises in that place of death beneath me.

II

In old days we had a great name as organisers. Then came a long period when we deliberately adopted a policy of individuality and "go as you please." Now once again in our sore need we have called on all our power of administration and direction. But it has not deserted us. We still have it in a supreme degree. Even in peace time we have shown it in that vast, well-oiled, swift-running, noiseless machine called the British Navy. But now our powers have risen with the need of them. The expansion of the Navy has been a miracle, the management of the transport a greater one, the formation of the new Army the greatest of all time. To get the men was the least of the difficulties. To put them here, with everything down to the lid of the last field saucepan in its place, that is the marvel. The tools of the gunners, and of the sappers, to say nothing of the knowledge of how to use them, are in themselves a huge problem. But it has all been met and mastered, and will be to the end. But don't let us talk any more about the muddling of the War Office. It has become just a little ridiculous.

✻   ✻   ✻   ✻   ✻

I have told of my first day, when I visited the front trenches, saw the work of "Mother," and finally that marvellous spectacle, the Ypres Salient at night. I have passed the night at the headquarters of a divisional-general, Capper, who might truly be called one of the two fathers of the British flying force, for it was he, with Templer, who laid the first foundations from which so great an organisation has arisen. My morning was spent in visiting two fighting brigadiers, cheery weather-beaten soldiers, respectful, as all our soldiers are, of the prowess of the Hun, but serenely confident that we can beat him. In company with one of them I ascended a hill, the reverse slope of which was swarming with cheerful infantry in every stage of dishabille, for they were cleaning up after the trenches. Once over the slope we advanced with some care, and finally reached a certain spot from which we looked down upon the German line. It was the advanced observation post, about a thousand yards from the German trenches, with our own trenches between us. We could see the two lines, sometimes only a few yards, as it seemed, apart, extending for miles on either side. The sinister silence and solitude were strangely dramatic. Such vast crowds of men, such intensity of feeling, and yet only that open rolling countryside, with never a movement in its whole expanse.

The afternoon saw us in the Square at Ypres. It is the city of a dream, this modern Pompeii, destroyed, deserted and desecrated, but with a sad, proud dignity which made you involuntarily lower your voice as you passed through the ruined streets. It is a more considerable place than I had imagined, with many traces of ancient grandeur. No words can describe the absolute splintered wreck that the Huns have made of it. The effect of some of the shells has been grotesque. One boiler-plated water-tower, a thing forty or fifty feet high, was actually standing on its head like a great metal top. There is not a living soul in the place save a few pickets of soldiers, and a number of cats which become fierce and dangerous. Now and then a shell still falls, but the Huns probably know that the devastation is already complete.

We stood in the lonely grass-grown square, once the busy centre of the town, and we marvelled at the beauty of the smashed cathedral and the tottering Cloth Hall beside it. Surely at their best they could not have looked more wonderful than now. If they were preserved even so, and if a heaven-inspired artist were to model a statue of Belgium in front, Belgium with one hand pointing to the treaty by which Prussia guaranteed her safety and the other to the sacrilege behind her, it would make the most impressive group in the world. It was an evil day for Belgium when her frontier was violated, but it was a worse one for Germany. I venture to prophesy that it will be regarded by history as the greatest military as well as political error that has ever been made. Had the great guns that destroyed Liège made their first breach at Verdun what chance was there for Paris? Those few weeks of warning and preparation saved France, and left Germany as she now is, like a weary and furious bull, tethered fast in the place of trespass and waiting for the inevitable pole-axe.

We were glad to get out of the place, for the gloom of it lay as heavy upon our hearts as the shrapnel helmets did upon our heads. Both were lightened as we sped back past empty and shattered villas to where, just behind the danger line, the normal life of rural Flanders was carrying on as usual. A merry sight helped to cheer us, for scudding down wind above our heads came a Boche aeroplane, with two British at her tail barking away with their machine guns, like two swift terriers after a cat. They shot rat-tat-tatting across the sky until we lost sight of them in the heat haze over the German line.

*   *   *   *   *

The afternoon saw us on the Sharpenburg, from which many a million will gaze in days to come, for from no other point can so much be seen. It is a spot forbid, but a special permit took us up, and the sentry on duty, having satisfied himself of our bona fides, proceeded to tell us tales of the war in a pure Hull dialect which might have been Chinese for all that I could understand. That he was a "terrier" and had nine children were the only facts I could lay hold of. But I wished to be silent and to think—even, perhaps, to pray. Here, just below my feet, were the spots which our dear lads, three of them my own kith, have sanctified with their blood. Here, fighting for the freedom of the world, they cheerily gave their all. On that sloping meadow to the left of the row of houses on the opposite ridge the London Scottish fought to the death on that grim November morning when the Bavarians reeled back from their shot-torn line. That plain away on the other side of Ypres was the place where the three grand Canadian brigades, first of all men, stood up to the damnable cowardly gases of the Hun. Down yonder is Hill 60, that blood-soaked kopje. The ridge over the fields was held by the cavalry against two army corps, and there where the sun strikes the red roof among the trees I can just see Gheluveld, a name for ever to be associated with Haig and the most vital battle of the war. As I turn away

I am faced by my Hull Territorial, who still says incomprehensible things. I look at him with other eyes. He has fought on yonder plain. He has slain Huns, and he has nine children. Could anyone better epitomise the duties of a good citizen? I could have found it in my heart to salute him had I not known that it would have shocked him and made him unhappy.

It has been a full day, and the next is even fuller, for it is my privilege to lunch at Headquarters, and to make the acquaintance of the Commander-in-chief and of his staff. It would be an invasion of private hospitality if I were to give the public the impressions which I carried from that charming château. I am the more sorry, since they were very vivid and strong. This much I will say—and any man who is a face reader will not need to have it said—that if the Army stands still it is not by the will of its commander. There will, I swear, be no happier man in Europe when the day has come and the hour. It is human to err, but never possibly can some types err by being backward. We have a superb army in France. It needs the right leader to handle it. I came away happier and more confident than ever as to the future.

Extraordinary are the contrasts of war. Within three hours of leaving the quiet atmosphere of the Headquarters Château I was present at what in any other war would have been looked upon as a brisk engagement. As it was it would certainly figure in one of our desiccated reports as an activity of the artillery. The noise as we struck the line at this new point showed that the matter was serious, and, indeed, we had chosen the spot because it has been the storm centre of the last week. The method of approach chosen by our experienced guide was in itself a tribute to the gravity of the affair. As one comes from the settled order of Flanders into the actual scene of war, the first sign of it is one of the stationary, sausage-shaped balloons, a chain of which marks the ring in which the great wrestlers are locked. We pass under this, ascend a hill, and find ourselves in a garden where for a year no feet save those of wanderers like ourselves have stood. There is a wild, confused luxuriance of growth more beautiful to my eye than anything which the care of man can produce. One old shell-hole of vast diameter has filled itself with forget-me-nots, and appears as a graceful basin of light blue flowers, held up as an atonement to heaven for the brutalities of man. Through the tangled bushes we creep, then across a yard—"Please stoop and run as you pass this point"—and finally to a small opening in a wall, whence the battle lies not so much before as beside us. For a moment we have a front seat at the great world-drama, God's own problem play, working surely to its magnificent end. One feels a sort of shame to crouch here in comfort, a useless spectator, while brave men down yonder are facing that pelting shower of iron.

✻　　✻　　✻　　✻　　✻

There is a large field on our left rear, and the German gunners have the idea that there is a concealed battery therein. They are systematically searching for it. A great shell explodes in the top corner, but gets nothing more solid than a few tons of clay. You can read the mind of Gunner Fritz. "Try the lower corner!" says he, and up goes the earth-cloud once again. "Perhaps it's hid about the middle. I'll try." Earth again, and nothing more. "I believe I was right the first time after all," says hopeful Fritz. So another shell comes into the top corner. The field is as full of pits as a Gruyere cheese, but Fritz gets nothing by his perseverance. Perhaps there never was a battery there at all. One effect he obviously did attain. He made several other British batteries exceedingly angry. "Stop that tickling, Fritz!" was the burden of their cry. Where they were we could no more see than Fritz could, but their constant work was very clear along the German line. We appeared to be using more shrapnel and the Germans more high explosives, but that may have been just the chance of the day. The Vimy Ridge was on our right, and before us was the old French position, with the labyrinth of terrible memories and the long hill of Lorette. When, last year, the French, in a three weeks' battle, fought their way up that hill, it was an exhibition of sustained courage which even their military annals can seldom have beaten.

✻　　✻　　✻　　✻　　✻

And so I turn from the British line. Another and more distant task lies before me. I come away with the deep sense of the difficult task which lies before the Army, but with a deeper one of the ability of these men to do all that soldiers can ever be asked to perform. Let the guns clear the way for the infantry, and the rest will follow. It all lies with the guns. But the guns, in turn, depend upon our splendid workers at home, who, men and women, are doing so grandly. Let them not be judged by a tiny minority, who are given, perhaps, too much attention in our journals. We have all made sacrifices in the war, but when the full story comes to be told, perhaps the greatest sacrifice of all is that which Labour made when, with a sigh, she laid aside that which it had taken so many weary years to build.

A Glimpse of the Italian Army

One meets with such extreme kindness and consideration among the Italians that there is a real danger lest one's personal feeling of obligation should warp one's judgment or hamper one's expression. Making every possible allowance for this I come away from them, after a very wide if superficial view of all that they are doing, with a deep feeling of admiration and a conviction that no army in the world could have made a braver attempt to advance under conditions of extraordinary difficulty.

First a word as to the Italian soldier. He is a type by himself which differs from the earnest solidarity of the new French army, and from the business-like alertness of the Briton, and yet has a very special dash and fire of its own, covered over by a very pleasing and unassuming manner. London has not yet forgotten Durando of Marathon fame. He was just such another easy smiling youth as I now see everywhere around me. Yet there came a day when a hundred thousand Londoners hung upon his every movement—when strong men gasped and women wept at his invincible but unavailing spirit. When he had fallen senseless in that historic race on the very threshold of his goal, so high was the determination within him that while he floundered on the track like a broken-backed horse, with the senses gone out of him his legs still continued to drum upon the cinder path. Then when by pure will power he staggered to his feet and drove his dazed body across the line it was an exhibition of pluck which put the little sunburned baker straightway among London's heroes. Durando's spirit is alive today. I see thousands of him all around me. A thousand such led by a few young gentlemen of the type who occasionally give us object lessons in how to ride at Olympia, make no mean battalion. It has been a war of most desperate ventures but never once has there been a lack of volunteers. The Tyrolese are good men—too good to be fighting in so rotten a cause. But from first to last the Alpini have had the ascendency in the hill fighting, as the line regiments have against the Kaiserlichs upon the plain. Cæsar told how the big Germans used to laugh at his little men until they had been at handgrips with them. The Austrians could tell the same tale. The spirit in the ranks is something marvellous. There have been occasions when every officer has fallen and yet the men have pushed on, have taken a position and then waited for official directions.

But if that is so, you will ask, why is it that they have not made more impression upon the enemy's position? The answer lies in the strategical position of Italy, and it can be discussed without any technicalities. A child could understand it. The Alps form such a bar across the north that there are only two points where serious operations are possible. One is the Trentino Salient where Austria can always threaten and invade Italy. She lies in the mountains with the plains beneath her. She can always invade the plain, but the Italians cannot seriously invade the mountains since the passes would only lead to other mountains beyond. Therefore their only possible policy is to hold the Austrians back. This they have most successfully done, and though the Austrians with the aid of a shattering heavy artillery have recently made some advance, it is perfectly certain that they can never really carry out any serious invasion. The Italians then have done all that could be done in this quarter. There remains the other front, the opening by the sea. Here the Italians had a chance to advance over a front of plain bounded by a river with hills beyond. They cleared the plain, they crossed the river, they fought a battle very like our own battle of the Aisne upon the slopes of the hills, taking 20,000 Austrian prisoners, and now they are faced by barbed wire, machine guns, cemented trenches, and every other device which has held them as it has held everyone else. But remember what they have done for the common cause and be grateful for it. They have in a year occupied some forty Austrian divisions, and relieved our Russian allies to that very appreciable extent. They have killed or wounded a quarter of a million, taken 40,000, and drawn to themselves a large portion of the artillery. That is their record up-to-date. As to the future it is very easy to prophesy. They will continue to absorb large enemy armies. Neither side can advance far as matters stand. But if the Russians advance and Austria has to draw her men to the East there will be a tiger spring for Trieste. If manhood can break the line then I believe the Durandos will do it.

"Trieste o morte!" I saw chalked upon the walls all over North Italy. That is the Italian objective.

And they are excellently led. Cadorna is an old Roman, a man cast in the big simple mould of antiquity, frugal in his tastes, clear in his aims, with no thought outside his duty. Everyone loves and trusts him. Porro, the Chief of the Staff, who was good enough to explain the strategical position to me, struck me as a man of great clearness of vision, middle-sized, straight as a dart, with an eagle face grained and coloured like an old walnut. The whole of the staff work is, as experts assure me, most excellently done.

So much for the general situation. Let me descend for a moment to my own trivial adventures since leaving the British front. Of France I hope to say more in the future, and so I will pass at a bound to Padua, where it appeared that the Austrian front had politely advanced to meet me, for I was wakened betimes in the morning by the dropping of bombs, the rattle of anti-aircraft guns and the distant rat-tat-tat of a maxim high up in the air. I heard when I came down later that the intruder had been driven away and that little damage had been done. The work of the Austrian aeroplanes is, however, very aggressive behind the Italian lines, for they have the great advantage that a row of fine cities lies at their mercy while the Italians can do nothing without injuring their own kith and kin across the border. This dropping of explosives on the chance of hitting one soldier among fifty victims seems to me the most monstrous development of the whole war, and the one which should be most sternly repressed in future international legislation—if such a thing as international law still exists. The Italian headquarter town, which I will call Nemini, was a particular victim of these murderous attacks. I speak with some feeling, as not only was the ceiling of my bedroom shattered some days before my arrival, but a greasy patch with some black shreds upon it was still visible above my window which represented part of the remains of an unfortunate workman, who had been blown to pieces immediately in front of the house. The air defence is very skilfully managed, however, and the Italians have the matter well in hand.

My first experience of the Italian line was at the portion which I have called the gap by the sea, otherwise the Isonzo front. From a mound behind the trenches an extraordinary fine view can be got of the Austrian position, the general curve of both lines being marked, as in Flanders, by the sausage balloons which float behind them. The Isonzo, which has been so bravely carried by the Italians, lay in front of me, a clear blue river, as broad as the Thames at Hampton Court. In a hollow to my left were the roofs of Gorizia, the town which the Italians are endeavouring to take. A long desolate ridge, the Carso, extends to the south of the town, and stretches down nearly to the sea. The crest is held by the Austrians and the Italian trenches have been pushed within fifty yards of them. A lively bombardment was going on from either side, but so far as the infantry goes there is none of that constant malignant petty warfare with which we are familiar in Flanders. I was anxious to see the Italian trenches, in order to compare them with our British methods, but save for the support and communication trenches I was courteously but firmly warned off.

The story of trench attack and defence is no doubt very similar in all quarters, but I am convinced that close touch should be kept between the Allies on the matter of new inventions. The quick Latin brain may conceive and test an idea long before we do. At present there seems to be very imperfect sympathy. As an example, when I was on the British lines they were dealing with a method of clearing barbed wire. The experiments were new and were causing great interest. But on the Italian front I found that the same system had been tested for many months. In the use of bullet-proof jackets for engineers and other men who have to do exposed work the Italians are also ahead of us. One of their engineers at our headquarters might give some valuable advice. At present the Italians have, as I understand, no military representative with our armies, while they receive a British General with a small staff. This seems very wrong not only from the point of view of courtesy and justice, but also because Italy has no direct means of knowing the truth about our great development. When Germans state that our new armies are made of paper our Allies should have some official assurance of their own that this is false. I can understand our keeping neutrals from our headquarters, but surely our Allies should be on another footing.

Having got this general view of the position I was anxious in the afternoon to visit Monfalcone, which is the small dockyard captured from the Austrians on the Adriatic. My kind Italian officer guides did not recommend the trip as it was part of their great hospitality to shield their guest from any part of that danger which they were always ready to incur themselves. The only road to Monfalcone ran close to the Austrian position at the village of Ronchi, and afterwards kept parallel to it for some miles. I was told that it was only on odd days that the Austrian guns were active in this particular section, so determined to trust to luck that this might not be one of them. It proved, however, to be one of the worst on record, and we were not destined to see the dockyard to which we started.

The civilian cuts a ridiculous figure when he enlarges upon small adventures which may come his way—adventures which the soldier endures in silence as part of his everyday life. On this occasion, however, the episode was all our own, and had a sporting flavour in it which made it dramatic. I know now the feeling of tense expectation with which the driven grouse whirrs onwards towards the butt. I have been behind the butt before now, and it is only poetic justice that I should see the matter from the other point of view. As we approached Ronchi we could see shrapnel breaking over the road in front of us, but we had not yet realised that it was precisely for vehicles that the Austrians were waiting, and that they had the range marked out to a yard. We went down the road all out at a steady fifty miles an hour. The village was near, and it seemed that we had got past the place of danger. We had in fact just reached it. At this moment there was a noise as if the whole four tyres had gone simultaneously, a most terrific bang in our very ears, merging into a second sound like a reverberating blow upon an enormous gong. As I glanced up I saw three clouds immediately above my head, two of them white and the other of a rusty red. The air was full of flying metal and the road, as we were told afterwards by an observer, was all churned up by it. The metal base of one of the shells was found plumb in the middle of the road just where our motor had been. There is no use telling me Austrian gunners can't shoot. I know better.

It was our pace that saved us. The motor was an open one, and the three shells burst, according to one of my Italian companions who was himself an artillery officer, about ten metres above our heads. They threw forward, however, and we travelling at so great a pace shot from under. Before they could get in another we had swung round the curve and under the lee of a house. The good Colonel B. wrung my hand in silence. They were both distressed, these good soldiers, under the impression that they had led me into danger. As a matter of fact it was I who owed them an apology, since they had enough risks in the way of business without taking others in order to gratify the whim of a joy-rider. Barbariche and Clericetti, this record will convey to you my remorse.

Our difficulties were by no means over. We found an ambulance lorry and a little group of infantry huddled under the same shelter with the expression of people who had been caught in the rain. The road beyond was under heavy fire as well as that by which we had come. Had the Ostro-Bosches dropped a high-explosive upon us they would have had a good mixed bag. But apparently they were only out for fancy shooting and disdained a sitter. Presently there came a lull and the lorry moved on, but we soon heard a burst of firing which showed that they were after it. My companions had decided that it was out of the question for us to finish our excursion. We waited for some time therefore and were able finally to make our retreat on foot, being joined later by the car. So ended my visit to Monfalcone, the place I did not reach. I hear that two 10,000-ton steamers were left on the stocks there by the Austrians, but were disabled before they retired. Their cabin basins and other fittings are now adorning the Italian dug-outs.

My second day was devoted to a view of the Italian mountain warfare in the Carnic Alps. Besides the two great fronts, one of defence (Trentino) and one of offence (Isonzo), there are very many smaller valleys which have to be guarded. The total frontier line is over four hundred miles, and it has all to be held against raids if not invasions. It is a most picturesque business. Far up in the Roccolana Valley I found the Alpini outposts, backed by artillery which had been brought into the most wonderful positions. They have taken 8-inch guns where a tourist could hardly take his knapsack. Neither side can ever make serious progress, but there are continual duels, gun against gun, or Alpini against Jaeger. In a little wayside house was the brigade headquarters, and here I was entertained to lunch. It was a scene that I shall remember. They drank to England. I raised my glass to Italia irredenta—might it soon be redenta. They all sprang to their feet and the circle of dark faces flashed into flame. They keep their souls and emotions, these people. I trust that ours may not become atrophied by self-suppression.

The Italians are a quick high-spirited race, and it is very necessary that we should consider their feelings, and that we should show our sympathy with what they have done, instead of making querulous and unreasonable demands of them. In some ways they are in a difficult position. The war is made by their splendid king—a man of whom everyone speaks with extraordinary reverence and love—and by the people. The people with the deep instinct of a very old civilisation understand that the liberty of the world and their own national existence are really at stake. But there are several forces which divide the strength of the nation. There is the clerical, which represents the old Guelph or German spirit, looking upon Austria as the eldest daughter of the church—a daughter who is little credit to her mother. Then there is the old nobility. Finally, there are the commercial people who through the great banks or other similar agencies have got into the influence and employ of the Germans. When you consider all this you will appreciate how necessary it is that Britain should in every possible way, moral and material, sustain the national party. Should by any evil chance the others gain the upper hand there might be a very sudden and sinister change in the international situation. Every man who does, says, or writes a thing which may in any way alienate the Italians is really, whether he knows it or not, working for the King of Prussia. They are a grand people, striving most efficiently for the common cause, with all the dreadful disabilities which an absence of coal and iron entails. It is for us to show that we appreciate it. Justice as well as policy demands it.

The last day spent upon the Italian front was in the Trentino. From Verona a motor drive of about twenty-five miles takes one up the valley of the Adige, and past a place of evil augury for the Austrians, the field of Rivoli. As one passes up the valley one appreciates that on their left wing the Italians have position after position in the spurs of the mountains before they could be driven into the plain. If the Austrians could reach the plain it would be to their own ruin, for the Italians have large reserves. There is no need for any anxiety about the Trentino.

The attitude of the people behind the firing line should give one confidence. I had heard that the Italians were a nervous people. It does not apply to this part of Italy. As I approached the danger spot I saw rows of large, fat gentlemen with long thin black cigars leaning against walls in the sunshine. The general atmosphere would have steadied an epileptic. Italy is perfectly sure of herself in this quarter. Finally, after a long drive of winding gradients, always beside the Adige, we reached Ala, where we interviewed the Commander of the Sector, a man who has done splendid work during the recent fighting. "By all means you can see my front. But no motor-car, please. It draws fire and others may be hit beside you." We proceeded on foot therefore along a valley which branched at the end into two passes. In both very active fighting had been going on, and as we came up the guns were baying merrily, waking up most extraordinary echoes in the hills. It was difficult to believe that it was not thunder. There was one terrible voice that broke out from time to time in the mountains—the angry voice of the Holy Roman Empire. When it came all other sounds died down into nothing. It was—so I was told—the master gun, the vast 42 centimetre giant which brought down the pride of Liège and Namur. The Austrians have brought one or more from Innsbruck. The Italians assure me, however, as we have ourselves discovered, that in trench work beyond a certain point the size of the gun makes little matter.

We passed a burst dug-out by the roadside where a tragedy had occurred recently, for eight medical officers were killed in it by a single shell. There was no particular danger in the valley, however, and the aimed fire was all going across us to the fighting lines in the two passes above us. That to the right, the Valley of Buello, has seen some of the worst of the fighting. These two passes form the Italian left wing which has held firm all through. So has the right wing. It is only the centre which has been pushed in by the concentrated fire.

When we arrived at the spot where the two valleys forked we were halted, and we were not permitted to advance to the advance trenches which lay upon the crests above us. There was about a thousand yards between the adversaries. I have seen types of some of the Bosnian and Croatian prisoners, men of poor physique and intelligence, but the Italians speak with chivalrous praise of the bravery of the Hungarians and of the Austrian Jaeger. Some of their proceedings disgust them, however, and especially the fact that they use Russian prisoners to dig trenches under fire. There is no doubt of this, as some of the men were recaptured and were sent on to join their comrades in France. On the whole, however, it may be said that in the Austro-Italian war there is nothing which corresponds with the extreme bitterness of our western conflict. The presence or absence of the Hun makes all the difference.

Nothing could be more cool or methodical than the Italian arrangements on the Trentino front. There are no troops who would not have been forced back by the Austrian fire. It corresponded with the French experience at Verdun, or ours at the second battle of Ypres. It may well occur again if the Austrians get their guns forward. But at such a rate it would take them a long time to make any real impression. One cannot look at the officers and men without seeing that their spirit and confidence are high. In answer to my inquiry they assure me that there is little difference between the troops of the northern provinces and those of the south. Even among the snows of the Alps they tell me that the Sicilians gave an excellent account of themselves.

That night found me back at Verona and next morning I was on my way to Paris where I hope to be privileged to have some experiences at the front of our splendid Allies. I leave Italy with a deep feeling of gratitude for the kindness shown to me, and of admiration for the way in which they are playing their part in the world's fight for freedom. They have every possible disadvantage, economic and political. But in spite of it they have done splendidly. Three thousand square kilometres of the enemy's country are already in their possession. They relieve to a very great extent the pressure upon the Russians who, in spite of all their bravery, might have been overwhelmed last summer during the "durchbruch" had it not been for the diversion of so many Austrian troops. The time has come now when Russia by her advance on the Pripet is repaying her debt. But the debt is common to all the Allies. Let them bear it in mind. There has been mischief done by slighting criticism and by inconsiderate words. A warm sympathetic hand grasp of congratulation is what Italy has deserved, and it is both justice and policy to give it.

18

↗

From *The Wanderings of a Spiritualist* (1921)

Chapter III

Mr. Hughes's letter of welcome.—Challenges.—Mr. Carlyle Smythe.—
The Adelaide Press.—The great drought.—The wine industry.—
Clairvoyance.—Meeting with Bellchambers.—The first lecture.—The
effect.—The Religious lecture.—The illustrated lecture.—Premoni-
tions.—The spot light.—Mr. Thomas's account of the incident.—
Correspondence.—Adelaide doctors.—A day in the Bush.—The
Mallee fowl.—Sussex in Australia.—Farewell to Adelaide.

I was welcomed to Australia by a hospitable letter from the Premier, Mr. Hughes, who assured me that he would do what he could to
make our visit a pleasant one, and added, "I hope you will see Australia
as it is, for I want you to tell the world about us. We are a very young
country; we have a very big and very rich heritage, and the great war has
made us realise that we are Australians, proud to belong to the Empire,
but proud too of our own country."

Apart from Mr. Hughes's kind message, my chief welcome to the
new land came from Sydney, and took the queer form of two independent challenges to public debate, one from the Christian Evidence
Society, and the other from the local leader of the Materialists. As the
two positions are mutually destructive, one felt inclined to tell them to

fight it out between themselves and that I would fight the winner. The Christian Evidence Society, is, of course, out of the question, since they regard a text as an argument, which I can only accept with many qualifications, so that there is no common basis. The materialist is a more worthy antagonist, for though he is often as bigoted and inaccessible to reason as the worst type of Christian, there is always a leaven of honest, open-minded doubters on whom a debate might make an impression. A debate with them, as I experienced when I met Mr. MacCabe, can only follow one line, they quoting all the real or alleged scandals which have ever been connected with the lowest forms of mediumship, and claiming that the whole cult is comprised therein, to which you counter with your own personal experiences, and with the evidence of the cloud of witnesses who have found the deepest comfort and enlarged knowledge. It is like two boxers each hitting the air, and both returning to their respective corners amid the plaudits of their backers, while the general public is none the better.

Three correspondents headed me off on the ship, and as I gave each of them a long separate interview, I was a tired man before I got ashore. Mr. Carlyle Smythe, my impresario, had also arrived, a small alert competent gentleman, with whom I at once got on pleasant terms, which were never once clouded during our long travels together upon our tour. I was fortunate indeed to have so useful and so entertaining a companion, a musician, a scholar, and a man of many varied experiences. With his help we soon got our stuff through the customs, and made the short train journey which separates the Port of Adelaide from the charming city of that name. By one o'clock we were safely housed in the Grand Central Hotel, with windows in place of port holes, and the roar of the trams to take the place of the murmurs of the great ocean.

The good genius of Adelaide was a figure, already almost legendary, one Colonel Light, who played the part of Romulus and Remus to the infant city. Somewhere in the thirties of last century he chose the site, against strong opposition, and laid out the plan with such skill that in all British and American lands I have seen few such cities, so pretty, so orderly and so self-suffing. When one sees all the amenities of the place, botanical gardens, zoological gardens, art gallery, museum, university, public library and the rest, it is hard to realise that the whole population is still under three hundred thousand. I do not know whether the press sets the tone to the community or the community to the press, but in any case Adelaide is greatly blessed in this respect, for its two chief papers, the *Register* and the *Advertiser,* under Sir William Sowden and Sir Langdon Bonython respectively, are really excellent, with a world-wide Metropolitan tone.

Their articles upon the subject in which I am particularly interested, though by no means one-sided, were at least informed with knowledge and breadth of mind.

In Adelaide I appreciated, for the first time, the crisis which Australia has been passing through in the shape of a two-years' drought, only recently broken. It seems to have involved all the States and to have caused great losses, amounting to millions of sheep and cattle. The result was that the price of those cattle which survived has risen enormously, and at the time of our visit an absolute record had been established, a bullock having been sold for £41. The normal price would be about £13. Sheep were about £3 each, the normal being fifteen shillings. This had, of course, sent the price of meat soaring with the usual popular unrest and agitation as a result. It was clear, however, that with the heavy rains the prices would fall. These Australian droughts are really terrible things, especially when they come upon newly-opened country and in the hotter regions of Queensland and the North. One lady told us that she had endured a drought in Queensland which lasted so long that children of five had never seen a drop of rain. You could travel a hundred miles and find the brown earth the whole way, with no sign of green anywhere, the sheep eating twigs or gnawing bark until they died. Her brother sold his surviving sheep for one shilling each, and when the drought broke had to restock at 50s. a head. This is a common experience, and all but the man with savings have to take to some subordinate work, ruined men. No doubt, with afforestation, artesian wells, irrigation and water storage things may be modified, but all these things need capital, and capital in these days is hard to seek, nor can it be expected that capitalists will pour their money into States which have wild politicians who talk lightly of past obligations. You cannot tell the investor that he is a bloated incubus one moment, and go hat in hand for further incubation the next. I fear that this grand country as a whole may suffer from the wild ideas of some of its representatives. But under it all lies the solid self-respecting British stuff, which will never repudiate a just debt, however heavily it may press. Australians may groan under the burden, but they should remember that for every pound of taxation they carry the home Briton carries nearly three.

But to return for a moment to the droughts; has any writer of fiction invented or described a more long-drawn agony than that of the man, his nerves the more tired and sensitive from the constant unbroken heat, waiting day after day for the cloud that never comes, while under the glaring sun from the unchanging blue above him, his sheep, which represent all his life's work and his hopes, perish before his eyes? A revolver shot has often ended the long vigil and the pioneer has joined his vanished flocks. I have just come in contact with a case where two young returned soldiers, demobilised from the war and planted on the land, had forty-two cattle given them by the State to stock their little farm. Not a drop of water fell for over a year, the feed failed, and these two warriors of Palestine and Flanders wept at their own helplessness while their little herd died before their eyes. Such are the trials which the Australian farmer has to bear.

While waiting for my first lecture I do what I can to understand the country and its problems. To this end I visited the vineyards and wine plant of a local firm which possesses every factor for success, save the capacity to answer letters. The originator started grape culture as a private hobby about 60 years ago, and now such an industry has risen that this firm alone has £700,000 sunk in the business, and yet it is only one of several. The product can be most excellent, but little or any ever reaches Europe, for it cannot overtake the local demand. The quality was good and purer than the corresponding wines in Europe—especially the champagnes, which seem to be devoid of that poison, whatever it may be, which has for a symptom a dry tongue with internal acidity, driving elderly gentlemen to whisky and soda. The Australian product, taken in moderate doses, seems to have no poisonous quality, and is without that lime-like dryness which appears to be the cause of it. If temperance reform takes the sane course of insisting upon a lowering of the alcohol in our drinks, so that one may be surfeited before one could be drunken, then this question of good mild wines will bulk very largely in the future, and Australia may supply one of the answers. With all my sympathy for the reformers I feel that wine is so useful a social agent that we should not abolish it until we are certain that there is no *via media*. The most pregnant argument upon the subject was the cartoon which showed the husband saying, "My dear, it is the anniversary of our wedding. Let us have a second bottle of ginger beer."

We went over the vineyards, ourselves mildly interested in the vines, and the children wildly excited over the possibility of concealed snakes. Then we did the vats and the cellars with their countless bottles. We were taught the secrets of fermentation, how the wonderful Pasteur had discovered that the best and quickest was produced not by the grape itself, as of old, but by the scraped bloom of the grape inserted in the bottle. After viewing the number of times a bottle must be turned, a hundred at least, and the complex processes which lead up to the finished article, I will pay my wine bills in future with a better grace. The place was all polished wood and shining brass, like the fittings of a man-of-war, and a great impression of cleanliness and efficiency was left upon our minds. We only know the Australian wines at present by the rough articles sold in flasks, but when the supply has increased the world will learn that this country has some very different stuff in its cellars, and will try to transport it to their tables.

We had a small meeting of Spiritualists in our hotel sitting-room, under the direction of Mr. Victor Cromer, a local student of the occult, who seems to have considerable psychic power. He has a small circle for psychic development which is on new lines, for the neophytes who are learning clairvoyance sit around in a circle in silence, while Mr. Cromer endeavours by mental effort to build up the thought form of some object, say a tree, in the centre of the room. After a time he asks each of the circle what he or she can see, and has many correct answers. With colours in the same way he can convey impressions to his pupils. It is clear that telepathy is not excluded as an explanation, but the actual effect upon the participants is, according to their own account, visual rather than mental. We had an interesting sitting with a number of these developing mediums present, and much information was given, but little of it could be said to be truly evidential. After seeing such clairvoyance as that of Mr. Tom Tyrell or others at home, when a dozen names and addresses will be given together with the descriptions of those who once owned them, one is spoiled for any lesser display.

There was one man whom I had particularly determined to meet when I came to Australia. This was Mr. T. P. Bellchambers, about whom I had read an article in some magazine which showed that he was a sort of humble Jeffries or Thoreau, more lonely than the former, less learned than the latter, who lived among the wild creatures in the back country, and was on such terms with our humble brothers as few men are ever privileged to attain. I had read how the eagle with the broken wing had come to him for succour, and how little birds would sit on the edge of his pannikin while he drank. Him at all cost would we see. Like the proverbial prophet, no one I met had ever heard of him, but on the third day of our residence there came a journalist bearing with him a rudely dressed, tangle-haired man, collarless and unkempt, with kind, irregular features and clear blue eyes—the eyes of a child. It was the man himself. "He brought me," said he, nodding towards the journalist. "He had to, for I always get bushed in a town."

This rude figure fingering his frayed cap was clearly out of his true picture, and we should have to visit him in his own little clearing to see him as he really was. Meanwhile I wondered whether one who was so near nature might know something of nature's more occult secrets. The dialogue ran like this:

"You who are so near nature must have psychic experiences."

"What's psychic? I live so much in the wild that I don't know much."

"I expect you know plenty we don't know. But I meant spiritual."

"Supernatural?"

"Well, we think it is natural but little understood."

"You mean fairies and things?"

"Yes, and the dead."

"Well, I guess our fairies would be black fairies."

"Why not?"

"Well, I never saw any."

"I hoped you might."

"No, but I know one thing. The night my mother died I woke to find her hand upon my brow. Oh, there's no doubt. Her hand was heavy on my brow."

"At the time?"

"Yes, at the very hour."

"Well, that was good."

"Animals know more about such things."

"Yes."

"They see something. My dog gets terrified when I see nothing, and there's a place in the bush where my horse shies and sweats, he does, but there's nothing to see."

"Something evil has been done there. I've known many cases."

"I expect that's it."

So ran our dialogue. At the end of it he took a cigar, lighted it at the wrong end, and took himself with his strong simple backwoods atmosphere out of the room. Assuredly I must follow him to the wilds.

Now came the night of my first lecture. It was in the city hall, and every seat was occupied. It was a really magnificent audience of two thousand people, the most representative of the town. I am an embarrassed and an interested witness, so let me for this occasion quote the sympathetic, not to say flattering account of the *Register*.

"There could not have been a more impressive set of circumstances than those which attended the first Australian lecture by Sir Arthur Conan Doyle at the Adelaide Town Hall on Saturday night, September 25th. The audience, large, representative and thoughtful, was in its calibre and proportions a fitting compliment to a world celebrity and his mission. Many of the intellectual leaders of the city were present—University professors, pulpit personalities, men eminent in business, legislators, every section of the community contributed a quota. It cannot be doubted, of course, that the brilliant literary fame of the lecturer was an attraction added to that strange subject which explored the 'unknown drama of the soul.' Over all, Sir Arthur dominated by his big arresting presence. His face has a rugged, kindly strength, tense and earnest in its grave moments, and full of winning animation when the sun of his rich humour plays on the powerful features.

"It is not altogether a sombre journey he makes among the shadows, but apparently one of happy, as well as tender experiences, so that laughter is not necessarily excluded from the exposition. Do not let that be misunderstood. There was no intrusion of the slightest flippancy—Sir

Arthur, the whole time, exhibited that attitude of reverence and humility demanded of one traversing a domain on the borderland of the tremendous. Nothing approaching a theatrical presentation of the case for Spiritualism marred the discourse. It was for the most part a plain statement. First things had to be said, and the explanatory groundwork laid for future development. It was a lucid, illuminating introduction.

"Sir Arthur had a budget of notes, but after he had turned over a few pages he sallied forth with fluent independence under the inspiration of a vast mental store of material. A finger jutted out now and again with a thrust of passionate emphasis, or his big glasses twirled during moments of descriptive ease, and occasionally both hands were held forward as though delivering settled points to the audience for its examination. A clear, well-disciplined voice, excellent diction, and conspicuous sincerity of manner marked the lecture, and no one could have found fault with the way in which Sir Arthur presented his case.

"The lecturer approached the audience in no spirit of impatient dogmatism, but in the capacity of an understanding mind seeking to illumine the darkness of doubt in those who had not shared his great experiences. He did not dictate, but reasoned and pleaded, taking the people into his confidence with strong conviction and a consoling faith. 'I want to speak to you to-night on a subject which concerns the destiny of every man and woman in this room,' began Sir Arthur, bringing everybody at once into an intimate personal circle. 'No doubt the Almighty, by putting an angel in King William Street, could convert every one of you to Spiritualism, but the Almighty law is that we must use our own brains, and find out our own salvation, and it is not made too easy for us.'"

It is awkward to include this kindly picture, and yet I do not know how else to give an idea of how the matter seemed to a friendly observer. I had chosen for my theme the scientific aspect of the matter, and I marshalled my witnesses and showed how Professor Mayo corroborated Professor Hare, and Professor Challis Professor Mayo, and Sir William Crookes all his predecessors, while Russell Wallace and Lombroso and Zollner and Barrett, and Lodge, and many more had all after long study assented, and I read the very words of these great men, and showed how bravely they had risked their reputations and careers for what they knew to be the truth. I then showed how the opposition who dared to contradict them were men with no practical experience of it at all. It was wonderful to hear the shout of assent when I said that what struck me most in such a position was its colossal impertinence. That shout told me that my cause was won, and from then onwards the deep silence was only broken by the occasional deep murmur of heart-felt agreement. I told them the evidence that had been granted to me, the coming of my son, the coming of my brother, and their message. "Plough! Plough! others will cast the seed." It is hard to talk of such intimate matters, but they were not given to me for my private comfort alone, but for that of humanity. Nothing could have gone better than this first evening, and though I had no chairman and spoke for ninety minutes without a pause, I was so upheld—there is no other word for the sensation—that I was stronger at the end than when I began. A leading materialist was among my audience. "I am profoundly impressed," said he to Mr. Smythe, as he passed him in the corridor. That stood out among many kind messages which reached me that night.

My second lecture, two nights later, was on the Religious aspect of the matter. I had shown that the phenomena were nothing, mere material signals to arrest the attention of a material world. I had shown also that the personal benefit, the conquest of death, the Communion of Saints, was a high, but not the highest boon. The real full flower of Spiritualism was what the wisdom of the dead could tell us about their own conditions, their present experiences, their outlook upon the secret of the universe, and the testing of religious truth from the viewpoint of two worlds instead of one. The audience was more silent than before, but the silence was that of suspense, not of dissent, as I showed them from message after message what it was exactly which awaited them in the beyond. Even I, who am oblivious as a rule to my audience, became aware that they were tense with feeling and throbbing with emotion. I showed how there was no conflict with religion, in spite of the misunderstanding of the churches, and that the revelation had come to extend and explain the old, even as the Christ had said that he had much more to tell but could not do it now. "Entirely new ground was traversed," says my kindly chronicler, "and the audience listened throughout with rapt attention. They were obviously impressed by the earnestness of the speaker and his masterly presentation of the theme." I cannot answer for the latter but at least I can for the former, since I speak not of what I think but of what I know. How can a man fail to be earnest then ?

A few days later I followed up the lectures by two exhibitions of psychic pictures and photographs upon a screen. It was certainly an amazing experience for those who imagined that the whole subject was dreamland, and they freely admitted that it staggered them. They might well be surprised, for such a series has never been seen, I believe, before, including as it does choice samples from the very best collections. I showed them the record of miracle after miracle, some of them done under my very eyes, one guaranteed by Russell Wallace, three by Sir William Crookes, one of the Geley series from Paris, two of Dr. Crawford's medium with the ecto-plasm pouring from her, four illustrating the absolutely final Lydia Haig case on the island of Rothesay, several of Mr. Jeffrey's collection and several also of our own Society for the Study of Supernormal Pictures, with the fine photograph of the face within a crystal. No wonder that the audience sat spellbound, while the local press declared that no such exhibition had ever been seen before in Australia. It is almost too overwhelming for immediate propaganda purposes. It has a stunning, dazing effect upon the spectators. Only afterwards, I think, when they come to turn it all over in their minds, do they see that the final proof has been laid before them, which no one with the least sense for evidence could reject. But the sense for evidence is not, alas, a universal human quality.

I am continually aware of direct spirit intervention in my own life. I have put it on record in my "New Revelation" that I was able to say that the turn of the great war would come upon the Piave months before that river was on the Italian war map. This was recorded at the time, before the fulfilment which occurred more than a year later—so it does not depend upon my assertion. Again, I dreamed the name of the ship which was to take us to Australia, rising in the middle of the night and writing it down in pencil on my chequebook. I wrote *Nadera,* but it was actually *Naldera.* I had never heard that such a ship existed until I visited the P. & O. office, when they told me we should go by the *Osterley,* while I, seeing the *Naldera* upon the list, thought, "No, that will be our ship!"

So it proved, through no action of our own, and thereby we were saved from quarantine and all manner of annoyance.

Never before have I experienced such direct visible intervention as occurred during my first photographic lecture at Adelaide. I had shown a slide the effect of which depended upon a single spirit face appearing amid a crowd of others. This slide was damp, and as photos under these circumstances always clear from the edges when placed in the lantern, the whole centre was so thickly fogged that I was compelled to admit that I could not myself see the spirit face. Suddenly, as I turned away, rather abashed by my failure, I heard cries of "There it is," and looking up again I saw this single face shining out from the general darkness with so bright and vivid an effect that I never doubted for a moment that the operator was throwing a spot light upon it, my wife sharing my impression. I thought how extraordinarily clever it was that he should pick it out so accurately at the distance. So the matter passed, but next morning Mr. Thomas, the operator, who is not a Spiritualist, came in in great excitement to say that a palpable miracle had been wrought, and that in his great experience of thirty years he had never known a photo dry from the centre, nor, as I understood him, become illuminated in such a fashion. Both my wife and I were surprised to learn that he had thrown no ray upon it. Mr. Thomas told us that several experts among the audience had commented upon the strangeness of the incident. I, therefore, asked Mr. Thomas if he would give me a note as to his own impression, so as to furnish an independent account. This is what he wrote:—

"Hindmarsh Square, Adelaide.

"In Adelaide, on September 28th, I projected a lantern slide containing a group of ladies and gentlemen, and in the centre of the picture, when the slide was reversed, appeared a human face. On the appearance of the picture showing the group the fog incidental to a damp or new slide gradually appeared covering the whole slide, and only after some minutes cleared, and then quite contrary to usual practice did so from a central point just over the face that appeared in the centre, and refused even after that to clear right off to the edge. The general experience is for a slide to clear from the outside edges to a common centre. Your slide cleared only sufficiently in the centre to show the face, and did not, while the slide was on view, clear any more than sufficient to

show that face. Thinking that perhaps there might be a scientific explanation to this phe-
nomenon, I hesitated before writing you, and in the meantime I have made several ex-
periments but have not in any one particular experiment obtained the same result. I
am very much interested—as are hundreds of others who personally witnessed the
phenomenon."

Mr. Thomas, in his account, has missed the self-illuminated appearance of the face, but otherwise he brings out the points. I never gave occasion for the repetition of the phenomenon, for in every case I was careful that the slides were carefully dried beforehand.

So much for the lectures at Adelaide, which were five in all, and left,
as I heard from all sides, a deep impression upon the town. Of course,
the usual abusive messages poured in, including one which wound up
with the hearty words: "May you be struck dead before you leave this
Commonwealth." From Melbourne I had news that before our arrival in
Australia at a public prayer meeting at the Assembly Hall, Collins Street,
a Presbyterian prayed that we might never reach Australia's shores. As we
were on the high seas at the time this was clearly a murderous petition,
nor could I have believed it if a friend of mine had not actually been
present and heard it. On the other hand, we received many letters of
sympathy and thanks, which amply atoned. "I feel sure that many mothers, who have lost their sons in the war, will, wherever you go, bless you,
as I do, for the help you have given." As this was the object of our journey it could not be denied that we had attained our end. When I say
"we," I mean that such letters with inquiries came continually to my wife
as well as myself, though she answered them with far greater fullness and
clearness than I had time to do.

Hotel life began to tell upon the children, who are like horses with
a profusion of oats and no exercise. On the whole they were wonderfully
good. When some domestic crisis was passed the small voice of Mal-
colm, once "Dimples," was heard from the darkness of his bed, saying,
"Well, if I am to be good I must have a proper start. Please, mammie,
say one, two, three, and away!" When this ceremony had been performed
a still smaller voice of Baby asked the same favour, so once more there
was a formal start. The result was intermittent, and it is as well. I don't
believe in angelic children.

The Adelaide doctors entertained me to dinner, and I was pleased to meet more than one who had been of my time at Edinburgh. They seemed to be a very prosperous body of men. There was much interesting conversation, especially from one elderly professor named Watson, who had known Bully Hayes and other South Sea celebrities in the semi-piratical, black-birding days. He told me one pretty story. They landed upon some outlying island in Carpentaria, peopled by real primitive blacks, who were rounded up by the ship's crew on one of the peninsulas which formed the end of the island. These creatures, the lowest of the human race, huddled together in consternation while the white men trained a large camera upon them. Suddenly three males advanced and made a speech in their own tongue which, when interpreted, proved to be an offer that those three should die in exchange for the lives of the tribe. What could the very highest do more than this, and yet it came from the lowest savages. Truly, we all have something of the divine, and it is the very part which will grow and spread until it has burned out all the rest. "Be a Christ!" said brave old Stead. At the end of countless æons we may all reach that point which not only Stead but St. Paul also has foreshadowed.

I refreshed myself between lectures by going out to Nature and to Bellchambers. As it was twenty-five miles out in the bush, inaccessible by rail, and only to be approached by motor roads which were in parts like the bed of a torrent, I could not take my wife, though the boys, after the nature of boys, enjoy a journey the more for its roughness. It was a day to remember. I saw lovely South Australia in the full beauty of the spring, the budding girlhood of the year, with all her winsome growing graces upon her. The brilliant yellow wattle was just fading upon the trees, but the sward was covered with star-shaped purple flowers of the knot-grass, and with familiar home flowers, each subtly altered by their transportation. It was wild bush for part of the way, but mostly of the second growth on account of forest fires as much as the woodman's axe. Bellchambers came in to guide us, for there is no one to ask upon these desolate tracks, and it is easy to get bushed. Mr. Waite, the very capable zoologist of the museum, joined the party, and with two such men the conversation soon got to that high nature talk which represents the really permanent things of material life—more lasting than thrones and dynasties. I learned of the strange storks, the "native companions" who meet, 500 at a time, for their stately balls, where in the hush of the bush they advance, retreat, and pirouette in their dignified minuets. I heard of the bower birds, who decorate their homes with devices of glass and pebbles. There was talk, too, of the little red beetles who have such cunning ways that they can fertilise the insectivorous plants without being eaten, and of the great ants who get through galvanised iron by the aid of some acid-squirting insect which they bring with them to the scene of their assault. I heard also of the shark's egg which Mr. Waite had raped from sixty feet deep in Sydney Harbour, descending for the purpose in a diver's suit, for which I raised my hat to him. Deep things came also from Bellchambers's store of knowledge and little glimpses of beautiful humanity from this true gentleman.

"Yes," he said, "I am mostly vegetarian. You see, I know the beasts too well to bring myself to pick their bones. Yes, I'm friends with most of them. Birds have more sense than animals to my mind. They understand what you like. They know what you mean. Snakes have least of any. They don't get friendly-like in the same way. But Nature helps the snakes in queer ways. Some of them hatch their own eggs, and when they do Nature raises the temperature of their bodies. That's queer."

I carried away a mixed memory of the things I had seen. A blue-headed wren, an eagle soaring in the distance; a hideous lizard with a huge open mouth; a laughing jackass which refused to laugh; many more or less tame wallabies and kangaroos; a dear little 'possum which got under the back of my coat, and would not come out; noisy mynah birds which fly ahead and warn the game against the hunter. Good little noisy mynah! All my sympathies are with you! I would do the same if I could. This senseless lust for killing is a disgrace to the race. We, of England, cannot preach, for a pheasant battue is about the worst example of it. But do let the creatures alone unless they are surely noxious! When Mr. Bellchambers told us how he had trained two ibises—the old religious variety—and how both had been picked off by some unknown local "sportsman" it made one sad.

We had a touch of comedy, however, when Mr. Bellchambers attempted to expose the egg of the Mallee fowl, which is covered a foot deep in mould. He scraped into the mound with his hands. The cock watched him with an expression which clearly said: "Confound the fellow! What is he up to now?" He then got on the mound, and as quickly as Bellchambers shovelled the earth out he kicked it back again, Bellchambers in his good humoured way crying, "Get along with you, do!" A good husband is the Mallee cock, and looks after the family interests. But what we humans would think if we were born deep underground and had to begin our career by digging our way to the surface, is beyond imagination.

There are quite a clan of Bellchambers living in or near the little pioneer's hut built in a clearing of the bush. Mrs. Bellchambers is of Sussex, as is her husband, and when they heard that we were fresh from Sussex also it was wonderful to see the eager look that came upon their faces, while the bush-born children could scarce understand what it was that shook the solid old folk to their marrow. On the walls were old prints of the Devil's Dyke and Firle Beacon. How strange that old Sussex should be wearing out its very life in its care for the fauna of young Australia. This remarkable man is unpaid with only his scanty holding upon which to depend, and many dumb mouths dependent upon him. I shall rejoice if my efforts in the local press serve to put his affairs upon a more worthy foundation, and to make South Australia realise what a valuable instrument lies to her hand.

Before I left Adelaide I learned many pleasing things about the lectures, which did away with any shadow cast by those numerous correspondents who seemed to think that we were still living under the Mosaic dispensation, and who were so absent-minded that they usually forgot to sign their names. It is a curious difference between the Christian letters of abuse and those of materialists, that the former are usually anonymous and the latter signed. I heard of one man, a lame stockman, who had come 300 miles from the other side of Streaky Bay to attend the whole course, and who declared that he could listen all night. Another seized my hand and cried, "You will never know the good you have done in this town." Well, I hope it was so, but I only regard myself as the plough. Others must follow with the seed. Knowledge, perseverance, sanity, judgment, courage—we ask some qualities from our disciples if they are to do real good. Talking of moral courage I would say that the Governor of South Australia, Sir Archibald Weigall, with Lady Weigall, had no hesitation in coming to support me with their presence. By the end of September this most successful mission in Adelaide was accomplished, and early in October we were on our way to Melbourne, which meant a long night in the train and a few hours of the next morning during which we saw the surface diggings of Ballarat on every side of the railway line, the sandy soil pitted in every direction with the shallow claims of the miners.

BIBLIOGRAPHY

Baker, Michael. *The Doyle Diary*. New York: Paddington Press, 1978.

Baring-Gould, William. *The Annotated Sherlock Holmes*. New York: Clarkson Potter, 1967.

Booth, Martin. *The Doctor, the Detective and Arthur Conan Doyle*. London: Hodder & Stoughton, 1997.

Brown, Ivor. *Conan Doyle*. London: Hamish Hamilton, 1972.

Carr, John Dickson. *The Life of Sir Arthur Conan Doyle*. New York: Harper, 1949.

Coren, Michael. *Conan Doyle*. London: Bloomsbury, 1995.

Cox, Don Richard. *Arthur Conan Doyle*. New York: Ungar, 1995.

Doyle, Adrian Conan. *The True Conan Doyle*. New York: Coward-McCann, 1946.

Edwards, Owen Dudley. *The Quest for Sherlock Homes*. Totowa, N.J.: Barnes & Noble, 1983.

Goldfarb, Clifford. *The Great Shadow: Arthur Conan Doyle, Brigadier Gerard and Napoleon*. Toronto: Simon & Pierre, 1995.

Green, Roger Lancelyn and John Michael Gibson. *A Bibliography of A. Conan Doyle*. New York: Oxford University Press, 1983.

Hall, Trevor. *Sherlock Holmes and His Creator*. New York: St. Martin's, 1977.

Hardwick, Michael and Mollie. *The Man Who Was Sherlock Holmes*. London: John Murray, 1964.

Higham, Charles. *The Adventures of Conan Doyle*. New York: Norton, 1976.

Jaffe, Jacqueline. *Arthur Conan Doyle*. Boston: Twayne, 1987.

Jones, Kelvin. *Conan Doyle and the Spirits*. Wellingborough, Northants: Acquarian Press, 1989.

Lamond, John. *Arthur Conan Doyle: A Memoir* (with an epilogue by Lady Conan Doyle). London: John Murray, 1931.

Lellenberg Jon, ed. *The Quest for Arthur Conan Doyle*. Carbondale: Southern Illinois University Press, 1987.

Nordon, Pierre. *Conan Doyle*. Trans. Frances Partridge. London: John Murray, 1966.

Orel, Harold, ed. *Critical Essays on Sir Arthur Conan Doyle*. New York: G.K. Hall, 1992.

———, ed. *Sir Arthur Conan Doyle: Interviews and Memoirs*. New York: St. Martin's, 1991.

Pearsall, Ronald. *Conan Doyle: A Biographical Solution*. London: Weidenfeld & Nicolson, 1977.

Rosenberg, Samuel. *Naked Is the Best Disguise: The Death and Resurrection of Sherlock Holmes*. Indianapolis: Bobbs-Merrill, 1974.

Stashower, Daniel. *Teller of Tales: The Life of Sir Arthur Conan Doyle*. New York: Henry Holt, 1999.

Symons, Julian. *Conan Doyle: Portrait of an Artist*. New York: Mysterious Press, 1979.

Other Cooper Square Press Titles of Interest

JOSEPH CONRAD
A Biography
Jeffrey Meyers
464 pp., 32 b/w photos
0-8154-1112-X
$18.95

KATHERINE MANSFIELD
A Darker View
Jeffrey Meyers
with a new introduction
344 pp., 29 b/w photos
0-8154-1197-9
$18.95

EDGAR ALLAN POE
His Life and Legacy
Jeffrey Meyers
376 pp., 12 b/w photos
0-8154-1038-7
$18.95

SCOTT FITZGERALD
A Biography
Jeffrey Meyers
432 pp., 25 b/w photos
0-8154-1036-0
$18.95

HEMINGWAY
Life into Art
Jeffrey Meyers
192 pp.
0-8154-1079-4
$27.95 cloth

GARY COOPER
American Hero
Jeffrey Meyers
404 pp., 32 b/w photos
0-8154-1140-5
$18.95

THE GREENWICH VILLAGE READER
Fiction, Poetry, and Reminiscences, 1872–2002
Edited by June Skinner Sawyers
708 pp., 1 map
0-8154-1148-0
$35.00 cloth

THE FAIRY TALE OF MY LIFE
An Autobiography
Hans Christian Andersen
New introduction by Naomi Lewis
610 pp., 20 b/w illustrations
0-8154-1105-7
$22.95

STEPHEN CRANE
A Critical Biography
Revised Edition
John Berryman
368 pp., 1 b/w photo
0-8154-1115-4
$18.95

**AMERICAN WOMEN
ACTIVISTS' WRITINGS**
An Anthology, 1637–2002
Edited by Kathryn Cullen-DuPont
692 pp., 15 b/w photos
0-8154-1185-5
$37.95 cloth

GEORGE ELIOT
The Last Victorian
Kathryn Hughes
416 pp., 33 b/w illustrations
0-8154-1121-9
$19.95

GRANITE AND RAINBOW
The Hidden Life of Virginia Woolf
Mitchell Leaska
536 pp., 23 b/w photos
0-8154-1047-6
$18.95

LOVECRAFT AT LAST
H. P. Lovecraft and Willis Conover
New introduction by S. T. Joshi
312 pp., 59 b/w illustrations
0-8154-1212-6
$27.95 cloth

THE GROTTO BERG
Two Novellas
Charles Neider
Introduction by Clive Sinclair
184 pp.
0-8154-1123-5
$22.95 cloth

TOLSTOY
Tales of Courage and Conflict
Edited by Charles Neider
576 pp.
0-8154-1010-7
$19.95

LIFE AS I FIND IT
A Treasury of Mark Twain Rarities
Edited by Charles Neider
with a new foreword
343 pp., 1 b/w photo
0-8154-1027-1
$17.95

**MARK TWAIN: PLYMOUTH
ROCK AND THE PILGRIMS**
and Other Speeches
Edited by Charles Neider
368 pp.; 1 b/w photo
0-8154-1104-9
$17.95

**THE TRAVELS OF
MARK TWAIN**
Edited by Charles Neider
448 pp., 6 b/w line drawings
0-8154-1039-5
$19.95

**THE SELECTED LETTERS OF
MARK TWAIN**
Edited by Charles Neider
352 pp., 1 b/w photo
0-8154-1011-5
$16.95

SHORT NOVELS OF THE
MASTERS
Edited by Charles Neider
648 pp.
0-8154-1178-2
$23.95

ESSAYS OF THE MASTERS
Edited by Charles Neider
480 pp.
0-8154-1097-2
$18.95

THE COMPLETE SHORT
STORIES OF MARCEL PROUST
Translated by Joachim Neugroschel
Introduction by Roger Shattuck
250 pp.
0-8154-1136-7
$25.95 cloth

SHAKESPEARE
The Man and His Achievement
Robert Speaight
416 pp., 24 b/w illustrations
0-8154-1063-8
$19.95

THE LANTERN BEARERS
AND OTHER ESSAYS
Robert Louis Stevenson
Edited by Jeremy Treglown
320 pp., 27 b/w maps
0-8154-1012-3
$16.95

THE LIFE AND DEATH OF
YUKIO MISHIMA
Henry Scott Stokes
318 pp., 39 b/w illustrations
0-8154-1074-3
$18.95

Available at bookstores; or call
1-800-462-6420

COOPER SQUARE PRESS
200 Park Avenue South
Suite 1109
New York, NY 10003-1503